Data
Transmission

Data Transmission

Dogan A. Tugal

Osman Tugal

Second Edition

McGraw-Hill Book Company

New York St. Louis San Francisco Auckland
Bogotá Hamburg London Madrid Mexico
Milan Montreal New Delhi Panama
Paris São Paulo Singapore
Sydney Tokyo Toronto

Library of Congress Cataloging in Publication Data

Tugal, Dogan A.
   Data Transmission/Dogan A. Tugal, Osman Tugal.   2nd. ed.

   Includes bibliographies and index.
   1. Data transmission systems.   I. Tugal, Osman.   II. Title.
TK5105.T785 1989   621.398—dc19   88-14067
ISBN 0-07-065447-6

1234567890   DOC/DOC   8954321098

ISBN 0-07-065447-6

*The editors for this book were Daniel A. Gonneau and Jim
Halston, the designer was Naomi Auerbach, and the production
supervisor was Suzanne W. Babeuf. It was set in Century
Schoolbook by Techna Type Inc.*

Printed and bound by R. R. Donnelley and Sons

*For more information about other McGraw-Hill materials,
call 1-800-2-MCGRAW in the United States. In other
countries, call your nearest McGraw-Hill office.*

To Belkis, understanding wife and mother

Contents

Preface / xi

Chapter 1. Communications and Communication Links / 1

1.1 Channels and Circuits / 4
1.2 Transmission Media / 8
1.3 Communication-Link Configurations / 14
1.4 Analog Transmission versus Digital Transmission / 16

Chapter 2. Transmissions over Voice-Grade Circuits / 21

2.1 Overall Attenuation / 23
2.2 Attenuation-Frequency Characteristics / 31
2.3 Echoes / 34
2.4 Return Loss / 41
2.5 Noise / 46
2.6 Delay Distortion / 59
2.7 Translation Errors in Carrier Systems / 66
2.8 Phase Jitter / 67
2.9 Harmonic Distortion / 75
2.10 Nonlinear Distortion / 76
2.11 Bias Distortion / 77
2.12 Characteristic Distortion / 79
2.13 CCITT Recommendations Referring to Data Transmission over Voice-Grade Circuits / 80
2.14 Estimating End-to-End Analog Transmission Performance / 82
2.15 Principles of Circuit Bridging / 86

Chapter 3. Modulation, Demodulation, Binary Basebands, and Modems / 89

3.1 Analog Modulation and Demodulation / 89
3.2 Pulse Modulation / 93
3.3 Binary Basebands / 97
3.4 Modems / 107

3.5   Short-Distance Digital Interconnections, Acoustic Couplers, Facsimiles, and Data Encryption / 122

3.6   Summary of CCITT Recommendations Relating to Modems / 130

Chapter 4. Channel-Capacity-Increasing Methods and Packet Switching / 133

4.1   Channel-Capacity-Increasing Methods on Data Transmission / 135
4.2   Analog Voice Compression Method / 138
4.3   Digital Voice Compression Methods / 139
4.4   Utilization of Idle Transmission Periods / 142
4.5   Packetized Speech / 144
4.6   Packet-Switching Data Networks / 145

Chapter 5. Multiplexing / 149

5.1   Multiplexing Techniques / 149
5.2   Comparison of Multiplexing Techniques / 161
5.3   Hierarchy of Analog Channels / 165
5.4   Hierarchy of Digital Channels / 173

Chapter 6. Synchronization / 177

6.1   Synchronization Techniques Used in Data Equipment / 177
6.2   Asynchronous and Synchronous Transmission / 182
6.3   Synchronization of Data Equipment in Different Transmission Networks / 184
6.4   Organization of International and National Digital Networks / 194

Chapter 7. Interfacing, Protocols, Information Codes, Error Correction / 197

7.1   Level 1 Protocols. Physical Interface between DTE and Network / 200
7.2   Interface Control Circuit Operations / 220
7.3   Level 2 (Data-Link) Protocols / 231
7.4   Level 3 (Network-Control) and Higher-Level (End-to-End) Protocols / 238
7.5   Information Codes / 243
7.6   Error-Detection and Correction Techniques / 247
7.7   Digital Services and Interfacing Units / 253

Chapter 8. Satellite Communications / 259

8.1   Description of a Satellite Communications System / 259
8.2   Forms of Operation / 264
8.3   Multiple-Access and Modulation Techniques / 268
8.4   Digital Data Transmission (in the United States) / 274
8.5   Propagation-Delay Problems and Error-Detection Methods / 276
8.6   The Marisat System / 279

8.7   Advantages and Future of Satellite Communications / 280
8.8   CCIR Recommendations and Reports for Data Transmission via
       Satellites / 282

Chapter 9. Monitoring and Testing on Operational Circuits / 285

9.1   Analog Technique, PAR Measurements / 286
9.2   Distortion Measurements on Digital Circuits / 288
9.3   Digital Monitoring and Testing / 294
9.4   Technical Control Center / 302

Chapter 10. Optical-Fiber Transmission / 313

10.1   System Configuration / 313
10.2   Optical-Fiber Cable / 315
10.3   Light Sources / 320
10.4   Optical Detectors / 322
10.5   Splicing and Connectors / 327
10.6   Fiber-Optic-Cable Installation Methods / 329
10.7   Testing and Test Instruments / 333
10.8   Advantages and Deterrents / 335
10.9   Recent Developments in Fiber-Optic Components and the Future / 337

Chapter 11. Shielding, Grounding, Protection of Systems, and Static
          Electricity / 341

11.1   Sources of Interference / 342
11.2   System and Circuit Protection / 345
11.3   Circuit Isolation / 372
11.4   Static Electricity in the Electronics Industry / 382

Chapter 12. Local-Area Networks / 389

12.1   Beginning of Local-Area Networks / 390
12.2   Network Topologies and Protocols / 391
12.3   Link Access Procedures / 392
12.4   Transmission Mediums for LANs / 395
12.5   Applications, Benefits, and Future of LAN / 401
12.6   Personal Computer Networks / 404

Appendix A. Organizations Involved in Telecommunications / 409

Appendix B. Telephone Signaling / 415

Glossary / 425
Index / 471

Preface

This book explains theories and concepts of analog and digital data transmission to engineers, managers, and technically oriented individuals in the telecommunications field. Only basic mathematical concepts are used, and virtually all the topics covered in the book can be used during the design, installation, and implementation stages of data transmission systems.

The communications industry has experienced a phenomenal growth during the past century. The social, political, and economic changes in society and the fantastic rate of economic progress recently experienced by some countries have resulted from successful developments in the telecommunications field. Telecommunications facilities are a prominent and integral part of the everyday life of a modern society. In fact, telecommunications plays a vital role in today's international relations. This industry influences the very nature of our existence. It will definitely influence our thinking, our behavior, our loves and hates, our passions and compassions, and above all world peace. Although still in its infancy, the telecommunications industry will remain a powerful entity that will shape our future, with an approximate annual growth of twenty percent.

Progress in the telecommunications field will force telecommunications engineers to continue their efforts to overcome the difficulties in finding a balance between cost and tolerance levels in their communications systems. This book is intended to help communication engineers overcome these difficulties.

In general, many technical issues must be considered and resolved during a communication system's design stage. Some of the critical questions that must be asked are given below.

- Which of the following network structures should be chosen for a telecommunication system: centralized, distributed, store-and-forward, packet-switching, looped, or a combination of these?
- Which of the following transmission facilities is appropriate for the system: voice-grade, wideband, digital, domestic satellite, radio, cable, or fiber-optic system?

- Which of the following devices should be chosen: conventional MUX, statistical MUX, or concentrator?

- How should the traffic be managed and controlled: via line disciplines, flow control, or routing strategies?

- What values should be assigned to the following as performance requirements of the system: response time, capacity, blocking probability, message error rate, reliability, and sensitivity?

- Which of the following system parameters and statistics should be monitored and measured: message size, line failure, traffic volume and pattern?

- How should the answers to the above questions be integrated to produce a cost-effective overall network?

Obviously, obtaining reliable answers to these questions is extremely difficult and often requires an experienced, dedicated team of specialists. It is virtually impossible to find comprehensive answers to all these questions in a single technical book. It is hoped that engineers and managers will use this book as a reference to learn briefly about topics concerning their technical problems before they refer to special sources for detailed information. With this intent, the contents of the book are outlined below by chapter.

In Chapter 1, analog and digital transmissions are discussed after a brief presentation on communication links and transmission media.

In Chapter 2, analog voice-grade circuits and their related problems are discussed. These problems include distortions, noise, phase jitters, trouble sources, and line conditioning. Also, amplitude- and angle-modulation vector representation are discussed when jitter-measurement methods are presented. Expected operational circuit test results and interpretation of these results are then presented.

In Chapter 3, analog and digital modulation and their transmission methods as well as demodulation and digital signals are discussed. Modems and related CCITT recommendations are also presented.

In Chapter 4, recent developments on compression of a speech into a bandwidth narrower than voice band, digital compression methods, utilization of idle transmission periods, and packet-switched networks are discussed.

In Chapter 5, several multiplexing techniques used in communication systems are explained and compared with computerized multiplexers.

In Chapter 6, synchronization techniques on transmission as well as between two digital networks are discussed.

In Chapter 7, protocol levels, EIA standards, and CCITT recommendations for interfacing on communication channels, with examples, and coding and error-detection techniques are presented.

In Chapter 8, satellite communication methods are discussed from an operational point of view.

In Chapter 9, analog and digital circuit quality measurements are discussed by utilizing sophisticated testing and monitoring equipment. Also operator efficiency and analog and digital meters are explained.

The rapid developments in optical fiber have introduced a new attractive medium to the data communication field. No data communication book would be complete without a discussion on optical-fiber transmission. So, in Chapter 10, a comprehensive discussion on optical-fiber transmission with basic mathematics is presented.

Ever since engineers attempted to provide communication service to humanity they have encountered an ever-present menace: noise. Although proper grounding and shielding procedures reduce the noise levels, they do not completely eliminate the problem. With the introduction of production quantities of MOS and CMOS devices, a unique reliability problem became manifest; the devices were becoming short-circuited after assembly on printed circuit boards. These failures were caused by static electricity, and their prevention became a major problem in the electronics industry. In Chapter 11, installation of reliable ground systems, and circuit and system protection methods are discussed, as are circuit isolation techniques, relays, and methods of protecting against static electricity.

Local-area networks (LANs) are pushing to the forefront on data communications. Rapid advances in coaxial and fiber-optic cable transmission, media, and related hardware, and computers in different shapes in offices and plants are fueling LAN development. In Chapter 12, LAN topology, operation, and protocols are explained.

In Appendix A, telecommunication organizations in the world as well as in the United States are briefly discussed.

In Appendix B, telephone signaling on loop lines and trunks as well as E and M signaling are explained.

Since this book is intended for engineers as a quick reference to solve their problems in their daily work, a comprehensive Glossary on transmission and communication terms is given in the end of the book. In the Glossary, classical terms and definitions studied in the standard college textbooks are not included.

The authors were assisted in their work by John Gulbenkian, Varian Associates Inc., Instrument Group, Walnut Creek, Calif., and Alfonse Acampora, RCA Laboratories, Princeton, N.J. Walter Geen, Nicholas DiSanti, and Jack Gold of RCA Global Communications, New York, are thanked for their vital technical information on transmission line theory. We would also like to thank Dr. H. Tugal, CTI-Cryogenics, Waltham, Mass., formerly with General Electric Co. MSTD, Lynn, Mass., who read the manuscript, provided many suggestions, and checked the calculations in this book.

Special thanks are owed to Mrs. B. F. Tugal, wife and mother, for her invaluable assistance, patience, and tolerance during the entire preparation of the manuscript.

D. A. Tugal
O. Tugal

Data
Transmission

Communications and Communication Links

Communication is the interchange of thoughts or opinions by words, letters, or messages. Communication between individuals or offices can be divided into two major categories: verbal and written. The major difference between the two is the speed of interaction.

In verbal communication, responses are immediate and one party can even interrupt the other if necessary. Written communications can have a response time of minutes, hours, or days.

Both methods of communication have their advantages and neither can completely replace the other. There are many applications, however, where verbal communication can be effectively replaced by written or message communication between offices.

Message communication and advantages

Message communication can be much more efficient than verbal communication in several ways. Anyone who has spent half a day dialing a number and getting only busy signals knows one of the ways: with message communication, both parties need not be simultaneously available for communication to take place. The message can be prepared at the originator's convenience, sent, and then read at the receiver's convenience. This improves worker efficiency.

An interesting and unexpected benefit occurs, however, when the two stations are in different time zones. Here message communication can actually be faster than the telephone. Consider the situation where a San Francisco-based office must send an important message to a London location. If sent in the afternoon, the message arrives after the London office has closed for the day. However, that urgent message is immediately available in London at the start of their next working day, long before the San Francisco office reopens. If the telephone had been used to relay this message, it would not be received until the San Francisco office opened on the next day, nearly half a day later than with the message delivery method. Realistically, message communication may be the only reasonable alternative between areas whose working hours may not overlap at all.

Another way in which message communication is more efficient is that it forces the originator to clarify and refine thoughts. Often, a person who starts to organize and write down a message sees holes or inconsistencies in logic that can be rethought and corrected; with the telephone, these problems are not discovered immediately. This can lead to further calls to clear up errors.

Moreover, message communication is generally less expensive than verbal communication, even beyond the savings afforded by its efficiency. Long-distance phone charges can be slashed by communicating via *electronic mail* on a message basis. With electronic message delivery over existing phone lines, the same amount of data can easily be transmitted 20 times (or 40 times) faster than in verbal communication. This assumes the use of a 1200 b/s (or 2400-b/s) modem, which transmits 1200 (or 2400) words per minute as compared to a verbal conversation rate of 60 words per minute.*

Another consideration is that messages can be batched; that is, they can be gathered together and sent on one call. This allows several short messages to be placed together so that the minimum call length on

---

*The 1200 and 60 words per minute is estimated as follows:

1 character = 8 information bits + 1 start bit + 1 stop bit = 10 bits

1 word = 6 characters = 60 bits

$$\frac{1200 \text{ bits/s}}{60 \text{ bits}} \times 60 \text{ s/min} = 1200 \text{ words/min}$$

The average person talks at a rate of 120 words per minute in a conversation, but pauses often to ponder a point and to talk about unrelated subjects. This leaves us with a speed of at most 60 words/min.

long-distance calls is not a factor. Also, lower-priority messages can be saved for overnight delivery to take advantage of lower rates.

Information is usually clearer and easier to understand when it is written. Where large amounts of information are concerned, message communication is the only practical method. Verbal communication is expensive in long-distance communication and very error prone. Message communication can easily be kept for reference; verbal communication is often forgotten. Message preparation involves putting the message into machine readable format that can be sent as data.

The term *data* refers to some kind of information in the form of machine language. Data can be obtained from punched cards, paper tapes, magnetic tapes, disks, computer memories, or directly from machines. The term *data transmission* refers to an electrical transmission of data from one point to another.

A *data communication link* can be defined as a path for electrical transmission between two or more stations or terminals, and it may contain a single wire, a group of wires, a coaxial cable, a special part of the radio-frequency spectrum, or an optical-fiber cable.

Electronic mail

The computer is invading the office environment, updating many functions that have remained relatively unchanged for the past century. Modern offices require not only data manipulation and processing capability, but a fast and efficient means to exchange information. Moreover, because offices are not populated with computer professionals, computer systems must be easy to use. To receive universal acceptance, a system must yield immediately measurable benefits in terms of office productivity and cost savings.

Electronic mail is merely the transmission of person-to-person written communications in electronic form; it is a computer-based mail service which enables customers to send, receive, and file messages electronically using a variety of data terminals and communicating word processors. The Telex network certainly qualifies as an electronic mail system, although constrained by outdated technology.

Voice-band or wider bandwidths are required to accommodate existing and new telecommunication services between various information processing units in the office of the future as well as for electronic mail service. Equipment in a typical office of the future will include:

- Electronic copiers
- High-speed duplicators
- Dictation units

- Automated text handlers
- Communicating word processors
- Computers
- Facsimile transmission systems and facilities
- Teleconferencing transmission systems and facilities
- Microfilm-microfiche readers
- Records of information processing
- Teleconferencing facilities

1.1 Channels and Circuits

A *channel* may be defined as a path within a line through which information flows, where *line* is defined as the physical equipment and configurations used in telecommunications. All channels have limitations on their information-handling abilities, depending upon their electrical and physical characteristics.

Types of channels

There are three basic types of channels: simplex, half-duplex, and full-duplex. As an example, of each channel, consider transmission between points A and B as shown in Fig. 1.1.

Transmission only from A to B and not from B to A describes a simplex channel. These channels are used in loop configurations, such as supermarket checkout terminals.

Transmission from A to B and then from B to A but not simultaneously describes a half-duplex channel. If a two-wire circuit is used, the line must be turned around to reverse the direction of transmission. Line turnaround can be eliminated with a four-wire circuit.

Transmission from A to B and from B to A simultaneously describes a full-duplex channel. Although four-wire circuits are most often used, a two-wire circuit can support full-duplex communications if the fre-

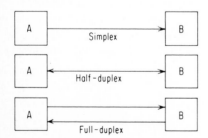

Figure 1.1 Types of channels.

quency spectrum is subdivided into receiving and transmitting channels.

Echoplex is a transmission mode used on full-duplex channels. When the operator presses a key and transmits a character to the computer or another terminal, the character is echoed back to appear on the printer or video display. The operator can see what the computer or terminal is receiving and make any necessary corrections. Echoplex cannot be used with half-duplex channels.

Types of circuits

Circuits are described in terms of two-wire, four-wire, switched (public), and leased (private).

Two-wire and four-wire circuits. A two-wire circuit is usually in the subscriber loop, between the telephone or data set and the local central office. It may be used as a balanced or unbalanced line (one wire is common or ground). A four-wire circuit is used between serving central offices for long-distance connections, with one pair being used for each direction of transmission. It is also used in the subscriber loop as a leased line when full-duplex operation is required. Several voice channels can be packed onto one four-wire voice-grade channel by using multiplexing techniques.

Four-wire circuits are also called single-ended or *unbalanced* circuits in that the data are carried over one wire of a pair. Confusion arises when wire terms are used in data communications. It should be remembered that four-wire is a term derived from the early days of telephones and that today it may not mean four physical wires. Two wires can form an equivalent four-wire circuit when different frequencies are used to convey information back and forth in the channel. In this way simultaneous transmission both ways is possible without the frequencies interfering with each other; the two directions are separated in frequency.

Switched circuits. The telephone network or Telex network used by the public is a switched network. It is called *switched* because a call is automatically switched through to its destination after dialing has been completed. It has the advantage of being universally available and is cheaper than leased lines when usage is low. A different circuit path is selected each time a call is placed. When a number is dialed, the call goes to the local serving central office where it is connected to the called location or transferred to another serving central office for completion.

Other services relate to switching methods used in public data networks. The switching method—i.e., *circuit switching* (or *line switching*), *message switching,* and *packet switching*—determines to a considerable extent the distribution of responsibilities or activities between the network and users.

Circuit switching is used in all telephone networks, in most telegraph networks, and in some data networks. The principle of circuit switching lies in creating one link (physical or virtual) between subscribers or end stations. Blocks are sent over this link without intermediate storing. The link is temporary.

Direct connection of subscribers by means of a tie data link is the advantage of circuit switching. But there are many disadvantages that show themselves especially in data transmission. Because the resulting data link is built from serially connected sections, the quality of the whole data link depends considerably on the quality of the worst section. This limits the speed and worsens the error rate. Although link establishment is normally automatic, the supervising is predominantly manual. When an unsuccessful attempt has been made to establish connection, the user decides if the attempt is to be repeated. An attempt may be unsuccessful not only because all lines are engaged, but also because the addressed station may not be available (it may be busy, not prepared, or failed). For these reasons, message switching and packet switching are being used more and more.

Message switching means that a network takes up the whole data message from a user and the network is fully responsible for delivery of the data message to the addressed station. A user need not trouble any more about the message. The network controls the hops of the message from one *store-and-forward switching* node to another. The message is temporarily stored in each intermediate node; this way better utilization of network resources is achieved. Message switching is used in some Telex or telegraph networks also.

Message-switching systems limit the message lengths and guarantee the delivery times. If the message lengths are not limited, the network operation is inefficient and slow, because many sections are blocked by long messages. This deteriorates the throughput substantially and makes the cost of such data transmission much higher. Therefore packet-switching systems were elaborated and put into operation, both experimental and routine.

Packet switching utilizes the same basic principle as does message switching, i.e., the store-and-forward principle. Packets are data blocks of reasonably limited length and of well-structured and agreed-on formats. The limited length and unified format make implementation much simpler and operation much more efficient.

Although not always practiced in packet-switching networks, sending packets of one message over different paths or routes through the network allows better utilization of partial data links and improvement of other performance measures. Allowing packets to travel via different routes brings some new problems, such as ensuring proper sequencing and reordering.

In this connection, two broadly discussed data transmission services have to be mentioned here. They are *datagram service* and the *virtual-circuit (virtual-call) service.*

In *datagram service,* the principle of using different routes for packets, called datagrams, is utilized. However, sequencing or reordering is not included in the subnetwork (i.e., in the packet-switching network), users are supposed to take care of the proper order of packets and some other matters. In this sense the datagram network transfers individual and independent packets.

In *virtual circuits,* different routes for packets are not used, or at least, are not made visible to users. There is no need to reorder the delivered packets, since they travel over the same virtual circuit and cannot become out of order.

There can be permanent virtual circuits created in the virtual-circuit network. These are analogous to leased lines in telephone or telegraph networks.

Figure 1.2 shows a survey of switching services that are used in public data networks.

Leased (dedicated) circuits. A leased line is a permanent circuit for private use within a communication network, with the line directly between the two locations or routed through a serving central office. In this office, which contains one or more wire centers (distribution frames), the leased line is physically connected to dedicated channels or equipment, independent of the public switching and signaling equipment in the office.

Where usage is high, leased lines are cheaper than switched lines. For some applications, the biggest advantage of a leased line is that no setup time is required. Just pick up a telephone set or throw a switch and the connection is made. This eliminates the setup time

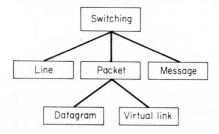

Figure 1.2 Services in public networks.

required on a switched line for addressing (dialing), switching (call routing), ringing, and obtaining billing information. Since the circuit is permanent, the same path is always used and conditioning can be applied to the cricuit to improve transmission quality.

While speeds of up to 4800 b/s are possible without conditioning, generally at speeds above 1200 b/s some form of conditioning is required to overcome the effects of delay and attenuation distortion. Line conditioning is discussed in Sec. 2.1.

Comparison of switched and leased channel links

From the point of view of communication control, the difference between switched links and leased links is twofold.

First, switched links must be selected from the set of all links available in the public network and assigned to subscribers for one call or for one session. When the subscribers finish their communication and have nothing more to say to each other, the link is returned to the network; i.e., the link is released.

Second, switched links have a substantially larger bit error rate than leased links, which means they require error control. Typical bit error rates in the existing public networks is given in Table 1.1. The reader must keep in mind that there are differences not only between public networks in various countries, and between different public networks in one country, but also between values measured at different time intervals (days, months, and hours). It should be emphasized that good error control is provided in packet-switching networks, resulting in low residual error rates.

1.2   Transmission Media

The early telegraph links carried signals at speeds up to about 30 words per minute, or about 15 b/s. Until the invention of carrier systems,

TABLE 1.1   Comparison of Error Rates in Typical Links and Paths

Type of link	Bit error rate
Switched-telephone lines	5×10^{-4}
Telex	10^{-4}
Leased telegraph	10^{-5}
Leased telephone	5×10^{-6}
Message-switched network	10^{-8}
Public line switched data network	10^{-9}
Packet-switched data network	10^{-12}

every telephone connection required an individual pair of wires. Today we are laying down cables which carry many thousands of voice channels, each with a capacity of 9600 b/s. This section briefly defines the transmission media of main interest today.

Open wire

In early years most telephone connections were made by means of wire pairs stretched between telephone poles. The wires were copper or steel-coated copper. One pair of wires might have carried up to 24 individual telephone channels.

Although many miles of open wire are still seen in rural districts and in under-developed countries, open wire is rarely seen today in urban areas.

Telephone cable

In the wire-pair cables which have replaced open-wire pairs, the conductors are insulated and brought close together. Many of them may be packed into one cable, which would tend to increase crosstalk considerably. To offset this, the conductors are twisted in pairs to minimize the electromagnetic interference between one pair and another. Different twist lengths are used for adjacent pairs. The group of conductors is wrapped in a tough protective sheath. Cables laid in cities have many hundreds of wire pairs in one cable.

The wires in cables are much smaller than the wires for open pairs. Because of this the resistance of the wires is higher and the signal needs to be amplified more frequently than with open-wire pairs.

Twisted-wire cable can carry more than one voice channel with multiplexing techniques. It is common for one wire pair on a trunk route to carry 12 voice channels simultaneously in two directions, using frequencies up to about 268 kHz.

Recent developments in repeater design permit frequencies of 1 MHz to be transmitted over wire pairs. Such repeaters would be spaced at intervals of about 2 km, allowing picturephone signals to be sent over wire pairs.

The capacitance between conductors is much greater in a cable pair than in open-wire lines, because the conductors are much closer together. This has a more serious effect at high frequencies than at low frequencies.

Submarine cable

The first submarine cables had no repeaters and carried telegraph signals. The transmission of multichannel speech over a submarine-cable system involves the provision of submerged repeaters and their associated special terminal and power-feeding equipment. Because of long spacing between amplifiers, the upper frequency at which the cables can be operated is lower than with land cables. The capacity of the first cables was therefore only 48 voice channels, and two cables were used for two-way talking. Cables laid recently carry more than 6000 two-way conversations in one cable. Cable capacity is increased by utilization of the TASI (time assignment speech interpolation) technique (discussed in Sec. 4.4).

Coaxial cable

A coaxial cable can transmit much higher frequencies than a wire pair. It consists of a hollow copper cylinder or other cylindrical conductor surrounding a single-wire conductor. The space between the cylindrical shell and the inner conductor is filled with an insulator. This may be plastic or may be air. Several coaxial tubes are often bound together in one large cable. A number of twisted wire pairs are packed in among the coaxial tubes and are usually used for control purposes. At higher frequencies there is virtually no crosstalk between the separate coaxial tubes in such a link because the current tends to flow on the inside of the outer shell and the outside of the inner wire. Because of this shielding from noise and crosstalk, the signal can be dropped to a lower level before amplification, which is not possible with telephone cables.

A very large number of telephone calls can be transmitted together on a coaxial-cable system. Whereas a single wire pair commonly carries 12 or 24 voice channels, one single coaxial tube commonly carries 3600 to 10,800 two-way conversations. The main reason for this higher capacity is that the signal attenuation does not become severe until very high frequencies.

Coaxial-cable circuits give a higher velocity of propagation that varies only very slightly with frequency, thus giving very little delay distortion. The propagation velocity along a coaxial cable at frequencies above 4 kHz is approximately equal to the velocity of light, or if the insulator is solid it is 25 to 45 percent lower than the air.

A loaded wire pair gives less distortion, but the transmission velocity is lower. It is normally about 15,000 to 32,000 km/s at voice frequencies. The signal in a coaxial cable can thus travel at 10 times the speed of an equivalent signal in a loaded wire pair. This is of value because it often removes the need for echo suppressors.

Waveguides

A waveguide is a metal tube which radio waves of very high frequency travel through. There are two main types of waveguide, rectangular and circular. Rectangular waveguides have been in use as the feed between microwave antennas and their associated equipment. They are rarely employed for distances over a few hundred meters. They consist of a rectangular copper or brass tube, 30 to 40 cm across or smaller. Radiation at microwave frequencies travels through this tube.

Circular waveguides are pipes about 5 cm in diameter. They are constructed with precision and are capable of transmitting frequencies much higher than rectangular waveguides. In the helical waveguide a fine enameled copper wire is wound tightly around the inside in a helix, surrounded by a layer of thin glass fibers and then by a carbon layer. The whole is encased in a strong steel case and bonded to it with epoxy resin. The purpose of this construction is to attenuate undesired modes of wave propagation. Waveguides are not flexible and cannot go around sharp bends.

The attenuation in waveguides actually becomes less as frequency increases up to about 100,000 MHz. A typical waveguide system carries about 230,000 two-way telephone calls simultaneously.

Radio

Each of the above means of transmission has used a metallic medium. Various circumstances, such as mountainous terrain and urban development, led to the consideration of radio as a transmission medium. The high-frequency band of the radio spectrum occupies 3 to 30 MHz, which is much lower than that of microwave. High-frequency radio transmission is reflected by the ionosphere. Because of the movement of and changes in the ionosphere, it is subject to fading, distortion, and periodic blackouts. Long-distance high-frequency telephone or telegraph circuits rarely form part of a computer data transmission system, except for transmitting telegraph signals from remote parts of the world. The data error rate is extremely high, and error detection and automatic retransmission are needed. It is still used for international telegraphy and for telephone to ships at sea.

The extremely low frequency radio (ELF) band occupies the 30- to 300-Hz part of the spectrum. It enables submarines to receive information while preserving their covert status. ELF signals penetrate hundreds of meters through seawater and permit one-way message transmission to deep-running subs that remain hidden from detection by hostile forces.

Microwave radio

Like coaxial cable, microwave links carry thousands of voice channels and are in widespread use for the transmission of television signals. A microwave route, however, carries much less traffic than the largest coaxial routes. Frequency bands for microwave transmission are allocated in the 1000–15,000 MHz spectrum. It needs line-of-sight transmission, and relaying antennas are all on towers within sight of one another. Relay towers are usually spaced 30 to 50 km apart. A long-distance microwave circuit has fewer amplifiers than a coaxial-cable link of the same length. The coaxial-cable system has amplifiers every 2 to 6 km. It is a disadvantage to have too many amplifiers because a slight defect in them is cumulative. For television transmission, for example, the amplification needs to be held constant within narrow limits for parts of the signal at different frequencies. If it has to pass through a thousand amplifiers with similar characteristics, each one of the thousand must be very exact indeed in this respect. This is difficult and expensive to engineer. Therefore, microwave links have come into wide use for television transmission. Fortunately the television peak hours do not coincide with the peak usage of telephones, so the same facility can be used by day for telephones. One television channel can carry 1200 telephone channels. Microwave antennas are fixed rigidly to focus a beam of the narrowest angle possible on their distant associated antennas. Beam angle is about 1°, and a typical antenna size is about 3 m in diameter. Microwave radio is scattered by hills and other objects. The beams from the antennas must clear trees and buildings, otherwise their reflections may cause echoes.

Different moisture and temperature layers can cause the beam to bend and vary in amplitude, just as we sometimes see light shimmering over a hot surface or causing minor mirages along a road surface in the sun. Occasionally these effects can cause fading. Rain can change the attenuation slightly, especially at the higher microwave frequencies, and occasionally trouble is caused by reflection from a flock of birds, helicopters, or new skyscrapers in a city. To a limited extent automatic compensation for changes in the radio attenuation is built into the repeaters. In addition to the long-haul trunks, many short microwave links of lower capacity are in use. Television companies use them for outside broadcasting. Telephone companies find it convenient in some locations to use them as feeders to the main exchange. The army uses a portable microwave receiver-transmitter as a field telephone.

A major problem with microwave is radio interference. Many cities are now congested with criss-crossing microwave beams. This congestion seriously restricts the siting of satellite earth stations which use the same microwave frequencies.

Tropo scatter

The troposphere is lower than the ionosphere and more stable. It extends up to about 10 km. The ionosphere is above 50 km. The troposphere scatters radio waves and this is used for telecommunication links of up to 1000 km where it is not possible or economic to construct other links. There are tropospheric scatter circuits in Alaska, from the United States to Nassau, from Scotland to the Shetland Islands in Britain's North Sea oil fields, and in NATO communication links. The tropospheric scatter circuit is used to transmit beyond the visible horizon. The received signal is the result of a multiplicity of reflections of different paths from the troposphere.

Tropospheric-scatter circuits use very large (18 to 36 m in diameter) antennas and a higher transmitter power than microwave circuits. Typically 72 voice channels can be sent on long links. Tropospheric-scatter circuits are subject to fading and are affected by atmospheric conditions; however, they are more dependable than high-frequency circuits using the ionosphere. Their operating cost is higher than that of the other media.

Satellites

A communication satellite provides a form of microwave relay. It is high in the sky and therefore can relay signals over long distances that would not be possible in a single link on earth because of the curvature of the earth, mountains, and atmospheric conditions. Today's communication satellites appear to remain stationary above the equator at a height of 35,800 km. Satellites are powered by solar batteries and handle several thousand voice channels. Because the high-power transmission from their earth stations interferes with terrestrial microwave links, the earth stations are located outside the cities.

A satellite link has a few differences when compared to a terrestrial link, as listed below:

1. A 257-ms transmission delay in each direction.
2. A very large number of terminals can share the facility.
3. The terminals can be scattered in a large portion of the world without additional transmission system installation.
4. A satellite channel is a broadcast facility, not a point-to-point link.
5. A transmitting station can monitor its own transmission by observing relayed satellite transmission.

Satellite communications are discussed in Chap. 8.

Optical communications

Optical communication links utilize optical-fiber waveguides, the atmosphere, and water as transmission media.

Optical fibers act like waveguides for the light frequencies of 10^{14} to 10^{15} Hz (3000 to 300 nm). These are more than 10,000 times the frequencies of microwaves and hence have the potential of providing an extremely wide bandwidth. Optical-fiber transmission and advantages are discussed in Chap. 10.

An optical beam propagating through the earth's atmosphere is altered by atmospheric absorption, scattering, and turbulence. These factors may act alone or collectively to change, often adversely, both the spatial and temporal intensity distribution of an optical beam. Atmospheric absorption is a spectrally selective phenomenon when the absorbent is gaseous in nature, and the principal gaseous absorbers are water vapor, carbon dioxide, and ozone. Since these gases absorb at narrow spectral lines rather than bands, the detailed transmissivity of the atmosphere as a function of wavelength is highly complex.

The temporal intensity distribution of an optical beam is altered by atmospheric turbulence. Since temperature changes the refractive index of the atmosphere, temperature gradients over an optical path will cause deviations in a ray as it passes between regions of differing refractive index. Intensity fluctuations are most pronounced when the optical beam passes near landforms which are good thermal absorbers and therefore good thermal emitters. Asphalt, rooftops, and other features can induce severe intensity fluctuations in an optical beam propagating nearby.

A series of aircraft-to-submarine tests have verified that a 1-W, short-pulse, high-repetition blue-green laser can penetrate clouds and seawater to a depth of several hundreds of meters without distortion and can transmit data in short bursts at data rates up to several kilobits per second.

1.3   Communication-Link Configurations

A communication link is intended to connect other channels or circuits. Data communication links are represented by modems, serial communication interface circuits, and the communication channels. Data-communication-link controls are required to operate a link but not the computers, terminals, or I/O devices at each end of the link.

The nature of the selected communication channel tends to dictate the selections of options in all other parts of the link. There are two basic communication-link configurations: point-to-point and multipoint. These are shown in Fig. 1.3.

Note

Modems are replaced with frequency-division or time-division multiplexing (FDM or TDM) for a baseband local-area network (LAN). Refer to Fig. 12.4.

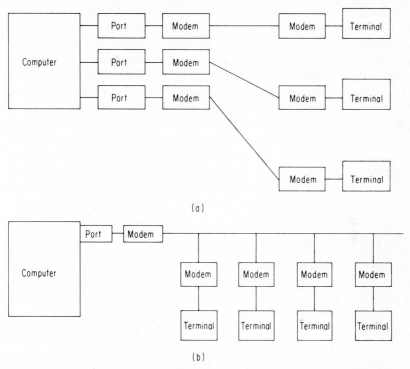

Figure 1.3 Communication-link configurations. (*a*) Point-to-point; (*b*) multipoint.

Point-to-point communication links

A point-to-point communication link is a communication facility between only two stations. All the transmissions over the links must be
between two stations operating on the link. The point-to-point link can
be established over leased (nonswitched) communication lines or a
switched network. On a leased line (permanent-type connection), the
transmission is always between the same two stations and may be full-
duplex or half-duplex. On a switched network, the link is disconnected
after the two stations complete their transmissions. A new link is
created for each subsequent transmission by standard dialing procedures which can be manual or automatic. The new link may be established with any other station in the network. Information flow is in
one direction at a time as in half-duplex on the switched network.

Multipoint communication links

For multipoint operation, often called *multidrop,* one station in the
network is always designated as the control or primary station. The
remaining stations are designated as tributary or secondary stations.

The control station controls all transmissions within the multipoint link, which is normally established over leased (nonswitched) lines. This is also called a *centralized multipoint operation*. The control station initiates all transmissions by selecting or polling a secondary station. Any transmission over the link is between the designated primary station and one of the secondary stations; the other stations in the network are in a passive monitoring mode.

Multipoint channels may be full-duplex or half-duplex. Frequently, only a primary station on a multipoint channel will operate full-duplex, while the secondary stations are half-duplex. This is known as *multi-multipoint operation*.

1.4 Analog Transmission Versus Digital Transmission

Basically there are two ways in which information of any type can be transmitted over a telecommunication medium: analog or digital. Analog means that a continuous range of frequencies is transmitted, like sound and light. If we wanted to transmit high-fidelity music along telephone wires, a continuous range of frequencies would be sent from 30 to 20,000 Hz. The current on the wire would vary continuously in the same manner as the sound humans hear. Concerned about the economics, we use only 300 to 3400 Hz on telephone lines, which is enough to make a person's voice recognizable and intelligible.

On the other hand, digital data transmission means that a stream of on-off pulses is sent, as in computer circuits. The pulses are referred to as *bits*.

Figure 1.4 shows an analog signal and a digital signal. A transmission path can be designed to carry either one or the other, as depicted in Fig. 1.5.

The telephone channel reaching our home today is an analog channel, capable of transmitting a certain range of frequencies. If computer

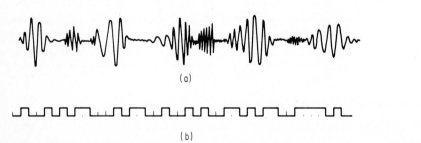

(a)

(b)

Figure 1.4 (*a*) Analog and (*b*) digital signals.

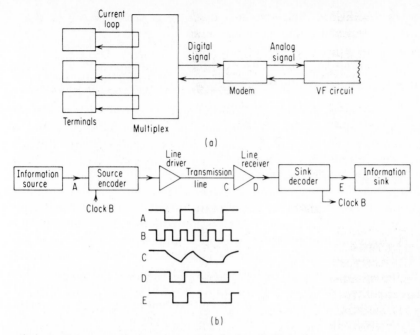

(a)

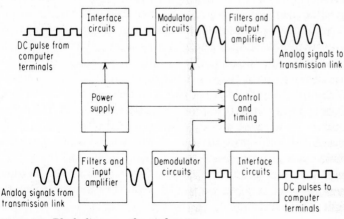

(b)

Figure 1.5 Data transmission systems. (a) Analog; (b) digital.

data are sent over a telephone channel, they must be digital bit streams
converted into an analog signal by using a device known as a modem
(Fig. 1.6). This allows the use of the world's analog channels for sending
digital data. On the other hand, where digital channels have been
constructed, it is possible to transmit the human voice over them by
converting it into a digital form. This technique is called *pulse-code*

Figure 1.6 Block diagram of a modem.

modulation (PCM). Similarly, any analog signal can be digitized for transmission in this manner. However, a television signal would need a much higher bit rate than sound transmission. The bit rate needed is dependent on the bandwidth or range of frequencies of the analog signal as well as the number of different amplitude levels desired to reproduce.

The economic circumstances favoring digital transmission stem from two main factors. First, it is becoming possible to build channels of high bandwidth that are high in information-carrying capacity. Indeed, it is now appreciated that many existing wire-pair channels which represent an enormous financial investment could be made to carry more information traffic than at present. However, a high-level multiplexing is needed to make use of high-capacity channels. The second advantage is that in analog transmission whenever the signal is amplified, the noise and distortion are also amplified; they are cumulative. With digital transmission, however, each repeater station regenerates the pulses. Therefore, the pulse train can travel through a dispersive noisy medium, but instead of becoming more and more distorted until eventually parts are unrecognizable, it is repeatedly reconstructed and thus remains impervious to most of the corrosion of the medium. Of course, an exceptionally large noise impulse may destroy one or more pulses so that they cannot be reconstructed by repeater stations.

A distinctive characteristic of digital transmission is that it requires a greater frequency bandwidth. To send a given quantity of telephone conversations, for example, a much higher bandwidth is needed than that used by today's systems. However, because the signal is regenerated frequently, the PCM signal can operate with a lower signal-to-noise (S/N) ratio. Thus there is a tradeoff between bandwidth and S/N ratio in the transmission of a given quantity of information. If, for example, a given pair of wires is used, then a wider range of frequencies can be employed for transmission because of the frequent regeneration of the signal, and only two states of a binary signal are needed to be detected, not a continuous range of amplitudes as in the analog signal.

An additional economic factor is the rapidly increasing use of data transmission. Although data transmission still employs only a small proportion of the total bandwidth in use, it is increasing much more rapidly than other uses of the telecommunication networks. Data are transmitted much more economically over a digital circuit than over an analog circuit. With the present state of the art, 10 times as much data can be sent over a digital voice line as over an analog voice line. As an example, one voice-grade line carries 24×50-Bd FDM analog channels; the same voice line can carry 176×50-Bd channels through a 9600 b/s digital transmission.

Thus four factors affect the economics in favor of digital transmission.

1. The trend to much higher bandwidth facilities

2. The decreasing cost of logic circuitry, which is used in coding and decoding the digital signals and in multiplexing and switching them

3. The increase in capacity resulting from the use of digital repeaters at frequent intervals on a line

4. The rapidly increasing need to transmit digital data on the networks

In terms of the immediate economics of today's common carriers, pressed for capacity, digital transmission is appealing for short-distance links, because with relatively low-cost electronics it can substantially increase the capacity of existing wire pairs. This is particularly important in congested city streets. An important long-term advantage is the fact that all signals, i.e., voice, television, facsimile, and computers, become a stream of similar-looking pulses. Consequently, they will not interfere with one another and will not make different demands on the engineering of the channels. In an analog signal format, television and data are much more demanding on the fidelity of transmission than on the speech and thus create more interference when transmitted with other signals. Eventually, perhaps, there will be an integrated network in which all signals travel together digitally.

Digital data may be transferred in serial or in parallel. In parallel transmission each bit of the character is transmitted on a single wire. Computers and high-speed data systems transmit parallel data wherever they are in close proximity. However, as the distance between these devices increases, multiwires become more costly and the drivers become more complex. Serial transmission is preferred to parallel transmission in data transmission.

Refer to the following CCITT recommendations for detailed information on parallel data transmission:

V.19   Modems for parallel data transmission using telephone signaling frequencies

V.20   Parallel data transmission modems standardized for universal use in the general switched telephone network

Classification of bandwidths and data speeds

Analog transmission can be divided into three ranges with respect to the bandwidth utilized. The *voice band* is assumed to occupy 300 to 3400 Hz in telephony, although the audible human hearing range is from 32 to 16,000 Hz. Frequency bands wider than voice band are referred to as *wideband,* although a communication channel with a bandwidth less than voice band is named *narrow band.* The various data transmission speeds are usually separated into three ranges:

Low speed	0–300 b/s	Usually used for teleprinters
Medium speed	600–4800 b/s	Used for minicomputer-to-printer or display-type terminals
High speed	Above 9600 b/s	Used for computer-to-computer communications

References

Martin, James: "Transmission Media," *Telecommunications and the Computer,* Prentice-Hall, Englewood Cliffs, N.J., 1976, chap. 9.

Hewlett Packard, Palo Alto, Calif.: *Training Manual Guidebook to Data Communications,* Manual Part No. 5955-1715. Channels and circuits.

Weisberger, Alan J.: "Communication Channels and Facilities," *Data Communications Handbook,* Signetics Corp., Sunnyvale, Calif., chap. 1.

Transmissions over Voice-Grade Circuits

A voice circuit consists of one or more facilities connected to provide a path for communicating at voice frequency between two or more points. The facilities may consist of metallic cable pairs, open-wire lines, coaxial cable, microwave radio link, fiber optic, or even a satellite circuit. The last connection in the chain is usually the local loop, provided by twisted cable pairs which connect the station equipment to the central office. Station equipment interfaces with the customer service requirements and the capabilities of the voice-frequency (VF) circuit. Conditioning (equalization), signaling, speech, speech plus data, alternate voice-data, and loopback are typical of station equipment functions; refer to Fig. 2.1.

To determine the suitability of a voice circuit for data transmission becomes more critical with the increase of data speed and the increase of distances between communication centers. Certain requirements for data circuits are less demanding than for voice circuits, whereas other requirements are more stringent.

Since a coherent conversation on a circuit does not necessarily mean that it is suitable for data transmission, another method must be used to evaluate the circuit. The speed at which data can be transmitted is a direct function of the available bandwidth. For example, the basic two-wire switched telephone channel is considered to have a usable

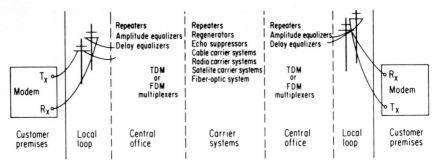

Figure 2.1   A complex data transmission circuit.

bandwidth of 300 to 3000 Hz. A basic four-wire voice-grade channel, dedicated to serve fixed sites on a continuous basis, is described as a 3002 channel in the United States. Dedicated lines may be used for alternate voice-data or data transmission only and will support data transmission usually at 2400 b/s without special line conditioners. Speeds 4800 b/s and higher can be achieved on a single voice channel by adding amplitude and delay equalization. Circuit parameters are controlled by attenuation distortion, envelope delay, signal-to-noise (S/N) ratio, nonlinear distortion, impulse noise, and phase-jitter characteristics. In many instances poor transmission performance may result from not one but a combination of line deficiencies. Performance is generally evaluated on the basis of a long-term error rate. Many types of data processing equipment are designed to detect the occurrence of a high percentage of errors or to correct the errors at the receiving terminal through error-correcting codes; therefore poorer transmission performance may be acceptable in these channels.

Various channel characteristics interact. A characteristic may have a value outside the suggested limits, with the overall system performance still meeting our requirements. The overall system, as a result, is rendered vulnerable to a slight deterioration of any other channel characteristics.

Most of the channel characteristics in this book are based upon the long-term probability of 1 error per 100,000 (10^{-5}) bits transmitted. Therefore recommended values are guides for well-engineered circuits. CCITT recommendations should be considered for international circuits, which may require slightly different values than domestic transmission requirements. Note that CCITT levels and measurements on voice-grade circuits always refer to 800 Hz unless otherwise stated.

Refer to CCITT Recs. M.1020 and M.1040 for characteristics of international leased circuits, to H.12 for transmission channels other than telephone signals, and to H.22 for international VF telegraph links which are summarized at the end of the chapter.

Tables summarizing CCITT recommendations concerning "Line transmissions for telephone circuits" are given in Table 1 of CCITT Vol. III, 1976.

In this book all values obtained at 1004 Hz are normally referred to as those obtained at 1000 Hz. The reader should keep in mind that all 1000-Hz tests are conducted with 1004 Hz.

2.1 Overall Attenuation

Overall attenuation, also called *insertion loss of transmission system,* has to be determined prior to the installation of data equipment for mixed-gage loaded and unloaded lines, and an approximation should be made by summing the individual insertion losses of equipment in the circuit.

There are short and long signal-level variations, mostly reductions, which affect data transmission channels and channel failures. As a quick reference, recommended attenuation values in a voice-grade channel are given below.

Recommended values
1. Overall attenuation from subscriber to subscriber not to exceed 16 dB for the frequencies in the band.
2. Attenuation of 10 dB at 1000 Hz is a typical value for 1200 b/s modems.
3. Marginal attenuation values:
   a. 30 dB at 1000 Hz
   b. 35 dB at 1700 Hz
4. Transmission circuit should be equipped with facilities which are able to adjust additional 8-dB losses at 1000 Hz.
5. Daily stability of the transmission system should be within ±4 dB.

Typical signal levels are depicted in Fig. 2.2.

Signal power, signal level, decibel, and neper

Basically, level is an expression of relative signal strength at various points in a communication circuit. Power, on the other hand, is an expresson of absolute signal strength at a specific point in a circuit.

In voice circuits the term *level* is used to express the relative amount of power at various points in a circuit. Power always designates a definite quantity, which is defined in electrical terms as the rate at

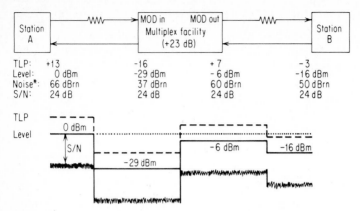

TLP:	+13	-16	+7	-3
Level:	0 dBm	-29 dBm	-6 dBm	-16 dBm
Noise*:	66 dBrn	37 dBrn	60 dBrn	50 dBrn
S/N:	24 dB	24 dB	24 dB	24 dB

Figure 2.2 Transmission levels on a voice circuit. (*C-notched noise level is shown as 53 dBrnc0 at all points for illustrative purposes only.)

which electric energy is taken from or supplied to a device. The most common unit for expressing power is the *watt*.

In practice, relative levels in a telephone circuit are expressed in dB (decibels) rather than in arithmetic ratios. If two powers p_1 and p_2 are expressed in the same units (watts, milliwatts, etc.), the definition of decibel is

$$D = 10 \log_{10} \frac{p_1}{p_2} \quad \text{dB}$$

$$= 10(\log_{10} p_1 - \log_{10} p_2) \quad \text{dB}$$

If power levels are related to a p_0 level, the equation can be written as

$$D = 10(\log_{10} p_1 - \log_{10} p_2 - \log_{10} p_0 + \log_{10} p_0)$$

$$= 10 \left(\log_{10} \frac{p_1}{p_0} \right) - 10 \left(\log_{10} \frac{p_2}{p_0} \right) \quad \text{dB}$$

Thus the value of this difference is independent of the value assigned to p_0.

It is convenient to use a value of 1 mW for p_0 in voice transmission, then p_1 and p_2 are expressed in milliwatts and relative level is expressed in dBm:

$$D_1 = 10 \log_{10} \frac{p_1}{1 \text{ mW}} \quad \text{dBm}$$

Note however that the level difference between p_1 and p_2 is measured in dB, not in dBm. Since the relation between power, voltage, and current may be written as

$$p = \frac{v^2}{R} = Ri^2$$

voltage and current levels can be obtained as

$$D = 10 \log_{10} \frac{v_1^2}{v_2^2} = 20 \log_{10} \frac{v_1}{v_2} \quad \text{dB}$$

$$D = 20 \log_{10} \frac{i_1}{i_2} \quad \text{dB}$$

Another level unit widespread in use is the *neper* (Np), defined as

$$N = \log_e \frac{i_1}{i_2} \quad \text{Np}$$

The relation between decibels and nepers can be written as

$$\text{dB} = 8.686 \text{ Np} = \frac{\text{Np}}{0.1151}$$

Transmission level point (TLP)

To specify the signal levels at various points along a channel, a common reference level should be used. To provide a common reference point, in the transmission direction at each end of a channel the zero dB transmission level point (0TLP) is designated; the 0TLP figure gives the maximum power applicable at this point. All other level points on the overall circuit should be referred to 0TLP. The abbreviation dBm0 is commonly used to indicate the signal magnitude in dBm referred to 0TLP.

The transmission level point is the ratio (in dB) of power of a signal at that point to the power of the same signal at the reference point:

$$\text{TLP (dB)} + \text{(dBm0)} = \text{signal power (dBm)}$$

The TLP value is given in dB, like -3 TLP.

CCITT recommends -13 dBmO (13 dB below 0TLP) for most cases of data transmissions. For example, for -3 TLP, the maximum allowable power is -3 dBm (0TLP); for -13 dBm0 operation, the actual level measured is -16 dBm at that point.

TABLE 2.1 Recommended TLP Values for Different Types
of Circuits in the United States

		Conditioned	Unconditioned
1. Overseas	X	0	+5
	R	0	+5 (+2, −7)
2. Intrastate	X	0	+13
	R	0	−3
3. Interstate	X	+5	+5
	R	−7	+1, −7
4. Local	X	+5	+5
	R	−7	+1, −7

Transmission levels for -13 dBm0 operation are given in Fig. 2.2. Recommended TLP values for different types of circuits in the United States are given in Table 2.1, CCITT recommendations of limiting power for each 50-Bd telegraph channel of a frequency-modulated voice-frequency telegraph (FMVFT) system are given in Table 2.2.

CCITT Rec. H.51 specifies data power levels on voice circuits as follows:

On multichannel carrier systems, the mean power of data circuits should be around -15 dBm0 for each direction of transmission; -10 dBm0 should not be exceeded. However -13 dBm0 is a reasonable figure for each data transmission direction.

The maximum power output of the subscriber's apparatus into the line shall not exceed 1 mW. For systems transmitting tones continuously, for example, in frequency-modulation systems, the maximum power level at the zero relative level point should be -10 dBm0. When transmission of data is discontinued for any appreciable time, the power level should be preferably reduced to -20 dBm0 or even lower.

For systems not transmitting tones continuously, as in amplitude-modulation systems, higher levels up to -6 dBm0 can be used.

For frequency-modulation phototelegraph transmission, -10 dBm0 is recommended. Refer to Sec. 3.5 and CCITT Recs. H.41 and M.880.

TABLE 2.2 Normal Limiting Power Per Telegraph Channel in a 50-Bd FMVFT

System	Permissible mean power per telegraph channel	
	μW0	dBm0
12 telegraph channels or less	11.25	−19.5
18 telegraph channels	7.5	−21.3
24 (or 22) telegraph channels	5.6	−22.5

SOURCE: CCITT Recs. H.23 and M.810.

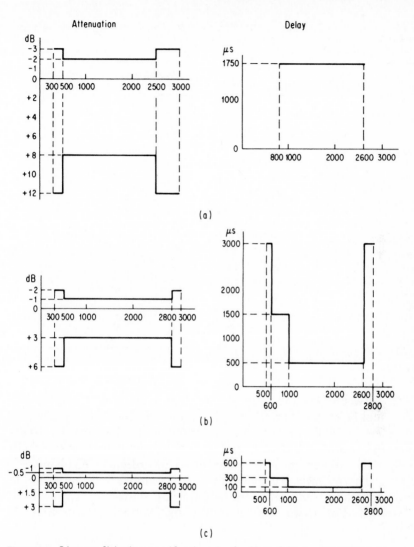

Figure 2.3 Line-conditioning specifications in the United States. (*a*) 3002 basic; (*b*) C2; (*c*) C5.

Line conditioning

Lines suitable for transmission of high-speed data are provided by conditioning the basic channel. A conditioned circuit must meet certain tariff specifications. In the United States, line-conditioning specifications of voice-grade channels are given in FCC Tariff 260 (refer to Fig. 2.3 and Table 2.3).

The basic 3002 line specifies that envelope delay distortion is less than 1750 μs from 800 to 2600 Hz. Attenuation varies between 0 and

TABLE 2.3 C1–C5 Line-Conditioning Specifications for Series 3002 Data Channels per FCC Tariff 260*

Characteristics	Uncond. 3002 chan.	C1	C2	C3 Access lines	C3 Trunks	C4	C5
				C3			
				Access lines	Trunks		
			Frequency response in dB				
0.3–3.2 kHz		−2 to + 6	−2 to +6			−2 to +5	
0.3–3.0 kHz	−3 to +12			−0.8 to +3	−0.8 to +2		
0.3–2.7 kHz							−1 to +3
0.5–3.0 kHz			−2 to +3			−2 to +3	
0.5–2.8 kHz				−0.5 to +1.5	−0.5 to +1		−0.5 to +1.5
0.5–2.5 kHz	−2 to +8						
1.0–2.4 kHz		−1.0 to +3					
2.7–3.0 kHz		−3 to +12					
			Max. envelope delay distortion in μs, any two freq. 200 Hz apart				
0.5–3.0 kHz						<3000	
0.5–2.8 kHz			<3000	650	500		600
0.6–3.0 kHz						<1500	
0.6–2.6 kHz			<1500	300	260		300
0.8–2.8 kHz						<500	
0.8–2.6 kHz	1750	<1750					
1.0–2.6 kHz			<500	100	80	<300	100
1.0–2.4 kHz		<1000					

*Each degree of line conditioning provides tighter specifications on envelope delay and frequency response.

15 dB between 300 and 2900 Hz, with an average of 7 dB; the S/N ratio must be better than 24 dB. The second-harmonic distortion must not exceed −25 dB, and the third harmonic must not exceed −30 dB.

CCITT recommends the overall loss limits between end-to-end offices. Group delay distortion is not mentioned in ordinary telephone-type circuits. These limits are shown in Figs. 2.4 and 2.5. As an example, C2 conditioning is described in the following words.

Type C2—For a two-point or multipoint channel (private-line service):

1. The envelope delay distortion shall not exceed:
   a. Between 1000 and 2600 Hz, a maximum difference of 500 μs
   b. Between 600 and 2600 Hz, a maximum difference of 1500 μs
   c. Between 500 and 2800 Hz, a maximum difference of 3000 μs
2. The loss deviation with frequency (from 1000-Hz reference) shall not exceed:
   a. Between 500 and 2800 Hz, − 1 to +3 dB
   b. Between 300 and 3000 Hz, − 2 to +6 dB

Note

On a multipoint channel arranged for switching, conditioning in accordance with the above specifications is applicable only when in the unswitched mode.

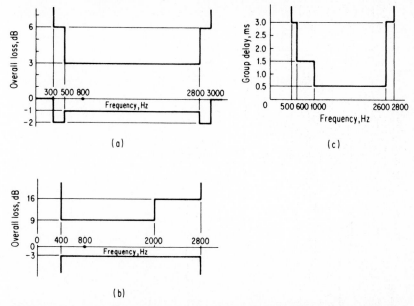

Figure 2.4 Limits for overall loss and group delay on a telephone-type leased circuit. (*a*) Limits for the overall loss relative to that at 800 Hz (H.12B, M.1020); (*b*) limits for the overall loss relative to that at 800 Hz (H.12A, M.1040); (*c*) limits for the group delay relative to the minimum measured group delay in the 500- to 2800-Hz band (H.12B, M.1020). [CCITT Recommendations. Ordinary circuits: H.12A and M.1040 (international); special-quality circuits: H.12B and M.1020 (international).]

D conditioning is an option introduced to handle 9600-b/s operation. Either D or C or both types of conditioning can be provided on the same unconditioned channel to limit impairments. The C conditioning controls attenuation and envelope delay distortion. The D conditioning controls the S/N ratio and nonlinear distortion. A high-speed data set with automatic equalizer may perform best on a 3002 (unconditioned) facility with D conditioning only.

Such channels meet the following specifications:

1. Signal-to-C-notched-noise ratio, 28 dB
2. Nonlinear distortion:
   a. Signal-to-second-order distortion, 35 dB
   b. Signal-to-third-order distortion, 40 dB

Most of the high-speed data sets of today will operate satisfactorily over C2 conditioned lines. Why, then, is there a need to condition lines to specifications tighter than C2? There are several reasons. Customers on leased circuits are constantly seeking improved performance or higher speeds or both. Many data circuits are cascaded or built up from a number of separate sections, and the entire tandem circuit must have

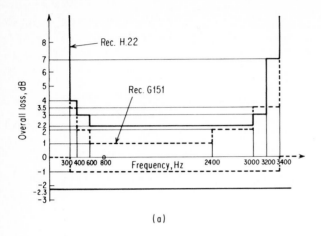

(a)

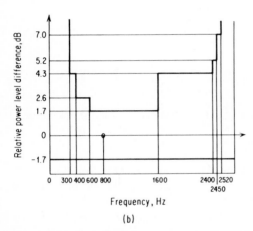

Frequency, Hz

(b)

Figure 2.5 Limits for overall loss on an international voice-frequency telegraph line relative to the value measured at 800 Hz (a) with 4-kHz end-to-end sections and (b) using the band 300 to 2600 Hz. (CCITT Rec. H.22.)

end-to-end C2 characteristic. This usually requires that the individual sections must be conditioned to C5 or equivalent to achieve C2 end to end. Another need occurs on international data circuits where noise and phase jitter may be severe. More stringent conditioning may be required to achieve satisfactory performance on such circuits.

Examples for level calculations in a voice-grade channel

Two types of level calculations are given in the following examples. They provide a good idea of the calculation of levels on a transmission line and of channel powers in an FMVFT system.

Example 1   The noise measured at the receive (RCV) line terminals is -46 dBm, with a line loss of 12 dB. Data are transmitted at -10dBm. The question is to determine a safe circuit set at S/N $= 10$ dB. At the RCV end,

$$\text{Level} = -10 - 12 = -22 \text{ dBm}$$

$$\text{S/N} = -46 - (-22) = 24 \text{ dB}$$

Operation margin of the system is then

$$24 - 10 = 14 \text{ dB}$$

A 14-dB margin of safety is enough to allow variations due to trouble conditions on the system.

Example 2   Find the level and power of a single telegraph channel in a 24-channel FMVFT system working at $+7$ TLP.

At 0 TLP (-13 dBm0):

$$-13 = 10 \log P_{\text{mWO}} \qquad \text{By definition } p_{\text{mWO}} \text{ is aggregate level}$$

$$P_{\text{mWO}} = 50 \times 10^{-3} \text{ mW} \qquad \text{Aggregate power}$$

For a single telegraph channel:

$$x_{\text{dBm0}} = 10 \log \frac{P_{\text{mWO}}}{24} = 10 \log P_{\text{mWO}} - 10 \log 24$$

$$= -13 - 13.8 = -26.8 \qquad \text{Level at 0 TLP}$$

$$P_{\text{ch}} = {}^{50}\!/_{24} = 2.08 \ \mu\text{W} \qquad \text{Power at 0 TLP}$$

At $+7$ TLP:

$$\text{Aggregate level} = +7 - 13 = -6 \text{ dBm}$$

$$-6 = 10 \log P_{\text{mW}}$$

$$P_{\text{mW}} = 0.250 \text{ mW} \qquad \text{Aggregate power}$$

$$P_{\text{ch}} = {}^{250}\!/_{24} = 10.4 \ \mu\text{W} \qquad \text{Single-channel power}$$

2.2   Attenuation-Frequency Characteristics

Amplitude distortion is a variation in signal attenuation or in power loss over a range of frequencies. Amplitude distortion, while caused by the same factors as envelope delay distortion, is affected somewhat differently. Typical behavior of the line attenuation and propagation velocity as a function of frequency is shown in Fig. 2.6 for a 22 AWG cable pair from frequencies 1 kHz to 10 MHz.

The change in resistance is the primary contributor to the attenuation increase as a function of frequency. For coaxial cables, this

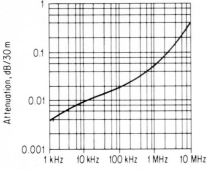 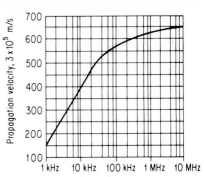

Figure 2.6 Attenuation and propagation velocity versus frequency curves in a 22 AWG (52 pF/m) twisted cable pair.

resistance increase is due primarily to the skin effect. For twisted pair and parallel wires, proximity effects and radiation losses make the curves less linear, but for high frequencies (over 100 kHz), the attenuation is a function of dc resistance plus the incremental resistance due to skin, proximity, and radiation loss effects. The signal propagation velocity is reduced at low frequencies but is almost constant at high frequencies. This variation in signal velocity as a function of signal frequency is called *dispersion*. Thus, in propagation of a very wide frequency band, high-frequency components with their faster propagation arrive first but their increased attenuation minimizes their effect, whereas the low-frequency signals arrive later but the reduced attenuation allows them a greater influence on the resultant signal.

The primary characteristics of amplitude distortion are band-edge roll-off and in-band ripple in VF band.

Band-edge roll-off is the name given to the sharp rise in attenuation in the frequencies near the upper and lower extremes of the bandwidth. The factors contributing to band-edge roll-off are voice multiplexing system filters, loaded cables, transformers, capacitors, and other frequency-selective power-absorbing equipment.

In-band ripple refers to nonuniform variations in amplitude at various frequencies across the midsection of the band. In-band ripple is caused primarily by signal reflection and interaction effects resulting from short lengths of lines with frequent impedance mismatches. Misadjusted equalizers on the line can also contribute to in-band ripple.

Attenuation-frequency measurements

The fact to be considered is that the measurements made at 1000 Hz may have only minor value in transmission. Most circuits will have different characteristics at other frequencies, so higher speeds of trans-

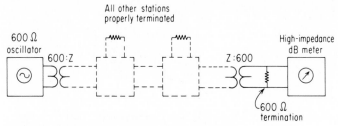

Figure 2.7   Attenuation-frequency measurements.

mission will be impossible without taking proper corrective and com-
pensating steps.

Data transmission via modem most commonly involves a band of
frequencies from about 800 to 2500 Hz.

Figure 2.7 illustrates the basic measurement principle involved.
Measurements should be made at about 100-Hz intervals by noting all
maximums and minimums in levels occurring at intermediate frequencies. On leased facilities − 10 dBm0 should be used in most cases
to avoid overloading intermediate equipment or causing disturbances
into other circuits. Higher levels may be used if other circuits are not
involved.

Measurements should be made in both directions between all points
as the data are being transmitted. Measurements made in one direction
may not be presumed to be the same for the other direction. Again,
proper terminations must be provided at all other terminal points while
tests are conducted. *Proper termination* means an equipment or a network (resistance plus capacitance) which has an impedance equal to
that of the facility to which it is applied. The recorded results should
not show excessive attenuation slope or variations across the voice
band.

Test results made over actual circuits and interpretations.   Figure 2.8
shows the spread of attenuation distortion referred to 800 Hz. Tests
were made on switched telephone networks with 1200-b/s modems.
Customer-to-customer distances are quite varied, and the curves in the
figure only give an idea of the attenuation distortion in the VF band.

Other kinds of test results are given in Figs. 2.32 and 2.33. If an
excessive but smooth slope is obtained with more than 4-dB difference
in the frequencies, equalization may be employed to overcome it. Large
peaks and valleys in the curve indicate impedance mismatches or
echoes. They may also be the result of certain open-wire line construction situations. This latter source of trouble generally results in nonsystematic variations.

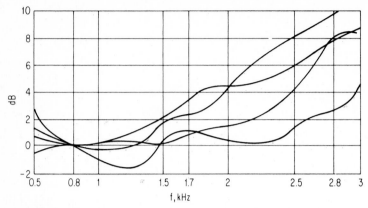

Figure 2.8 Attenuation distortion in the telephone network referred to the value at 800 Hz.

The echoes produce periodic variations across the frequency spectrum, although the combined result of multiple echoes can create confusing results. Consequently any variations in the voice band should be investigated.

Recommended values. Attenuation-frequency variations should be within 4 dB in 800 to 2300 Hz.

The nominal value of the input and output impedances of the signal receiver is 600 Ω. Z_E and Z_S, which are respectively the measured values of the input and output impedance of the signal receiver, should meet the following condition throughout the 300- to 3400-Hz frequency band:

$$\frac{Z_E - 600}{Z_E + 600} \leq 0.35 \quad \text{and} \quad \frac{Z_S - 600}{Z_S + 600} \leq 0.35$$

per CCITT Rec. Q.114.

Amplitude equalizers. Information for amplitude equalizers is given in Sec. 2.6, together with delay equalizers. See Fig. 2.35 for amplitude equalization on a voice channel of a submarine cable.

2.3 Echoes

Echoes, similar to acoustical echoes, occur in electrical transmissions whenever the signals encounter an impedance irregularity in the facility. Impedance-matching techniques can be used to reduce the magnitude of the irregularity and the resulting echo. Echoes are a major

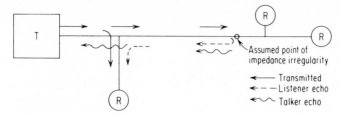

Figure 2.9 Echo paths.

source of trouble in data transmission. They are most predominant on two-wire facilities but can also give trouble on some four-wire circuits.

Most data sets are operated so that transmission is in one direction at a time. While transmitting, the receiver is generally disabled and held disabled for a few milliseconds after the transmission is over to make it insensitive to echoes of its own transmission. These are known as *talker echoes,* i.e., echoes heard at the transmitting point. Data sets, however, are more frequently disturbed by *listener echoes,* i.e., echoes heard at a receiver point. Figure 2.9 illustrates the echo paths. While in voice transmission the tolerance to echoes is related to the delay experienced (the longer the delay, the less tolerance), in data transmission this is not the case.

The effect of echoes on data reception is basically twofold. First, the echo signal will add to or subtract from the original signal voltage, depending upon the phase relationship between the signals. The phase relation will in turn be dependent upon the frequency, the distances involved to reflection points, and the velocity of propagation. Second, when the originating data signal frequency is shifted, the echo signal will not be shifted at the receiver at the same time as the direct signal. This delay in the shift of the signal would create confusion (jitter) in the receiver if the echo is about the same magnitude as the direct signal. Consequently, for most data sets, the listener echo must be at least 12 dB below the received level of the direct signal.

It is not possible to separate two signals (direct and echo) to measure them individually. To measure this difference however, the first of the two above effects can be used. In case of echoes, when making attenuation-frequency measurements, the received signal level will change in a rather uniform periodic manner through maximum and minimum values as the frequency is changed across the band, thus changing the resulting phase relation between the echo and the direct signal. This change in level is an indication of the relative magnitudes of the two signals. The curve of Fig. 2.10 can be used to determine the difference between the two signals. For example, if the variation between maximum and adjacent minimum on the attenuation-frequency curve (up-

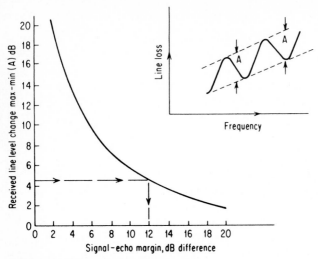

Figure 2.10 Listener-echo measurement.

per right of Fig. 2.10) is 4.5 dB, the difference between the two signals (direct and echo) will be 12 dB.

Recommended value.   Listener echo should be at least 12 dB lower than the direct signal between 800 and 2300 Hz (or level variations of about 4.5 dB or less). Refer to CCITT Rec. G.131 for echoes on international telephone lines.

Test results made over actual circuits and trouble locations.   Refer to Fig. 2.8 and notice the fluctuations on some curves which are due to echoes at the ends of the four-wire circuit. The echo ratio of each connection was determined with the help of these curve fluctuations.

Trouble locations.   Echoes are always caused by inadequate matching of impedances at some junction point in the circuit. The point may be at:

1. The junction of a data set

2. The junction of a branch circuit

3. The junction of two types of facilities joined to make a longer circuit

4. A hybrid system, where a carrier channel converts its four-wire circuit to two-wire

Singing

Power reflected at a single frequency may result in the circuit going into sustained oscillations. This is known as *singing* and may occur at any frequency in the voice band but usualy in the 200–500 or 2500–3200 Hz ranges. Singing depends upon the degree of balance at both ends of a circuit, on the facility loss, on the frequency response, and on the phase relationships between the original and reflected power. Singing margin tests are required when two-wire data sets terminate circuits that are provided in part over four-wire facilities.

A system called VODAS (voice-operated device antisinging) is used to prevent singing by disabling one direction of transmission at all times. Refer to CCITT Rec. G.463 for VODAS characteristics.

Hybrid coupler

To reduce the possibility of transmission impairments, networks are designed to match the impedance of two-wire lines to four-wire lines. These networks are called *balancing networks*. The resultant degree of impedance is called *balance,* and the system is called a *hybrid coupler* (see Fig. 2.11). Echo in any two-wire or combination of two- and four-wire telephone circuits is caused primarily by the imbalance in the hybrid couplers located at the interface of two-wire (local loops) and four-wire (long-haul) circuits. The ideal hybrid coupler passes the incoming signal from its four-wire in-port to its two-wire port, attenuating it by 3 dB, and does not pass anything to the four-wire out-port. Conversely it passes signals with 3-dB attenuation from the two-wire port to the four-wire port, without reflecting any energy back into the two-wire line. However this ideal performance is obtained only if the balancing impedance is equal to the impedance presented by the two-

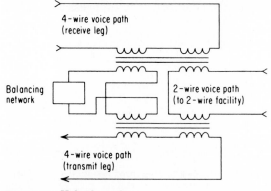

Figure 2.11 Hybrid coupler.

wire line. In practice, the impedance is not constant from line to line, and in fact the impedance of a particular line may exhibit a frequency characteristic that is not easily reproduced. Therefore, the practical balancing network is a design compromise which, in turn, leads to a variable performance not always satisfactory. The attenuation from the four-wire in-port to the four-wire out-port of the hybrid coupler (ideally infinite) is actually observed to have an average value of about 15 dB with a standard deviation of about 3 dB. This loss is called *echo return loss* (ERL) (refer to Sec. 2.4). Echo results because signals from the distant telephone arrive at the four-wire in-port, pass directly across the hybrid to the four-wire out-port, with a nominal 15-dB loss, and are retransmitted back to the distant telephone.

In the terrestrial telephone plant, echo can be made tolerable to the subscriber by simply inserting loss, if the circuit is not too long, i.e., the one-way propagation delay does not exceed 25 ms. The problem is solved by this method in the direct-distance-dialing (DDD) network on trunks as long as about 2500 km. For longer circuits, however, echo control devices must be used.

The rate of tolerable loss for delayed echo signals is given in Fig. 2.12.

Echo control devices

Within the switched service networks and on some dedicated circuits there are often separate paths for the two directions of transmission over a portion of the circuit. In voice communication, at least one of the paths is usually idle at any given time. To prevent the person who is talking from hearing a disturbing echo of his voice on long-distance calls, echo is either attenuated or removed completely by echo control devices utilizing this idle path.

There are two types of echo control devices, echo suppressor and echo canceller.

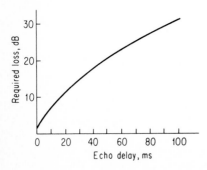

Figure 2.12 Required loss for delayed echo signals.

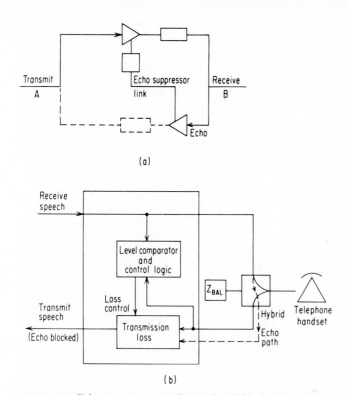

Figure 2.13 Echo suppressor. (*a*) Principle; (*b*) block diagram.

Echo suppressor. The receive path signal is attenuated more than 50 dB on the idle transmit path by a device called an *echo suppressor*. As a result, voice signals may be transmitted in one direction at a time under normal conditions. If duplex operation is desired, the echo suppressor must be disabled. (Refer to Fig. 2.13*a*.)

In voice transmission, required attenuation in echo signals increases by the increase in time delay (see Fig. 2.12). In Fig. 2.13*b* a block diagram of an echo suppressor is given. An echo suppressor is basically a pair of voice-operated switches which, while the subscriber is talking, insert a loss of 50 dB or more in the echo return path. It is initiated automatically whenever the signal level through the receive channel exceeds both the suppression threshold (typically -30 dBm0) and the signal level through the transmit channel.

There are two basic types of echo suppressor, the full and the split. The full echo suppressor controls both directions of transmission. It seldom is located at the midpoint of the circuit. The full echo suppressor does not satisfy operations in most cases, since a typical delay between the near talker and the echo suppressor is 5 to 10 ms, while there may be as much as a 35-ms delay between the distant talker and the echo suppressor. This imbalance is avoided in the split echo suppressor, which provides a sensing circuit and switch near each talker. Normally switch operation is controlled by the distant talker and introduces high loss in the return (echo) path. This blocks transmission from the talker nearer the switch. However, the sensing circuit continually compares signal levels in the transmitting and receiving paths, and in the case of simultaneous talking, gives the low-loss path to the louder talking, which causes some speech to be blocked or chopped and some echo to remain. Although this kind of suppression may work satisfactorily on telephone transmission, echo suppressors cause serious problems for data transmission.

First, any business machine or data set using voice circuits equipped with echo suppressors must allow about 100 ms for turnaround time, the time it takes to reverse transmission directions. Second, and more important in many cases, if the echo suppressor is activated by a transmission from machine A, any attempt by machine B to send back a signal to A will be blocked.

A device called a *disabler* deactivates the echo suppressor by applying a 2025- or 2100-Hz tone at -5 dBm0 for about 300 ms from either end of the circuit. No other signals should be transmitted during this disabling period. Any interval of 100 ms or more will reactivate the echo suppressor. Enabling can be assured by a signal interruption greater than 500 ms.

In half-duplex operation the time required for turnaround should be included in the delay between Request to Send being turned on and Clear to Send coming on.

Refer to CCITT Rec. V.25 for disabling procedures of echo suppressors. Characteristics of echo suppressors are given in CCITT Recs. G.161 and G.164. CCITT Recs. V.21, V.23, V.26*bis,* and V.27 recommend utilization of a 2100-Hz disabling tone at the -12 ± 6 dBm0 level for at least 400 ms; any signal of 200 to 3400 Hz at -36 dBm0 should release at more than 100-ms duration. Recommendations Q.115 and G.131 refer to stability and control of echoes.

Echo canceller. If the delay were not too long, if the echo return loss (ERL) were not too low, and if the subscribers would not frequently interrupt each other, then a conventional echo suppressor would do the job on satellite circuits. Unfortunately the effective ERL can vary considerably from connection to connection. The requirement to provide satisfactory service under such adverse circumstances has generated much interest in the echo canceller using a digital technique.

As shown in Fig. 2.14, an echo canceller contains complex signal-processing circuits that compare the signals in both directions of transmission and generate a replica of the echo and subtract it from the real echo. Residual echo is further removed by an adaptive clipper.

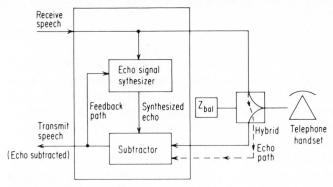

Figure 2.14   Echo canceller.

This precisely cancels the echo but allows speech to pass essentially unimpaired. This improved performance, however, is more complex and more expensive than an echo suppressor. At present the cost of an echo canceller is at least three or four times higher than that of a conventional analog echo suppressor. CCITT recommendations for echo cancellers are given in Rec. G.165.

2.4   Return Loss

The degree of balance is usually expressed in terms of return loss in dB, at a specified frequency or band of frequencies. Echo return loss is a weighted average on a power basis of the return losses at all frequencies in the echo range 500 to 2500 Hz. Since the main concern at a junction is not the magnitude of an impedance but the difference between the two impedances being connected, this difference is checked first. Hence the definition of return loss is

$$R_L(\text{dB}) = 20 \log \frac{A + B}{A - B}$$

After possible junction points for the impedance mismatch have been checked and after the trouble spot has been located, a measurement may be necessary to determine the type of impedance-matching network or repeating coil to be used. The location causing the trouble can sometimes be located by using impedance measurements made at one terminal point.

Recommended values.   A return loss of at least 42 dB at all frequencies between 800 and 2300 Hz is recommended. This corresponds to an impedance of $600 \pm 10 \ \Omega$, or a ratio better than 98 percent. Any return loss below this limit indicates an excessive impedance irregularity and should be investigated. In most cases 12-dB listener echo also satisfies the return-loss value.

Utilization of a hybrid for return-loss measurement

A hybrid test circuit is given in Fig. 2.15. Use the configuration of Fig. 2.16a. If the data set is not yet available, a series network (resistor and condenser) should be made according to the specifications of the set. In the case of using a repeating coil between the line and the data set, the same repeating coil should be used on the line at the termination. All data sets must be connected to the line (or simulated) at all other points, and all data transmitters are to be turned off.

First, short out the line terminals and increase the oscillator output until the dB meter reads 0 dBm; now the dB meter is calibrated to read directly the return loss. Remove the short across the line terminals and read the dB meter for the frequency band 800 through 2300 Hz by keeping the oscillator output constant. Repeat similar tests at all branching points, as illustrated in Fig. 2.16b.

Note

When tests are made on a leased telephone circuit, continuous tone level should not exceed −10 dBm0 for single-tone (half-duplex) transmission or −13 dBm0 for simultaneous two-tone transmission (for duplex systems on a telephone switching system, according to CCITT Rec. V.2).

Analysis of test results.   Note that a high return loss indicates a good impedance match and is therefore desirable. A low return loss will indicate an inadequate impedance match at the data-set-line junction. A faulty data-set internal-impedance termination may be detected by substituting an *RC* network for the data set. If the return loss is still low, though relatively uniform across the frequency band, a different repeating coil in the line side is needed; i.e., the line impedance is not what it was presumed to be. If the return-loss measurement varies considerably in a rhythmic manner, this will be the result of talker echoes from an impedance mismatch at some other point in the circuit.

It is also possible to have a high return loss, i.e., good impedance

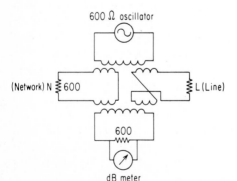

Figure 2.15 Hybrid test circuit.

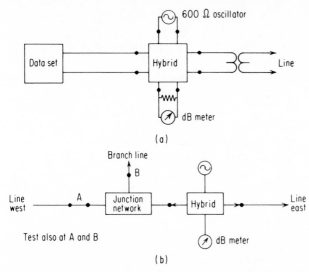

Figure 2.16   Return-loss measurement. (*a*) Data set to line; (*b*) junction point to line.

match, at a terminal location and still have excessive listener echo due to a low return loss at some other terminal out on a branch line or elsewhere in the line circuit. It has been determined that whenever there is an excessive listener echo, the above return-loss measurements should be checked at all stations, and then similar tests should be performed on all intermediate sections of the circuit, especially at all branching points, to isolate the trouble area. Such a test configuration is illustrated in Fig. 2.16*b*. Of course, if the facilities are leased, the telephone company would be responsible for these intermediate tests.

As the frequency is changed across the voice band, the impedance will vary. When impedance irregularities are present, the frequency at which each maximum and minimum point occurs should be determined.

The data set should very closely match the average impedance value within the data frequency band. A repeating coil of proper turns ratio may be used. However, if the line impedance varies too widely between maximum and minimum values, a repeating coil cannot prevent a return loss which is too low. Since repeating coils are rarely available to make an exact impedance match between the data set and the average line impedance, the variations in the line impedance must be held to still closer limits.

Therefore, variations in the line impedance are the result of an impedance mismatch elsewhere in the facility. Such variations can be reduced by improving the impedance matching at the other end of the circuit.

Trouble at one location can be confirmed by referring to the imped-
ance-frequency curve of Fig. 2.10. If the minimum points occur at
regular intervals, the distance of trouble can be computed from the
formula

$$d = \frac{V}{2(f_2 - f_1)}$$

where d = distance, km
     V = velocity of propagation, km/s
  $f_2 - f_1$ = difference in frequency of adjacent minimum points, Hz

Typical V values are as follows:

Microwave carrier circuit	225,000 km/s
Cable carrier circuits	177,000 km/s
No-load cable circuits	64,000 km/s
H88 loaded cable circuits*	22,500 km/s

*Coils of 88 mH at spacing about 2 km.

Impedance measurements

Different types of measurement techniques are used in impedance
measurements. They range from very accurate laboratory-type instruments to simple derives for use in the field. The measurement principles
of the two methods given in the following paragraphs provide satisfactory and quick results in most operations.

Impedance measurement with a hybrid.   In analyzing the possible causes
and treatments of impedance irregularities, impedance measurements
can be of considerable value. For this purpose only the magnitude is
generally needed, and the following simplified procedure can be used.
As shown in Fig. 2.17, a decade resistor box is connected to the network
side of the hybrid. With the oscillator set for the frequency of the test,
the resistance R is changed to provide a minimum reading on the meter.

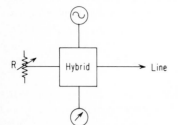

Figure 2.17 Impedance measurement with a hybrid.

The value of the meter reading is not significant; it is the value of R which results in the lowest meter reading that is important. The value of R is the equivalent of the line impedance. It is recognized that actual impedance is usually a complex value of resistance plus a negative reactance. Consequently, both resistance and capacitance should be used in the network (usually a 2-μF capacitor in series). However, for the purpose of these tests, a resistance only is a sufficient approximation.

Impedance measurement with an oscillator and a dB meter.   Referring to Fig. 2.18, a 600-Ω terminated dB meter is connected to an oscillator and the oscillator output level is adjusted to 0 dBm. With the meter still connected, the unknown impedance, line or data set, is bridged across the oscillator output. The reduction in signal level is observed on the meter and is converted to impedance by the curve shown.

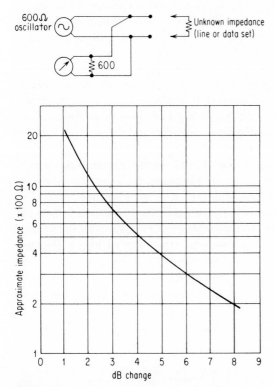

Figure 2.18 Impedance measurement with a dB meter.

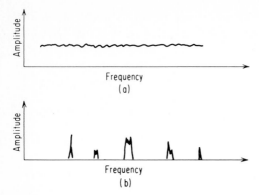

Figure 2.19 (*a*) White noise and (*b*) impulse noise.

2.5 Noise

Although the definition of noise is unwanted electric signals, two types of noise are considered in order to distinguish noise from unwanted signals created by signal distortions. Hissing or background noise, frequently referred to as white noise, is not frequency-selective and is fairly constant in magnitude (see Fig. 2.19). The second type, called *impulse noise,* has more effect on data circuits and will be discussed later.

Noise measured on a circuit which is correctly terminated but not carrying any traffic is called *white noise* (refer to Fig. 2.20). Generally if the circuit meets normal white noise limits in voice communications, it will be satisfactory for data. Specifying the noise in a test channel as a noise power provides a relative indication of interference. An alternative is to express the noise in decibels relative to a signal level in the test channel; this way, the S/N ratio is defined as follows: S/N is the decibel ratio of the level of the standard test tone (0 dBm0) to the noise in a 3100-Hz bandwidth within the test channel.

In analog transmission, noise is cumulative; an increase in the number of links decreases the S/N ratio. Results of tests conducted on a 24-channel FM-carrier telephone system are given in Fig. 2.21; after 10 repeaters the S/N ratio decreases 7 dB.

In digital transmission systems, the signal is regenerated by repeaters; thus the idle noise is mostly due to noise generated in the receiving

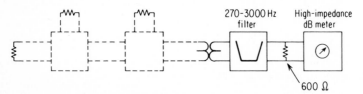

Figure 2.20 Definition of white noise.

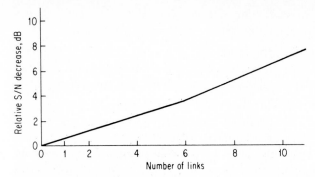

Figure 2.21   Effect of number of links on the S/N ratio (for 24-channel carrier system).

terminal and is reduced to insignificant values. However, the quantizing, i.e., reducing the sampled level to discrete levels, leads to noise generation not present in frequency-division-multiplex (FDM) systems. This type of noise is called *quantizing distortion noise* and must be measured while a signal present. In a typical PCM system, the signal-to-quantizing-noise ratio is around 22 dB. Refer to Sec. 3.3 for further discussions on this subject.

Crosstalk

Crosstalk refers to one channel picking up some of the signal that is traveling in another channel. It occurs between cable pairs carrying separate signals, or in multiplex links where several channels are transmitted over the same facility, or in microwave links where one antenna picks up the reflected portion of the signal for another antenna on the same tower.

Recommended crosstalk limits are given by CCITT G.151 as follows:

- 43 dB Near end (between the go and return telephone channels)
- 58 dB Between the link and other carrier circuits

Refer to CCITT Rec. G.116 for detailed crosstalk effects on telephone circuits.

In digital data transmission, to reduce the possibility of crosstalk between various leads, the following recommendations are made regarding the cable-pair assignments for a twisted pair cable:

1. The greatest crosstalk problems are between the control and signal circuits. It is recommended that one twisted pair be used for each control signal, with one lead of the pair tied to signal ground at the connector of the cable.

2. The amount of crosstalk depends on the cable, the cable driver characteristics and the cable terminator input impedance.

3. To minimize crosstalk, the balanced data and clock signals should be assigned to pairs in the center of the cable. The cable pairs around the outside of the cable should be assigned to the control signals.

4. An extra twisted pair with both leads tied to signal ground at the connector of the cable should be used between each control pair to provide isolation. This arrangement with extra ground wires around the outside of the cable also provides some shielding from interfering signals in the outside environment.

Intermodulation noise

On a multiplexed channel many different signals are amplified together, and slight departures from linearity in the equipment cause intermodulation noise. The signals from two independent channels intermodulate with each other to form a product which falls into a separate band of frequencies reserved for another signal. Such products arising from large numbers of pairs of channels combine to form a low-amplitude babble that adds to the background noise in other channels. However, if one signal were a single frequency, then when it modulates a voice channel on another channel, this voice might become clearly audible in a third channel.

Intermodulation noise rates on PCM audio channels are given in CCITT Rec. G.712.

Compandors

Compandors first compress the dynamic range of voice signals for transmission over the carrier facility, then expand the range back to the original scale, from which derives its name. The advantage is that dynamic range is reduced; thus the signal is moved above the system ambient noise level. This results in a quieter talking path (see Fig. 2.22). This type of compandor is called a *syllabic compandor*.

A compression ratio of 2 with a corresponding expansion ratio of 1:2 provides satisfactory performance for compandors used in most telephone circuits. This means that the speech energy traveling in the circuit between the compressor and the expandor will have an intensity range of one-half its original value. A companding range of 50 to 60 dB is usually sufficient to avoid distortion and to provide the optimum signal-to-noise improvement. Compression and expansion of speech energy in the compandor occurs around a *focal point* known as the *unaffected level*. The focal point refers to that energy level within the companding range that is not affected by compandor action. Energy at

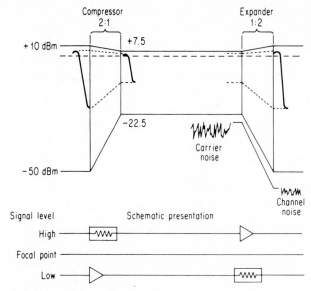

Figure 2.22   Compandor operation.

the focal point level passes through the compressor and the expandor with zero loss or gain. In Fig. 2.22 the focal point is shown with a dashed horizontal line.

The characteristics of compandors are given in CCITT Rec. G.162.

Next the operation of a syllabic compandor is examined. Assume a noise intensity of -51 dBm at the input to the receiving carrier terminal; signal intensity varies between $+5$ dBm and -20 dBm; line loss is 30 dB.

Without a compandor, the low-intensity signal reaches the input of the receiving carrier terminal at -50 dBm, only 1 dB above the noise level. Eventually noise reaches the listener only 1 dB below the low-intensity speech level. For intelligible voice, noise power should be 20 dB below the weakest speech level. In a carrier channel equipped with a compandor, the weakest signal leaves the compressor at -10 dBm and reaches the input of the receiving carrier terminal at -40 dBm, with a -51 dBm noise level. After 30-dB amplification, the signal enters the expandor with -10 dBm intensity and noise with -21 dBm. After expansion the signal levels are attenuated inversely proportional to their power; the weakest signal becomes -20 dBm and noise -47 dBm. In this manner the margin between the weakest signal and the noise is increased to 27 dB.

This type of compandor is used in voice circuits, but is not recommended for data circuits since it offers little or no noise improvement for data signals.

Another type of compandor, known as an *instantaneous compandor,* is used to reduce quantizing noise in PCM transmission systems. In this method, the amplitude range of pulse samples is compressed before uniform quantization and then expanded back to normal range at the receiving end of the circuit. Note that a syllabic compandor responds to the envelope of analog speech signals directly, whereas the instantaneous compandor responds to pulse-amplitude-modulation samples of the analog signals. Signal compression modifies the normal distribution of speech amplitudes by imparting more gain to weak signals than to strong signals. Using certain compression characteristics to reduce the speech ranges from about 60 dB to about 36 dB and one that varies logarithmically with signal amplitude, the number of quantum steps can be reduced while maintaining the same quantizing noise performance.

Note

The normally experted signal-to-quantizing-noise ratio is 22 dB (refer to CCITT Rec. H.12).

Noise Measurements

White noise measurement is generally performed while attenuation measurements are being made. To measure message circuit noise, a *quiet termination,* which is a resistor matching the impedance of the line, is placed at the transmitting end to prevent extraneous noise from entering the system, and then at the receiving end the amount of background noise is measured (see Fig. 2.23).

Refer to CCITT Rec. G.228 for measurement of circuit noise in cables.

On the other hand, if the compandor is used in the circuit, in the presence of no signal the expandor inserts maximum loss; thus an idle noise reading would be very low. To get a true measure of the noise level, it is necessary to remove the compandor action by transmitting

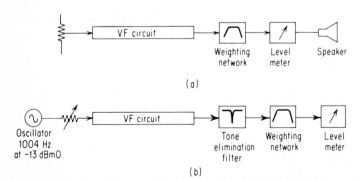

Figure 2.23 (*a*) Idle noise and (*b*) notched noise measurements.

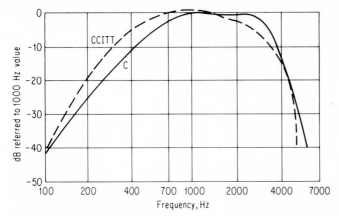

Figure 2.24 Frequency characteristics of psophometric and C weighting filters.

a *holding tone* equal in level to the focal point (refer to Fig. 2.22), then measuring the noise after the tone is filtered out. Since there might be amplifiers and echo suppressors as well as compandors within the circuit that is activated, only when there is a signal present will the preferred measurement, be *noise with tone* because data always have a carrier present.

In the United States noise measurements for voice circuits are generally made through a C-message-type weighting filter. This takes into account the weighted response of telephone instruments and the human ear (refer to Fig. 2.24).

The circuit should always be monitored with a speaker while making C-message noise measurements. The purpose is to detect intelligible crosstalk or single-frequency tone interference.

For data circuits a "flat measurement" is made since the response curve of data sets are flatter than human ear response (see Fig. 2.26). Noise-with-tone or C-notched noise measurement determines the unwanted power present when the channel is carrying a normal signal. A C-notched filter is given in Fig. 2.25.

To make this measurement, a 1004-Hz tone simulating data is sent to activate the devices in the circuit. At the receiving end the tone is filtered out with a very narrow-band filter and the remaining background noise level is measured (Fig. 2.23). Thus it actually measures the S/N ratio, which is the most important item to be measured with respect to the transmission. This is a true measurement of noise in circuits and is the same as that used to make idle noise measurements except that a narrow-band elimination filter (55-dB deep) is used to eliminate the 1004-Hz holding tone.

The noise-with-tone measurement not only tells whether the line

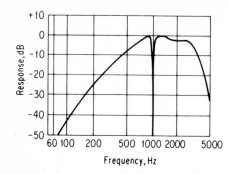

Figure 2.25 C-message weighting with notch characteristic.

has excessive noise but also provides an important clue to other problems that may exist on the line. This measurement can alert one to nonlinear distortion or harmonic distortion. For example, if a signal at 1004 Hz is sent and a high noise reading is received, it may be caused by excessive harmonic distortion. Investigating further, excessive energy at 3012 Hz may be found, which indicates that high third-order harmonic distortion is present.

Noise units (United States).   Noise reading would have negative values if a 10^{-3} W (0 dBm) reference level is used. In telephony the chosen reference is 10^{-12} W or -90 dBm, and noise measurements are expressed in decibels above reference noise level (dBrn). A 1000-Hz tone at 10^{-12} W (a level of -90 dBm) will give a 0 dBrn reading regardless of which weighting network is used. For other measurements the weighting network must be specified. The notation dBrnC is commonly used when readings are made using the C-message weighting network. This way a -40 dBm noise level is 50 dBrn; 20 dBrnCO means that the noise level is 20 dB above the reference noise level, that the measurement was made with a C-message filter, and that the number is referred to 0TLP.

Example   Let us calculate the S/N ratio on a circuit per the following test conditions:

Test frequency	1004 Hz
Transmit level	0 dBm
Line loss	16 dB
C-notched reading	39 dBrnC

Thus S/N = 0 $-$ 16 $-$ (39 $-$ 90) = 35 dB.

Psophometric noise weighting.   Although the dBrnC has become a standard unit of message circuit noise in the United States, it is not

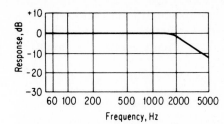

Figure 2.26 Frequency characteristics of a flat filter.

an international standard. The International Telegraph and Telephone
Consultative Committee (CCITT) has defined noise as measured on a
psophometer which includes a specified weighting that differs slightly
from the C-message weighting used in the United States (Fig. 2.24).
For general conversion purposes, it is usually sufficient to assume that
the psophometric weighting of 3-kHz white noise decreases the average
power by about 2.5 dB compared to the 2.0-dB factor for C-message
weighting. The term *phophometric voltage* refers to the rms weighted
noise voltage at a point and is usually expressed in millivolts. It has
become common to refer to average noise power rather than to noise
voltage. This power is often expressed in picowatts psophometric (pWp):

$$\text{pWp} = \frac{\text{psophometric } V^2}{600} \times 10^{12}$$

In decibels,

$$\text{dBp} = 10 \log (\text{pWp})$$

For flat noise from 0 to 3 kHz, the relation between two weightings is

$$\text{dBp} = \text{dBrnC} - 0.5$$

This relationship is not exact for other noise shapes because of the
differences between psophometric and C-message weighting. Figure

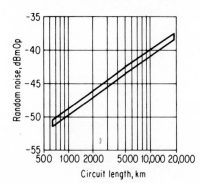

Figure 2.27 Random noise performance (CCITT Recs. H.12 and
M.1020).

2.27 displays random noise versus circuit length and is presented as a guide to the random noise performance which may be found on an international leased circuit. A satellite circuit contributes approximately 10,000 pW0p (-50 dBm0p).

Example Find the total psophometric noise level of a system composed of a satellite circuit and terrestrial networks with 20,000 pW0p of psophometrically weighted noise.

Solution By definition

$$dBm0p = 10 \log \frac{pW0p}{10^{-3}} \times 10^{-12}$$

	Power, pW0p	Level, dBm0p[*]
Satellite link	10,000	$-50 = 10 \log \frac{10,000}{10^{-3}} \times 10^{-12} = 10(-5)$
Terrestrial link	20,000	$-47 = 10(-5 + 0.3)$
Total	30,000	$-45.2 = 10(-5 + 0.48)$

[*]See Sec. 2.14.

Noise level at $+7$ TLP is

$$+7 - 45.2 = -38.2 \text{ dBm}$$

The S/N ratio for -13 dBm0 operation is

$$45.2 - 13 = 32.2 \text{ dB}$$

Recommended noise levels. A low-level background noise of 20 to 25 dBrnC0 is actually desirable in a voice channel. A high-level noise above 40 dBrnC0 may not be usable for a low-level talker. For example, if a C-message reading of 31 dBrnC is obtained at the input to the modem at -3 TLP, the noise level is actually 34 dBrnC0.

Message circuit noise objectives are given below.

Circuit length, km	dBrnC0
0–80	31
160–640	37
1600–2400	43
4000–6400	47
13,000–25,000	53
Satellite channel	44

The S/N ratio must be 24 dB or greater.

CCITT Recommendations for noise levels. Recommendation G.123 is about "Circuit noise in national networks."

■ Total induced noise should not exceed 1 mV (approx. 16,000 pWp).

■ Noise in the channels should not exceed 2 pW0p/km.

■ Noise level in a 10,000-km open-wire line should not exceed 50,000 pW (-43 dBm0p).

Recommendation G.152 gives the "Characteristics appropriate to long-distance circuits of a length not exceeding 2500 km," and G.222 covers "Noise objectives for design of carrier transmission system of 2500 km." Recommendation G.153 gives the "Characteristics appropriate to international circuits more than 2500 km in length." Figure

TABLE 2.4 Noise Objectives for More than 2500-km-long Circuits

Psophometric power		Type of objective or limit	
pW0p	dBm0p	For a connection, a chain of circuits, or a leased circuit	For a circuit which may form part of a switch connection
40,000	-44		Limit for a telephone circuit used without a compandor (Rec. G.143B).
50,000	-43	Objective for a chain of 6 international circuits, obtained in practice by a combination of circuits of 1, 2, or 4 pW/km (Rec. G.143A).	
80,000	-41	Limit for FM v.f. telegraphy, in accordance with CCITT standards (Rec. G.143C).	
100,000	-40	Objective for data transmission over a leased circuit [(Rec. G.143D.*)].	
250,000	-36		Tolerable for data transmission over the switched network (Rec. G.143D$^+$). A circuit exceeding this limit without a compandor cannot be used in a chain of 6 telephone circuits even if it is equipped with a compandor (Rec. G.143B).
10^6	-30	Tolerable for a certain system of synchronous telegraphy (Rec. G.143C.).	

*Only the mean psophometric power over 1 h has been indicated, referred to a point of zero relative level of the international circuit, or of the first circuit of the chain.
$^+$Limits or objectives determined according to the minimum requirements of each service.
SOURCE: CCITT Rec. G.153, Orange Book.

2.27 and Table 2.4 give noise objectives for very long circuits. Noise calculation in telephone circuits is given in CCITT Rec. G.223.

Noise figure.   All networks, whether passive or active, and transmission media contribute noise to a transmission system. *Noise figure* is a measure of the noise produced by a network compared to an ideal (noiseless) network. For a linear system, the noise figure NF is expressed by

$$NF = \frac{S/N_{in}}{S/N_{out}}$$

It simply relates the S/N ratio of output signal from the network to the S/N ratio of the input signal. Common procedure is to specify both the S/N ratio and the noise figure in dB:

$$NF \text{ (dB)} = S/N_{in} \text{ (dB)} - S/N_{out} \text{ (dB)}$$

Example   Consider an S/N ratio of 60 dB at the input to an amplifier and an output S/N ratio of 50 dB.

$$NF \text{ (dB)} = 60 - 50 = 10 \text{ dB}$$

As a rule of thumb, a 0.12-dB rise in NF occurs for each 10°C rise in operating temperature.

Impulse noise

Impulse noise is a household name in data transmission. It appears in short duration with high peaks and is more troublesome to data bits than to voice transmission. It is generally accepted that noise peaks are approximately 12 dB above the rms noise level (refer to Figs. 2.28 and 2.29). The very short duration of the pulses as well as their sporadic appearance in the circuits make the use of ordinary noise-measuring meters impractical. Consequently, impulse noise is generally measured in terms of the number of pulses occurring in a given period of time that exceed the reference magnitude. The reference level of 8 dB below the signal level is generally accepted, which becomes −18 dBm0 for a −10 dBm0 half-duplex signal level. For more information refer to CCITT Recs. M.81 and V.55.

Measurement of impulse noise.   Impulse-noise-measuring instruments are designed to ignore all pulses below an adjustable preset level and to actuate a counter for each pulse which exceeds that value and comes after 125 μs for a specific period of time (usually 15 min).

When such a test set is not available, an oscilloscope may be em-

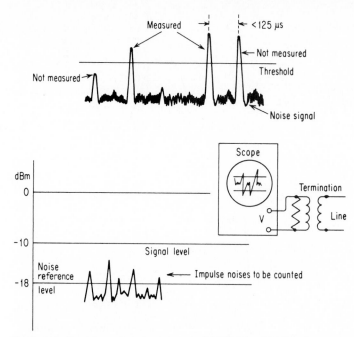

Figure 2.28 Impulse noise measurement (CCITT Rec. H.13) and counts.

ployed to detect noise impulses as follows. A filter should be used to limit the bandwidth to 3000 Hz and the line should be terminated at both ends by characteristic impedances (refer to Fig. 2.28). Utilizing the square calibration lines on the screen and applying a signal from an oscillator to the vertical plates, for example, the signal (-18 dBm) can be adjusted to the limiting value of noise above which impulses are to be counted. When the line is connected to the vertical terminals of the oscilloscope, any impulse spikes that exceed the limiting magnitude will show above or below the signal level on the scope. By counting the pulses an evaluation of the impulse noise rate may be obtained; the measurements are to be conducted for 15 min.

The measurements should be made at the receiving data locations. The average readings of many tests over several days at different times of the day should be used, rather than considering a single test.

Recommended impulse noise rate. In leased circuits, with a -21 dBm0 impulse limiting level, 18 impulse counts in 15 min is an admissible limit (refer to CCITT Recs. H.12 and H.13). It should be noted that the limiting level and impulse count values are subject to variations depending upon the data speed and type of data set detection technique used, since some transmission techniques are less sensitive to impulse noise than others.

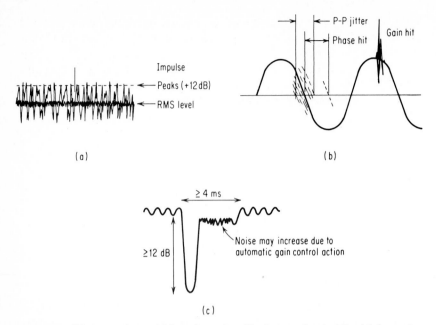

Figure 2.29 Line transients. (*a*) Impulse noise; (*b*) phase and gain hits; (*c*) dropouts.

Phase and gain hits and dropouts

Gain and phase changes may occur rapidly due to switching to standby facilities, fading in microwave paths, and noise transients which may couple into carrier supplies. A gain or phase hit is registered when the change lasts for 4 ms or longer. The threshold level at which the hit is registered is adjustable, as follows:

Gain hit: $+1$ to $+6$ dB

Phase hit: 5 to 45°

The impulse noise counter is inhibited when a gain or phase hit occurs.

Phase-hit measurements are made using a method similar to that for phase jitter. A test tone of 1004 Hz (United States) or 1020 Hz (CCITT Rec. 0.91) is used.

Phase hits of less than about 15° do not normally cause severe problems.

Gain hits are measured using the 1004- or 1020-Hz holding tone. A *dropout* is a short interruption of service lasting 4 ms or more. A 12-dB reduction in level of a received signal is interpreted as an interruption. Note that in a switched telegraph network a 300-ms interruption of the current would be translated into a release of switches; then the duration of interruption should in no case exceed 150 ms.

When a 12-dB reduction in level occurs, the background noise may rise to a level which activates impulse and hit counters. These are erroneous counts; thus it is best to measure transients with a composite hit counter which inhibits all other counts when a dropout occurs. Impulse noise, phase and gain hits, and dropouts together are also called *line transients* (refer to Fig. 2.29). Sources of line transients and protection methods are given in Secs. 11.1 and 11.2.

Recommended values

Phase hit: Two hits greater than 15° in 15 min

Gain hit: Two hits above 12 dB in 15 min

Refer to CCITT Recs. Q.29–Q.33 for noise in telephone exchanges.

2.6 Delay Distortion

Voice channels equipped with bandpass devices (filters) do not provide uniform transmission speed in all frequencies. This allows a relative phase difference between frequencies. As transmission speeds increase and bit lengths shorten, it becomes increasingly important that the various frequencies within the data band take about the same time to reach the distant end.

The phase characteristics of a channel would be very difficult to measure directly since a phase reference cannot easily be established at the receiving end. Thus the variation of phase with frequency ($\Delta\Theta/\Delta f$) is measured instead. This is the envelope delay (or group delay), and it is common practice to indicate the envelope delay instead of the phase delay (Θ/f) (refer to Fig. 2.30). This is to be attributed to the following reasons:

1. In the case of carrier telephone channels employing single-sideband transmission with suppressed carrier, the phase between the input and the output of channel gets lost. Direct assessment of phase distortion is therefore not possible.

2. When a signal is modulated on a carrier and is transmitted over a voice circuit, it is in practice sufficient to indicate attenuation distortion and envelope delay distortion for the assessment of the circuit quality with regard to its linear distortion.

It becomes evident that envelope delay distortions are almost exclusively caused by carrier frequency channels and that the overall subscriber-to-subscriber group delay is therefore practically proportional

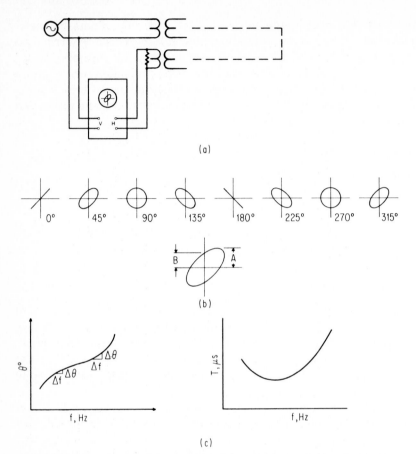

Figure 2.30 Delay calculations. (*a*) Test circuit. (*b*) Phase angles; sin $\Theta = B/A$. (*c*) Graphical solution.

$$\text{Delay} = \frac{\Delta\theta}{\Delta f} \times \frac{1}{360} \times 10^6 \ \mu\text{s} = \frac{\Delta\theta}{\Delta f} \times 2778$$

to the number of carrier frequency channels connected in tandem in the circuit. Compared with that, the influence of loaded and unloaded circuits is but slight, particularly when such circuits are relatively short in length. In most cases the complete speech band (300–3400 Hz) is available even with loaded circuits. This is another reason why the increase of envelope delay distortion at the upper limit of the frequency band (which is typical of loaded circuits) is of little effect to the telephone network.

In short, above 1000 Hz the envelope delay distortion is primarily due to loading coils as well as channelgroup and supergroup filters of the carrier systems.

Delay distortion measurements

In practice all known envelope-delay-measuring instruments operate in accordance with the method proposed by Nyquist in 1930. According to this method, the phase shift, which the envelope curve of an amplitude-modulated signal suffers on traversing a transmission system, is a measure of the absolute envelope delay of that system at the carrier frequency.

The actual measuring technique is to determine the phase-shift difference experienced by the two sidebands of a low-frequency-modulating signal. The difference in this shift measured at some test frequency and that measured at the reference frequency is defined as the *envelope delay distortion*.

Specification for an envelope-delay-measuring set for audio circuits is given in CCITT Rec. 0.81. Test sets are available for measuring the delay distortion on an end-to-end basis. Since the delay distortion of a circuit does not change very much with time, the delay measurements would be made at the time of initial installation. In the case where two legs of a four-wire circuit do not follow the same routings, delay measurements should be made for each leg.

By assuming equal delay characteristics in both directions, measurements may be made on a loopback basis, using a delay-measuring set, or an oscilloscope if four-wire facilities are available. Figure 2.30a and b shows the general hookup for such a test and the method of determining the phase angle between the two signals as observed on the scope's screen. This angle is plotted against frequency, and the slope of this curve is translated into time delay (Fig. 2.30c).

The standard Nyquist technique for measuring envelope delay is to transmit a carrier with a low-frequency amplitude-modulated signal (25 or 83⅓ Hz) forward on one line, recover the modulation at the distant end, and modulate a returning carrier with this envelope. The original modulating signal is used to establish the phase reference in measuring the phase delay of the returning signal. Most of the delay sets have provision to zero set the reading at any frequency; thus the point of minimum delay is set to 0 μs. The maximum time difference using 83⅓ Hz as the measuring base is 12 ms ($^1/_{83.33}$) and is more than sufficient for most applications.

In CCITT standards, a reference frequency and a measuring frequency are transmitted alternately. The receiver recovers the modulating envelope (41⅔ Hz) and locks a phase detector to the reference frequency segment. The difference between the phase of the reference and that of the measuring frequency is measured and displayed in terms of delay in microseconds. This technique does not use a return line; however, it is not flexible in application to complex communication systems.

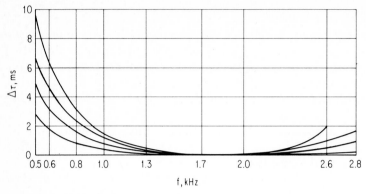

Figure 2.31 Delay distortion in a telephone network referred to the value
at 1700 Hz.

Recommended values.   The tolerable distortion varies with the acceptable error rate, data speed, type of data set, and other limiting characteristics. If the circuit exceeds these limits, apply sufficient
equalization to reduce the distortion to within these limits.

Less than 1-ms difference between any two frequencies in the 800–
2300 Hz band is recommended. Refer to "Line Conditioning" in Sec.
2.1, Table 2.3, and Fig. 2.3 for C1–C5 line-conditioning requirements
and Fig. 2.4 for CCITT recommendations.

Test results obtained from actual circuits.   Figure 2.31 gives the dispersion range of the group delay distortion referred to a value at 1700 Hz.
Notice that these curves do not indicate the fluctuations in the fine
structure caused by echoes. Other test results are given in Figs. 2.32
and 2.33.

Delay figures in various mediums.   Limiting values for group delays at
800 Hz are:

1. National extension: 12 + (0.004 × dist. in km) ms
2. International circuits:
    a. For terrestrial lines, submarine cables: 160 km/ms
    b. For others utilize the velocity figures given in Sec. 2.4
3. For satellites:
    a. 14,000 km high, single hop: 110 ms
    b. 35,000 km high, single hop: 260 ms

Equalizers

Although envelope delay will always be present in communications
circuits, it is important to flatten this delay across the frequency band-

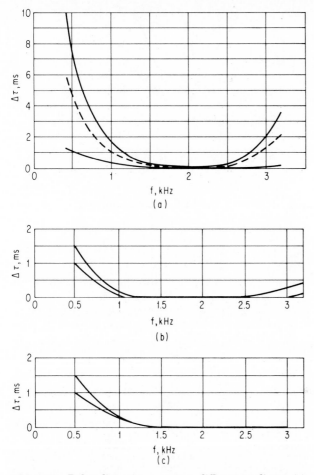

Figure 2.32 Delay distortion curves on different mediums. (*a*) Deviation range of delay distortion Δτ in the switched telephone network (connections comprising up to five carrier telephone channels in tandem, but no heavily loaded circuits). (*b*) Deviation range of delay distortion Δτ of several connections simulating typical connections comprising unloaded local circuits and loaded regional circuits, but no carrier channels. (*c*) Deviation range of delay distortion Δτ of several connections simulating typical connections in the local network comprising unloaded circuits only.

width of the channel to minimize delay distortion. This is done by adding *delay equalizer networks* to the channel (see Fig. 2.34). The usual procedure is to calculate the delay distortion in the circuit and prescribe an equalizer which will sufficiently compensate for the distortion. This requires obtaining the delay characteristics for each section of the circuit so they can be added together to determine the overall delay distortion; see Sec. 2.14.

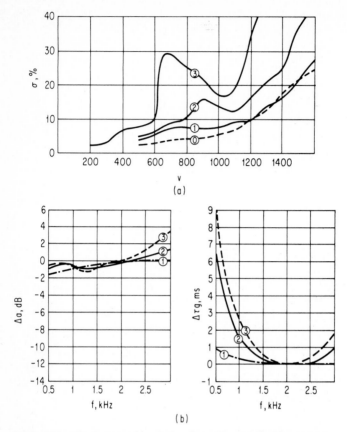

Figure 2.33 Effect of envelope delay distortion. (*a*) Isochronous tele-graph distortion σ as a function of modulation rate *v*. Modem: FM (1700 ± 400 Hz). ⓪ : without line; ① : short nonloaded local lines without carrier section; ② : short nonloaded local lines with three carrier sections; ③ : short nonloaded local lines with five carrier sections. (*b*) Attentuation distortion Δa(*f*) and envelope delay dis-tortion Δτg(*f*) of the lines measured.

Provision of amplitude and delay equalization does not completely eliminate those distortions on the line but reduces them to below certain limits, as shown in Fig. 2.35.

Amplitude equalization is accomplished by selecting a narrow frequency band and attenuating the middle frequencies or amplifying the frequencies at the edges. By connecting these types of circuits in series to the transmission line, equalization is achieved in the voice band.

A similar process is performed for envelope delay characteristics except that the frequencies in the middle of the selected frequency band are delayed more than the frequencies on the edges.

There are several types of equalizers in use. In a typical equalizer,

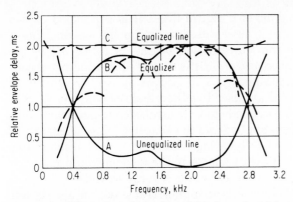

Figure 2.34 Flattening of envelope delay by using delay equalizer (dashed lines show practical equalization).

the operating range is 250 to 3400 Hz and is divided into 14 resonant sections spaced at 200-Hz intervals from 600 to 3200 Hz. Delay inserted per section varies from 500 to 2200 μs, and amplitude varies per section from $+3$ to -3 dB.

Usually, equalization is performed at the receiver side. In some transmission circuits equalization is provided on the transmit circuit also. It is called *predistortion equalization,* and the signal is distorted in such a way that the line itself acts as an equalizer. Another kind of equalization, called *midpoint equalization,* combines the effects of post- and predistortion equalization; refer to "Equalization" in Sec. 3.4.

Digital equalization. A regenerator in a digital transmission system reduces the equalization problem, and all that may be needed is a simple digital filter. When the distortion is severe or when it varies so much that a digital filter would not cope unless it could be adjusted automatically, then the process of correcting the line distortion digitally, called *digital equalization,* is needed. Digital equalization con-

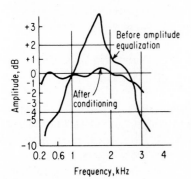

Figure 2.35 Amplitude distortion before and after equalization (3-kHz link of a submarine cable).

sists of setting up the gains of a digital filter. It is performed in two ways. A special sequence of pulses used to set up the system, like a training session before the transmission begins, is called *automatic equalization*. In *adaptive equalization,* the digital filter is adjusted continuously during transmission.

In practice both methods are used together, and the adaptive system often relies on a training session before transmission to get nearly into adjustment. Data are then applied and the adaptive phase of operation started. If there happened to be a big change in line characteristics which closed the "eyes" in the eye pattern, the modem would start the training sequence and be out of action for several seconds.

Modems operating at 4800 b/s or higher transmission speeds are equipped with digital line equalizers. Refer to "Modem Features" in Sec. 3.4 as well as to CCITT Recs. V.27 and V.29 for equalization in the modems.

2.7 Translation Errors in Carrier Systems

Carrier systems are frequently employed in long-distance circuits. The voice (or data) frequencies are translated through a modulation process to higher frequencies and then returned to the voice-frequency (VF) band at the other end of the circuit. Several steps of such a translation may take place. If in these processes the demodulating carrier frequencies do not exactly match the modulating frequencies, the tone at the receiving end may differ from that injected into the transmitting end by several cycles. For example, a transmitted 1100-Hz tone may be received as an 1105-Hz tone. This is called *carrier shift.* Some carrier systems may have considerable drift, whereas some systems employ absolute synchronizing techniques which assure no frequency error.

Depending upon the method of data set modulation and detection, requirements regarding frequency errors may be more or less important. Refer to data set instruction books of the system you are using for specific objective values.

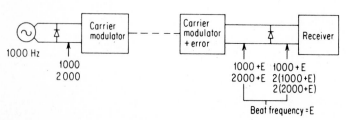

Figure 2.36 Carrier shift error.

Measurements of frequency error. The accurate measurement of frequency error may be quite involved and difficult. If two separate paths are available, one is a physical circuit or has no frequency error, and tone transmitted over both may be compared at the receiving end on an oscilloscope. Today, an accurate frequency counter is more commonly used to measure the received frequency directly.

Another method, shown in Fig. 2.36, employs a single tone such as 1000 Hz fed through a harmonic generator (a bridged low-voltage diode). The 1000-Hz tone and its harmonics are transmitted to the distant end. Assuming a +5-Hz error, the tones will be received as 1005 and 2005 Hz. These are passed through another similar harmonic producer, and the second harmonic of 1005 Hz is produced as 2010 Hz. By watching the circuit, a beat frequency of 5 Hz will be observed as a result of the 2005 and 2010 Hz mixing. Although it is difficult to judge accurately the exact error rates, it is possible to use this technique periodically to readjust the carrier oscillators to produce a low error rate, less than 1 Hz.

Recommended error rate. The recommended error rate is ±6 Hz (CCITT) Rec. V.23). The carrier-frequency tolerance allowance at the transmitter is ±1 Hz, and assuming a maximum frequency drift of ±6 Hz in the connection between the modems, then the receiver must be able to accept errors of at least ±7 Hz in the received signal frequency.

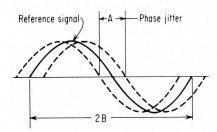

Figure 2.37 Phase jitter. Percent jitter $= (A/2B)100$.

2.8 Phase Jitter

Phase jitter is a variation in time of the received sequence of tone transitions as compared to the time sequence in which they are transmitted (refer to Figs. 2.29 and 2.37).

Note

Amplitude jitter is unwanted vibrations in the amplitude of a signal and may be observed in circuits. Amplitude jitter does not affect data circuits unless it exceeds the signal-level limits. Phase hits and gain hits, which are different from jitter, may also frequently occur in a circuit. They represent a short duration of phase-shift and gain changes in the signal. Phase jitter, phase hit, and gain hit are shown in Fig. 2.29.

Phase jitter has a negligible effect on voice transmission but a potentially disastrous impact on high-speed data transmission. The traditional definition of phase jitter is simply *unwanted angle modulation*. This means an instantaneous change in frequency from cycle to cycle. It often occurs when noise frequency modulates a carrier frequency. Jitter as small as 1° ($^1/_{360}$ c) can have a noticeable effect on high-speed data transmission. Many circuits now in use show 5 to 7° of jitter. The effect is easy to understand by considering data transmission as basically a series of binary pulses. As the transmission speed increases, these pulses become narrower and closer together. Eventually, a small displacement of one of the pulses due to jitter can cause the receiving equipment to see a pulse where it should see the absence of a pulse, or vice versa.

More technically, phase jitter describes any unwanted variations in the zero crossings of the received signal (refer to Fig. 2.37).

In earlier studies it was found that the jitter was caused mainly by power supply ripples modulating the master-frequency generator. As the frequencies were multiplied up in the carrier modulation scheme, the magnitude of this "hum modulation" jitter increased in proportion to the frequency modulation. The resultant jitter of each carrier was imparted to all signals affected by that carrier. Thus signals transmitted over channels in the higher supergroups suffered the most. The jitter frequency was the same as the modulating frequency, in this case the 60-Hz power line frequency and its several harmonics. Another jitter source was 20-Hz ringing and its several harmonics. The jitter from these two sources was concentrated in the band from 20 to 300 Hz.

Noise, crosstalk, and other kinds of signals infiltrating the voice band also contribute to jitter readings. For this reason, Bell standard jitter measurements limit the jitter measurements to 300–1800 Hz.

Jitter is a major fact in data errors, but it is not independent. It is closely related to other types of transmission impairments. Furthermore, the modulation technique used in a particular modem has a great deal to do with its tolerance to jitter, noise, and other impairments.

Occasionally, a long-haul circuit will have trouble indicating a transmission problem, although all transmission parameters test satisfactorily. The problem could be low-frequency phase jitter, between 3 and 20 Hz. This type of jitter is known as *phase wobble*. It sometimes causes temporary loss of clock synchronization. If trouble persists, although all other parameters check good, phase wobble may be the cause. Phase wobble can be measured by using several available test sets.

Phase-jitter measurement techniques

While jitter measurements can be made by measuring the carrier- (test tone) to-sideband ratio, the process is cumbersome and there is no convenient method to distinguish between angle modulation and amplitude modulation of sidebands. A more convenient measurement technique is to use a zero-crossing detector to check for any disturbance in the periodicity of the received signal, as indicated in Fig. 2.37.

Zero-crossing detection is the standard technique used in modern phase-jitter measurement instruments. The term *phase jitter* is now used to describe any unwanted variations in the zero crossings of the received signal. Since data modems also look for zero crossings, the zero-crossing technique seems like a straightforward test to identify and measure phase jitter. Unfortunately, it is not quite that simple. To understand why, it is useful to examine some of the factors that affect zero crossings and some of the factors that don't.

CCITT recommendations for instruments to measure phase jitter are given in Rec. 0.91.

Signal modulation. *Modulation* is defined as the modification of some characteristics of carrier signal. When a carrier is modulated by a second tone, sidebands are generated at the carrier frequency (plus and minus the modulating frequency). The effect of these sidebands on the composite received signal depends on the modulation process. Figure 2.38 shows the vector diagram for amplitude modulation. The upper and lower sideband vectors are rotating synchronously in opposite directions around the carrier vector (which is itself rotating). The resultant of the two sideband vectors is always in phase or 180° out of phase with the carrier vector. Thus the composite signal amplitude varies but its phase is not affected by the sidebands. In other words, the periodicity of the carrier's zero crossings is unaffected and no phase jitter is produced.

As shown in Fig. 2.39a the case of angle modulation is similar except that the resultant of the sideband vectors is always 90° out of phase with the carrier vector. Since the sideband resultant lies at any instant somewhere along the dashed line, the peak phase excursions occur when the two sidebands are in phase. The signal varies through the total angle $2\Delta\Theta$ at the modulating frequency. Thus $\Delta\Theta$ is a measure of the peak total phase jitter, and $2\Delta\Theta$ is the peak-to-peak total jitter.

The angle $\Delta\Theta$ depends only on the relative magnitudes of the carrier and its sidebands and is independent of the relative frequencies of the carrier and sidebands.

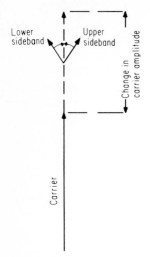

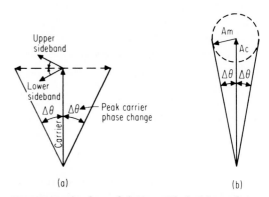

(a)   (b)

Figure 2.38 In amplitude modulation, the resultant of contrarotating sideband vectors is always in phase or 180° out of phase with the carrier vector. This causes amplitude changes, but not phase change.

Figure 2.39 Angle modulation with double- and single-sideband vectors. (a) Resultant of contrarotating sideband vectors in angle modulation is always 90° out of phase with the carrier vector. This causes phase changes, but does not cause a change in amplitude. (b) Interfering-tone vector Am creates a resultant (dashed circle), which represents both amplitude and angle modulation of carrier vector Ac. 2Δθ is peak-to-peak phase jitter.

Single-frequency interference.   Assume now that instead of a sideband pair, a single interfering tone is under consideration. The vector of the interfering tone rotates around the carrier vector at a rate equal to the difference in their frequencies. As shown in Fig. 2.39b, the composite signal always lies somewhere on the dashed circle. In other words, both the phase and the amplitude of the carrier signal vary. The interfering tone is introducing both angle modulation and amplitude modulation. If the amplitude modulation of the interfering signal is eliminated, the circle is reduced to a straight line. The interfering signal has been split to a pair of coherent sidebands. Thus the composite signal now varies in the same way as the two-sideband case shown in Fig. 2.29a. The phase varies at a rate equal to the difference between the carrier frequency and the interfering tone. As this frequency is increased, the effective modulation frequency increases, but ΔΘ remains constant. After limiting, this carrier-plus-interfering-tone case assumes the same characteristics as a phase-modulated signal.

The magnitude of the angle ΔΘ produced by a sideband pair or by a second signal depends on the relative magnitudes of the carrier Ac and the modulating signal Am. From Fig. 2.39b we get

$$\Delta\Theta = \sin^{-1}\frac{Am}{Ac}$$

Following the above procedure the phase jitter value for a given interfering-tone level can be calculated. For example, take a 20-dB low single-tone interference.

$$20 \text{ dB} = 20 \log\frac{Ac}{Am}$$

$$\frac{Am}{Ac} = \frac{1}{10}$$

$$\sin\Delta\Theta = 0.1$$

$$\Delta\Theta = 5.7°$$

or

$$2\Delta\Theta = 11.4° \qquad \text{(peak-to-peak value)}$$

For a 30-dB difference:

$$2\Delta\Theta = 3.6°$$

For a 10-dB difference:

$$2\Delta\Theta = 36.9°$$

The two-tone procedure has been accepted as a calibration test for phase-jitter meters.

Note that the same 11.4° phase jitter value can be produced by two separate interfering tones, each 26 dB below the carrier:

$$26 \text{ dB} = 20 \log\frac{Ac}{Am_1}$$

$$\frac{Am_1}{Ac} = \frac{1}{20}$$

$$\Delta\Theta_1 = \frac{5.7°}{2}$$

For the other tone, Am_2,

$$\Delta\Theta_2 = \frac{5.7°}{2}$$

For $Am_1 + Am_2$,

$$\Delta\Theta = \Delta\Theta_1 + \Delta\Theta_2 = 5.7° \qquad \text{(for small angles)}$$

$$2\Delta\Theta = 11.4°$$

As more tones are added, the situation becomes more complex. Each tone acts not only on the carrier but on all the tones as well. If a very large number of tones spaced at random frequencies are considered, then an approximation of white noise can be obtained.

Phase-jitter figures. The following figures are given for a single interfering signal and help to evaluate test results. For a data circuit, less than 15° peak-to-peak jitter is recommended (CCITT Recs. H12 and M 1020). Phase-jitter eye patterns are given in Figs. 9.3 and 9.6.

Tone/Carrier	Jitter value	
	Peak-to-peak	Percent
10 dB	34.8°	9.6
20 dB	11.4°	3.2
30 dB	3.6°	1.0

Jitter on digital circuits

As the use of PCM transmission systems and switching grows, more and more attention is being paid to the amount of jitter contained in digital signals. The clock oscillator of a system provides a jitter component even if it is stabilized by a crystal. Interference such as noise or mechanical effects and power-supply variations can cause phase variations at this point.

In the digital signal path, additional jitter can be produced in the regenerator. One cause of variations is changes in the decision threshold of a regenerator (due, for example, to the instability of the power supply). Additionally, noise signals or interference due to crosstalk are added to the input at the regenerator, resulting in the signal transitions not being detected at the correct time. Figure 2.40 shows such a case with the resulting jitter.

In digital systems each separate regenerator derives the necessary

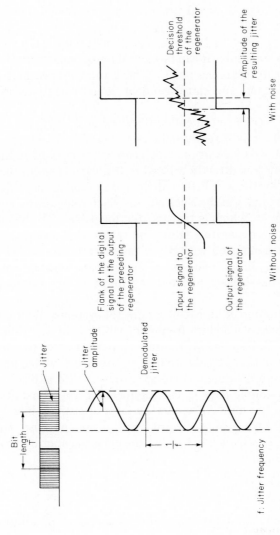

Figure 2.40 Generation of jitter by noise in a regenerator (the normally existing propagation time is ignored in order to simplify the illustration).

Jitter

Jitter amplitude

Bit length T

Demodulated jitter

$\frac{1}{f}$

f: Jitter frequency

Flank of the digital signal at the output of the preceding regenerator

Input signal to the regenerator

Output signal of the regenerator

Decision threshold of the regenerator

Amplitude of the resulting jitter

Without noise

With noise

clock signal from the incoming pulse pattern. If the pattern contains a long sequence of zeros, the clock oscillator of the regenerator is no longer synchronized and runs freely. At the end of the zero sequence, the clock oscillator synchronizes itself once again. This operation can cause a jitter which is termed *pattern-dependent jitter.*

Two types of digital signal jitter are distinguished; nonsystematic and systematic jitter.

Nonsystematic jitter has no fixed relationship with the received bit pattern and its structure. It can be caused by noises within the channel or by external interference noises. These interference noises are overlaid on the signal and cause random phase variations in each regenerator.

This type of jitter is often called *intrinsic* or basic jitter.

Systematic jitter is directly dependent on the structure of the bit pattern. The phase modulation which can be recognized on the leading and trailing edges is directly related to the variations in the pattern. The causes for systematic jitter can be, for example, incomplete equalization and mistuning of the clock circuit. Each regenerator contributes a jitter component, which is transmitted together with the digital signal to the next regenerator. Here, the received jitter component and the component generated within the regenerator are added together. In extreme cases, linear addition of the jitter amplitudes must be expected, since the series-connected regenerators are correlated jitter sources.

In the construction of higher-order digital systems, the input signals must be sampled with a clock frequency which is higher than the sum of the input clock frequencies in order to permit error-free multiplexing. In the case of the typical secondary system (T2) which multiplexes four (T1) 1544-kb/s signals, this increased bit rate is 6312 kb/s. The resulting unavoidable gaps in the input buffer are transmitted to the receiver side of the multiplexer in the form of stuffing bits.

The multiplexer prevents onward transmission of these stuffing bits and bridges the resulting gap with a time pattern generated by a phase-controlled oscillator.

Insertion and removal of the stuffing bits also cause jitter.

Jitter suppression.   In many cases, the regenerators of a digital transmission path not only generate jitter but also suppress existing jitter to a great degree. A regenerator synchronizes itself to the input signal with a certain inertia. This means that it follows slow phase shifts of the digital signal and regulates itself to an average value. In other words, a regenerator acts on the input jitter like a low-pass filter.

The ratio between output and input jitter of a regenerator is called the jitter suppression curve. Such a curve is shown in Fig. 2.41.

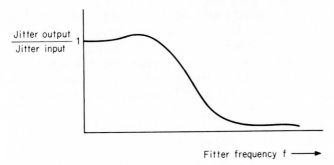

Jitter output / Jitter input   1

Fitter frequency f ⟶

Figure 2.41 Jitter suppression curve of a regenerator.

2.9 Harmonic Distortion

Harmonic distortion, which is the production of harmonic frequencies, is due to nonlinearities in the amplitude transfer characteristics of a device. The typical output contains not only the fundamental frequency but integer multiples of the fundamental frequency. Harmonic content is related to the amount of oscillator output power at frequencies other than the fundamental. In the voice band the second and third harmonics are the most concerned (see Fig. 2.42).

Measurement. The frequency most commonly used is 704 Hz, which allows a reasonably accurate measurement of the harmonics. The second (1408 Hz) and the third (2112 Hz) harmonics are measured with a frequency-selective voltmeter. The distortion ratio in dB is equal to the difference between the measured harmonic and the received level of the fundamental (refer to Fig. 2.43).

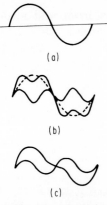

(a)

(b)

(c)

Figure 2.42 Harmonic distortion. (*a*) Fundamental; (*b*) third harmonic; (*c*) second harmonic.

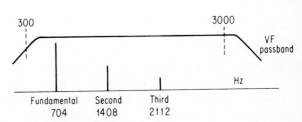

300   3000

                                          VF
                                          passband

                                   Hz

Fundamental   Second   Third
   704   1408   2112

Figure 2.43 Harmonic distortion measurement.

If there is only one source of distortion in the channel, this is a valid measurement. In a typical telephone circuit there may be several such sources, with filters which introduce envelope delay between them. This delay will change the phase relationships such that the distortion products will not be purely additive; they might even cancel out. Note that distortion is still present; it just is not being measured under these circumstances.

Recommended values

Second harmonic (1408 Hz): 25 dB

Third harmonic (2112 Hz): 30 dB

2.10   Nonlinear Distortion

Nonlinearities in amplifiers or other devices cause the generation of signal components from an input signal that add to the output signal in an undesirable manner, i.e., phase relation in the band changes. Phase distortion has an insignificant effect on voice transmission because the human ear is relatively insensitive to phase distortion. However, phase distortion can seriously affect data transmission. For example, with data transmitted at speeds greater than 2400 b/s over a voice-grade channel without proper delay equalization, data bits tend to overlap each other, producing errors. An ideal circuit which has a linear phase-shift characteristic will produce a straight-line slope, i.e., a linear relationship between a change in frequency and a corresponding change in phase, as shown in Fig. 2.44. The practical circuit however, is never ideal and will produce a nonlinear phase-shift characteristic as shown in the same figure.

If an amplifier is not exactly linear, considerable distortion and noise will be introduced into all carrier channels in a carrier system, i.e.,

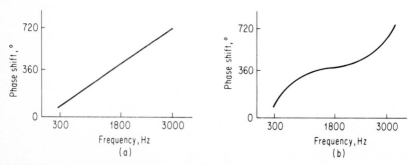

Figure 2.44 (*a*) Ideal linear phase characteristic and (*b*) practical nonlinear phase characteristic of an amplifier.

intermodulation products are generated. For example, a strong signal in one channel of a 24-channel cable carrier may cause an amplifying stage to operate in its nonlinear region and degrade the transmission features of all 24 channels. In fact, the principal limitation of the number of channels in FDM systems is not bandwidth but the loading or linearity characteristics of amplifiers. Nonlinear distortion attenuation between end offices of 30 dB or higher is recommended.

Measurement.   Two pairs of tones are transmitted, centered at 860 and 1380 Hz. Second-order distortion products are measured in two narrow bands and third-order products in one band. It is similar to noise-loading tests made to measure distortion performance of wideband systems, but instead of using a white noise slot, it uses four discrete frequencies. The technique correlates well with the harmonic distortion measurement, it is not overly sensitive to delay, the noise content in the measurement may be separated, and no products are placed near the band edges.

Two equal-level tone pairs are transmitted at a combined level to the data level (see Fig. 2.45). Second-order distortion products $B \pm A$ are measured in two bands, third-order $2B - A$ in one band; all in the voice band. The combined power of the products is measured and compared to the received signal level.

The distortion measurement will also contain a component due to C-notched noise. The level of this may be determined by the S/N check incorporated in nonlinear distortion measurements. When this check is made, one of the tone pairs is removed and the other is increased 3 dB at the transmitter. The measurement is repeated; this time only C-notched noise is present. The difference in readings is an indication of the power ratios, i.e., distortion plus noise to noise, and is used to correct the first measurement (see Fig. 2.45).

2.11 Bias Distortion

The shape of the received digital signal is not the same as the original transmitted signal because distortion occurs in the transmission media. Mark-to-space and space-to-mark transitions are not instantaneous and create a time delay on received signals. Refer to Fig. 2.46.

The dashed line indicates the decision threshold or slicing point. Voltages above that threshold level produce one logic state output, while voltages below the threshold produce the other logic state at the receiver output. If the decision threshold point is misplaced from its optimum value, distortion can occur at the received signal. If the receiver threshold is shifted up to the broken line, toward the 1 signal level, then the time duration of the 1 bits shortens with respect to the

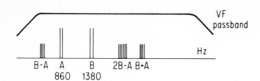

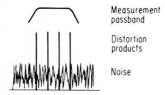

Figure 2.45 Nonlinear distortion measurement and noise.

duration of the 0 bits; this is called *positive bias* or *marking bias*. *Negative bias* or *space bias* shifts the receiver threshold toward the 0 signal level which the time duration of 0 bits shortens. This is called *bias distortion* in telegraphy and can be due to receiver threshold offset.

Percent distortion is defined as

$$\% \text{ distortion} = \frac{T_M - T_S}{T_M + T_S}$$

where T_M = 1 bit mark
      T_S = 1 bit space

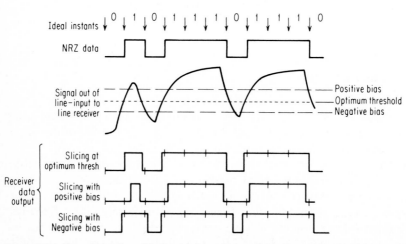

Figure 2.46 Bias distortion. (*Redrawn from Kenneth M. True,* Interface, *Fairchild Semiconductor Co., Mountain View, Calif., 1975, fig. 4–8.*)

2.12   Characteristic Distortion

Comparing the original data in Fig. 2.47 to the received data shows that the actual recovered data transitions are displaced from their original instants. This time displacement of the transitions is due to a new wave arriving at the receiver before the previous wave has reached its final value. Since the wave represents the present data bit, this phenomenon is called *intersymbol interference* or *characteristic distortion* in telegraphy. This distortion can be reduced to zero by making the unit interval of the data signal quite long in comparison to the rise-fall time of the signal at the receiver, either by reducing the modulation rate or by reducing the line length. Here the effect is not reversed when 1 and 0 are interchanged but is similar for either of them. For example, a single 1 may be shortened in transmission, whereas an adjacent 0 may lengthen. This may be caused by some nonlinear characteristics of the transmission media.

Isochronous distortion is discussed in Sec. 9.2.

Regenerators are devices that improve the distortion rate of dc signals. A typical regenerator receives a 300-Bd signal with up to 45 percent distortion and delivers it with less than 2 percent distortion. Most of the data communication equipments (DCEs) and data terminal equipments (DTEs) perform the generation as a supplement to their designated function, although regenerators are also available as a separate unit.

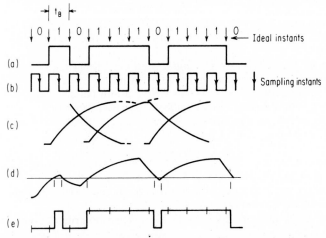

Figure 2.47   Characteristic distortion. (*a*) NRZ data; (*b*) clock; (*c*) wavefronts due to each data transition; (*d*) resultant load signal; (*e*) line receiver data output. (*Redrawn from Kenneth M. True,* Interface, *Fairchild Semiconductor Co., Mountain View, Calif., 1975, fig. 4–7.*)

2.13 CCITT Recommendations
Referring to Data Transmission over
Voice-Grade Circuits

H.12   Characteristics of telephone-type leased circuits.
   A. (also M.1040). Ordinary international circuits.
   Receive level at the end office should not be less than -15 dB; maximum loss in any part of circuit should not exceed 28 dB.
   Loss-frequency distortion curve is given in Fig. 2.4b.
   Psophometric noise power limit is given in Fig. 2.27; satellite circuit between earth stations contributes 10,000 pW0p (-50 dBm0p) of noise.
   B. (also M.1020). Special-quality leased circuits.
   Receive level, overall loss, and random circuit noise are as given in paragraph A above.
   Loss-frequency distortion curve is given in Fig. 2.4a.
   Group-delay distortion is given in Fig. 2.4c.
   Level variations: Short term (in a few seconds), ±3 dB
   Long term (daily and seasonal), ±4 dB
   Impulsive noise exceeding -21 dBm0 should not be more than 18 in 15 min.
   Phase jitter: Maximum 15° peak to peak
   Quantizing noise: If any section of the circuit is routed over a PCM system, minimum signal-to-quantizing-noise ratio normally expected is 22 dB.
   Single-tone interference shall not exceed the value which is 3 dB below the circuit noise of Fig. 2.27.
   Frequency error: Maximum ±5 Hz
   Harmonic distortion: 700 Hz injected at -13 dBm0 will be at least 25 dB below fundamental frequency

H.22   Transmission requirements of international VFT links (at 50, 100, and 200 Bd).
   Variation of insertion loss with time should not exceed 1 dB.
   Overall loss-frequency deviation curve is given in Fig. 2.5.
   The mean psophometric noise power referred to a point of zero relative level should not exceed 80,000 pW0p (-41 dBm0p).
   The number of impulsive noise peaks exceeding -18 dBm0 should not be more than 18 in 15 min.
   The crosstalk ratio between the go and return channels of the link should be at least 43 dB, and 58 dB between carrier circuits.
   It is not necessary to recommend limits for group delay distortions for 50-Bd VFT links; experiments are recommended for higher-speed telegraph systems.
   Frequency drift introduced by the link must not be greater than 2 Hz.

H.41   Phototelegraph transmissions on telephone-type circuits.
   Overall loss: The same conditions apply as used for telephony.
   Transmit signal power: 0 dBm0 for amplitude-modulation (AM) pho-

totelegraph transmission and -10 dBm0 for frequency-modulation (FM) transmission. In the case of AM, the level of the signal corresponding to black is usually about 30 dB lower than the white signal.

Attenuation-frequency distortion is given in Fig. 2.5a in dashed lines and marked as G.151. In AM transmission, less than 8.7 dB is recommended between two stations.

Variation of circuit overall loss with time should not exceed 1 dB; 1.5 dB may be accepted in some cases.

Phase distortion limits the range of satisfactory phototelegraph transmissions; thus the carrier frequency (where AM is used) or mean frequency (where FM is used) must be chosen in such a way that it is as near as possible to the frequency which has the minimum group delay on the telephone circuit; for more information see Rec. H.42.

H.42   Range of phototelegraph transmissions on a telephone-type circuit. Contains information and gives curves for drum speed and range of phototelegraphy.

H.51   Data signals on telephone-type circuits.

Channel loading: -15 dBm0 is recommended; -10 dBm0 is allowable. -13 dBm0 on an international carrier system for each direction.

On carrier systems, the maximum power output of the subscriber's apparatus is 1 mW. For systems transmitting tones continuously, for example, FM systems, maximum power shall be -10 dBm0. When transmission of data is discontinued for any appreciable time, the power should be reduced to -20 dBm0. For systems not transmitting tones continuously, for example, AM systems, -6 dBm0 may be used.

Over switched telephone network, in systems continuously transmitting tone, such as FM and PM systems, maximum power at the international circuit input shall not exceed -10 dBm0 (simplex systems) or -13 dBm0 (duplex systems). In systems not transmitting tones continuously, -15 dBm0 (64 μW) is recommended.

In switched connections the loss between subscribers' telephones may be high; 30 to 40 dB. These signals may suffer disturbance from dialing pulses sent over other circuits. Hence the transmission level should be as high as possible.

M.590   Setting up a circuit fitted with a compandor

M.660   Periodical in-station testing of echo suppressors

M.670   Maintenance of a circuit fitted with a compandor

M.1015   Types of transmission on leased circuits

M.1020   Characteristics of special-quality international leased circuits (similar to Rec. H.12B)

M.1040   Characteristics of ordinary-quality international leased circuits (similar to Rec. H.12A)

2.14   Estimating End-to-End Analog Transmission Performance*

This section provides examples of the estimation of end-to-end analog transmission performance based on sectional measurements of a two-point service, instead of tedious calculations.

1. Attenuation distortion

The sectional loss with respect to 1000-Hz (or 800-Hz) measurements should be added algebraically for each frequency.

Example

Freq., Hz	Link A, dB	Link B, dB	Total, dB
300	1	−0.3	+0.7
1000	0	0	0
3000	1.3	1.4	2.7

2. Envelope delay distortion

The sectional envelope delay measurements should be added algebraically.

Example

Freq., Hz	Link A, μs	Link B, μs	Total, μs
500	410	380	790
800	180	170	350
1800	0	−30	−30
2800	290	260	550

3. C-message noise, psophometric noise, C-notched noise, and signal-tone interference

Combine the sectional measurements on a power basis.

Example 1   Refer to "Psophometric Noise Weighting" in Sec. 2.5.

Link *A*	−50 dBm0p
Link *B*	−47 dBm0p

*Condensed from "Bell System Practices," sec. 314-410-500, issue 4, July 1972, appendix B, AT&T, New York.

For a 3-dB difference, we read 1.8 dB from Table 2.5. Add this combining power to the lower figure (higher noise level):

$$-47 + 1.8 = -45.2 \text{ dBm0p} = \text{overall noise}$$

Example 2

Link A	50 dBrnCO
Link B	55 dBrnCO

TABLE 2.5 Combining Powers and Voltages

Difference between two quantities	Power-combining term	Voltage-combining term
0–0.1	3.0	6.0
0.2–0.3	2.9	5.8
0.4–0.5	2.8	5.6
0.6–0.7	2.7	5.4
0.8–0.9	2.6	5.2
1.0–1.2	2.5	5.0
1.3–1.4	2.4	4.8
1.5–1.6	2.3	4.6
1.7–1.9	2.2	4.4
2.0–2.1	2.1	4.2
2.2–2.4	2.0	4.0
2.5–2.7	1.9	3.8
2.8–3.0	1.8	3.6
3.1–3.3	1.7	3.4
3.4–3.6	1.6	3.2
3.7–4.0	1.5	3.0
4.1–4.3	1.4	2.8
4.4–4.7	1.3	2.6
4.8–5.1	1.2	2.4
5.2–5.6	1.1	2.2
5.7–6.1	1.0	2.0
6.2–6.6	0.9	1.8
6.7–7.2	0.8	1.6
7.3–7.9	0.7	1.4
8.0–8.6	0.6	1.2
8.6–9.6	0.5	1.0
9.7–10.7	0.4	0.8
10.8–12.2	0.3	0.6
12.3–14.5	0.2	0.4
14.6–19.3	0.1	0.2
19.4–up	0	0

For a 5-dB difference, we read 1.2 dB from Table 2.5. Add this combining power to the higher figure (higher noise level):

$$55 + 1.2 = 56.2 \text{ dBrnCO} = \text{overall noise}$$

4. Harmonic distortion

Combine the sectional second-harmonic measurements on a power basis; combine the sectional third-harmonic measurements on a voltage basis using Table 2.5.

Example 1.   Ratio of Second Harmonic to Fundamental

Link A	35 dB
Link B	38 dB

$$\text{Difference} = 38 - 35 = 3 \text{ dB}$$

From Table 2.5, the combining term is 1.8 dB. Subtract the combining term from the lower number (higher distortion):

$$35 - 1.8 = 33.2 \text{ dB}$$

is the overall second-harmonic-to-fundamental-frequency ratio.

Example 2.   Ratio of Third Harmonic to Fundamental

Link A	37 dB
Link B	41 dB

$$\text{Difference between quantities} = 41 - 37 = 4 \text{ dB}$$

From Table 2.5, the voltage-combining term is 3 dB. Subtract the combining term from the lower number (higher distortion):

$$37 - 3 = 34 \text{ dB}$$

is the overall third-harmonic-to-fundamental-frequency ratio.

5. Phase jitter

Table 2.6 may be used to add phase-jitter measurements expressed in degrees.

Example

Link A	3°
Link B	5°

TABLE 2.6 Combining Two Phase-Jitter Measurements Expressed in Degrees Peak to Peak

Link B	Link A									
	1	2	3	4	5	6	7	8	9	10
1	2	3	4	4	5	6	7	8	9	10
2	3	3	4	5	6	7	8	9	10	11
3	4	4	5	6	7	8	9	10	11	12
4	4	5	6	7	8	8	9	10	11	12
5	5	6	7	8	8	9	10	11	12	13
6	6	7	8	8	9	10	11	12	13	14
7	7	8	9	9	10	11	12	13	13	14
8	8	9	10	10	11	12	13	13	14	15
9	9	10	11	11	12	13	13	14	15	16
10	10	11	12	12	13	14	14	15	16	17

From Table 2.6, the overall phase jitter would be expected to approximate 7°.

6. Impulse Noise

Algebraically add the number of impulses recorded in 15 min on each section to obtain the overall counts.

Example

Link A	5 counts
Link B	2 counts
Overall	7 counts

7. Frequency shift

Add the frequency shift for each section algebraically. Note whether the shift for each link is plus or minus with respect to the source.

Example

Link A	+1 Hz
Link B	−2 Hz
Overall	−1 Hz

2.15 Principles of circuit bridging

A bridging network can be used in a variety of ways. Two of the most common applications allow the addressing of several receivers by one transmitter and the combining of slow-speed FDM channels with medium-speed data on a single VG line.

In digital circuits a high-impedance repeater relay is used.

In analog circuits, bridging may be accomplished simply with a passive network or high-impedance configuration, which require amplification. The passive bridge network matches line impedance and introduces a specific insertion loss.

In Fig. 2.48 a two-wire/three-way bridge through 15-way network is illustrated for a 600-Ω line. Values of insertion losses between legs and network resistors are given for a sequentially expanding network.

A two-wire/three-way bridge network connection for duplex operation is shown in Fig. 2.49.

A four-wire *conference bridging network* enables any transmitter to address any receiver in the system. In Fig. 2.50, four-wire/four-way

Unit description	Total legs (input + output)	Insertion loss in dB ±1.0 dB	Impedance of each leg in ohms ±10%	Value	Resistor numbers
2-wire, 3-way brdg.	3	6.0	600 balanced	100 Ω	R1 through R6
2-wire, 4-way brdg.	4	9.5	600 balanced	150 Ω	R1 through R8
2-wire, 5-way brdg.	5	12.0	600 balanced	180 Ω	R1 through R10
2-wire, 6-way brdg.	6	14.0	600 balanced	200 Ω	R1 through R12
2-wire, 7-way brdg.	7	15.6	600 balanced	220 Ω	R1 through R14
2-wire, 8-way brdg.	8	17.0	600 balanced	220 Ω	R1 through R16
2-wire, 9-way brdg.	9	18.0	600 balanced	240 Ω	R1 through R18
2-wire, 10-way brdg.	10	19.0	600 balanced	240 Ω	R1 through R20
2-wire, 11-way brdg.	11	20.0	600 balanced	240 Ω	R1 through R22
2-wire, 12-way brdg.	12	20.8	600 balanced	240 Ω	R1 through R24
2-wire, 13-way brdg.	13	21.5	600 balanced	240 Ω	R1 through R26
2-wire, 14-way brdg.	14	22.3	600 balanced	240 Ω	R1 through R28
2-wire, 15-way brdg.	15	22.9	600 balanced	260 Ω	R1 through R30

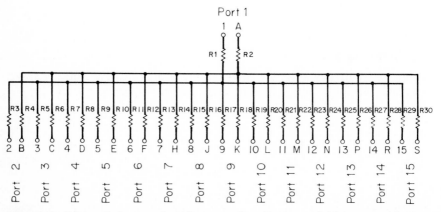

Figure 2.48 Schematic for two-wire/(three-way through 15-way) bridging network.

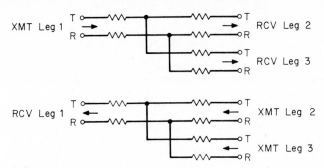

Figure 2.49 Two-wire/three-way connection. All resistors are 100-Ω for 600-Ω line impedance.

and six-way conference bridging networks with insertion losses and resistor values for 600-Ω line impedance are given. These two bridges are readily available in the market.

Note that each leg must be terminated with a 600-Ω resistor if the leg is not used or the transmitter or receiver is disconnected.

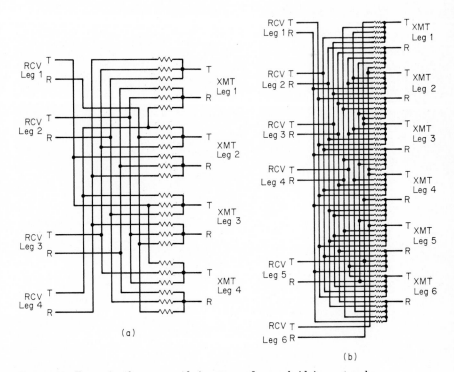

Figure 2.50 Four-wire/four-way and six-way conference bridging networks.

References

"Bell System Practices," sec. 314-410-500, issue 4, July 1972, appendix B, AT&T, New York.
CCITT, Geneva: *Orange, Yellow,* and *Red Books.* Volume III, "Line Transmission"; vol. IV, "Line Maintenance," "Specifications of Measuring Equipment"; vol. VIII, "Data Transmission."
Digital Communications Corp., Gaithersburg, Md.: "Digital Echo Canceller," fig. 2 and portions.
GTE Lenkurt, San Carlos, Calif.: "Demodulator," July/August 1980, pp. 11, 22.
Halcyon Inc., San Jose, Calif.: "Data Line Testing," Application Note AP-520-01.
Tugal, Dogan A.: "Data Transmission over Voice Circuits," RCA Global Communications, Anchorage, Alaska, 1972.
W&G Instruments, Inc., Livingston, NJ.: Application Note 307.

Modulation, Demodulation, Binary Basebands, and Modems

Modulation can be defined as the modification of some characteristics of an otherwise continuous signal called a *carrier*. Usually, a carrier is a single-frequency electronic wave which serves as a means of propagation. It is modified in some way that can be accurately detected at the receiving end by a signal containing the information which is transmitted, and this signal is called a *baseband signal*.

In this chapter analog and pulse modulation, demodulation, binary basebands, and pulse-code modulation are discussed. Modems, acoustic couplers, facsimile transmission, and data encryption are reviewed.

3.1 Analog Modulation and Demodulation

Whenever dial-up networks or leased lines are used, to a great extent they are dependent on how the modem modulates data prior to sending them over the phone lines. Certain modulation techniques permit higher rates of transmission than others, and all modulation techniques directly affect the maximum data rate and the error performance. Three analog-modulation techniques are frequency-shift keying, amplitude modulation, and phase modulation. They are illustrated in Fig. 3.1, and vector diagrams are given in Sec. 2.8.

Frequency-shift keying (FSK)

The most popular form of frequency modulation is known as FSK. In this system, the carrier frequency, say 1700 Hz, is modulated plus or minus 500 Hz to represent binary 1 or binary 0. Thus a frequency of 1200 Hz represents a 1, while a frequency of 2200 Hz represents a binary 0. FSK techniques are generally quite suitable for low-speed devices such as teleprinters and allow operation at speeds as high as 1800 b/s.

Amplitude modulation (AM)

Amplitude modulation enables a modem to transmit and receive analog equivalents of binary 1s and 0s. This technique involves varying the

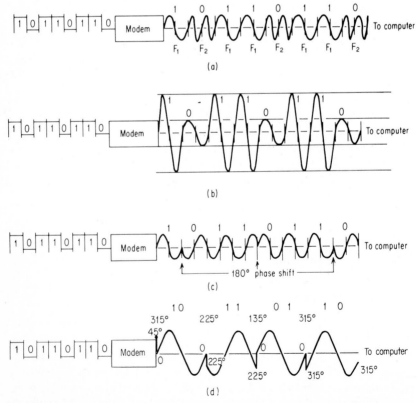

Figure 3.1 Analog modulation techniques. (a) Frequency-shift keying (FSK); (b) Amplitude modulation (AM); (c) Phase-shift keying (PSK); (d) Differential phase-shift keying (DPSK) for dibit coding per Table 3.1, Alternative B.

amplitude of the line's carrier frequency. Several levels of AM are possible, allowing twice as much data to be sent in the same time frame (refer to Sec. 4.1). Both AM and FSK are quite suitable for data transmission. FSK, however, has a noise advantage over AM, but AM allows more efficient use of the available bandwidth.

Vestigial-sideband modulation (VSBM). This is a technique used with AM to reduce bandwidth requirements, conserve power, and increase speed. It does this by using most of the lower sideband and a small part (vestige) of the upper sideband. Sideband frequencies exist on either side of a carrier wave and represent the sum (upper) or difference (lower) of the baseband and carrier wave.

Phase modulation (PM) [or phase-shift keying (PSK)]. In this technique, the transmitted signal is shifted a certain number of degrees in response to the pattern of bits coming from the terminal or computer. For example, in a two-phase PM modem, if the analog signal generated by the transmitting modem is shifted 180°, a change in the binary value is indicated. If there is no shift, then the signal will be interpreted as a series of 0s (or 1s) until such a shift is sensed. Generally PM modems operate in four and eight phases, permitting up to two or three times the data to be sent over the line in the same bandwidth also called differential phase-shift keying (DPSK). Most 2400–9600 b/s modems use PM (refer to Sec. 4.1). CCITT recommendations for phase arrangements are given in Tables 3.1 and 3.2. DPSK dibit coding signals are shown in Fig. 3.1d.

Four-phase modulation is merely a phase shift of 0, 90, 180, and 270° (or 45, 135, 225, and 315°), depending on the sequence of values of the modulating quaternary signal. A pair of binary digits can combine in only four ways: 00, 01, 11, and 10. We can assign each of these pairs

TABLE 3.1 Two Alternative Phase Arrangements for Dibit Coding

Dibit	Phase change	
	Alternative A	Alternative B
00	0°	+45°
01	+90°	+135°
11	+180°	+225°
10	+270°	+315°

SOURCE: CCITT Rec. V.26.

TABLE 3.2 Phase Arrangements for Tribit Coding

Tribit values	Phase change
001	0°
000	45°
010	90°
011	135°
111	180°
110	225°
100	270°
101	315°

SOURCE: CCITT Rec. V.27.

a phase-shift value, as seen on Table 3.1. Then we can transmit a carrier that shifts phase for each pair of bits in a sequence of message bits.

A message with bit sequence 0010110110 was divided into the dibit sequence 00 10 11 01 10 which modulated a carrier once per cycle and produced the PM wave shown in Fig. 3.1. This modulation allows transmission of 2 bits per cycle of carrier. Actual throughput is considerably less, however, to allow for sample detection time in the receiver.

Demodulation

When a modulated waveform reaches the demodulator, a detection (*demodulation*) process must convert it back to the original signal.

Detection of frequency-shift keying.   The frequency-modulated signal is transmitted at constant amplitude. A circuit called the *limiter* converts zero crossings of shift frequencies (for example, 1700 ± 500 Hz) into a square wave. The output of the limiter can then be converted by different types of circuits to produce the original bit pattern.

Detection of amplitude modulation.   There are two main types of detection, *synchronous* (also called *coherent* or *homodyne*) and *envelope detection*. *Synchronous detection* involves the use of a locally produced source of carrier which has the same frequency and phase as that bringing the received signal. In conjunction with the reference carrier signal at the output of the balanced demodulator, coherently demodulated signals are obtained together with even harmonics of the carrier frequency. The harmonics are rejected by a low-pass filter. These binary signals are interpreted as being either 1 or 0 at the decoder, similar to the original bits.

In synchronous detection, to produce the reference carrier signal of the same frequency and phase as the received carrier, it is normally necessary to transmit some information with the signal. Such a signal can be extracted from the carrier, and so the carrier may not be completely suppressed. It is usually partly suppressed because of its relatively high energy content.

Envelope detection involves rectifying the signal to obtain its envelope. The original bit pattern is obtained by regeneration of these rectified signals.

Envelope detection does not require the reference signal to be produced, and so it is considerably less expensive than synchronous detection technique. Envelope detection does, however, need both sidebands and amplitude carrier.

Detection of phase modulation. There are two methods of detection in PM systems: *fixed-reference detection* and *differential detection*. The receiver has no absolute sense of phase. It is therefore necessary either to use the signal in some way to generate information about the phases at the source or else to manage without it and operate by examining the changes in phase that occur.

The former approach needs a *fixed reference* providing the source phase. To achieve this it is desirable to transmit the carrier information. The phase information may be sent in bursts at intervals in the transmission. This *reference-phase signal* is used to detect phases of the received signal and convert them into the original bit stream.

Differential detection does not attempt to generate a fixed-reference phase at the receiver. Instead the data are coded by means of changes in phase. The detector now looks for changes in phase and does not need a *reference-phase signal*. If the phase of the signal slips or drifts, the system recovers without aid. To carry out the detection, the received signal is delayed one symbol interval and compared with the signal being received. This comparison indicates the phase change that occurred between the symbol intervals. The detected phase change is then converted into the original bit pattern.

Because of the delaying one-symbol interval, the speed of the transmission cannot easily be varied. Furthermore, it is difficult to use this type of detection for other than *synchronous transmission* in which the bits of characters are sent in a continuous, equally spaced stream, with no start and stop bits or gaps between characters.

3.2 Pulse Modulation

In pulse modulation the unmodulated carrier is usually a series of regularly recurrent pulses. Modulation results in sampling the baseband signal at regular intervals and converting the sample results into *pulse-amplitude, pulse-width,* or *pulse-position modulation.*

Sampling

Sampling is the process of obtaining a sequence of instantaneous values of a signal at regular or intermittent intervals. The output of a sampled circuit is a series of discrete values representing the values of the input signal at a series of points in time. One method uses samples of the signal near the midpoint of the duration of each pulse. Another method uses circuits that will change state each time the signal level advances or retreats across the decision level. If the properties of the baseband signal are such that rather than changing from a zero to a positive value it changes from a negative to a positive value, then another method of sampling involves the detection of zero crossing of the signal. In summary, the purpose of sampling is to determine the value (1 or 0) of a portion of a received signal.

Pulse-amplitude modulation (PAM)

In PAM the amplitude of a pulse carrier is varied in accordance with the value of the modulating wave, as shown in Fig. 3.2a. It is convenient to look upon PAM as modulation in which the value of each instantaneous sample of the modulating wave is caused to modulate the amplitude of a pulse.

Pulse-width modulation (PWM or PDM)

Pulse-width modulation, sometimes referred to as *pulse-duration modulation* (PDM) or *pulse-length modulation,* is modulation of a pulse carrier in which each sampled pulse is a constant in amplitude and time position but may vary in width (refer to Fig. 3.2b).

Pulse-position modulation (PPM)

In PPM each sampled pulse is of the same width and amplitude, but its pulse time position with respect to a uniform time scale varies (refer to Fig. 3.2c).

Pulse-code modulation (PCM)

Pulses produced by pulse-modulation methods still carry their information in an analog form where the amplitude (or width or position) of the pulse is continuously variable. If the pulse train were transmitted over a long distance and subjected to distortion, it may not be possible to reconstruct the original pulses. To avoid this a second process is employed which converts those pulses into unique sets of equal-am-

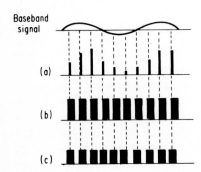

Figure 3.2 Pulse-modulation techniques. (a) Pulse-amplitude modulation (PAM); (b) pulse-width modulation (PWM); (c) pulse-position modulation (PPM).

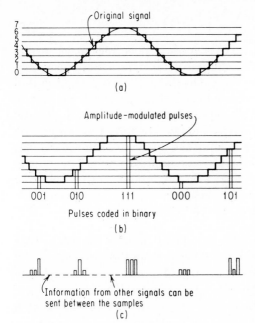

Amp.	Tribits
0	000
1	001
2	010
3	011
4	010
5	101
6	110
7	111

Figure 3.3 Pulse-code modulation (PCM). (*a*) The signal is first "quantized" or made to occupy a discrete set of values (eight levels). (*b*) It is then sampled at specific points. The PAM signal that results can be coded for PCM. (*c*) The coded pulse may be transmitted in a binary form ($2^3 = 8$).

plitude pulses so that the presence or absence of a pulse, not its size, is only detected. The PAM pulses themselves are used in certain switching equipment in which the switching is done electrically, controlling the flow of PAM pulses.

The amplitude of a PAM pulse can assume an infinite number of possible values ranging from zero to its maximum.

It is normal with pulse modulation to transmit not an infinitely finely divided range of values but a limited set of specific discrete values. In other words, the input signal is quantized. This process is illustrated schematically in Fig. 3.3. Here the signal amplitude can be represented by any one of eight values shown. The amplitude of the pulses will therefore be one of these eight values. An inaccuracy is introduced in the reproduction of the signal by doing this, analogous to the error introduced by rounding a value in a computation. If there were more values, the "rounding error" would be less. In systems in actual use today, 128 pulse amplitudes are used, or 127 to be exact since the zero amplitude is not transmitted.

After a signal has been quantized and samples taken at specific points, as in Fig. 3.3, the result can be coded. If the pulses in the figure are coded in binary, as shown, 3 bits is needed to represent the eight possible amplitudes of each sample. A more accurate sampling with 128 quantized levels would need 7 bits to represent each sample. In general, if there were N quantized levels, $\log_2 N$ bits would be needed per sample. the process producing the binary pulse train is referred to as *pulse-code modulation* (PCM).

The mere presence or absence of a pulse can be recognized easily even when distortion is present, whereas determination of pulse magnitude would be more prone to error. On the other hand, the original voice signal can never be reproduced exactly because of the quantizing errors. This deviation from the original signal is sometimes referred to as *quantizing noise*. It is of known magnitude and can be reduced at the expense of bandwidth. Increasing the number of sampling levels to 128, needing 7 bits per sample, is enough to produce telephone channels having an S/N ratio of 22 dB, comparable to that achieved on today's analog channels; refer to Sec. 2.5.

Related CCITT recommendations for PCM are given at the end of this section.

It can be shown mathematically that if the signal is limited so that the highest frequency it contains is W hertz, then a pulse train of $2W$ pulses per second is sufficient to carry it and allow it to be completely reconstructed. This is called the *Nyquist theorem*. The human voice, therefore, if limited to frequencies below 4000 Hz, can be carried by a pulse train of 8000 PAM pulses per second. The original voice sounds below 4000 Hz can be completely reconstructed.

In telephone transmission, the frequency range encoded in PCM is 200 to 3500 Hz, and 8000 samples per second are used. Each sample is digitized using 7 bits so that $2^7 = 128$ different volume levels can be distinguished. This gives $7 \times 8000 = 56,000$ b/s. High-fidelity music with five times this frequency range would need five times as many bits per second. Table 3.3 shows the bandwidth needed for four types of signals for human perception plus the digital bit rate used or planned for their transmission with PCM.

CCITT Recommendations for PCM

G.703   General aspects of interfaces, deals with interconnection of 1544 kb/s, 6312 kb/s, 32,064 kb/s, 44,736 kb/s, 2,048 kb/s, 8,448 kb/s, 34,368 kb/s, 139,264-kb/s, and 64-kb/s signals; gives the definition of the HDB3 code.

G.711   Pulse code modulation (PCM) of voice frequencies, recommends 8000 samples per second, eight binary digits per sample for international circuits. Two encoding laws are recommended, and these are commonly referred to as the A-law and the μ-law; definitions and relationship between the encoding laws are also mentioned.

G.712   Performance characteristics of PCM channels at audio frequencies, specifies attenuation-frequency distortion limits, envelope delay specifications for 64 kb/s transmission, together with return loss, different types of noise, quantizing distortion figures.

G.721   Hypothetical reference digital paths.

TABLE 3.3 Bandwidth and Digital Bit Rate Requirements of Signals

Type of signal	Analog bandwidth, kHz	No. of bits per sample	Needed digital bit rate, kb/s
Telephone voice	4	7	$4 \times 2 \times 7 = 56$
High-fidelity music	20	7	$20 \times 2 \times 7 = 280$
Picturephone*	1000	3	$1000 \times 2 \times 3 = 6000$
Color television	4600	10	$4600 \times 2 \times 10 = 92,000$

*In picturephone encoding, a smaller number of bits is used to code each sample. It is not necessary to distinguish as many separate levels of brightness. The ratio between the bit rate and the bandwidth used is therefore smaller. On high-fidelity services such as color TV network, however, a larger number of bits is employed to minimize quantizing noise.

3.3 Binary Basebands

The baseband signal used to modulate a sinusoidal carrier in digital modulation is digital. At the receiver end either coherent detection, where the receiver is phase-locked with the transmitter, or noncoherent detection, where the receiver is not phase-locked with the transmitter, is used. The receiver is always synchronized to the transmitter signals in digital systems.

An example of a binary baseband (pulse code) signal is given in Fig. 3.4. Figure 3.4a shows a signal produced by a data source. In Fig. 3.4b the reproduced signal is given. The dashed line indicates the *decision level* or *slicing point* which has been drawn at the appropriate middle of the signal's magnitude. The binary value of the signal at any instant is determined by its presence above or below the decision level.

Types of binary baseband signals

Various types of binary baseband (pulse code) signals have been developed to meet the following special needs:

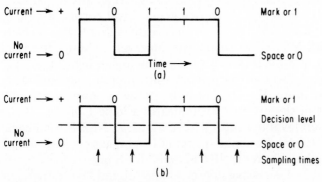

Figure 3.4 An example of a binary baseband signal.

- Compressing the overall bandwidth normally required to adequately transmit the signal yet still ensure recovery of the binary data
- Eliminating the need for a dc response in the transmission medium so that transformer coupling can be used for phantom power distribution on repeated lines
- Providing a clocking scheme within the signal so that no separate channel is required for synchronization
- Providing built-in error detection

In general, the binary class of pulse codes can be grouped into four categories:

1. Nonreturn to zero (NRZ)
2. Return to zero (RZ)
3. Phase-encoded (PE), sometimes called split phase
4. Multilevel binary (MLB)

A secondary differentiation among the pulse codes is concerned with the algebraic signs of the signal levels. If the signal levels have the same algebraic sign for their voltages or currents and differ only in their magnitudes, then they are called *unipolar*. The complement of unipolar signaling is *polar* signaling, where one logic state is represented by a signal voltage or current having a positive sign and the other logic state is represented by a signal with a negative sign. For binary signals, the magnitude of both signals should be ideally equal, and their only difference should be in the algebraic signs. This allows the receiver to use ground as its decision threshold reference.

1.   Nonreturn-to-zero (NRZ) pulse codes.   There are three NRZ pulse codes: NRZ-level (NRZ-L), NRZ-mark (NRZ-M), and NRZ-space (NRZ-S).

In NRZ-L signaling, data are represented by a constant signal level during the bit time interval, with one signal level corresponding to one logic state and the other signal level corresponding to the opposite logic state. In NRZ-M or NRZ-S signaling, however, a change in signal level at the start of a bit interval corresponds to one logic state, and no change in signal level at the start of a bit interval corresponds to the opposite logic state. For NRZ-M pulse codes, a change in signal level at the start of the bit interval indicates a logic 1 (mark), while no change in signal level indicates a logic 0 (space), NRZ-S is a logical complement to NRZ-M. A change in signal level means a logic 0, and no change means logic 1. With NRZ-M and NRZ-S pulse codes, therefore, there is no direct correspondence between signal levels and logic states as there is with NRZ-L signaling. Any of the NRZ pulse codes may, of course, be used in unipolar or polar form. The NRZ codes are shown in Fig. 3.5a.

Briefly, the NRZ signal is discussed as follows. When the bit interval t_B is less than the 0 to 50 percent rise or fall time of the signal at the line end, the open space in the eye pattern closes (refer to Figs. 9.2 and 9.3), thereby indicating that error-free data transmission is unlikely. When t_B is less than the 10 to 90 percent rise or fall time of the line end signal, some intersymbol interference is present, and thus some jitter in the transitions of the recovered data will be present.

NRZ codes are simple to generate and decode because no precoding or special treatment is required. This simplicity makes them probably the most widely used pulse codes, with NRZ-L the leader by far. NRZ-M has been widely used in digital magnetic recording, where it is usually called NRZI for nonreturn to zero, invert-on-ones. Since NRZ codes do possess a strong dc component and have neither intrinsic clocking nor error detection features, none of the NRZ codes appeals to transmission design engineers.

2. Return-to-zero (RZ) pulse codes. The RZ pulse codes are usually simple combinations of NRZ-L data and its associated single- or double-frequency clock. By combining the clock with data, all RZ codes possess some intrinsic synchronization feature. Three representative RZ pulse codes are shown in Fig. 3.5b. Unipolar RZ is formed by performing a logic AND between the NRZ-L data and its clock. Thus a logic 0 is represented by the absence of a pulse during the bit time interval, and a logic 1 is represented by a pulse as shown.

Pulse-position modulation (PPM) uses a pulse of $t_B/4$ duration beginning at the start of the bit interval to indicate a logic 0 and a $t_B/4$ pulse beginning at the middle of the bit interval to indicate a logic 1. Pulse-duration modulation (PDM) uses a $t_B/3$ duration pulse for a logic 0 and a $\frac{2}{3} t_B$ pulse for a logic 1, with the rising edge of both pulses coinciding with the start of the bit interval. PDM with $t_B/4$ pulse widths is also used, but better results are usually obtained with the $t_B/3$ and $2t_B/3$ schemes.

The reason for differentiating between information rate and modulation rate can now be further clarified. Each of the RZ pulse codes in Fig. 3.5b has the same information rate, that is, $1/t_B$ b/s. Their respective minimum signaling elements (unit intervals), however, are all less than t_B, so the "modulation rate" for the RZ pulse code is greater than the "information rate." Remember that with an NRZ signal the unit interval and the bit time interval are equal in duration and the information rate in bits per second is equal to the modulation rate in baud. For isochronous NRZ signaling, the measures bits per second

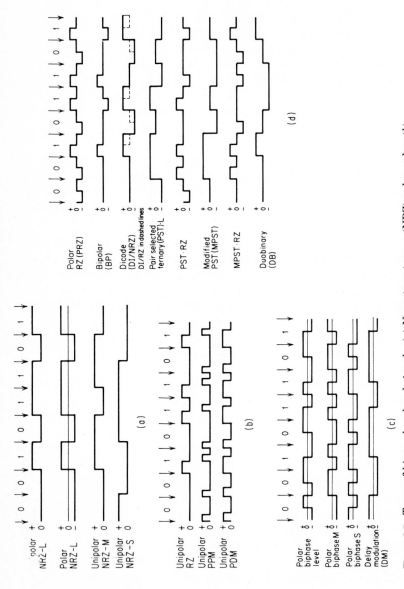

Figure 3.5 Types of binary baseband signals. (*a*) Nonreturn-to-zero (NRZ) pulse codes; (*b*) return-to-zero (RZ) pulse codes; (*c*) phase-encoded (PE) pulse codes; (*d*) multilevel-binary (MLB) or pseudoternary pulse codes. (*Redrawn from Kenneth M. True, Interface, Fairchild Semiconductor Co., Mountain View, Calif., 1975, chap. 4.*)

and baud are both synonymous and interchangeable. Inspection of unipolar RZ signaling reveals that the unit interval is a ½-bit interval. When this unit interval is less than the 0 to 50 percent rise or fall time of the line, the data are likely to be unrecoverable. With a fixed modulation rate, the price paid to include clocking information into unipolar RZ is reduced information rate over that for NRZ signaling. Likewise, for PPM with its unit interval of $t_B/4$, the information rate reduces to one-fourth that of NRZ data under the same conditions, because maximum modulation rate is determined by the 50 percent rise time of the line, which is constant for a given length and type of line. PDM has a unit interval of $t_B/3$, so for a given maximum modulation rate the resulting information rate is one-third that of NRZ data.

With PPM and PDM, the maximum time that the line signal can be in one state is quite reduced from the NRZ case. For PPM, this time is $1.25\ t_B$, while for PDM it is $0.67\ t_B$. With PPM and PDM, then, the signal may never reach the final signal levels that it does with NRZ data. The PPM scheme appears to be a poor trade in comparison, since PDM allows a greater information rate while retaining the self-clocking feature. Unipolar RZ, because it provides no clocking for a logic 0 signal, is not generally as useful as PDM for baseband data transmission. However unipolar RZ is used in older digital magnetic tape recorders. Examination of RZ codes shows only one more desirable feature than NRZ codes, which is the clocking. RZ codes still have a dc component and their bandwidth is extended over that of NRZ. RZ codes also do not have any intrinsic error-detection features.

3. Phase-encoded (PE) pulse codes.   The PE group of pulse codes uses signal-level transitions to carry both binary data and synchronization information. There are four types of PE pulse codes: BiΦ-L (*biphase-level*), BiΦ-M (*biphase-mark*), BiΦ-S (*Biphase-space*), and DM (*delay modulation*). Each of the codes provides one signal-level transition per bit interval, aiding synchronous recovery of the binary data. Simply stated, BiΦ-L code is binary phase-shift keying (PSK) and is the result of an EXCLUSIVE-OR logic function performed on the NRZ-L data and its clock. It further requires that the resultant signal be phase-coherent. BiΦ-M and BiΦ-S codes are essentially phase-coherent binary frequency-shift keying (FSK) signals. In BiΦ-M, a logic 1 is represented by a constant level during the bit interval, while a logic 0 is represented by one-half cycle of the higher frequency. In BiΦ-S, however, the logic states are reversed from those in BiΦ-M. Another method distinguishing between BiΦ-M and BiΦ-S is given as follows:

- Changes signal level at the end of each bit interval regardless of the logic state of the data

- Changes signal level at the middle of each bit interval to mean a particular logic state

In BiΦ-M (sometimes called *diphase*), a midbit interval change in signal level indicates a logic 1 (mark), while no change indicates a logic 0. In BiΦ-S, no signal-level change in the middle of the bit interval means a logic 1, while a change means a logic 0.

In BiΦ-L (also called *Manchester code*), a positive-going transition at the middle of the bit interval means a logic 0, while a negative-going transition there indicates a logic 1. The appearance of the Manchester code is such that when 1 and 0 are adjacent to one another, the joining pulses appear as a double-width pulse. If a 1 or 0 repeat, normal-width pulses occur at the clock rate.

The fourth member of the PE family is *delay modulation* (DM), sometimes referred to as *Miller code*. Here logic 1 is represented by a midbit interval signal-level change, and a logic 0 is represented by a signal-level change at the end of the bit interval if the logic 0 is followed by another logic 0. When the logic 0 is immediately followed by a logic 1, no signal-level transition at the end of the first bit interval is used. The waveforms for the PE pulse code family are shown in Fig. 3.5c.

A brief inspection of the signal waveforms for the three biphase pulse codes reveals that their minimum signaling element has a duration of a ½-bit interval; that is, $t_{ui} = t_B/2$. The longest duration of either signal level is a 1-bit interval. Similarly, DM is seen to have a minimum signaling element of a 1-bit interval $t_{ui} = t_B$, and the maximum duration of either signal level is 2-bit intervals produced by the 101 pattern. Biphase codes would not be recoverable without equalization when t_{ui} was less than 0 to 50 percent rise time. So, a 50 percent jitter on NRZ signaling approximately corresponds to the biphase codes nonoperation point. Biphase codes, therefore, provide half the information rate of NRZ signals at a given maximum modulation rate. This is in exchange for synchronization information and a dc-free spectrum when used in polar form.

DM should have essentially the same intersymbol interference characteristics as NRZ, since the unit interval is the same for both codes. DM may perform slightly better than NRZ, because the maximum duration of either signal level is 2-bit intervals. Overall, DM is a better coding scheme than the biphase. It also does not require as much bandwidth as the biphase and still possesses the desirable dc response and synchronization qualities. Both biphase and DM are good choices for digital magnetic recording; biphase is widely used in disk memory equipment, and DM is rapidly gaining acceptance whenever high bit-packing densities are desired. PE pulse codes have bandwidth compression, no dc component, and intrinsic synchronization features.

The biphase family does not possess any intrinsic error-detection scheme. DM does possess the capability of detecting some, but not all, single-bit errors. This detection process is accomplished by checking if a single level persists longer than 2-bit intervals, in which case an error is indicated. DM detection also requires two samples per bit interval.

A better utilization of time and space is the feature of the biphase codes. They overcome the disadvantages of other codes where a series of 0s produce a zero resultant. This means that if noise is present, it will fill the empty spaces with noise pulses and possibly produce an erroneous 1 signal.

4. Multilevel-Binary (MLB) pulse codes. The pulse codes in the MLB group discussed have a common characteristic of using three signal levels $(+, 0, -)$ to represent the binary information. However each receiver decision yields only 1 bit of information. These are sometimes called *pseudoternary codes* to distinguish them from true ternary codes where each receiver decision can yield 1.58 information bits.

The most straightforward pulse code in the MLB group is polar or PRZ (see Fig. 3.5d). Some authors place PRZ in the RZ group, but since PRZ uses three signal levels, it is better to place it in the MLB group as done here. A logic 1 is represented by a positive polarity pulse, and a logic 0 is represented by a negative polarity pulse. Each pulse lasts for a ½-bit interval. PRZ has excellent synchronization properties since there is a pulse present during every bit interval.

Bipolar (BP) coding uses a $t_B/2$ duration pulse to signify a logic 1 and no pulse during the bit interval to signify a logic 0. The polarity of the pulses for a logic 1 is alternated. Bipolar coding is also known as *alternate mark inversion*. BP is widely used in T1-PCM carrier systems as a pulse code transmitted along a regenerative repeated transmission line. Since BP has no dc component, the regenerative repeaters along the span line may be transformer-coupled and powered by a phantom constant-current power loop from the central office.

The synchronization properties of BP are excellent if the number of 0 bits transmitted in series is constrained. This constraint on the number of sequential 0s allow clock circuits in each repeater to remain in synchronization. A scheme called *binary-with-6-zeros-substitution* (B6ZS) was developed to replace six 0s with a given signal sequence to offset any loss of synchronization.

In dicode (DI), a polar pulse (either t_B for DI-NRZ or $t_B/2$ for DI-RZ) is sent for every input data transition. The limiting constraint is that the successive pulses must alternate in sign (see Fig. 3.5d). As in NRZ-M and NRZ-S, the actual polarity of the pulses does not necessarily correspond to the logic state of the data. A positive pulse may represent either a 0 to 1 or a 1 to 0 transition of the input data. The power spectrum for DI is the same as for BP; it does not contain a dc component. Bit synchronization for DI can be obtained in the same manner as for BP; however with DI, the number of bits of the same logic must be controlled for the receiver to maintain bit synchronization. DI also has the intrinsic capability of detecting single-bit errors, via two successive positive or negative signal levels, all odd, and some errors in even numbers.

Pair-selected ternary (PST) and modified PST (MPST) were proposed to minimize the BP coding advantages in loss of synchronization with long strings of 0s and timing jitter. PST and MPST maintain strong features of BP as in dc-free spectrum and in single-error detection. To produce PST or MPSt, the incoming bits are grouped into pairs and the signal produced on the line is governed by a coding table. The features of PST and MPSt thus include:

- No dc spectral component
- No loss of synchronization with long strings of 0s
- Intrinsic error detection
- Simplification of requirements for timing extraction circuits with respect to BP

MPST coding was developed primarily to speed up the framing process, i.e., selecting which two successive pulses constitute a valid pair, when the probabilities for a 0 and a 1 are not equal.

Duobinary is an example of a correlative-level coding technique, where a correlation exists between successive signal levels. Duobinary uses three signal levels, with the middle level corresponding to a logic 0, and the other two levels corresponding to a logic 1. The pseudoternary signal is generated by precoding the input data which results in constraining the line signal to change only to the neighboring level; i.e., the $(+)$ to $(-)$ and $(-)$ to $(+)$ level changes are not allowed. This precoding process uses controlled intersymbol interference as part of the coding scheme. The benefit of this is an effective doubling of the bit rate for a given bandwidth and a concentration of the power spectrum toward the dc component. Duobinary has the capability to detect single errors which violate the encoding rules. In terms of bandwidth utilization, duobinary ranks first among all the binary and MLB codes, but its strong dc component prohibits the use of ac-coupled transmission media. Synchronization properties are similar to NRZ; thus external clocking must be used to recover the data.

Digital filter

Digital filtering is a computational process or algorithm by which a sampled signal or sequence of numbers, acting as an input, is transformed into a second sequence of numbers called the output. The computational process may correspond to high-pass, low-pass, bandpass, or bandstop filtering, integration, differentiation, or something else. The second sequence can be used for further processing or it can be converted to an analog signal, producing a filtered version of the original analog signal.

The digital approach offers many advantages over analog approaches, as listed below:

1. Changes resulting from variations in component values (normally associated with filter capacitors and resistors as a result of temperature or aging) are nonexistent.

2. Periodic calibration is eliminated.

3. The performance from unit to unit is stable and repeatable.

4. Great flexibility is available since filter response can be altered by changing arithmetic coefficients.

5. Arbitrarily high precision can be achieved, limited only by the number of bits involved.

6. Very small size, low power, and low cost are possible by large-scale integration (LSI).

Example Let us consider the following practical situation: the need to reject very strong 60-Hz interference contaminating a 10-Hz signal. The obvious solution is to build a bandstop or notch filter that rejects the 60-Hz component while passing the 10-Hz signal with no alteration.

First, a familiar analog RC notch filter will be examined. A commonly used RC notch filter network is the twin-T shown in Fig. 3.6. From the input and output waveforms shown, it can be seen that the twin-T circuit rejects all the 60-Hz interference and leaves the desired 10-Hz signal.

Changing the center frequency of the notch requires changes in the values of all three capacitors, all three resistors, or the two shunt elements R' and C' together. The position and depth of the notch is very sensitive to parameter changes in the components of the twin-T, so precision components must be used in building the filter if good rejection at exactly 60 Hz is to be maintained. The digital filter solution to this problem is simple yet just as effective as the linear filter and is considerably more flexible. In this case the input signal is sampled by an analog-to-digital converter at a rate of 500 samples per second. That is, the input signal level is measured at intervals of 2 ms, and the result forms the input sequence to our digital filter.

Figure 3.7 shows the digital counterpart to the twin-T notch circuit. This filter is made using two registers, a digital multiplier, and a three-input adder. As

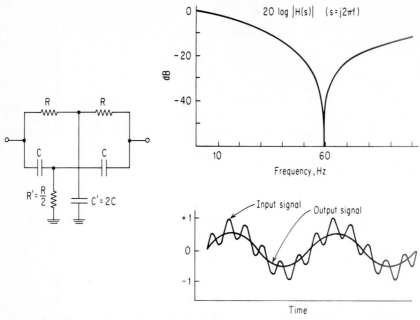

Figure 3.6 RC notch filter. (*Lyon A. Schmidt, "What Is a Digital Filter?"* HP Journal, *September 1977.*)

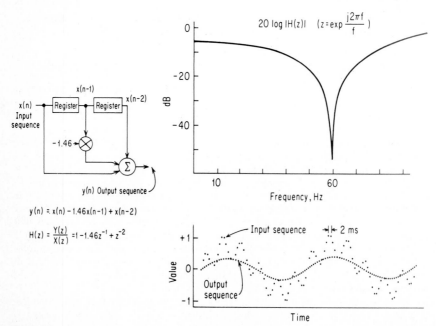

$$y(n) = x(n) - 1.46x(n-1) + x(n-2)$$

$$H(z) = \frac{Y(z)}{X(z)} = 1 - 1.46z^{-1} + z^{-2}$$

Figure 3.7 Digital filter. (*Lyon A. Schmidt, "What Is a Digital Filter?"* HP Journal, *September 1977.*)

the difference equation in Fig. 3.7 shows, the current-output sample word $y(n)$ is formed by summing the current-input sample word $x(n)$ with the previous input $x(n - 1)$ multiplied by the constant -1.46 and with the second previous input $x(n - 2)$. When this filter is fed sample words at a rate of 500 samples per second, the 60-Hz components in the analog input signal will be eliminated from the regenerated analog output signal.

Figure 3.7 also shows two cycles of the sampled 10-Hz input signal, which is contaminated as before by 60-Hz interference. Passing this input sequence through the digital bandstop filter results in the output sequence as shown. It is evident that the filter has rejected all the 60-Hz interference, leaving the desired 10-Hz signal.

One advantage that the digital filter has in this application is that the position and depth of the bandstop notch will remain constant and will not drift with temperature or age.

The notch center frequency can be changed in two ways. The first way is simply to change the multiplication coefficient. For example, changing the -1.46 coefficient to -1.62 changes the notch center frequency to 50 Hz. The second way is to change the sample rate. In this particular example, the notch center frequency is 12 percent of the sample rate. Reducing the sample rate to 417 Hz reduces the notch center to 50 Hz.

In summary, for certain applications digital filters offer advantages in terms of flexibility, stability, and simplicity of control when compared to their analog counterparts.

3.4 Modems

Modem is a contraction word of modulator-demodulator, which describes its function. The digital output of a terminal equipment is modulated to form an analog signal for easier transmission over communication lines; conversely, an analog signal is demodulated to change it back to a digital signal.

Theory of operation

A block diagram of a four-wire 2400-b/s modem is given in Figs. 1.5 and 3.8, and the theory of operation is explained below as an example of modem operation.

Transmitter. (Refer to Table 7.1 for interface signals.) At the start of transmission, as illustrated in Fig. 3.9, the terminal turns Request to Send (105) on, thus turning the Data Carrier Detect (109) on and initiating the Clear to Send (106) with a delay to the terminal. During the delay time Transmit Data (103) is inhibited and a steady mark signal is transmitted to the VF line. After (typical) 8.5 ms, Clear to Send (106) is turned on and transmit data are applied to the phase encoder.

The phase encoder groups the incoming data into dibits, used to generate the differential phase-shift-keyed (DPSK) four-phase car-

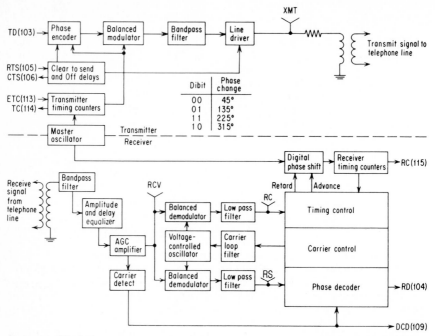

Dibit	Phase change
00	45°
01	135°
11	225°
10	315°

Figure 3.8 Block diagram of a modem. (*Intertel Inc., Burlington, Mass., "Modem, 2400 b/s, Model 2010, Theory of Operation."*)

rier signal. The four possible combinations of dibits have the corresponding carrier changes as shown in Table 3.1 and Fig. 3.10. Refer to Sec. 4.1 for more information.

The length of mark and space frequencies is determined by the transmit clock. The output of the phase encoder is applied to a balanced modulator, which performs the carrier envelope shaping required for compatibility of standards and receiver timing recovery.

The analog output of a balanced modulator is a complex-frequency waveform and feeds a bandpass filter. The output of the bandpass filter

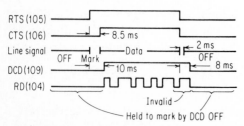

Figure 3.9 Timing diagram of a modem. (*Intertel Inc., Burlington, Mass., "Modem, 2400 b/s, Model 2010, Theory of Operation."*)

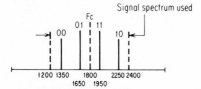

Figure 3.10 Dibit pattern and line signal spectrum for a modem. (*Intertel Inc., Burlington, Mass., "Modem, 2400 b/s, Model 2010, Theory of Operation."*)

is coupled to a line driver which provides transmit level adjustment and passes the data under the control of Request to Send (105). The transmit signal is transformer-coupled to the two-wire VF line.

When transmission is complete, the terminal turns Request to Send (105) off, and, as shown in Fig. 3.9, after a 2-ms delay the signal is removed from the line.

Internal transmitter timing is supplied via the master oscillator and related timing counters. Operation with external timing is obtained through a buffer via a strap selection.

Receiver-demodulation.   At the receiver, the telephone-line signal is coupled via a line-matching transformer to a bandpass filter which eliminates band noise. The filter output is connected to an amplitude and delay equalizer. From the equalizer, the signal is applied to an AGC (automatic gain control) amplifier which compensates for different received signal levels.

After the adjustment is made for operational level, the AGC circuit will automatically compensate for changes in received signal level of up to ±15 dB from the nominal setting. As shown on the block diagram, the output of the AGC amplifier is fed to three circuits, two of which are balanced demodulators.

The balanced demodulators in conjunction with the reference carrier signals generated by the voltage-controlled oscillator (VCO) provide coherently demodulated signals. After low-pass filtering, in-phase (RC) and quadrature- (RS) demodulated signals provide data as well as timing and carrier recovery information. The phase decoder determines the phase change of the received signal between successive dibits via the demodulated signals. The operation is the inverse of that performed by the phase encoder in the transmitter and results in Receive Data (104).

The filtered demodulated signals are also used by the carrier control circuit to generate a correction signal for controlling the VCO through the carrier loop filter. This correction guarantees that the reference carrier is properly aligned in both phase and frequency with the incoming signal. In this manner, a clean reference signal is available for demodulation rather than the noisy reference signal used in incoherent demodulators.

Receiver-carrier detection. The carrier detection circuit monitors the level of the received signal versus the nominal received level established by the setting of the received level adjustment. If the incoming signal drops below the nominal level by more than 15 dB, Carrier Detect (DCD) is turned off after 8 ms. This clamps Receive Data (104) to a mark and prevents erroneous data from entering the receiver terminal during loss of signal. When the received signal level returns to within 15 dB of nominal, DCD turns back on and RD is enabled. Note that by referencing the DCD threshold to the received level setting a more reliable indication is obtained than would be possible if a fixed threshold were used for all times.

Receiver-data-derived timing. The in-phase (RC) and quadrature-demodulated signals (RS) are also used to recover timing information. The timing control circuit observes these signals and adjusts receiver timing alignment to minimize the error rate in Receive Data (104). By continually adjusting the timing alignment, the receiver timing signal is forced into synchronization with the incoming signal and thus with the transmitter. This technique is known as *data-derived timing* since the timing information is determined directly from the demodulated data signal and improves the error rate by 10 to 100 times.

Another feature of the timing recovery technique is the use of a digitally controlled loop for timing alignment. As shown in Fig. 3.8 the receiver timing is aligned by the digital phase-shift circuit through the use of advance-retard control signals generated by the timing control circuit. Whenever there is a loss of signal and DCD goes off, the digital phase-shift circuit is inhibited and the receiver timing will remain in alignment for line outages of a second or more.

The receiver timing counter accepts the output from the digital phase-shift circuit and provides timing signals required for operation

Bit rate	2400 b/s
Operation mode	Synchronous
Transmit level	0 to −15 dBm (switch-selectable)
Receiver level	0 to −48 dBm
Carrier detect response	10 ± 2 ms (switch-selectable)
Transmit clock (internal or external)	1200, 2000, or 2400 Hz
Receiver clock	1200, 2000, or 2400 Hz
Internal clock stability	1 part in 10,000 per year
Power consumption	20 W

of the receiver, as well as receiver timing (115). For two-wire operation, the Clear to Send (106) delay must be strapped for 150-ms operation.

The modem described above, with data-derived timing, narrow-band filtering, and coherent demodulation, has an error rate less than 10^{-6} operating at S/N = 15 dB with 20° peak-to-peak phase jitter measured at 180 Hz.

Typical modem characteristics are given in the table; they may change, however, with application and data rate.

Modem features

While all modems perform the prime function of modulation-de-modulation, there are other functions that can add to their capability or in some situations restrict their performance to better accomplish a specialized task. There are also several operational options that may be included in the modem, although they do not improve the modem's performance. These features are:

Secondary channel	Attended-unattended operation
Equalization	Forward error control
Soft carrier disconnect	Switching to lower speed
Scrambling	Elastic buffer storage
Testing	Alternate voice-data operation
Transmit only-receive only	Multiplexing
Originate only-answer only	Line protection
	Data compression

Secondary channel. A feature with some modems is an optional secondary channel. The primary channel is the channel having the highest signaling rate capability of all the channels sharing a common interface connector. The secondary channel is the data transmission channel having a lower signaling rate capability than the primary channel in a system in which two channels share a common interface connector. A secondary channel may be either one way only, half-duplex (HDX), or full-duplex (FDX). Pin assignments for a secondary channel in a 25-pin connector are given in Table 7.1; note that they come with an S prefix.

Data terminal equipment do not transmit data on the secondary channel unless an on condition is present on all the following four circuits:

1. Circuit SRTS (pin 19): Secondary Request to Send
2. Circuit SCTS (pin 13): Secondary Clear to Send

3. Circuit DSR (pin 6): Data Set Ready

4. Circuit DTR (pin 20): Data Terminal Ready

Two classes of secondary channels are defined as *auxiliary* and *backward*. Auxiliary-channel transmission direction is independent of the primary channel and is controlled by secondary control interchange circuits. The transmission direction of a backward channel (also called a *reverse* channel) is always opposite to that of the primary channel. The direction of transmission of the backward channel is restricted by the control interchange circuit 105 (RTS) that controls the direction of the primary channel. Circuit SRTS shall be interconnected with circuit RTS within the data communication equipment.

When secondary channels are used only for circuit assurance or to interrupt the flow of data in the primary channel, they transmit no actual data and depend only on the presence or absence of the secondary channel carrier. For this application only, circuits STD (Secondary Transmitted Data), SRD (Secondary Received Data), and SCTS (Secondary Clear to Send) are not provided. Circuit SRTS turns secondary channel carrier on and off as required, and Circuit SDCD (Secondary Data Carrier Detector) recognizes its presence or absence.

During HDX operation, while the transmitting modem is operating, the receiving modem generates a signal which by being on or off indicates a go or no-go condition to the transmitting modem. It is usually a supervisory signal for error detection and control. Other purposes are to inform the transmitting modem that the signal is being received, or that the receiving modem is inoperable, e.g., that a paper tape reader has run out of tape.

An auxiliary channel can be used as a talker circuit for service communications between operating centers. A secondary channel is offered with the Bell 202 modems with a maximum bit rate of 5 b/s; CCITT V.23 (also V.26, V.27, V.27 *bis,* and V.27*ter*) recommends a backward channel with a modulation rate up to 75 Bd, mark 390 Hz, and space 450 Hz; refer to Fig. 3.11.

Equalization.   Usually modems operating at 1200 b/s or higher speeds are equipped with line equalizers that provide satisfactory operation for these modems. These equalizers can be fixed, manually adjusted, or automatic.

Fixed equalizers.   Some modems are equipped with equalizers that provide some equalization in the circuit by manually selected switches. Their use is based on the fact that most of the unconditioned lines have similar amplitude and envelope delay characteristics. In these circumstances equalization is provided on the average values of line char-

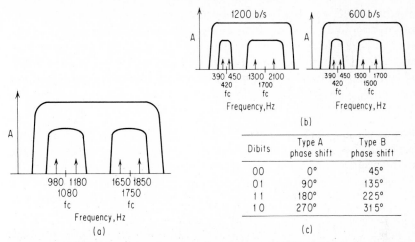

Figure 3.11   CCITT channel assignments for modems. (*a*) V.21 channel assignments; (*b*) V.23 channel assignments; (*c*) V.26 data encoding. V.21, 0 to 300 b/s, is similar to the Bell 103/113 modem; V.23, 0 to 1200 b/s, is similar to the Bell 202 modem; V.26, 2400 b/s, is similar to the Bell 201 modem.

acteristics across the frequency band. This type of equalization is used in modems operating at 3600 b/s or less.

Manual equalizers.   Several continuously adjustable controls provide the equalization required by utilizing a minimum reading meter. Some modems are equipped with two sets of equalizers and test circuits. If desired an operator can perform equalization on FDX circuits in both directions.

Automatic equalizers.   Automatic equalization is initiated and performed by selecting several built-in equalizers. Circuit conditioning and equalization are generally accomplished by active or hybrid analog circuits. In modems working above 4800 b/s speeds, digital equalization is performed. Digital equalization is rather a proprietary right of modem manufacturers and is relatively complex. As an example, in the digital built-in automatic equalizer in 9600 b/s modems, the initial equalization sequence time required is about 120 ms, and adaptive adjustments occur 2400 times in a second. An adaptive process allows an equalizer to follow or track the frequently occurring channel variations which occur during data transmission without interrupting traffic.

Equalization in the transmit modem (predistortion equalization).   Usually equalization is performed in the receiver by removing the distortions. When the equalizer is in the transmit modem, the signal is distorted in such a manner that the line compensates the distortion; i.e., the line itself acts as an equalizer.

Predistortion equalization is generally used in multidrop polled systems, particularly with modems equipped with manual or fixed equalizers. Thus it eliminates the requirement to readjust equalizers each time a signal is received from a different location. Note that on a 2400-b/s transmission link with light equalization, RTS/CTS delay is about 8 ms, while on a 4800-b/s modem equipped with automatic equalizer, delay is around 50 ms in FDX operation.

Mop-up (middle-point) equalization.   Middle-point equalization combines the effects of post- and preequalization. The equalizer compensates for the attenuation and delay distortion introduced by the preceding facility section, and introduces additional predistortion which, when summed with the response of the succeeding facility section, results in a flat response at the remote receiving end.

It must be noted that, more often than not, the tandem legs making up long-haul circuits which have been individually conditioned to meet the accepted industry standards (AT&T-C2, CCITT-M1020, and DCA-S1), will not adequately support the transmission of high-speed data when interconnected to provide point-to-point service. For this reason, the concept of midpoint equalization is common practice. The organization having technical responsibility for the complete end-to-end circuit will install data line conditioning equipment (amplitude/delay equalizers) at a fixed junction point in the circuit to accomplish the "mop-up" equalization necessary to condition the complete link for high-speed data service.

Soft carrier.   Carrier detector off-time is a problem in system operation. Since the communications line tends to ring (damped oscillations) after the remote-site transmitted signal has been removed, the central modem receiver is unable to determine the exact instant when the opposite-end remote modem transmitter has turned off. This effect can cause potential delays in carrier signal turn-off. In the worst-case condition, it can prevent the carrier from turning off at all, thereby allowing the central processing unit (CPU) to receive erroneous data (line noise). A common technique used to solve carrier turn-off problems is to employ a soft carrier tone—a 900-Hz signal sent from the remote modem transmitter—at the end of a data transmission. When the remote-end transmitter is turned off, the soft carrier tone is automatically turned on for a short span of time (10 to 25 ms). This signal causes two effects in the central modem receiver; it forces the received data signal to mark and causes the carrier detector to turn off more rapidly. In leased channel networks, carrier detector turn-off time can also be minimized by decreasing the sensitivity of the central site modem receiver. This is practical since telephone company leased lines have a maximum signal loss of 18 dB from end to end. An alternate approach is sending an end-of-transmission (ETX) code at the end of each transmitted message. When host logic (not part of the modem) receives the ETX, received data can be gated off for a short time. This function is more fail-safe than use of a soft carrier tone and allows better performance than decreasing the host modem receiver sensitivity. In addition, ETX allows time delays to be set via logic circuitry and eliminates time wasted due to carrier-detector-off delay.

Scrambling.   Scrambling is a coding technique applied to digital signals and produces a random data pattern. At the receiving end, signals are decoded. This technique maintains a more nearly constant transmitted power level and makes receiver timing recovery insensitive to the data pattern.

CCITT Recs. V.27 and V.29 recommend that a self-synchronizing scrambler-descrambler be included in the 4800 and 9600 b/s modems, respectively.

Testing.   Modems are equipped with loop-testing facilities which are very helpful in troubleshooting. These loops allow local or remote tests at the analog or digital transmission side. For more information on loop tests refer to Sec. 9.1 and CCITT Rec. V.54.

Modems operating on 4800 b/s or higher speeds that use the quadrature-amplitude-modulation (QAM) technique are equipped with an eye pattern generator, which allows testing of modem performance as well as of transmission line quality. An eye pattern is produced on an oscilloscope by plugging it into a special connector on the modem. Normal eye pattern figures which are to be observed in an associated scope are shown in Fig. 4.2, while several line impairments are shown in Fig. 9.6.

Modems may be equipped with a test-tone oscillator at 800 Hz (CCITT recommendation) or 1000 Hz.

Transmit only–receive only.   There are modems that can only transmit or receive, not both. While this is equivalent to simplex mode, actually an HDX channel is used. However, simplex operation is frequently used in a local hardware application such as in-plant data collection.

Originate only–answer only.   Some modems can only initiate calls, while others can only answer to a call. However, once the call is received or placed, the modem can operate in the FDX or HDX mode (F1/F2 modems).

Attended-unattended operation.   When a modem requires an operator to place or receive a call and switch it from voice to data, it is called *attended operation.* Unattended operation, however, is when a modem turns on its associated terminal and commences operation from a distance. This is very useful, especially in batch transmission from data collection terminals when a central computer operating at night could collect data from many such terminals at scattered geographic locations.

Forward error control/correction (FEC).   The FEC feature is an option in the modems that tries to correct errors without referring back to the transmitter terminal. As many redundant bits as there are data bits are added to the transmission stream to achieve an acceptable degree of correction at the receiver. The FEC technique in conjunction with the ARQ (automatic request to repeat) technique provides an excellent error rate on high-speed data transmission. Refer to Sec. 7.6 for error-correcting procedures.

Switching to lower speed.   In some cases, when the transmission line performance deteriorates and the BER (bit error rate) falls below a threshold, the modem switches to lower-speed data transmission automatically in conjunction with the distant-end modem. A status indicator lights together with the switching action. Resetting to normal-speed operation is performed manually rather than automatically after the line is restored. This prevents the modem from switching between high-speed and low-speed transmissions in the event that line deterioration is intermittent.

Elastic buffer storage.   Modems may be equipped with an elastic-buffer-storage or a buffer-storage option. Explanations of buffer storage and elastic buffer storage are given in Secs. 6.3 and 8.4, respectively. For the buffer-storage or memory unit, the first-in, first-out (FIFO) terminology is also used. The term is self-explanatory. The first data in are the first data available at the outputs.

Alternate voice-data (AVD) operation.   This is an option for modems to provide voice communication capability. For example, a telephone set is installed at the modem to provide end-to-end voice communication. The set is equipped with ringer and amplifier as well as switches for data or alternate voice use. The voice-data switch automatically inhibits data transmission and connects the telephone circuit to the modem when the voice mode is selected. However, reversing to the data mode at both locations restores normal data communication after a training period, where *training period* is defined as the time required to equalize the line and to recover timing from the received data on synchronous modems. This time is often referred to as RTS/CTS delay or poll response, and it varies from 8.5 to about to 240 ms for a 9600-b/s modem equipped with a digital equalizer. For a typical 4800-b/s modem, the 140-ms training period consists of:

40 ms: AGC setup, timing, and frequency acquisition

80 ms: equalizing training and providing QAM pattern for data

20 ms: scrambler synchronization

Multiplexing.   The built-in four- or two-channel multiplexing is another option in the modem. This option allows more effective use of the communications systems by allowing four or two lower-speed channels to be multiplexed into one high-speed data stream which is fed to the modem. Interface units at the channel side are usually equipped with a 4- to 8-bit buffer storage for phasing of external and internal clocking signals.

Line protection.   Telephone-line protection may be provided by installing a fuse and zener diode as an option.

Data compression.   Data compression is an approach which is based on the strategy of maximizing the usefulness of the bit rate available. The key benefits of this approach are that it does not increase the sensitivity to noise and it does not increase modem cost significantly. Principles of data compression are given for intelligent time-division multiplexing in Sec. 5.1.

Broadband (or wideband) modems

Modems for broadband systems are available in many types and performance ranges. Basic units operate with RS 232C interfaces up to 9600 b/s asynchronously, and may occupy from 100 to 400 kHz of the spectrum. Synchronous modems are available for data ranges of 19.2, 56, and 512 kb/s.

Frequency-agile modems can off-load traffic to alternate channels during peak activity periods. Packet communication units (PCUs) are intelligent modems supporting broadband-based packet networks with rates up to 3 Mb/s per channel.

Data paths may be assigned to broadband channels in 9.6-kb/s, 56 kb/s, 230.4 kb/s, 1 Mb/s or 3 Mb/s slots up to the capacity of each cable in the network. The number of links that can be accommodated in each cable depends upon the data rate. Thus, at 9.6 kb/s, 10,500 simplex or asynchronous data links can be accommodated, each taking 10 kHz of the 105-MHz bandwidth available. (Divide by 2 for full-duplex operation.)

A broadband network is protocol transparent. Interfaces for radio-frequency modems may be procured in all normal conventions: RS 232C, 422, 423, V.24, V.35, DS-1, teleprinter, and even parallel TTL.

Bell equipment used with modems

Data-access arrangement (DAA). Connecting a non-Bell modem to the switched network requires the use of a protective device called a *data-access arrangement*. This is a network protection device and can be either manual or automatic. However, it is not required for leased lines. Some non-Bell modems may be authorized by the telephone company for use without a DAA if they have a suitable protective device similar to a DAA.

Automatic calling unit (ACU). Where traffic volume between a remote site and the CPU cannot satisfy a dedicated circuit, automatic dialing is used. The Bell 801-type automatic calling unit (ACU) works with a computer and provides the called number to allow automatic dialing connect and disconnect in a switched network, which is usually performed by an attendant.

The ACU assumes control of the line after receiving a dial tone until a valid connection is established, which is indicated by a tone received from the distant, answering modem. The line is then transferred from the ACU to the originating modem, which goes into data mode.

With pulse dialing, a typical 10-digit number takes 15 s to dial. Pulses are 100 ms wide with a 61 percent duty cycle; the interdigit period for pulse dialing is 600 to 1700 ms. With Touch-Tone dialing, a 10-digit number takes 1 s, the tone pair is present for 40 ms, and the interdigit period is 60 ms minimum; refer to Appendix B.

CCITT recommendations for modems

Outside the United States, data transmission standards are recommended by the International Telegraph and Telephone Consultative Committee (CCITT), a part of the International Telecommunications Union (ITU) in Geneva, Switzerland.

Recommendation V.21 covers 200-Bd modems for use in the general switched telephone network. It can obviously be used on leased networks. However modems to this recommendation may operate also at modulation rates of up to 300 Bd, but reliable transmission cannot be guaranteed in all cases. It may therefore be necessary to carry out tests to verify whether operation at rates up to 300 Bd is possible.

Synchronous or asynchronous transmission can be used. Two channels are available in the voice band. When both channels are used for simultaneous both-way data transmission, channel no. 1 is used for transmission of the caller's data while channel no. 2 is used for transmission in the other direction. When one channel is used for data transmission and the other is used for transmission of check signals, service signals, etc., then it is no. 1 which is used for transmission.

For channel no. 1, the nominal mean frequency is 1080 Hz; for channel no. 2 it is 1750 Hz (refer to Fig. 3.11). The frequency deviation for 200 Bd is ± 100 Hz (most 300-Bd modems use ± 120 Hz). In each channel the higher characteristic frequency F_A corresponds to the symbol 0, space.

The counterparts of the V.21 recommendation are the Bell 103 and 108 modems. The Bell 103 modem is designed for Data-Phone service over switched lines. It operates at speeds up to 300 b/s and is asynchronous and uses FSK keying. During the operation it is in the data mode. Otherwise it is in the auto, local, test, or talk modes, which can be selected by the operator. The modem has two frequency modes: one for originating calls and one for answering calls. Normally it is in the originating mode. When a ringing signal is received, the modem switches to the answering mode. It remains in this mode for the duration of the call.

Two frequency bands designated as $F1$ and $F2$ are used in each mode. $F1$ is the lower-frequency band and $F2$ is the higher-frequency band. The originating modem transmits at $F1$ and receives at $F2$, while the answering modem transmits at $F2$ and receives at $F1$. Within each band two frequencies are used: one for mark and one for space. Corresponding space and mark frequencies for CCITT Rec. V.21 and Bell 103 modems are given in Table 3.4. Channel establishment and disconnect sequences in the Bell 103A modem are given in Sec. 7.2.

Recommendation V.22 concerns the 1200-b/s modem for use on two-wire switched and point-to-point circuits. Channel separation is frequency division. Differential phase-shift modulation is utilized in each channel, and the modulation rate is 600 Bd. The modem includes a scrambler-descrambler and loop-test facilities. Carrier frequencies are 1200 Hz for the low channel and 2400 Hz for the high channel. A guard

TABLE 3.4   Mark and Space
Frequencies for 0–300 b/s Modems

	CCITT V.21	Bell 103
Channel 2:		
Space	1180 Hz F_A	2025 Hz $F2$S
Mark	980 Hz F_Z	2225 Hz $F2$M
Channel 1:		
Space	1850 Hz F_A	1070 Hz $F1$S
Mark	1650 Hz F_Z	1270 Hz $F1$M

tone of 1800 Hz shall be transmitted at all times when the modem is transmitting in the high channel. A fixed-compromise equalizer shall be included in the modem and equally shared between transmitter and receiver. Data signaling rates shall be 1200 and 600 b/s. At 1200 b/s, four-phase shift keying is used; at 600 b/s, two-phase keying is utilized.

Recommendation V.23 is about 600- to 1200-Bd modems, and modulation rates and frequency characteristics are as follows (refer to Fig. 3.11):

	F_Z (symbol 1, mark)	F_0	F_A (symbol 0, space)
Up to 600 Bd (± 200 Hz)	1300 Hz	1500 Hz	1700 Hz
Up to 1200 Bd (± 400 Hz)	1300 Hz	1700 Hz	2100 Hz

For teleprinter utilization a backward channel is defined with modulation rate and characteristics as follows:

	F_Z (symbol 1, mark)	F_A (symbol 0, space)
Up to 75 Bd	390 Hz	450 Hz

In the absence of any signal on the backward-channel interface, the condition Z is to be used for transmission.

CCITT Rec. V.26 concerns 2400 b/s modems for use on four-wire leased telephone-type circuits and the carrier frequency is to be 1800 Hz. If the simultaneous transmission of the forward and backward channels occurs in the same direction, a backward channel should be 6 dB lower than the data channel.

The transmitted data stream is divided into pairs of dibits. The phase relation between dibits is given in Table 3.1. In this case the data signaling rate should be 2400 b/s, the modulation rate 1200 Bd, and the bandwidth should be 1200 to 2400 Hz. Also, a fixed-compromise equalizer should be incorporated into the receiver. CCITT V.26*bis* recommends that on switched networks the data signaling rate should be 1200 b/s and the modulation rate remains at 1200 Bd. Coding and modulation used are two-phase differential modulation with binary 0 for $+90°$ and binary 1 for $+270°$.

The Bell 201 series modems operate at 2400 b/s with a 1200-Bd modulation rate and are also called *dibit modems*.

CCITT Rec. V.27 is about the 4800-b/s modem with a manual equalizer for use on leased telephone-type circuits, and the carrier frequency is 1800 Hz.

Tribit coding is given in Table 3.2. Data signaling rate should be 4800 b/s, the modulation rate 1600 Bd, and the bandwidth 1000 to 2600 Hz. Backward-channel characteristics are as recommended in CCITT V.23.

Recommendation V.27*bis* covers a 4800-b/s modem with an automatic equalizer, standardized for use on leased telephone-type circuits. The data rate can be reduced to 2400 b/s, using the 1200–2400 Hz frequency band.

Recommendation V.29 concerns 9600 b/s modems and is discussed in Sec. 4.1. For this case an automatic equalizer should be provided in the receiver.

In modems, the carrier frequency tolerance at the transmitter is ±1 Hz, and assuming a maximum frequency drift of ±6 Hz in the connection between the modems, the receiver must be able to accept errors of at least ±7 Hz in the received frequencies. In a typical modem the transmit level is adjustable between 0 to −15 dBM, and the receiver sensitivity is 0 to −48 dBm.

Recommendation V.35 is on wideband modems at 48-kb/s data channels using 60–108 kHz group band circuits. The baseband signal should be translated to the 60–104 kHz band as an "asymmetric sideband suppressed carrier AM signal" with a carrier frequency of 100 kHz. Interfacing is made via a 34-pin connector.

Recommendation V.36 is on modems using 60–108 kHz group band circuits and is applicable to 48-, 56-, 64-, and 72-kb/s data rates.

A summary of CCITT modem characteristics is tabulated in Table 3.5. A list of CCITT recommendations relating to modems is given in Sec. 3.6.

TABLE 3.5 Summary of CCITT Modem Characteristics

Speed, b/s	Mod.rate, Bd	Ctr.freq, Hz	Mode, PSK	Bandwidth, Hz	Freq.,spectr., Hz	CCITT Rec.
600	600	1200 low 2400 high	2	600	900–1500 2100–2700	V.22
1200	600	1200 low 2400 high	4	600	900–1500 2100–2700	V.22
max. 600	max. 600	1500	(FSK)	400	1300–1700	V.23
max.1200	max. 1200	1700	(FSK)	800	1300–2100	V.23
1200	1200	1800	2	1200	1200–2400	V.26 *bis*
2400	1200	1800	4	1200	1200–2400	V.26, V.27*bis*, V.27*ter*
4800	1600	1800	8	1600	1000–2600	V.27
4800	2400	1700	4	2400	500–2900	V.29
7200	2400	1700	8	2400	500–2900	V.29
9600	2400	1700	8	2400	500–2900	V.29

3.5   Short-Distance Digital Interconnections, Acoustic Couplers, Facsimiles, and Data Encryption

A convenient, though somewhat arbitrary, dividing line within a single building or a complex of buildings falls between computer-to-computer interconnections and computer-to-peripheral or multiplexer interconnections.

In intra- or inter-building applications, there are two types of peripheral-to-computer interconnections: close-grouped and remote. Close-grouped peripherals include card readers, memory disks, and high-speed parallel-driven printers. They are called *close-grouped peripherals* because they are normally found in a group configuration within 15 m (50 ft) of the computer. Since close-grouped devices are usually located in an environmentally controlled room and their distance from the computer is short, cable interference problems can usually be solved with simple metallic cable.

However, remote peripherals on a local data network can be located hundreds of meters from a central processor and are not usually housed in any special environment. Terminals fitting the remote description can be used for applications ranging from low-speed remote job entry (RJE) card-reading chores to interactive graphic-display tasks. Data rates on those kinds of terminals are commonly as high as 19.2 kb/s. As a result, interference problems for remote terminals require more effort to solve. Currently, five methods are widely used to interconnect such terminals:

1. Direct connection by ordinary copper cable

2. Direct connection by a special cable

3. The use of line drivers and cables

4. Limited distance (or local) modems and cables

5. Connection via fiber-optic cable

As a general rule, the greater the distance, the more sophisticated the interface and the greater the price.

Direct connections.   In a direct EIA RS 232C connection, the only hardware required is a cable comprising 3 to 25 wires. It is apparent that if the system requirements relating to data rate and separation distance are within RS 232C and RS 423A limitations, a less expensive interface could not possibly be found. Special low-capacitance cables (with less than 20 pF/m) can extend the interconnection distance to 200 m (660 ft).

Line drivers. For distances greater than 30 m (100 ft), line- or cable-driving techniques are commonly employed for interconnecting local terminals to a central processor or multiplexer. Line drivers are required because of signal distortion (which limits distance and speed) inherent in the electrical characteristics of cables. Extended-distance transmission produces pulse rounding, a condition in which the edges of a square-wave pulse are distorted because of the loss of high-frequency elements. In addition to pulse rounding, transmission over extended distances increases signal attenuation, resulting in marginal reception and lost or erroneous bits.

A typical synchronous line driver consists of a transmit and receive clock section; a transmitter which diplexes data, clock, and control signals; a receiver to recover the data, clock, and control signals.

Line drivers typically operate at speeds of up to 19.2 kb/s. Special units are available that will operate at data speeds of up to 1.5 Mb/s. Distances may range from 30 m to several kilometers. As might be expected, there is an almost direct tradeoff between higher speed and longer distance in any line-driver interface.

Limited-distance modems (local modems). If line drivers cannot do the job, the next consideration is the limited-distance modems (LDMs). These devices are simpler and less-expensive versions of conventional telephone modems. They do not utilize conventional modulation-demodulation techniques that characterize normal modems used in data communications systems.

The LDM concept assumes that the inherent bandwidth of an all-metallic circuit is not limited by the channelization of a carrier system and is strictly a function of the impedance of the metallic circuit and any components used to configure that circuit. As a result, the normal carrier-derived voice-grade channel cannot be used with an LDM; local exchange loops or unloaded cables are then required.

Any bandwidth limitation of a metallic circuit can be overcome by merely increasing the output power of the LDM. This would easily create a broadcasting situation as the metallic circuit continued to radiate the majority of the LDM's output power. If the metallic circuit can be established as an unloaded circuit, the upper bandwidth frequency limitation would be sufficient to permit only a low output power, such as 40 to 50 mW (17 dBm), from the LDM to achieve reliable data transmission.

A wide spectrum of data transmission rates is provided by these modems depending on the actual gage of the cable that comprises the metallic circuit. As shown in Table 3.6, a representative LDM can provide essentially wideband transmission data rates on a local metallic circuit.

TABLE 3.6 **Communication Ranges of LDMs**

Data rate, b/s	Range, km	
	AWG 19	AWG 24
1,800	30.5	18.3
2,400	30.5	18.3
4,800	24.4	13.7
9,600	21.3	9.1
19,200	16.2	6.7

TABLE 3.7 **Communication Ranges of High-Speed LDMs**

Bit rate, kb/s	Maximum distance, km		
	Coaxial	19 AWG	24 AWG
19.2		16	6.5
56	13		5.0
230.4	8		3.2

LDMs are available in both synchronous and asynchronous models. The purchase price difference between the two types is sufficient to lead prospective users to select an asynchronous model. Both versions specify essentially the same data rate capabilities. The basic difference is that the synchronous model provides the transmit and receive clock or timing source. In addition, this timing source is complemented with the necessary circuitry to maintain both LDMs at each end of the metallic circuit in bit-timing synchronization. The asynchronous model depends on the occurrence and recognition of a start and stop bit time associated with each data byte to reset and synchronize the data timing clocking sources.

At low-speed rates the cost difference is not great, but at higher speeds the difference can be thousands of dollars. System cost savings can be readily recognized when a proposed 4800 b/s data communications applications is considered.

In addition to economic advantages, the resulting data reliability can also be expected to improve.

High-speed LDMs are used for the transmission of 19.2 kb/s to 1 Mb/s digital data up to 15 km. They can operate on balanced or unbalanced lines or coaxial cables. Operating distances for a typical high-speed LDM are given in Table 3.7.

Advantages of limited-distance modems. The traditional modem must modify the digital bit stream to construct and transmit samples or states whose maximum rate of change does not exceed the available frequency bandpass of the channel. This data-compression procedure requires that the traditional synchronous modem interpret and reconstruct the digital bit stream. The conversion is dependent on the timing accuracy as well as on the demodulator's signal recovery capabilities. Many transmission data errors can be traced to the fact that the transmitted signal has been distorted beyond the limits of its capability in the associated demodulator. The LDM transmits a single state for each digital bit value; the value of bits per second is equal to the value of baud. Since the usual complex and error-prone conversion is no longer required, the resulting data transmission can be expected to be more accurate with respect to these factors. Second, the LDM is immune to frequency offset. As explained in Sec. 2.7, if the modulation-demodulation carriers are not precisely at the same frequency and phase, then the received signal is offset, causing modulation errors. Third, noise rejection is relaxed by the LDM. This factor often plays an important role in dictating the modulation technique of a telephone modem and tends to make it costly.

Connection via fiber-optic cable.   Besides direct connections, line drivers, and LDMs, fiber-optic cable connection is available for 9600 b/s and higher data speeds in both synchronous and asynchronous modes. The fiber-optic data link takes an Electronic Industries Association (EIA) interface signal and converts it to optical information, which is then transmitted over a fiber-optic waveguide and converted from an optical signal back to EIA standard.

In addition to increased bandwidth and total isolation of the equipment (refer to Sec. 10.8), fiber optics offer a significant cost advantage in certain installations. The fiber-optic link can be less costly in not only the initial installation but in future expansion of the system (see Fig. 10.17).

Acoustic couplers

An acoustic coupler is a popular device which couples data signals acoustically to the modem signal circuit. This device avoids DAAs, yet affords asynchronous communications on the dial network. Top speed on these devices is 1200 Bd, half-duplex.

As a general rule these devices can suffer from any audible noise, vibration, and limitations on the frequency response of the handset microphone and earpiece. Since the user must go through the motions of inserting the handset, a carrier-detect lamp or indicator shows whether the connection is adequate for data transmission.

There is usually some performance degradation due to the distortion introduced by transducers reducing the maximum speed capability and receiver sensitivity (8 to 13 dB) of acoustic couplers compared with hard-wired modems.

Refer to CCITT Rec. V.15, "Acoustic coupling for data transmission," for detailed information.

Operational characteristics of a typical acoustical coupler are as follows:

1. Transmission speed of 450 Bd
2. Half-speed and full-speed operation

3. A 20-mA current loop or an RS 232C (CCITT V.24) interface using acoustic or hardware coupling
4. Sound seal cushions that minimize external interference
5. Sensitivity:
    a. -40 dBm in acoustic mode
    b. -48 dBm in hardware mode
6. *a.* 1270 Hz and/or 2225 Hz for mark
    b. 1070 Hz and/or 2025 Hz for space
7. A transmission level of -16 dBm

Facsimile transmission

Facsimile is a system for the transmission of images. The image is scanned at the transmitter, reconstructed at the receiver, and duplicated on some form of paper.

Figure 3.12 shows a block diagram of a facsimile transmitter and receiver on analog transmission. The original page is placed on a drum or the page passes a scanning slit. The synchronizer controls the rate of motion of the scanner. In the case of a drum, it drives a synchronous motor. The synchronizer at the receiver may be controlled by the transmitting end or runs independently. Phasing, the process of assuring that both scanning and recording devices are at the same location along the scanning lines, is required in both cases. Phasing signals are usually sent prior to scanning of the original copy. These signals consist of pulses of a given duration which are repeated once per scanning line for a specified duration of time, for example, 15 s of phasing pulses, each consisting of 12 ms of black signal occurring once per scanning line.

The modulator accepts the photocell signals and converts to AM or FM signals. Various types of modulation have been used and vestigial-sideband amplitude modulation (VSBAM) seems to be the most popular on analog systems.

At the receiver end, the demodulator is incorporated in the recording

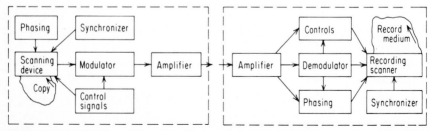

Figure 3.12 Analog facsimile block diagram. (*Donald H. Hamsher,* Communication System and Engineering Handbook, *McGraw-Hill, New York, 1967, p. 2–67, fig. 31.*)

device. For example, a gaseous recording lamp used for photographic recording may act as a half-wave rectifier.

A variety of recording media have been utilized for facsimile transmission. These employ electrothermal, electromechanical, electrostatic, photographic, thermal, pressure, and ink transfer techniques.

The electrothermal technique consists of a process whereby a stylus is in contact with a special paper which acts as a semiconductor. When voltage is applied to the stylus, the heat generated by current flow causes a dissipation of a top white surface layer of the paper, exposing a black sublayer. In some systems the white layer forms a surface on a carbon-impregnated vinyl material. The passage of current through the material not only dissipates the white surface material but creates small holes in the vinyl.

The electromechanical process usually involves a wet or damp electrolytic paper and the passage of current through the paper, causing the formation of a dye.

Pressure-type recording may be accomplished with special papers having surfaces that are pressure-sensitive or by the use of ordinary paper with a carbon paper between the recording device and the paper.

The most popular speed of early transmission was approximately one 8.5×11 in page in 6 min using a voice circuit of 4-kHz nominal bandwidth.

In AM operation, the level of the output signal of the transmitter shall be greatest for white and least for black. It is desirable to have the ratio of nominal white signal to nominal black signal be approximately 30 dB. For audio-frequency telephone circuits, the frequency of the picture carrier current is fixed at about 1300 Hz. This frequency gives the least delay distortion on lightly loaded underground cables. In the case of carrier telephone circuits providing a transmission band from 300 to 3400 Hz, a carrier current frequency of about 1900 Hz is recommended.

In FM operation, the characteristics of the frequency-modulated output should be:

Mean frequency	1900 Hz
White frequency	1500 Hz
Black frequency	2300 Hz

The stability of the transmission must be such that the frequency corresponding to a given tone does not vary by more than 8 Hz in a period of 1 s and by more than 16 Hz in a period of 15 min. The receiving apparatus must be capable of operating correctly when the drift of black and white frequencies received does not exceed their nominal value by more than ±32 Hz.

Refer to CCITT Rec. T.1 for standardization of phototelegraph apparatus.

For detailed information on facsimile transmission, refer to the EIA RS 357 standard and to CCITT Vol. VII, T Recommendations. The functional electrical characteristics of EIA RS 357 are given in Fig. 3.13.

To avoid the risk of disturbing phototelegraph signals (for example, by dial pulses transmitted over adjacent channels or by noise), it is important that the sending level should be as high as permissible. However, it should not exceed − 10 dBm0 on the multichannel system, and the power at the output of the transmitting equipment shall not exceed 1 mW. This value of − 10 dBm0 is in accordance with CCITT Rec. V.2, since in all cases the phototelegraph transmissions are operated in simplex. For more information on phototelegraph transmission, refer to CCITT Rec. M.880 on international circuits and to H.41 for FM phototelegraph transmission on voice-grade circuits.

High-speed wideband systems are also available. One system, using

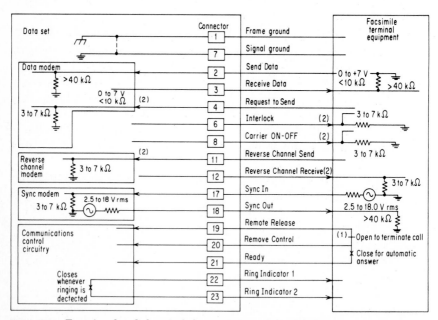

Figure 3.13 Functional and electrical characteristics of the EIA RS 357 standard. Notes: (1) Must be closed or Data Set cannot be placed in data mode.

(2)	Receiver sensitivity	On +3 to +25 V	Off −3 to −25 V
	Source	+5 to +25 V	−5 to −25 V

digital techniques to encode the analog facsimile signal, is capable of transmitting an 8.5 × 11 in page in 6 s. The speed is 60 times faster but the bandwidth required is also 60 times as much—240 kHz instead of 4 kHz. A super high speed wideband system capable of transmitting an 8.5 × 11 in page in 1 s is also available.

Recently, a digital facsimile system designed to operate over digital facilities up to 19.2 kb/s or over the public switched telephone network at 4.8 kb/s became available. Transmission speeds and resolution for an 8.5 × 11 in page in a digital facsimile system are as follows:

Modem	High speed	Standard	Fine detail
Internal, 4.8 kb/s	35 s	50 s	90 s
External, 9.6 kb/s	20 s	25 s	45 s
External, 19.2 kb/s	20 s	20 s	28 s

Either in analog or in digital mode, fast facsimile service equipment is equipped with buffer storage so that white spaces between lines of the message are skipped and only the content is transmitted.

Data encryption

Communications security has been linked in the public imagination with military secrets. But the commercial sector has its secrets too. They may not be as sensitive as military ones but they often revolve around important marketing strategies, contract bids, and the disposition of large sums of money. With business offices becoming increasingly electronic in operation, companies are looking for better ways to protect their dealings from competitors and disloyal employees. The banking and financial communities are another prime encryption market. Fortunes are handled by means of electronic transmission and computer manipulation, and reports appear regularly of the clever new ways people have devised to get money by electronic fraud. Other security markets include common carriers and service bureaus.

Transmission of data can be protected against unauthorized interceptions, additions, changes, and deletions by cryptography techniques. Data encryption dynamically alters transmitted data by rearranging the bit pattern. This new bit pattern renders the data useless except to authorized locations. Encrypted text starts with a special start-encrypted-text character and ends with stop-encrypted-text characters.

Cryptosystems do not require programming and are transparent to the users. Each cryptosystem user issues a "secret key" to encrypt a message, and only those intended receivers who know that secret key can decrypt the user's message. Cryptosystems can be used in asynchronous or synchronous data channels.

In the United States, data-encryption systems utilize a Data Encryption Standard (DES) algorithm as approved and published in 1977 by the U.S. National Bureau of Standards under the title "Federal Information Processing Standards" (FIPS), Pub. 46. It is complex ciphering algorithm or defined set of rules. It is based on both substitution and transposition techniques, neither of which are at all new in concept. Substitution codes involve the substitution of one character or symbol for another. Transposition techniques involve rearranging the order of the characters or symbols according to some control pattern or key known only to the sender and the intended recipient.

The DES defines a set of operations to be performed on a 64-bit block of information (the plain text) to encrypt it into an 84-bit block of scrambled information (encrypted text). This is done under the control of a 56-bit key block chosen by the sender with the knowledge of the recipient. Eight parity bits used for internal checking make the actual entered key word 64 bits long; these 8 bits are removed before the key is used. In this manner it is possible to convert one 64-bit piece of plain text into any of 2^{56} (or about 70×10^{15}) possible versions of 64-bit encrypted text. The feasibility of deriving a particular key in this way is extremely unlikely in typical threat environments. Moreover, if the key is changed frequently, the risk of this event is greatly diminished. However, users should be aware that it is theoretically possible to derive the key in fewer trials and should be cautioned to change the key as often as practical. When correctly implemented and properly used, this standard provides a high level of cryptographic protection to computer data.

To summarize, data encryption has become popular because:

- Utilization of satellite and microwave transmission exposes messages to eavesdropping.

- Spreading the use of distributed processing exposes more sensitive data to possible interception.

- Interception of communications becomes very risky because of increased international trade, which is highly competitive.

- In bank-to-bank transmission involving fund transfers, it is mandatory to utilize data encryption.

3.6 Summary of CCITT Recommendations Relating to Modems

Refer to the Glossary for a complete list of V recommendations.

V.21   0 to 200 (300) b/s; similar to Bell 103 and 108. Defined for FDX switched network operation.

V.22   1200 b/s; similar to Bell 212A. Defined for FDX switched network operation and dedicated circuits.

V.23   600 to 1200 b/s, similar to Bell 202. Defined for HDX switched network operation; 75-Bd secondary channel optional.

V.24   Definition of interchange circuits, similar to EIA RS 232C.

V.25   Automatic calling units, similar to Bell 801.

V.26   2400 b/s, identical to Bell 201 B; defined for four-wire dedicated circuits.

V.26*bis* 2400 b/s, similar to Bell 201 C; defined for switched network.

V.27   4800 b/s, similar to Bell 208A. Defined for leased circuits using manual equalizers.

V.27*bis* 4800 b/s. Defined for leased circuits using automatic equalizers.

V.27*ter* 4800/2400 b/s modem standardized for use in the general switched telephone network.

V.28   Electrical characteristics for unbalanced, double-current interchange circuits operating below 20,000 b/s.

V.29   9600 b/s. Similar to Bell 209, using an automatic adaptive equalizer and QAM technique.

V.35   48 kb/s. Interfacing with 34-pin connector, using 60–108 kHz group band circuits.

V.36   48 to 72 kb/s synchronous data transmission, using 60–108 kHz group band circuits.

V.54   Loop test devices for modems.

References

CCITT, Geneva: *Orange, Yellow,* and *Red Books.* Volume VIII, "Data Communication Over the Telephone Network."

Davenport, William P.: *Modern Data Communication,* Rochelle Park, N.J., Hayden, 1972.

Department of Commerce, National Bureau of Standards: "Data Encryption Standard," Pub. 46, Jan. 15, 1977, Federal Information Processing Standards, Springfield, Va.

Disanti, N., F. Oster, and O. Tugal: "4800 b/s Modem Evaluation," Report, RCA Global Communications, New York, November 1977.

Hamsher, Donald H.: *Communication System and Engineering Handbook,* McGraw-Hill, New York, 1967, pp. 2–67, 2–68, fig. 31.

Hewlett Packard, Palo Alto, Calif.: *Training Manual Guidebook to Data Communications,* Manual Part No. 5955-1715. Modem features.

Hindin, Harvey J.: "LSI-based Data Encryption Discourages the Data Thief," *Electronics,* June 21, 1979.

Intertel Inc., Burlington, Mass.: "Modem, 2400 b/s, Model 2010, Theory of Operation." Excerpts and schematics.

Martin, James: *Future Developments in Telecommunications,* Prentice-Hall, Englewood Cliffs, N.J., 1971, p. 75, fig. 6–3.

———: *Telecommunications and the Computer,* Prentice-Hall, Englewood Cliffs, N.J., 1976, pp. 213, 221, 226.

Motorola Inc., Government Electronics Div., Scottsdale, Ariz. "Advanced Techniques in
   Network Security—Infoguard."
Schmidt, Lyon A.: "What Is a Digital Filter?" *HP Journal,* September 1977.
True, Kenneth M.: *Interface,* Fairchild Semiconductor Co., Mountain View, Calif., 1975.
Weisberger, Alan J.: *Data Communications Handbook,* Signetics Corp., Sunnyvale,
   Calif., 1977.

4

Channel-Capacity-Increasing Methods and Packet Switching

The growth of data communications has impelled users to search for cost-effective means of employing telecommunication facilities. Multiprocessors have allowed the insertion of more channels into existing channels by using digitization of analog signals or analog modulation of digital signals or a combination of both techniques. In this chapter compression of digital and analog signals as well as utilization of idle periods and packet switching are discussed. Multiplexing, a classical version of line-capacity-increasing technique, will be discussed in Chap. 5.

Transmission Rate

The transmission rate is generally expressed in baud (Bd). Although in most systems it is equivalent to bits per second (b/s), the baud transmission rate must not be confused with the information rate, bits per second, the rate at which actual data are transmitted. One baud signal may carry one or more bits of the data. The following examples are given to distinguish these two concepts.

Example 1 In a 9600 b/s system which utilizes the QAM (quadrature amplitude modulation) method, the transmission rate is 2400 Bd; i.e., the quantity of discrete signals transmitted in a second is 2400. Since every discrete signal represents a combination of 4 bits, the information or communication rate is 9600 b/s. For more information refer to Sec. 4.1.

Example 2 If a one-unit stop and start bit and an eight-level ASCII code are used, the byte becomes 10 bits long. If the transmission rate is 4800 Bd, the actual information rate is 0.8 × 4800 = 3840 b/s. Hence 960 b/s is lost due to synchronization. If parity is considered, another 480 b/s is also lost due to parity detection. As a result 1440 b/s, or 30 percent of the original bits, is not used for carrying information.

Therefore, it can be seen from these examples that the information rate bits per second and the transmission rate baud are not equivalent. Low-speed transmission rate also has another expression—wpm (words per minute) or cps (characters per second). For example, 100 wpm can mean either 75 Bd using a five-level (7.42-unit) code or 110 Bd using an eight-level-plus-three-pulses code. Note that one word equals six characters.

The most-utilized telegraph and data codes in the communication field are given in Table 4.1.

TABLE 4.1   Start-Stop Telegraph and Data Codes

Unit code (total pulses per character)	Code level (information pulses per character)	Transmitting speeds			Pulse lengths, ms		Maximum modulation rate, Bd
		Characters per second	Characters per minute	Words per minute	Start and code pulses	Stop or rest pulse	
7-unit	5	6.5	390	65	22	22	45.45
7-unit	5	10.6	636	106	13.47	13.47	74.2
7.42-unit	5	6.13	368	61.33	22	31	45.45
7.42-unit	5	6.73	404	67.33	20	28.4	50
7.42-unit	5	7.67	460	76.67	17.57	25	56.88
7.42-unit	5	10.0	600	100	13.47	19.18	74.2
7.5-unit	5	6.67	400	66.67	20	30	50
8-unit	6	6.13	368	61.33	20.4	20.4	49.06
8-unit	6	8.33	500	83.33	15	15	66.67
9-unit	7	8.33	500	83.33	13.33	13.33	75
9-unit	7	14.8	888	148	7.5	7.5	133.33
9-unit	6	15	900	150	7.41	14.81	135
9-unit	7	66.67	4004	666.67	1.67	1.67	600
10-unit	8	10	600	100	10	10	100
10-unit	8	15	900	150	6.67	6.67	165
11-unit	8	6.67	400	66.67	13.64	27.72	73.33
11-unit	8	10	600	100	9.09	18.18	110
11-unit	8	15	900	150	6.06	12.12	165

TABLE 4.2   Data Speeds for Computer and Peripheral Equipment

Bits per second	Characters per second, 1 char. = 8–11 bits	Characters per minute	Words per minute, word = 6 char.	Cards per minute, 80-col. card	Boxes per hour, 1 box = 2000 cards	Lines per minute, 132 char./line	Pages per hour, 1 page = 63 lines
110	10	600	100	7		4	4
150	15	900	150	11		7	7
600	60	3,600	600	45	2	30	30
1,000	100	6,000	1,000	75	2	46	40
1,200	120	7,200	1,200	90	3	50	50
1,300	130	8,000	1,300	100	3	60	60
1,500	150	9,000	1,500	112	3	70	70
1,800	180	10,800	1,800	135	4	80	80
2,000	250	15,000	2,500	188	4	80	80
2,100	270	16,000	2,700	200	6	120	120
2,400	300	16,000	3,000	225	7	140	130
4,000	500	30,000	5,000	375	11	230	220
4,200	530	32,000	5,300	400	12	240	230
4,800	600	36,000	6,000	450	13	270	260
5,300	660	39,600	6,600	495	15	300	290
10,600	1300	79,200	13,000	990	30	600	570
19,400	2400	145,000	24,000	1800	54	1100	1050
40,800	5100	306,000	51,000	3080	92	2300	2200
64,000	8000	480,000	80,000	6000	180	6000	5700

Table 4.2 depicts data communication speeds and card reader, paper reader, and line printer speeds for computers.

4.1   Channel-Capacity-Increasing Methods on Data Transmission

The Nyquist theorem states that over a band-limited channel at most two independent data pulses per second per cycle of bandwidth can be transmitted. For data transmission over a voice channel, the usable bandwidth is 2400 Hz. This then indicates that a maximum baud rate of 4800 b/s is allowable. To accomplish a 9600 b/s data rate, therefore, 2 bits/Bd must be transmitted.

Multilevel bit transmission

One of the simplest methods of increasing the rate of bits through a channel is to combine pairs of adjacent bits into dibits (pronounced "die-bits") and let each baud carry one dibit. For example, the bit sequence shown in Fig. 4.1 is divided into dibits. These dibits are the only four combinations that bits can assume if taken two at a time. The objective is to send each dibit as one multilevel signal element or baud. If converted, a different voltage is assigned to each of the four combinations; then each dibit is converted to its respective voltage before sending it out on the channel, and bits can then be transmitted at twice the channel's capacity.

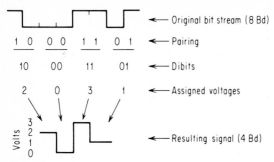

Figure 4.1 Dibits presented to channel as variable voltages.

If the possible dibit combinations are assigned to the voltages as given in Table 4.3, then the same sequence of bits can be converted to dibits, which in turn are presented to the channel as variable voltages. Sent at the same bit rate as before, these 8 bits require only half the previous amount of time. Instead of voltages, four tones of different frequencies (FM) or four different phases (PM) could have been used; FM and PM are used extensively in modems. Being analog signals, tones have the advantages of being able to pass through the dialed telephone network and of being less susceptible to attenuation and noise.

Digital baseband signals produce sets of sidebands displaced from the carrier. Higher-order sidebands are filtered out, and only the first-order sidebands are used.

Bell modems 201A and 201B utilize the PM technique. Since there are four distinct dibits, each one might be represented by phase values of 90, 180, 270, and 0°. Refer to CCIT V.26 for phase modulation in 2400 b/s modems.

By similar consideration, the data stream might be divided into

TABLE 4.3

Dibit	Voltage
11	3
10	2
01	1
00	0

TABLE 4.4 Phase Assignments for Tribit Combinations

Tribits	Phase change
001	0°
000	45°
010	90°
011	135°
111	180°
110	225°
100	270°
101	315°

SOURCE: CCITT Rec. V. 27.

TABLE 4.5

Absolute phase	$Q1$	Relative signal element amplitude
0°, 90°, 180°, 270°	0	3
	1	5
45°, 135°, 225°, 315°	0	$\sqrt{2}$
	1	$3\sqrt{2}$

groups of three consecutive data bits (tribits) to give eight different phase changes. The CCITT V.27 phase change assignments for 4800 b/s modems are given in Table 4.4.

A modulation technique of 9600 b/s is now discussed which gives a comprehensive idea about multilevel bit transmission as well as the QAM technique. For 9600 b/s transmission, a modulation technique combining phase and amplitude modulation is used and is known as *quadrature amplitude modulation* (QAM). The structure is similar to a four-phase, four-level structure, although eight phases are used in all. The baud rate is 2400, and 4 bits are transmitted per baud, which requires 16 locations, to give a total of 9600 b/s. CCITT V.29 describes 9600 b/s modems for use on "Leased channel circuits given by CCITT M.1020."

The transmitted data stream is divided into four consecutive data bits (quadbits). The first, $Q1$, is used to determine the transmitted signal element amplitude. The second, third, and fourth bits ($Q2$, $Q3$, $Q4$) are encoded as a phase angle relative to the $Q1$ phase. This phase value is identical to Rec. V.27. The relative amplitude and the absolute phase of the transmitted signal element is determined by $Q1$ (refer to Table 4.5). At the receiver the quadbits are decoded and the data bits are reassembled in correct order. It should finally be noted that for this transmission the center frequency is 1700 Hz and the modulation rate is 2400 Bd.

An exercise is given in Chap. 6 for QAM signals. QAM is a double-sideband modulation technique and is economical in channel bandwidth usage while not requiring excessively sharp filters at the band edges. It has a good S/N ratio and imperviousness to phase jitter as its advantages.

Signal space diagrams for 4800, 7200 fallback and 9600 b/s data inputs to a 9600 b/s (V.29) modem are given in Fig. 4.2. Bandwidth utilization of the modems at different data speeds, using different modulation rates, is given in Table 4.6.

Some modems are equipped with an *eye pattern generator* which produces a description of the telephone-circuit status and the modem

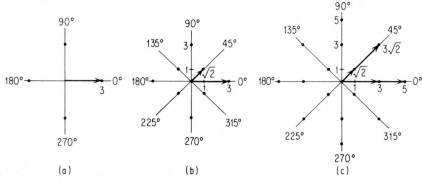

Figure 4.2 Signal space diagrams. (*a*) 4800 b/s; (*b*) 7200 b/s; (*c*) 9600 b/s. (Redrawn from CCITT Rec. V.29.)

performance in a QAM operation, i.e., twin carrier signals operating at 90° (or quadrature) relationship to each other. Eye patterns for different data speeds are similar to the diagrams given in Fig. 4.2.

4.2 Analog Voice Compression Method

This method converts a voice-grade channel into a channel with dual-voice capability and four 74.2-Bd narrow-band teletype channels (see Fig. 4.3). It is an analog technique, and a special bandwidth compression method, *analytic routing,* is used. The speech bandwidth is clipped to 300–2700 Hz and is divided into four contiguous passbands, each containing no more than one formant (formant stands for characteristic of a sound). Each band passes through a 90° phase splitter, an envelope detector, and a square router. These four signals are summed and form a compressed transmitter output. The other speech channel is also processed in the same manner, and two channels are mixed with a 1650-Hz frequency. The lower side for voice 1 and the upper side for voice 2 are extracted and are mixed. At the receiver, voice 1 and voice

TABLE 4.6

Speed, b/s	Mod. rate, Bd	Mode, PSK	Bandwidth, Hz
1200	600	4	600
1200	1200	2	1200
2400	1200	4	1200
4800	1600	8	1600
4800	2400	4	2400
7200	2400	8	2400
9600	2400	8	2400

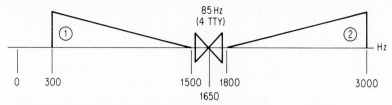

Figure 4.3   Analog speech compression system (2 speech + 4 teleprinter).

2 are separated and mixed with 1650 Hz. Each composite signal is divided into four formant channels, and each channel passes through a 90° phase splitter, a squarer, and an algebraic summer, and then four passband channels are summed to give the original voice.

Four 74.2-Bd (or three 110-Bd or two 150-Bd) teleprinter outputs are character-interleaved at a 250 b/s rate and converted to 85 Hz through a modem and placed between two sidebands.

4.3   Digital Voice Compression Methods

Although the digitized voice generally requires more bandwidth for transmission than the voice, it provides for the following items:

1. Far lower susceptibility to noise interference during transmission
2. Multiplex operation of many channels on a single wideband channel with inexpensive digital hardware
3. Reduced crosstalk
4. Easier encryption for secure communication

A typical digital voice transmission circuit is given in Fig. 4.4. Digital voice compression methods are different than PCM. In conventional PCM, the transmitted data stream consists of a series of words, each representing the voice signal level at the instant of sampling. PCM has an advantage in that it can respond to very abrupt level changes. Refer to Fig. 4.5.

Delta modulation

Delta modulation is a variation of the PCM method. It compares successive signal samples and transmits only their differences, thus re-

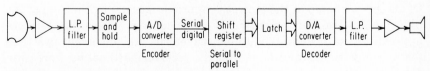

Figure 4.4   Digital voice transmission circuit.

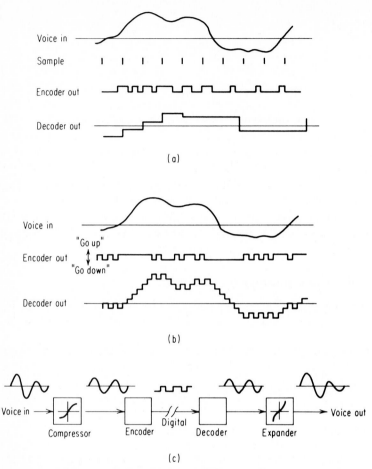

Figure 4.5   Digital conversion of voice. (*a*) PCM waveforms; (*b*) delta modulation waveforms; (*c*) simplified companding.

ducing the number of bits required to code speech. The principle of delta modulation is shown in Fig. 4.5. The continuous signal is sampled at periodic intervals of time. The sampled value is then compared with a staircase approximation of the output signal. If the sampled waveform exceeds the staircase approximation, a positive pulse is generated. If the sampled waveform is less than the staircase approximation, a negative pulse is generated. This output pulse, positive or negative, forms the next step in the staircase approximation; i.e., the sum of the binary pulse train at the output of the encoder produces the staircase approximation or delta-modulated waveform. An important practical feature of delta modulation is that the receiver need not be more complicated than a simple integrator.

Continuously variable slope delta modulation (CVSD)

CVSD takes advantage of the fact that voice signals do not change abruptly and that there is only a small change from one sample to the next. Therefore, a reasonably good reproduction can be obtained by transmitting in a given time interval the information of whether the output signal should increase or decrease. Since the low-level signals are distorted in this procedure, the voice input is companded. In the CVSD system, the companding scheme is optimized for the characteristics of the human voice.

Compared to PCM, CVSD allows lower data rates; therefore more channels can be multiplexed at the same bit rate. PCM requires 56 kb/s per voice channel; CVSD gives comparable voice at 32 kb/s. CVSD also exhibits less serious sound degradation in the presence of digital noise interference.

Linear predictive coding technique

This system allows four simultaneous conversations over a single voice-grade channel together with four 74.2-Bd teleprinter channels. Basically the technique is digital and is based upon a linear predictive coding technique, where each channel is digitized and passed through digital filters called *resonating filters*. Here only the digits corresponding to fundamental frequencies are selected and converted to a 2400 b/s data stream. An adult male's pitch is in the range of 50 to 150 Hz; for women, 90 to 450 Hz, and for children, 125 to 575 Hz. A telephone circuit has a range of 300 to 3000 Hz; most of the fundamental pitches are cut off by the phone system. For example, an energy at a frequency of 360 Hz could be the second harmonic of 180 Hz or the third harmonic of 120 Hz. Vocal cords of the human body can be considered as the source of speech and produce the voiced portion of the speech. In this system, the fundamental pitch is determined from the harmonics and is mixed with voiced and unvoiced sources of the speech in the proper proportions required for natural voice simulation. Digital simulation of an unvoiced speech is white noise.

Formants are simulated by a series of digital filters, called resonating filters, and through a data-compressing process are converted into a 2400 b/s data stream. Four 2400 b/s data streams can be multiplexed into a 9600 b/s stream and connected to a voice-grade channel via a modem.

Bath technique

Digital speech encoding would take a giant step forward if time-encoding techniques could pack four speech channels into a conventional

64,000 b/s digital link. Moreover, where voice quality of less than the international standards is acceptable, for example, in military or mobile radio applications, it could achieve 5400 b/s data rates at a cost much less than that of other coding techniques.

The basic principle of the Bath technique is as follows. It has been discovered that male speech at every second has around 900 segments, each occurring between successive real zeros of the waveform. It can be represented with 200 basic types, such as half-sine waves. A mapping technique was able to reduce these 200 shapes to 23 symbols, each of which can be represented by a 5-bit word. The encoder produces a new word after every zero crossing, producing around 900 b/s, so the basic data rate is 4500 b/s. If speech is to be modulated for loudness, an 8-bit word defining amplitude can be added after every eight symbols, giving a 5400 b/s data rate.

The Bath technique allows encoding in real time with little more than a microprocessor, whereas the other techniques require an extremely fast and expensive minicomputer.

4.4   Utilization of Idle Transmission Periods

Only one customer transmits in an HDX telecommunication, which keeps the FDX channel idle in one direction on trunk cables. Furthermore, on any given channel, the data activity in either direction of a data transmission invariably ranges from 50 down to 10 percent or even less.

It is often assumed that voice traffic is characterized by a long (60–300 s) holding time. Furthermore, during conversations actual active speech is followed by periods of silence and thus utilizes the channel only a fraction of the time. A voice source is characterized by active speech periods separated by silent intervals of approximately equal duration. Also, only one speaker is usually active at any specific time. Hence, dedicating an end-to-end circuit to a pair of subscribers for an entire interval of communication wastes channel capacity.

Several techniques developed to utilize these idle data or speech periods economically are discussed below.

Statistical time-division multiplexers

A statistical time-division multiplexer (STDM), also called an *intelligent time-division multiplexer* (ITDM), takes advantage of the statistics of data activity by reassembling or retransmitting variable-length data blocks composed of only the actual data characters from individual channels. STDMs are different from conventional multiplexers and are discussed in Sec. 5.1.

Computer data concentrators

Computer data concentrators compress and store data coming from several remote terminals and send them over a high-speed trunk to the host computer. Computer data concentrators are distinguished from the multiplexers in the following manner:

- The single facility on the output side carries one channel, whose capacity is less than the sum of all the capacities on the input side of the concentrator.

- A multiplexer is transparent to the channel structure of a network, whereas a concentrator is not transparent. Since a computer data concentrator is intimately related to the host computer, it permits its user to off-load actual data processing tasks from the host CPU.

The percentage of time a channel is used is called *utilization*. Many terminals generate data for transmission at an average rate much less than the capacity of the channel, resulting in channels with low utilization. A concentrator achieves economic advantage by replacing several low-utilization channels with one highly utilized channel. Note that the output channel capacity of a concentrator will not be greater than the sum of the data rates of the terminals on its input. A concentrator has more time slots arriving on its input side than leaving on its output side. Each time slot carrying information must be assigned a time slot on the output side. Thus a concentrator must be able to identify which time slots are in fact transferring information. Furthermore, it must be able to assign output time slots to this information in such a manner as to be understood by whatever device is on the other end of the output channel. Although the average number of time slots carrying information on the input will be less than the number available on the output, the random nature of terminal use may result in the number of slots carrying information arriving over a brief interval being greater than the number of slots available on the output. Hence the concentrator must also have the ability to buffer the arriving information as it waits for available slots. The requirements of intelligence and storage for a concentrator invariably lead to its implementation with a minicomputer.

The actual operation of concentrators varies considerably but is usually much more sophisticated than the simple bit packing noted above. By performing such local operations as polling, error checking, line control, etc., and transferring information to the computer with efficient high-speed transmission techniques, the concentrator can achieve an apparent output channel utilization in excess of 100 percent.

The major disadvantages of the computer concentrator are that such a system is significantly more complex and almost certainly less reliable than the relatively simple general-purpose communications hardware of a frequency- or a time-division multiplexer. The greater unreliability results from the imperfections typically found during the initial operational phase of a specially written computer program. The computer concentrator is also several times more expensive than a corresponding multiplexer equipment.

Utilization of idle voice transmission periods

Numerous analog and digital techniques for compressing the conversations of a number of speakers onto a smaller number of channels have been developed. The earliest strategy was the AT&T TASI (time assignment speech interpolation), in which channel capacity is allocated only when appropriate hardware detects that a subscriber is actively speaking. Once the channel is seized, the speaker is given uninterrupted access to it. During periods of silence, the channel is relinquished and becomes available to other speakers. The above systems "freeze-out" speakers when the number of active speakers temporarily exceeds the available channel capacity. This results in the clipping and segmenting of certain conversations with an associated loss in intelligibility. Refinements of the TASI concept, based on digital encoding techniques, whereby the bandwidth per active speaker is systematically reduced to accommodate additional speakers, have also been implemented. Two such techniques are APCM (adaptive pulse-code modulation) and VRAM (variable-rate adaptive multiplexing). In these systems, when the number of active speakers exceeds the channel capacity during "overflow periods," performance degradation is shared among all speakers by reducing the sampling rate per conversation. Thus no single speaker suffers excessive degradation.

4.5   Packetized Speech

Despite the bandwidth savings achieved by deploying such voice compression systems, their use is restricted to one link. The addressing-routing problems which must be solved for systems of this nature are adopted in a distributed communications network, which naturally leads to a packet-type family of operational procedures. Thus packetized-voice represents a viable scheme for multiple-class traffic integration and speech compression within a distributed network.

Packet transmission of speech is recognized as an opportunity to increase the utilization of transmission capacity. A combination of *variable-quality coding* and *time interval modification* can load a transmission circuit efficiently and also accommodate fluctuating demands upon the circuit.

A voice switch detects speech energy bursts, distinguishes each as a packet, time stamps it, and discards the silent intervals. After encoding, successive packets are assembled in a transmit buffer and transmitted, as shown in Fig. 4.6. Packets arriving at the receiver are buffered, decoded, and reassembled in temporal order, with the silent bits reinserted artificially but acceptably. Research results indicate that the benefits of packetized speech are:

1. Fifteen percent of total sentence duration can be eliminated.

2. Digital coding at a rate of 20 kb/s is reasonably acceptable.

3. Interval modifications of the order of 50 percent are tolerable.

Packet voice communications is always cheaper except for very short distances (less than 25 km) from a low-density central office location. For distances 150 km or more, the savings range from 70 to 80 percent for low-density locations. Note that the cost savings of packet communications are lost when a communications terminal is a long distance from the packet central office.

4.6 Packet-Switching Data Networks

With the available electronics technology today, equipment required to concentrate data traffic is considerably less expensive than the cost of the transmission lines which otherwise would have been required. World data carrier organizations have taken advantage of this and established networks to concentrate their data traffic into packages. Packages are sent to their destination through the fastest available link, where the message is reassembled and delivered as one piece to the receiving terminal.

The definition of *packet* is a group of binary digits including data and call control signals which are switched as a composite whole. The control signals and error-correction information are arranged in a specific format.

A packet-switching network does not provide an end-to-end physical link to the user. Nevertheless, it appears to the user either as a leased

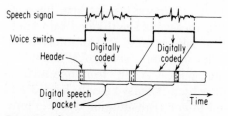

Figure 4.6   Speech packetizing. Speech is digitally coded and formed into packets.

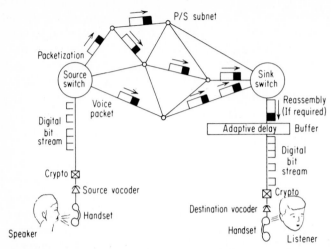

Figure 4.7   Information flow in a packet-voice-data network.

channel service using a permanent connection or as a switched data service. The economics of packet switching are the same as other switched communication systems and utilize hold-and-forward switching techniques. An example of a packet-switching data network is shown in Figs. 4.7 and 4.8.

Operation of a packet-switching data network

A packet-switching data network must conform to the protocols used by the data terminal. The user also utilizes standard network interface protocols.

Packet network systems operate central offices or utilize central offices of common carriers to which the users bring their circuits through terrestrial links. Computerized interfacing and switching equipment connect the user circuit to the packet network. The precise nature of the interface protocol is specified for the network depending upon the nature of subscriber-service specifications. In addition to interfacing, the computer formats the received data into packets and determines the transmission routes. There is a maximum packet size for each network—typically 1024 bits. Long messages are divided into slices and sent in several packets. Each packet contains control information for communication between network computers. The packet is held for transmission by the computer. Each packet is sent from one node to another via the most suitable link which is least heavily loaded and without faults. In this manner, end-to-end transmission delay is minimized. At each node the packet is checked for ARQ criteria. At the terminal computer, control and service information is removed, and the message is reassembled and transmitted to its final destination. The packet-switching network is virtually transparent to the user.

Protocols used in packet-switching network operations are:

- User to network: level 1 and level 2 protocols
- Network to network: level 3 protocols
- User to user: higher-level protocols, such as file transfer and transaction application

CCITT Rec. X.25 outlines the protocols for block transfer between the host computer and the packet-switching network. With this protocol the network appears to be a concentrator to the host computer.

Interconnect standards between packet networks are developing in CCITT Rec. X.7X. Refer to CCITT Vol. VIII-2, Recommendations Series X for public data and packet networks. Brief descriptions of some X Recommendations are provided in Sec. 7.4.

Distinctive advantages of packet-switching networks are:

- Rapid exchange of short messages
- High network availability because of distributed routing
- Ability to adapt to rapidly changing demands with near-real-time network operation
- Ability to communicate with terminals using incompatible codes
- Cost-effective for large networks having varying message lengths

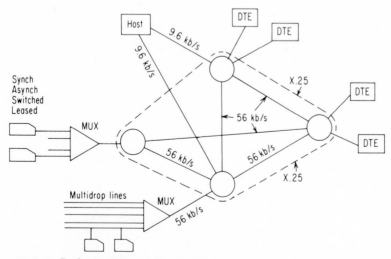

Figure 4.8 Packet-switching data network.

The present backbone trunk speed of packet-switching networks is 56 kb/s with a 100- to 200-ms delay. It is expected that traffic demand will increase and a 1.544 Mb/s (T1) speed with decreased time delay will be used in the network. A considerable price decrease on the user costs will accompany these networks.

References

CCITT, Geneva: *Orange, Yellow,* and *Red Books.* Volume VIII, "Data Communication over the Telephone Network," "Interfaces," and "Signaling."

Davenport, William P.: "Dibits," *Modern Data Communication,* Hayden, Rochelle Park, N.J., 1972, chap. 5.

Harris Semiconductor, Melbourne, Fla.: I.C. Update Brochure. May 1977.

Puckhoff, Steven J.: "9600 b/s—A Five Year History," *Telecommunications,* August 1973.

Richards, J. R., W. F. Meeker, and A. L. Nelson: "Conferencing in Digital Speech Communication Network—Delta Modulation," *RCA Engineer,* March 1979.

Multiplexing

In a network of data terminals communicating with a central computer over telephone lines, attempts must be made to put more than one terminal on each line so that the cost of the telephone lines does not exceed that of the computer. This is achieved by multiplexing the channels. Costs associated with typical data communication networks are often described as 65 percent transmission media and 35 percent equipment. All multiplexing techniques provide a "transparent" connection between low-speed terminals located remotely from the computer ports to which these low-speed terminals are normally directly attached. The word *transparent* means that the multiplexer system does not in any way interrupt the flow of data and the interface signals which are normally passed across the cable; neither the computer nor the modem nor the terminal knows that the multiplexer system is being used. In other words, no additional character is visible in the received message inserted by the transmission system.

5.1 Multiplexing Techniques

Two types of multiplexing techniques are in use today: frequency-division multiplexing (FDM) and time-division multiplexing (TDM). Multiplexing concepts of FDM and TDM are illustrated in Fig. 5.1. In FDM, several simultaneous signals, 1 through N, are multiplexed onto one line containing N channels, each channel discrete in a narrow

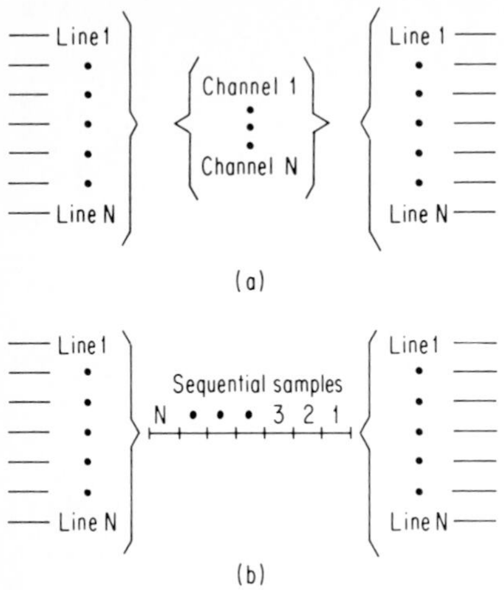

(a)

(b)

Figure 5.1 Techniques of (*a*) frequency-division multiplexing (FDM) and (*b*) time-division multiplexing (TDM).

frequency range. In TDM, samples of several simultaneous signals are transmitted sequentially on a single higher-speed circuit. A small increment of time is allocated for transmission of a sample from each input signal or channel. The samples are transmitted in sequence until all signals have been sampled, and then the cycle is repeated.

Note:

Recent publications include *space-division multiplexing* among multiplexing techniques. It is accomplished by simply binding the metallic wires or coaxial pairs together to form a single cable. It is a useful and economical technique when relatively few channels are to be transmitted in a short distance within a building or in an exchange area for local customer connections.

Frequency-division multiplexing

FDM is the oldest and most common type of multiplexing. It takes advantage of the fact that the bandwidth of a voice-grade telephone line is significantly greater than that required by a low-speed data channel, and by using a different center frequency for each channel, it allows several data channels to share the same line without interfering with each other. Refer to Fig. 5.2.

Filters of exact prescribed characteristics and highly linear amplifiers are indispensable elements of FDM systems. If an amplifier is not exactly linear, considerable distortion and noise will be introduced into all carrier channels.

The number of repeaters that are used also has a limiting effect on FDM carrier systems. Each repeater amplifies the noise, crosstalk, and other distortion products that may have accumulated in the previous cable section. Precise filters are also required in each repeater when the "frequency frogging" method is employed to compensate for the increased attenuation in the cable with frequency increase.

Improvements in the state of the art and the introduction of solid-state devices substantially reduced the costs of carrier equipment. As a result, the use of FDM carriers was extended to short-haul toll circuits and even to subscriber lines in rural areas. Economic considerations, however, still exclude the application of FDM-type carrier systems to interoffice trunk cables as a means of supplanting VF circuits.

Time-division multiplexing

TDM is a digital technique. It interleaves bits or characters, one from each attached channel, and transmits them at higher speed down the high-speed line, where the other multiplexer separates the bit trains or character frame, presenting one bit or character to each low-speed channel just as they were originated.

A TDM can be compared to a rotary switch in operation. Each switch position can be thought of as a low-speed channel. As the arm of the switch passes each position, that channel's data are sampled and placed onto a common bus. The resulting stream consists of a piece of information from each channel. To this, frame information must be added in order for the distant receiver to synchronize its "rotary switch." Refer to Fig. 5.3.

The length of time that the rotary switch remains on each channel depends on the TDM technique utilized. In a character-interleave TDM

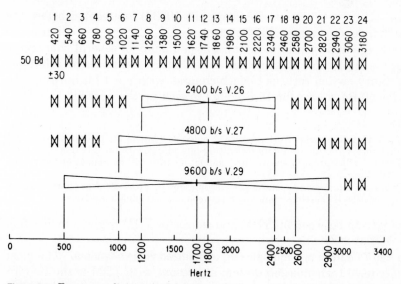

Figure 5.2 Frequency-division multiplexing of low-speed channels and combined operation with higher-speed data channels.

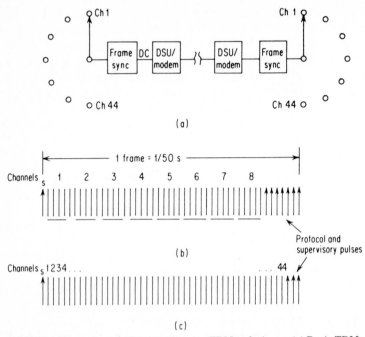

Figure 5.3 Character- and bit-interleaving TDM techniques. (*a*) Basic TDM technique; (*b*) character interleaving, 2400 b/s; (*c*) bit interleaving, 2400 b/s. Notes: (1) 1 character = 5 information + 1 start + 1½ stop pulses. (2) Start and stop pulses are deleted at (*b*).

a full character (150 ms, for five-unit, 50 Bd) is accepted before the switch indexes to a new channel. This requires a great deal of hardware for storage and results in a transmission delay of several characters, which is intolerable for some networks. In the bit-interleave technique, the rotary switch returns to each channel within a 1-bit duration (20 ms for 50 Bd, 13 ms for 75 Bd, etc.) to pick up the next bit.

Notes:

1. The 7.42-unit signal of a teleprinter is treated as 8 bits in the bit-interleave TDM.
2. Bit interleaving requires data formatting into blocks with the addition of internal framing information to ensure that channel identity will be maintained at the receiver.
3. Character interleaving requires the transmission of a periodic sync character. Synchronization is therefore maintained between each terminal scan cycle.

Comparison between bit TDM and character TDM is given in Sec. 5.2.

The Bell T1 carrier and multiplexing of digitized voice channels. The most widely used transmission system at present with TDM is the Bell T1 carrier in the United States. This carrier uses wire pairs with digital repeaters spaced 6000 ft (1800 m) apart to carry approximately 1.5

million b/s. Into this bit stream 24 speech channels are encoded using PCM and TDM techniques. Eight thousand frames per second travel down the line, and each frame contains 24 samples of 8 bits. (Refer to Fig. 5.4.) Seven bits are the encoded sample, and the eighth forms a bit stream for each speech channel containing network signaling and routing information. (Refer to the PCM technique discussed in Sec. 3.2.)

There are a total of 193 bits in each frame, so the T1 line operates at $193 \times 8000 = 1,544,000$ b/s. The last bit in the frame, the 193d bit, is used to establish and maintain synchronization. The sequence of these 193 bits from separate frames is examined by the logic of the receiving terminal. If this sequence does not follow a given coded pattern, then the terminal detects that synchronization has been lost. If

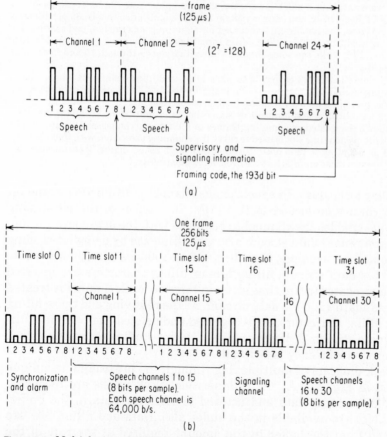

Figure 5.4 Multiplexing of PCM voice signals. (a) T1-PCM carrier format. For speech, $2^7 = 128$ levels. (b) 2048 kb/s PCM format. (CCITT Rec. G.732.)

synchronization does slip, then the bits examined will in fact be the bits from the channels that will not exhibit the required pattern.

There is a chance that these bits will form a pattern similar to the pattern being sought. The synchronization pattern must therefore be chosen so that it is unlikely that it will occur by chance. If the 193d bit was made to be always a 1 or always a 0, this could occur by chance in the voice signal. It was found that an alternating bit pattern 010101 . . . never occurs for long in any bit position. Such a pattern would imply a 4-kHz component in the signal, and the input filters used would not pass this. Therefore, the 193d transmitted bit is made alternately 1 and 0.

Notes:

1. In T1-PCM format, for five frames out of six, the full 8 bits of a channel is used for voice encoding. But in every sixth frame only 7 bits is used for voice. The eighth bit is used for dial pulsing or supervisory information. Since these control functions have to be transmitted at a much lower rate, their sampling rate can be much lower, too.
2. In CCITT Rec. G.732, the carrier system uses 32 eight-bit channels, 30 of which are used for voice, the remaining 2 reserved for signaling, supervision, and alarms. The result is a $64,000 \times 32 = 2048$ Mb/s rate. Signaling channels are located in time slots 0 and 16, while the voice channels have time slots 1 through 15 and 17 through 31 (see Fig. 5.4).
3. Recommendation G.733 covers 1544 kb/s PCM multiplex equipment which carries 24 telephone channels. Carrier format is similar to T1-PCM format with the exception that the first bit is used for framing instead of the 193d bit. The first bit of the format is used for multiframe alignment or signaling. In a multiframe structure, frames 6 and 12 are designated as signaling frames (a multiframe comprises 12 frames). The eighth bit in each time slot is used to carry the signaling associated with that channel.
4. AT&T is adopting a new optical-fiber-based, high-speed digital transmission and interface specification to achieve European compatibility.

Bit-stuffing technique. In synchronous channel multiplexing, if the bit stream cannot be locked to the TDM, utilization of the bit-stuffing technique enables the channel to be mixed with the aggregate stream.

An isochronous data stream also is multiplexed by using bit-stuffing techniques. For example, to multiplex four 1000 b/s data channels into a 4800 b/s data stream, filling bits or filling characters are inserted in the aggregate stream time slots. In this way each channel is treated like a standard 1200 b/s data stream. At the receiving end these filling bits or filling characters are recognized and deleted from the demultiplexed data stream. A disadvantage of the bit-stuffing technique is that transmission efficiency is reduced.

A block diagram of multiplexing through the bit-stuffing technique is given in Fig. 5.5. At the channel side, clock pulses are recovered from the incoming data and utilized to store the data in the buffer. Filling bits are available in the buffer also. Data and filling bits are extracted from the buffer in the amount required at the rate of the TDM clock. At the receiving end, filling bits are recognized and re-

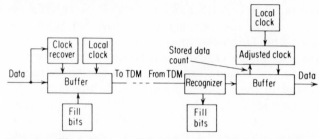

Figure 5.5 Block diagram of the bit-stuffing technique in TDM.

moved from the demultiplexed data. The data are stored in a buffer, and the data rate is reestablished by checking the amount of the stored data in the buffer. Then the data are extracted from the buffer by using this clock pulse. If the buffer storage is low, the output clock is automatically slowed down, and vice versa.

High-speed time-division multiplexing. High-speed (also called *wideband*) transmission facilities are available from the common carriers at rates of 56 kb/s, 1.5 Mb/s (T1), 6.3 Mb/s (T2), 46 Mb/s (T3), and 281 Mb/s (T4) in the United States. The digital transmission media are given in Fig. 5.11.

High-speed transmission media are different from the voice-band facilities both in speed and in error rate. They usually provide transmission between computers, computers and terminals, and data concentrators or between two central offices of a common carrier company.

High-speed multiplexers multiplex synchronous data and are bit-interleaved. The lower transmission efficiency of bit-interleaving techniques in reference to asynchronous data multiplexing does not apply to high-speed TDM. High-speed TDMs are relatively simple and are almost 100 percent efficient. Channels are multiplexed by assigning one or more time slots in the frame in proportion to their speeds; i.e., if a 2400 b/s channel uses one bit slot, a 9600 b/s channel uses four time slots. No stuffing bits are used, as only a small portion of bits is utilized for supervisory purposes. A typical 56 kb/s TDM system multiplexes 21 × 2400 b/s synchronous channels or a combination of different speed channels such as 5 × 4800 + 2 × 9600 + 3 × 2400 b/s.

The remaining 5600 bits are utilized for local loopback, remote loopback commands and status, synchronization and its status, longitudinal redundancy checks, and others. Normally, digital data on the channel are synchronized to the clock of a high-speed TDM. However, when the data channel is clocked independently, a small-capacity buffer unit is provided at the channel interface to compensate for clock slippage. At the channel side EIA RS 232C and CCITT V.24/28 standards are conformed, and at the aggregate side EIA RS 422A and CCITT V.35 (balanced-line) standards are conformed.

Most of the high-speed TDMs provide multipoint operation, which saves transmission line and modem expenses. Data can be extracted and other data inserted in the vacated channel while the rest of the channels can bypass the midpoint. In this way one TDM communicates with other TDMs.

In Fig. 5.6 a multipoint high-speed TDM network versus voice-grade point-to-point operation is shown. For example, assume:

2 × 9.6 kb/s circuits between Ⓐ and Ⓒ

5 × 4.8 kb/s circuits between Ⓐ and Ⓑ

3 × 4.8 kb/s circuits between Ⓑ and Ⓒ

3 × 2.4 kb/s polling between Ⓐ and Ⓑ and Ⓒ

Via voice-grade transmission channels this system uses the following:

2 × 9.6 kb/s channel and 4 × 9.6 kb/s modem between Ⓐ and Ⓒ

5 × 4.8 kb/s channel and 10 × 4.8 kb/s modem between Ⓐ and Ⓑ

3 × 4.8 kb/s channel and 6 × 4.8 kb/s modem between Ⓑ and Ⓒ

3 × 2.4 kb/s channel and 9 × 2.4 kb/s modem between Ⓐ, Ⓑ and Ⓑ, Ⓒ

The same communication can be provided by utilizing a digital transmission network and multipoint high-speed TDMs, which require the following:

2 × DDS between Ⓐ, Ⓑ and Ⓑ, Ⓒ

4 × DSU (for TDM interfacing to DDS)

3 × 56 kb/s high-speed TDM

Statistical time-division multiplexing. In a conventional TDM, the multiplex link is the aggregate sum of the channel data rates. However, a statistical TDM (STDM), also called an *intelligent TDM* (ITDM) or a *statistical MUX* (SMUX), permits the sum of the channel data rates to be higher than the multiplex link data rate (see Fig. 5.7).

ITDM systems are character TDMs, since character-oriented systems are more efficient for multiplexing asynchronous channels. In ITDM, character time slots are available to all channels and are assigned on a channel activity basis, whereas inactive ones are ignored. If the channel activity rate becomes greater than the multiplex data rate, the channel characters are temporarily stored in a buffer memory and

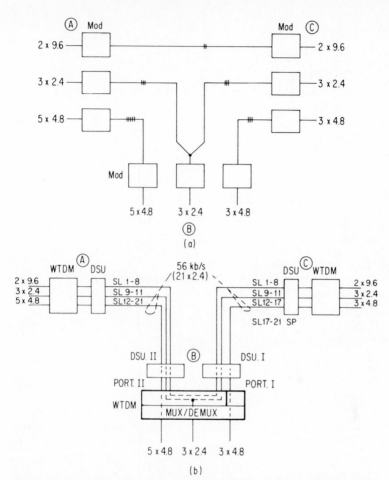

Figure 5.6 Comparison of a digital data network (*a*) via voice-grade circuits and (*b*) via wideband TDMs on DDS. Notes: (1) All data speeds are in kilobits per second. (2) One channel 9.6 kb/s occupies four time slots in a frame; one channel 4.8 kb/s occupies two time slots in a frame; one channel 2.4 kb/s occupies one time slot in a frame. (3) Minimum channel speed is 2.4 kb/s.

are sent over the multiplex link when a time slot becomes available. ITDM may be designed with buffer storage either on the channel or on the aggregate ports.

Typically, 200 percent multiplexing efficiency (the ratio of the channel data rates sum to the MUX data rate) is achieved. Efficiency as high as 400 percent is also achievable in networks with low data traffic. The ITDM also stores all aggregate link information in a buffer memory for possible retransmission of line errors and to meet the load peak activity periods. Here a typical buffer capacity is a 12-kbyte RAM.

A new multiplex link format is required for an ITDM to handle the

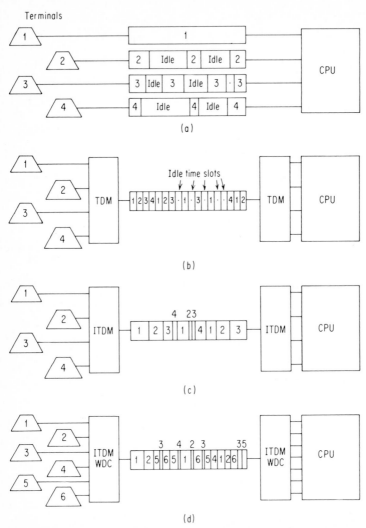

Figure 5.7 Time slot savings by using intelligent TDM. (a) Four 1200 b/s lines without multiplexing; (b) one 4800 b/s line with conventional TDM; (c) one 2400 b/s line with ITDM; (d) one 2400 b/s line with ITDM with Data Comp.

increased number of channels. The multiplex link frame is variable. Short frames are used during periods of low activity, and longer frames are used as the traffic volume increases. A two-character CRC (cyclical redundancy check) is added to the end of all frames. The receiving ITDM uses this CRC for ARQ operation. If an error is detected in a received frame, retransmission is requested and this provides a BER (bit error rate) better than 1 in 10^{12}.

There are several options available for controlling data flow in the ITDM, but only buffer overflow operation on the aggregate side is mentioned in the following discussion. Although a large data buffer storage is provided, a potential for buffer overflow exists due to either excessive retransmissions or the prolonged peak channel data activity or a combination of both. When utilization of buffer storage reaches, typically, 90 percent, a terminal restraint is initiated in one of two ways as selected by a configuration switch. If the CTS method of flow control is selected, the EIA RS 232C control signal Clear to Send (CTS) is turned off to all channels when the buffer-storage utilization reaches 90 percent. This causes terminals or computer ports which respond to EIA control signals to suspend transmission. CTS is turned on again when buffer-storage utilization reduces to 65 percent. If the XON/ XOFF method of flow control is selected, the ITDM sends the ASCII XOFF control character (DC3 or CTL-S) to all attached terminals or computer ports when buffer-storage utilization reaches 90 percent. This control character causes the data terminals or computer ports to cease transmission. When the buffer-storage utilization reduces to 65 percent, the ASCII XON control character (DC1 or CTL-Q) is sent to the attached terminals or computer ports, causing them to resume transmission.

Two fundamental types of statistical multiplexers exist. The first might be described as an intelligent switching device that routes live data inputs into idle channel time slots (refer to Fig. 5.7). But these units' intelligence is limited in the sense that they do not alter the data since they are not information-sensitive. The second type of statistical multiplexer not only statistically averages data flow among the ITDM channels that have data to transmit, but also achieves even greater data link efficiency by compressing the data. In this respect, this type of ITDM is information-sensitive.

Statistical time-division multiplexer with data compression. The data transmitted over computer networks are usually redundant in a number of ways. One of the less obvious ways is that different characters are used with different frequencies. The data-compression technique used in ITDM reduces this sort of redundancy by a variable-length coding technique that assigns short code words to represent commonly used characters and longer code words to represent less commonly used characters.

In a given code set, such as ASCII, the different characters will occur with different frequencies. While to some extent these frequencies will depend on the application, typically the space character, the more common letters, the numerics, etc., will be much more common than most of the control characters, punctuation marks, and so forth. These uneven statistics can be exploited by translating from the original code set to a new code set with variable-length code words, with the short words assigned to the more frequent characters and the longer to the rarer characters. The result is that fewer bits need to be sent, and thus data compression is achieved. Clearly, variable-length codes raise some questions which do not arise with fixed-length codes.

First, there is word synchronization. If words are sent consecutively in an undifferentiated bit stream, how can the receiver or decoder establish code-word boundaries? This does not turn out to be a problem as long as the code has what is called the *prefix property,* namely, no code word is the prefix (first part) of another code word. When this is true, the code can always be described by means of a code tree. Each code word is assigned a unique terminal node in the tree and can be reached in a unique way by starting from the root of the tree by a series of binary choices corresponding to the successive bits in the code word.

An additional feature to character TDM (removal of start and stop bits) is that parity bits and the idle and filler bits of Binary Synchronous Communication (BSC) data are stripped from asynchronous communication.

A final advantage of variable-length coding is that the transmitted characters are translated into a form which is extremely difficult to interpret if intercepted, and thus a high degree of inherent data security and privacy is attained.

In conclusion, the data compression scheme used by ITDM provides communication efficiency and data security.

Trends in statistical multiplexers

As users increase their dependence on data communication networks for making vital business decisions, the demand for methods to reduce communication line costs and to provide network control likewise increases. Accordingly, statistical multiplexers, generally accepted as the answer to the problem of reducing line costs, are now becoming nodal processors.

Through the use of multiple microprocessors, monitoring and control functions previously handled by the host or front-end processor can now be off-loaded to the nodal processor/statistical multiplexer (statmux). In addition, functions of stand-alone network components such as protocol converters, data switches, and data link monitors are being assigned to statistical multiplexers. Improvements like these have kept the statmux market segment growing faster than the overall computer industry.

To integrate a long-haul network and gain more and more control of that network, users need sophisticated nodal processors that move data efficiently, monitor reliability, and centrally manage system performance. To achieve this end, the new generation of statistical multiplexers will incorporate such functions as data PBX support, distributed processing storage, remote polling, multiple gateway interfacing, digitized voice, reliability through redundancy, and network control.

Statmuxes will be called nodal processors, and they will have multiple functions, with statistical multiplexing being only one of the primary functions.

5.2 Comparison of Multiplexing Techniques

When multiplexing techniques are compared against seven general criteria, as shown in Table 5.1, frequency-division multiplexing does not seem to have many benefits, as indicated below.

1. It is inefficient because the channels have to be separated across the band to prevent crosstalk, and this wastes bandwidth.
2. It is inflexible because a change in the channel speed or number of channels may demand that the center frequencies of all other channels must be redefined.
3. Channel capacity is physically limited by the available bandwidth on a voice-grade line.
4. FDM is unsuited to multiplexing of synchronous channels because of the difficulty of driving clocks and maintaining bit timing of frequency modulation on the high-speed line.

Comparison of FDM and TDM techniques

Although there is practically no cost difference between FDM and TDM equipment, TDM has a much greater channel capacity than FDM. TDM

TABLE 5.1 Comparison of Multiplexing Techniques

	FDM	Bit TDM	Char. TDM	ITDM	Computer concentrator
Efficiency:					
Asynchronous channels	Poor	Good	Very good	Excellent	Excellent
Synchronous channels	N/A	Good	Good	Excellent	Excellent
Channel capacity	Poor	Good	Good	Excellent	Excellent
Flexibility	Poor	Good	Good	Very good	Very good
Reliability	Good	Very good	Very good	Good	Poor
Complexity	Good	Good	Good	Good	Poor
Purchase price	Very good	Good	Good	Good	Poor

also allows very considerable flexibility to change the number and speed of channels as the requirements of the data network change. This is possible because the TDM is independent of the data modem or DSU attaching it to the high-speed line. The following example can help to clarify this picture. Most data networks link terminals to the host computer through leased voice-grade FDX lines which have a useful bandwidth of about 300 to 3200 Hz. A 300-Bd terminal requires a 480-Hz FDM channel, and six terminals can be multiplexed with an FDM system and still remain within phone-line bandwidth. But only one 1200 b/s terminal which requires an 1800-Hz channel could be used with such an FDM equipment. On the other hand, a 9600 b/s TDM system which operates on a voice-grade line can accommodate eight 1200 b/s channels. Furthermore, with a 200 percent multiplexing efficiency an ITDM can multiplex sixteen 1200 b/s terminals on a voice-grade line.

Comparison of character TDM and bit TDM techniques

The primary area where character TDM offers an advantage over bit TDM is its efficiency when multiplexing asynchronous channels. Because a character multiplexer buffers a complete character before transmitting it to the high-speed line, it is possible to remove start and stop bits from the character before transmission, adding start and stop bits during demultiplexing at the other end. Thus in the case of an eight-unit teleprinter it is only necessary to transmit 8 bits for every 11 bits received (1 start and 2 stop bits are removed). The net result is that the high-speed line is used more efficiently and channel capacity is greater on a given speed of high-speed line with character TDM than with bit TDM. In the descriptive example given in Fig. 5.3, the character-interleaving technique transmits 64 characters in eight frames, while the bit-interleaving technique transmits only 44 characters in eight frames in 5-unit teleprinter signals.

But the character buffering required in a character TDM does make it somewhat more expensive than bit TDM. As a result, bit TDM is more economical for multiplexing synchronous channels where there are no redundant start and stop bits. It also provides less transmission delay than character TDM, which is essential for Telex operation. Furthermore, Telex signaling on the customer line may require special handling in TDMs. This modification is more expensive in character TDMs in comparison to bit TDMs.

The bit-interleaved multiplexer stores a maximum of only 1 low-speed channel bit at the input and 1 bit at the output multiplexer terminal. The channel propagation delay is consequently held to a minimum. However, loss of synchronization may result in the loss of several characters. The loss of synchronization in the character-interleaved system will result in the loss of only a single character from each terminal.

Comparisons of TDM and ITDM techniques

The very special advantages of the ITDM and the computer concentrator are in their ability to buffer data prior to transmission, to transmit variable-length data blocks according to the loading on individual channels, and to check data blocks received on the high-speed line and request transmission in the event of errors.

However, the simplicity of the TDM technique results from the fact that multiplexers communicate with each other by transmitting a constant stream of bits (bit TDM) or characters (character TDM) with a regularly recurring sync character. A constant number of time slots is inserted between sync characters; each time slot contains a predefined number of bits or characters for a specific channel. At the receiving end, the demultiplexer can recognize which characters belong to which data channel as a function of their time relationship to the sync character. These data frames are transmitted continuously, even when no active data are being transmitted from a terminal; thus dummy or idle characters fill the frames, and the bandwidths assigned to the idle channels are wasted. In ITDMs and concentrators, however, the character time slots are available to all channels, and idle periods are well-utilized. Furthermore, there is no possibility of retransmission even if the receiving end detects errors since transmission is continuous in TDM.

Comparison of ITDMs and computer concentrators

In a transmission medium, multiplexed channels operate simultaneously through their permanently assigned links. The number of multiplexed channels is equal to the number of links desired between two locations.

A concentrator is used when the number of channels on the terminal side is more than the links available between two locations. A link is assigned as it becomes available, while a terminal may wait if all the links are in use. However, this does not occur often in properly designed concentrator systems.

Computer data concentrators can impose software-related operating complications such as the need to reload programs upon system failure. The microcomputer controlling an ITDM incorporates semiconductor

RAMs (random-access memories) for data buffer storage and a PROM (programmable read-only memory) for the microcomputer control firmware storage. This combination in essence forms a small-scale concentrator as powerful as one based on a minicomputer. Since the operating program is stored in the PROM, the ITDM is transparent to the network and unaffected by system failure. However, the more expensive computer data concentrators do offer capabilities not available in ITDMs.

A computer data concentrator is not system-transparent. It is a remote front end operating in concert with the main computer. Demultiplexing of the various data channel inputs from this remote concentrator occurs via software in the host (refer to Fig. 5.8).

For example, suppose 100 lines are demultiplexed by ITDM and connected to a computer. The process requires 100 computer ports. An equivalent system using a computer data concentrator requires only one computer port at the host computer site. Furthermore, while using a computer data concentrator at a remote site costs more than installing a statistical multiplexer with comparable line capacity, the data concentrator approach usually requires only one extra piece of equipment, whereas a multiplexer system always needs two, one at each end of the link.

The computer concentrator can offer significant advantages in efficiency and channel capacity but at considerably increased cost and greater complexity and less reliability. On the other hand, although ITDM contains a microprocessor, the cost is compatible with a conventional TDM.

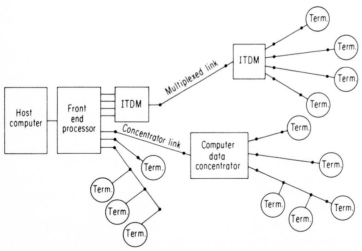

Figure 5.8 Connection of a computer concentrator and an ITDM to a computer.

5.3   Hierarchy of Analog Channels

The basic building block of the hierarchical scheme is the message channel. The basic message channel, although originally intended for voice transmission, can be used for data transmission. In this channel, several low-speed voice-frequency telegraph (VFT) channels operated at various nominal modulation rates and having different passband spacings are utilized. Since the same system may include channels with different characteristics, a numbering system has been recommended by CCITT Rec. R.70; refer to Table 5.2.

For a 50-Bd modulation rate, the nominal mean frequency series are formed by odd multiples of 60 Hz with 120-Hz spacings, and the lowest frequency is 420 Hz. Refer to CCITT Recs. R.31 for AMVFT and to R.35 for FMVFT channel spacing.

Telegraph circuits with 75 Bd can obviously be used over 100-Bd channels and in some cases over 50-Bd channels. Similarly the rate of 150 Bd can obviously be used over a 200-Bd channel and in some cases over a 100-Bd channel. Refer to CCITT Recs. R.35, R.36, R.37, and R.38 for telegraph circuits with modulation rates 50, 75, 100, 150, and 200 Bd.

Channel assignments for different modem speed rates are given in Fig. 3.11. An example of a mixture of modems and 50/75 Bd channels is given in Fig. 5.2.

Data signals requiring more bandwidth than that provided by the voice or message channel are called *wideband data*.

The first multiplexing step for the message channels combines them into a set of 12 channels called a *group* (refer to Figs. 5.9 and 5.10). A channel is said to be *erect* within a group when the frequencies in the group-frequency band corresponding to the audio frequencies in the channels ascend in the same relative order as those in the channels forming a group. Similarly, a channel is said to be *inverted* within a group when the frequencies in the group-frequency band descend in the same relative order as the ascending order of the frequencies in the channels. A group, supergroup, etc., is said to be erect when all its channels are erect and is said to be inverted when all its channels are inverted.

CCITT Rec. M.320 gives the 8-, 12-, and 16-channel group-numbering schemes. Only the 12-channel group is shown in Fig. 5.9. Twelve inverted sidebands occupy the 48-kHz bandwidth and are filtered to the 60–108 kHz band. The group then defines another basic building block in the FDM scheme. Any other signal whose spectrum occupies the 48 kHz between 60 and 108 kHz could be treated as a group in further multiplexing steps.

The next step in the FDM hierarchy is the combination of five groups into a 60-channel supergroup. The numbers are allocated in the as-

TABLE 5.2 Numbering Scheme of Frequency-Modulation Voice-Frequency Telegraph (FMVFT) Channels

In accordance with Recs. R.31 and R.35: 50 Bd/120Hz

Mean frequency, Hz	420	540	660	780	900	1020	1140	1260	1380	1500	1620	1740
Channel no.	001	002	003	004	005	006	007	008	009	010	011	012
	101	102	103	104	105	106	107	108	109	110	111	112

Rec. R.37:50, 100 Bd/240 Hz

Mean frequency, Hz	480	720	960	1200	1440	1680
Channel no.	201	202	203	204	205	206

Rec. R.38A: 200 Bd/480 Hz

Mean frequency, Hz	600	1080	1560
Channel no.	401	402	403

Rec. R.38B: 200 Bd/360 Hz

Mean frequency, Hz	540	900	1260	1620
Channel no.	301	302	303	304

One example of application of Rec. R.36: 2 chan., 200 Bd/480 Hz; 3 chan., 100 Bd/240 Hz; 10 chan., 50 Bd/120 Hz

Mean frequency, Hz	420	540	660	780	900	1020	1140	1260	1560
Channel no.	101	102	103	104	105	106	107	108	403

SOURCE: CCITT Rec. R.70.

cending order of frequency in the basic supergroup, 312 to 552 kHz, and in descending order in the other supergroups (CCITT Rec. M.330).

The position of a supergroup within a mastergroup is identified by a number in the series from 4 to 8. This also refers to one of the numbers of the supergroups constituting the basic mastergroup in the 4-MHz coaxial system (CCITT M.340).

The position of a mastergroup within a supermastergroup is identified by numbers 7, 8, and 9 (CCITT M.350).

The hierarchy of analog channels in the United States is given in Figs. 5.10 and 5.11 as well as in Table 5.3. A group combines a set of 12 voice channels and is the basic building block. A group occupies the 48-kHz frequency spectrum between 60 and 108 kHz. The basic

1860	1980	2100	2220	2340	2460	2580	2700	2820	2940	3060	3180
013	014	015	016	017	018	019	020	021	022	023	024
113	114	115	116	117	118	119	120	121	122	123	124

1920	2160	2400	2640	2880	3120
207	208	209	210	211	212

2040	2520	3000
404	405	406

1980	2340	2700	3060
305	306	307	308

2040	2340	2460	2640	2880	3120
404	117	118	210	211	212

supergroup consists of 60 voice channels. Five inverted group channels are combined to form a 240-kHz supergroup occupying the 312–552 kHz frequency band. High-speed data of 64 kb/s can enter the FDM system through a modem as a group, occupying the 60–108 kHz bandwidth, while high-speed data of up to 240 kb/s can enter the FDM system through a modem in the basic supergroup spectrum, as shown in Fig. 5.11.

The combination of 10 supergroups forms the L600 mastergroup and occupies the 60–2788 kHz band of frequencies. It is the broadband signal used on the L1 coaxial system.

Another signal that enters the FDM hierarchy above the supergroup level is commercial television. Although the television baseband spec-

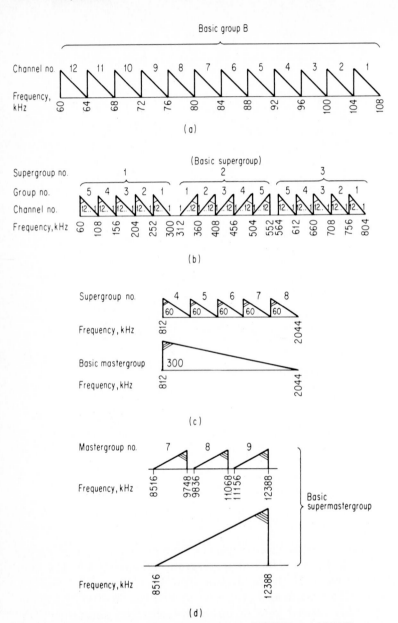

Figure 5.9 Numbering of analog carrier systems. CCITT Rec. (*a*) M.320, numbering of channels in a 12-channel group; (*b*) M.330, numbering of 12 circuit groups and channels in supergroups; (*c*) M.340, numbering of supergroups within the basic mastergroup; (*d*) M.350, numbering of mastergroup within a supermaster group.

(a)

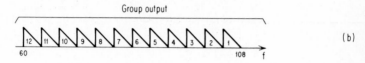

(b)

(c)

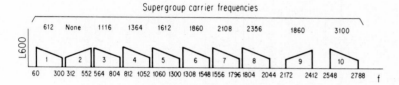

(d)

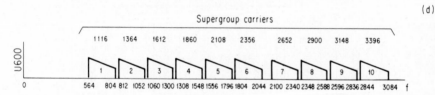

(e)

Figure 5.10 Creation of carrier systems by frequency-division multiplexing, United States system. (*a*) Voice band, 1 channel; (*b*) group, 12 channels; (*c*) supergroup, 60 channels; (*d*) mastergroup (L1), 600 channels; (*e*) L3 system, 1860 channels. Note: All frequencies are in kilohertz.

trum has almost twice the bandwidth of a mastergroup, the radio systems are designed to accommodate it.

In the United States, the U600 mastergroup occupies slightly higher frequencies (564–3084 kHz) than the L600 mastergroup and is used as a building block for even larger groupings. Both L600 and U600 mastergroups have gaps between supergroups as a result of design considerations and limitations which were taken into account when the frequency allocations were adopted.

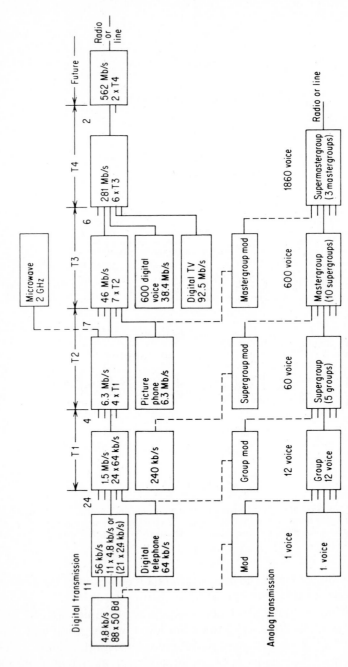

Figure 5.11 Digital and analog transmission media, United States system.

For an L3 carrier, three mastergroups and one supergroup comprising 1860 message channels are combined.

In the L4 system, six U600 mastergroups multiplexed to form 3600 message channels are utilized. Since these larger groups are rather specialized and restricted to specific systems, there is no universal name for them.

A summary of United States analog carriers is given in Table 5.3.

Pilot tones

Pilot tones in FDM carrier equipment have essentially two purposes:

- Control of levels
- Frequency synchronization

Separate tones are used for each application. However, it should be noted that on a number of systems frequency-synchronization pilots are not standard design features, owing to the improved stabilities now available in master oscillators. Secondarily, pilots are used for alarms.

TABLE 5.3 Summary of United States Telephone Carriers

Carrier system	Transmission medium	Line frequency band	Equivalent telephone circuits	Long or short haul*	Max. mileage
Single voice band	Wire or cable (1 pair)	300–3300 Hz	1	Short	
C	Open wire (1 pair)	4.6–30.7 kHz	1	Short	500
J	Open wire (1 pair)	36–143 kHz	12	Short	800
N	Cable (2 pairs)	44–260 kHz	12	Short	200
O	Open wire (1 pair)	2–156 kHz	16	Short	150
P	Open wire	8–100 kHz	4	Short	25
ON	Cable	36–268 kHz	24	Short	200
ON/K	Cable	68–136 kHz	14	Short	200
TJ	Radio	10.7–11.7 GHz	1200	Short	200
K	Cable (2 pairs)	12–60 kHz	12	Long	
LI	Coaxial cable	68–2788 kHz	600	Long	
L3	Coaxial cable	312–8284 kHz	1860	Long	
L4	Coaxial cable	564–17,548 kHz	3600	Long	
TD-2	Radio	3700–4200 MHz	600	Long	
TH	Radio	5925–6425 MHz	1860	Long	

*Short-haul systems vary from 25 to 800 mi, but usually are about 100 to 200 mi.

Level-regulating pilots. The nature of speech, particularly its varying amplitude, makes it a poor prospect as a reference for level control. Ideally, simple, single-sinusoid, constant-amplitude signals with 100 percent duty cycles provide simple control information for level-regulating equipment. Multiplex level regulators operate in the same manner as AGC circuits on radio systems, except their dynamic range is considerably smaller. Modern carrier systems initiate a level-regulating pilot tone on each group at the transmit end. Individual level-regulating pilots are also initiated on all supergroups and mastergroups. The intent is to regulate the system level within ±0.5 dB. Pilots are assigned frequencies that are part of the transmitted spectrum yet do not interfere with voice-channel operation. They usually are assigned a frequency appearing in the guard band between voice channels, or they are residual carriers (i.e., partially suppressed carriers). CCITT Rec. G.241 assigns the regulation pilots as given in Table 5.4.

The operating range of level control equipment activated by pilot tones is usually about ±4 or ±5 dB. If the incoming level of a pilot tone in the multiplex receiver drops outside the level-regulating range, then an alarm will be indicated.

Frequency-synchronization pilots. End-to-end frequency tolerance on international circuits should be better than 2 Hz. To maintain this accuracy, carrier frequencies used in FDM equipment must be very accurate or a frequency-synchronizing pilot must be used.

The basis of all carrier-frequency generation for modern FDM equipment is a master-frequency source. On the transmit side, called the *master station,* the frequency-synchronizing pilot is derived from this source. It is thence transmitted to the receive side, called a *slave station.*

TABLE 5.4 Frequencies and Levels of Pilots

	Freq., kHz	dBm0
Basic group B	84,080	−20
	84,140	−25
	104,080	−20
Basic supergroup	411,860	−25
	411,920	−20
	547,920	−20
Basic mastergroup	1,552	−20
Basic supermastergroup	11,096	−20
Basic 15 supergroup assembly (no. 1)	1,552	

SOURCE: CCITT Rec. G.241.

TABLE 5.5   System Capacity (Alternative B) for 2400
b/s TDM

| Modulation rate, Bd | Character structure | | No. of channels, homogeneous configuration |
	Character length, units	Stop element, units	
50	7.5	1.5	46
75	7.5	1.5	30
100	7.5 or 10	1.5 or 1	22
110	11	2	22
134.5	9	1	15
150	10	1	15
200	7.5, 10, or 11	1.5, 1, or 2	10
300	10 or 11	1 or 2	7

SOURCE: CCITT Rec. R.101.

The receive master oscillator is phase-locked to the incoming pilot tone. Thus for any variation in the transmit master-frequency source, the receive master-frequency source at the other end of the link is also varied.

CCITT recommendations for the numbering of analog carrier systems*

M.320   Numbering of channels in a group (60–108 kHz)

M.330   Numbering of groups within a supergroup (312–552 kHz)

M.340   Numbering of supergroups within a mastergroup (812–2044 kHz)

M.350   Numbering of mastergroups within a supermastergroup (8516–12,388 kHz)

M.380   Numbering of coaxial systems

M.390   Numbering in systems on symmetric-pair cables

CCITT recommendations on "General characteristics common to all analog carrier transmission systems" are given in G.211 through G.243.

5.4   Hierarchy of Digital Channels

In this network voice, television, facsimile, picturephone, and computer data travel in digital form and are intermixed. Digital and analog transmission media for the United States are given in Fig. 5.11.

---

*Also refer to Fig. 5.9.

Economic transmission of large numbers of telegraph and data services over a single telephone-type circuit may be achieved by using TDM techniques. The TDM system is capable of operating as a submultiplexer within a higher-order TDM hierarchy as well as on analog telephone-type circuit in association with standard data modems. The minimum duration of signal transfer delay through the TDM system could be achieved by the transmission of interleaved elements. Bit-interleaved TDM systems are used for telegraph and data transmission, with an aggregate bit rate of 2400 b/s.

A description of digital channels in the United States is as follows: 22 × 2400 b/s TDM channels are multiplexed into a 56 kb/s system (some systems use 21 × 2400 b/s multiplexing).

The T1 system carries 24 voice, or 24 × 56 kb/s, channels with TDM at 1.544 Mb/s and is in widespread use.

The next step to be analyzed is the T2 system, which carries a pulse stream of 6.3 Mb/s. It should be noted that the T2 system has a potential to carry the required signal for one picturephone.

The T3 system is seven T2 lines interleaves to form a signal at 46 Mb/s. The mastergroup of the FDM system can be digitized as a unit to form a signal of 46 Mb/s. Color television needs twice this bit rate and could be carried on two such pulse streams.

At the next higher level, six 46 Mb/s signals are combined to form a signal at 281 Mb/s. This signal may travel over microwave or coaxial-cable links with digital repeaters and is named the T4 link.

One great advantage of a digital system is its ability to carry all types of digital signals without having them interfere with each other.

CCITT R.101 recommends that the capacity of the 2400 b/s system shall be 46 channels at 50 Bd, with 7.5 units including 1 unit of a start element and 1.5 units of stop elements.

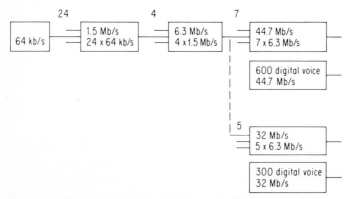

Figure 5.12 Basic multiplex arrangements for 1544 kb/s derived networks. (CCITT Rec. G.752.)

The TDM system shall be capable of multiplexing the eight different modulation rates simultaneously, as shown in Table 5.5. Figure 5.12 illustrates the basic multiplex arrangements recommended by CCITT G.752, using 1544 kb/s primary multiplex equipment. It is very similar to the digital transmission media of the United States described above. CCITT Books, Vol. III, covers digital networks, transmission systems, and multiplexing equipment.

Whenever practicable a bit rate of either 32,064 or 44,736 kb/s is recommended to allow for the efficient and economical coding of wideband signals in the networks, using primary systems 1544 and 6312 kb/s. For instance, for a 300-voice-circuit mastergroup 32,064 kb/s is appropriate, while for a 600-voice-circuit mastergroup 44.736 kb/s coding is recommended.

CCITT recommendations for digital multiplexing equipment

G.703   General aspects of interfaces, deals with interconnection of 1544 kb/s, 6312 kb/s, 32,064 kb/s, 44,736 kb/s, 2048 kb/s, 8448 kb/s, 34,368 kb/s, 139,264 kb/s, and 64 kb/s signals

G.721   Hypothetical reference digital paths.

Recommendations G.731 to G.734 relate to primary multiplex equipment.

G.732   Characteristics of primary multiplex PCM equipment operating at 2048 kb/s, recommends utilization of the encoding A-law, specifies thirty-two 64 kb/s channels, 256 bits per frame and 800 frames per second, activation of fault indication when BER = 10^{-3}, allocation of time slots, and 64 kb/s channel electrical characteristics. See Fig. 5.4.

G.733   Characteristics of primary PCM multiplex equipment operating at 1544 kb/s, recommends utilization of the μ-law, 24 channel time slots per frame, 8 bits per time slot, 1 bit added for frame alignment, 193 bits per frame, 8000 frames per second; similar to multiplexing given in Fig. 5.4.

G.734   Characteristics of 2048 kb/s frame structure for use with digital exchanges.

Recommendations G.741 to G.746 relate to second-order multiplex equipment.

G.741,   Digital multiplex equipment operating at 8448 kb/s, deals with 132
G.742,   time slots, 120 telephone channels.
G.745,
G.746

G.743   Digital multiplex equipment operating at 6312 kb/s, is intended for use with 1544 kb/s multiplex equipment.

Principal characteristics of higher-order multiplex equipment.

G.751   Digital multiplex equipment operating at the third-order bit rate of 34,368 kb/s and the fourth-order bit rate of 139,264 kb/s.

G.752   Characteristics of digital multiplex equipments based on a second-order bit rate of 6312 kb/s, recommends that bit rates of terrestrial systems can be either 32,067 or 44,736 kb/s.

G.911–G918   Cover 1544 kb/s–139, 264 kb/s digital lines on cables.

References

Bell Telephone Laboratories-Western Electric Co. Inc., Winston-Salen, N.C.: "Frequency Division Multiplex," *Transmission Systems for Communications,* 4th ed., 1971, chap. 6.

Evans, R. L.: "Cost Savings with Multiplexers and Concentrators," *Telecommunications,* May 1976.

Freeman, Roger L.: *Communication Transmission Handbook,* Wiley, New York, 1975, par. 3.5, Compandors.

General Data Communication, Danbury, Conn.: "Statistical TDM 1241."

Infotron Systems, Cherry Hill, N.J.: "Supermux 480—Users Manual."

McDermott, Jim: "Statistical Time Division Multiplexers," *EDN,* April 20, 1979.

Synchronization

Synchronization in a telecommunication system acts to operate the transmitting and receiving equipment at the same rate and fixed-phase relationship. As noted earlier, synchronous transmission does not use start-stop bits to frame characters and therefore makes more efficient use of the communication channel than asynchronous transmission. Most protocols use synchronous transmission to realize this efficiency.

6.1 Synchronization Techniques Used in Data Equipment

A distinction must be made between bit synchronization, block (character) synchronization, and message synchronization when using synchronous transmission.

Bit synchronization is achieved through a received clock signal which is coincident with the received seriel data stream. Most modems or terminals drive this clock by means of phased lock loops from the 0 to 1 and 1 to 0 transitions occurring in the received data. This technique, called *self-clocking*, overcomes the effect of propagation delay between distant stations and the tendency of electronic circuits within the modem to drift. If the DLC (data-link control) protocol is implemented on an HDX channel, bit transitions will not occur during the line turnaround and synchronization will be lost. To assist the initial establishment of bit synchronization following each line turnaround, a pattern of alternating 0s and 1s is often sent to precede each transmission. This pattern is called an *opening PAD character.*

Character synchronization is accomplished by recognizing one or two *phasing characters*, often called SYN or *sync characters*. The receiver senses these SYNs and phases its receive logic circuits to recognize the beginning and end of each subsequent character by bit count.

To ensure character synchronization throughout a message, SYN sequences are sometimes inserted in the transmitted data stream at 1- or 2-s intervals. This technique is called *message synchronization* and permits receiving stations to verify that they are in synchronization. If a SYN is not received within the prescribed time interval, the receiver will reject the message and begin searching for the SYN sequence that will precede the next message.

Block and message synchronization is more a matter of framing or recognizing the beginning and end of a block or message than it is of exact time dependency. It is directly dependent on the DLC procedure.

Synchronization signals in the modems

Transmission of synchronizing signals may be initiated by the modem or by the associated terminal equipment. When circuit 105 (RTS) is used to control the transmitter carrier, the synchronizing signals are generated during the interval between the off-to-on transition of circuit 105 (RTS) and the off-to-on transition of circuit 106 (CTS); this interval is called *turnaround time.* When the receiving modem detects a circuit condition which requires synchronizing, it shall turn circuit 106 (CTS) off and generate a synchronizing signal.

Modems require periodic transitions to maintain their timing integrity. Since long space and mark periods will not create transitions, a scrambling technique is utilized in the modems. This is a coding technique applied to the digital signals which makes receiver timing recovery insensitive to the data stream. Refer to CCITT Recs. V.26, V.27, and V.29 for more information about synchronizing signals on 2400, 4800, and 9600 b/s modems, respectively.

Note:

The following information about synchronizing signals in modems is derived from CCITT Rec. V.29.

The synchronizing signals for all data rates are divided into four segments as in Table 6.1.

Segment 2 of the synchronizing signal consists of alternations between two signal elements. The first element A has a relative amplitude of 3 and defines the absolute phase reference of 180°. The second signal element B depends on the data rate. Figure 6.1 shows the B

TABLE 6.1

	Segment 1	Segment 2	Segment 3	Segment 4	Total of segments 1, 2, 3, and 4
Type of line signal	No transmitted energy	Alternations	Equalizer conditioning pattern	Scrambled all data 1s	Total synchronizing signal
Number of symbol intervals	48	128	384	48	608
Approximate time in ms*	20	53	160	20	253

*Approximate times are provided for information only. The segment duration is determined by the exact number of symbol intervals.

signal element at each of the data rates. Segment 2 alternates $ABAB\cdots ABAB$ for 128 symbol intervals.

Segment 3 of the synchronizing signals transmits two signal elements according to an equalizer conditioning pattern. The first element C has a relative amplitude of 3 and absolute phase of 0°. The second signal element D depends on the data rate. Figure 6.1 shows the D signal element at each of the data rates. The equalizer conditioning pattern is a pseudo-random sequence generated by the polynomial

$$1 + x^{-6} + x^{-7}$$

Each time the pseudo-random sequence contains a 0, point C is transmitted. Each time the pseudo-random sequence contains a 1, point D is transmitted. Segment 3 begins with the sequence $CDCDCD\cdots$ according to the pseudo-random sequence and continues for 384 symbol intervals.

Segment 4 commences transmission with continuous data 1s, applied to the input of the data scrambler. Segment 4 duration is 48 symbol intervals. At the end of Segment 4, circuit 106 (CTS) is turned on and user data are applied to the input of the data scrambler.

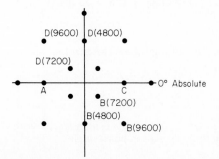

Figure 6.1 Signal space diagram showing synchronizing signal points (CCITT-V.29).

The time between the off to on transition of circuit 105 (RTS) and the off to on transition of circuit 106 shall be optionally 15 ms ± 5 ms or 253.5 ms ± 0.5 ms. The short delay is used when curcuit 105 does not control the transmitter carrier. The long delay is used when circuit 105 controls transmitter and a synchronizing signal is initiated by the off to on transition of circuit 105.

The time between the on to off transition of circuit 105 and the on to off transition of circuit 106 shall be suitably chosen to ensure that valid signal elements have been transmitted.

A self-synchronizing scrambler/descrambler having the generating polynomial $1 + x^{-18} + x^{-23}$ shall be included in the modem.

Exercise   Trace the analog synchronizing signals at the output of a 9600 b/s (QAM) modem, described at segment 2 above.

Solution   Synchronizing signals are given as A and B in Fig. 6.1.
  A: 3/180° (Amp 3/phase 180°)
  B: 3√2/315° (Amp 3√2/phase 315°)
Referring to Table 4.4 for QAM, find that 180° corresponds to 111 for Q_2, Q_3, Q_4 bits. Q_1 bit (for 180° and amplitude 3) is 0. Thus, we obtain

$$A = 0111 \qquad Q_1Q_2Q_3Q_4$$

$$B = 1101 \qquad Q_1Q_2Q_3Q_4$$

$$\text{Bit length} = 1000/9600 = 0.104 \text{ ms}$$

$$\text{Duration } A \text{ or } B = 4 \times 0.104 = 0.416 \text{ ms}$$

$$\text{Modulation rate} = 2400 \text{ Bd}$$

$$\text{Modulation cycle length} = 1000/2400 = 0.416 \text{ ms}$$

$$\text{Carrier frequency} = 1700 \text{ Hz}$$

$$\text{Sine cycle length} = 1000/1700 = 0.588 \text{ ms}$$

$$\text{Length of segment 2} = \left(\frac{1}{9.6} \times 4 \text{ bits}\right) \times 128 = 53 \text{ ms}$$

On the basis of these findings, the analog and digital synchronization signals are as shown in Fig. 6.2.

Note:

Compare Figs. 6.2 and 3.1 and notice that, in QAM, phase angle is an assigned value for each tribit, while the DPSK signal phase shifts by a given phase angle.

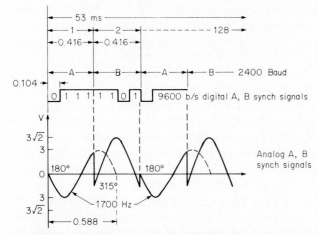

Figure 6.2 *A* and *B* synchronization signals per CCITT-V.29.

Synchronization of demultiplexed signals in a multipoint link

Demultiplexing is the reverse operation of multiplexing. The most popular form of TDM is pulse-code modulation (PCM). A PCM receiver consists of one or more decommutators which demultiplex and decode the signal. The PCM decommutator must sync the arriving data channels with respect to time. If there is a time displacement of the data stream, all the data become destroyed. Included in this timing process are bits, characters, frames and subframes, or groups. Timing, which is inherent in the received data stream, must be accurately detected. An internal local clock is used with its phase synchronized to the input signal to clock the output signals. The regeneration, the detection, and the clocking are all performed by the synchronizer, often referred to as the *PCM signal conditioner*.

The conditioned PCM signal is passed through a low-pass filter. If NRZ is used, for example, the filter removes half the bit rate. The bit is sampled and detected as either 1 or 0.

The synchronizer determines the start of the sequence of the serial data words or characters that constitute the frame. In the search mode, the receiver must explore the PCM bit stream to see if it can identify the sync code pattern. It is desirable for the synchronization pattern to be long enough so that the start of the data frame could be identified, yet it should not occupy more than is necessary for sync identification. As a rule, only 3 to 5 percent of the data bandwidth should be devoted to frame synchronization.

A pattern recognizer is used to acquire frame sync. It looks at serial PCM bit streams in parallel with succeeding bit streams. At the same time, the pattern recognizer scans the serial PCM input to seek a frame sync which will pinpoint where the data frame begins.

After correlation is found, the pattern recognizer reevaluates the pattern immediately. This is called the *check mode.*

A number of searches and checks may be made before the true sync pattern is located. When this occurs, the system locks in on the sync pattern and remains locked until disrupted. Subframes are occasionally used with either identification (ID) sync patterns or inversion techniques. Sync with subframes requires that a greater portion of an entire frame be used to carry subframe-related data and sync data. With this method the pattern recognizer needs only to search the subframe sequentially (bit by bit) for each subchannel until the acceptable pattern is detected. By means of the inversion technique, the frame sync pattern is electronically inverted and used to represent subframe sync. Complementary patterns exhibit the same correlation properties as the noninverted patterns. Also subframe sync recognition indicates the presence of a prime frame sync pattern.

6.2 Asynchronous and Synchronous Transmission

Asynchronous data are typically produced by low-speed terminals with bit rates up to 1200 b/s. In asynchronous systems, the transmission line is in mark (binary 1) condition in its idle state (refer to Fig. 6.3). As each character is transmitted it is preceded by a start bit or transition from mark to space (binary 0), which indicates to the receiving terminal that a character is being transmitted. The receiving device

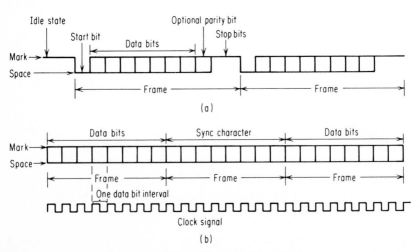

Figure 6.3 (*a*) Asynchronous and (*b*) synchronous transmissions.

detects the start bit and the data bits that make up the character. At the end of the character transmission, the line is returned to mark condition by 1 or more stop bits and becomes ready for the beginning of the next character.

This process is repeated character by character until the entire message has been sent. The start and stop bits permit the receiving terminal to synchronize itself to the transmitter on a character-by-character basis.

An asynchronous character varies in length depending on the information code employed—5 bits for Baudot code, 7 for ASCII (American standard code for information interchange) plus an optional parity bit, and 8 for EBCDIC (extended binary-coded decimal interchange code).

The whole set of start, stop, and data bits is called an *envelope*. An asynchronous modem does not itself transmit binary digits because there is no built-in clock to indicate that a 1 or 0 digit is being sent.

Synchronous transmission via an analog circuit usually makes use of a clocking source within the modem to synchronize the transmitter and receiver. Once a synchronization character (SYN) has been sensed by the receiving terminal, data transmission proceeds character by character (or byte by byte) without the intervening start and stop bits (refer to Fig. 6.3). The incoming stream of data bits is interpreted on the basis of the receive clock supplied by the modem. This clock is usually derived from the received data through a phase-locked loop.

The receiving device accepts data from the modem until it detects a special ending character or a *character terminal count*, at which time it knows that the message is over.

The message block is usually composed of one or two SYNs, a number of data and control characters (typically 100 to 10,000), a terminating character, and one or two error control characters. Between messages, the communication line may idle in SYNs or be held to mark.

Note that synchronous modems can be used to transmit asynchronous data, and conversely, asynchronous modems can be used for synchronous data if the receiving terminal can drive the clock from the data. Asynchronous transmission is advantageous when transmission is irregular (such as that initiated by a keyboard operator's typing speed). It is also inexpensive due to the simple interface logic and circuitry required. Synchronous transmission, on the other hand, makes better use of the transmission facility by eliminating the start and stop bits on each character. Furthermore, synchronous data are suitable for multilevel modulation which combines 2 or 4 bits in one signal element (baud). This can facilitate data rates of 4.8 or 9.6 kb/s over a bandwidth of 2.4 kHz (refer to Sec. 4.1). Synchronous modems offer higher transmission speeds but are more expensive because they require precisely synchronized clock and data.

Isochronous transmission is a combination of both synchronous and asynchronous transmission. The data are clocked by a common timing base, and bytes are also framed with start-stop bits.

Note:

The terms *anisochronous, isochronous,* and *isochronous start-stop* are used in CCITT and European literature for the *asynchronous, synchronous,* and *isochronous* terms, respectively, used in this book and in American publications to describe transmissions, channels, and signals. The term synchronous applies to two or more operants; for example, two signals are synchronous.

6.3 Synchronization of Data Equipment in Different Transmission Networks

Synchronization is clearly important with digital transmission. It is essential for the receiving machine to know which bit is which. This section describes several methods of providing the synchronous transmission facilities between two digital media.

Analog transmission

The simplest case with respect to synchronization is one where analog transmission media are used end to end. Figure 6.4*a* shows the general case of modems at both ends of the circuit. Both modems are clocked externally by the terminal on the transmit side, and the modems supply receiver timing (derived from the received data) to the terminal device. In this method, both ends of the system are independent in that they both can be considered master clocks. That is, the transmit and receive clocks may be slightly different at any one terminal end.

Although this is a workable configuration, modems generally have more stable and accurate clocks. Figure 6.4*b* shows a configuration which takes advantage of this fact, yet still maintains the autonomy of clocking at each end. Here, the modem supplies the transmit clock both to the terminal and to itself. In this case, either terminal transmits under the control of its associated modem.

There are cases, however, where certain terminal devices require the same clock for both transmit and receive functions. In Fig. 6.4*c* terminal 1 supplies the clock to the associated modem 1. The received timing from the far end, modem 2, is not only used to clock data into terminal 2 but also to clock data out of terminal 2, as shown. In this way, the receive clock at terminal 1 is identical in frequency to the transmit clock at this terminal. Figure 6.4*d* is practically the same as Fig. 6.4*c* except modem 1 provides the total system timing.

In practice, the configurations of Fig. 6.4*b* and *d* are preferred be-

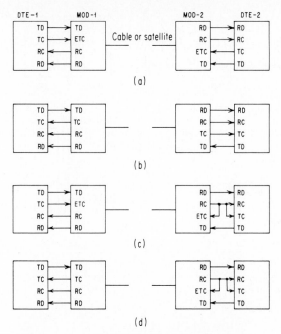

Figure 6.4 Various synchronization configurations. (*a*) Terminal control at both ends; (*b*) modem control at both ends; (*c*) terminal control at one end; (*d*) modem control at one end. TD: transmit data; RD: receive data; TC: transmit clock; RC: receive clock. [Read TC to modem (DCE) as ETC (external transmit clock).]

cause modem clocks are usually more stable than terminal equipment clocks.

Digital transmission

The area of digital transmission systems can be basically split into two types of operation: mixed digital-analog systems and totally digital systems. Although digital data service is provided in some areas of the United States by Data-Phone digital service (DDS), digital networks are not available in other countries. This has forced the utilization of mixed digital-analog networks.

Mixed analog-digital network. An example of a mixed analog-digital network at 9.6 kb/s (or less) is given in Fig. 6.5. It shows a network where DDS is used between two domestic offices and then carried on analog voice-grade facilities to the overseas end. Unlike the analog modem operation which affords either external or internal timing, this leads to the forced utilization of buffers as shown. Because of this fact, the DSU (data service unit) cannot be clocked externally.

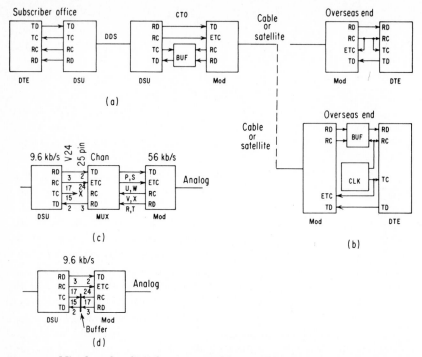

Figure 6.5 Mixed analog-digital system, 9.6 kb/s. (a) DDS timing controls overseas end; (b) independent clock at overseas end; (c) multiplexer at CTO; (d) digital/analog conversion at CTO.

Figure 6.5a is the simplest configuration which can exist. The terminal is dependent on the DDS clock, which is provided at the DSU interface. This clock is passed through a modem pair to the distant-end terminal equipment. Here, the clock is looped around, which causes the overseas modem-terminal to be dependent on the DDS clock. Notice, however, that the modem-DSU interface at the domestic side requires a buffer on the receive leg to account for clock phasing. This buffer is of modest size.

In this system, everything is dependent on the DDS clock so there is no possibility of bit slippage. To effectively divorce the overseas equipment from the DDS clock requires two things:

1. A clock of comparable accuracy to the DDS clock (2×10^{-9} or better). See note 5, page 188.

2. Buffer of suitable capacity at the domestic DSU-modem interface and the overseas modem-terminal interface.

This way a suitably long time interval between bit slips can be achieved; such an arrangement is shown in Fig. 6.5b.

In Fig. 6.5*c* another case is shown. 9600 b/s data are brought via a synchronous modem or DSU to the CTO (central telecommunications office) where they are multiplexed to 56 kb/s. A buffer unit is required at the channel port of the multiplexer.

Figure 6.5*d* depicts a digital-to-analog (analog-to-digital) conversion of a 9.6 kb/s circuit with a buffer unit.

Interface cables are given for modem/DSU/MUX connections in Fig. 6.8.

Bit slippages will create a bit or block error for each slip and will result in errored data in conventional synchronus systems or packet retransmission in packet-switching systems. When digital networks are configured for 56 kb/s, then effective utilization can be made of a single channel per carrier (SCPC) via satellite which can benefit the system from both economic and performance viewpoints. Similar to the operation at lower speeds, advantage can be taken of the DDS network for interconnection between subscribers and central offices. However, if DDS is not presently available to cableheads and earth stations, then a configuration using a DDS off-net extension must be used, as depicted in Fig. 6.6. DDS off-net is basically an analog group facility terminated in the conventional DSU interface. Small-capacity B1 buffers are used to phase the DDS and off-net clocks. Although the clock is shown looped around at the overseas modem, a buffer is required at the American earth station to account for satellite orbital variations. Refer to Sec. 8.5 for more information on satellite propagation delay problems.

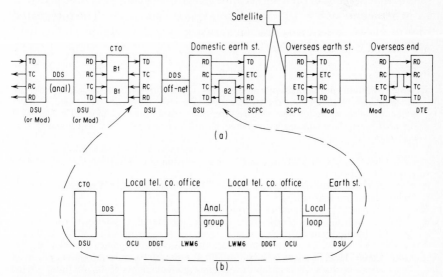

Figure 6.6   (*a*) Mixed analog-digital system, 56 kb/s. (*b*) Details of off-net DDS extension. OCU: office channel unit; DDGT: digital data group terminal.

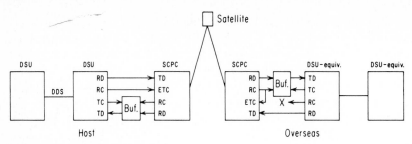

Figure 6.7 Total digital service.

Total Digital Network.   As the overseas correspondents develop digital network equivalents to the DDS, it will be possible to enjoy high-performance digital transmission systems. The basic problem of isolating two internally timed networks can be solved, as shown in Fig. 6.7. The approach is to pass the transmit clock and data through the SCPC equipment in both directions and provide buffers on both receive legs as shown. A buffer is needed to account for the differences in clock accuracy and orbital effects at the overseas end and orbital effects only in the host country.

Conclusions.   Modem operation over analog circuits is an effective means of data communications. In such systems, it is usually best to have the modems supply the timing clock. Performance of analog facilities (with error rates of 10^{-5}) is not as good as digital systems, such as DDS which offers 99.5 percent error-free seconds (EFS) operation; this is equivalent to an error rate of 5×10^{-7} for 56 kb/s system operation. The integrated digital network requires precise network synchronization and control of jitter on digital signals.

Notes:

1. When two data communications equipments (DCEs) are connected back to back, the received data of one become the transmitted data of the other, and vice versa. Control and clock supply circuits also require attention. Pin connections of CCITT V.24 (EIA RS 232C) interface circuits among modem, multiplexer, and DSU are given in Fig. 6.8.
2. Reduce crosstalk between data and control circuits by properly assigning wires in a cable. Refer to "Crosstalk" in Sec. 2.5 for prevention of crosstalk in the digital data interface cables.
3. The buffer unit is usually included in the TD input portion of DCE unless a separate buffer storage unit is utilized.
4. Transmit clock (TC) is supplied by the DCE.
5. There are two features of an oscillator to be considered: *Accuracy* is the ratio of measured frequency error to the nominal frequency of the oscillator (example: 1,000,000 Hz oscillator with a 10^{-6} accuracy may actually deliver a frequency between 999,999 and 1,000,001 Hz.); *Stability* is the ratio of fluctuations in the output frequency derived from various perturbations of inputs and associated elements of the oscillator circuit to the nominal frequency of the oscillator (example: with $\pm 2.10^{-6}$ stability, 1,000,001 Hz measured frequency of an oscillator may vary between 1,000,003 and 999,999 Hz).

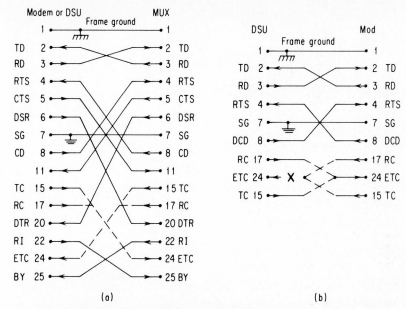

Figure 6.8 Typical DCE-to-DCE [EIA RS 232C (CCITT V.24)] interface circuits. Optional wirings per local requirements shown by dashed lines. (*a*) Modem/DSU/ multiplexer interface circuits. Note that some pins are tied together per circuit requirements; DSU does not receive ETC; pins 11-5 are wired so that cable can be reversible. (*b*) DSU/modem interface circuits.

Buffer-synchronizer unit.   The *buffer-synchronizer* (also called the *buffer-storage*) *unit* compensates for frequency drift, phase shift, and jitter between the receive and the local clocks. The unit receives the data in synchronism with a received clock and automatically phases and regenerates the incoming data in synchronism with a local clock.

The buffer-storage unit provides a digital interface between communication links where timing is derived from accurate but separate unsynchronized clocks or data-derived sources. The unit compensates for differences in clock rates or changes because of changes in propagation delay. This is accomplished through the storage of data bits at the receive clock rate and the release of stored data at the local clock rate. The synchronization of received incoming data allows all outputs to be in synchronism with the local clock and, therefore, with each other to permit a reliable retransmission or multiplexing. A simplified diagram of a ±32-bit buffer-storage unit which operates at 4.8 to 19.2 kb/s is given in Fig. 6.9.

Received (input) data are applied to a 64-bit shift register for storage. The received clock is used to shift the data bits 1 bit at a time within the register up to the point where data are to be extracted for resynchronization with the local clock. If both clocks are already in syn-

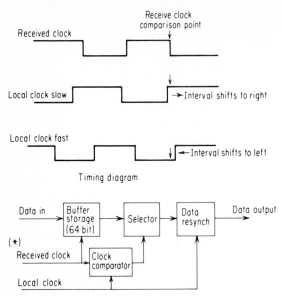

Timing diagram

Figure 6.9 Block diagram and retiming of buffer-synchronizer unit. [*On the received clock, ETC (pin 24) for DCE; RC (pin 17) or TC (pin 15) for DTE.]

chronism or the buffer has just been recentered, the data are extracted from the storage register at the 33d bit. If the local clock is operating faster than the received clock, the data are extracted from successively earlier bits and the total number of data bits in storage will be gradually depleted. If the clock is slower than the received clock, the data are extracted from successively later bits, gradually filling the storage register toward its overflow point.

If the storage register becomes depleted or overflows, audible and visual alarms come on and the storage register recenters automatically, causing a loss or duplication of received data if the communication channel is active at that time.

Because of filling and depletion capability (which acts as a spring in satellite communications), the buffer-synchronizer is also called an *elastic-buffer-storage unit* (refer to Sec. 8.4).

Examples for leased-network synchronization. In the following examples, all channels of the network have a common timing clock in a continuous carrier system, with phase differences due to transmission delays and instantaneous tracking error. The phase differences are eliminated by the buffers where the external timing clock (ETC) is compared with the internal clock (TC) of the device and received data (TD) are clocked with the corrected timing.

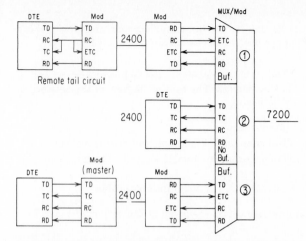

Figure 6.10 Timing diagram of a leased network. (Remote-tail modem provides network timing.)

Example 1 The configuration of system timing when a modem is at a remote location determines the timing clock; a high-speed modem at the technical control center is equipped with a three-channel MUX and buffer at each channel. The system consists of one local data terminating equipment (DTE) and two remote-tail circuits. The overseas end has a similar system. A timing diagram of the system is given in Fig. 6.10. Refer to Table 7.1 and Fig. 6.8, respectively, for DTE/DCE and DCE/DCE interfaces.

Notes:

- MUX/MOD receives clock (ETC) at each channel of tail circuit.
- Interface of modem/local DTE is EIA RS 232C (CCITT V.24).
- Each tail modem is loopback-timed at the distant end.
- All modems are externally timed (ETC) at the overseas end if the network uses overseas clock.

Example 2 In the following point-to-point leased circuit, several interfacing and timing problems are covered; refer to Fig. 6.11.

Technical control center A provides the following:

- Twelve asynchronous 50-Bd teleprinter channels for loop-current terminals.
- Three asynchronous 50-Bd teleprinter channels via CCITT V.21 modems.
- Two 1200 b/s to two computers via modem.
- One 2400 b/s to computer via modem.
- One 1200 b/s to local computer.
- Two TDMs, two remote-tail circuit modems, one 7200 b/s MUX/MOD with buffers at channels, one FDM, one CPU and two local printers are used at the technical control center.

Technical control center B provides the following:

- Fifteen asynchronous 50-Bd channels to local computer.
- Three 1200 b/s to local computer (two are not shown).

- One 2400 b/s to computer via modem.
- Two TDMs, two computers, one remote-tail circuit modem, and one 7200 b/s MUX/MOD with buffers are used at the technical control center.

Timing of the network.   The 7200 b/s modems of the technical control centers provide the timing clock for the network. The timing diagram of the network is given in Fig. 6.11. Note the following:

- Remote modems are loopback-timed.
- Cable 1 interfaces the TDM channel to the remote-tail circuit modem.
- Cable 2 interfaces a CPU to a modem at a remote location, which modem then loops back the timing.
- Cable 3 is DTE/DCE, EIA 232C (CCITT V.24) interface cable.

Pin-to-pin connections of interface cables are given at the bottom of Fig. 6.11.

Connection of low-speed asynchronous channels.   Three channels operate via CCITT V.21 modems. Twelve 50-Bd channels are converted to 20-mA polar cur-

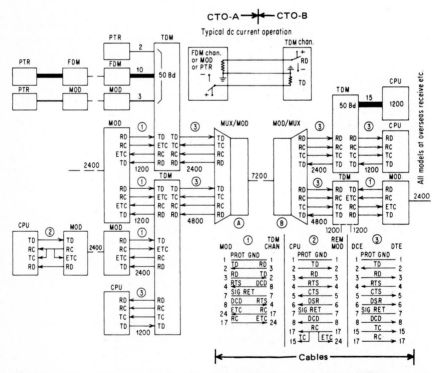

Figure 6.11   Timing diagram of a leased network. (High-speed modem provides network timing.)

rent; ten of them use FDM channels for transmission to remote locations, while two channels are connected to local printers. A typical polar dc circuit is given at the top of Fig. 6.11.

Example 3   How many clock corrections (resulting in bit loss) will occur within a 1-year period, between two independent digital networks?
Circuit parameters:

- Data speed, 9600 b/s
- Relative clock accuracy, 10^{-9}
- Buffer size, ±64 bits

Solution:

- Nr of seconds in one year = $3,15.10^7$
- Total number of bits transmitted in one year = 3.10^{11}
- Based on the relative clock accuracy of 10^{-9} the bit slippage will be $3 \cdot 10^{11} \cdot 10^{-9}$ = 300 bits. A 64-bit buffer will then be filled $300/64$ = 4.7 times each year, resulting in a clock correction and corresponding loss of bits.

Synchronization of byte control protocols (BISYNC)

Bit synchronization.   All BISYNC transmissions are synchronous. Before valid data may be received, a modem-supplied or DTE-supplied clock must be synchronized so that valid bits are being received. Modem bit sync is taken care of automatically; however, DTE clock recovery requires that a minimum of 16 data transitions occur before any actual transmission characters will be recovered correctly. This is accomplished by sending two 5/5 or four SYN characters just ahead of the character sync pattern.

Character syncronization.   BISYNC character synchronization is achieved by recognition of a special and unique data pattern (SYN SYN) prior to the information or link control character sequence. Only the reception of the SYN SYN character framing pattern is used to signal the system that a transmission is being received. Each transmission must begin with at least two contiguous SYNs, but may begin with any number. Some point-to-point duplex systems send SYNs continuously in lieu of any other transmission. This is called *synchronous idle.*

The first non-SYN character is accepted as the beginning of the data. Character sync is retained until a line turnaround character or a receive (loss of sync) time-out occurs. Loss of sync is a particular problem as transmission block size increases. Failure to recognize data link control characters can result in unreliable operation. To help prevent such problems, and to assure that a DTE modem retains bit sync, BISYNC uses a *transmit time-out* to assure that SYN SYN is sent at least once each second. A station failing to receive SYN SYN within a 2.6- to 3.9-s *receive time-out* interval assumes that sync is lost and begins searching for new sync. This scheme requires a sending station to insert SYNs into its data stream at 1-s intervals. Likewise, a receiving station must remove these SYNs from the data stream before it is delivered to the system. Since the link control and text characters are never in the same binary patterns, basic mode transmission works well with the two types intermixed.

6.4 Organization of International and National Digital Networks*

The national reference clock has to be located at an international exchange and other international exchanges within the same country might have been operated by clocks which are synchronized to the reference clock by means of a national synchronization system.

International digital links will be required to interconnect a variety of national networks. The national networks may be of the following forms:

1. A wholly synchronous network controlled by a single reference clock

2. A set of synchronous subnetworks each controlled by a reference clock but with plesiochronous operation between the subnetworks

3. A wholly synchronous network with two or more reference clocks which are mutually synchronized by national links

4. A wholly plesiochronous national network (two signals having the same nominal digit rate, but not stemming from the same clock)

The international plesiochronous network should be organized so that the rate of occurrence of slips in any 64 kb/s channel is not greater than 1 bit in every 70 days per exchange. All clocks controlling exchanges with international links must have a long-term frequency inaccuracy of not greater than 1×10^{-11}. Recommended mean time between failures for the catastrophic failure is better than 50 years.

Reference-clock (a clock which is used to govern the frequency of a network clock of lower stability; the failure of such a clock does not cause loss of synchronization) accuracy of an exchange will be better than 1×10^{-9} for a 200-s period.

CCITT Rec. G.811 is directed toward limiting slip in the national networks participating in international links. G.822 specifies slip-rate objectives for a hypothetical international end-to-end connection comprising 13 time-division switches, and G.823 defines maximum per-

---

*Condensed from CCITT Rec. G.811.

missible levels of jitter at the interface of digital transmission systems and time-division exchanges.

References

CCITT, Geneva: *Orange, Yellow, and Red Books*, Volume VIII-1, "Series V Recommendations. Data Communication over the Telephone Network."
Versitron Inc, Washington, D.C.: "Model SB-2 Data Synchronizer/Buffer."
Weisberger, Alan J.: "Modems," *Data Communications Handbook*, Signetics Corp., Sunnyvale, Calif., 1977.

Interfacing, Protocols, Information Codes, Error Correction

Several hardware elements are necessary to interface the terminal equipment to the communications channel. These include a baud rate generator to provide receive and transmit clocks, control (or handshaking) signals to coordinate receive and transmit operations, and level-shifting line drivers–receivers and loopback facilities for off-line self-testing. Line-break generation and echoplex (autoecho) capability are features for asynchronous communication, while protocol support hardware is necessary for synchronous communications. A complete communications channel interface is shown in Fig. 7.1.

Transparency

Transparency is the concept of a function or process occurring without the user knowing how it is accomplished. From the time data leave a terminal equipment until they are delivered to their destination terminal, many functions unknown to the user have to take place. In an ideally transparent medium the following functions may take place:

1. Buffering: data are stored and retransmitted.

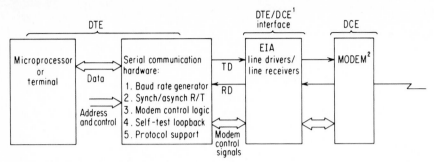

Figure 7.1   Computer-communication interface. Notes: (1) RS 232C, RS 422/423. (2) Synch modems provide RC and TC to DTE.

2. Speed and transmission mode changes and code conversions: data are multiplexed, converted from analog to digital (or vice versa) transmission; code formatting may be required in the network.

3. Queuing and routing: data may be queued and routed in a switched network.

Transparency prevents a potential user from considering voltage levels at interfacing points as well as bit formats between devices in a distributed data processing network. A network with transparency allows different computers and terminals to be connected.

Bit-sequence transparency is the ability to convey any sequence of bits. The task of a binary transmission channel is to convey a sequence of bits from the sender to the receiver. It therefore has an interface at each end, capable of transferring binary digits in sequence. If certain sequences of bits are not conveyed correctly by the channel, it is not bit-sequence-transparent. An example of nontransparency would be the inability to recover the clock if a long series of 1s is sent.

The scrambler

The scrambler is another measure to preserve transparency. The Fourier spectrum of a data signal depends on the binary sequence it represents. Periodic or repeated sequences can give rise to peaks in the power spectrum. These are undesirable when the telephone network is used for transmission, and, at the worst, they might cause breakthrough to neighboring channels. It would be better to have a binary sequence which appeared to be random. But repeated sequences do happen in data, particularly strings of 0s.

The adaptive equalizer works best with a random data sequence, and a random bit sequence sometimes helps the recovery of the block at the receiving end. For these reasons, in some modems a scrambler is employed which encodes the input binary sequence so that it is unlikely to have repeated sequences. It is not possible to prevent repeated sequences with absolute certainty, but at least the common repetitions in incoming data can be removed. The scrambler at the transmitting end is matched by an unscrambler at the receiving end.

Utilization of scramblers alters the error performance. Consider a single, isolated error bit. It can be considered as passing through the unscrambler to cause an output error. But at least there is no permanent "loss of synchronism" between two devices, causing errors to continue. A scrambler recommended by CCITT guards against sending long strings of 0s or 1s which could give difficulties with clock recovery in certain kinds of modems.

CCITT V.27 and V.29 recommend self-synchronizing scrambling to be included in the 4800 and 9600 b/s modems, respectively.

Hierarchy of protocols

A data transmission facility must conform to the interface definition which covers the electric and physical connection procedures between DTE and DCE; additional coordination procedures (protocols) must take place in a communication system for establishing links between terminals and networks. For computer networks the International Standards Organization (ISO) has proposed a seven-layer architecture called the Reference Model of Open Systems Interconnection; the palindromic acronym is ISO-OSI. Protocol levels are shown in Fig. 12.2. These protocols deal with synchronization, error control and recovery, addressing, logic connections, device control, file access, and application-to-application control.

Level 1.   Physical interface between the DTE and the network (the DCE is considered to be part of the network). Defines the linking characteristics and procedures used to establish, maintain, and disconnect the communication channel between the DTE and the network or between DTE units.

Level 2.   Data-link control for the exchange of data between the DTE and the network or between DTE units.

Level 3.   Network control protocol. Communications control for defining the formatting of messages or packets and the control procedures for the transfer of data through a communications network.

For higher levels, system and user control within an operating system are explained in Sec. 7.4.

7.1   Level 1 Protocols. Physical Interface between DTE and Network

Once the parallel data of the computer or terminal have been serialized, it must meet EIA (Electronic Industries Association) interface standards in the United States or CCITT (International Telegraph and Telephone Consultative Committee) interface standards. These standards encompass data interchange and control circuits, electric voltage levels, impedance, transmission speed, slew rate (volts/microseconds), and distance between the terminal or processor (DTE) and the data communications equipment (DCE).

EIA and CCITT standards for interface circuits

For data speeds up to 20 kb/s the accepted standards for interfacing DTE and DCE are EIA RS 232C and CCITT V.24 (functional characteristics) and V.28 (electrical characteristics). However, other related standards, RS 422A and CCITT V.35 and X.27 for balanced lines and RS 423A and CCITT X.26 for unbalanced lines, provide increased speed and distance. These standards apply to synchronous and asynchronous transmission, switched or dedicated phone lines, and simplex HDX and FDX operating modes.

Notes:

1. The signal quality is the most important factor limiting the distance in balanced circuits; near-end crosstalk is the principal limiting factor for unbalanced circuits.
2. In CCITT Recommendations, associated V and X standards are equivalent, where the X version is for public data network interfaces and the V version for modems of the V series.
3. The RS 232C standard defines signal levels and a pinout on a connector for many types of equipment but not for the teleprinter. The serial transmission concepts for the teleprinter are the same; start and stop bits, data bits, and parity bits, but the signal interface is a current loop, not a voltage level. Instead of voltage levels to represent logic 0 and logic 1 levels, the current loop uses the presence or absence of a current. The current may be 20 or 60 mA, neutral or polar, with supply voltages 24, 48, 60, or 120 V. Some European countries utilize 40- or 80-mA polar loop currents.

EIA standards for digital interfacing.   In the United States, the EIA recommends standards including interfaces designed for use between manufacturers and purchasers of electronic products. Related digital interfacing standards are explained in the following paragraphs. A list of EIA standards is given in the Glossary of this book, under RS.

EIA RS 232C. Interface between DTE and DCE employing serial binary data interchange.   The EIA RS 232C is a first-level protocol standard as well as an electrical standard specifying handshaking and functions between the DTE and the DCE over short distances (up to 15 m) at low-speed data rates (upper limit of 20,000 b/s). The specified interface circuit is a single-ended, bipolar-voltage, and unterminated circuit. A positive voltage between $+5$ and $+25$ V represents a logic 0, and a negative voltage between -5 and -25 V represents logic 1. The load impedance R_L at the terminator side shall have a dc resistance between 3000 and 7000 Ω, and the voltage measured across R_L shall not be less than 5 V nor more than 15 V. The effective shunt capacitance C_L across R_L shall not exceed 2500 pF.

CCITT counterparts of EIA RS 232C are Recs. V.24 and V.28. The EIA and CCITT standards have essentially the same electrical specifications but differ in signal lead nomenclature. CCITT recommendations are given following the EIA standards. For functions of circuits and connector pin numbers, refer to Table 7.1; a 25-pin connector is a standard for RS 232C circuits.

Single-ended circuits are susceptible to all forms of electromagnetic interference. Noise and crosstalk susceptibility are proportional to length and bandwidth. The RS 232C places restrictions on both. It limits slew rate of the drivers to 30 V/μs to control radiated emission on neighboring circuits and allows bandwidth limiting on the receivers to reduce susceptibility to crosstalk.

EIA RS 422A. Electrical characteristics of balanced-voltage digital interface circuits. EIA RS 422A is a differential balanced-voltage interface standard, capable of significantly higher data rates over longer distances than specified in RS 232C (refer to Fig. 7.2). It is fully compatible with CCITT Recs. V.11 and X.27. It can accommodate rates of 100 kBd over a distance of 1200 m or rates up to 10 MBd over a maximum distance of 12 m (40 ft) (refer to Fig. 7.3). These performance improvements stem from the advantages of a balanced configuration which is isolated from ground noise currents. It is also immune to fluctuating voltage potentials between system ground references and common mode electromagnetic interference.

While the balanced interface is intended for use at the higher data signaling rates, it may generally be required where any of the following conditions prevail:

1. The interconnecting cable is too long for effective unbalanced operation.

2. The interconnecting cable is exposed to extraneous noise sources that may cause an unwanted voltage in excess of ± 1 V. The unwanted voltage is measured differentially between the signal conductor and common conductor at the load end of the cable with a 50-Ω resistor substituted for the generator.

3. It is necessary to minimize interference with other signals.

TABLE 7.1   Pin Assignments for EIA RS 232C (CCITT V.24) and CCITT V.35 Interface Circuits

	EIA RS 232C (CCITT V.24) interface					V.35 interface				
Pin	Name	DTE/DCE	Function	CCITT	EIA	Pin	Name	DTE/DCE	Spec.	Function
1	FG		Frame Ground	101	AA	A	FG		RS-232	Frame (or Protective) Ground
2	TD	↑	Transmitted Data	103	BA	B	SG			Signal (or Reference) Ground
3	RD	↓	Received Data	104	BB					
4	RTS	↑	Request to Send	105	CA	C	RTS	↑	RS-232	Request to Send
5	CTS	↓	Clear to Send	106	CB	D	CTS		RS-232	Clear to Send
6	DSR	↓	Data Set Ready	107	CC	E	DSR		RS-232	Data Set Ready
7	SG		Signal Ground	102	AB	F	RLSD		RS-232	Received Line Signal Det.
8	DCD	↓	Data Carrier Detect	109	CF	H	DTR	↑	RS-232	Data Terminal Ready
9		↓	Pos. DC Test Voltage			J	RI		RS-232	Ring Indicator
10		↓	Neg. DC Test Voltage			K	LT	↑	RS-232	Local Test
11		↓	Equalizer Mode	Bell 208A						
12	SDCD	↓	Sec. Data Carr Det.	122	SCF	R	RD	↓	V.35	Received Data (Sig. A)
13	SCTS	↓	Sec. Clear to Send	121	SCB	T				Received Data (Sig. B)
14	STD	↑	Sec. Transmitted Data	118	SBA					
15	NS	↑	New Sync	Bell 208A		V	SCR	↓	V.35	Serial Clock Receive (Sig. A)
	TC	↓	Transmitter Clock	114	DB	X				Serial Clock Receive (Sig. B)
16	SRD	↓	Sec. Received Data	119	SBB					
17	DCT	↓	Divided Clock Trans.	Bell 208A		P	SD	↑	V.35	Send Data (Sig. A)
	RC	↓	Receiver Clock	115	DD	S				Send Data (Sig. B)
18	DCR	↓	Divided Clock, Recv.	Bell 208A						
19	SRTS	↑	Sec. Request to Send	120	SCA	U	SCTE		V.35	Ser. Clock XMT EXT (Sig. A)
20	DTR	↑	Data Terminal Ready	108/2	CD	W		↑	V.35	Ser. Clock XMT EXT (Sig. B)
21	SQ	↓	Signal Quality Det.	110	CG					
22	RI	↓	Ring Indicator	125	CE	Y	SCT	↓	V.35	Ser. Clock Transmit (Sig. A)
23			Data Rate Selector	111	CH	a				Ser. Clock Transmit (Sig. B)
		↓	Data Rate Selector	112	CI					
24	ETC	↑	Ext. Transmit. Clock	113	DA					
25		↑	Busy							

Positive voltage equals binary 0, Signal space control on, LED on.
Negative voltage equals binary 1, Signal mark control off, LED off.
Binary 0, signal space or control on equals balance. V.35, A positive with respect to B; RS 232C positive voltage.
Binary 1, signal mark or control off equals balance. V.35, A negative with respect to B; RS 232C, negative voltage.

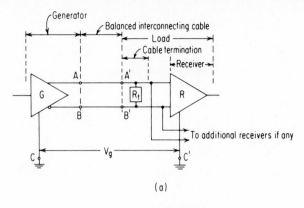

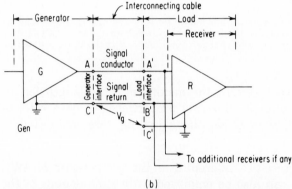

Figure 7.2   (a) Balanced digital interface circuit (EIA RS 422A). R_t = optional cable termination resistance; V_g = ground potential difference; A, B = generator interface points; A', B' = load interface points; C = generator circuit ground; C' = load circuit ground. The physical connections of multiple receivers are not defined. (b) Unbalanced digital interface circuit (EIA RS 423A). A, C = generator interface; A', B' = load interface; C' = load circuit ground; C = generator circuit ground; V_g = ground potential difference. The physical connections of multiple receivers are not defined.

4. Inversion of signals may be required; e.g., plus mark to minus mark may be obtained by inverting the cable pair.

When preparing the EIA RS 422 standard, tests were conducted with 24 AWG twisted-pair wire. The resulting length versus data rate is published as a guideline in Fig. 7.3. This shows two important results:

1. NRZ binary baseband signaling is not recommended at distances greater than 1200 m (4000 ft); as the data signaling rate is reduced below 90 kb/s, the cable length has been limited to 1200 m by the assumed maximum allowable 6-dBV signal loss.

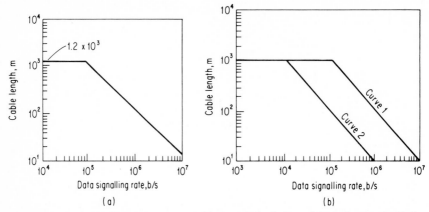

Figure 7.3 Data signaling rate versus cable length for balanced interchange circuit for 24 AWG (0.51-mm wire diameter) twisted-pair cable. (*a*) EIA RS 422A; (*b*) CCITT V.11. In (*b*), curve 1 is the terminated interchange circuit; curve 2 is the unterminated interchange circuit.

2. At data rates above 100 kHz, the maximum cable length for acceptable signal quality is inversely proportional to data rate; at operation over 60 m (200 ft), the signaling rate is limited to 2,000,000 b/s.

Cables having characteristics different from the twisted-pair 24 AWG 52.5 pF/m (16 pF/ft) can also be employed within the bounds of the curve in Fig. 7.3. First determine the absolute loop resistance and capacitance values of the typical 24 AWG cable provided by the cable length associated with the data signaling rate desired from Fig. 7.3. Then convert those values to equivalent lengths of the cable actually used. For example, longer distances would be possible when using 19 AWG, whereas shorter distances would be necessary for 28 AWG cable.

The characteristic impedance of twisted-pair cable is a function of frequency, wire size, and type as well as the kind of insulating materials employed. For example, the characteristic impedance of average 24 AWG, copper conductor, plastic-insulated twisted-pair telephone cable to a 100-kHz sinus wave will be on the order of 100 Ω.

In general, reliable operation of the balanced interface circuit is not particularly sensitive to the presence or absence of the cable termination at lower speeds (below 200 kb/s), or at any speed where the signal rise time at the load end of the cable is greater than four times the one-way propagation delay time of the cable. At other speeds and distances, where signal reflections are of negligible significance, terminating the cable with a resistor ranging in value from 90 to 150 Ω tends to preserve generated signal rise time but at the expense of signal amplitude. At lower data signaling rates, where zero-crossing ambiguity and signal rise time are not critical, the cable need not be terminated.

The RS 422A standard is compatible with other standards, such as CCITT Recs. V.11 and X.27. The electrical characteristics of the balanced-voltage digital interface are designed to allow use of both balanced and unbalanced circuits within the same interconnection cable sheath. For example, the balanced circuits may be used for data and timing, while the unbalanced circuits may be used for low-speed control functions.

Since the basic differential receivers of RS 423A and RS 422A are electrically identical, it is possible to interconnect an equipment using RS 423A receivers and generators on one side of the interface with an equipment using RS 422A generators and receivers on the other side of the interface, if the leads of the receivers and generators are properly configured to accommodate such an arrangement and the cable is not terminated. The balanced interface circuit is not intended for interoperation with other interface electrical characteristics such as RS 232C, MIL STD 188C, MIL STD 188-100, and CCITT Recs. V.28 and V.35. Under certain conditions, interoperation with circuits of some of the above interfaces may be possible but may require modification in the interface or within the equipment.

EIA RS 423A. Electrical characteristics of unbalanced-voltage digital interface circuits. Like EIA RS 232C, EIA RS 423A is also a single-ended, bipolar, unterminated voltage circuit (refer to Fig. 7.2). It extends the distance and data rate capabilities to distances up to 1200 m (4000 ft) at a data rate of 3000 Bd or at higher rates of up to 300 kBd over a maximum distance of 12 m (40 ft).

The curve of signal rise time versus cable length and data signaling rate is given in Fig. 7.4. These curves are based upon calculations and empirical data using 24 AWG twisted-pair, copper telephone cable with a shunt capacitance of 52.5 pF/m (16 pF/ft), a 50-Ω source impedance, a 12-V peak-to-peak source signal, and allowing a maximum near-end crosstalk of 1 V peak. The abscissa is the rise time of the signal, from 0.1 V_{SS} to 0.9 V_{SS} from the generator (V_{SS} stands for difference in steady-state voltages). Curves are given for both linear and exponential rise times. By reading up to the appropriate cable length curve and over to the left-hand ordinate scale, the associated maximum data signaling rate can be determined. Thus, for any specific rise-time value, both the maximum cable length and maximum data signaling rate can be determined. For example, for a 5-μs linear rise time, the maximum cable length would be 150 m and the maximum data signaling rate would be 60 kb/s to ensure that near-end crosstalk does not exceed 1 V peak under the conditions previously presented.

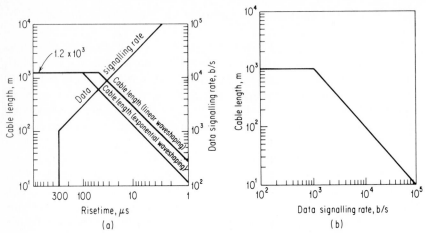

Figure 7.4 Data signaling rate versus cable length for unbalanced interchange circuit for 24 AWG (0.51-mm wire diameter) twisted-pair cable. (*a*) EIA RS 423A; (*b*) CCITT V.10.

Using the guidelines of RS 423A, operation over 60 m (200 ft) of cable limits the maximum signaling rate of unbalanced interchange circuits to 60 kb/s with exponential waveshaping or to 138 kb/s with linear waveshaping.

For any equipment design, the tolerance of components must be considered in determining the specific maximum data signaling rate and maximum cable length that can be employed.

Cables having characteristics different from the twisted-pair 24 AWG 52 pF/m can also be employed; however, the user should determine that the crosstalk will be held to the suggested value of less than 1 V. The type and length of cable used must be capable of maintaining the necessary signal quality needed for the particular application. Where twisted-pair cable is used with an unbalanced circuit and the two wires serve as signal conductors for two different interchange circuits, the information flow in both wires should be in the same direction.

Generators and receivers meeting the requirements of RS 423A are compatible with those meeting CCITT Recs. V.10 and X.26. The electrical characteristics of the unbalanced-voltage digital interface are designed to allow use of both balanced and unbalanced circuits within the same interconnection cable sheath. For example, the balanced circuits may be used for data and timing, while the unbalanced circuits may be used for low-speed control functions.

Since the basic differential receivers of RS 423A and RS 422A are electrically identical, it is possible to interconnect equipment using RS 423A receivers and generators on one side of the interface with equipment using RS 422A generator and receivers on the other side of the interface if the leads of the receivers and generators are properly configured to accommodate such an arrangement.

It is also possible for the unbalanced interface circuit to interoperate with RS 232C interface circuits. The requirements and suggested implementations for such interoperation are provided by EIA Industrial Electronics Bulletin No. 12.

The waveshape must be controlled to limit near-end crosstalk coupled to adjacent circuits. Typically, for most applications implementing IC technology, a linear-type waveshape may be derived by using slew rate control. In other applications, particularly at low modulation rates where rise times are 100 μs or longer, an exponential rise time may be implemented by using RC waveshaping.

EIA RS 357. This standard defines the electrical, functional, and mechanical characteristics of the interface between analog facsimile equipment to be used for data transmission and data sets used for controlling-transmitting the data. Figure 3.13 summarizes the functional and electrical characteristics of RS 357.

EIA RS 366. This standard defines the electrical, functional, and mechanical characteristics of the interface between automatic calling equipment for DCE and DTE. The electrical characteristics are encompassed by RS 232C.

EIA RS 408. This standard recommends the standardization of the two interfaces between the numerical control equipment (tape reader, etc.) and the serial-to-parallel converter with less than 40 ft (12 m) distance.

Comparison of EIA RS 232C and RS 422A, RS 423A standards. A system implemented with the RS 422A differential output cannot be used to drive an RS 232C system directly. An RS 423A single-ended driver may be used, provided certain precautions are observed.

1. Although the RS 423A driver output specification of between 4 to 5 V does not meet the RS 232C specification of 6 V, operation is usually satisfactory with RS 232C receivers. This is achieved because the short cable lengths permitted by RS 232C cause very little signal degradation and because of the low source impedance of RS 423A driver.

2. RS 232C specifies that the rise time for the signal to pass through the ±3-V transition region shall not exceed 4 percent of the signal element duration. RS 423A requires a much slower rise time, specified from 10 to 90 percent of the total signal amplitude, to reduce crosstalk for operation over longer distances. Therefore the RS 423A

driver in the equipment must be equipped with wave-shaping components.

3. RS 423A specifies two common return grounds for each direction of transmission; RS 232C requires one only. Care must be taken to ensure that a return ground path has been created when interfacing between the two systems.

4. RS 232C does not require termination, whereas it may be necessary for RS 422A (refer to Fig. 7.2).

5. RS 422A and RS 423A specify that receivers should not be damaged by voltages up to 12 V, whereas RS 232C allows drivers to produce output voltages up to 25 V.

Table 7.2 compares the key characteristics required by drivers and receivers intended for these applications. Since RS 232C has been in use for many years, RS 422A and RS 423A parameter values have been selected to facilitate an orderly transition from existing designs to new equipment.

EIA RS 449. General-purpose 37-position and 9-position interface for DTE and DCE employing serial binary data interchange. Developed to provide a functional interface between DTE and DCE, EIA RS 449 retains all functional capabilities of EIA RS 232C and introduces 10 new interchange circuits to enhance interface capabilities. RS 449 provides standardized 37-pin and 9-pin interface connectors together with latching arrangements for these connectors.

The interface is compatible with the current state of the art of IC technology, offers greater immunity to noise, increases the data signaling rate to 2 Mb/s, and permits an increase up to 200 m in the length of interconnecting cable.

The 10 new interchange circuits defined in RS 449 not appearing in RS 232C include three circuits for control and status of testing functions in the DCE (circuit LL, Local Loopback; circuit RL, Remote Loopback; and circuit TM, Test Mode), two circuits for control and status of the transfer of the DCE to a standby telecommunication facility (circuit SS, Select Standby, and circuit SB, Standby Indicator), and a circuit for DCE transmit and receive frequency selection (circuit SF, Select Frequency). The standard also defines a circuit providing an out-of-service function under the control of the DTE (circuit IS, Terminal in Service) and a circuit to provide a new signal function (circuit NS, New Signal) and two common wires (refer to Table 7.3). Interconnection between interface circuits using RS 449 and RS 232C is given in EIA Industrial Electronics Bulletin No. 12.

The electrical characteristics of the interchange circuits in RS 422A and RS 423A are applicable to RS 449.

TABLE 7.2 Key Parameters of EIA Specifications

Characteristics	EIA RS-232C	EIA RS-423-A	EIA RS-422-A
Form of operation	Single-ended	Single-ended	Differential
Max. cable length	15 m*	600 m	1200 m
Max. data rate	20 kBd	300 kBd	10 MBd
Driver output voltage, open circuit	± 25 V (max.)	± 6 V(max.)	6 V (max.) between outputs
Driver output voltage, loaded output	± 5 to ± 15 V (min.)	± 3.6 V (min.)	2 V (min.) between outputs
Driver output resistance, power off	$Ro = 300 \, \Omega$ (min.)	100 μA between -6 to $+6$ V (min.)	100 μA between $+6$ and -0.25 V (min.)
Driver output short circuit current I_{sc}	± 500 mA (max.)	± 150 mA (max.)	± 150 mA (max.)
Driver output slew rate	30 V/μs max.	Slew rate must be controlled based upon cable length and modulation rate	No control necessary
Receiver input resistance R_{in}	3 to 7 kΩ	$\geqslant 4$ kΩ	$\geqslant 4$ kΩ
Receiver input thresholds	-3 to $+3$ V (max.)	-0.2 to $+0.2$ V (max.)	-0.2 to $+0.2$ V (max.)
Receiver input voltage	-25 to $+25$ V (max.)	-12 to $+12$ V (max.)	-12 to $+12$ V (max.)

Interconnecting cable type	Twisted-pair wire or flat cable conductor pair
Conductor size:	
Copper Wire (solid or stranded)	24 AWG or larger
Other (per conductor)	$R \leqslant 10 \, \Omega/100$ m
Capacitance:	
Mutual Pair	$C \leqslant 66$ pF/m
Stray	$C \leqslant 130$ pF/m
Pair-to-pair crosstalk (balanced) attenuation at 150 K Hz	$A \geqslant 40$dB

*Cable length can be extended, if the capacitance at the interface does not exceed 2500 pF.

The following 10 interchange circuits are classified as category I circuits (refer to Table 7.4):

SD	Send Data	RS	Request to Send
RD	Receive Data	CS	Clear to Send
TT	Terminal Timing	RR	Receiver Ready
ST	Send Timing	TR	Terminal Ready
RT	Receive Timing	DM	Data Mode

TABLE 7.3   Equivalency Table of EIA RS 232C, EIA RS 449, and CCITT Rec.

DTE/DCE	EIA RS 449		EIA RS 232C		CCITT Rec. V.24	
	SG	Signal Ground	AB	Signal Ground	102	Signal Ground
→	SC	Send Common			102a	DTE Common
←	RC	Receive Common			102b	DCE Common
→	IS	Terminal in Service				
←	IC	Incoming Call	CE	Ring Indicator	125	Calling Indicator
→	TR	Terminal Ready	CD	Data Terminal Ready	108/2	Data Terminal Ready
←	DM	Data Mode	CC	Data Set Ready	107	Data Set Ready
→	SD	Send Data	BA	Transmitted Data	103	Transmitted Data
←	RD	Receive Data	BB	Received Data	104	Received Data
→	TT	Terminal Timing	DA	Transmitter Signal Element Timing (DTE Source)	113	Transmitter Signal Element Timing (DTE Source)
←	ST	Send Timing	DB	Transmitter Signal Element Timing (DCE Source)	114	Transmitter Signal Element Timing (DCE Source)
←	RT	Receive Timing	DD	Receiver Signal Element Timing	115	Receiver Signal Element Timing (DCE Source)
→	RS	Request to Send	CA	Request to Send	105	Request to Send
←	CS	Clear to Send	CB	Clear to Send	106	Ready for Sending
←	RR	Receiver Ready	CF	Received Line Signal Detector	109	Data Channel Received Line Signal Detector
←	SQ	Signal Quality	CG	Signal Quality Detector	110	Data Signal Quality Detector
→	NS	New Signal				
→	SF	Select Frequency			126	Select Transmit Frequency
→	SR	Signaling Rate Selector	CH	Data Signal Rate Selector (DTE Source)	111	Data Signaling Rate Selector (DTE Source)
←	SI	Signaling Rate Indicator	CI	Data Signal Rate Selector (DCE Source)	112	Data Signaling Rate Selector (DCE Source)
→	SSD	Secondary Send Data	SBA	Secondary Transmitted Data	118	Transmitted Backward Channel Data
←	SRD	Secondary Receive Data	SBB	Secondary Received Data	119	Received Backward Channel Data
→	SRS	Secondary Request to Send	SCA	Secondary Request to Send	120	Transmit Backward Channel Line Signal
←	SCS	Secondary Clear to Send	SCB	Secondary Clear to Send	121	Backward Channel Ready
←	SRR	Secondary Receiver Ready	SCF	Secondary Received Line Signal Detector	122	Backward Channel Received Line Signal Detector
→	LL	Local Loopback			141	Local Loopback
→	RL	Remote Loopback			140	Remote Loopback
←	TM	Test Mode			142	Test Indicator
→	SS	Select Standby			116	Select Standby
←	SB	Standby Indicator			117	Standby Indicator

For applications where the signaling rate on the data interchange circuits (SD and RD) is 20,000 b/s or less, the individual category I circuits shall use either the balanced electrical characteristics of RS 422A, without the cable-terminating resistance (R_T), or the unbalanced electrical characteristics of RS 423A. All interchange circuits not classified as category I circuits are classified as category II circuits. For all applications, the category II circuits shall use the unbalanced electrical characteristics of RS 423A.

Pin assignments for 37-pin and 9-pin connectors are given in Table 7.4.

Two major benefits of RS 449 are the increased cable distances permitted by the interface and improved diagnostic capabilities. RS 449 gives the host computer and terminal a great deal of control over the modem, much more than RS 232C permitted. Most of that control involves diagnostic and reliability issues in terms of checking out a channel in the modem. The drawback is that a 37-pin and 9-pin connector plus the connector that couples to the data jacks occupy a sizable area and the unit may run out of space.

TABLE 7.4 Connector Pin Assignments for EIA RS 449

Contact Number	Circuit	Contact Number	Circuit	Circuit Category	DTE/DCE
		37-pin connector			
1	Shield				
2	SI	20	RC	II	←
3	Spare	21	Spare		
4	SD	22	SD	I	→
5	ST	23	ST	I	←
6	RD	24	RD	I	←
7	RS	25	RS	I	→
8	RT	26	RT	I	←
9	CS	27	CS	I	←
10	LL	28	IS	II	→
11	DM	29	DM	I	←
12	TR	30	TR	I	→
13	RR	31	RR	I	←
14	RL	32	SS	II	→
15	IC	33	SQ	II	←
16	SF/SR*	34	NS	II	→
17	TT	35	TT	I	
18	TM	36	SB	II	←
19	SG	37	SC	I	→
		9-pin connector			
1	Shield				
2	SRR	6	RC	II	←
3	SSD	7	SRS	II	→
4	SRD	8	SCS	II	←
5	SG	9	SC	II	→

*Circuits SF and SR share the same contact number.

CCITT Recommendations for digital interfacing

CCITT Rec. V.10 (also X.26).   This recommendation deals with the electrical characteristics of unbalanced double-current interchange circuits operating at data rates up to 100 kb/s. At the receiver lower than -0.3 V corresponds to binary 1, or off (control and timing); higher than $+0.3$ V corresponds to binary 0, or on (control and timing). The receiver is identical to that specified in Rec. V.11. The generator output impedance is equal or less than 50 Ω. The recommendation also specifies measurement and test methods as well as interconnecting conditions with V.11 and V.28 circuits.

The recommendation is similar to RS 423A except that in RS 423A the driver output voltage is specified at a load resistance of 450 Ω. The required waveshaping may be accomplished either by providing a slew-rate control in the generator or by inserting an RC filter at the generator output. A combination of these methods may also be employed.

The electrical characteristics of Rec. V.10 are designed to allow the use of balanced and unbalanced circuits within the same interface. For example, the balanced circuits may be used for data and timing, while the unbalanced circuits may be used for associated control circuit functions.

The basic differential receiver specifications of Recs. V.10 and V.11 are electrically identical; it is therefore possible to interconnect equipments using V.10 and V.11 generators and receivers. The unbalanced electrical characteristics of V.10 have also been designed to permit limited interworking, under certain conditions, with generators and receivers of V.28.

No electrical characteristics of the interconnection cable are specified in this recommendation. However, guidance is given concerning operational constraints imposed by cable length and near-end crosstalk.

The maximum operating distance for the unbalanced interchange circuit is primarily a function of the amount of interference (near-end crosstalk) coupled to adjacent circuits in the equipment interconnection. Additionally the unbalanced circuit is susceptible to exposure to differential noise resulting from any imbalance between the signal conductor and signal common return at load. Increasing the physical separation and interconnection cable length between the generator and the load might increase the exposure to common-mode noise and the degree of near-end crosstalk. The curve of cable length versus signaling rate given in Fig. 7.4 may be used as a guide; it is very similar to the curve given in the RS 423A interfacing standard. This curve is based upon calculations and empirical data using twisted-pair telephone cable with a shunt capacitance of 52 pF/m, a 50-Ω source impedance, a 6-V source signal, and maximum near-end crosstalk of 1 V peak. The rise time of the signal at signaling rates below 1000 b/s is 100 μs, and above 1000 b/s it is 0.1 of nominal duration of the signal element. Experience has shown that in most practical cases the operating distance at the lower signaling rates may be extended to several kilometers.

The point-to-point interchange circuit arrangement of one generator and one load might be expanded to a multipoint arrangement by adding generators, receivers, and cables along the interconnecting cable. The combined load impedance presented to any active generator by other generators, receivers, and cable must not be less than 50 Ω. When the generator is in the high-impedance state, the output resistance shall be greater than 10,000 Ω. It is recognized that where coaxial cables are used for interconnecting purposes it may be desirable to include a terminating resistance at the receiver end of the cable. This is considered to be a special case for which special generator characteristics are required. The terminating resistance shall in no case be less than 50 Ω. The screen of the coaxial cable shall be connected to ground, only at the generator end.

CCITT Rec. V.11 (also X.27). The recommendation deals with the electrical characteristics of balanced double-current interchange circuits, operating with data signaling rates up to 10 Mb/s. Receiver sensitivity and test measurement specifications are similar to those given in Rec. V.10. This standard is similar to RS 422A with the exception that the receiver sensitivity at the specified maximum common-mode voltage (±7 V) shall be ±300 mV versus ±200 mV for RS 422A.

The maximum permissible length of cable separating the generator and the load in a point-to-point application is a function of the data signaling rate. It is further influenced by the tolerable signal distortion and the environmental constraints such as ground potential difference and longitudinal noise. Increasing the distance between generator and load might increase the exposure to ground potential difference.

As an illustration of the above conditions, the curves of cable length versus data signaling rate in Fig. 7.3 may be used for guidance; these curves are similar to the curve given in the RS 422A interfacing standard. These curves are based upon empirical data using twisted-pair telephone cable 24 AWG (0.51-mm wire diameter) both unterminated and terminated in a 100-Ω resistive load. The cable-length restrictions shown by the curves are based upon the following assumed signal quality requirements at the load:

1. Signal rise and fall time equal to or less than one-half the duration of the signal element.
2. Maximum voltage loss between generator and load of 6 dB.

At the higher signaling rates, the sloping portion of the curves shows the cable-length limitation established by the assumed signal rise and fall time requirements. The cable length has been arbitrarily limited to 1000 m by the assumed maximum allowable loss of 6 dB. Experience has shown that in many practical cases the operating distance at lower signaling rates may extend to several kilometers.

The use of cable termination is optional; at signaling rates above 200 kb/s or at any signaling rate where the cable propagation delay is of the order of half the signal element duration, a termination should be used to preserve the signal rise time and minimize reflection. The terminating impedance should match as closely as possible the cable characteristic impedance in the signal spectrum. Generally, termination resistance in the range of 100 to 150 Ω will be satisfactory, the higher values leading to lower power dissipation. At the lower signaling rates, where distortion and rise time are not critical, it may be desirable to omit the termination to minimize power dissipation in the generator.

The electrical characteristics of V.11 are designed to allow the use of unbalanced and balanced circuits whithin the same interface; see Rec. V.10. Equipment having interchange circuits according to V.11 is not intended for interworking with equipment having interchange circuits according to electrical characteristics of V.35.

In multipoint configuration, the combined load impedance presented to any active generator by generators, receivers, cable, and terminators must be less than 100 Ω.

CCITT Rec. V.24. It gives the list of definitions for interfacing circuits between DTE and DCE for transfer of binary data and control and timing signals; the definitions are applicable to synchronous and asynchronous data communications. The recommendation gives definitions for the 100-series interchange circuits and 200-series for automatic calling together with operational requirements. A list of the 100-series interchange circuits which are applicable to EIA 232C is given in Table 7.1.

CCITT Rec. V.28. This recommendation gives the electrical characteristics for unbalanced double-current interchange circuits. Electrical characteristics specified are applicable to interchange circuits operating with data signaling rates below 20,000 b/s.

Binary 1 (off) corresponds to lower than -3 V.

Binary 0 (on) corresponds to higher than $+3$ V.

It limits the instantaneous rate of voltage to 30 V/1 μs to reduce the crosstalk.

CCITT Rec. V.35. This recommendation defines interface circuits similar to EIA RS 232C and Rec. V.24, with balanced lines on (103) Transmit Data, (104) Receive Data, (114) Transmit Clock, and (115) Receive Clock; however it does not mention (113) External Transmit Clock at all.

The recommendation specifies the source impedance to be in the range 50 to 150 Ω, the resistance between short-circuited terminals and dc return to be 150 $\pm$ 15 Ω, and the input load impedance to be in the range 100 $\pm$ 10 Ω. The rise time between the 10 and 90 percent points of any change of state when terminated by a 100-Ω resistive load should be less than 1 percent of the nominal duration of a signal element or 40 ns, whichever is the greater.

Although the recommendation specifies circuit characteristics for modems operating at 48 kb/s and never mentions connector size, a 34-pin Winchester connector has become a standard for interface circuits operating on 48, 56, and 64 kb/s data transmission in the United States; also the balanced External Transmit Clock circuit is assigned to connector pins, as depicted in Table 7.1.

CCITT Rec. V.36. It covers the synchronous data transmission modems using 60–108 kHz group band circuits and is applicable to the extension of a PCM channel at 64 kb/s, extension of an SCPC circuit from a satellite earth station, and the transmission of a multiplex aggregate bit stream for telegraph and data signals. Data signaling rates are synchronous 48, 56, 64, and 72 kb/s. Interfacing control circuits 105, 106, 107, and 109 comply with the electrical characteristics of Rec. V.10; interchange circuits 103, 104, 113, 114, and 115 comply with the electrical characteristics of Rec. V.11.

CCITT Rec. V.57. This recommendation gives the measuring equipment characteristics for higher than 20,000 kb/s data transmission.

CCITT X Recommendations for protocols are given in Sec. 7.4. CCITT V and X Recommendations are given in the Volume VIII.

Other interface standards

There are military and other commonly encountered interfaces that have become standardized; some of them are given below.

The U.S. Military interface standards. The military standards for the communication links are more stringent than the commercial standards. The military standards are issued by the U.S. Department of Defense and its agencies for application to the military communication systems and its subsystems.

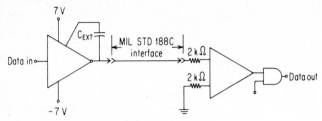

Figure 7.5 MIL STD 188C interface circuit.

Most equipments which operate under EIA and CCITT standards may satisfy military requirements.

MIL STD 188C (low level). The military equivalent of RS 232C is MIL STD 188C. Equipment intended for RS 232C can be applied to MIL STD 188C by use of external waveshaping components on the driver end and input resistance and threshold tailoring on the receiver end. Refer to Fig. 7.5 and Table 7.5.

MIL STD 188-114 balanced. This standard is similar to RS 422A with the exception that the driver offset voltage level is limited to ±0.4 V versus ±3 V allowed in RS 422A.

MIL STD 188-144 unbalanced. This standard is similar to RS 423A with

TABLE 7.5   MIL STD 188C Summary

	Parameter	Conditions	Low-level limits	
			Min.	Max.
V_{OH}	Driver output voltage open circuit	*	5 V	7 V
V_{OL}			−7 V	−5V
R_O	Driver output resistance power ON	$I_{OUT} \leq 10$ mA		100 Ω
I_{OS}	Driver output short-circuit current		−100 mA	100 mA
	Driver output slew rate, all interchange circuits, control circuits, rate & timing circuits	†	5% IU	15% IU
R_{IN}	Receiver input resistance	Mod. rate ≤ 200 kBd	6 Ω	
	Receiver input threshold:			
	Output = MARK	‡		100 μA
	Output = SPACE		−100 μA	

*Ripple < 0.5 percent, V_{OH}, V_{OL} matched to within 10 percent of each other.
†Waveshaping required on driver outputs such that the signal rise or fall time is 5 to 15 percent of the unit interval at the applicable modulation rate.
‡Balance between marking and spacing (threshold) currents actually required shall be within 10 percent of each other.

TABLE 7.6   MIL STD 1397 Summary

	Parameter	Conditions	Comparison limits 1397 (slow)	Comparison limits 1397 (fast)
	Data transmission rate		42 kb/s	250 kb/s
V_{OH}	Driver output voltage		± 1.5 V	0 V
V_{OL}			-10 to -15.5 V	-3 V
I_{OH}	Driver output current		≥ -4 mA	
I_{OL}			1 mA	
R_S	Driver power OFF impedance		≥ 100 kΩ	
V_{IH}	Receiver input voltage	Fail-safe open	≤ 4.5 V	≤ -1.1 V
V_{IL}		Circuit	≥ -7.5 V	≥ -1.9 V

the exception that the loaded circuit driver output voltage at $R_L = 450$ Ω must be 90 percent of the open-circuit output voltage versus ± 2 V (at $R_S = 100$ Ω) for RS 422A.

MIL STD 1397 (slow and fast).   This standard is summarized in Table 7.6.

Computer-to-peripheral interface standards.   At present, the only standards dealing with the interface between processors and other equipment are the de facto standards. One of them, IBM specification GA-22-6974-0, covers the electrical characteristics, the format of the information, and the control sequences of the data transmitted between the IBM 360/370 unit and up to 10 of the I/O ports (refer to Table 7.7).

The interface is an unbalanced bus using 95 Ω, terminated coax cables. Devices connected to the bus should feature short-circuit protection, hysteresis in the receivers, and open-emitter drivers. Pay careful attention to line lengths and quality to limit cable noise to <400 mV.

IEEE Standard 488-1978. Digital interface for programmable instrumentation.   IEEE 488 defines a general-purpose interface. Designed for instrumentation systems requiring only limited-distance communications (about 20 m), the standard defines as many variables in an interface as possible, without defining the actual use of the interface.

In addition, IEEE 488 defines the interface without reference to the hardware used to implement it. This allows new products to take advantage of new technologies, thus permitting faster, less-expensive construction of devices and systems. It also precisely specifies the connector pin functions as well as signal levels (both voltage and current) and signal timings. IEEE 488 defines the hardware of interconnection in such a way that two interconnected instruments can talk to each

TABLE 7.7   IBM 360/370 Unit Interface Summary

	Parameter	Conditions	IBM 360/370 Min.	IBM 360/370 Max.
V_{OH}	Driver output voltage	$I_{OH} = 123$ mA		7 V
V_{OH}		$I_{OH} = 30$ μA		5.85 V
V_{OH}		$I_{OH} = 59.3$ mA	3.11 V	
V_{OL}		$I_{OL} = -240$ μA		0.15 V
V_{IH}	Receiver input threshold			1.7 V
V_{IL}	Voltage		0.7 V	
I_{IH}	Receiver input current	$V_{IN} = 3.11$ V		-0.42 mA
I_{IL}		$V_{IN} = 0.15$ V	0.24 mA	
	Receiver input voltage range:			
V_{IN}	Power ON		-0.15 V	7 V
V_{IN}	Power OFF		-0.15 V	6 V
R_{IN}	Receiver input impedance	0.15 V $\leq V_{IN}$ ≤ 3.9 V	7400 Ω	
I_{IN}	Receiver input current	$V_{IN} = 0.15$ V		240 μA
Z_O	CABLE impedance		83 Ω	101 Ω
R_O	CABLE termination	$P_D \geq 390$ mW	90 Ω	100 Ω
	Line length (specified as noise on signal and ground lines)			400 mV

other. Unlike parallel interfaces, which are designed to connect specific devices to specific computers, IEEE 488 is a generalized non-computer-specific interface that makes possible the interconnection, via a bus, of as many as 15 peripheral devices of any type. The bus is similar in concept to an I/O bus into which interface cards plug on the computer.

On an I/O bus, two entities reside: the computer and the interface. The computer always controls the I/O bus and the interfaces react to commands from the computer. On the IEEE 488 bus, however, three types of devices can exist: listeners, talkers, and controllers.

It is a bit-parallel–byte-serial interface; its 8-bit-byte structure makes it well-suited to the test and measurement instrument field. In this document physical lines fall into two categories:

- Eight bidirectional lines that provide for the transfer of either address or data information between devices connected on the bus

- Eight housekeeping lines (three handshake, five control signals) that provide control information to all devices communicating on the bus to specify the nature of the use of the bidirectional bus lines (refer to Fig. 7.6)

Operations in the bus.   Basically, the bus operates in one of two major modes at a given time. In one of these modes, a system controller establishes which device on the bus will "talk" and which one or more of the other devices will "listen." When the system controller device terminates this network establishing process, the talker takes over the bus and begins to send data, one 8-bit byte at a time to each of the listeners.

In general, active talkers drive the data lines in the data bus, and active listeners read the information. To avoid conflicts, only one talker at a time is allowed to be active, but several listeners may be active simultaneously.

Handshake and control signals. The potential existence of several active listeners receiving data simultaneously presents a problem: the active listeners may not be capable of accepting data at the same rates. Thus the slowest active listener must control the speed of data transfer so that data are not lost.

Data bus information. The type of information carried by the 8-bit data bus includes bus commands, listener addresses, talker addresses, and secondary addresses. The 32 bus commands directly control devices on

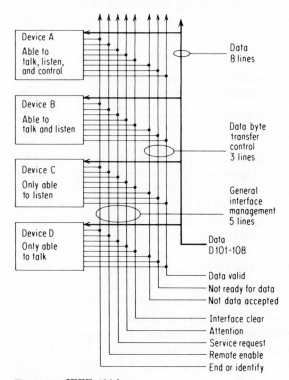

Figure 7.6 IEEE 488 bus.

TABLE 7.8 IEEE 488 Bus and Connector Pin Assignments

Pin no.	Signal line	Pin no.	Signal line	Pin no.	Signal line	Pin no.	Signal line
1	D101	7	NRFD	13	D105	19	Gnd (7)
2	D102	8	NDAC	14	D106	20	Gnd (8)
3	D103	9	IFC	15	D107	21	Gnd (9)
4	D104	10	SRQ	16	D108	22	Gnd (10)
5	EOI (24)	11	ATN	17	REN (24)	23	Gnd (11)
6	DAV	12	Shield	18	Gnd (6)	24	Gnd (logic)

the 488 bus; listener and talker addresses (31 each) activate the appropriate listeners and the talker; secondary addresses control subunits within any peripheral capable of performing two or more functions simultaneously.

Pin assignments for IEEE 488 standard. The connector itself is physically similar to the RS 232C, 25-pin connector. The ground (return) for eight data lines and for EOI and REN are via pin 24, the logic ground; the return lines for six other functions on pins 6–11 are via pins 18 to 23, as shown in Table 7.8.

Interface mediums and application fields of different first-level standards are given in Table 7.9.

7.2   Interface Control Circuit Operations

The purpose of interface control circuit operations is to ensure that certain control information supplied by one device is understood by the other. Refer to Table 7.1 for circuit designations and Table 7.10 for their utilization on different systems.

1. Altering. Circuit CE (Ring Indicator) (125) is the basic circuit for alerting data stations of an incoming call. This is primarily used on the switched telecommunication network, where typically the ringing signal on the carrier line is 2 s of 20-Hz voltage applied by the serving central office every 6 s. In autoanswer stations this signal is detected by the DCE, which converts the ringing signals to a dc voltage that appears on circuit CE (RI) (125) with approximately 2 s on (positive) and 4 s off (negative). When the DTE is ready, circuit CD (Data Terminal Ready) (108/2) is on; the DCE will go off-hook when it detects a 20-Hz (2 s of 20-Hz voltage, in every 6 s) signal. The DCE will then respond with answer tone, data carrier, or silence according to the system design. DTEs which do not use the alerting signal may keep circuit DTR (108/2) on and ignore indications on circuit RI (125). Circuit CC (Data Set Ready) (107) may then be used to start operations concerned with answering a call.

2. Equipment readiness. Circuits CC (Data Set Ready) (107) and CD (Data Terminal Ready) (108/2) indicate the readiness of the station equipment to operate. Circuit DSR (107) is specified as a basic interchange circuit for all types of interfaces. Circuit DTR (108/2) is required for switched services.

In some dedicated-line DCEs, circuit CC (Data Set Ready) (107) is turned on when power is on and the DCE is not in the test mode; in others, circuit DSR (107) comes on when the DCE starts transmission of its line signal.

Circuit CD (Data Terminal Ready) (108/2) is not specified for dedicated-line service because the DCE does not require this information, there being no on-hook–off-hook switching functions, and a DTE that is not ready will not attempt to transmit data. Certain DCEs are de-

TABLE 7.9 Standards for Interface Circuits

Interface area	Application	Standard	Remarks
DCE to DTE	EIA (U.S. industrial)	RS 232C	Unbalanced short lines
		RS 422A	Balanced long lines
		RS 423A	Unbalanced RS 232 upgrade
		RS 449	Syst. standard covering use of RS 422/423
	CCITT	V.24	Similar to RS 232
		V.10	Similar to RS 423
		V.11	Similar to RS 422
	U.S. military	188C	Unbalanced short lines
		188-114	Similar to RS 422/423
		1397 Slow	42 kb/s
		1397 Fast	250 kb/s
Computer to peripheral	IBM 360/370	System chan. I/O	Unbalanced bus
Instrument to computer	Automatic test system lab. instrumentation	IEEE 488	Unbalanced bus
Facsimile to DTE	EIA facsimile transmission	RS 357	Incorporates RS 232
Automatic calling equipment to DTE	EIA impulse dial. and multitone equipment	RS 366	Incorporates RS 232
Numerical control equipment to DTE	EIA numerical control equipment	RS 408	Short lines (< 40 ft) (12m)

TABLE 7.10 Standard Interface for Selected Communication Systems Configuration

Interchange circuit	A	B	C	D	E	F	G	H	I	J	K	L	M	N
	Transmit only	Transmit only*	Receive only	Duplex*/half duplex	Duplex	Prim. chan. transmit only*/sec. chan. receive only	Prim. chan. receive only/sec. chan. transmit only*	Prim. chan. transmit only/sec. chan. receive only	Prim. chan. receive only/sec. chan. transmit only	Prim. chan. transmit only*/half-duplex sec. chan.	Prim. chan. receive only/half-duplex sec. chan.	Half-duplex prim. chan./half-duplex sec. chan. Duplex prim. chan.*/duplex sec. chan.*	Duplex prim. chan./duplex sec. chan.	Special (circuits specified by supplier)
AA Protective Ground	—	—	—	—	—	—	—	—	—	—	—	—	—	—
AB Signal Ground	X	X	X	X	X	X	X	X	X	X	X	X	X	X
BA Transmitted Data	X	X		X	X	X		X		X		X	X	o
BB Received Data			X	X	X		X		X		X	X	X	o

CA Request to Send		X	X	X	X	X	X	X	X	X	X	X	o
CB Clear to Send		X	X	X	X	X	X	X	X	X	X	X	o
CC Data Set Ready	X	S	S	S	S	S	S	S	S	S	S	S	o
CD Data Terminal Ready	S	S	S	S	S	S	S	S	S	S	S	S	o
CE Ring Indicator	S	S		S	S	S		S		S	S		o
CF Received Line Signal Detector		X	X	X	X	X	X	X	X	X	X	X	o
CG Signal Quality Detector	X			X	X		X			X			o
CH/CI Data Signaling Rate Selector (DTE) (DCE)							X	X	X	X	X	X	o
DA/DB Transmitter Signal Element Timing (DTE) (DCE)	t		t	t	t	t	t						o
DD Receiver Signal Element Timing (DCE)		t	t	t	t	t	t	t			t	t	o
SBA Secondary Transmitted Data						X	X		X	X	X	X	
SBB Secondary Received Data			X			X	X	X	X	X	X	X	o
SCA Secondary Request to Send				X	X	X	X		X	X	X	X	o
SCB Secondary Clear to Send					X	X	X		X	X	X	X	o
SCF Secondary Received Line Signal Detector			X	X	X	X	X		X	X	X	X	o

o: To be specified by the supplier

—: Optional

S: Additional interchange circuits; required for switched service

t: Additional interchange circuits; required for synchronous channel

X: Basic interchange circuits; all systems

*Indicates the inclusion of circuit CA (Request to Send) in a one-way only (transmit) or duplex configuration where it might ordinarily not be expected, but where it might be used to indicate a nontransmit mode to the data communication equipment to permit it to remove a line signal or to send synchronizing or training signals as required.

signed to provide a switched network backup capability in event of failure of the dedicated facility to provide a terminator for circuit DTR (108/2). Where the system does not use alternate switched-network capability, circuit DTR (108/2) should be strapped to a permanent on condition either in the DTE or, if provided by a strapping option, in the DCE.

3. Data-channel readiness.   Preparation of the data channel to transmit is controlled by circuits CA (Request to Send) (105) and CB (Clear to Send) (106). Indication of readiness to receive is given by circuit CF (Received Line Signal Detector) (109).

Circuit CTS (106) is required in all transmitting DCEs, just as circuit DCD (109) is required in all receiving DCEs. If circuit RTS (105) is not implemented in the DCE, it is assumed to be on at all times and circuit CTS (106) must respond appropriately. The on condition of circuit CTS (106) is a response to the occurrence of a simultaneous on condition on circuits CC (Data Set Ready) (107) and circuit CA (Request to Send) (105). A delay may be appropriate to the DCE for establishing a data communication channel to a remote DTE. The on condition on circuit CTS (106) does not guarantee that the remote receiver is listening; circuit assurance cannot be obtained from this interchange circuit. Where a synchronous DCE is used, the on condition of circuit CB (Clear to Send) (106) implies that the clock at the remote DCE is synchronized and that the transmitting DTE is free to start transmitting data. Thus, during the time-out interval between the on condition of circuit CA (Request to Send) (105) and the on condition of CB (Clear to Send) (106), the two clocks must achieve synchronization.

4. Handshaking.   A handshaking technique is used predominantly on the switched telecommunication network. DCEs used on dedicated point-to-point circuits with alternate voice capability may also use this technique. The DCEs transmit signals to each other and perform certain time-outs to establish the data communication channel and provide circuit assurance prior to turning the channel over to the DTE for data transmission. Where the DCE includes the handshaking function, it guarantees initial circuit assurance, and circuit CB (Clear to Send) (106) and circuit CF (Received Line Signal Detector) (109) must mean exactly what their names imply. Each DCE has communicated with the other end of the telecommunication channel and knows that it is ready to transmit and receive data. In the design of some DCEs this philosophy is carried even further in that the DCE will turn circuit CB (Clear to Send) (106) off if the received line signal disappears from the telecommunication channel. This is based on the logical deduction, "If I can't hear him, he probably can't hear me either; therefore, stop transmitting." Certain types of data sets will, after a line signal disappears for a certain length of time, cause the switched network call to be disconnected.

5. Circuit assurance.   An on condition on interchange circuit CF (Received Line Signal Detector) (109) normally indicates that the DCE at the other end of the channel is transmitting a line signal, and this provides circuit assurance where data carriers are simultaneously transmitted in both directions. Where a carrier is transmitted in one direction at a time, assurance for establishment of the channel requires exchange of information in each direction. This may be performed at the beginning and at the end of each message, or the successful receipt of data may be acknowledged on a block-by-block basis during the message. Between acknowledgements there is no continuous assurance of circuit continuity in such systems.

In practice there is a delay between the appearance of the line signal on the telecommunication channel and the resultant on condition on circuit CF (Received Line Signal Detector) (109). Similarly there is a delay between the disappearance of the line signal and the off condition of circuit CF (109), although the turn-off delay is usually a small fraction of the turn-on delay. However, the DTE may be exposed to spurious signals on circuit BB (Received Data) (104) during this turn-off interval.

Procedures on typical links

There are various first-level protocols utilized in the communication links. A communication center may have links with some or all of these line protocols. Details of these first-level protocols are provided in the following paragraphs.

1. Dedicated service: Duplex four-wire.   This is possibly the simplest of all configurations. In some systems the only interchange circuits provided between the DTE and the DCE are circuits AB (Signal Ground) (102), BA (Transmitted DATA) (103), and BB (Received Data) (104). With these three circuits it is possible to communicate; however, there is no information on the status of the associated equipment across the interface nor is there any circuit assurance. Interface types D or E of EIA RS 232C are recommended for this application (refer to Table 7.10). There is no specific idle state for this type of service. In a type D interface, circuit CA (Request to Send) (105) has to be on before circuit CB (Clear to Send) (106) can be turned on. In a type E interface, circuit CA (Request to Send) (105) is not implemented and circuit CB (Clear to Send) (106) will be turned on when the DCE is ready to send data. Note that use of a DTE having a type D interface with a DCE having a type E interface is not recommended. The DCE with a type E interface presents a permanent on condition on circuit CB (Clear to Send) (106), while the DTE with a type D interface cannot turn circuit CA (Request to Send) (105) on during intervals when circuit CB (Clear to Send) (106) is already on. Thus the DTE can never go to a transmit mode of operation.

2. Dedicated service: Multipoint. The dedicated multipoint network is a relatively permanent, nonswitched communication network serving three or more data stations. The use of this arrangement is particularly popular in system applications where a central location must rapidly exchange relatively short messages with a multiplicity of remote stations and where the long connect times encountered on a switched telecommunication network would reduce the system efficiency below an acceptable level.

In general, multipoint networks fall into two general categories, *centralized* and *noncentralized*. In the centralized category, the remote stations communicate only with the central or controlling station, and traffic between remote stations must be relayed by the central station. In noncentralized multipoint operation, remote stations can communicate directly with each other; however, because of contention problems, one of the stations may be given the authority to control the flow of traffic.

Multipoint networks can be configured as one-way only (broadcast), two-way alternate, or two-way simultaneous. Two-way alternate systems are discussed in the following lines.

3. Dedicated service: Multipoint two-way alternate systems. This configuration operates in a half-duplex mode but may be implemented on a duplex or half-duplex communications channel. Duplex implementation permits more rapid turnaround of the link between the central station and the selected remote station and offers an increase in system efficiency.

Centralized operation. The following discussion assumes centralized operation on a duplex communication channel. The central station may leave its line signal turned on at all times because it is the only transmitter on the outbound circuit (type E interface). In cases where the DCE transmits training signals, the use of circuit CA (Request to Send) (105) by the DTE is required. In this case a type D interface is used. Since all the transmitters of the remote stations share the inbound telecommunication channel, the use of circuit CA (Request to Send)

(105) is mandatory to permit removal of the data signal from the tele-communication channel when the remote terminal is not transmitting. The central terminal selects a remote terminal by transmitting the address to which that terminal must respond. The selected terminal transmits a response. There is normally an exchange of additional messages between the two terminals; however, at this point the remote terminal may operate either in half-duplex mode and turn circuit CA (Request to Send) (105) off after each transmission or it may leave circuit CA (Request to Send) (105) on, establishing a duplex telecom-munication channel between two terminals until it is commanded by the central terminal to circuit RTS (105) off and go into standby mode. Note that the central terminal rigidly controls which of the remote terminals may send at any one time.

Noncentralized operation.   Noncentralized operation on multipoint net-works uses a half-duplex telecommunication network. With this ar-rangement, all stations receive everything that is transmitted on the network. This has the advantage that any station on the network can be selected as the control station without requiring modification to the network. This characteristic of the network makes direct transmission between remote stations possible, which is the basic purpose of non-centralized operation. The most serious disadvantage of the half-duplex multipoint network is the exposure to third-party contention. The con-trol terminal selects one of the other terminals and establishes com-munication with that terminal. If during the transmission of data be-tween the two, the sequence of codes transmitted as part of the data coincides with the address of one of the other terminals, that terminal will interpret this as a command to respond and will start to transmit. The result will be garbled traffic and a serious recovery problem. A defense against this is to use a positive response from the selected terminal to effectively "turn-off" all the other terminals so they will no longer respond to their address until the control terminal restores them by commanding the originally selected terminal to end the cur-rent exchange with the control terminal. This is effective unless one of the terminals fails to receive the positive response and consequently does not get "shut off." This defense materially reduces third-party contention but does not completely eliminate it.

4.   Switched network.   Before the data can be transmitted the two mo-dems must be in the data mode and a tone exchange is performed. Refer to "CCITT Recommendations for Modems" in Sec. 3.4 for modem characteristics given in the Bell 103A modem and in CCITT Rec. V.21, a 200-Bd modem standardized for use in the general switched telephone network.

Channel establishment. The sequence for establishing a channel is described below and shown in Fig. 7.7.

1. Operator presses talk button and dials the number of the distant modem. Originator modem is on mark-hold on Received Data circuit (104), and Data Terminal Ready (108/2) is on.

2. At the distant modem the Ring Indicator (125) turns on to inform the called DTE that the modem has received a ringing signal. We assume that the distant modem automatically answers a call.

3. The distant modem receives a Data Terminal Ready (108/2) signal from the called DTE. The distant modem Received Data (104) circuit turns to mark-hold.

4. The distant modem turns on Data Set Ready (107), meaning that modem enters the data mode. The data push button lights at the modem.

5. After a 1.5-s time delay, the distant modem transmits an F2M tone to disable echo suppressors and initialize the telephone company's billing equipment.

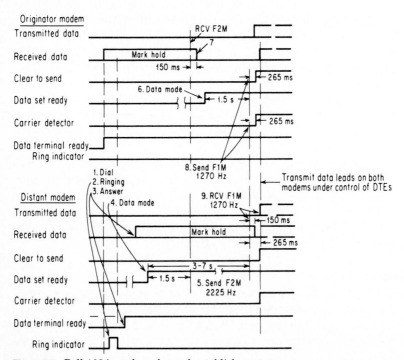

Figure 7.7 Bell 103A modem channel-establishment sequence.

6. At the originating modem, the operator hears the tone and presses the data pushbutton. Data Set Ready (107) turns on and the data push button lights. The original modem is now in data mode.

7. Received Data (104) which was in mark-hold condition at the original modem, goes to a nonhold condition 150 ms after receiving the F2M tone from the distant modem.

8. After Data Set Ready (107) has been on for 1.5 s, the original modem starts an F1M tone. Clear to Send (106) and Carrier Detector (109) are turned on after a 265-ms delay. This places the modem's transmit circuit under the control of the calling DTE. The 265-ms delay assures that the distant modem has adequate time to recognize the F1M tone.

9. At the distant modem, 150 ms after F1M is received, the mark-hold is removed from Received Data (104). After 265 ms, Clear To Send (106) and Carrier Detector (109) are turned on, placing Transmitted Data (103) under the control of the DTE. With Clear to Send (106) signals turned on at both modems, the answering DTE can send a coded GO AHEAD line-protocol character, indicating it is ready to receive data.

Disconnect. At the completion of a call, the operator (if attended operation) or the ACU on a signal from the DTE (if unattended operation) breaks the connection and goes on-hook. Since we have assumed the distant modem is in auto mode, it will automatically break the connection. With attended operation at both modems, the operator can end the data mode but maintain the connection for voice communication by pressing the talk push button. (For ACU see p. 118.)

A disconnect can be a long or a short space. With a long space the modem will disconnect and return to idle after receiving a 1.5-s spacing signal. With a short space, it will disconnect after a 400-ms spacing signal. We will describe a long space as an example of a disconnect, as shown in Fig. 7.8.

1. A long-space disconnect sequence starts when the originator DTE turns off Data Terminal Ready (108/2) for at least 50 ms. Three seconds later, Data Set Ready (107) will be turned off.

2. Transmitted Data goes to a 3-s space.

3. After 1.5 s of the above space, the distant modem releases the line and turns off Data Set Ready (107).

4. Thirty milliseconds after Data Set Ready (107) goes off, Clear to Send (106) and Carrier Detector (109) turn off, disconnecting the distant modem. Received Data (104) goes to a mark-hold.

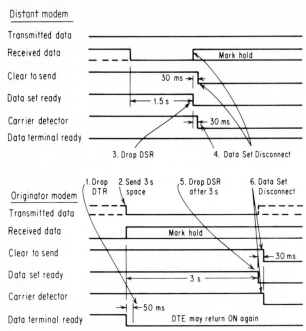

Figure 7.8 Bell 103A modem long-space disconnect sequence.

5. Three seconds after initiation, the originator's Data Set Ready (107) turns off when the line is released.

6. Thirty milliseconds later, Clear to Send (106) and Carrier Detector (109) turn off, disconnecting the originator modem.

Both modems are now in a nondata mode, and the Received Data (104) line is on mark-hold.

Notes

1. CCITT Rec. V.24 defines circuit 108/1 (Connect Data Set to Line) and 108/2 (Data Terminal Ready) on pin 20 of a 25-pin connector. There is no EIA equivalent to circuit 108/1. Signals on this circuit control switching of the signal conversion equipment to and from the line; direction is toward the DCE. This lead is used by European countries.

   In a switched network, after receiving the Ring Indicator (125) signal at the terminal, Data Terminal Ready (108/2) turns on, which prepares the DCE to be connected to the communication channel. However the DTE is normally permitted to present an on condition on the circuit DTR (108/2) whenever DTR is ready to transmit or receive data.

   The function of circuit 108/1 is essentially the same as the Data Terminal Ready (108/2) lead except that no interlocking with the Ring Indicator (125) circuit is involved. Thus assertion of the lead in advance of the call reception is not permitted; it must wait to receive the Ring Indicator (125) signal before asserting Connect Data Set to Line (108/1).

2. The off condition of Data Terminal Ready (108/2) causes the DCE to be removed from the channel after completion of the transmission. It is not automatically terminated

by the modem; the modem has no control to put the transmission over; the program which has the control of the Data Terminal Ready (108/2) decides when to bring it to off. The off condition shall not disable the operation of Ring Indicator (109).

3. When the Data Terminal Ready (108/2) is turned off, it shall not be turned on again until the Data Set Ready (107) circuit is turned off by the DCE.

7.3 Level 2 (Data-Link) Protocols

Generally a master station or central processing site controls the reception and transmission of the remote stations by the addition of nonprintable characters to the data to be transmitted.

A data-link control (DLC), sometimes called *line discipline* or *second-level protocol,* is a set of rules that is followed by interfaced computers or terminals to orderly transfer information. The basic functions of a DLC are:

1. To establish and terminate a connection between two stations

2. To assure the message integrity through error detection, request for retransmission, and positive or negative acknowledgments

3. To identify the sender and the receiver through polling or selection

4. To handle special control functions such as requests for status, station reset, reset acknowledge, start, start acknowledge, and disconnect

One of the key functions of any link-control procedure is to provide for data transparency, which involves either distinguishing data bits from control bits or providing a means for telling where a particular data block begins and ends without restricting the content of the data blocks. Two general methods for achieving data transparency are in widespread use. The first, known as *byte stuffing,* is used in the binary synchronous communications (BSC or BISYNC) protocol. The second is known as *bit stuffing* and is used in high-level data-link control (HDLC). In the byte-stuffing case it is a pair of characters; in the bit-stuffing case it is a series of 8 bits. To achieve data transparency the receiver removes these special bytes or bits, preserving the original data pattern.

Operation of second-level protocol. In most data communications environments, a number of terminals interact with one or more CPUs. For this to happen, the transmitting and receiving devices must be able to tell each other such things as:

▪ This is station A transmitting.

▪ I have a message for station B.

▪ Are you ready to receive?

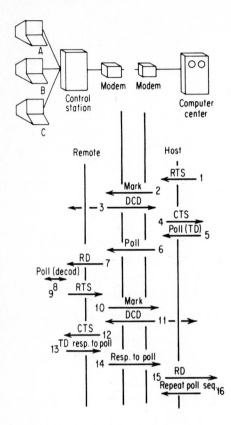

Figure 7.9 Interaction in a computer system.

- I received your last message.
- I am finished; now it is your turn to transmit.
- Do you have anything to send me?
- I cannot listen now, so do not send me anything.
- I do not hear you, so I am hanging up.

Figure 7.9 is a typical example of a system which requires a protocol in order for the computer center to select (or poll) a remote terminal so that it can send data to or receive from that terminal. One terminal (with a special built-in apparatus) may act as a control for the other terminals. The control station then receives all the digital information from its modem, decodes it, and sends it to the proper terminal. In this way, the control station can receive information in large quantities at one time from a number of terminals at once, rather than making the computer wait for data from a single terminal.

Data-link-control operation through a modem is given as an example in a leased-line, multidrop network, when the central site, made up of computer and modem, sends out a short series of characters—a code referred to as a poll—that uniquely identifies one particular remote site consisting of modem and associated terminal. The poll sequence is received by the modem and passed to its terminal. In common use is a polling sequence requiring 16 discrete steps (refer to Fig. 7.9):

1. Host computer (computer center) raises Request to Send (RTS) (105).

2. Mark frequency is transmitted from host modem to remote modem.

3. Remote modem raises Carrier Detector (DCD) (109); also sends an indication to remote terminal.

4. Host modem raises Clear to Send (CTS) (106) with a time delay to host computer.

5. Host computer sends poll to host modem on Transmit Data (TD) (103).

6. Host modem transmits poll on telephone line.

7. Remote modem receives poll and relays it on Receive Data (RD) (104) lead to remote terminal.

8. Remote terminal receives and decodes poll.

9. Remote terminal raises RTS (105) to remote modem.

10. Mark frequency is transmitted on line from remote modem to host modem.

11. Host modem raises DCD (109); also sends an indication to host computer.

12. Remote modem raises CTS (106) to remote terminal.

13. Remote terminal sends response to poll to remote modem on TD (103) lead.

14. Remote modem transmits response to poll on telephone line.

15. Host modem receives response to poll and relays it on RD (104) lead to host computer.

16. Host computer receives response to poll. Then host computer repeats polling sequence.

Remote terminal logic decodes and recognizes the preset poll code. If data follow the correct poll code, they are accepted by the remote terminal. If the terminal has data to transmit, these data are passed to the remote modem for transmission to the central polling site. If no information is ready, the remote terminal sends a negative acknowledgement and the central site polls the next remote terminal on its polling list. Exact operation of a polling system is determined by its software and hardware. Therefore, many operating variations are possible in a specific leased-line multidrop network.

There are many ways to configure a data communication system and nearly as many types of protocols. Basically, however, protocols may be divided into byte-controlled protocols (BCP) and bit-oriented protocols (BOP).

Some BOP examples are the SDLC (synchronous data-link control) of IBM, the ADCCP (advanced data communication control procedures) of ANSI, the HDLC (high-level data-link control) of ISO, and the BDLC (Burroughs data-link control).

Some BCPs include the DDCMP (digital data communications message protocol) and the BISYNC (binary synchronous communications) of IBM. Refer to Table 7.11.

Bit-oriented protocols (BOP)

In general bit-oriented protocols are less dependent on control characters and rely instead on the position of bits within specific fields or blocks of bits. There is one standard field format of fixed bit length. Perhaps the most widely known bit-oriented protocol is IBM's *synchronous data-link control* (SDLC). In SDLC, information is sent by frames. With each frame are fields which have specific functions (refer to Fig. 7.10).

The *flag field* is a unique combination of bits (01111110) which lets the receiving device know that a field in SDLC format is about to follow.

The *address field* defines the sender and the receiver; for polling a specific station, a predefined character in the information will be used.

The *control field* consists of 8 bits and determines the nature of the accompanying message of that field. The control field is used by the

TABLE 7.11 Types of Level 2 Protocols

	Reference
Bit-oriented:	
ANSI's ADCCP	BSR X.3.66
ISO's HDLC	3309, 4335
CCITT's LAP/LAPB	Rec. X.25
IBM's SDLC	
Byte-controlled:	
ANSI	X.3.28—ASCII
ISO	1745—ASCII
IBM's BISYNC	
DDCMP	

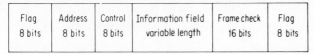

Flag 8 bits	Address 8 bits	Control 8 bits	Information field variable length	Frame check 16 bits	Flag 8 bits

Figure 7.10   BOP(SDLC) frame format.

primary station (which maintains control of the data link at all times) to tell the addressed station what it is to do—to poll devices, transfer data, or retransmit faulty data among other things. The addressed station can use the control field to respond to the primary station—to tell which frames it has received or which it has sent. The control field is also used by both the primary and secondary stations to keep track of the sequence number of the frames transmitted and received at any one time. SDLC frames which contain information fields have sequence numbers. Frames which only serve to control the line are typically unnumbered.

The *information field* may be at any length and may be composed of any code structure (EBCDIC or ASCII, for example) and carries the message text. It may carry supervisory messages (request for retransmission, etc.) and frame check computations.

The *frame check sequence* is 16 bits long and contains a cyclical redundancy check (CRC). All the data transmitted between the start and stop flags (including address control flags) are checked by the frame check sequence.

The flag field marks the end of a standard frame and has the same bit configuration of the opening flag. Flag fields at the beginning and at the end of the format accomplish synchronization.

Byte-control protocols (BCP)

Byte-control protocol messages are transmitted in units called *blocks*. The sample protocol that we will use to show how a data link is operated will be IBM's binary synchronous communications (BSC or BISYNC) protocol. To go into a detailed explanation of all the line protocols in existence is beyond the scope of this book.

In BCP, the special characters or character sequences that control link operation consist of three different types: communication characters, peripheral control characters, and graphic characters.

Communication characters provide synchronization to determine where the start of a particular field is within a block. They include:

SOH	Start of header	ENQ	Inquiry
STX	Start of text	ACK	Acknowledge message
ETX	End of text	NAK	Not acknowledge message—Disavow
EOT	End of transmission		

EOH End of header

ITB Intermediate transmission block

ETB End of transmission block

DLE Data-link escape (for transparent text)

Peripheral control characters control the operation of peripheral devices. They include:

CR Carrier or carriage return

LF Line feed or index

BS Backspace

Graphic characters are generally the information characters that can be seen on a cathode-ray tube (CRT) screen:

Alpha characters (uppercase and lowercase)

Numeric characters

Special characters and symbols

The transparent text mode requires that we distinguish between the three types of characters. In BISYNC, the transparent mode is entered with the DLE-STX character and ends with the DLE-ETX character. The block format for BCP-BSC is given in Fig. 7.11.

During idle time, the line will appear as follows:

$$\text{FF   FF   FF   FF   FF   FF   FF}$$

A series of hexadecimal Fs is all 1s in binary; BISYNC protocol may require the insertion of SYN characters at distinct time intervals. Two SYN characters are inserted to assure proper synchronization at the beginning of the format. Each SYN character consists of 8 bits.

SOH is a communication control character of 8 bits, used at the beginning of a sequence of characters that constitute a machine-sensible address or routine information. Such a sequence is referred to as the *header*. The header is the control information prefixed in a message text, e.g., source or destination code (address), priority or message type, acknowledgment. Also called *heading* or *leader*.

STX is a communication control character which precedes a sequence of characters that is to be treated as an entity and entirely transmitted through to the ultimate destination. Such a sequence is referred to as

Error checking

S Y N	S Y N	S O H	Header	S T X	Text	ETX, ETB, ITB	B C C L R C – 8 C R C – 16 8/16 bits

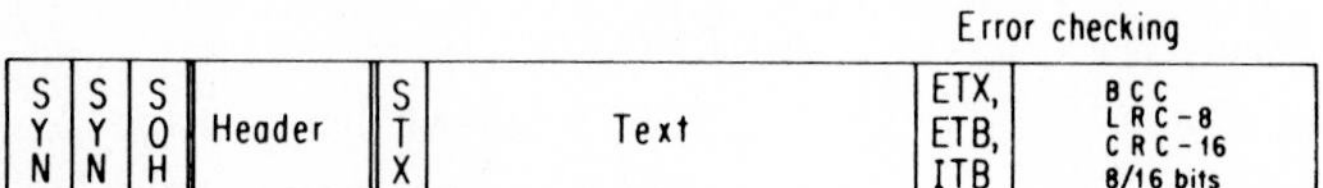

Figure 7.11 BCP-BSC block format.

text. STX may be used to terminate a sequence of characters started by SOH.

TEXT is the message to be conveyed; it is in variable length and may have transparent data. The text portion of the message block is identified by a preceding STX character.

ETX indicates the end of message which precedes the error-checking field.

The error-checking field (or trailer) consists of BCC (block check characters) which perform verification of block transmission and is normally appended at the end of the block. Block checking in BISYNC may be in the LRC (longitudinal redundancy check) or CRC (cyclic redundancy check) technique, which are discussed in Sec. 7.6.

Long messages are broken into a series of blocks for transmission. Each block of text, except the last, is followed by an ETB (end of transmission block) character or an ITB (end of intermediate transmission block) character. ETB requires a response from the receiver and causes line turnaround and the BCC to be sent and compared. ITB divides the message for error-checking purposes and does not require a response from the receiver. The last intermediate block is followed by an ETX or ETB character. As each intermediate block arrives, its BCC is compared with the receiver's BCC. If an error is detected in any intermediate block, no action can be taken until ETB is received; then all intermediate blocks must be retransmitted.

Comparison between BCP and BOP

BCP is generally characterized by HDX behavior. After a BCP format is sent, it must be acknowledged by the receiver. This reduces the communication speed. Furthermore there are many control characters for line configuration, peripheral equipment control, and other graphics in the BCP. Transparency is achieved only through use of escape mechanisms.

There are two or three control characters in the BOP; for example, peripheral equipment control is functioned between the host computer and remote terminals; it is not a part of the protocol function. There is one standard format for information, supervisory and nonsequenced frame types. Transparency is provided through 0 insertion and deletion. Furthermore, in BOP, the receiver does not have to acknowledge reception of each frame. The receiver receives the entire message and acknowledges when it is ready to transmit.

BOP may be used in FDX or HDX operation; BISYNC operates in HDX only, although DDMCP can be used in the FDX or HDX mode.

There are no restrictions on the data codes used in the BOP. Also error checking and correction is available on a complete frame in the BOP.

The disadvantages of BOP are that the header of a BOP is relatively short and a buffer of appropriate size must be made ready by the operating system on relatively short notice. It may become necessary to limit the message length to a maximum number of characters. In addition, the transmitting station cannot transmit an idle in the middle of a message because it will cause an incorrect count and produce a bad CRC check. One of the advantages of BISYNC is that it can transmit idle characters, which is impossible by using other protocols.

BOPs have several advantages over BCPs, including reduction of overhead, higher integrity of transmission, and simpler hardware, since they only handle one bit at a time rather than a full character as in BSC.

Satellite communications also present problems for BCPs. The inherent long delays in this type of communications cause major bottlenecks for half-duplex BCPs. The full-duplex nature of BOPs and their allowance for multiple transmission frames awaiting for acknowledgment make these more modern protocols better suited here.

BOPs have made feasible the expansion of packet-switched networks, also.

7.4 Level 3 (Network Control) and Higher-Level (End-to-End) Protocols

Level 3 protocol is the communications-control level that defines format and control procedures for the transfer of user data through a communications network. This level performs many of the same functions as the lower levels, such as addressing and flow control, but the scope of concern is broader. For example, level 2 link control procedures are used for reliable transmission of information across a data link, while level 3 procedures are used on the same link to multiplex several streams of data across the link, with individual addressing and selective flow control. In general, while levels 1 and 2 are implemented through hardware, level 3 protocols are software functions. Protocol levels are depicted in Fig. 12.2.

The major reason for the development of level 3 protocols was the introduction of public data networks, especially packet-switching networks. CCITT Rec. X.25 covers necessary level 3 protocols and also deals with levels 1 and 2 as they pertain to packet-switching networks. It proposes an interface for host computers and data terminals intelligent enough to format data in accordance with the interface specifications, as well as to respond to the interface's complex control signaling requirements. The interface is designed for multichannel use; that is, it provides communication with a multiple independent process within a single terminal (or computer). CCITT Rec. X.25 is explained at the end of this section.

Detailed information on packet-switching networks is given in Sec. 4.6.

Higher-level protocols

User-level logical protocols (those above level 3) deal with data exchange on a totally end-to-end basis from operating system to operating system or from application program to application program.

Levels 3 and 4 are strictly transportation-oriented levels, while 5, 6, and 7 are referred to as the *higher-level protocols*. Messages traveling across an interface are wrapped in a control envelope (for example, a header and trailer) and become information for the next preceding level. The lower levels handle these data in a transparent manner; the highest level represents all the possible service applications that are offered by the lower levels.

Level 4 handles message reconstruction from data blocks (loss, duplication, and misdelivery sequencing) and data-block/virtual-message channel association. This may be the busiest of all architectural levels in a local-area network (LAN). Its protocol establishes network connections for a given transmission; for example, whether several parallel paths will be required for high throughput, whether several paths can be multiplexed onto a single connection, or whether the transmission should be broadcast.

Level 5, called the *session level,* is primarily used to initialize, run, and terminate sessions. It controls logging on and off, user identification, and billing.

Level 6 is called the *presentation level.* Interpretation of data exchanged, control of data structure, display of data, character codes, and formats are all handled here. The 8-bit ASCII code for CRT terminals is an example of a standard at this level.

Level 7 is the *application level,* which is used for deadlock recovery, file access, industry standards, and protocols. Operational procedures are flexible. They depend on the organization and the functions performed, for example, remote batch-processing control, file-transfer protocol, and civilian-aviation protocol.

CCITT recommendations for protocols

CCITT Rec. X.3. This recommendation describes the basic functions and user-selectable functions of the PAD. PAD stands for *packet assembly-disassembly facility* and applies to exchange of serial data streams with the character-mode terminal, and packetizes-depacketizes the corresponding data exchanged with the X.25 terminal. In addition, the characteristics of PAD parameters are given, along with their possible values. Among the basic functions of the PAD are:

- Assembly of characters into packets destined for the X.25 DTE
- Disassembly of the user data field of packets destined for the start-stop mode DTE
- Handling of virtual call setup and clearing, resetting, and interrupt procedures
- Generation of service signals
- A mechanism for forwarding packets when the proper conditions exist, such as when a packet is full or an idle time expires
- A mechanism for transmitting data characters, including start, stop, and parity elements as appropriate to the start-stop DTE
- A mechanism for handling a "break" signal from the start-stop DTE

User-selectable functions include management of the packet assembly and disassembly and a limited number of additional functions related to the operational characteristics of the start-stop DTE.

CCITT Rec. X.20. Recommendation X.20 applies to the DTE/DCE interface for start-stop operation on public data networks. It covers switched data circuits and leased channel services employing either point-to-point or multipoint connections. X.20 employs a character-oriented protocol, using International Alphabet No. 5 per CCITT Rec. V.3, which is essentially the same as ASCII.

CCITT Rec. X.21. This recommendation applies to the DTE/DCE interface for synchronous operation on public data networks. It defines functions at all three lower levels of the networks. At level 1, it specifies all the functional circuits designed by X.24 with the exception of common return. It is character-oriented and follows the basic four phases of operation in level 2 protocols: idle, call establishment, data transmission, and disconnection. In level 3, it specifies "call establishment procedures of switched service operations between networks."

Recommendation X.21*bis* describes how a public data network should interface with existing DTEs using synchronous V-series modems on leased and switched circuits.

The electrical characteristics of the interchange circuits at the DCE side of the interface comply with Rec. V.28 by using a 25-pin connector and pin allocation standardized by ISO IS-2110. The electrical characteristics of the interchange circuits at the DTE side of the interface may be applied according to V.28 or X.26(V.10), specified in the ISO IS-4902 (standard for the assignment of the 37-pin interface connector).

For applications of the data signaling rate of 48 kb/s, indications concerning the connector and electrical characteristics at both the DTE side and the DCE side of the interface are given in ISO IS-2593 (standard for the assignment of the 34-pin interface connector) and in V.35, respectively.

CCITT Rec. X.24.   Recommendation X.24 gives the list of definitions for DTE/DCE interface circuits on public data networks.

CCITT Rec. X.25.   This recommendation applies to the DTE/DCE interface for terminals operating in the "packet mode on public data networks." Refer to Sec. 4.6 for an operational description of packet-switched networks.

Two types of operations are specified. The first is *virtual call service,* which establishes a logical end-to-end path through the packet network. This connection is held for the duration of the communication and then released. The other type is *permanent virtual circuit service,* which effectively provides a continuous connection between two users through the network. In this case, there are no call establishment and clearing procedures. In essence, the two services simulate dialed circuit-switched connections and leased circuits, respectively.

For level 1, Rec. X.25 specifies level 1 of X.21, with the provision for accepting X.21*bis* as an interim measure.

For level 2, a link-access procedure (LAP) is defined, using the principles of high-level data-link control. Level 2 provides the function of error and flow control for the access link between the DTE and the network. Each frame has a check sequence to detect errors, and error frames are retransmitted when requested by the receiving end. Flow control is accomplished through the sending of receiver ready and receiver not ready commands.

Level 3 of X.25 defines the packet formats and control procedures for exchange information between a DTE and the network. The establishment of a virtual circuit is initiated from a calling DTE by a call request packet. The called DTE is notified that a circuit is being established by an incoming call packet. In turn, the called DTE answers by returning a call accepted packet. Subsequently, the calling DTE is notified that the circuit is established by a call connected packet. Data packets are then exchanged between DTEs. On the completion of the call, the circuit can be disconnected by either a DTE clear request packet or a DCE clear indication packet, whichever is appropriate, followed by a clear confirmation packet response.

Recommendation X.25 provides for the capability of multiplexing up to 4096 logical channels, or virtual circuits, on a single access link. Each channel can be used for virtual calls or a permanent virtual circuit. Each packet exchanged across the interface has its associated logical channel number identified, and each logical channel operates independently of the others. The data packets are also identified by sequence numbers, which are used for flow control within individual logical channels. The sequence numbering scheme may be based upon either modulo 8 for normal operation or modulo 128 for extended transmission delay conditions. Data packets are limited to a maximum data field length. All networks must allow a maximum of 128 octets, but some networks may also support maximum lengths of 16, 32, 64, 256, 512, and 1024 octets.

CCITT Recs. X.26 and X.27.   These recommendations are given in Sec. 7.1.

CCITT Rec. X.28.   Recommendation X.28 defines the interface for the start-stop mode terminals accessing the PAD on a public data network. It specifies procedures for establishing an access information path between a start-stop DTE and PAD and for character interchange and service initialization between them, as well as for the exchange of control information. It also summarizes PAD commands and service signals.

CCITT Rec. X.29.   This recommendation specifies the procedures for the exchange of control information and user data between an X.25 DTE and a PAD.

CCITT Rec. X.75.   This recommendation outlines protocols for interconnecting national public networks as well as private networks.

International user classes of data services.   The establishment of data networks in various countries created a need to standardize the signaling rates, the terminal operating modes, and the address selection and call progress signals. The user classes of service are given in Table 7.12. They are divided into three types:

1. Terminals operating in the start-stop mode (as typified by printers used for message transfer)

2. Terminals operating in a synchronous mode

TABLE 7.12   User Classes of Service for Public Data Networks

User class of service	Data signaling rate and code structure	Address selection and call progress signals
	1. Terminal operating mode—start-stop	
1	300 b/s, 11 units/character	300 b/s, International Alphabet No. 5
2	50–200 b/s, 7.5–11 units/character	200 b/s, International Alphabet No. 5
	2. Terminal operating mode—synchronous	
3	600 b/s	600 b/s, International Alphabet No. 5
4	2,400 b/s	2,400 b/s, International Alphabet No. 5
5	4,800 b/s	4,800 b/s, International Alphabet No. 5
6	9,600 b/s	9,600 b/s, International Alphabet No. 5
7	48,000 b/s	48,000 b/s, International Alphabet No. 5
	3. Terminal operating mode—packet	
8	2,400 b/s	2,400 b/s
9	4,800 b/s	4,800 b/s See Rec. X.25
10	9,600 b/s	9,600 b/s for user packet format
11	48,000 b/s	48,000 b/s

SOURCE: CCITT Rec. X.1.

3. Terminals operating in the packet mode

For more information, refer to CCITT Rec. X.1.

7.5 Information Codes

To allow communications between the various computers and terminals composing a data link, a uniform method of exchanging information is needed. This requires the establishment of a character code structure for operation of bits as characters, a message syntax to form characters into messages, and data communications control procedures for exchange of the messages.

A number of different coding schemes are used to represent characters in data communications systems. The codes differ primarily in the number of bits used to represent characters and the particular pattern of bits corresponding to the characters. Characters are divided into *graphic characters,* representing symbols, *control characters,* which are used to control a terminal, and *communication characters* to control computer functions. BCP characters are given in Sec. 7.3. Among the many codes used in communications today is the 7-bit-plus-parity ASCII (American standard code for information interchange) code.

TABLE 7.13   American National Standard Code for Information Interchange

Bits $b_7b_6b_5$		000	001	010	011	100	101	110	111
Bits $b_4b_3b_2b_1$	Col. Row	0	1	2	3	4	5	6	7
0000	0	NUL	DLE	SP	0	@	P	`	p
0001	1	SOH	DC1	!	1	A	Q	a	q
0010	2	STX	DC2	"	2	B	R	b	r
0011	3	ETX	DC3	#	3	C	S	c	s
0100	4	EOT	DC4	$	4	D	T	d	t
0101	5	ENQ	NAK	%	5	E	U	e	u
0110	6	ACK	SYN	&	6	F	V	f	v
0111	7	BEL	ETB	'	7	G	W	g	w
1000	8	BS	CAN	(	8	H	X	h	x
1001	9	HT	EM	)	9	I	Y	i	y
1010	10	LF	SUB	*	:	J	Z	j	z
1011	11	VT	ESC	+	;	K	[	k	{
1100	12	FF	FS	,	<	L	\	l		
1101	13	CR	GS	—	=	M	]	m	}
1110	14	SO	RS	.	>	N	∧	n	~
1111	15	SI	US	/	?	O	—	o	DEL

ASCII was introduced by the USA Standards Institute and has been accepted as the U.S. federal standard. Special characters are set aside for the purpose of communications control (see Table 7.13).

The international counterpart of ASCII is given as *International Alphabet No. 5* in Table 1 (basic code) and Table 2 (international reference version) of CCITT Rec. V.3, which has been established jointly by the CCITT and the International Organization for Standardization (ISO). The international reference version of Alphabet No. 5 is similar to ASCII. The only difference is that the currency sign at position col. 2, row 4 in ASCII is replaced by $ letter. ASCII (or Alphabet No. 5) contains a set of 128 characters (control characters and graphic characters such as letters, digits, and symbols) with their coded representation. Most of the characters of Alphabet No. 5 are unchangeable and mandatory, but provision is made for some flexibility to accommodate special national and other requirements.

Special characters are set aside for the purpose of communications control. These control functions include synchronization, message handling, and control. Within any one character the bits are identified by $b_7, b_6, \ldots, b_1$, where b_7 is the highest order or *most significant bit* and b_1 is the lowest order or *least significant bit*.

Any one position in the table may be identified either by its bit pattern or by its column and row numbers.

Example   The bit representation for character F, positioned in col. 4, row 6, is:

	Column 4			Row 6			
	b_7	b_6	b_5	b_4	b_3	b_2	b_1
Binary	1	0	0	0	1	1	0
Decimal equiv.	4	2	1	8	4	2	1

The code table for character F may also be represented by the notation col. 4, row 6, or as 4/6. The decimal equivalent of the binary number formed by bits b_7, b_6, and b_5 (4,2,1) collectively forms the column number, and the decimal equivalent of the binary number formed by bits b_4, b_3, b_2, and b_1 (8,4,2,1) collectively forms the row number.

A variation of the ASCII code is the *data interchange code*. Primarily this code differs from ASCII in that some printing characters are replaced by nonprinting control characters and the parity is specified to be odd. This code is now readily adaptable to computer-to-computer communications.

Of the other existing codes, the more widely used ones are the *extended binary-coded decimal interchange code* (EBCDIC), the *5-bit Baudot code* (CCITT version Alphabet No. 2) found in old teleprinter equipment, the *four-of-eight code,* the IBM punched-card *Hollerith code,* the *binary-coded decimal* (BCD) *code,* and the *6-bit transcode.*

EBCDIC is an eight-level code similar to ASCII. EBCDIC uses the eighth level for an information bit which extends the range of characters to 256. ASCII uses its eighth level for a parity bit (odd for synchronous transmission, even for asynchronous transmission). Refer to Table 7.14 for the EBCDIC code.

Example   The binary and hexadecimal representation for character F, positioned in col. 6, row C, is

	B_7	B_6	B_5	B_4	B_3	B_2	B_1	B_0
Binary	1	1	0	0	0	1	1	0
Hexadecimal		C				6		

TABLE 7.14 EBCDIC Chart

High bits $B_7 B_6 B_5 B_4$ = Row, Low bits $B_3 B_2 B_1 B_0$ = Col

Row \ Col	0 (0000)	1 (0001)	2 (0010)	3 (0011)	4 (0100)	5 (0101)	6 (0110)	7 (0111)	8 (1000)	9 (1001)	A (1010)	B (1011)	C (1100)	D (1101)	E (1110)	F (1111)
0 (0000)	NUL	SOH	STX	ETX	PF	HT	LC	DEL		RLF	SMM	VT	FF	CR	SC	SI
1 (0001)	DLE	DC1	DC2	DC3	RES	NL	BS	IL	CAN	EM	CC		ITS	IGS	IRS	IUS
2 (0010)	DS	SOS	FS		BYP	LF	EOB/ETB	ESC/PRE						ENR	ACK	BEL
3 (0011)			SYN		PN	RS	UC	EOT			3M		DC4	NAK		SUB
4 (0100)	SP										¢	●	<	(	+	|
5 (0101)	&										!	$	*	)	;	¬
6 (0110)	−	/									¦	,	%	_	>	?
7 (0111)										`	:	#	@	'	=	"
8 (1000)		a	b	c	d	e	f	g	h	i						
9 (1001)		j	k	l	m	n	o	p	q	r						
A (1010)		~	s	t	u	v	w	x	y	z		[				
B (1011)												]				
C (1100)	{	A	B	C	D	E	F	G	H	I						
D (1101)	}	J	K	L	M	N	O	P	Q	R						
E (1110)	\		S	T	U	V	W	X	Y	Z						
F (1111)	0	1	2	3	4	5	6	7	8	9						

246

The letter f is represented by the binary number 10000110. The hexadecimal equivalent is col. 6, row 8, or 6/8. On the other hand, the hexadecimal form of line idle which consists of 1s, is FF, and its binary representation is 11111111. Note that since the EBCDIC is based upon base 16, binary representation of numbers 0 through 15 is as follows:

0	0000	4	0100	8	1000	C	1100
1	0001	5	0101	9	1001	D	1101
2	0010	6	0110	A	1010	E	1110
3	0011	7	0111	B	1011	F	1111

Binary representation of line idle is

$$\underbrace{1\ \ 1\ \ 1\ \ 1}_{F}\ \ \underbrace{1\ \ 1\ \ 1\ \ 1}_{F}$$

7.6   Error Detection and Correction Techniques

Because of noise on communications mediums, there will be errors in received data. It is practically impossible to prevent the errors occurring, but it is possible to detect them and somehow to correct them. There are two ways to control errors:

1. Detect the error and have the erroneous message retransmitted.

2. Use a technique for correcting the error without retransmission.

In many systems errors are simply ignored (i.e., in 50-Bd Telex transmission). In some systems, received messages are retransmitted to the transmitter and compared with the transmitted text.

In several communication systems, messages are retransmitted upon a verbal request or each message is transmitted twice. This kind of communication is used on short-distance circuits without heavy traffic or on in-plant operations of an institution. The most common is the ARQ (automatic request for repeat) method. In this technique, retransmission of the message is automatically requested upon detection of an error by the receiver.

Error detection

For error detection, bits are added in the frames or in the formats; in other words, redundancy is built into the messages. The most commonly used error-detection techniques are *parity checks* and *redundancy checks*.

Parity checks. With parity checking, the transmitter counts the number of 1s in each character. With odd parity, if the number of 1s in the character is even, then the parity bit is made of 1 to make that number odd. With even parity, if the number of 1s in the character is odd, then the parity bit is made a 1 to make that number even. The receiving device counts the 1s. If an even number of bits shows up in a character when the system is set for odd parity, then an error is counted.

In the following examples, ASCII D and T codes are shown with 7-bit even parity:

	8	7	6	5	4	3	2	1
D	0 parity bit	1	0	0	0	1	0	0
T	1	1	0	1	0	1	0	0

Note that parity only counts for one error; if there are two errors, a parity bit may still show even, even though a second bit has slipped.

Redundancy checks. In this technique, a block check character (BCC) is used for error checking in the block. It may be in the LRC (longitudinal redundancy check), VRC (vertical redundancy check), or CRC (cyclical redundancy check) method.

When a parity bit is added to each group of bits forming a character, it is called *vertical parity*. This comes from the relative position of the bits if they are observed on a paper tape held lengthwise. b_1, b_2, ... , b_7 bits and the P parity bit in Table 7.15 are the verticals.

Horizontal (or *longitudinal*) *parity* results in an extra bit being placed at the end of a block of bits along the length of the tape. b_1 bits and the P_1 parity bit in Table 7.15 are the horizontals.

LRC performs as follows: Data bits are grouped into a block containing a specific number of characters. A count of 1 parity bits added in the characters of the format forms an LRC character for this format and is called BCC. Each transmitting and receiving terminal generates a separate count for the format. The LRC character generated in the transmitter is sent to the receiver (refer to Fig. 7.12) and is compared to the LRC character generated in the receiver. If they are equal, an ACK character is sent back to the transmitter; if they are not equal, a NAK character is sent back to the transmitter.

The CRC technique is similar to LRC. Instead of generating a check character by adding the bits in each character of a block, it divides all

TABLE 7.15   Redundancy Checks

	Longitudinal redundancy parity $\longrightarrow$																
b_1	b_1	b_1	b_1	b_1	b_1	b_1	b_1	b_1	b_1	b_1	b_1	b_1	b_1	b_1	b_1	b_1	P_1
b_2	b_2	b_2	b_2	b_2	b_2	b_2	b_2	b_2	b_2	b_2	b_2	b_2	b_2	b_2	b_2	b_2	P_2
b_3	b_3	b_3	b_3	b_3	b_3	b_3	b_3	b_3	b_3	b_3	b_3	b_3	b_3	b_3	b_3	b_3	P_3
b_4	b_4	b_4	b_4	b_4	b_4	b_4	b_4	b_4	b_4	b_4	b_4	b_4	b_4	b_4	b_4	b_4	P_4
b_5	b_5	b_5	b_5	b_5	b_5	b_5	b_5	b_5	b_5	b_5	b_5	b_5	b_5	b_5	b_5	b_5	P_5
b_6	b_6	b_6	b_6	b_6	b_6	b_6	b_6	b_6	b_6	b_6	b_6	b_6	b_6	b_6	b_6	b_6	P_6
b_7	b_7	b_7	b_7	b_7	b_7	b_7	b_7	b_7	b_7	b_7	b_7	b_7	b_7	b_7	b_7	b_7	P_7
P	P	P	P	P	P	P	P	P	P	P	P	P	P	P	P	P	P

(Left margin label: Vertical redundancy parity, with downward arrow)

the serial bits in a block by a predetermined binary number. The remainder of this division is the check character. In a similar way a check character is generated at the receiver. The check character is added in the block and transmitted; it is compared with the check character of the receiver at the receiver. An example of encoding and generation of a check character is given in the paragraph following "CCITT Recommendations for Error Detection."

A 16-bit CRC is used in synchronous protocols. LRC is used with end-to-end protocol. Since end-to-end asynchronous error protection requires an intelligent terminal or terminal control unit, the cost may be excessive in some cases. In most cases, LRC and VRC are used together.

Echoplex or *echo-back* is another error-correction method that is often used; a character received at the receiving end is sent back (echoed) to the originating terminal; the operator reenters erroneous characters. This method of error protection has shortcomings:

- Users must verify data entry.

- Echoed characters are unprotected.

- Data from a computer to the user are not verified, unless the receiving user knows what the output should be or suspects the received results.

CCITT recommendations for error detection.   Recommendations on error detection are given in CCITT Recs. V.40 (for electromechanical equipment) and V.41 (code-independent error control system).

CCITT V.41 recommends provision of simultaneous forward and

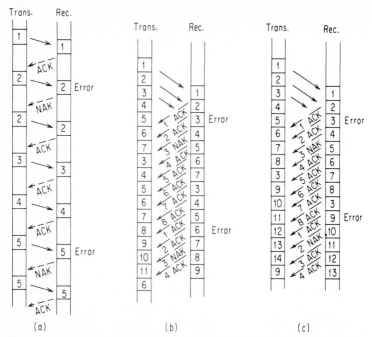

Figure 7.12 Types of ARQ operations. (*a*) Stop-and-wait ARQ (HDX). (*b*) Continuous ARQ with pullback (FDX). Continuous ARQ uses 3-bit binary (8-modulo) count. (*c*) Selective repeat ARQ (FDX). (*James Martin*, Communications Satellite Systems, *Prentice-Hall, Englewood Cliffs, N.J., 1978, p. 265, fig. 17-5. Reprinted by permission of Prentice-Hall Inc.*)

backward channels in the modem for error-correction transmission. The system uses synchronous transmission on the forward channel and asynchronous transmission on the backward channel. The system employs block transmission of information in fixed units of 240, 480, 960, or 3840 bits; a 3840-bit block length is suitable for circuit operation via satellite. If error correction is achieved by ARQ, storage for data blocks must be provided at the transmitter.

The forward bit stream is divided into blocks, each consisting of 4 service bits, the information bits, and 16 error-detection (or check) bits. Thus each block transmitted to the line contains 260, 500, 980, or 3860 bits. Check bits are generated in a cyclic encoder. This technique is also called CRC-CCITT (cyclic redundancy check). Refer to CCITT *Yellow Book* Recs. Q.277 and 703 for error controls.

Encoding of the block and generation of the check character. The service bits and information bits correspond to the coefficients of a message polynomial having terms from x^{n-1} down to x^{16}; n is the total number of bits in a block. For example, in a 3860-bit block, x^{n-1} corresponds to the 3860th bit. It is termed as x^{3859}; if this bit is zero, the coefficient of the term is zero and it does not appear at the polynomial.

This 3844-bit block is converted to 16 bits, and the corresponding 16-term polynomial is divided by the polynomial $x^{16} + x^{12} + x^5 + 1$, per CCITT Rec. V.41 (or $x^{16} + x^{15} + x^2 + 1$ per ANSI X3.28.1976). The coefficients of the terms x^{15}, x^{14}, ..., x^0 in the remainder polynomial are the check bits. This 16-bit check character is added to the 3844 service and information bit stream to complete the 3860-bit block.

Example Define the check character per CCITT recommendation when the service and information bit stream in a countdown to 16 bits is in the following bit pattern:

$$1111 \quad 1010 \quad 0110 \quad 0001$$

solution

$$
\begin{array}{cccc}
x^{15}x^{14}x^{13}x^{12} & x^{11}x^{10}x^9x^8 & x^7x^6x^5x^4 & x^3x^2x^1x^0 \\
1\ 1\ 1\ 1 & 1\ 0\ 1\ 0 & 0\ 1\ 1\ 0 & 0\ 0\ 0\ 1
\end{array}
$$

The 16-bit polynomial is

$$P(x) = x^{15} + x^{14} + x^{13} + x^{12} + x^{11} + x^9 + x^6 + x^5 + 1$$

$$G(x) = x^{16} + x^{12} + x^5 + 1 \qquad \text{Generated polynomial}$$

$$\frac{P(x) \cdot x^{16}}{G(x)} = Q(x) + R(x)$$

where $Q(x) =$ quotient polynomial
$R(x) =$ remainder polynomial

After a simple mathematical operation, we obtain

$$\frac{P(x) \cdot x^{16}}{G(x)} = \frac{x^{31} + x^{30} + x^{29} + x^{28} + x^{27} + x^{25} + x^{22} + x^{21} + x^{16}}{x^{16} + x^{12} + x^5 + 1}$$

$$Q(x) = x^{15} + x^{14} + x^{13} + x^{12} + x^{10} + x^8 + x^5 + x^3 + x^2 + 1$$

$$R(x) = x^{15} + x^7 + x^3 + x^2 + 1$$

Then the check-bit pattern is

$$1000 \quad 0000 \quad 1000 \quad 1101$$

This bit pattern is reversed to facilitate the calculation. The proper order of the check character is

$$1011 \quad 0001 \quad 0000 \quad 0001$$

The check character in EBCDIC is (B/1), (0/1).

Notes:

The verification of the polynomial division is an easy mathematical exercise if the reader considers the following hints:

1. The dividend is a 31st-degree polynomial.
   The divisor is a 16th-degree polynomial.
   Then the quotient is a 15th-degree polynomial.
2. In mathematics, $x^m \cdot x^n = x^{m+n}$.
3. In modulo arithmetics in this case, $x^m + x^m = 0$ $(1 + 1 = 0)$.
4. Term signs are always positive on either side of the equal sign, although in mathematics the $+$ sign changes to the $-$ sign when the term moves to the other side of the equal sign.

Error correction

Once errors are detected, retransmission of the erroneous message is automatically requested by the receiver. Only one character or several characters or many messages may be retransmitted depending upon the system design.

Retransmission of a small quantity of bits saves time and does not require large storage. But this is not efficient; furthermore, redundant bits in a short interval reduce the communication speed.

ARQ technique. When the receiver detects an error, the block is automatically retransmitted upon the request of repeat from the receiver. This necessitates a storage at the transmitter.

There are two types of ARQ systems:

1. Stop-and-wait ARQ

2. Continuous ARQ

In stop-and-wait ARQ, the transmitter stops after sending a block and waits to receive a positive (ACK) or negative (NAK, if the block contains error) acknowledgment. If ACK is received the transmitter sends the next block and stops for acknowledgment; if NAK is received, it retransmits the previous block and stops for the acknowledgment of this block. Data transmission codes, such as ASCII or EBCDIC, contain ACK and NAK characters.

In continuous ARQ, the transmit terminal sends blocks continuously while examining the stream of acknowledgments. ACK or NAK specifies the sequence number of the last good block received. With a 3-bit binary number (modulo or base 8) seven blocks are counted. The numbering system on high propagation delay links (such as satellites) may permit up to a 255 (8-bit binary) acknowledgment count. On receiving NAK, the transmitter will then retransmit all blocks after the block specified in the NAK; this procedure is called *pullback*.

Note

A problem arises when the ARQ storage space is not large enough and a frame is knocked out because of an overflow before the ACK or NAK is returned.

Error-correcting codes. Error-correcting codes try to correct errors in the block by using redundant bits. This does not require a return path that the ARQ technique uses; it is often called the *forward-error-correction* (FEC) technique. Codes may be designed to correct up to a given number of random errors or a burst of errors which does not exceed a certain span. Forward error correctors add sufficient redundancy to the message to allow both detection and correction of errors at the receiver. The FEC technique needs as many redundancy bits as data bits to achieve acceptable levels of error correction. Although this reduces the transmission speed, it improves the error rate by a factor of 10^2 to 10^3. On channels with a low S/N ratio, which causes a large number of errors, the FEC technique may upgrade the line efficiency. This error-correcting technique is also valuable on one-way transmission, such as TV and data broadcasting operations.

When the error rate is high and the retransmission time is long, the ARQ technique lowers the overall throughput of the channel. In such cases FEC and ARQ techniques may be used together. In this manner some errors are caught before the ARQ action. Certain modems come with an FEC option which is recommended for operation on a high-speed data transmission together with an ARQ system. Refer to Sec. 8.5 for error correcting methods in satellite transmission.

7.7   Digital Services and Interfacing Units

In this section Data-Phone digital service (DDS) and Data-Phone II service of the United States system are explained briefly, together with two types of digital interface units. A functional description of these units is very valuable to give the reader an idea of digital system operation in a communication office.

Data-Phone digital service (DDS)

In the United States Data-Phone digital service is provided over the digital data system, with 56, 9.6, 4.8, and 2.4 kb/s data speeds. Synchronous signals are accepted at these rates from a customer terminal and combined with other digital data signals through TDM techniques.

Two types of equipment are used at a customer office to connect the terminal unit to the digital transmission circuit: the *channel service unit* (CSU) and the *data service unit* (DSU) instead of a modem.

The CSU is a basic customer interface unit for a DDS channel. The unit provides for testing a DDS channel up to the customer interface point. Electrical characteristics of interface leads are different from EIA RS 232C and are used in special cases.

The DSU provides service between two customer equipments and operationally is equivalent to CSU. Data signals of customer equipment must conform to the interface requirements of EIA standards and CCITT recommendations for connection to a DSU. The baseband signal is a bipolar, return-to-zero, 50 percent duty cycle format and is similar to the baseband signal given in Fig. 3.5d. A functional description of a DSU is given below.

The DSU or CSU transmits data over cable pairs to a DDS office where it is terminated by an *office channel unit* (OCU). The OCU reshapes and regenerates the incoming signals and reassembles the data into a format suitable for multiplexing.

Data service unit (DSU)

At the customer's premises, a standard interface between the customer's terminal and the DDS is provided by the data service unit (DSU). Timing information required at the station is derived from the network through the DSU. The DDS synchronous timing network is based on the use of one master clock, with several subordinate clocks located at cities throughout the country. These clocks are configured such that all elements of the DDS including the DSU are maintained at the same time base.

On rare occasions, disruptions in the timing distribution system may isolate certain geographical segments. During these rare occasions the resulting subnetworks will run independently. This may result in the deletion or repetition of customer bits (a slip) without any indication to the DSU. (In a multiple-DSU installation, this effect may occur simultaneously to all DSUs.) However, the accuracy and configuration of the clocks is such that the time between the occurrence of a disruption and the first slip between the subnetworks is on the order of several days. The DSU consists of two basic sections: a channel terminator and an encoder-decoder. The channel terminator provides basic loop equalization, network protection, and a maintenance loopback. The encoder-decoder contains the transmitter, the receiver, the clock recovery circuitry, the interface loopback, and the necessary EIA and CCITT drivers and terminators required to interface with the customer's data terminal equipment (refer to Fig. 7.13). The basic function of this unit is the conversion of EIA RS 232C or CCITT V.35 interface signals to baseband bipolar line signals, and vice versa.

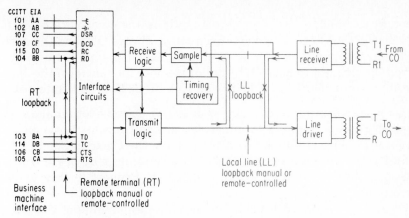

Figure 7.13 Block diagram of a data service unit, United States system.

System operation.   The DDS provides four-wire duplex private line digital data transmission. In describing the various DSU operations the DSU can be thought of as comprising separate transmitter and receiver portions. There are three modes of operations common to both portions: data (transmission), idle, and test. A fourth mode, out-of-service, is applicable to the receiver portion. The out-of-service mode is the result of the DSU receiving the out-of-service control code or the loss of received line signals from the network. The transmitter of the DSU can attain the data or idle mode independent of the state of the receiver. Similarly the receiver can attain the data, idle, or out-of-service mode independent of the state of the transmitter. The test mode involves both the transmitter and receiver.

The transmitting data mode is achieved by turning on the Request to Send (105) circuit, after which the DSU responds by turning on the Clear to Send (106) circuit. When the Request to Send (105) circuit is off, the transmitter is in the idle mode and produces a control idle signal on the line. In the receiving data mode, noncontrol data signals are being received and the received Line Signal Detector (109) circuit is on. In the receiving idle mode, control idle signals are being received and the Signal Detector (109) circuit is off. In the out-of-service mode, either control signals indicating a trouble condition are being received or no signals are being received; in both cases the Signal Detector (109) circuit is off. In the remote terminal test mode, both the Signal Detector (109) and the Data Set Ready (107) circuits are off.

Duplex operation.   Simultaneous transmission in both directions is one of the basic premises around which the digital data system was designed. The DSU provides, in addition to terminal control of the Request to Send (105) circuit, a permanent ON option that holds the

Request to Send (105) circuit permanently in the on condition. With this option the Clear to Send (106) circuit is always ON, and the data terminal equipment should have an EIA RS 232C type E interface. When the Request to Send (105) circuit is under the control of the data terminal equipment, the DSU has an EIA RS 232C type D interface.

Half-duplex operation. In half-duplex operation only one terminal transmits at a time. The data terminal desiring to transmit turns on its Request to Send (105) circuit. After a delay the Clear to Send (106) circuit turns on, indicating that the data terminal may begin transmission. The receiving data terminal has its Request to Send (105) circuit off.

Figure 7.14 shows the signal on the interface circuits of the local and remote DSU during a turnaround sequence when the transmitting local DSU(A) enters the receive data mode. To change directions of transmission, the transmitting data terminal equipment should turn its Request to Send (105) circuit off. The receiving data terminal equipment turns the Request to Send (105) circuit on and after a short delay receives a Clear to Send (106) on signal. If the permanent ON Request to Send option is used (which is provided in the DSU), the receiving terminal may start transmitting immediately after an end of transmission code is received. The transmission delay between terminals consists of the propagation delay of the specific circuit and a fixed delay

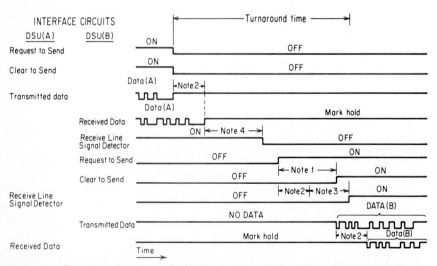

Figure 7.14 Turnaround sequence for HDX operation of DSU. Notes: (1) Request to Send-Clear to Send delay; (2) Transmission delay (not to scale; generally under 50 ms); (3) Receive Line Signal Detector turn-on time; (4) Receive Line Signal Detector turn-off time.

through the DSUs. The transmission delay for one-way transmission will generally be less than 50 ms in DDS.

Testing. The DSU contains two loopbacks; both can be operated either manually or remotely. The first loopback is referred to as the *local-line loopback* and provides a loopback both toward the line and toward the customer. The second loopback, referred to as the *remote-terminal loopback,* disconnects the customer equipment and loops toward the line at the interface connector. This loopback can also be utilized by the customer to verify that the customer's remote terminal is operating properly, and it also permits the operations center to verify whether the circuit meets the quality objective for the digital data system (refer to Fig. 7.13). When the DSU is in either of the test modes, the Data Set Ready (107) circuit is off; therefore, the terminal should be designed to recognize this condition to utilize the DSU's test features. The local loop test connects the transmitter section of the DSU to the receiver section in both directions. For this position of the test switch, the Data Set Ready (107) circuit is off; the Request to Send (105), Clear to Send (106), and Signal Detector (109) operate as in the control idle or data mode.

In the remote loopback position of the switch, the local transmission path is interrupted and data transmission is looped back toward the other station. At this position the Data Set Ready (107), Signal Detector (109), and Clear to Send (106) circuits are off.

Data-Phone II service

AT&T has recently introduced Data-Phone II, an advanced data service. This is a synchronous, serial-binary data transmission system which allows users to utilize advanced services with minimal inconvenience. Test, monitoring, and control functions are also included.

Data-Phone II provides level 1, level 2, and level 3 data transmission services.

Level 1 uses four modems: the 2024A and 2048 for 2400 b/s and 4800 b/s operation, respectively; the 2048C for quick (20 ms) start-up; and the 2096A for multiplexed 9600 b/s operation. The 2400 and 4800 b/s units work with basic four-wire private lines. Lines for the 9600 b/s set require high-performance D1 and D2 data conditioning.

The level 1 units offer built-in real-time diagnostics: they employ a control modem working with one or more tributary modems, which are all microprocessor-based.

Level 2 augments level 1 at the central site with a diagnostic console that continuously monitors each set in the network.

Level 3 runs complex data transmission systems by means of a communications management center. In this center, a network controller responds to instructions from a keyboard display terminal and reports on an optional teleprinter.

Network monitoring and testing features of Data-Phone II are given in Sec. 9.3.

References

Adlerstein, Sidney; "Modular Three-level Data Communication Network Looks Like the Standard for 1980s," *Electronic Design,* vol. 24, Nov. 22, 1979.

CCITT, Geneva: *Orange, Yellow,* and *Red Books.* Volume VIII, "Data Communication over the Telephone Network." "Interfaces," and "Signaling."

"Digital Data System–Data Service Unit Interface Specifications," Bell System Data Communications, March 1973, Pub. 41450.

"Industrial Electronics Bulletin No. 12," EIA Standards RS 232C, 422A, 423A, and 449, Electronic Industries Association, Engineering Dept., Washington, D.C.

Laws, David A., and Roy L. Levy: "Use of the Am261s 29, 30, 31 and 32. Quad Driver/ Receiver Family in EIA RS 422 and 423 Applications," National Semiconductor, Plattsburg, N.Y.

Tarver, Don: "Interface Standards for Line Drivers and Receivers," *Electronic Products Magazine,* March 1979.

Tektronix Inc., Poughkeepsie, N.Y.: "Essentials of Data Communications."

Satellite Communications

A satellite at a height of 35,800 km above the earth in a circular equatorial orbit, appearing stationary relative to the earth, is called a *geostationary satellite*. After expensive experimental studies, an active geostationary satellite was finally established, and transmission of commercial traffic through communication satellites commenced in 1965. With a few exceptions all operating systems use this type of satellite.

The minimum number of satellites that will give world coverage, not including the poles, is three. Because communication satellites must be at least 3.5° apart, so that ground stations can separate satellite signals, there is room for only some 114 equatorial satellites.

Note:

The FCC has plans to space the satellites 2° apart which will be phased in over a period of 10 years.

8.1 Description of a Satellite Communications System

In a satellite communications system the satellite is a node, i.e., a junction point where the earth stations are interconnected (see Fig. 8.1). The major functional elements of the communications satellite system are the earth stations with an associated central terminal office (CTO), a demand-assignment control center, the communication sat-

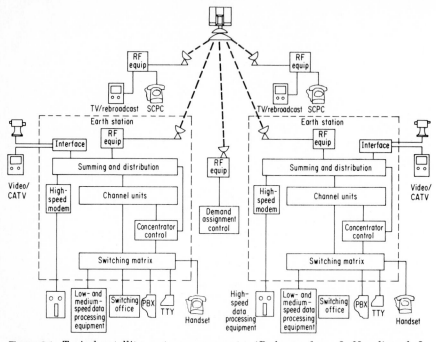

Figure 8.1 Typical satellite system components. (*Redrawn from J. Napoli and J. Christopher, "RCA Satcom System," RCA Engineer, vol. 121, no. 1, June/July 1975.*)

ellites, and the supporting terrestrial links. Telephone access lines and other communication circuits from the user's locations are connected by terrestrial links to the earth station. These earth stations in turn are interconnected through satellite channels to provide long-haul telecommunications transmission.

A typical system accommodates any combination of video, switched or point-to-point voice, teleprinter, data, and facsimile facilities. Built-in automatic maintenance monitoring features help to locate and isolate faulty circuits before the customer is aware of difficulty. Automatic switchover to standby facilities is provided, and monitoring facilities are made accessible 24 hours a day to customers.

Earth stations

The initially small number of earth stations has now increased considerably, with stations in operation on all continents. Typical earth station characteristics are 5 to 10 kW of transmitter power radiated from an antenna having a reflector of between 10 and 32 m in diameter. Reception is by the same antenna. The overall receiving system noise temperature is between 50 and 200 K at a 5° elevation angle.

A very suitable characteristic indicative of the quality of a receiving system (earth or satellite system) is the figure of merit G/T, that is, the ratio of the receiving antenna gain to the system noise temperature in kelvins, expressed in dB/K. A large earth station, having an antenna diameter of about 25 m and a system noise temperature of about 50 K, operating at 4 GHz, has a G/T figure of about 41 dB/K. (Similarly a geostationary satellite, having an antenna with full earth coverage and a system noise temperature of 1200 K will have a G/T value of about -14 dB/K.) In smaller earth stations the G/T figure decreases. For example, an earth station with an antenna diameter of 9 m and a system noise temperature of 150 K would have a G/T figure of about 27 dB/K.

Satellites

A description of a typical spacecraft which carries 24 transponders is given below. Like a microwave relay station, the satellite uses different frequencies for receiving and transmitting. The equipment which receives a signal frequency, amplifies it, and retransmits it in another frequency is called a *transponder*. In this system, frequency reuse establishes 24 independent 34-MHz channels within the 500-MHz allocated band. The channels are spaced on 20-MHz centers but are transmitted via alternately horizontal and vertical polarizations to isolate adjacent channels. Greater than 33-dB polarization discrimination is provided between channels. Each transponder carries a separate receiver for each polarization so that 12 out of 24 channels are supported by each receiver. The 12 channels in each receiver output are separated, amplified, and recombined through the input multiplexers, 24 nonredundant traveling-wave-tube (TWT) amplifiers, and the output multiplexers.

Capabilities of these channels are as follows:

- Single-carrier FDM/FM or TDMA for 900-voice channels
- SCPC with demand-assigned routing capability
- Single-carrier FM-TV
- 50 Mb/s data stream

Technical characteristics of spacecraft are as follows:

Mass in orbit	40–700 kg
Size:	
Diameter	75–250 cm
Height	60–540 cm
Antenna gain:	
Spot beam	25–30 dB
Global	12–18 dB
Transmitter power output	30–50 W

Noise

Noise in a space communications system affects the capability of the link to carry information. The noise in a voice-grade channel originates from the following sources:

- Thermal noise arising on the earth-to-satellite and satellite-to-earth paths
- Interference noise from terrestrial systems and possibly other satellite systems
- Intermodulation noise
- Clicks when operation is near the threshold point

Additionally, for digital transmission:

- PCM quantizing noise
- Idle channel noise when PCM signals are transmitted

A satellite system contributes approximately 10,000 pW0p (-50 dBm0p) noise to the system. Noise allocation in an FDM/FM/FDMA system is as follows:

1. 1000-pW0p interference from terrestrial system
2. 1000-pW0p group delay and intermodulation noise arising in the earth station
3. 3000-pW0p thermal noise in the up-link and intermodulation noise arising in the common repeater
4. 5000-pW0p thermal noise in the down-link

Note:

Bit error probability of 10^{-4} corresponds to a noise power of approximately 50,000 pW0p in a voice-grade channel.

Transmission losses

In a 4/6 GHz system, by assuming 41,300 km distance between the earth station and the satellite, free space loss is 200.6 dB for a 6-GHz up-link and 196.8 dB for a 4-GHz down-link. The first number in each case refers to the frequency of the down-link; the second number refers to the frequency of the up-link. Gains and losses in a typical satellite communications system are given in Table 8.1 and Fig. 8.2.

Order-wire system between earth stations

Order-wire systems provide facilities for voice and/or data communications between operation centers. They have been used as mainte-

TABLE 8.1   Transmission Path Losses and Gains of a Typical Satellite Communications System

Transmitting earth station		
Amplification		73 dB
Transmitter power	20 kW	43 dBW*
Antenna gain		62 dB
e.i.r.p.†		105 dBW
Up-link loss (6 GHz)		200 dB
Satellite		
RCV antenna gain:		
Spot beam		29 dB
Global		17 dB
Amplification		92 dB
Transmitter power	400 W	26 dBW
XMT antenna gain:		
Spot beam		26 dB
Global		14 dB
Down-link loss (4 GHz)		196 dB
Receiving earth station		
Antenna gain		59 dB
Amplification		55 dB

*dBW refers to 1 W.
†e.i.r.p. stands for *effective isotropic radiated power* and is the power of a transmitter over an isotropic antenna that would achieve the same result as the transmitter and the antenna in question; i.e., e.i.r.p. = antenna gain + transmitter power.

nance service and party line teleprinter terminals. They are also utilized for control and switching of multiple satellite down-links and transmit ports.

The order-wire system between earth stations provides voice and data communication over a four-wire line with required amplification and filtering units. Most earth station order-wire circuits are arranged for "speech plus" operation. Typically a voice service channel occupies the 300–2400 Hz spectrum; up to five 50-Bd teleprinter channels can be used on the 2400–3400 Hz spectrum in addition to a voice channel. A similar spectrum division is given in Fig. 5.2 for modem and teleprinter operation in the voice spectrum.

Dual-tone multifrequency (DTMF) signaling may be used for selective calling. The DTMF encoder at the transmitter and the address decoder at the receiver provide separate voice and teleprinter communication. For example a two-digit station code is assigned for voice call, while a three-digit code is assigned for teleprinter operation.

The teleprinter call codes can also be used to operate teleprinters during unattended periods.

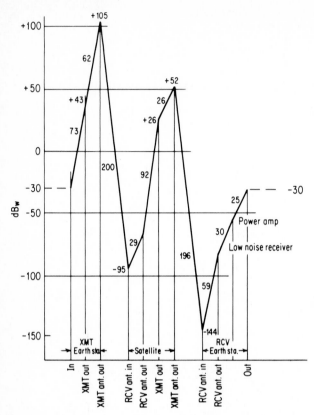

Figure 8.2 Power levels of a typical satellite communication path (⁴⁄₆ GHz).

In high-capacity order-wire systems, automatic switch selection can be provided for voice channels as well as for data channels.

8.2   Forms of Operation

Interconnection of the earth stations at the satellite by means of satellite channels can be accomplished by several forms of operation, e.g., preassignment, time-assignment, and demand-assignment.

In *preassignment operation,* satellite channels are preassigned permanently between the earth stations, based on the busy-hour traffic in Erlangs and the grade of service measured by the probability of lost calls (for instance, 0.01, one lost call per 100 calls). Preassignment operation has the drawback that a number of the assigned channels become idle during nonbusy hours. These idle channels are unavailable to other stations that have heavy traffic at these hours, since satellites, particularly those in geostationary orbits, have wide coverage on earth, and the busy hours of one region do not necessarily occur at the same hours as those of other regions. This results in an inefficient utilization of the satellite channels.

In *time-assigned operation,* satellite channels are preassigned, not permanently, but on a fixed time schedule between two earth stations, based on the time-varying (hourly, daily, or long-term) traffic of the stations. This form of operation improves the utilization of the satellite channels to some extent, but there are still times when channels are idle and unavailable to other stations.

In *demand-assignment operation,* satellite channels are instantaneously assigned between two earth stations on demand, based on the actual traffic as it occurs. When the demand for a channel ends, the channel becomes available for interconnection between any other two earth stations. This permits full utilization of all satellite channels. Refer to Sec. 4D of the Consultative Committee on International Radio (CCIR) *Green Book,* Vol. IV, for more information about methods of modulation and multiple access recommendations and reports.

CCIR recommendations and reports related to data transmission via satellites are listed in Sec. 8.8.

SCPC technique

SCPC (*single channel per carrier*) is the assignment of one radio carrier to each voice or data channel. It is an efficient satellite transmission technique. In this way larger numbers of independent circuits can be accommodated within an allocated satellite transponder using SCPC versus conventional FDMA service. Even remote areas with light traffic loads can now have low-cost communications with high interconnectivity to larger networks.

Conventional satellite service for medium to heavy communications routes uses multidestination carriers occupying the allocated bandwidth on a preassigned frequency-division access scheme, with voice channels being multiplexed in frequency as well. This FDM/FM/FDMA system normally uses standard-size carriers of 24, 60, 90, or 132 channels. Each earth station receives and demodulates carriers of interest and then demultiplexes those channels from each carrier which are destined to that station. When considering lighter routes, with a reduced number of channels in each multidestination carrier, the total transponder capacity is significantly reduced. Consider a typical 36-MHz transponder. Seven 5-MHz FDM carriers (each containing 60 channels) can be accommodated, for a total of 420 channels. If the FDM carrier is reduced to 2.5 MHz (24 channels), then 14 carriers can be assigned to one transponder, for a total of 336 channels. Hence, the capacity decreases with an increasing number of carriers. Furthermore, the carriers are normally assigned in standard sizes, but each carrier is rarely completely occupied. This *fill factor* is usually on the order of 80 to 90 percent; a satellite's transponder capacity is therefore not wholly used. SCPC allows for a fill factor of 100 percent. Channels are usually assigned at spacings from 25 to 60 kHz across the transponder bandwidth. A diagram of the Intelsat frequency plan is shown in Fig. 8.3. Here 800 channels at 45-kHz intervals are accommodated in a 36-MHz transponder bandwidth.

Pulse-code modulation is used for channel encoding, and coherent (quadrature) four-phase shift keying is used to modulate each carrier; the total coded bit rate is 64 kb/s.

For light to medium traffic between fixed stations, carriers are normally preassigned channel frequencies in the transponder. When there is no channel activity, the carrier is disabled, thus economizing satellite power and permitting increased capacity. Networks with high interconnectivity requirements among light traffic routes have employed *demand-assigned multiple-access* (DAMA) techniques, allowing automatic assignment of carriers on an as-needed basis. An additional capacity advantage is obtained when call statistics are taken into account. The effective traffic-handling capability of the satellite can be tripled. In our example, 2400 subscribers could be serviced using DAMA with SCPC. The Intelsat SPADE system exemplifies this operating method. (SPADE stands for single channel per carrier pulse-code modulation multiple-access demand-assigned equipment.) SPADE permits utilization of the satellite system on an occasional as-needed basis in lieu of a full-time allotment for whatever number of channels is required without a central control. Hence with SPADE, one country can communicate with another country for the time required without having to maintain a full-time circuit.

The success of Intelsat's SCPC programs has stimulated the planning and installation of several domestic SCPC networks. A diagram showing functional blocks of a one-channel SCPC/PCM system is given in Fig. 8.4. A key feature of the installation is the deemphasis upon

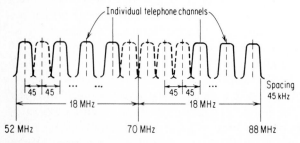

Figure 8.3 Intelsat frequency plan.

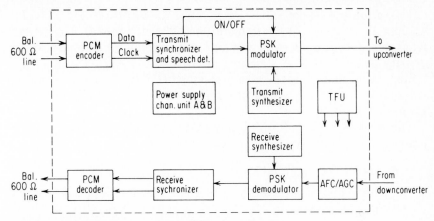

Figure 8.4 Block diagram of a PCM/SCPC channel unit.

common equipment support; that is, the channel unit is a self-sufficient element; it can be added at any one site as traffic demands increase. A PCM voice encoder interfaces directly to the analog voice channel input. The audio signal is encoded into a 56 kb/s digital stream and passed onto the transmit synchronizer for insertion of start-of-message (SOM) or synchronization words. The resulting bit stream is passed to the PSK modulator. The modulator is tuned to transmit a specific ratio carrier supplied by a frequency synthesizer. The modulator IF (intermediate frequency) interface to the upcounter is in the 52–88 MHz band. (A 36-MHz transponder bandwidth is assumed).

A voice switch is used to detect the beginning of speech, initiate the modem preamble (used for acquisition by the receiver), and enable the carrier. A digital delay for the voice signal is used to eliminate speech clipping while the carrier is being turned on. The channel unit input from the earth station downconverter is at 70 MHz also. A pilot reference signal is received and used to phase-lock a loop in the AFC/AGC module, thus providing automatic correction of frequency offsets and link power fluctuations. The corrected and translated frequency spectrum is passed onto the PSK demodulator which, by using a frequency synthesizer as a first local oscillator, "tunes" the receiver to select the desired channel. Once carrier acquisition and symbol timing recovery have been achieved, the demodulated digital stream is fed to the receiver synchronizer when SOMs are recognized and removed. The 56 kb/s stream is converted back to an audio signal in the PCM decoder.

Timing signals and reference frequencies are generated and distributed by the timing and frequency unit (TFU). These signals are provided for automatic frequency control–automatic gain control (AFC-AGC) references, synthesizer references, and modem local oscillators.

The recent Intelsat specification requires the inclusion of PCM-SCPC equipment in standard B earth stations. The standard B concept satisfies the continuing need to provide low-cost communications to light-density traffic routes. A standard B earth station uses a smaller antenna (11 m) and operates with a specified G/T (gain-to-temperature) ratio of 31.7 db/K compared to standard A stations requiring a G/T ratio of 40.7 dB/K.

The terminal channel units may take on three functional configurations:

1. Digitized voice using 56 kb/s PCM

2. Wideband digital data at 48 or 50 kb/s using a rate of 3/4 forward-acting error correction

3. Wideband data at 56 kb/s using a rate of 7/8 encoding

At standard B installations, channel units are usually single-function units serving one of the above operations, although one station can easily implement all three, as the modulation schemes and common equipment support are compatible.

The scope of current activity in SCPC applications is widening because of decreased system costs, effective satellite transponder utilization, and adaptability to fixed as well as mobile communications. Demand assignment is most easily implemented using SCPC. Voice communications using PCM or adaptive delta modulation is available, in addition to error-coded wideband data or narrow-band telegraphy.

8.3   Multiple-Access and Modulation Techniques

To achieve as high a degree of flexibility of interconnection between the earth stations as may be desired, multiple access is an operational requirement of utmost importance. *Multiple access* refers to techniques which allow more than two earth stations to enter a single satellite transponder, providing real-time interconnection for simultaneous two-way communications between any two stations.

There are three basic multiple-access techniques: frequency-division (FDMA), time-division (TDMA), and code-division (CDMA). They differ in the utilization of the satellite power, time, and frequency (bandwidth). All can be used for any of the three forms of operation, namely, preassignment, time-assignment, or demand-assignment operation.

In *frequency-division multiple access* (FDMA), the satellite frequency domain (bandwidth) is divided into n discrete frequency channels. Each earth station can use one or more channels. Each frequency channel has full use of satellite time but shares the satellite frequency and power with all other frequency channels.

In *time-division multiple access* (TDMA), each interval of T seconds (called a *frame period*) of the satellite time domain is divided into n discrete time slots. Each earth station can use one or more time slots. Satellite time, frequency, and power are shared by all time slots.

In *code-division multiple access* (CDMA), neither the satellite frequency nor the time domain is divided among the earth stations. Instead, each earth station has common usage of the full satellite bandwidth and time slots by employing a special coding-decoding technique. Each station uses a code different from the others. The satellite power, however, is shared by all earth stations.

The three basic multiple-access techniques can be combined to generate several hybrids. Most noteworthy are FD/TDMA, FD/CDMA, TD/CDMA, and FD/TD/CDMA.

TDMA technique*

Let us scrutinize TDMA closer since it is becoming more popular than other access techniques. TDMA is a technique whereby stations communicate with each other on the basis of nonoverlapping transmission bursts through a common satellite repeater. (Refer to Fig. 8.5). Since there is no overlap, the same carrier frequency may be assigned to all earth stations sharing the same transponder.

TDMA is characterized by the durations of the time frame and the time slot (see Fig. 8.6). The time slot allocated to an earth station

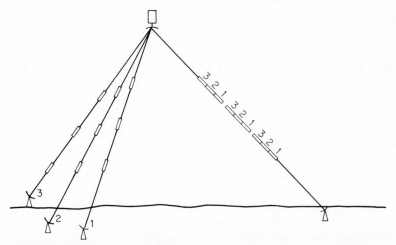

Figure 8.5 TDMA concept. Traffic bursts are transmitted in a periodic TDMA frame.

---

*Refer to CCIR Vol. IV, Rep. 213-3 for more information.

consists of a guard time, a preamble, and the information to be trans-mitted. The preamble contains auxiliary information for system organ-ization such as synchronization and routing information. The time allocated to the guard time and the preamble is to a high degree de-pendent on the principle used for system organization. The message information may consist of a number of basic channel units. A basic channel unit is an encoded sample of a telephone channel or a digital baseband signal. In a system in the fixed-satellite service employing TDMA, each participating earth station is assigned one time slot. One complete sequence of earth station transmission is the time frame. The time slots of different earth stations can differ in their time duration, depending on the traffic to be transmitted. The smallest increment in time-slot duration is governed by the duration of the basic channel unit.

A particular earth station receiver identifies the desired transmis-sion by observing the information in the periodically recurring time slots associated with the corresponding earth station. Considerations of synchronization and timing, associated with the use of time division in a multiaccess system in a fixed-satellite service, set a minimum limit for the duration of the time assignment to an individual earth station. This limitation plus the necessity for time compression of the baseband signals for discontinuous transmission leads to a time-division tech-nique in which many pulses are transmitted during each time slot. Duration of the time frame is limited by maximum permissible trans-mission delay, and duration of the time slot is limited by the number of stations and the guard time. The time slot content is limited only by the modulation formats which can be transmitted therein. Propa-gation time is the largest delay factor in the case of the geostationary satellite. Geostationary satellite systems handling voice traffic cannot allow excess delays from other sources which approach an appreciable

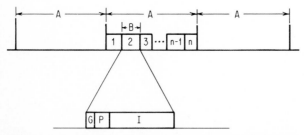

Figure 8.6 Format of a TDMA system. A = recurring time frame; B = time slot allocated to an earth station—within the time slot the earth station transmits information as a burst of pulses; G = guard time, separating successive transmissions from earth stations; P = preamble containing auxiliary in-formation for system organization; I = information. (CCIR, Geneva, 1974, vol. IV, Rep. 213-3.)

fraction of the transmission delay. This determines a maximum value of the time frame. However in practice, the optimization of the time frame, from the standpoint of access efficiency versus buffer cost in a multiple-access system, at the present time leads to time frames much less than this maximum value.

If the duration of the time frame is equal to the sampling interval (typically 125 μs for CCITT quality of speech) or an integral divisor thereof, then no buffer store is required and the system can be operated as a real-time system; in TDMA systems, however, preamble requirements cause a decrease in the available telephone capacity.

Within the time frame (Fig. 8.6) the first time slot is designated as the reference time slot. A reference time is provided to permit sequential interleaving of time slots. Transmitted time slots are synchronized to the frame reference by correcting for path variations at a rate equal to the derivative of the path delay. The method of modulation and modulation rate within a particular time slot is independent of the others except for frame synchronization and addressor-addressee compatibility.

PSK modulation and coherent detection present advantages which give the minimum BER for a given satellite power. An appropriate number of synchronization bits is normally assigned to the beginning of each burst, and reference carrier and clock timing are recovered during this synchronization time interval. For example, in one PCM/ TDMA system, 6 to 40 bits is used for synchronization. Recently a new PCM/TDMA system, especially suitable for a geostationary satellite, has been developed which effectively utilizes the full frame and avoids a decrease in the information transmission capacity due to guard time. To implement a system without guard time, the transmitting clock of each station in the network is controlled by clock pulses received from a reference station through the satellite; in this way the earth station time slots will be perfectly synchronized at the satellite. In each time slot two sets of 7 bits each are transmitted for supervisory information; the rest of the time slot is used for the communication information.

In the first set of 7 bits, the first bit allows for overlap of the carrier burst, the next bit is used as a reference for PSK delay detection, and the remaining 5 bits is used for control in DAMA. The next 7 bits is used for synchronization of the time slots and for station identification.

In this system, acquisition is achieved by the use of a *pseudorandom noise code*. Initially, the pseudorandom noise (PN) code pulses are transmitted from a slave station continuously at a level 15 to 25 dB lower than normal. Its PCM clock pulses are then synchronized by comparing the PN code clock pulses with the clock pulses of the master station received through the satellite. After the synchronization has been established, the level of the pulses transmitted by the earth station is raised to normal and connection is achieved.

In a TDMA system any time slot in the frame is available to any station. Especially in a demand-assigned system where the number of traffic channels within the time slot can be varied, this flexibility is limited only by the overall capacity of the system and requires the establishment of general network discipline. Depending on the system organization, this function can be performed by a central network control station or in a decentralized system by the ground terminals in a prearranged network discipline. In either network organization, there must be order-wire communications between the participating earth stations. The fraction of time allocated to order-wire need is quite small, of the order of 0.5 percent.

TDMA systems can take full advantage of the application of digital speech interpolation; refer to CCIR Vol. IV, Rep. 211-3. Although intermodulation noise is absent in a TDM system, quantizing noise (or distortion) is present, a common phenomenon occurring in most time-division systems (refer to Sec. 3.2). Advantages of TDMA may be briefly noted as follows:

1. In a TDMA system, the full power of the satellite repeater is available at a particular instant of time for the repeating of signals from any earth station. It is independent of all the others; the satellite repeater output is a constant envelope signal. Because of this, a variety of types of stations may be mixed in an operating system.

2. Stations with different receiving sensitivities (G/T) and/or transmitter powers can employ the same repeater provided they transmit at rates appropriate to the sensitivities of the intended receivers. With the consideration that the frame synchronization signal must be receivable by all stations, each station of a given size may communicate with other larger or smaller stations. Further, communications between stations of different size can be achieved by adjusting the average power received from the satellite repeater (by adjusting the width and rate of the pulses in a constant envelope signal) to values commensurate with the receiving sensitivity of the smaller station. The basic frame parameters such as guard time and burst synchronization should be compatible with the lowest-sensitivity station sharing the repeater.

3. TDMA systems accommodate easily to changes and growth in traffic patterns since the capacity of any station is proportional only to the allocated time it may access the satellite. Thus by simple control and redistribution of burst lengths (a digitally controlled element), an entire network may be reconfigured statistically or, if desired, dynamically.

4. Accommodation of digital traffic is very easy; a change in a channel speed does not require a new filter.

5. Dynamic monitoring of system performance is easy.

6. Reliability is increasing; cost of digital hardware is decreasing.

7. Implementation of automatic diagnostics is very easy.

Methods of modulation and multiplexing

Since the satellite transponder operates at radio frequencies, the multiple access is preferably done at these frequencies. Many methods of modulation and multiplexing at baseband and at radio frequencies can be used.

The baseband signal may be in any conventional form such as a frequency-division multiplex (FDM) of voice channels, or it may be put into a pulse format. The pulse format may be a time-division multiplex (TDM) of samples of each voice channel, or samples of an FDM group of voice channels. The samples may use an analog representation such as pulse-amplitude modulation (PAM), pulse-width modulation (PWM), or pulse-position modulation (PPM), or they may use a digital representation such as pulse-code modulation (PCM). PCM is attractive for pulse formats because it is less susceptible to interference and intermodulation. So far both FDM and PCM have been principally used.

Any conventional form of amplitude modulation (AM) or angle modulation (FM or PM) at radio frequencies may be used with the baseband signals discussed above. Angle modulation has been used, following the practice of terrestrial radio relay systems, because of the S/N improvement factor. If the baseband signal is in pulse-code format, phase-shift keying (PSK) has been advocated because of its better noise performance. A pulse format at baseband is necessary for TDMA and CDMA at radio frequencies. There are several combinations of modulation methods at baseband and at radio frequencies for various techniques of multiple access.

Comparison of multiple-access techniques

Numerous studies have been made on the comparative merits of various multiple-access techniques, based on the same system parameters and performance. There are pros and cons in all techniques. The difference in satellite power requirement among various techniques is not great. However, the access capability in terms of number of satellite channels is quite different among access techniques. For satellite bandwidth, both FDMA and TDMA require about the same, whereas CDMA requires 10 to 20 times as much. CDMA is therefore bandwidth-limited if large numbers of satellite channels are to be provided. From the interference and antijamming point of view, CDMA outperforms both FDMA and TDMA, with tradeoffs in equipment complexity and perhaps high cost. FDMA and TDMA have little antijamming capability. For commercial use, either FDMA or TDMA is preferred. TDMA transmission requires complex modulation and filtering equipment and precise centralized synchronization compared with simpler ground-station equipment for FDMA that Intelsat and many others use. But a key advantage of TDMA is that it is almost a digital time-division switch itself.

There are other problems, such as the backoff satellite power due to multiple radio carrier operation of FDMA; accuracy of bit and network time synchronization in TDMA and equipment complexity, high cost, and limited channel capacity in CDMA present problems. If antijam is not involved one can summarize approximately by noting that FDM/FM seems optimum if a single carrier can be used; that TWT backoff with multiple carriers makes TDM more attractive if more accesses are needed; and finally that SCPC is preferred if many accesses and light traffic characterize the network.

8.4 Digital Data Transmission (in the United States)

Digital satellite data transmission has centered around the design and implementation of dedicated-user low-cost earth stations, using SCPC digital transmission equipment. To minimize overall interconnect costs, as well as ensure high end-to-end performance, the earth terminals have been collocated with the users' facilities, thus providing true direct satellite communications exclusive of intervening terrestrial carrier interconnections. The guaranteed link performance has been designed to be at least P_{BE} (probability of bit error) $= 1 \times 10^{-7}$ with nominal operation at $P_{BE} = 1 \times 10^{-9}$, and the system reliability has been designed to exceed 99.9 percent operating with unmanned earth stations. Measured performance data to date confirm that the design objectives have been met. The system's initial purpose is to transmit 1.544 Mb/s (T1) data streams over long- and medium-range distances and connect remote data collection terminals to centrally located computer processing equipment.

The earth stations were designed to be relatively low cost, easily deployable, and to provide high service performance and reliability, equipped with 10- or 5-m-diameter antennas. A typical baseband equipment consists of SCPC channel equipment using four-phase-coherent PSK modulation and a rate of 3/4 (for 48–50 kb/s service) or 7/8 (for 56 kb/s) forward-acting error-correction codes for a 64 kb/s transmission rate. A 7/8 rate corresponds to the ratio of 56 kb/s service to 64 kb/s transmission rate; 8000 stuffing bits are error-coded to enhance the bit error rate from 10^{-4} to 10^{-7}. PSK modulation and error coding together are also called *convolutional encoding—threshold decoding,* which multiplies the available system capacity for the SCPC network as well as requiring 3 dB less power per carrier.

A unique synchronizing system is used which provides PSK phase-ambiguity resolution and digital bit synchronization by using the inherent characteristics of the convolution coder. This technique provides synchronization without adding additional overhead bits to the data stream. The system is also designed to monitor the nominal channel error rate during on-line transmission of user data, without adding an external pseudorandom BER sequence. Monitoring of the on-line channel error rate is a key element in the design of the channel unit automatic switchover logic. The interface to the user is a simple digital interface consisting of clock and data.

Digital data transmission through satellites offers a number of advantages:

1. Satellite transmission of digital data over medium to long distance and to multipoint locations is less costly than the use of terrestrial microwave. The quality and reliability of satellite transmissions are generally superior to wire-line and terrestrial microwave circuits.

2. Higher-speed satellite data systems to handle the rapidly increasing volume of information demanded by business involve less capital expenditure than the expansion of terrestrial microwave systems.

3. Satellites can provide digital data communications to remote areas which are not served by digital wire-line circuits.

4. In areas served by digital wire-line circuits, satellite communications compete economically when several channels are required.

5. Satellites can also provide higher data rates than are available via wire-line.

6. Utilization of 5-m-diameter antennas, made possible to install low-cost digital earth stations on the user's premises, eliminates the interconnection to the carrier's regional earth station.

7. It can tolerate smaller S/N than the analog system can.

8. TDM techniques can be employed which can lead to much greater spectrum utilization efficiency.

Elastic buffering

A satellite launched into synchronous orbit does not stay exactly over the equator. It is inclined at a small angle to the equator and no longer appears stationary in the sky. In addition, because of the attraction of the sun and the moon, it appears to move in a figure eight (see Fig. 8.7).

Figure 8.7 Satellite in a circular synchronous orbit inclined with respect to the equator appears to move in a figure eight.

Daily cyclic moves of a satellite change the total path length up to 15,000 m, and hence the propagation time can change by 50 μs in a day. This corresponds to a speed of 0.6 m/s to or from the earth, or 2×10^{-9} s change in propagation time.

Digital data transmission via satellite requires frequent resynchronization because of this movement. This slow time shift accumulates a fixed number of timing bits up to a maximum; thereafter procession reverses direction and the accumulation is depleted to a minimum number of bits. Usually at earth stations $\pm$ 64 bits of elastic buffering is needed to permit interfacing of 56 kb/s multiplexer channels to satellite links as independently synchronized links. Refer to "Buffer Synchronizer Unit" in Sec. 6.3 for more information. In practice, buffer overloading is not permitted, and a control signal is transmitted when three-fourths of buffer capacity is used in order to hold the data flow.

The satellite starts to trace larger figure eights toward the end of its life span. Larger elastic buffer capacity is needed in the earth station to utilize the satellite's longer time. The Doppler effect of satellite swing also changes the 6-GHz transmission frequency by ± 13 Hz.

8.5 Propagation-Delay Problems and Error-Correction Methods

Transmission via satellite severely lowers the throughput efficiency of a data circuit if certain terrestrial protocols are used without any modification. On a satellite link it will take about 700 ms to travel the 80,000 km to a receiving station and for acknowledgment to travel back 80,000 km to the transmission station. If the frame size is large, the transmitting end waits most of the time, which degrades the utilization efficiency of the circuit. (Note that one-way propagation delay on a satellite path is 257 ms.)

There are two basic modes of data transmission in satellite communications: continuous ARQ and stop-and-wait ARQ. ARQ (automatic request for repeat) is an error-detecting scheme which allows a receiver to detect an error, notify the originator, and have the error portion of the message automatically retransmitted by the transmitter. In a stop-and-wait ARQ, the transmit terminal stops after sending a block and waits to receive an ACK (confirmation) or NAK (if the block contains an error) control character. This waiting period consists of the round-trip propagation time of the satellite link plus modem terrestrial link turnaround times (if the channel operates in a half-duplex mode) plus the duration of the forward and return of ACK, NAK codes. Therefore, direct substitution of a terrestrial link with a satellite link lowers throughput substantially in this type of data operation.

In continuous ARQ mode, the transmit terminal sends a definite number of frames before receiving a response. The most popular number is seven; i.e., transmission is continuous except for the retransmission of the last seven frames when an error is detected in a frame. For a 9600 b/s data speed, the frame length is 1200 bits. A seven count uses 3 bits (111 binary) to number each frame. By extending numbering to 7-bit binary, 127 frames can be sent before a response is received. A satellite circuit working on a low-error-rate circuit with higher data speed uses a 127-frame count with shorter frame length. At 56 kb/s, frame length is around 400 bits. Degradation of a circuit by the substitution of a satellite link depends upon the transmission rate, frame size, and the size of the count used for the error acknowledgment. However, if these parameters are selected appropriately (frame size big and data rate small), the throughput of a satellite circuit is the same as that of a terrestrial circuit.

The second type of continuous ARQ mode is called *selective repeat* ARQ, which is most efficient on the satellite circuits. It is similar to continuous ARQ in concept and operation. Instead of retransmitting all seven frames together with the erroneous frame, only the frame in error is retransmitted. In this mode, utilization of smaller frames is more efficient. See Sec. 7.6 for ARQ technique.

The satellite circuits are designed to have better error rates than the similar terrestrial links, in general. The errors in terrestrial links often come in bursts, whereas satellite bit errors are distributed randomly and the bits are damaged independently of one another. The error correction process linked to the modulation process in a satellite circuit is most effective to recognize and correct errors. Thus, the error-detecting codes will provide more superior performance on satellite links than on terrestrial links. However, circuits contain terrestrial and satellite links. Therefore, error control must be able to handle both terrestrial and satellite circuit errors.

Although utilization of expensive earth stations provides an admissible error rate on a satellite link, it is not economically feasible. Systems equipped with ARQ circuits are much cheaper in provision of higher transmission quality. But when the error rate is worse than

10^{-4}, the error detection alone is not satisfactory and needs to be supplemented with error-correcting codes. An error-correcting code attempts to correct errors without requesting retransmission. It is also called the *forward-error-correction* (FEC) method. Although the FEC method improves the error rate 10^3 times, it is not so safe and some errors may remain uncorrected. Furthermore FEC utilizes a greater portion of redundant bits than does the error-detection method. FEC needs to be backed up by the use of ARQ methods.

Satellite delay compensation unit (SDCU).   A device designed to perform continuous ARQ functions is called a *satellite delay compensation unit* (SDCU). Figure 8.8 is a simplified block diagram of a typical implementation of such a device. Internally, the SDCU restructures the data blocks for efficient transmission over the satellite link. At the remote end the data blocks are restored to their original format for presentation to the terminal. The business machine (or other data source) provides a data stream to the unit, which arranges the bits in blocks of a predetermined size. As long as no ARQs are received, the data continue to be transmitted block by block. Whenever an ARQ is received, the controller asks the data source to stop and causes the multiplexer to select the data buffer output rather than the block formatter output.

If the go-back-N approach were used, the last N blocks in the buffer would be transmitted. Assuming that no ARQs are generated during this time, the system would switch back to the transmission of current data blocks after the transmission of the N previous blocks. If, on the other hand, a selective repeat scheme were used, only the block identified as being in error would be transmitted. The performance of either of these two basic schemes as well as any of the possible variations is, of course, governed by the interrelationship between several key pa-

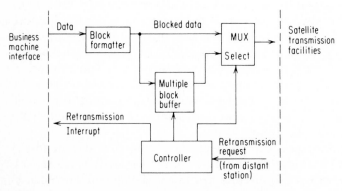

Figure 8.8 Block diagram of a satellite delay compensation unit.

rameters, including error rate, data rate, block size, and required throughput efficiency.

8.6 The Marisat System

Since 1976, the Marisat system has been using satellites to provide up-to-date Telex, telephone, facsimile, and data services to ships and offshore facilities equipped with appropriate terminals. The Marisat system provides global commercial services through Atlantic, Pacific, and Indian Ocean region stationary satellites. Each Marisat satellite operates at three different frequencies to serve varying needs: UHF for the American Navy and C band (6/4 GHz) and L band (1.6/0.4 GHz) for commercial users.

Mobile terminals are installed on merchant ships and offshore equipment to operate with Marisat. The terminal units include an above-deck portion enclosed in a fiberglass radome consisting of a 1.22-m stabilized antenna equipped with ship motion sensors and gearless servo drive that automatically keep the antenna locked on the satellite at all times. The system is operated by Comsat General Corporation of the United States.

Coverage of earth by three Marisat satellites is given in Fig. 8.9. The DAMA technique is used in conjunction with SCPC carriers to provide voice and Telex transmission. The signaling control and Telex operation are implemented using TDM and TDMA techniques. Basically, requests for service are transmitted on 1.6/4 GHz from ship-to-shore using an open-loop TDMA channel, while control (frequency assignment, broadcast messages, and so on) is provided in the shore-to-ship TDM channel on 1.5/6 GHz. Speech, facsimile, and data are carried by analog FM channels on an SCPC basis, i.e., without multiplexing.

Communication via Marisat is established as follows. The operator on a ship requests a Marisat communications channel by sending a short burst of signaling pulses to shore via a satellite. The signaling pulses, which are at the same carrier frequency for all ships, identify the requesting ship and the type of channel required. When the shore

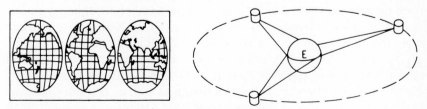

Figure 8.9 Coverage of earth by three Marisat satellites.

station receives the request, it selects a pair of frequencies and assigns them to the requesting ship. When the call is completed, the frequency pair is released and made available for another call. Teleprinter messages, by contrast, are carried by digital TDM channels. The shore-to-ship carrier is modulated by a bit stream at 1.2 kb/s. The ship-to-shore carrier is occupied by pulse bursts transmitted in a predetermined sequence by up to 22 ships. Each burst is modulated at 4.0 kb/s and contains up to 12 characters of message text. The ship transmissions are synchronized by the continuously received carrier from shore. Time intervals are automatically allocated between bursts to allow for propagation-delay differences between terminals at the center and those at the edge of the satellite coverage area.

International satellite organizations are given in Appendix A.

8.7   Advantages and Future of Satellite Communications

The first international communications satellite system was inaugurated in 1965 with Intelsat I, which carried two (one working and one protecting) transponders with 240 telephone circuits and single access by only two earth stations at one time. Intelsat V, launched in December of 1980, provides 12,000 circuits plus two TV channels. Design life is 7 years. Capacity was achieved by the use of the 14/11 GHz frequency bands in addition to the 6/4 GHz frequency bands. The 6/4 GHz frequencies are used four times and the 14/11 GHz frequencies are used twice by employing advanced techniques. The 27 transponders of the Intelsat V satellite come in three different bandwidths: 40, 80, and 240 MHz.

Presently all real-time transoceanic television is transmitted via satellite. The standard earth station is equipped with 30-m-diameter antennas. A substandard station with a 13.5 m antenna may also be used on some occasions.

Communications satellites provide point-to-multipoint or broadcast capability, which facilitates electronic mail and other business applications. Also, satellites make available high-speed digital links, which open up new uses for communications such as teleconferencing among several dispersed computers. Further, satellites virtually eliminate distance as a constraint in the design of communications networks, giving users greater flexibility in their implementation options and easing the overall network design task. The satellite's broadcasting capability even allows parallel processing as well as the simultaneous update of data bases at different locations. Attention has been given

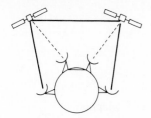

Figure 8.10 Transmission by intersatellite link.

to the capability of satellite systems for integrating voice, data, video, and image communications; this way satellites provide users with an integrated network, not just a group of circuits.

Also, a user can continually reassign satellite capacity to meet its varying needs, both geographically and in terms of the mix of voice, data, video, and image communications. This is in contrast to terrestrial networks which are usually dedicated to one communications mode and where unused links on the West Coast, say, cannot help meet peak traffic demands on the East Coast. With satellite service, an organization needing excess capacity at one time of the day for the New York–Miami corridor and at another time for Los Angeles–San Francisco communications will be able to switch its capacity between the two areas instead of having to purchase the capacity twice.

Direct-broadcasting satellites are now in the experimental stage. The transmitter sweeps the area with a highly directive beam which covers only a small portion of the entire area, and the subscriber receives the program directly from the satellite, in a manner similar to an oscilloscope beam sweeping the screen.

The first steps toward the establishment of an intersatellite communications link via traveling-wave tube (TWT) have been taken by Intelsat. This way communications bound for destinations outside the single-satellite coverage area will be switched directly from the first satellite to the second. One down- and one up-link transmission path will be saved (refer to Fig. 8.10). This will allow more efficient use of the system as a whole. It will also enable one earth station to communicate through more than one satellite in each area, thus improving the system flexibility.

Utilization of laser beams to transmit data from satellites is in the experimental stage. This technique would conserve power and reduce weight. Utilization of laser-optical frequency instead of radio frequency in the crowded frequency bands will offer big advantages to satellite communications.

8.8   CCIR Recommendations and Reports for Data Transmissions via Satellites*

Recommendations

352.2   Fixed-satellite service systems for telephony and/or television

353.2   Systems in the fixed-satellite service for FDM telephony

354.2   Systems in the fixed-satellite service carrying television

446.1   Carrier energy dispersal in systems in the fixed-satellite service

464   Systems in the fixed-satellite service for multiplex telephony

465.1   Reference earth station radiation pattern for use in coordination and interference assessment in the frequency range from 2 to about 10 GHz

466.1   Systems in the fixed-satellite service for telephony using FDM (interference levels)

481   Systems in the fixed-satellite service for telephony using FDM (noise measurement)

482   Systems using FDM in the fixed-satellite service for telephony (performance measurement)

483   Systems for television using FM in the fixed-satellite service

484   Station keeping of geostationary satellites using frequency bands allocated to the fixed-satellite service

Reports

204.3   Terms and definitions relating to space radiocommunications

206.3   Technical characteristics of systems in the fixed-satellite service

207.3   Active communication satellite systems (characteristics)

208.3   Systems in the fixed-satellite service for FDM telephony and television

211.3   Active communication-satellite systems (modulation and multiple access)

212.3   Systems in the fixed-satellite service for FDM telephony and television

213.3   Factors affecting multiple access in systems in the fixed-satellite service

383.2   Systems in the fixed-satellite service (transmission delay)

390.2   Earth station antenna for the fixed-satellite service

553   Fixed-satellite service (operation and maintenance)

559   The effect of modulation characteristics on the efficiency of use of the geostationary satellite orbit

---

*CCIR *Green Book*, Vol. IV, 1974.

References

Bargellini, Pier L.: "Commercial U.S. Satellites," *IEEE Spectrum,* October 1979.

CCIR, Geneva: vol. IV, Rep. 213-3, "TDMA Technique," 1974.

Communications Satellite Corporation, Washington, D.C.: "Guide to the Intelsat, Marisat, and Comstar Satellite Systems," 1980.

Martin, James: "Nonstationary Satellites," *Future Developments in Telecommunications,* Prentice-Hall, Englewood Cliffs, N.J., 1971, chap. 15, p. 243.

Napoli, J., and J. Christopher: "RCA Satcom System," *RCA Engineer,* vol. 21, no. 1, June/July 1975.

Puente, J. G., and E. R. Cacciamani: "A Dedicated User 1.344 Mb/s Satellite Data Transmission Network," *Telecommunications,* September 1975.

Salamoff, Steven; "SCPC Is Efficient Satellite Technique," *Communications News,* February 1978.

Yeh, Leang, P., P.E.: "Dial a Channel," *Telecommunications,* March 1975.

—— "Satellite Communications and Terrestrial Networks," *Telecommunications,* October 1977.

Chapter

9

Monitoring and Testing on Operational Circuits

Today's complex business world is demanding more and more widespread use of data communications for order entry, inventory control, on-line banking, insurance claims processing, and so forth. The trend is for more sophisticated systems, faster speeds, and efficient utilization of the many communication links. The modern teleprocessing user today requires hundreds or even thousands of telephone circuits and modems to conduct business to move great amounts of data from place to place. Collectively, those circuits comprise a network.

When considering access to the network, it is wise to differentiate between the analog and digital parts of the system. Analog testing provides a confidence in the transmission line and is generally performed before inaugurating a new circuit or accepting a line for operations as well as for troubleshooting purposes. Digital monitoring on data circuits gives operators a general idea about the quality of the circuit without interrupting it for long durations.

The kind of monitoring and testing required must be considered at the time of network planning and design. The thresholds of quality variation should be set so that warning will be given of an impending transmission-line failure. LED indicators and an audible alarm give a definite indication of trouble in the operation center. It is always recommended to obtain qualitative information by monitoring the performance of the circuit before moving to quantitative measurements.

An operator must have a basic idea about the kind of result to expect before beginning the tests, as well as the knowledge to interpret those results obtained. In this way, interruption of operations is minimized and quick remedial steps can be taken. Analog measurements are covered in detail in Chap. 2. Analog PAR measurement, digital monitoring-testing, and the function of a technical control center are explained in this chapter.

9.1   Analog Technique, PAR Measurements

As indicated earlier, the measurements of attenuation-frequency and delay-distortion characteristics are a time-consuming process and are generally performed during detailed studies on systems. They are not daily routine. An analog measurement that is a rapid and accurate way to measure the quality of circuits for data transmission is called *PAR* (peak-to-average-ratio) *measurement*. The PAR technique utilizes a generator and a receiver connected in either end-to-end or loop-around configuration. The generator transmits a closely controlled, repetitive pulse through the system, and the receiver further processes the pulse train. Loss and phase distortions in the system disperse the energy, reducing the ratio of the pulse envelope peak (E_{pk}) to envelope full-wave average (E_{FWA}). This ratio serves as the basis for the PAR rating, which is

$$\text{PAR} = \left(2\frac{E_{pk}}{E_{FWA}} - 1 \right) 100$$

Thus an undistorted signal with a PAR of unity has a rating of 100; a distorted signal with a normalized ratio of 0.75 has a rating of 50, which is suitable for speeds of up to 2400 b/s. The PAR is sensitive to attenuation distortion (bandwidth-limiting), envelope delay distortion, and some other characteristics such as high background noise, poor return loss, and harmonic and nonlinear distortion.

Recommended values.   Tentative overall requirements for circuit facilities are listed below; if these requirements are met, it is a strong indication that the circuit envelope delay distortion is within limits.

Circuit conditioning	Minimum PAR
Basic channel	45
C1	48
C2	78
C4	87
C5	95

The PAR measurement requires minimal technical skill to perform and little knowledge of analog measurement techniques to identify line problems.

The PAR rating is affected most significantly by envelope delay distortion, which causes the data signal to spread in time, resulting in intersymbol interference, and by attenuation distortion which may result in a high error rate in some modems. To a lesser degree, PAR is also affected by noise, gain ripples, and nonlinearities such as compression or clipping.

How to Use PAR

Application of the PAR test may be found in the three phases of analog testing: *commissioning, troubleshooting,* and *preventive maintenance.*

In the commissioning phase, a PAR test should be performed on a new line when it is initially installed. This measurement serves a twofold purpose: to ensure that the line meets the minimum requirements for that particular grade of conditioning and to provide a benchmark reading to be recorded and used as a reference for future testing.

If a problem develops at a later date, the benchmark reading may be used in the troubleshooting phase. Another PAR test is conducted on the line and the result is compared to the benchmark made at commissioning. A change of ±4 units would indicate that a significant change has taken place in the line. Thus, with a single measurement, the network manager can, with a reasonable level of confidence, either eliminate or pinpoint the line as the source of the problem.

Finally, PAR can be a valuable tool when used as a part of a preventive maintenance program. Measurements are periodically made and the results recorded on a test card. With this program, line degradation can be noted and corrective action taken at a convenient time before service is affected.

The PAR measurement may be performed in either the end-to-end or the loop-around configuration. There are advantages and disadvantages to each technique.

End-to-end testing is the recognized method for testing analog circuit parameters. This technique involves placing a test instrument at each end of the line and performing the PAR measurement using one instrument as the transmitter and the other one as the receiver. The advantages of this method are that it requires only a single two-wire circuit and it is the technique used for testing to common-carrier specifications. Obviously, the disadvantage is the requirement for two test instruments.

Using the loop-around technique overcomes the requirement for two test instruments, although it does require a four-wire circuit. This method is not recognized for testing to specifications since impairments on the transmit side of the circuit could cancel out or add to impairments on the receive side to give erroneous readings. Despite this limitation, loop-around readings are very powerful when used as a benchmark to isolate line problems when they occur.

Limitations of PAR

While certainly a powerful testing tool, PAR is by no means a panacea for all line problems. Impairments such as impulse noise and frequency shift which may be troublesome to data transmission will have no effect on the PAR rating of the line. In addition, PAR does not provide any specific information about the nature of the problem. For example, a user who encounters a low PAR reading cannot determine from the PAR test alone whether the problem is due to poor frequency response, delay distortion, or noise.

On the other hand, most network managers are not concerned with the specific nature of a problem but simply whether the line is capable of passing data. This information may be readily obtained by a PAR test. Tests such as attenuation distortion, signal-to-noise ratio, and impulse noise may be used to identify a specific failure.

9.2 Distortion Measurements on Digital Circuits

A very effective method of measuring distortion in a data transmission system is based on the *eye pattern*. By observing the eye pattern, signal quality curves can be constructed also, which gives the jitter rate as a function of the line length.

The eye pattern

The quality of a detected data signal may be observed by means of an eye pattern. If the data bit rate is used to trigger the horizontal sweep of an oscilloscope and a pseudorandom data word is applied to the vertical deflection plates, a distinctive pattern, such as the one illustrated in Fig. 9.2, will appear on the screen. The detection cross hairs are centered in the opening or "eye." Impairments to the signal transmission will have the effect of closing this eye, thus reducing the margin or even producing errors if the pattern overlaps the cross hairs. Formation of eye pattern in a digital circuit is simply the superposition over one unit interval of all the 0 to 1 and 1 to 0 transitions, each preceded and followed by various combinations of 1 and 0 levels.

The name *eye pattern* comes from the resemblance of the open pattern

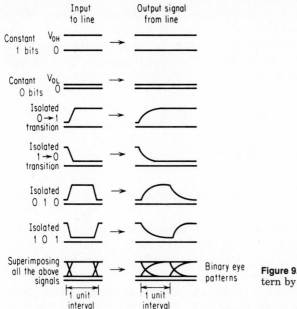

Figure 9.1 Formation of eye pattern by superposition.

center to an eye. The diagramatic construction of an eye pattern is shown in Fig. 9.1.

Several features of the eye pattern makes it a useful tool for measuring data signal quality. Figure 9.2 shows a typical binary eye pattern for NRZ data. The spread of traces crossing the receiver threshold level is a direct measure of the peak-to-peak transition jitter of the data signal. The rise and fall time of the signal can be conveniently measured by using the built-in 0 and 100 percent references produced by long strings of 0s and 1s. The height of the trace above or below the receiver threshold level at the sampling instant is the noise margin of the system. If no clear transition-free space in the eye pattern exists, the eye is closed. This indicates that error-free data transmission is not possible at that data rate and line length with that particular transmission line without resorting to equalizing techniques. In some

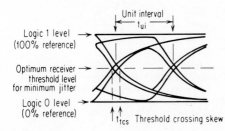

Figure 9.2 NRZ data eye pattern, using a 640 m terminated 24 AWG twisted-pair cable with PVC insulation. Peak-to-peak jitter $= (t_{tcs}/t_{ui}) \times 100\%$. (*Redrawn from Kenneth M. True,* Interface, *Fairchild Semiconductor Co., Mountain View, Calif., 1975, fig. 4-13.*)

extreme cases error-free data recovery may not be possible even when using equalizing techniques.

Figure 9.3 shows different jitter values in an eye pattern for NRZ signals with various amounts of isochronous distortion. Isochronous distortion (ID) is defined as

$$ID = \frac{t_{tcs}}{t_{ui}} \times 100\%$$

where tcs = threshold crossing skew
      ui = unit interval

Isochronous distortion as a function of modulation rate is given in Fig. 2.33.

The eye pattern can also be used to find the characteristic resistance of a transmission line. Figure 9.4 shows the NRZ eye patterns for $R_T > R_0$, $R_T = R_0$, and $R_T < R_0$, where R_T = termination resistance and R_0 = characteristic resistance.

The eye pattern gives the minimum peak-to-peak transition jitter for a given line length, type, pulse code, and modulation rate, because the eye-pattern transition spread is the result of intersymbol interference and reflection effects. This minimum jitter is only obtainable if the following conditions are met:

1. The 1 and 0 signal levels produced by the line driver are symmetrical, and the line receiver's decision threshold (for NRZ signaling) is set to coincide with the mean of those two levels.

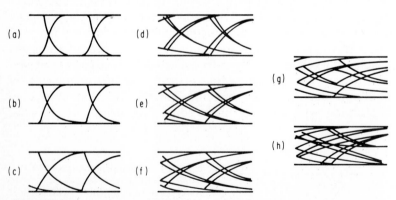

Figure 9.3 Eye patterns for NRZ data corresponding to various peak-to-peak transition jitter. (*a*) No intersymbol interference, $t_{ui} = 4t_r$; (*b*) no intersymbol interference, $t_{ui} = 2t_r$; (*c*) 5 percent jitter; (*d*) 10 percent jitter; (*e*) 20 percent jitter; (*f*) 30 percent jitter; (*g*) 50 percent jitter; (*h*) 100 percent jitter. (*Redrawn from Kenneth M. True*, Interface, *Fairchild Semiconductor Co., Mountain View, Calif., 1975, fig. 4-16.*)

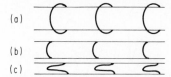

Figure 9.4 Using eye pattern to determine characteristic resistance of line. (*a*) Undertermination, $R_T > R_0$; (*b*) terminated case, $R_T = R_0$; (*c*) overtermination, $R_T < R_0$. (*Redrawn from Kenneth M. True,* Interface, *Fairchild Semiconductor Co., Mountain View, Calif., 1975, fig. 4-14.*)

2. The line is perfectly terminated in its characteristic resistance to prevent reflections from altering the signal threshold crossings.

3. The time delays through driver and receiver devices for both logic states is symmetrical and there is no relative skew in the delays; i.e., the difference between $L \rightarrow H$ and $H \rightarrow L$ propagation delays is 0. This is especially important when the device propagation delays become significant fractions of the unit interval for the applicable modulation rate.

If any one of these conditions is not satisfied, the signal quality is reduced; i.e., distortion increases. The effects of receiver bias or threshold ambiguity and driver offset can be determined by location of the decision threshold(s) on the oscilloscope of the eye pattern. Bias distortion and characteristic distortion are given in Secs. 2.11 and 2.12. For eye patterns displaying more than 20 percent isochronous distortion, the slope of the signal in the transition region is relatively small. Therefore, a small amount of bias results in a large increase in net isochronous distortion. See Fig. 9.5 for a graphic illustration of this effect.

In the interest of conservative design practices, systems should al-

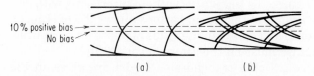

Figure 9.5 Receiver bias effect on total isochronous distortion. (*a*) 320 m, 1 MBd; (*b*) 640 m, 1 MBd. Isochronous distortion $ID = (t_{tes}/t_{ui}) \times 100\%$.

Bias	320 m	640 m
0%	5% ID	20% ID
10%	12% ID	36% ID

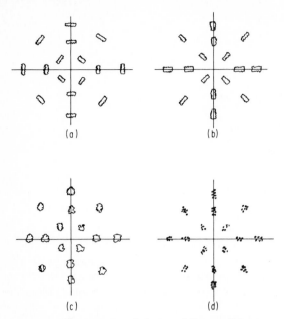

Figure 9.6 Eye patterns of abnormal line conditions on a QAM system, 9600 b/s. (*a*) 20° phase jitter; (*b*) gain jitter; (*c*) noise; (*d*) gain hit.

ways be designed with less than 5 percent transition spread in the eye pattern. This allows the detrimental effects due to bias to be minimized, thus simplifying construction of line drivers and receivers.

Some modems are equipped with an eye-pattern generator which converts digital quadrature data to analog voltage levels and displays them on an oscilloscope. The QAM technique is explained in Sec. 4.1, and eye patterns for different data speeds are given in Fig. 4.2. Although with the QAM technique the oscilloscope pattern bears no resemblance to an eye, the term has stuck. This method allows the operator to quickly diagnose the line status without interfering with data reception. The appearance of the signal pattern allows the operator to determine the presence and approximate value of phase and amplitude jitter, hits, and impulse noise on the communication line.

Transient disturbances on a transmission media are given in Fig. 9.6. A random noise causes the eye patterns to be dispersed around their proper positions; phase jitter causes the dots to oscillate back and forth; gain jitter is characterized by amplitude errors.

Digital Signal-Quality Graphs By using the eye pattern to measure signal quality at the load end of a given line, a graph can be constructed. An example graph for NRZ data is shown in Fig. 9.7. The graph was

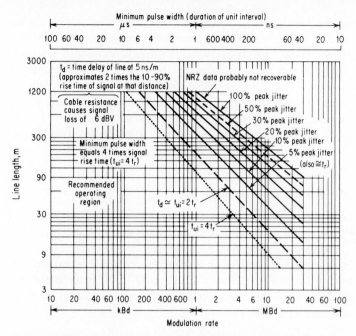

Figure 9.7 Signal quality as a function of line length and modulation rate for a terminated 24 AWG twisted pair (PVC insulation). $Z_0 = 96$; $t_d = 5$ ns/m. Data from cables of 45 to 1130 m. (*Redrawn from Kenneth M. True*, Interface, *Fairchild Semiconductor Co., Mountain View, Calif., 1975, fig. 4-15.*)

constructed using eye-pattern measurements on a 24 AWG twisted-pair line, with peak-to-peak jitter as a function of line length and modulation rate for a specific pulse code.

Since the twisted-pair line used was not specifically constructed for pulse service, the graph represents a reasonable case condition insofar as signal quality versus line length is concerned. Twisted-pair lines with polyethylene or Teflon insulation have shown better performance at a given length than the polyvinyl chloride insulation. Likewise, larger conductors like 20 AWG or 22 AWG also provide better performance at a given length. Thus the graph in Fig. 9.7 can be used to estimate feasibility of a transmission system when the actual cable to be used is unavailable for measurement purposes. The arbitrary cutoff of 1200 m (4000 ft) on the graph was due to an observed signal amplitude loss of 6 dBV (half voltage) of the 24 AWG line at that distance.

EIA RS 422A and 423A graphs of cable length limits versus transmission speeds are shown for both balanced and unbalanced digital interface circuits in Figs. 7.3 and 7.4. Field experience has shown that twisted-pair transmission systems using RS 422A and 423A drivers have operated essentially error-free when the line length and modulation rate are kept to within the shaded recommended operating region shown in Fig. 9.7. This has not precluded operation outside this region for some systems, but these systems must be carefully designed with particular attention paid to defining the required characteristics of the line, the driver, and the receiver devices.

The use of coaxial cable instead of twisted-pair lines always yields better performance, i.e., greater modulation rate at a given line length and signal quality, because coaxial cable has a wider bandwidth and reduced attenuation at a given length than twisted-pair line.

9.3 Digital Monitoring and Testing

In practice *"out-of-service" testing* and *"in-service" error measurements* and *monitoring* have to be distinguished. In out-of-service testing the live traffic is replaced by a known test pattern.

Digital monitoring and testing on a communication system include DCEs and transmission lines as well as EIA (CCITT) interfacing circuits. EIA (CCITT) interfacings consist of three electrically and operationally different circuits:

- Signal circuits
- Control circuits
- Timing circuits

Testing procedures are also different on these circuits.

Monitoring

Integrity of an EIA (CCITT) interface is more a function of monitoring than of testing. There are many different types of test equipment available with some form of LED (light-emitting diode) status lights to provide this monitoring; refer to Fig. 9.8. Two-color LEDs are preferred because they distinguish the current polarity in double-current circuits. For example, if a signal is higher than $+3$ V, it triggers a red light; if it is less than -3 V, it triggers a green light; if it is at an undefined level (between -3 and $+3$ V), no light is triggered.

Most DCEs are equipped with alarm warnings together with LED status indicators and built-in test facilities. These enable the operator to respond and solve the problem quickly. When the trouble is indicated, the operator switches to next-step monitoring and testing.

LED indicators in a typical DCE monitor the following:

- *Good-Bad Data.* When the averaged error is below a threshold (say 10^{-5}) or above a threshold (10^{-4}).

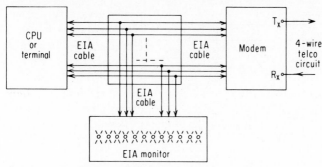

Figure 9.8 Monitoring of EIA lines using LED indicators.

- *Carrier Loss.* The received signal from the remote transmitter is lost.

Loop tests*

The locating of faults can be facilitated in many cases by looping procedures in DCEs. These loops allow local or remote measurements in analog or digital forms to be carried out optionally. A number of routine tests can be initiated from a central office without the involvement of any operator at the remote site. Remote testing signals may be included in the data stream, or a separate channel is used for testing purposes. The operator may monitor the data stream on a CRT (cathode-ray tube).

Four loops are defined in CCITT V.54; refer to Fig. 9.9. Loop 1 is used as a basic test on the operation of the DTE by returning transmitted signals to the DTE for checking. During the loop 1 test condition:

- Transmitted Data circuit (103) is connected to Received Data circuit (104) within the DTE.
- Data Terminal Ready (108/2) must be in the same condition as it was before the test.
- Request to Send (105) must be in the off condition.
- Ring Indicator (125) should continue to be monitored by the DTE so that an incoming call can be given priority over a routine loop test.
- Transmitted Data (103) must be in the binary 1 condition.

Loop 2 is designed to check the satisfactory working of the telephone line and of the local and remote DCE. It can only be used in the duplex

---

*Refer to CCITT Rec. V.54 for detailed loop testings on modems.

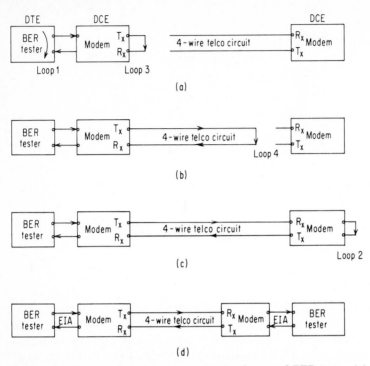

Figure 9.9 Circuit-quality measurements using loops and BER tester. (*a*) Local loop tests; (*b*) remote loop tests; (*c*) remote loop tests through both modems; (*d*) end-to-end tests.

operation and is established by sending a command signal to remote modem. During the loop 2 test condition:

- Received Data (104) is connected to Transmitted Data (103) within the DCE.
- Data Carrier Detect (109) is used to activate Request to Send (105).
- Receiver Clock (115) is connected to External Transmit Clock (113).

Loop 3 is a local loop established in the dialog mode to check the satisfactory working of the local DCE. The loop should include the maximum number of circuits used in normal working conditions, which may in some cases necessitate the inclusion of devices for attenuating signals, for example.

Loop 4 arrangement is only considered in the case of four-wire lines. Loop 4 is designed for the maintenance of lines by using analog-type measurements. In the loop position the two pairs are disconnected from the remote DCE and are connected to each other through a symmetrical attenuator designed to prevent oscillation of the circuit; the value of the attenuator should be of the order of 6 dB for stability reasons.

Loop 4 may be established inside the DCE or in a separate unit; when the loop is inside the DCE, it presents circuits Data Set Ready (107) and Data Carrier Detect (109) to the DTE in the off condition. This signal is not equalized, decoded, or regenerated at the distant end. The distortion of the received loopback signal will therefore be approximately double that of a normal received signal. Thus this loop test provides an indication of the receiver equalizer's ability to provide usable received output data with double the normal amount of telephone-line distortion.

In performing circuit-quality tests we have to make a tradeoff between end-to-end testing or loop-around testing. End-to-end testing is superior because it locates problems to the send or receive side of the line. With loop-around testing, we will know if the line is faulty but never determine which side is at fault. Obviously end-to-end tests mean twice the test equipment investment.

Most of DCEs are equipped with unattended remote loopback facilities, either as an option or an integral part of the DCE. In a very popular modem, for example, a 1.92-kHz tone is sent (1–4 s) for Dc Busback loop 2; Audio loop 4 is initiated by sending a 2.4-kHz tone (refer to Fig. 9.10). Remote loopback commands may be initiated externally from a data terminal, with loopback-initiate and clear signals via the EIA interface.

To perform testing that includes the modems, the basic figure of merit is the bit error rate (BER). A typical BER tester has the capabilities of EIA RS 232C (CCITT V.28), CCITT V.35, and other most-utilized physical interface connections together with LED indications on the interface wires. Several test patterns can be delivered: alternate 1s and 0s, 511, 2047, 32,767, 65,535 bits. It can simulate a modem with external transmit and transmit and receive timing features. Some bit patterns are pseudorandom, which simulate random bit patterns associated with normal data transmission. Pseudorandom bit sequences are generated by using a special algorithm. The receiving portion of the test equipment generates the identical pattern, and comparison is performed in the tester. The number of bits received in error divided by the number of bits transmitted is the BER. The block error rate is the number of blocks where the bits are received in error divided by the number of blocks transmitted. Blocks are usually 1 kb long, and a block error constitutes at least 1 bit error per block. CCITT V.52 recommends the standard 511-bit pattern and defines the pseudorandom bit pattern and BER tester specifications. The BER test is the basic test relied on because, with one simple test, an operator can move rapidly toward isolating the fault between the modem and the telephone line. As with analog testing, a BER tester does off-line testing. The sequential events shown in Fig. 9.9 indicate how the process is

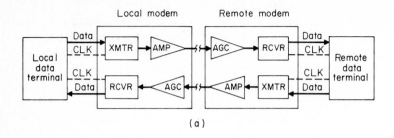

(a)

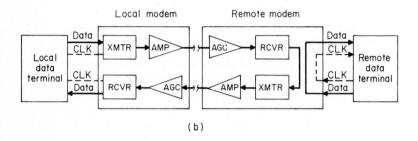

(b)

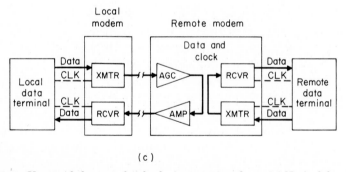

(c)

Figure 9.10 Unattended remote loopbacks in remote modems. (a) Normal data mode; (b) dc bussback—loop 2; and (c) audio—loop 4.

performed with BER testing. It is important to conduct BER tests during peak hours of communications on a transmission line, rather than on weekends or at night; CCITT Rec. V.51 also specifies this requirement. Otherwise, satisfactory test results would be obtained for unsatisfactory transmission lines. Figure 9.11 shows that the BER is 11 times lower at off-peak periods than peak hours.

CCITT Rec. V.53 gives the maximum bit error rates for telephone-type circuits. For 200-, 600-, and 1200-Bd modulation rates on leased lines, maximum BER is 5×10^{-5}; for 200-Bd switched lines, maximum

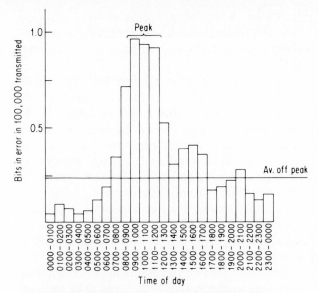

Figure 9.11   Daily BER fluctuations of a Telex trunk.

BER is 10^{-4}, and for 600- and 1200-Bd switched lines maximum BER is 10^{-3}.

Another term for describing the error performance in digital transmission is the *error-free second*. This quantity originates from the requirement of digital data transmission and is more suitable than error ratio for defining the quality of those systems. An error-free second is a period during which no errors are observed in a digital signal.

In addition to the terms defined above, the absolute number of errors observed during a certain period of time is used for specifying the error performance of digital systems, especially in such cases where the error ratio is very small and only few errors occur.

In addition to pseudorandom patterns, periodic sequences can serve as test signals. Because the input signal applied to the object under test is known in both cases, the output from the test object can be compared with a reference signal which is identical with the original input signal. This permits the detection of any error in the data stream. Therefore, this way of assessing digital errors is often called a *true error measurement*.

Testing of a system by utilizing protocols

BER testing stems from the DCE and involves proper transmission and reception of bit sequences. Other types of tests may be originated from the DTE; this is protocol testing and deals primarily with the proper character reception. Protocol testing gives the network manager a window into the data that are going back and forth in the system. The protocol tester is a test equipment which displays protocol information in symbols on a CRT.

The protocol instrument lets an operator monitor both the actual traffic that the front-end processor (FEP) or terminal is sending and the response from the far end. In effect this is a monitoring of the exchange of data between computers and seeing the control symbols that control the communications link, the information which the FEP adds to the row data coming from the computer. It lets an operator see data formatting and in a gross sense, the timing of the system; in essence, it gives an overview of the system's operation.

As a troubleshooter for data communication networks, a protocol analyzer connects to the digital interface of a computer or terminal, which may be data terminal equipment (DTE) or data circuit equipment (DCE), usually a modem (Fig. 9.12).

A protocol analyzer either monitors or simulates network activity. As a monitor, it passively and nonintrusively captures data that are moving across the interface. The data are displayed in the code being used by the communicating terminals, ASCII or EBCDIC, or in hexadecimal notation. Since control circuits govern the movement of data, the analyzer must also display the status of the control lines in real time.

While the instrument monitors the data and control leads, it stores their states in a circular buffer memory, which can be a combination of volatile random-access memory (RAM) and a nonvolatile magnetic floppy disk or tape. After being captured, the data are evaluated offline by examining the contents of the buffer memory or sometimes by processing the data later using the instrument's analysis capabilities.

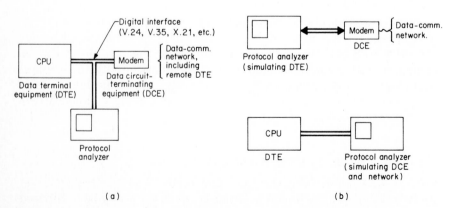

Figure 9.12   Utilization of protocol analyzer as (a) monitor and (b) simulator.

In the simulation mode, the protocol analyzer interacts with the remote DTE or DCE by simulating the local counterpart. Simulation is primarily used for developing or debugging network software, but may also functionally test a DTE upon installation or while troubleshooting complex network problems. The designer employs the instrument as a low-cost, more versatile alternative to providing the connection environment for the DTE or DCE. Most sophisticated protocol analyzers can interact with the network up to and including level 3 protocols.

A protocol analyzer may be installed in a computer room or in the technical control center as a complement to digital and analog test equipment.

AT&T has introduced a new service for data network control, called *Data-Phone II*. Data-Phone II is a synchronous data transmission system with a line of microprocessor-based modems, monitored by an outband automatic line and modem control system. Diagnostics are designed to eliminate tedious and wasteful fault-location techniques used with other data sets, which minimizes disruption and downtime. As explained in Sec. 7.7, Data-Phone II provides level 1, level 2, and level 3 data transmission services.

In level 1 systems, the control modem continuously polls all tributary modems in accordance with a polling list entered by the user. If a tributary modem requests a maintenance test, the control modem runs the test.

Level 2 augments level 1 at the central site with a diagnostic console that continuously polls each set in the network with expanded test and command capabilities.

The network controller brings several features to a level 3 system, including continuous monitoring that yields up-to-date status records, later execution of tests, and storage on a tape cartridge of test routines. Level 3 service provides for a number of disruptive and nondisruptive modem tests. Disruptive tests range from loopback and end-to-end error tests to the inbound and outbound circuit loss measurements. Nondisruptive tests utilize the out-of-band channel and include signal-level measurements, EIA interface status. If the user wishes, network trouble can be reported automatically to an AT&T test center.

Network troubleshooting

Correcting a problem in a data communications network can eat up valuable staff time and talent. Finding the problem is often more difficult than resolving it. The error may not recur except at the most awkward hours, and, when it does occur, it may be so obscure and fleeting that there is little time to learn how to reproduce it and even less time to correct it.

In today's worldwide communications networks, automated switching equipment makes it possible to operate remote hubs with few or no trained communications engineers and technicians.

Subtle errors may occur in a network which degrade performance and reduce efficiency without completely shutting down any portion. Excessive NAKs and resultant retransmission on a data link or frequent time-outs of terminals will slow or interrupt work.

The causes of errors can lie in many different network components. Faulty EIA-standard signal timing can be one cause. Protocol problems on a data link can be another. Ascertaining all the causes requires sophisticated test equipment and highly trained personnel. Sending technicians to remote sites to perform tests can be quite costly.

Network problems can also be annoyingly random and troublesome to reproduce. When this occurs, valuable staff time is lost waiting for the condition to repeat itself. Also, convincing the manufacturer whose equipment is at fault of the accuracy of the expert's analysis is difficult.

However, if serial data transmissions are recorded, when errors occur they can be played back at slow or intermediate speeds to capture the exact character of the signals transmitted and to accommodate the limitations of test equipment.

Placed at a remote network node, a recorder can record data on a troublesome channel and later transmit the information back to the central location for duplication. Systems analysts can then do their work at the central site without expensive and lengthy trips to the field sites. Even unmanned remote sites can be serviced this way.

Recording and playback rates are usually selectable from 50 b/s to 56 kb/s to match the rates of almost any installation.

Note the difference between *system restoration time* and *circuit repair time*. The system can be restored very fast with sparing and other backup techniques, some of which can be easily automated. Problem determination usually takes a bit longer, and corrective action, e.g., replacing a modem, may take quite a while.

9.4   Technical Control Center

The primary purpose of a technical control center is to provide responsive and dependable communications support for the user. This task is best accomplished when the center can perform diagnostic monitoring and testing over the entire communications link. For this purpose, control centers have begun to be equipped with systems which provide continuous monitoring and isolate faults on analog and digital transmission systems without interrupting the service. Since a communication office provides its service via analog and digital facilities, a control center has to be equipped with analog and digital test systems.

A typical analog system samples the signal on lines at preset (typically 1 s) intervals, identifying the type of traffic present, and determines the characteristics; it starts minor or major alarms by recognizing the preset tolerance limits and prints on a trouble report printer. In addition, a control operator can call for the display of all measured values and can cause the system to monitor a selected line continuously.

The principal functions of such an automatic monitoring system include:

- Continuous in-service monitoring of large numbers of voice-band lines

- Line-by-line limit tests based upon traffic recognition and multidimensional signal analysis

- Alarming of out-of-specification and degraded line conditions

- Monitoring of data from remote signal acquisition facilities in a telecommunication network

- Out-of-service tests to aid in fault isolation and remedial maintenance

- Loopback, end-to-end, and midpoint-to-midpoint tests with local and remote signal injection and measurement

- Conversational system operation using video terminals located at one or more technical control sites

- Reporting facilities

Table 9.1 shows the measurements made within the analysis time for each facility type in a typical automatic monitoring system. Also, once in each scan sequence and upon fault verification the system performs a self-check using a calibrated test signal. Failure of this system validation check will result in a system alarm, and a trouble report will be printed.

Once a line fault is verified and the system validates its own operation, a trouble report is printed and observation of the faulty line is discontinued pending operator attention. The out-of-service measurement provides the operator with the ability to perform the full complement of tests typically associated with the characterization of voice-band data lines. The out-of-service measurement can also be performed with the addition of a portable test unit at the end office. The technical control center or end office can inject signals, and the other end acquires this test signal. If measurement is made at another point in the net-

TABLE 9.1   Type of Measurements Performed by Automatic Monitoring System

Measurement	Facility type				
	Modem	VFCT	AVD	Speech plus*	Idle
Aggregate signal power	X	X	X	X	X
Spectral center frequency	X	X	X	X	X
Spectral width	X	X	X	X	X
Spectral median frequency	X	X	X	X	X
Derived C-message noise	X	X	X	X	
Signal/C-message noise (derived)	X	X	X	X	
Power, each VFCT channel†		X		X	
Max./min. VFCT channel power		X		X	
Power, SF tone			X	X	
Power, VFCT band				X	
Power, speech band				X	
SF-VFCT power				X	
Power, test tone					X
Harmonic distortion					X
Notched C-message noise					X
Power, single-frequency interference					X
Frequency, single-frequency interference					X
White noise					X

*Speech plus teleprinter channels.
†VFCT stands for voice-frequency carrier telegraphy.

work, the technical control center provides point-to-point measurement coordination and analyzes the signals. The system performs the following measurements within its 1-s scan analysis time in the out-of-service mode:

Net loss	Frequency error	Frequency response
Envelope delay	White noise	Notched noise
C-message noise	Notched C-message noise	Phase jitter
Amplitude jitter	Harmonic distortion	Intermodulation distortion

Time-requiring tests for transients are conducted at the receiving end of a line. Using looping facilities the system permits the operator to perform a full series of out-of-service loop measurements.

An automatic analog monitoring system can be flexibly introduced into a variety of network management and administration. This significantly reduces the operational costs by providing an improved technical control with fewer and lower skilled operators. Organization of the maintenance of international telephone-type circuits used for data transmission is given in CCITT Rec. V.51. As mentioned before, that master controller at the technical center communicates with a special electronics module added to each modem in the network. This module is responsible for gathering status and operational data from its associated modem and responding to commands from the controller. Communication takes place over the regular data network, normally over a secondary channel, without interrupting regular network operations. For 9.6 kb/s modems the channel operates at 75 b/s; for lower-speed modems the data rate is 150 b/s, typically.

Although an analog technical control system performs a superb job, it is not capable of identifying intermittent failures and is not effective for monitoring digital circuits. For this reason a digital control system has been developed.

Digital technical control centers also have limitations; they cover only digital links, such as the CTE/DTE portion and channel ports of the circuits which extend to relatively short distances. Although this can be compensated for by using digital repeaters, it also increases the system cost considerably. Furthermore, digital operators need more training and are paid more than analog operators.

The answer to the problem is a hybrid analog-digital technical control center that provides the ability to perform quick digital diagnostics and complete circuit monitoring as well as takes advantage of the economies of analog patching and switching. A digital-analog technical control center employs two relatively simple concepts: monitoring digital data on the analog level (by using modems) and a digital-analog pushbutton bus structure. Several synchronous and asynchronous modems are used to cover the 200 to 56,000 b/s spectrum in a typical technical control center. These modems are functionally identical to the replaced operational unit. This way the suspected portion of the link can be tested as though it were in a normal operating mode.

EIA RS 232C interface conditions on individual circuits are displayed by two-color LEDs (to cover double-current interface circuits). The quantity of digital test equipment at the center is dictated by the operational requirements.

A BER tester is utilized when performing off-line tests, and a high-speed tape unit is used to record and play back the digital data at a slower rate to check the data stream visually for errors.

Another useful device is a programmable *communication network analyzer* which exercises the line, looks for errors, and performs a number of programmed functions to analyze the error conditions by utilizing both byte-controlled and bit-oriented protocols. Normally a technical control center is equipped with several CRT units and one large overhead monitor.

Several network control systems have been developed for use in a technical control center. Some systems use a separate minicomputer to handle the data base and to function as a CPU for the master controller. Some systems gather performance data such as response times and BERs and produce daily management reports on line utilization.

Intelligent terminal

An intelligent terminal is used in some control centers in connection with programming supplied via a CPU, or the terminal itself can be programmed to perform a limited number of predetermined functions.

Although the adjectives "smart" and "intelligent" are used to describe similar TDM equipment in the book, the distinction between a smart terminal and intelligent terminal was introduced in the industry to identify some functions performed in one terminal which are not available in the other type of terminal.

Smart terminals have the capability to edit and store data as well as perform unattended operations. These can include management of peripherals such as cartridges, floppy disks, or printers. A major disadvantage with the smart terminal is that its capability is limited and it must eventually rely on the "brain power" of the host CPU for sophisticated operations. As a consequence, only a limited number of smart terminals may access the CPU at one time, severely restricting simultaneous terminal activity within a production environment. The *intelligent terminal,* however, has that capability, allowing extended editing, and forms handling capabilities at various workstations, further freeing the CPU for additional duties. Intelligent terminals not only boast extended editing capabilities and possibilities for interfacing but can also be programmed by the user. Consequently, the user can determine the terminal's functions based on particular requirements and, whenever the need arises, change the programs to meet the new requirements. The intelligent terminal, by virtue of its superior versatility and extended capabilities, is one of the driving forces in the growth of distributed data processing.

One of the most dynamic aspects of intelligent terminals occurs in the area of communications. Intelligent terminals can be adapted to communicate with one host computer after another simply by changing the protocol of the terminal rather than by adapting the host for a terminal.

Most typical intelligent terminal configurations make use of either an EIA RS 232C or an RS 422/423 type of interface or a current loop interface.

Description of units.   An intelligent terminal may be defined as a processing engine with the appropriate human and communications interfaces. Figure 9.13 depicts a block diagram of an intelligent terminal

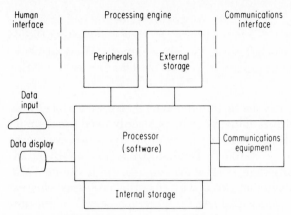

Figure 9.13 Block diagram of an intelligent terminal.

which is also applicable to a smart terminal, since the difference between the two lies in the microprocessor capabilities.

Data input unit. This unit is the principal interface between the operator and terminal for programming and interactive operations and in many instances is the only input device. It may have a typewriter, teletypewriter, or keypunch layout. It is the main factor in determining operator effectiveness and should be detachable to allow positioning flexibility for operator convenience and comfort and to make best use of space. Minimizing operator fatigue is a key factor in reducing input errors.

Display. This is a high-quality television monitor using a raster scan which covers the screen area 60 times per second with the displayed data being refreshed from an internal buffer. The display itself can lead to fatigue and a high error rate if poorly designed. Character size, brightness, screen size, spacing, and phosphor color are the factors that influence readability. Alternate display technologies include LEDs, liquid crystals, and gas or plasma panels.

Processor. This may be a single microprocessor or several, with each one controlling a specific function. For the slight additional cost of using multiple microprocessors, flexibility and ease of system design and overall increase in processing speed and efficiency may be achieved.

Internal storage. Two types of memory are commonly used: core and solid-state. Random-access memory (RAM) is the principal memory, where the stored bits are changed by deletion or by writing over the existing data. Read-only memory (ROM) is used primarily for the storage of fixed instruction sequences since the data content cannot be changed. Programmable read-only memory (PROM) is a particular type of ROM. Programs for PROMs are generally developed on a computer which produces a paper tape output; the tape is fed into a PROM burner and the memory is burned or made permanent. There are erasable PROMs where the data can be erased by deletion or by writing over the data.

Software. For ease of use, the terminal generally comes with the bulk of the programming already done, so that users only need program for specific applications. High-level languages simplify programming by allowing operations to be stated in Englishlike terms. COBOL, the most commonly used language, is ideal for business applications. FORTRAN, the second most popular, excels with scientific problems, whereas BASIC is currently the most popular language for small computers. APL is a newer and more powerful language that is easy to learn and code, but difficult to debug or to modify other people's code, and requires a large, fast processor to run. When written to conform with ANSI standards, COBOL, FORTRAN, and BASIC programs are portable; that is, they will run on a variety of machines without modification.

External storage. This unit can be characterized as unit record or mass storage and as serial or random access. Punched cards, for example, represent a unit record and serially accessed storage medium. Punched tape and magnetic tape are also serially accessed, whereas disks may be accessed serially or randomly. Both serial- and random-access storage devices may be used in a single terminal system.

Peripherals. In addition to storage devices, the intelligent terminal may use a printer for hard-copy output and a variety of other peripherals such as badge readers and low-cost optical character readers. Character printers are popular for interactive and data-entry applications, while line printers find use for batch jobs.

Communications equipment. Besides providing an electrical interface to the DCE, the terminal may operate with one of many line disciplines or communications protocols. In clustered configurations, it may perform limited multiplexing or concentration functions.

Recommendations for operator efficiency. Studies have been performed to determine the maximum comfort levels for operators working with a CRT. Figure 9.14 illustrates the critical dimensions affecting musculoskeletal comfort of an operator seated at a CRT workstation.

Furthermore, to ease visual and muscular strain and fatigue the following major factors are to be considered for a CRT terminal:

- Display dark characters on a light background. It has been found that unavoidable reflections are less disturbing with this method. In

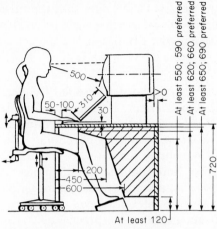

Figure 9.14 Critical dimensions for comfort of an operator seated at a CRT work station. (Taken from a West German labor union report. "Sicherheitsregein für Bildschrim-Arbeitsplätze im Burobereichl," October 1980.)

Note: All measurements are in millimeters

addition, closer luminance levels between paper documents and the screen are achieved, easing eye adjustment when the user switches between the two media. Further, the legibility of the characters is improved, simply because of the positive contrast in relationship to the rest of the room.

- Provide a 38-cm (15-in) screen.
- Use a nonreflecting housing.
- Include the ability to scroll.
- Use detached keyboards with sculptured clustered key zones.
- Provide tilting and swivel controls.
- Use a character dot matrix of 7 by 12.

Analog and digital meters

In communications, measurements are expressed in logarithmic units, such as decibels. Meters measure dB volts, dB watts, or dB milliwatts, and come in analog and digital types.

Analog meters. An ordinary ac meter is designed to have equal spacing on equal increments. If such a meter is calibrated to read in decibels, the marks on the scale for successive units above or below zero will be spaced increasingly close together. With a specially shaped coil magnet, flux across the air gap increases logarithmically as the coil moves from zero position. Thus equal spacing is obtained for a logarithmic increase in sinusoidal current values.

Note that when a dB meter reads zero, it means only that the ratio between the power being measured and reference power is 1. This reference power is 1 mW for measuring in dBm, and the measured current is sinusoidal.

Volume unit. Since speech waves contain several sinusoidal frequencies, and vary with time in a complex manner, it is not possible to measure their precise values in decibels except on an instantaneous basis. A method of expressing the average amplitude of complex non-periodic signals measures volume. A volume indicator, calibrated in volume units, is used for this purpose. Note that the volume indicator is not frequency-weighted. Volume is a logarithmic unit that measures signal strength above or below a specified reference level. In general, this reference level, designated 0 vu, indicates no precise electrical quantity, but the volume indicator is calibrated to read 0 vu on 1 mW of 1000 Hz power dissipated in a 600-Ω resistance. The volume unit (vu) represents the same power ratio as the decibel, and the volume indicator may therefore be used to measure transmission losses or gains when the current being measured is a 1000-Hz sine wave, although its primary purpose is to measure the volume of complex waves.

In other words, the volume meter is designed to measure the approximate root-mean-square (rms) voltage averaged over a syllabic interval. As a consequence, the meter gives no indication of the activity of a talker but only tells how loud the talker is when speaking. Relating volumes in vu to average power is usually done by first converting a continuous talker from vu to average dBm by the relation

$$\text{Average power} = \text{vu} - 1.4 \text{ dBm}$$

where the 1.4-dB conversion factor is the result of empirical tests with a variety of talkers reading text.

Talker volumes in the telephone plant have been found to be normally distributed in vu with a mean between -14 vu and -25 vu at 0TLP and a standard deviation between 4 and 6.5 dB depending upon the geographical area and type of talker. From these considerations, it would not be unusual to expect a transmission system to accommodate a -40-vu talker having an average power of -41.4 dBm and not distort on a $+10$ dBm peak due to a louder talker.

Refer to CCITT Recs. O.51 and P.52 for volume indicator characteristics.

Digital meters. For applications in which readings tend to fluctuate or oscillate and in which rates of change and trends must be monitored, analog meters are preferred. There are, however, a few digital meters with graphic displays that can compete with their analog equivalents when trends need to be indicated. One such instrument has a luminous bar graph made of discrete segments and marked in decades so that the rate of change of an input signal can be recognized at a glance.

When accuracy and resolution are paramount, however, digital panel meters perform much more satisfactorily than analog ones. Although readings from analog meters are typically in error by 1 to 5 percent, those displayed on digital panel meters are typically within 0.5 to 0.005 percent of true signal value. Further, the display of a digital meter can usually be read up to 12 ft (3.5–4 m) from the instrument under poor lighting conditions, without the parallax or repeatability problems associated with analog equipment.

Another important feature of digital panel meters is their ability to supply an auxiliary BCD output that can be used to run printers and for input to external data-acquisition systems. These outputs usually present parallel data and are accompanied by a status or data-ready signal that indicates to a printer that the digital panel meter output is valid after each update.

CCITT Recommendations relating to maintenance and technical control centers for data transmission*

M.80	Control stations
M.82	Circuit control station, leased and special circuits
M.90	Subcontrol stations
M.92	Subcontrol station, leased and special circuits
M.95	Transmission Maintenance Point-International Line (TMP-IL)
M.100	Service circuits
M.110	Circuit testing
M.130	Operational procedures in locating and clearing transmission faults
M.160	Transmission stability
M.201	Transmission path restoration for service protection
M.221	Exchange of information for planned outages of transmission systems
M.820	Periodicity of routine tests on international VFT links
M.830	Routine measurements to be made on international VFT links
M.1060	Maintenance of international leased circuits

*Orange Book, Vol. IV-1 and 2.

Series O Recommendations refer to specifications of measuring equipment.

References

Coenning, Frank: "Digital System Error Performance," *Telecommunications,* July 1983.

Pineau, Albert J.: "Network Troubleshooting," *Telecommunications,* September 1982.

Stein, Maurice I., and John Capobianco: "Communications Quality Monitor," *Telecommunications,* July 1979.

True, Kenneth M.: "Long Transmission Lines and Data Signal Quality," *Interface,* Fairchild Semiconductor Co., Mountain View, Calif., 1975, chap. 4.

Tugal, Dogan A.: "Data Transmission over Voice Circuits," RCA Global Communications, Anchorage, Alaska, 1972.

Wright, Douglas H.: "Is Your Network up to PAR?," *Telecommunications,* June 1982.

10

Optical-Fiber Transmission

The concept of communicating via a light beam in air has been known for many years. Range, dependability and general usefulness, were limited by atmospheric absorption of light and the need for line-of-sight transmission paths. The use of glass fibers as optical waveguides for conducting light waves has been limited to rounding corners. However, it was not until the development of a low-loss glass fiber with an attenuation of 20 db/km that large-scale developments in fiber-optic communication systems got under way.

Another necessary ingredient for a practical fiber-optic communication system is a highly concentrated but convenient-to-use light source. Developments in solid-state light sources coupled with the availability of solid-state optical detectors contributed toward the realization of practical optical-fiber communication systems.

Today electronic engineers are aware of the great advantages that optical fibers have over other transmission mediums, namely, a drastic reduction in weight and size for a given bandwidth, electrical isolation, immunity to electromagnetic interference, and a capability for secure transmission.

10.1 System Configuration

A typical fiber-optic communications system is shown in Fig. 10.1. For illustrative purposes, it is assumed that the original information is an

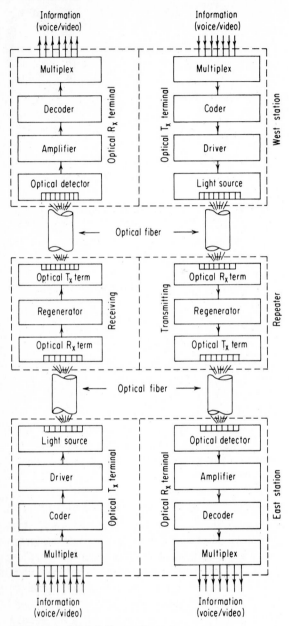

Figure 10.1 Digital fiber-optic system.

analog telephone signal converted to digital form by conventional terminal equipment (because of the large bandwidth available, the digital technique is preferred, although low-capacity links may use analog modulation). At the transmitting terminal, the digital signals are used to modulate the current of a light source, an injection laser or an LED. The laser could be switched on and off at gigabit rates, if the driver unit were designed carefully. It can couple a few milliwatts of light power into an optical fiber. On the other hand, an LED can couple only a few hundred microwatts of light power with modulation speeds limited to around a few hundred megahertz or less (see Fig. 10.4).

At the repeater site, the fiber terminates on an optical detector, such as a photodiode which converts the light back to digital signals for amplification and regeneration. After regeneration, the digital signals modulate the current of an optical source for coupling to the fiber again. At the receiving terminal, the light is again converted back to digital signals by an optical detector for amplification and decoding into the original analog telephone signal.

The above description is for the outgoing path of a full-duplex transmission circuit. The incoming path is exactly the reverse of the outgoing path. Except for some differences in the components and subsystems, the configuration of a fiber-optic system is very much similar to that of a conventional cable or wire system.

10.2   Optical-Fiber Cable

An *optical fiber* is a dielectric waveguide used for the propagation of electromagnetic energy at optical frequencies. Transmission of information is achieved by the modulation of the optical flux. An optical-fiber cable in simple form is shown in Fig. 10.2. It has a circular core of diameter d with a uniform refractive index n_1, surrounded by a cladding layer of refractive index n_2. Light launched at angles up to θ_1 will be propagated within the core at angles up to θ_2 to the axis. Light at launched angles greater than θ_1 will not be reflected internally but refracted into cladding or even out of the cladding into the air. The maximum launch and propagation angles are related mathematically to the numerical aperture N.A., a number that expresses the light-gathering power of an optical-fiber cable:

$$\text{N.A.} = (n_1^2 - n_2^2)^{1/2} = \sin \theta_1 = n_1 \cdot \sin \theta_2$$

As in any electromagnetic waveguide propagation, only certain modes can propagate in an optical-fiber cable. The number of modes M is

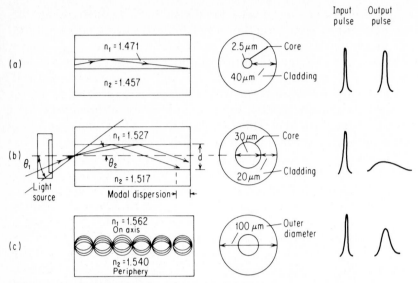

Figure 10.2 Optical-fiber cable parameters. (*a*) Single mode; (*b*) multimode step index; (*c*) multimode graded index.

$$n\text{(refractive index)} = V_{\text{vacuum}}/V_{\text{medium}}$$
$$n_{\text{air}} = 1$$
$$n_{\text{water}} = (300{,}000 \text{ km/s})/(225{,}000 \text{ km/s})$$
$$n_1 = \text{refractive index of core}$$
$$n_2 = \text{refractive index of cladding, } n_2 < n_1$$
$$\theta_1 = \text{maximum acceptance angle of the fiber}$$
$$\theta_2 = \text{propagation angle in the core of } \theta_1$$
$$\text{N.A.} = \sqrt{n_1^2 - n_2^2}/n_{\text{air}} = \sin \Theta_1 = n_1 \sin \Theta_2$$

related to the light wavelength λ as follows:

$$M = 0.5 \left(\frac{\pi d \text{N.A.}}{\lambda}\right)^2$$

where d = core diameter. Thus for a given N.A. or refractive index and light wavelength the number M decreases as the diameter of the core is reduced. When the core diameter approaches the light wavelength, only a single mode will propagate.

Optical fibers can be classified as either *single-mode* or *multimode*. Single-mode fibers offer the potential of extremely wide bandwidths and low losses. To achieve propagation in one mode, however, the fiber core must be no more than 2 to 4 μm in diameter, and there is the rub. At the present time, the technology has not been developed to provide sources, connectors, and detectors for use with these microscopic fibers.

In multimode fibers, the fiber-core diameter is large enough to permit propagation in several modes (each having characteristic velocities and propagation times). As an optical signal travels along a fiber, it suffers a reduction in bandwidth and amplitude. Bandwidth reduction is caused by dispersion that arises from two sources: *mode dispersion* and *material dispersion*. Modal dispersion is pulse spreading caused by the different path lengths of light rays in a multimode fiber. Material dispersion arises from the nonlinear dependence of the core refractive index over the wavelength band of the source. Material dispersion is obviously worse with broadline sources.

Dispersion or bandwidth reduction increases with fiber length and is usually expressed in megahertz per kilometer (MHz/km). It increases linearly with length to approximately 1.5 km and as the square root of the length beyond that point. For pulse signals, dispersion results in time spreading, which is given in nanoseconds per kilometer (ns/km).

Multimode fibers are characterized as *step-index* or *graded-index*. In step-index fibers, the core has a uniform index of refraction providing an abrupt change in refraction index at the core-cladding interface. Step-index fibers have relatively high dispersion, leading to a bandwidth reduction of approximately 30 ns/km. In graded-index fibers the core index decreases parabolically from the center outward. In these fibers light rays are propagated by refraction so they are bent in a sinusoidlike curve about the fiber axis (Fig. 10.2). The increased velocity of the rays away from the axis (in the lower-index region) compensates for the increased path length and therefore results in much lower dispersion. Although dispersion values in graded-index fibers vary to some extent with different fibers, values as low as 1 ns/km can be obtained with premium fibers.

Signals traveling along an optical fiber also suffer a loss in amplitude. This attenuation is caused principally by scattering due to metal ions and by absorption due to water in the OH radical form. Fiber attenuation depends strongly on wavelength and is usually given in decibels per kilometer (dB/km) at a specific wavelength. Fibers range in attenuation from high-loss (greater than 100 dB/km) plastic types to low-loss (less than 20 dB/km) graded-index silica fibers manufactured

TABLE 10.1 Characteristics of High-, Medium-, and Low-Loss Fiber-Optic Cables

Fiber type	Attenuation, dB/km	Transmission length, m	N.A.
Plastic or commercial glass, step index	High: 100–1000	< 30	0.5
Plastic-coated silica and glass-glass, step index	Medium: 20–100	30–500	0.25–0.5
Silica, graded index	Low: 1–20	500–10,000	0.1–0.25

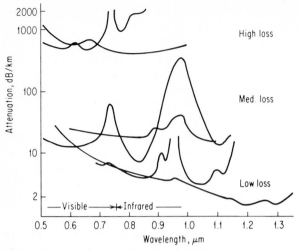

Figure 10.3 Attenuation characteristics of fiber-optic cables.

by the chemical vapor-deposition process; graded index is achieved by varying the level of dopants in successive layers of the vapor-deposited material. Typical characteristics of high-, medium-, and low loss fibers are given in Table 10.1 and in Fig. 10.3.

The transfer of light power into a fiber-optic cable from a source is a function of the numerical aperture of the fiber cable. Source power versus N.A. curves are provided in Fig. 10.4.

Manufacturers are hopeful of developing a commercially accessible fiber-optic cable working on the 1250-nm (1.25-μm) wavelength region with dispersion and attenuation minimized; less than 0.01 dB/km dispersion has already been achieved at that frequency in the laboratory. Present technology can manufacture a low-loss (less than 4 dB/km) with high N.A. (greater than 0.5) and wideband (1 GHz/km) fiber-optic cable in continuous lengths exceeding 25 km.

Basically only two cable design philosophies exist: the *loose tube* and

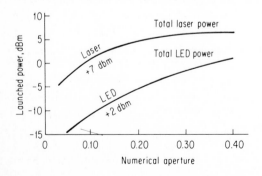

Figure 10.4 Launched power versus N.A. curves in sources.

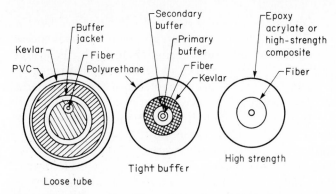

Figure 10.5   Fiber-optic-cable configurations. (Corning)

the *tight buffer*. In the tight-buffer cable, each fiber is encased in resilient padding that protects against external forces. The optical loss of the fibers is sensitive to tensile loading and temperature changes and is usually increased by the cabling process. Tight-buffer cable is best suited for indoor, short-distance applications. A variation of tight-buffer cable is high-strength cable (see Fig. 10.5).

In the loose-tube approach, each individual fiber is carried in a jacket which has an inside diameter considerably larger than the fibers' outside diameters. As a result the fiber is immune to external influences. Furthermore, loose-tube cable can be made with the fiber length slightly in excess of the cable length so that the cable can elongate under tensile loading without applying stress to the fiber. By allowing for significant cable elongation, less Kevlar is needed for tensile strength, resulting in lower material costs.

If packing of fibers is necessary, particularly if a need arises for coupling to a broad-area source, a number of individual fibers are put together in a fiber bundle enclosed in a protective jacket. In bundles, the fibers must be arranged in a closely packed array when coupling from a source to a bundle or from one bundle to another because only the light striking the active core area is transmitted. The ratio of the core area to the overall bundle diameter is called the *packing fraction;* the higher the packing fraction, the more efficient the bundle. The packing fraction depends on the core-to-cladding ratio of the individual fibers as well as the density of fiber packing. The highest core-to-cladding ratio consistent with adequate core isolation between fibers will help to provide a high packing fraction. For a given fiber, the optimum packing fraction occurs when a number of fibers, typically 7 or 19, is arranged in a hexagonal configuration.

CCITT has initiated studies on optical-fiber cables. See Recs. G.651, Characteristics of 50/125 μm Multimode Graded Index Optical Fiber

Cables, and G.652, Characteristics of a Single-Mode Optical Fiber Cable. The fibers described in these recommendations have been chosen because most administrations are considering them for initial use in their public networks. The recommended multimode graded-index optical fiber has a core diameter of 50 μm and a reference surface diameter (generally that of the cladding) of 125 μm and can be used for both analog and digital transmission. The main transmission characteristics are defined for the wavelength region 0.8–0.9 μm.

CCITT also studies digital optical fiber systems. It was recognized that these systems should be in agreement with Recs. G.911 through G.915 giving the general characteristics for the digital line sections operating at various hierarchical bit rates in order to ensure their international interconnection.

10.3 Light Sources

Light-emitting diodes (LEDs) and *injection laser diodes* (ILDs) are the most commonly used light sources. Both LEDs and ILDs use GaAs as the basic semiconductor material, with appropriate dopants to achieve emission in the range of 800 to 1300 nm. In the double-heterojunction laser structure, a GaAs active laser is surrounded by a *p*-type GaAlAs layer and an *n*-type GaAs layer deposited by epitaxial growth. Light emission takes place at the *pn* junction when an external voltage drives both electrons and holes into the junction. These holes and electrons recombine rapidly by transitions from the conduction band. In recombining, the electrons emit at a wavelength proportional to the energy drop. Thus the light emitted from an LED is relatively incoherent and has a spectral width of about 40 nm (see Fig. 10.6). In an ILD the thin layers or heterojunction surrounding the active region have a lower refractive index, creating a resonant cavity perpendicular to the plane of the *pn* junction. Light rays traveling back and forth within the cavity stimulate other transitions until all the light is oriented in the same direction. The width of the heterojunction is kept well under 1 μm to restrict operation to the fundamental transverse modes. A stripe-contact geometry is used to confine lateral radiation and limit operation to one or several lateral modes. A typical ILD operating in several longitudinal modes has a spectral line width of only 1 to 3 nm (see Fig. 10.7). Both LEDs and ILDs are modulated by varying the injection current. ILDs, however, emit much higher power levels with small changes in the driving current above threshold. The *quantum efficiency* for double-heterojunction lasers ranges from 10 to 50 percent, in contrast with values of about 3 percent for LEDs. [Quantum efficiency, the ratio of emitted photons to injected electrons, is given by P_o (optical power)/I_f (drive current).]

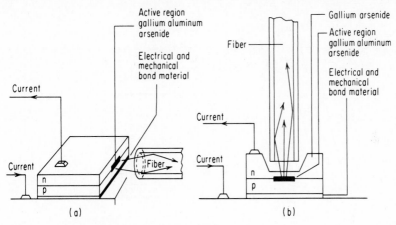

Figure 10.6 Light sources. (*a*) Laser; (*b*) LED.

The laser, a semicoherent source in its present form, can couple a few milliwatts of light power into a fiber. Linearity in the curve of light power versus driving electrical current is not good, even around an operating point above threshold. Therefore, lasers are considered more appropriate for digital applications. Since their optical bandwidth is much less than that of LEDs (2 nm versus 20 nm), material dispersion is not a problem. Thus, they can be modulated by a driving current at up to gigabit-per-second rates.

Lifetime and driver complexity are more serious disadvantages of the laser with respect to the LED. Although laser lifetime of 1 million hours at room temperature is common, its variation with temperature (lifetime drops as temperature increases) is still of concern to designers.

Continued improvements in performance are making LEDs a more viable light source for medium-range communication application. An InGaAsP LED that emits 1.27 μm has been developed, which is a

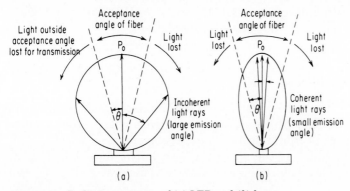

Figure 10.7 Radiation patterns of (*a*) LED and (*b*) laser.

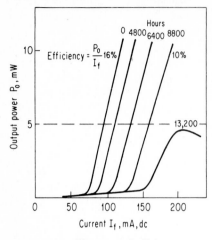

Figure 10.8 Change of light power versus current characteristics during aging of a laser.

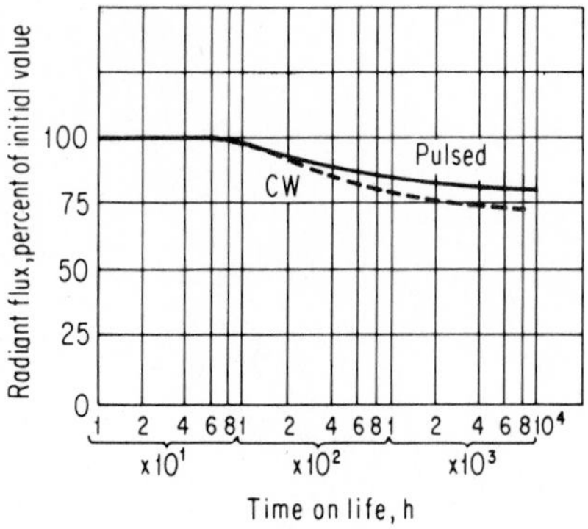

Figure 10.9 Typical life test data for an infrared LED.

minimum attenuation region for silica fibers; in fact by varying the doping, a diode to emit any wavelength between 1.05 and 1.35 μm can be designed; typical rated output power is 500 μW and modulation can occur at up to 50 MHz.

The life of ILDs and LEDs extends over 10,000 h under normal operating conditions. This is a function of driver current density, duty cycle, and metallurgy.

Aging reduces the efficiency of a light source considerably. Figure 10.8 shows that a 90-mA driver current produces 5 mW in a new laser diode with 16 percent efficiency (P_o/I_f). After 8800 h of operation, a 5-mW output is obtained by a 160-mA driver current and efficiency drops to 10 percent. An ILD is not capable of providing a 5-mW output after 13,200 h of operation, despite a substantial increase in driver current.

Figure 10.9 shows that direct current deteriorates LED output power faster than pulsed driver current. Recently an ILD with a 60,000-h operating life has been introduced to the market.

10.4 Optical Detectors

When the junction of a semiconductor is illuminated and a connection is made to both sides of the junction, a current will be seen to flow during the period of illumination. This phenomenon is called the *photovoltaic* effect, which is the operating mechanism for solar cells. In this case, there is no external bias and the cell generates an emf when illuminated.

The *photodiode dark current* is the current that flows through the photodiode biasing circuit when no light is incident on the photodiode. If external bias is applied in the reverse direction at the *pn* junction, current will also flow under illumination. The current generated is composed of photocurrent and dark (reverse-leakage) current. The dark current will remain constant for fixed-bias and fixed-temperature conditions. The photocurrent will vary linearly with the intensity of the incident light. A good approximation for the temperature coefficient of dark current is that the dark current doubles for every 10°C increase in operating temperature.

Figure 10.10 shows a typical spectral response curve for a PIN (*positive-intrinsic-negative*) photodiode at a normal operating bias. The spectral range is from 0.35 to 1.13 μm, or from the *near ultraviolet* to the *near infrared*. The sensitivity (or responsivity) typically peaks at 0.9 μm, with a response of approximately 0.5 μA/μW.

Quantum efficiency for a typical PIN photodiode is

$$\text{Q.E.} = 124\,\frac{S}{\lambda}\quad \%$$

where S = sensitivity, μA/μW
λ = wavelength, μm

In plain words, the quantum efficiency is the ratio of primary photoelectrons generated to photons incident on the detector. Sensitivity is the minimally required input light power needed to achieve a given performance level, i.e., the S/N ratio for analog systems and the error rate for digital systems. For example, for $\lambda = 0.9$ and $S = 0.5\ \mu$A/μW, we obtain Q.E. = 80 percent.

The noise equivalent power (NEP) figure of merit defines the minimum incident power required to generate a photocurrent equal to the total photodiode noise current. In formula form,

$$\text{NEP (W/}\sqrt{\text{bandwidth}}) = \frac{\text{noise current (A/}\sqrt{\text{bandwidth}})}{\text{sensitivity (A/W)}}$$

where bandwidth is the utilized bandwidth in hertz.

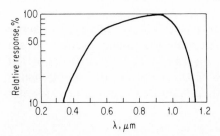

Figure 10.10 Typical spectral response of a photodiode.

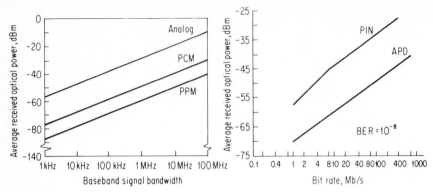

Figure 10.11   Received power level versus bandwidth and bit rate in optical detectors.

Optical detectors are well-developed. The most ideally suitable for systems operating in the 800–1200 nm wavelengths are two main silicon types, the PIN diode and the *avalanche photodiode* (APD). These detectors convert light power input to electric current output with excellent quantum efficiency in the order of 90 percent, fast response time in the order of 10 ns, and low-noise power in the order of −54 dBm.

PIN devices are simple devices, easy to use, but their sensitivity is not high. Thus their performance is limited by the thermal noise in subsequent amplifiers after detection (see Fig. 10.11). APDs give better sensitivity because the avalanche process provides large amplification, as much as 100 times, within the detector, thus giving a large output current and thereby reducing the effect of subsequent after-detector amplifier noise. However, the avalanche process also generates noise within the detector. The overall improvement in the S/N ratio of an APD compared to a PIN diode is about 10-fold. The drawbacks of an APD are the high bias (about 100 V) requirements and the temperature dependence in performance.

Noise and distortion are responsible for signal degradation, and the receiver is the major source of noise in a fiber-optic system. Nonlinearities in a light source's (output power/drive current) characteristic harmonically distort a signal. In particular, an ILD has a strong nonlinearity and requires proper biasing to avoid clipping.

Even though the photodetector receives the prescribed optical power with the specified S/N ratio, nonlinear distortion can degrade system performance. Digital systems can tolerate more harmonic distortion and exploit the advantages of the ILD. However, in analog-modulated systems, nonlinear distortion components are produced by the source.

System rise time

Material and modal dispersion cause pulse-spreading distortion in digital systems or band-limited amplitude distortion in analog systems. With LED sources material dispersion measures about 3.5 ns/km, but this component is negligible when an ILD is used.

Pulse spreading due to fiber modal dispersion is about 15 ns/km for step-index fiber but only 2.5 ns/km for graded-index fiber. Source and photodetector rise times must be considered because they can also distort the shape of a signal. Typically they range from 5 to 15 ns for LEDs and 0.1 to 2 ns for ILDs. PINs and APDs have rise times 1 and 4 ns, respectively.

Total rise time for a system must include the individual rise times of the source, fiber-optic cable, and photodetector. It has been determined that rise time due to modal dispersion and material dispersion contribute to the total distortion of the system.

A method to verify the distortion limits in analog and digital systems is given as follows. Rise time for the system is given as

$$T_{\text{system}} = 1.1\sqrt{T_{\text{source}}^2 + T_{\text{modal}}^2 + T_{\text{material}}^2 + T_{\text{detector}}^2}$$

All T values under the square root sign correspond to 10 to 90 percent of the rise time.

The 3-dB bandwidth of an analog system is calculated by

$$\text{Bandwidth} = \frac{0.35}{T_{\text{system}} \text{ (in s)}} \quad \text{Hz}$$

Upper limits of T_{system} should be less than 70 percent of the bit interval for NRZ data and less than 35 percent for an RZ format in a digital system.

Fiber-optic-link design examples

For illustration purposes two kinds of system design examples are given.

Example 1 We would like to have a fiber-optic system for a T3 digital telephone network with the following requirements:

$$\text{Bit rate} = 44.7 \text{ Mb/s (22.35 MHz, NRZ format)}$$

$$\text{Distance} = 4 \text{ km}$$

$$\text{BER} = 10^{-8}$$

$$\text{S/N ratio} = 12 \text{ dB (optical), 24 dB (electrical)}$$

$$\text{Total bandwidth} = 50 \text{ MHz; 200 MHz/km}$$

Solution

a. Source

	ILD (injection laser diode)	LED (only for information)
Average output power	10 dBm at 300 mA	−3 dBm (0.5 mW)
Coupling loss (ILD/fiber)	8 dB	15 dB
Power coupled into fiber	+ 2 dBm	(−18 dBm)

b. Detector—APD (avalanche photodiode)
   NEP (noise equivalency power) for 50 MHz = −58 dBm
   S/N ratio for required BER = 12 dB
   Fiber coupling loss = 1 dB
   Receiver sensitivity = −45 dBm

c. Fiber cable
   Cable attenuation = 6 dB/km
   Cable loss = 24 dB
   Connector losses = 3 dB
   Splicing losses = 1.5 dB
   Total link loss = 28.5 dB

d. Margin allowances

	Temperature	Time	Radiation
Source	2 dB	3 dB	1 dB
Receiver	1 dB	3 dB	0.5 dB
Fiber	0.5 dB	1 dB	0.5 dB
Total	3.5 dB	7 dB	2 dB
	Total margin = 12.5 dB		

e. Calculation of excess power

$$\text{Optical level at the receiver } a - c - d = \quad -39 \text{ dBm}$$
$$\text{Receiver sensitivity} = -(-45) \text{ dBm}$$
$$\text{Excess power} = \quad +6 \text{ dB}$$

Note

A 6-dB increase in received optical power at 44.7 Mb/s causes an S/N increase to 18 dB from 12 dB and a BER decrease to $<10^{-12}$ from 10^{-8}.

f. Calculation of system rise time

	Rise-time	
	ns/km	Total
Source, ILD		2
Fiber rise time due to multimode dispersion	2	8
Fiber rise time due to material dispersion (typically 3.5 ns/km for LED; negligible for ILD)	0	0
Detector, APD		2

$$T_{\text{system}} = 1.1\sqrt{2^2 + 8^2 + 2^2} = 9.33 \text{ ns}$$

$$70\% \text{ bit interval} = 0.70 \times 22 = 15.2 \text{ ns} = T_{\text{system}}$$

Rise time provided by the fiber-optic system satisfies the 15.2-ns requirement of the 44.7 Mb/s operation.

Let us verify the 3-dB bandwidth in an analog system:

$$\text{Bandwidth} = \frac{0.35}{T_{\text{system}}} = 37.5 \text{ MHz}$$

Bandwidth provided is larger than 22.35 MHz.

Example 2 Let us consider a high-grade fiber-optic link operating at 50 Mb/s with a BER of 10^{-9}, which is equivalent to a peak signal-to-rms-noise ratio of 12:1. The required signal power would be about -44 dBm (40 nW) for a PIN diode receiver and one-tenth (-54 dBm) of that for an avalanche diode receiver. Assuming a laser with 5-mW (7 dBm) output power and 50 percent (-3 dB) coupling efficiency, the loss in the cable could be 48 dB for the PIN diode receiver. Allowing -3 dB for splices, this represents a 9-km repeater spacing with a 5 dB/km cable. With an avalanche diode receiver, repeater spacing could be 11 km. Pulse dispersion is not a limiting factor if the cable is a silica fiber with a material dispersion of 0.2 ns/km (because of the laser) and with a graded-index profile that gives a modal dispersion of 1 ns/km.

For optimum system performance, the source's *emission peak wavelength* should match the valleys in the fiber's attenuation-wavelength characteristics. Additionally, the detector must be responsive in this wavelength range.

A system working on 830 nm (0.83 μm) is given in Fig. 10.12; it depicts that a wavelength of the laser source matches the bottom of the attenuation curve of the fiber optic; the photodiode also operates efficiently at that wavelength.

10.5 Splicing and Connectors

Any mechanical connector may be used for fiber splicing if it is designed for splicing single fibers of 125 μm in diameter. Any type of splice case

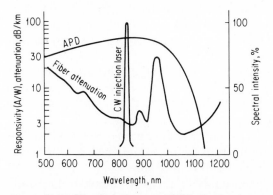

Figure 10.12 Wavelength compatibility in a system.

which is suitable for telephone cables with polyethylene jackets may be used with fiber-optic cable if an appropriate size of case is chosen.

The additional attenuation introduced at a splice between two fibers cannot be less than the loss corresponding to the dimensional mismatch between the fibers. The loss in the splices between fibers lies between 1.3 and 0.5 dB. To this loss must be added the losses introduced by misalignment due to mechanical imperfections of the connector, by foreign material located in the space between the fibers, and by reflections due to disparities of refractive index; the total loss recommended for a splice is 1.5 dB. Nevertheless each splice may present the equivalent of several hundred meters of cable. Fortunately fiber-optic cables are relatively lightweight and available in long lengths.

Optical-fiber splices with the lowest possible loss and greatest reliability can be obtained by heating the ends of the fibers so that they melt and become fused together. Because the splice is made in a sealed chamber, fused splicing can be employed in manholes and other places where explosive gases may congregate.

The alignment of fibers as a preliminary step before fusing is performed by making transmission measurements and adjusting for minimum transmission loss. In this manner it is the cores of the fibers which are brought into line, securing important advantages over most other methods which align fibers from their external surfaces. The use of fused splices does not restrict the employment of mechanical splices, if desired, when temporary cable repairs are necessary on an emergency basis. Handling of many separate fibers is difficult and introduces a serious hazard in respect to breaking during splicing operations. The handling of all fibers together as a single ribbon greatly simplifies splicing problems.

In general, connector losses can be divided into four main areas: axial misalignment, angular misalignment of core axes, end separation between fibers, and imperfect fiber-end finishes. Even if the connectors were perfect, there are still other loss mechanisms within a connector splice. These variations include numerical aperture variations, core and cladding diameter variations, eccentricity of core and sometimes of the cladding, and core ovality.

A lensed fiber-optic connector for assembly in the field and connectors which are fully capable of interfacing with card-edge, bulkhead, and PC mounting assemblies and can be installed with standard crimping and cleaving tools have been available in the industry.

Although repeated connector engagements have shown excellent reproducibility of the same light transmission quality, 0.5 to 0.8 dB reading differences can be expected in connections.

High-efficiency connectors (those having through-connector losses of less than 1 dB) have demanding criteria, such as:

- Optimum alignment must be easily achieved every time connectors are joined, without special engagement or tuning.
- The connector must maintain alignment under a variety of hostile conditions.
- Repeated connect-disconnect operations must not adversely affect the fiber or its end-face finish.
- The interface must be sealed so that the fiber-to-fiber junction remains free of contaminants that would lower efficiency.
- Connectors must be low in cost and easy to use.

Connector manufacturers have been studying fiber-optic connector problems; they have already increased coupling efficiency considerably by using resilient alignment mechanisms.

10.6   Fiber-Optic-Cable Installation Methods

Fiber-optic cables demand more delicate treatment than conventional metal-conductor transmission lines and conductors. Engineers cannot merely designate cable runs because technicians are not yet familiar with this new transmission medium and its special electromechanical installation and maintainability constraints. Thus, ever-increasing use of more delicate glass-fiber transmission links has spurred the development of protective handling and of installation techniques. Successful fiber-optic system design will depend greatly on engineers mastering these methods.

Cross sections of typical optical-fiber cables expose from 1 to 10 or more individually jacketed fibers, each approximately 0.4 mm in diameter with an overall cable diameter of approximately 6 mm. Cable-jacketing materials vary with the application: indoors, outdoors in aerial installation, or for direct burial. Although development of glass fibers stronger than steel wire of the same diameter has been achieved, an optical cable may contain one or more strengthening members to absorb shock and tensile loads during installation and handling.

For ease of test and handling, terminate each fiber within the cable with an optical connector before installing it in the field; this process is call *connectorizing* (Fig. 10.13). Terminating optical cables, however, requires more time and money than connecting standard copper cables.

Initially, consider long-term protection of installed cables.

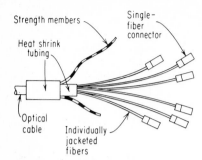

Figure 10.13 Connectorizing of fiber cable.

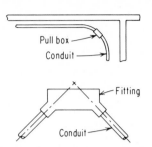

Figure 10.14 Rounding of optical cables in interior and exterior corners.

Indoor installation

Quite often cables will be installed in existing wireways or conduit systems that provide ample protection. Other cases, such as high-traffic areas, locations under raised floors, or harsh environments, could require special dedicated-conduit systems.

Conduit or wireway systems must meet the mechanical restrictions that the chosen cable imposes; the critical constraint is generally the cable bend radius. The final installation must not contain any bends or fittings with less than the minimum cable bend radius. A 25- to 30-cm (10- to 12-in) radius meets the mechanical requirements of most currently available optical cables (Fig. 10.14).

Pull boxes should sit at all corners in the conduit run as well as on straight runs at 80 to 100 m. This arrangement lets the installer pull cable in short sections, which lessens the chance of damage from high tensile load during installation. Also pull boxes should be located in runs where the sum of all bends equals 90° or more; this condition often occurs where the conduit makes several short bends to clear minor obstacles; additionally, pull boxes should allow working room for pulling and feeding cable without undue stress. Finally, pull boxes and fittings should be carefully selected since they must allow for straight pulls and should not require sharp bends at entry and exit ports. When choosing fittings and in-line pull boxes, again attention must be paid to minimum cable bend radius to ensure that the cable does not experience excess stress. Pull box length must equal four times the bend radius (Fig. 10.15).

In long vertical runs the weight of the cable itself creates a tensile load. This tensile load must be considered to determine the minimum bend radius at the top of the vertical run. Long vertical runs should be clamped at intermediate points (preferably every 1 or 2 m) to prevent

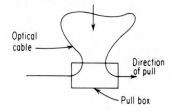

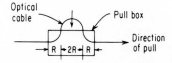

Figure 10.15 Pulling of optical cables.

excessive tensile loading of the cable. Clamping force should be no more than is necessary to prevent the possibility of slippage and is best determined experimentally since it is highly dependent on the type of clamping material used and the presence of surface contaminants on both the clamp and the jacket of the optical cable. The clamping force must not exceed 10 kg/cm^2 and must be applied uniformly across the full width of the cable. The clamping surfaces should be made of a soft material, such as rubber or plastic.

Fiber-optic cables are pulled by using many of the same tools and techniques used to pull a wire cable. The connectors are usually preinstalled on the fiber-optic cable, causing a departure from the standard cable-pulling methods. Smaller pull forces and minimum bend-radius requirements are applicable to fiber-optic cables than to those of standard copper cables. The pull tape must be attached to the optical cable in such a way that the pulling forces are applied to the strength members of the cable and the connectors are protected from damage. The connector should be wrapped in a thin layer of foam rubber and inserted in a stiff plastic sleeve for protection. During pulling of the cable, the pulling force should be constantly monitored, using a mechanical gage.

During pulling-in, the cable should be continuously lubricated as it enters the duct or conduit, in the same manner as is standard procedure for wire cables. At points such as pull boxes and manholes, where the cable enters the conduit at an angle, a pulley or wheel should be used to ensure that the cable does not scrape against the end of the conduit and/or make sharp bends.

As the cable emerges from intermediate-point pull boxes, it should be coiled in a figure-eight pattern with loops at least 1 ft in diameter. When all the cable is coiled and the next pull is to be started, the figure-eight coil can be turned over and the cable laid out again from the top. This will eliminate twisting of the cable.

Outdoor installation

Optical cables can be suspended by using a messenger wire, but in most cases they are buried or put in an underground conduit system because it offers greater protection or room for additional cables. No additional protection for the cable is necessary for either application except that in rocky ground the usual bed of sand or screened earth should be prepared and the cable should be covered with the same material for 30 cm.

For direct burial, special cables are available which are able to withstand the forces imposed by plowing in and by earth displacements after installation. Standard cable can be used underground by burying below the frost line. In general, the methods and procedures commonly employed for installation of telephone cables with copper conductors are entirely suitable also for fiber cables.

The handling of longer lengths and the method of measuring the pulling tension require special attention. It has been shown to be possible under favorable circumstances to pull a continuous length of 1 km of cable into ducts. As this is a considerably greater length than the average separation between manholes, the cable must be pulled through several manholes that are intermediate on its route; this can only be done if the ducts on opposite sides of each manhole are reasonably at the same level and in the same line. Should these conditions not apply or should the ducts themselves have sharp bends or obstructions, it will be necessary to reduce the length of the pull, cut the cable, and introduce additional splices. However, it is possible to make a turn of 90° or more in a manhole if appropriate guides are provided for the cable; a convenient form for such a guide is a quadrant provided with several rollers, as such a piece of equipment can be introduced with ease into a manhole and will provide a bending radius of 100 cm or more.

Cable which is pulled into duct should be supported by a flexible guide or "elephant's trunk" from the reel to the face of the duct so that sharp bends are avoided. The cable should be well-lubricated with a compound such as Vitalife or polywater; the bentonide compounds are not recommended as lubricants. To provide slack for forming cable in manholes, the cable should be pulled back, starting at the manhole nearest to the center of the pull. A minimum radius of 30 cm may be used in forming cable.

If the cable enters a terminal station from below ground level, it is desirable to avoid a splice in the vault or basement. Bypass the main distribution frame by threading the cable into the building as far as is necessary to reach the equipment room and particular location where the terminal equipment will be situated.

For a typical cable the maximum permitted pulling tension is 400 kg, and this value must not be exceeded; on long pulls it is essential to use a tensiometer.

Although the discussion has been limited to cable installed in ducts, similar considerations apply to cable directly buried in the ground, especially if the cable is pulled into a trench. If it should be necessary to remove cable from the reel to negotiate obstacles which cross its path by threading the cable beneath them, the greatest possible care must be taken to avoid accidental sharp bends in the cable which is off the reel. It is recommended that the cable should not be unwound from the reel but that the reel of cable should be placed in a reel carrier, so that the cable can be laid into the trench as the reel carrier advances along the cable route.

Cable should be kept under pressure during the installation period, and the pressure should be monitored as the installation proceeds. Alternatively the pressure may be removed from the cable and the individual fibers may be monitored for breakage.

Another cable installation method is to utilize a mechanical rodder. The rodder rods the ducts and pulls the cables during the rod-retrieval process. This method is preferred where long pulls or numerous corners apply excess stress on the ducts and twist the cables. The stretching will cause surging of the cable. Therefore, this method should be used where possible.

A simple and economical method of extracting the metal conductors from buried telecommunication cables without damaging the cable's conduit has been developed. Once the original conductors have been removed, optical fibers can be inserted at about 20 percent of the cost of laying new optical fiber cable.

Tests have indicated that the method is practical for cable lengths of up to 1500 m provided that there are no splices or turns between the two chosen points. For greater lengths, the amount of friction generated in extracting the conductors makes the process impractical.

10.7 Testing and Test Instruments

The employment of fiber cable makes it necessary to conduct testing at optical frequencies. The principal tests conducted on reels of cable at the completion of manufacture are the measurements of attenuation, pulse dispersion, and numerical aperture. Testing of cable during installation requires that optical tests be available and be suitable for field operation. The measurement of attenuation is the principal test conducted under field conditions.

At first glance, the status of fiber-optics test instrumentation appears bleak. This equipment often is not readily available, sometimes requires considerable operator skill and technical knowledge, and is relatively expensive.

One apparent bright note for fiber-optics test instrumentation is the similarity in testing techniques between fiber optics and conventional coaxial cables. Specifically, if both ends of a cable are available, it is possible to use relatively unsophisticated equipment to measure continuity, attenuation, bandwidth, and other parameters. With only one cable end available, more complicated equipment, such as *optical time-domain reflectometers* (OTDRs) are needed.

A comparison tester, like most instruments that perform measurements, requires access to both ends of the fiber. That is, the manufacturer supplies a reference cable, which is used to calibrate the instrument; the cable to be tested is measured and compared to the reference cable. Accuracy is better than 1 percent; it can measure cable losses between 0 and 60 dB for a wide variety of cable diameters.

In the more complex attenuation-measurement instrument, dual light is incorporated; a HeNe laser implements gross cable measurements, while a white light source with a monochromatic filter allows measurement of fiber spectral response (attenuation versus wavelength). Another important instrument, the power meter, measures the output power from such sources as LEDs or lasers. It can also measure source emittance angle, optical fiber and connector losses, and optical fiber numerical aperture.

An optical time-domain reflectometer needs only one end of a fiber-optic cable to characterize a tested system. Utilizing an OTDR, an operator can check the integrity of splices, connectors, and cable lengths in addition to measuring cable-attenuation properties. Most important of all, cable characteristics as a function of frequency characteristics that include phase, bandwidth, delay, and distortion can be determined. An OTDR utilizes backscattering and far-end reflection effects in an optical fiber to determine the fiber's length, the location of breaks, the nature of splice and connector losses, the amount of fiber attenuation, and the status of any manufacturing defects (e.g., bubbles).

An OTDR closely resembles the time-domain reflectometer employed in coaxial-cable measurements. Light pulses from a laser diode or laser are launched into the tested fiber; any defects in that fiber send back reflections, which are picked up by a light detector. An examination of the timing of these reflected pulses relative to the output pulse permits an operator to determine the distance each defect lies from the source. An OTDR requires a high-speed oscilloscope for display. A 10-ns pulse allows an operator to ascertain a break's location to within 0.5 to 1 m, but reflected power is so low that reflections could get lost in the noise. A 0.5-m resolution is achieved by using the reflected pulse out of the noise by means of *phase-locked-loop* (PLL) techniques. EIA Standard RS-4555-5 gives the test procedures for fiber-optic cables.

10.8   Advantages and Deterrents

The advantages of fiber optics are many, and its potential is very promising. For example, 200 kg of weight can be saved in an aircraft by using fiber optics instead of copper wiring; in the medical field it can be used to light a very small area of a patient's body during a delicate operation.

Figure 10.16 compares attenuation in coaxial and fiber-optic cables on the left, while on the right side it depicts that, for the same information-carrying capacity, a fiber-optic cable replaces up to 80 times its size in copper pairs.

While fiber optics can be performance-competitive and, in fact, offers performance advantages over conventional technologies, cost competitiveness of fiber-optic systems is today a major consideration. It turns out, however, that fiber-optic systems can be most competitive with conventional trunking methods. Figure 10.17 shows a comparison of the relative cost per circuit-kilometer for fiber-optic systems and conventional systems.

As can be seen in the figure, fiber optics can be significantly lower in cost, especially at the higher capacities, in T3 and T4 systems. In fact, from a cost and performance point of view, fiber optics is the preferred approach for the T4 system. It is also interesting to note that fiber optics are competitive at capacities less than T3—672 voice-grade circuits.

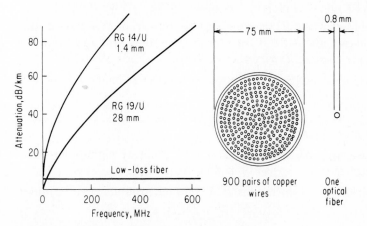

Figure 10.16   Comparing fiber-optic, coaxial, and copper cables.

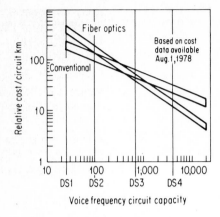

Figure 10.17 Cost comparisons: fiber optics versus conventional trunking system.

On the other hand, there is the usual reluctance of reliability minded engineers to abandon highly developed, well-proven systems for a totally new technology.

Advantages

Advantages of fiber optics are as follows:

1. High-speed data transmission capability.

2. Cost savings in conductor weight and size.

3. Relative immunity to electromagnetic and radio-frequency interferences.

4. Low crosstalk.

5. Higher degree of communication security; systems cannot be tapped by electromagnetic induction or by surface conduction.

6. Optical fiber with LED carries 50,000 voice-grade channels; coaxial cables carry about 5400 voice-grade channels, and ordinary two-conductor telephone wire carries 48 voice-grade channels.

7. Low signal-strength loss; the use of repeaters every kilometer is not necessary.

8. The transmission signal can be seen in some cases, thereby aiding circuit monitoring.

9. Only the capacity of a light source to generate signals for transmission limits the capacity of fiber channels.

10. Ground loops and shifts caused by common grounds are eliminated.

11. Transmitters and receivers are isolated.

12. Fiber-optic cable breaks cause no shorts since optical transmission medium involves guides for light waves instead of conductors for electrons; this allows use of this technology in hazardous environments, e.g., explosive chemical facilities.

13. No damage to equipment is expected because of current surges on open lines.

14. Large reduction of the BER in data processing.

15. Improved signal quality.

16. Fiber-optic cable does not radiate electromagnetic energy nor disturb other communication mediums.

Deterrents

Since fiber-optic communications is a totally new approach, not a refinement of an existing technique where only a small part of the system would be subject to innovation, this reflects in a lack of standardization in fibers, cable connectors, wavelengths, and power levels. Without standardization, communication is possible only between equipment of common origin.

Furthermore, it becomes a time-consuming process to replace one of the optical parts in the system, since a direct replacement is not a shelf item and requires a special order to be prepared, with the ensuing delivery cycle. With the active light source in the transmitter being particularly suspect, material defects appear to be the major limiting factor on the life of LEDs and lasers.

Any damage inflicted on a fiber-optic cable is not easily repairable. In most cases it necessitates replacement of the entire cable.

10.9   Recent Developments in Fiber-Optic Components and the Future

Wide-scale use of optical communications is coming not only for data and telephone transmissions, cable TV, and distributed computer networks but also for short-haul applications such as PC-board-to-PC-board signal transfer within an instrument. Most transmitters and receivers now are designed for specific bit rates and link lengths. Large-scale integration and possibly tradeoffs in receiver sensitivity and maximum bit rates will result in compact circuits that will be able to accommodate a wide range of link lengths and bit rates without requiring any adjustments. This will facilitate the economical application of fiber optics to a wide range of applications. In the immediate future we can see further developments in splices and connectors. To avoid undue loss of power, the faces of the adjoining fibers must be of equal size, in line, parallel, and as close to each other as possible. This leads to strict diameter control in fiber production and a precision in the micrometer range for the connectors and splices. At present, the optical power loss in a typical connector is 0.5 to 2 dB, equivalent to a substantial length of low-loss fiber cable.

Fusion equipment for connecting single-mode fiber-optic cables has been developed in the laboratory and 0.1-dB optical power loss has been achieved. This fusion equipment automatically makes a precision connection between 10-μm-diameter fiber cores with only 0.1-μm error.

Further in the future we anticipate developments in single-mode fibers and also in integrated optics, the optical equivalent of semiconductor ICs. These will consist of solid-state components, usually based on thin-film technology, in which optical rather than electric signals are switched, amplified, modulated, and processed directly without conversion to electric signals.

Recently researchers have come up with an experimental process that yields a single-mode fiber-optic cable with attenuation as low as 0.38 dB/km at 1300 nm and 0.2 dB/km at 1500 nm. The cable exhibits a standard deviation of measured attenuation of 0.05 dB/km at 1300 nm and water content of less than 100 parts per billion.

Bidirectional transmission on a single fiber will certainly cut the costs of transmission systems. With a total loss of 3.7 dB, providing more than 44-dB separation between transmit and receive channels, directional couplers have already been developed. The problem to overcome is that the characteristics of the fiber have to match the characteristics of the coupler pigtail.

In optical linear amplifiers, researchers have devised an optical amplifier that eliminates the need for conventional repeaters in baseband fiber-optic communication systems. The amplifier consists of an optical isolator that provides the amplifier with unidirectional performance and a semiconductor laser for the actual amplification. Operating at wavelengths of 850, 1300, and 1500 nm, the amplifier has yielded gains of 20 dB minimum after isolator and coupling losses are subtracted; it is 1/1000 the size of existing devices and requires only 1/100 of the power (approximately 0.03 W).

Researchers have also developed a diode that can serve either as a transmitting LED source or as a receiving photodiode. Termed EROS (emitter-receiver for optical systems), this diode eliminates the costly separator requirement for bidirectional transmission over a single fiber.

A liquid-crystal device has been developed for switching light energy between multimode optical fibers. The system exhibits an optical insertion loss of 1.6 dB in the 0.4- to 2.5-μm wavelength region.

A *continuously variable optical attenuator* has been developed which can be used for loss measurement of the optical-fiber cable. The *optical filter* has been developed and is used for the wavelength division of the multiplexer-demultiplexer. At present, four to five optical waves can be transmitted together with an insertion loss of 3 to 4 dB.

A 16-channel fiber-optic multiplexer/demultiplexer for asynchronous data transmission is also available in the market. This equipment has obvious attractions of flexibility in meeting future growth in circuit requirements while minimizing initial investment. High system capacities will be achieved without involving very high speed digital circuitry; also the need for additional higher-order multiplexing and demultiplexing equipment will be avoided.

As optical technology becomes established, and with the prospect of very long repeater spacings promised by operation at long wavelengths, submerged optical-fiber cable systems become economically attractive. Submerged systems will need single-mode fiber at wavelength of 1.3– 1.55 μm to achieve repeater spacings exceeding 50 km. With the development of high-speed digital repeaters, a fiber-optic system can be extended as a transoceanic transmission system.

TAT-8 is a trans-Atlantic fiber-optic cable scheduled to be installed by 1988. The Japanese have announced their intentions to lay a fiber-optic cable between Japan and Hawaii, also by 1988. We may expect that most of the industrialized world and the major centers of developing countries will be connected through a vast optical-fiber matrix by the end of this century.

Researchers have developed an aluminum-coated fiber cable that withstands high temperatures, strain, and heavy doses of cobalt radiation under which plastic-coated fibers would have melted, snapped, and lost their ability to transmit light.

References

Andreiev, Nikita: "Newest Fiber Optics Test Instruments," *EDN,* November 1978.

Canoga Data Systems, Canoga Park, Calif.: "Fiber Optic Cable Installation Techniques and Specifications," Application Note 103.

Cole, James A.: "Mix and Match Components for the Best Optical Link Design," *Electronic Design,* Jan. 22, 1981.

"Designers Guide to Fiber Optics" *EDN,* Feb. 20, 1978, p. 3, figs. 1 and 8.

Edwards, Morris: "Fiber Optic Links," *Communications News,* February 1978, p. 32.

Eppes, Tom A., Jim E. Goell, and Charles Kao: "Use of Optical Fibers for Long Range," *Electronic Design,* Apr. 2, 1976, p. 91, fig. 3.

Fagenbaum, Joel: "Fiber Optic Tradeoffs," *Electronic Engineering Times,* February 1978.

File, Pete: "Fiber Optic Installation Methods," *EDN,* Feb. 20, 1978, figs. 1 to 4.

General Cable Corporation, Colonia, N.J.: "Outdoor Cable Installation," Issue AT-5, September 1977.

Hewlett Packard Components, Palo Alto, Calif.: *Opto Electronics Applications Handbook,* p. 2.4, figs. 2.5, 5.2.

Howell, Dave: "Optical Communications Systems," *Telecommunications,* September 1978.
Jones, J. R., C. R. Patisaul, P. W. Casper, and D. F. Hemmings: "Live Traffic over AGT's Optical T4 Trunking System," *Telephone Engineer & Management,* Feb. 15, 1979.
Yeh, Leang P., P. E.: "Fiber Optic Communications Systems," *Telecommunications,* September 1978.

11

Shielding, Grounding, Protection of Systems, and Static Electricity

In electrical communication, virtually any type of disturbance which impairs communication by obscuring the signal has come to be termed *noise*. It is a very broad term which now includes hum, crosstalk, spurious signals, and, of course, thermal noise. Any of these tends to limit the quality and permissible length of a communications circuit.

One of the effective ways of reducing the noise is to intercept the interference energy with shielding and carry it away by grounding the shield.

In a conventional telephone system, speech or carrier signals are carried on a *balanced transmission line* consisting of two conductors. Signals are transmitted as a current that travels down one conductor and returns on the other, thus forming a *transverse* or *metallic circuit*. Both conductors are at the same electrical potential in reference to ground.

A second type, the *unbalanced transmission line*, normally uses a single conductor to carry the signal, with ground providing the return path. Ground may take the form of another conductor which is grounded or common to several circuits. All early telegraph and telephone lines were of the unbalanced type, since only half as much wire was required. Because the unbalanced line is very vulnerable to interference, however, its use has been generally limited to coaxial circuits.

A balanced line is basically free of external interference. Signal currents travel in opposite directions on the two conductors as they complete the loop. Ideally, interference acts equally on the two conductors, inducing equal voltages which travel in the same direction on the two wires and thus oppose and cancel each other.

Although externally induced voltages tend to cancel their flow around the transverse circuit, they do seek a return path through ground, thus forming a so-called *longitudinal circuit* as shown in Fig. 11.1. If the interfering voltages induced in two parallel conductors are unequal, perhaps because of circuit imbalance or because the source of the disturbance is closer to one conductor than the other, a net transverse current may result, thus introducing interference into the circuit. Most interference enters a circuit this way.

11.1   Sources of Interference

When a current flows through a conductor, it sets up two distinct fields around the conductor: the *electrostatic* or *electric field* and the *magnetic field*. Both are capable of inducing longitudinal voltages in adjacent conductors and both increase in proportion to the power and frequency of the current from which they result. They differ greatly, however, in how they affect nearby circuits. That is, the higher the line impedance, the less voltage that can be induced by a magnetic field. Line impedance is usually determined by the reactance of the line itself and the nature of the terminating equipment. The voltage induced by the electric field, however, increases in direct proportion to line impedance. Thus the higher the impedance, the greater the electric or capacitive pickup and the lower the magnetic or inductive coupling. Figure 11.2 shows an equivalent circuit for both types of coupling. Note that magnetic coupling is equivalent to being in series with the line, thus requiring a low impedance to be effective. Electric coupling is

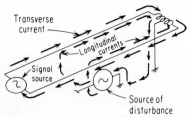

Figure 11.1   Balanced line and disturbance currents.

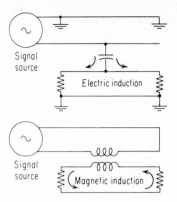

Figure 11.2 Comparison of electromagnetic and electric coupling.

capacitive and requires a very high impedance to develop maximum potential.

Interference to communication equipment can take several forms; *electromagnetic radiation* (EMR), *electromagnetic interference* (EMI), *radio-frequency interference* (RFI) and *electromagnetic pulse* (EMP).

EMR is radiation generated by electrical means. It ranges from electrostatic fields to high-frequency changing fields and to transmitted waves of radio frequency.

EMI is EMR that causes an undesirable response in the function of electrical equipment in the low-frequency range of 1 Hz to 10 kHz.

There are two forms of RFI: *conducted* and *radiated*. Both are forms of EMR that cause an undesirable response at high frequency (10 kHz and above). In conducted RFI, interference is fed back to ac power lines from a device; the power lines act as transmitting antennas. In radiated RFI, a device and its interconnected cables act as an antenna, radiating interference into the atmosphere.

Electromagnetic pulse is EMR of large magnitude resulting from the detonation of nuclear weapons.

An *electromagnetic compatibility* (EMC) test measures the ability of equipment to tolerate EMR produced by other devices while not itself producing EMR.

Line transients

Transients in electric circuits result from the sudden release of previously stored energy. Transients may occur either in *repeatable fashion* or as *random impulses*. Repeatable transients such as commutation voltage spikes, inductive load switching, etc., are more easily observed, defined, and suppressed. Random transients are more elusive. They occur at unpredictable times at remote locations and require the installation of monitoring instruments to detect their occurrence. Line transients affect communications equipment in the forms of EMR and RFI.

Sources of line transients. Sources of line transients may be divided into two categories: artificial, which are due to industrial and advanced living requirements, and natural sources.

Artificial sources
- Switching of reactive loads; opening and closing of switches and relays
- Fuse and circuit breaker interruptions and resettings
- Generator and motor operation (overspeed and hunting, start-up, control, and shutdown)
- Ignition system, arc welder, particle-precipitator operation
- Fluorescent light operation
- Reflected waves
- Electromagnetic pulse from nuclear blasts or large chemical explosions
- Current inrush
- Thyristor switching; power control circuit operation
- In close proximity to line pairs carrying dc keying currents

Natural sources
- Lightning
- Static charges on personnel, work surfaces, tools, etc.
- Static charges on long transmission lines

Static electricity and prevention in the electronics industry is discussed in Sec. 11.4.

Lightning. *Static electricity* is electricity at rest. Lightning serves as an example of what static electricity is and how it behaves. Static electricity in the atmosphere remains at rest until the potential gradient between clouds reaches a level that causes the air to break down or fail. A lightning bolt is then generated to equalize this potential gradient.

Telecommunication equipment has become more vulnerable to overvoltage due to lightning because of the introduction of solid-state devices into the telecommunications industry as well as the increase in equipment installed in rural areas.

Telecommunication networks are composed of various transmission systems, whether wired or wireless, on land or underwater. As most of the installations in these systems include metallic material and have grounding systems, they are apt to suffer from lightning. Telecommunication equipment is fed by electrical power distribution lines, and lightning surges may appear on these lines. Thus, lightning surges induced in telecommunication installations can be divided into two kinds:

- Those caused by bolts of lightning directly striking telecommunication installations.

- Those caused by electromagnetic induction from the lightning discharge to the telecommunication lines.

In a summit microwave relay station, the electric potential of the station ground rises sharply with a direct lightning strike to a lightning rod or lightning current penetrating from a power distribution line. In such cases, abnormal voltages are produced between ground equipment in the station and the entrance cable connecting the station and other facilities having a different ground potential.

Surges from radiated RFI, however, occur frequently in overhead telecommunication lines. Among the various kinds of transmission lines, overhead subscriber lines in rural and suburban areas are the most apt to be exposed to lightning. A typical lightning surge wave across a paired line and ground, measured at the subscribers terminal, is given in Fig. 11.3. Lightning surge currents measured on subscriber lines, power distribution lines, and lightning rods for microwave stations are about 1 kA, several kA, and 10 kA respectively.

11.2   System and Circuit Protection

Protection can be provided either by eliminating the transients at the source with shielding and grounding methods or by locating a protector between the noise source and the load or by isolation of the system being protected. Static electricity and prevention methods are covered in Sec. 11.4.

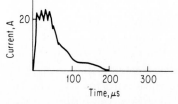

Figure 11.3 The surge current caused by lightning.

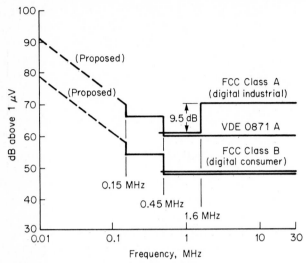

Figure 11.4   RFI limits by FCC and VDE.

Any electronic device or system, including devices utilizing digital techniques, create a major RFI suppression problem for both manufacturers and users. The magnitude of the problem has made it necessary for government to increase its role in regulating and controlling radio-frequency interference. As a result, equipment generating disruptive RFI is now required to have sufficient filtering to meet specific emission requirements as defined in various agency standards. In the United States, such standards include FCC Rules, Part 15 (for communication devices) and Part 18 (for industrial, scientific, and medical equipment); in Germany, they include VDE 0871A (industrial) and VDE 0875. (VDE stands for Verband Deutsher Electrotechniker, a West Germany government agency.)

The standards establish two levels of noise emission limits: A, a level for industrial equipment, and B, a level for consumer devices such as personal computers and TV games. FCC and VDE regulation limits are given in Fig. 11.4 and Table 11.1.

Shielding techniques

The most effective method of eliminating unwanted coupling is to isolate the disturbed circuit from the source of interference by some form of shielding. In principle, either the disturbing circuit, the disturbed circuit, or both are surrounded by a metallic covering that intercepts the interfering fields and provides an alternate path for the longitudinal currents which are induced. The nature of shielding varies greatly, depending on the nature of the interference, its strength, and

TABLE 11.1 RFI Limits

FCC radiated RFI		
	Maximum field strength, μV/m	
Frequency, MHz	Class A (distance = 30 m)	Class B (distance = 3 m)
30–88	30	100
88–216	50	150
216–1000	70	200

FCC conducted RFI		
	Maximum RF line voltage, dB above 1 μV	
Frequency, MHz	Class A	Class B
0.45–1.6	60	48
1.6–30	69.5	48

VDE conducted RFI*		
	Maximum RF line voltage, dB above 1 μV	
Frequency, MHz	A level	B level
0.15–0.50	66	52
0.50–30	60	48

*VDE conducted limits in the frequency range 10–150 kHz are recommended values, not regulations. The West German VDE test procedure is very similar to that for the U.S. FCC. There is one significant difference in the procedures—the receiver bandwidth. The FCC specifies a broader bandwidth in the lower frequencies, essentially making the conducted emission limits tougher than the VDE limits. Bandwidth: tolerance in cycles per second (hertz) expressing the difference between its limiting frequencies.

frequency. A good shield against electric fields may be ineffective against a magnetic field. Essentially, some sort of magnetic material such as iron or steel is required to block interference due to magnetic fields. Electric fields are best shielded by excellent conductors such as aluminum or copper.

At the audio frequencies (EMI) magnetic coupling can be minimized by enclosing the conductors in a braid or in a steel tape which tends to absorb magnetic fields. Electric coupling is usually negligible at these frequencies, so that magnetic shielding is usually all that is needed.

At carrier frequencies (RFI), braid, tape, or a solid sheathing of copper, aluminum, or lead is somewhat effective against magnetic fields because induced eddy currents within the shield oppose and partially neutralize the fields that produce them. The effectiveness of these materials against electric fields increases with frequency and with their conductivity and thickness. As frequency rises, the electric coupling remains much less than the magnetic coupling across the whole frequency range.

Another class of shielding that uses a covering of steel wool or a paper or fabric impregnated with carbon or some powdered metallic substance converts radio or other electromagnetic radiation into heat and effectively dissipates interfering fields. This form of shielding is particularly effective against high-powered high-frequency radio interference, which may be capable of filtering through the gaps on braided or overlapped shielding materials. In this respect a laminated shield of two different materials is a far more effective shield than a solid shield of the same thickness made of only one material, due to reflective losses and introduced at each interface.

At 1 MHz a double braid of copper provides about 25 dB better shielding than single braid, and a triple braid is 30 dB better than the double. Coaxial cable with conventional copper braiding encased in an outer copper braid provides a very effective shield for coaxial circuits from 10 kHz up to several megahertz.

Although these generalities concerning shielding materials can be helpful, it is necessary to identify the exact nature of the interference to achieve maximum shielding effectiveness. Since magnetic and electric coupling cause different effects, shielding will have to be tailored to the type of interference encountered in the specific application.

By means of a simple test, it is possible to identify the nature of the coupling between two lines, as shown in Fig. 11.5. A variable-frequency

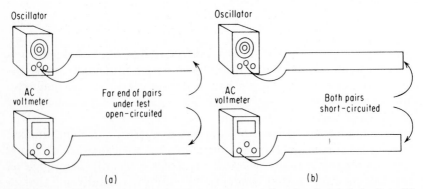

Figure 11.5 Identification of the type of coupling. (*a*) Test for electric induction; (*b*) test for magnetic induction.

oscillator is connected to one circuit and a sensitive voltmeter is connected to the other circuit to measure the induced voltage. The oscillator is adjusted to a normal operating frequency and the far ends of both lines are short-circuited. Since voltages induced by magnetic coupling are inversely proportional to the line impedance, the short circuit will result in a much reduced voltage if the principal coupling is electric. Conversely, if the principal fields are electromagnetic, the induced voltage will increase with a short circuit. The test should be repeated with the far ends of both lines open. The induced voltage will be the result of electric coupling. Once the type of field has been identified, the most appropriate shielding method can be specified.

Unbalanced circuits present special shielding problems, since the shielding serves as the return path for the signal, thus helping to carry the signal. Even though part of the signal return may travel through other ground paths, a portion of it will travel through the shield, where it may be subject to interference caused by induced longitudinal voltages.

When coaxial cables are grounded at both ends, a longitudinal path or ground loop may be established which makes the cable vulnerable to interference from external magnetic fields (Figs. 11.6). Even though the inner conductor may be shielded from the external field, longitudinal currents induced into the shield are in effect in series with the signal current flow through the shield, thus directly affecting the signal. Note that the low impedance of the ground loop restricts its effect on magnetic pickup. As a result, the shield should be grounded at the load only and the ground circuit resistance should be kept as low as possible.

In voice-grade circuits, interference primarily consists of lower frequencies, such as ac hum from power supplies and other low-frequency inductive components. In a run consisting of two or more coaxial cables, the possibilities of intercable coupling are great, simply because all shields are normally grounded at each end of the cable and the shield of one cable could quite easily become the return path for the inner conductor of its neighbor, at least for some part of its full length. This

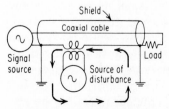

Figure 11.6   Longitudinal currents of a coaxial cable grounded at both ends.

can be reduced by enclosing the coaxial cable in heavy copper tubing or braiding which serves as a ground path for neighboring coaxial circuits.

Filtered connectors

Filtered connectors are becoming a cost-effective way to control electromagnetic interference in computer applications. With built-in low-pass filters, the connectors prevent external EMI from compromising system performance and data integrity, protect against damage and downtime due to electrostatic discharge, and help designers meet government requirements on maximum levesls of conducted and radiated EMI.

Filtered connectors are physically compatible with nonfiltered devices. They are fully interchangeable in terms both mating and mounting.

Tests show that, if the cable radiates beyond the limits set by the FCC for class B computing devices, there are two ways the radiation can be reduced. The offending interconnection can simply be replaced with a shielded cable, which typically adds $10 to the cost of the system. The alternative is to use a filtered connector which directly replaces the conventional connector and adds $5 at most to the system cost. AC power line filters are discussed in "AC power supply protection" in this section.

Grounding

A *ground* is an assumed arbitrary point of zero potential, and a *ground connection* is a tie to a point as close as possible to zero potential. The objective of any grounding technique is to provide a path to earth of as low a resistance or impedance as possible, because the flow of current causes a voltage drop that is directly proportional to the resistance of the path to ground. Any resistance that results in an unwanted difference of potential is the source of coupling to other circuits.

In a telecommunications system it is necessary to provide a good ground for a wide variety of currents that may range from direct currents to very high radio frequencies. This is not easy to accomplish, since a low-resistance path for direct current is not necessarily a low-resistance path at radio frequencies. For example, the dc resistance of any conductor is inversely proportional to its cross-sectional area and directly proportional to its length. However, because of the self-inductance of the conductor, alternating currents tend to concentrate near the surface of the wire, rather than flowing uniformly through the whole conductor as in direct currents. This effect, called the *skin effect,* increases as frequency and wire size become greater.

As a result, a typical solid copper conductor of 24 gage shows a resistance of approximately 26 Ω/1000 ft (8.2 Ω/100 m) to direct current and 37 Ω/1000 ft (12 Ω/100 m) at 500 kHz. At 10 MHz, the same wire shows a resistance of 170 Ω/1000 ft (57 Ω/100 m). Since any resistance to a flow of current creates a difference of potential and a standing difference of potential contributes noise to the communications circuit, it is advantageous to provide the greatest possible conducting surface for any ground path. Thus, for direct current, a solid copper ground conductor is chosen which has a total current-carrying capacity substantially higher than the sum of all internal currents that share this ground. For alternating current, stranded conductors are preferred, since the perimeter of each strand provides a separate path for high-frequency currents, resulting in a much greater surface or skin area for the whole conductor and hence less resistance. Since we must accept the fact that every ground path has some resistance or impedance, it is apparent that the total resistance to ground can be reduced by adding parallel paths.

Grounding system of a communication center.   The grounding system of a communication center or a telephone office may be inadequate for electronic switching systems due to high voltage and current spikes during make-break of the relay contacts or wiper switches. Therefore the decision to improve or add a new grounding system must be faced at the time of installation. Telecommunication offices may have four different ground connections (see Fig. 11.7): ac neutral, protection ground, dc return (dc neutral), and logic ground.

1. The ac neutral is provided as a reference for the ac power system and is the current-carrying conductor of an ac power distribution system.

2. The protective or potential ground is a safety measure and equalizes the potential difference between equipment in the telecommunication center. The protective ground system reduces noise by intercepting interference energy and providing a low-resistance path to the ground potential. This system of ground is achieved by equipment grounding, framework grounding, and relay rack grounding and is normally specified by the manufacturer. Any ground lead that is not normally used in a current-carrying capacity can be considered a protective and/or potential ground. For ac wiring in a telecommunication center, a separate grounding conductor enclosed in a metallic raceway with the phase and neutral conductors is required in the United States. This conductor, called the *green wire,* is solidly connected to the protective ground bus at the power distribution closet. The fault current path relies entirely on this wire.

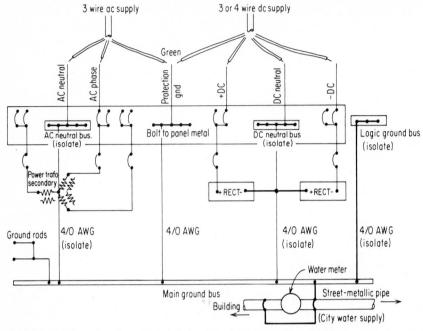

Figure 11.7   Ground and neutral systems for a communication center.

The *National Electrical Code®*, local building codes, and fire prevention codes define requirements for conductor sizes.

3. The battery return ground is a path designed to carry dc return current to the source of power.

4. The logic ground stays floating or comes directly from the main grounding system of the building and is assigned to low potentials (less than 10 V) of circuits in the system (see Fig. 11.7) or connected to signal return (see Fig. 11.8c).

All points of systems ground should remain at approximately the same potential while carrying a range of fault and steady-state currents. Four different grounding systems should be kept separated in the building, i.e., *never* to be interconnected. In a small or a private telecommunication center, the logic ground may not be needed and dc neutral and protective ground are not separated; in this case a ground system with very low resistance should be installed and ground connections should be made carefully. In a communication center the system ground resistance should not exceed 5 Ω under all conditions. Wired connections should be made using two-hole solderless or equivalent terminal lugs to facilitate inspection and testing.

Grounding arrangements in digital interfacing circuits. Proper operation of the EIA (CCITT) interface circuits, whether using balanced, unbalanced, or a combination of both, requires the presence of a signal ground path between the circuit grounds of the equipment at each end of the interconnection. The signal ground lead shall be connected to the circuit ground (or common) which shall be connected to protective ground by any one of the following methods, as required by the specific application. Refer to Fig. 11.8.

In configuration *A*, the circuit ground of the equipment is connected to protective ground, at one point only, by a 100-Ω $\pm$ 20 percent $\frac{1}{2}$-W resistor.

In configuration *B*, the circuit ground shall be connected directly to protective ground or to logic ground if it is available. The same configuration need not be used at both ends of an interconnection; however, care should be exercised to prevent establishment of ground loops carrying high currents. Under certain ground-fault conditions in configuration *A*, high ground currents may cause the resistor to fail; therefore, a provision shall be made for inspection and replacement of the resistor.

Some interface applications may require the use of shielded interconnecting cable for radio-frequency interference or other purposes.

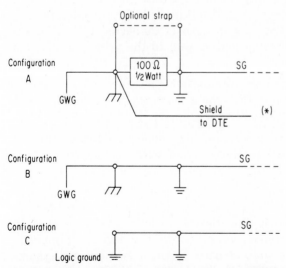

Figure 11.8 Optional ground arrangements for CCITT and EIA interface circuits. /77 = protective ground or frame ground; $\equiv$ = circuit ground or circuit common; SG = signal ground interchange lead; GWG = green wire ground of power system; * = normally no connection to shield in DCE.

When employed, the shield shall be connected only to protective ground at either or both ends depending on the specific application.

In a telecommunication center where a logic ground is provided, configuration C is recommended; i.e., signal return is connected to logic ground.

Grounding and noise control guidelines for digital operating area

- Use dedicated power feeders and, if possible, dedicated transformers for critical loads. Do not allow other nonessential or power-disturbing loads to share the same power feeder and associated ground conductors.

- If the critical load is spread out over a significant area with distances of more than 10 m (30 ft) for high-data-rate cables, provide the system with a signal reference grid. This may be a sheet of copper foil, a mesh of bonded copper wires, or a suitably bonded supporting steel structure for a raised floor, connected to the same system grounding point. The impedance of the foil or grid at high frequencies is much lower than that of a single conductor. The grid should be used to supplement the normal grounding means and as an addition to, rather than a replacement for, equipment ground conductors. Interfacing a power center with an isolating transformer on the reference grid allows the secondary derived voltage to be grounded to the grid at the transformer. The grid in turn is connected to the nearest qualified ground, and connected as well to the principal electrical ground of the building.

- For circuits which have an automatic bypass through an uninterruptible power supply (UPS), the power source grounding point should not change as the power is changed.

- Voltage step-down, if required, should be done close to the computer room, preferably in the computer room with a shielded isolation transformer.

- In interconnections between very large systems, each system, with its own grounding reference conductor, may have a voltage difference with respect to the other. This may be a continuous ac voltage difference or may be a random impulse voltage difference. Simply installing a heavy-gage ground path between two ground systems keeps noise currents from flowing in any data cable interconnections.

- Signal wire cables lying upon a subfloor in a computer room can pick up noise signal voltages by capacitive or inductive coupling with surrounding structural steel and conductors. At the system central grounding point, connection should be made with the building steel wherever possible. If the reinforcing steel or mesh is inaccessible, a

130 × 130 cm (4 × 4 ft) sheet of conducting metal such as copper, aluminum, or galvanized steel may be placed directly upon the concrete subfloor and connected electrically to the system central grounding point. Capacitance between the plate and the reinforcing steel or mesh will provide a bypass current path, reduce the voltage difference, and reduce coupling into the underfloor cables. This arrangement is known as a *transient trap*.

- Review and plan the underfloor cable routing to provide the maximum isolation between circuits which can carry disturbances and those which can be disturbed. Avoid parallel and nearby runs in which both electromagnetic and capacitive coupling will occur. If one set of conductors must cross another, the possible intercoupling will be minimized if they cross at right angles and they are separated instead of lying one upon the other.

- Be aware of the possibility of interference from conductors which extend outside the computer area. These include refrigerant pipes, water pipes, fire alarm or water detector circuits and conduit, fire extinguishing system pipes and control wires, and both power and control wires for heating, ventilation, and air conditioning. In addition, there may be metallic air ducts. In many instances, the pipes and ducts can be installed with an insulating joint. This allows the portion under the computer room be grounded to the computer system rather than to be a continuation of a virtual antenna extending outside the area. An example might be coolant pipe from a penthouse which is exposed to lightning in addition to being closely coupled to elevators and neon signs or other equipment which often create substantial radio-frequency noise (RFI).

- When providing surge arrestors to clip or bypass surge voltages of significant magnitude (typically 250 V or more on a 120-V ac line or 10 V or more on a 5-V signal line), remember that traveling voltage or current impulse waves cannot be absorbed by such devices; most of the energy will be reflected or diverted to another path provided for the purpose. Lightning arrestors do not belong in the computer room. They belong on utility poles and on the input high-voltage-winding side of transformers (above 4000 V, typically), or just inside the buildings they are intended to protect.

- The connection from a surge arrestor to the nearest earth ground creates an electromagnetic field during a voltage surge. It is possible to arrange the conductors to minimize unwanted couplings from such surge impulses.

- Ground the equipment covers and racks and distribution frames.

- Do not power the lights and appliances on or off frequently in the office.

- Keep the openings in an enclosure smaller than one-twentieth of the wavelength of the highest critical frequency for commercial products and one-fiftieth of the wavelength for military products. As an example, to provide 20 dB of shielding at a critical frequency of 100 MHz, the maximum opening dimension must not exceed 15 cm (6 in). In general, keep all openings as small as possible.

- Put a steel magnetic shield around the 60-Hz ac line transformer to reduce magnetic radiation to acceptable levels; also the transformer must have internal noise shields, to keep electromagnetic noise out of sensitive circuitry. Connect them to ground.

- Put a high-frequency capacitor directly across the computer input terminal, to reduce audio rectification, radiation, and susceptibility. More effective than this are filter connectors or filter circuits on inputs and outputs of the cable connections.

- Place ceramic capacitors in parallel with the electrolytics to reduce switching noise.

- Shielded and double-shielded and twisted pair cables are a necessity for digital communication links.

- Tie outer shields of a multipair cable directly to ground at both ends when the cable is 2 m or shorter, to avoid ground loops and maximize high-frequency shielding. If longer cable runs are used or ground loops are present, one end (preferably the receiving end) of the outer shield should be tied to ground, with the other end tied to ground through a capacitor that will pass high-frequency noise but adequately block 60-Hz currents.

- Terminate idle pairs of cables with characteristic impedances or connect the other end to ground.

- Do not operate 60-V or higher dc keying and high-speed-data circuits with pairs of the same cable.

Installation of ground system.   Achievement of the desired ground resistance normally requires installation of a multiple grounding connection. The connection may be to existing underground metallic structures, metal piping, steel pilings, well casings, or to an intentionally designed ground electrode system.

Traditionally, metallic water pipe has been used as one of the principal grounds for most installations.

Galvanized steel, stainless steel, brass, or copper rods have long been used in a matrix formation around the periphery of buildings. The curve of Fig. 11.9 shows the resistance in ohms of various-diameter ground rods versus driven depth. Note that the relation of resistance to depth is not a linear function; instead, the greater the depth, the

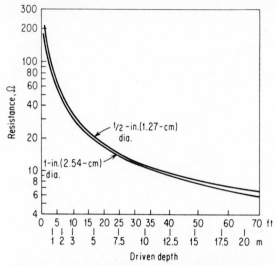

Figure 11.9 Ground resistance versus ground rod depth.

$$R = \frac{\rho}{191.5D}\left(\log_e \frac{96D}{d} - 1\right)$$

where R = resistance of soil, Ω; ρ = Ω/cm^3; D = depth, ft; d = diameter, in.

$$R = \frac{\rho}{627D}\left(\log_e \frac{800D}{d} - 1\right)$$

where D = depth, m; d = diameter, cm.

less the resistance changes. The rods should be buried to a depth where the moisture of the soil is permanent.

A single driven rod is an economical and simple means of making a grounding electrode. In general, however, a single driven rod does not provide sufficiently low resistance, and consequently several rods must be driven and connected in parallel by a cable. Although these rods are connected as would be for parallel resistance, their total resistance does not follow the usual law for computing resistances in parallel. To attain the full effect of resistances in parallel, these rods would have to be spaced at such distances that the effective resistance areas immediately surrounding them would not overlap. The extent to which the areas overlap determines how much of their effectiveness is lost. The curves of Fig. 11.10 show a change in resistance for two, four, and eight parallel rods with various spacing. When two, three, or perhaps four rods are used in parallel, they are usually driven in a straight line and connected together. In cases where more than four are used, they are usually driven in a hollow-square formation and connected in parallel. Distances between the rods are usually made equal, as in

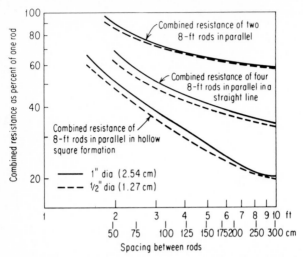

Figure 11.10 Combined resistances of 8-ft (244-cm) parallel
ground rods. Solid curves are for 1-in-(2.54-cm-) diameter
rods; dashed curves are for ½-in-(1.27-cm-) diameter rods.

the hollow-square formation of eight rods. The distance between rods
should be approximately twice the depth of the deepest rod. Moreover
all rods must be located at least 2 ft (60 cm) from any wall.

Concrete-encased grounding electrodes are utilized in locations
where stones or rock make it difficult to drive long ground rods
and where water-pipe grounding cannot be relied upon. Electrodes
(No. 4/0 AWG bare copper wire) placed in concrete forms, spaced
about 2 in (5 cm) above the base of the footing, have been used. Ground
resistance tests show that this method provides lower resistance values
than an equivalent amount of driven ground rods. Concrete in the earth
tends to draw moisture from the soil and keeps its own water content
high, a condition which accounts for its own consistent low resistivity.

Concrete-enclosed reinforcing rods also can be used. The reinforcing
frame-work of footings for the columns of structural steel buildings
provides equivalent ground resistance to those of conventional electrodes in low- and medium-resistivity soil and lower resistance in high-
resistivity soil. The only cost of making electric connections to the
reinforcing bar is that of connecting an anchor bolt to the vertical
reinforcing bars. Thus the complete steel superstructure and the internal reinforced bars provide a ground resistance which is found to
be below 0.5 Ω. Care must be exercised during the laying and typing
of the reinforcing bars so that a good continuous electric connection is
obtained.

In locations where all the previous methods fail, a well drilled to the
water table with a No. 4/0 AWG copper wire conductor enclosed in

concrete or in a well housing and suspended in water will serve in addition to the other systems.

Sometimes referred to as the *single-ground concept* or the *ground-tree concept* is a method of integrating the system ground with the equipment ground. The trunk of the tree is a continuous vertical riser busbar bonded to the system ground at one point and centrally located. It is the reference ground point. The branches connect all bay lineups and frames to the trunk on the same floor. All other grounds, such as additional ground rods, must be bonded to the reference point only. A physical separation or insulation must be provided between the two switching systems as well as the other communication systems in a central office to avoid flashover from ground potential difference. Patch bays associated with these two types of equipment must be separately grounded and each brought to the reference ground point. No closed loops are permitted in the ground system.

System protection

Elimination of the noise and transients at the source is the preferred approach, but access to the transient source for tinkering is often limited to unrewarding (like being between the clouds and ground during an approaching lightning storm). In addition, access to systems that generate transients is frequently impractical, and the transient energy encountered may vary widely.

It appears then, that insertion of protection between the source and the area affected is the best way to go. Protection devices may be installed in series and/or in parallel. Series overvoltage protection would require the protective device to swing from full conduction (with a very small voltage drop) to a virtual open circuit in a very short time, like a fuse. While the energy-handling capability could be rather small, the holdoff voltage rating would have to be considerable. The drawback is that if a device failure occurred, the load would still be destroyed.

Shunt overvoltage protection is almost universally employed because protective devices can operate rapidly and handle significant amounts of energy. If a shunt protection device fails, it generally fails as a short, which still affords some protection to the load. Combined methods of protection generally employ a shunt device to protect the load while it is causing a series protective device (fuse or circuit breaker) to disconnect the load from the transient (and power) source.

Carrier system protection.   Communication cables are usually run along the power lines in rural areas, exposing the communication system to power line disturbances as well as to lightning. A lightning strike may sometimes cause a power fault, which in turn induces current surges on the transmission line (see Fig. 11.3). At other times, power line surges may occur for unrelated reasons. These factors put tremendous demands on the electrical protection techniques for carrier systems.

A carrier system is protected by devices which may be of the carbon-block or, more often, the gas-tube type. The protectors are connected between the conductors and the grounded shield of a signal carrier cable to offer an easy path to ground for electric disturbances.

Carbon-block protectors. Carbon-block protectors operate in the following manner. When a high potential appears between the conductors and ground, the electric energy strikes an arc across the gap and flows to ground. The dimensions of the gap are such that the protector will fire at a potential of less than 1 kV, preventing damage to the carrier equipment from most lightning strikes.

Carbon-block protectors have several undesirable characteristics. After several discharges across the air gap, dislodged carbon particles can bridge the gap, creating a leakage path for the signal to ground. If the impedance of this path is low enough, the electrical balance of the pairs will be disturbed, making them susceptible to induced voltage which appears as excessive noise. The carbon particles may also induce a noisy and/or intermittent short in the transmission loop which is very difficult to locate.

Gas-tube protectors. An alternate protector device is the gas tube; its metal electrodes are separated by a glass or ceramic sleeve. The gas inside is typically at a pressure of one-tenth normal air pressure to allow a relatively large spacing between the electrodes while still maintaining a reasonable breakdown voltage. The large gap is desirable to prevent metal from bridging the gap after being sputtered off the electrodes by the arc. When a high potential is applied across the two electrodes, the arc conducts a current across the gas-filled space be-

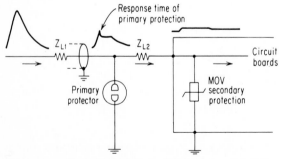

Figure 11.11 Protection system with gas tube and varistor.

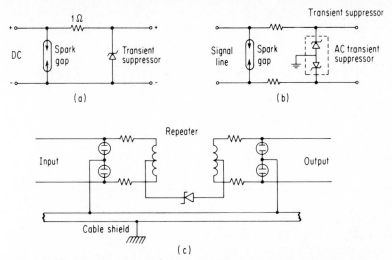

Figure 11.12 Protection system with resistors, zener diode, and protectors. (*a*) Lightning spark gap, zener protection; (*b*) lightning spark gap, suppressor protection; (*c*) repeater protection.

tween them like the carbon-block protector. The gas tube is connected between the wire pairs and ground, creating a path to ground when a high voltage is applied (see Figs. 11.11 and 11.12). Gas tubes can be designed to operate at various voltages, such as 90 V, 350 V, and 3 kV, and come in modules for installation on distribution frames.

Tubes with three or more electrodes can be used to improve protection levels in certain cases; for example, a single three-element device can replace two two-electrode gas tubes for grounding a pair of wire conductors at the input or output of a repeater. The operation of the three-electrode tube is such that once it fires across the gap between the first pair of electrodes, a much lower voltage is needed to initiate the arc across the second gap. Therefore it prevents unsymmetrical operation of the protectors and hence a potentially damaging sequence of protector operation.

Modern solid-state communications circuitry can be damaged even if the primary (high-voltage) protection is working normally. It is often advisable to provide a secondary protection system to further reduce the voltage transient. As shown in Figs. 11.11 and 11.12, the secondary protection removes the overvoltage spike that is passed by the primary protector.

Solid-state circuit protection. Transient voltages present hazards to the solid-state equipment. System voltages and currents can surge to levels many times greater than the steady-state values when the transients are present. For protection against these transients the following precautions are utilized.

Thyristors. Thyristors are also sometimes configured to conduct upon the application of a triggering gate voltage, derived from the unwanted transient, thus sinking destructive current pulses. Thyristor circuits permit variable-gate thresholds. However, relatively high shunt capacitance limits their application versatility, particularly in high-frequency circuits.

Metal-oxide varistors. Tin, zinc, or bismuth oxide voltage-dependent resistors (VDRs), often referred to as *metal-oxide varistors* (MOVs), offer a cost-effective means of dealing with high-, medium-, and low-level transients. Most MOVs are electrically symmetrical, resembling back-to-back zener diodes, and are thus useful elements in both ac and dc circuits. Protection of a transistor switching circuit with a varistor is given in Figs. 11.11 and 11.13.

In Fig. 11.14, the noise suppression efficiency of a MOV is given. The highest breakdown voltage recorded is about 1020 V. The varistor installed directly across the switch terminals completely eliminates the relaxation oscillations by responding in a few milliseconds and holding the voltage below the gap breakdown voltage (about 300 V) while dissipating the stored energy in the system.

Diodes and zener diodes. When specifying low-level, fast-acting protective devices, such as those required on logic data lines, *avalanche diodes* are a common choice. Ordinary diodes and especially zener diodes are also often used for their clamping capabilities in low-voltage circuits. Sensitive gates found in today's logic devices are susceptible to damage from surprisingly low energy pulses.

Zeners provide a low-cost, readily available solution to the problem. Their prime advantage rests in their ability to protect very low voltage circuits from deadly voltage excursions. However, their reasonably

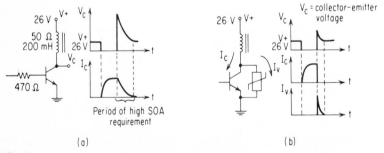

Figure 11.13 Protection of transistor with a varistor. (*a*) Basic solenoid circuit; (*b*) solenoid circuit with varistor protection. (SOA = safe operating area.)

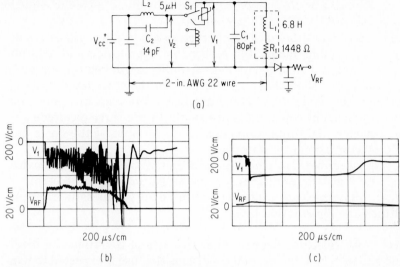

Figure 11.14 Noise suppression with a MOV. (*a*) Switch circuit; (*b*) unprotected contacts; (*c*) MOV-protected contacts.

sharp, well-defined knees, rapid response times, and low leakage currents are additions to performance. Zeners may be installed in parallel to provide bidirectional protection.

It should be pointed out that only the junction-type avalanche suppressors offer the advantage of polar operation. Recently, optimized avalanche-diode overvoltage protectors have become available; they are specifically designed and manufactured for transient suppression. They have lower dynamic impedances and much sharper avalanche breakdown "knees."

Avalanche-type zeners respond to transients in about 10^{-12} s. Because of their miniature size, zener diodes can be installed on circuit boards.

Protective devices such as MOVs and spark gaps have a slow response to transients. In many cases zener transient-voltage suppressors and MOVs and spark gaps are used together. A zener transient-voltage suppressor keeps the voltage at an acceptable level until another circuit protector device acts. This way, the circuit protector protects both the solid-state circuit as well as the zener suppressor.

The lightest-duty gas tube (or gas-discharge tube) is a simple *neon tube*, such as the common type NE-2. Gas-tube protectors were described earlier.

Silicon controlled rectifiers (SCRs), *triacs*, and *diodes* are used in dc-to-ac inverters, rectifiers, and regulators.

Frequency and phase controllers are usually protected by means of selenium stacks or RC networks. However, silicon avalanche-diode suppressors can be efficient alternatives.

Table 11.2 shows the various characteristics of these protective devices. As the table shows, the carbon block protector and gas-tube protector have large surge current capabilities, but require a certain amount of time before they can respond. On the other hand, the thyristor and zinc oxide varistor feature fast surge response times, but their surge current capabilities are small. In the three-electrode gas-tube protector, lightning protection characteristics of the basic gas-tube protector have been improved.

In the subscriber equipment area recently, the number of devices using power distribution lines has increased, making it necessary to develop countermeasures against lightning surges in both transmission lines and distribution lines.

Fuses. Fuse selection requires that two sets of conditions be determined and satisfied: the normal conditions the fuse is expected to handle and the fault conditions it must protect against.

The normal conditions include both normal operating current and ambient temperature. Generally, for long and trouble-free life, the operating current should not exceed 75 percent of the fuse's rated current established at 25°C. Ambient temperature above 25°C requires additional derating, since the fuse's current-carrying capacity will decrease as ambient temperature rises (see Fig. 11.15).

The required fault-condition description should include the circuit voltage and the time by which the fuse must open when subjected to a specific fault current. Since fuses are current-sensitive devices, they can be used in circuits with voltages up to their rated value.

Proper protection and elimination of nuisance blowing requires selection of the appropriate blowing characteristic: fast-acting, medium-acting, or slow-blow (Fig. 11.16).

Fast-acting fuses were developed for the protection of instruments and other sensitive devices by quick response to current overloads.

Medium-acting fuses, the most widely used in general applications, will normally be the least expensive.

Slow-blow fuses provide a built-in time lag for applications in which the initial current is normally several times greater than the stabilized running current: motor starting, capacitor charging, and highly inductive circuits, for example. The time lag in slow-blow fuses is a result of their greater thermal inertia at slight overloads.

AC power supply protection. The increased dependence of commercial and industrial organizations on electronic equipment is coupled with a decline in the quality and availability of utility-provided power. Of

TABLE 11.2 Protection Device Characteristics

Protection device	Surge response time, μs	Sparkover voltage, V	Surge current capacity, A	Electrostatic capacity, pF	Application
Carbon-block protector	~10	10^2–10^3	10^4 ($100\ \mu s$)	~50	Outdoor/indoor links
Gas-tube protector	~1	10^2–10^3	10^5 ($100\ \mu s$)	~1	Outdoor/indoor links
Thyristor	~0.001	1–10^2	10^3 ($10\ \mu s$)	~10	Circuits in equipment
Zinc oxide varistor	~0.05	10–10^3	10^5 ($20\ \mu s$)	~10^4	Outdoor/indoor links, I/O part of equipment

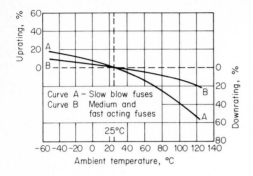

Figure 11.15 Effect of ambient temperature on current carrying capacity of fuses.

all the problems which affect data processing, telecommunications, and other sophisticated devices, the most unpredictable and most frequently encountered are related to the ac power supply.

Modern high-speed digital equipment is sensitive to a wide variety of perturbations on the power line, not just interruptions or scheduled power reductions. These would have created only a minor perturbation in previous years, but they now affect the user equipment.

For example, variations in the voltage and frequency of the source of carrier frequency due to variations in the power supply are liable to disturb all kinds of data channels. Noise riding on the power line, voltage drift beyond tolerance limits, momentary high- or low-voltage transients, dips, and surges can cause errors, shutdowns, or even equipment damage, depending on their magnitude and duration.

There are a variety of devices available, each designed to solve some of the ac power problems; they include the *isolation transformer, voltage regulator, ac line conditioner, motor generator,* and *uninterruptible power systems* and are briefly discussed below.

Power lines act as antennas, picking up all sorts of electric noises generated by appliances, machine tools, street cars, and other power-absorbing equipment (RFI). Two types of noise are encountered on a

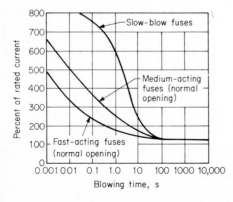

Figure 11.16 Percent of rated current versus blowing time.

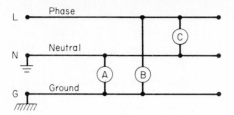

Figure 11.17 Common-mode noise (A and B) and transverse-mode noise (C).

power line: *common-mode* noise appears between both sides (line and neutral) of a power line and ground, and *transverse-mode* (also called *differential-mode* or *normal-node*) noise appears from line to line (Fig. 11.17). This common-mode noise can run through voltage regulators and transient suppressors with very little if any attenuation and can even work its way through the filters in most power supplies. It can be removed, however, by the installation of a *multishielded isolation transformer* with around 10,000-MΩ isolation resistance, less than 0.005-pF interwinding capacitance, and with a 120-dB range of noise attenuation or RFI filters, both of which are discussed in succeeding pages.

A relatively inexpensive solution to the voltage-drift problem is the installation of an *automatic voltage regulator* with an output range within the acceptable input range of the power supplies being used.

Voltage regulators come in many forms. Two of the most popular are the *switched multitap transformer* and the *motor-driven variable transformer*. Switched transformer types use both a buck-boost transformer placed in series with the hot input line and voltage-detector–electronic-switch circuits to automatically connect the output terminal to the transformer tap that provides the required output. As the ac input rises and falls, the taps are changed to provide a stable output. Complete correction can be achieved in less than 35 ms. Accuracy at the output terminals is around 3 percent for most applications. Motor-driven transformers work on a similar principle. An auxiliary transformer is connected in series with the hot power lead and fed with the output of an autotransformer connected across the line. A voltage detector at the output terminals monitors the regulated voltage and automatically commands the motor to reset the variable transformer's output to add or subtract the required voltage from the input. Single-phase regulators correct at a rate well under 0.2 s/V and can hold the output to within 0.75 percent of the nominal voltage setting.

Incoming ac supply lines may be cleaned up with *line-conditioner networks*. These networks range from simple *LC/RC* noise and spark suppressors to more elaborate integrated filters and regulators. A line conditioner eliminates distortion as well as line transients, usually responds faster than conventional ac regulators, and has a very high (70–100 dB) line isolation at 60 Hz. A line conditioner is also called an *RFI filter*.

A *motor-generator* eliminates line noise, keeps a constant voltage, but is vulnerable to power failure.

RFI power-line filters. The filter can be used to reduce the equipment's internally generated RFI below the level of an applied emission standard or used to reduce the susceptibility of that equipment to malfunction due to external conducted RFI.

Filters are designed to take care of either the common mode or differential (transverse) mode or both components of the noise.

Filters are generally built with two-pole (L-type) or three-pole (T-type) filter networks. It has been generally recommended that a two-pole network be used for linear power supplies and three-pole networks for switching power supplies and synchronous motors.

The selection of a suitable filter can best be based on the type of power supply or input impedance of the equipment and on the type of offending mode; also leakage current, insertion loss, and line frequency have to be considered. In Fig. 11.18 some filter designs and their application fields are given.

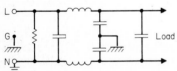

(L) Common mode applications

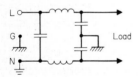

(L) Differential mode plus common mode applications

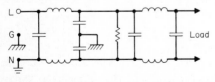

Figure 11.18 Power line filters and application fields.

(T) Capacitive and low-impedance loads

Uninterruptible power supply (UPS).   Unfortunately most of the problems exist at least some of the time in the devices previously discussed, except uninterruptible power supply systems.

A UPS is a continuously on-line device accepting utility-grade ac input and providing precise, computer-grade ac output. The primary goal of a UPS is to provide power to the load for enough time after utility power failure to allow for orderly system shutdown or transfer to an auxiliary power source for continued system operation.

When the ac line is operating, the system protects the load from transients, surges, faults, and brownouts. In the event of commercial ac line failure, the system supplies uninterrupted power from the battery bank and continues to provide regulation and isolation plus transient, surge, and fault protection.

It has four basic elements (refer to Fig. 11.19):

1. Rectifier-charger which converts the normal utility power to dc.
2. DC-to-ac inverter to convert the dc power supplied either by the rectifier-charger or a storage battery to precise ac power.
3. Storage battery, connected between the rectifier-charger and inverter to sustain the ac power output from the UPS whenever utility power is out of tolerance or unavailable.
4. Bypass switch to automatically transfer the critical load equipment from the inverter output back to the utility in the event of internal UPS malfunction, in a few milliseconds.

The ac output frequency from the UPS is phase-locked to the ac input under normal conditions. When there is no ac input, the output frequency is automatically determined by the internal oscillator.

The heart of the UPS is the inverter, which converts dc power into ac power. The inverter is required to produce a constant regulated ac output voltage even though the dc input varies considerably when the

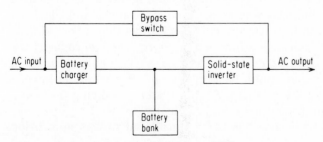

Figure 11.19 Block diagram of solid-state UPS.

battery is supplying power. Various pulse-width-modulation techniques are available to control the magnitude of this output voltage. Another more basic technique is to use a *ferroresonant transformer.*

UPS units are usually categorized by the type of inverter used.

Most commonly used pulse-width-modulation techniques are *single-pulse modulation, multiple-pulse modulation, sinusoidal-pulse modulation,* and *true harmonic-reduction pulse modulation.*

A *ferroresonant constant-voltage transformer* (CVS) is simple, reliable, and practical in low output ranges, no higher than 15–30 kVA; in larger power applications the CVS becomes impractical. UPS units that incorporate ferroresonant transformers in the inverter offer the advantage of excellent voltage stability without feedback circuitry as required in pulse-width-modulation designs.

Batteries, which determine the time reserve of the UPS output, offer two basic choices: wet or gelled cells. Wet-cell batteries are available in nickel-cadmium or lead-acid types. Nickel-cadmium types are generally considered too costly for UPS applications. Lead-acid batteries may be either lead-calcium or lead-antimony types, lead-calcium being the most widely used today in UPS units. Gelled-cell batteries are considered maintenance-free because they use an immobilized electrolyte instead of a wet electrolyte. Gelled batteries are generally used in tight, restricted areas where wet-cell maintenance would be difficult.

Standard UPS units are equipped with a *solid-state transfer device* that can switch from inverter to bypass fast enough to accomplish a "no-break" transition. To do this, the inverter must have circuits to make sure that the ac wave produced by the inverter is synchronous with and phase-locked to the ac wave of the bypass line. If a transfer is caused by the inverter or is manually initiated, the solid-state switch will be locked on bypass and must be manually returned to UPS. If the critical load is able to withstand up to 50–100-ms transfer time, an electromechanical transfer switch is available and may reduce the system cost.

For larger power requirements, usually higher than 50 kVA, a hybrid UPS (HUPS) rotary-type converter (ac/dc) and inverter (dc/ac) is used.

In Table 11.3, effectiveness of each power conditioning device is given. Isolation transformers are discussed in details in Sec. 11.3.

Battery backup power is a function of energy storage capacity and load and can be expressed in kilowatt-hours (kWh). For example, a 10-kW system with a maximum backup time of 15 min would have 10 kW × 0.25 = 2.5 kWh capacity. Such a system used on a 5-kW load would give backup time of 30 min, practically.

Emergency lighting also has to be considered in communications offices and plants.

TABLE 11.3 Effectiveness and Cost of Each Power Conditioning Device Varies Considerably

Power conditioning device	% Effectiveness*	Installed cost†	Operating cost	Cost of unresolved power problems	Total cost ($1000s)
High-isolation transformer	18%	13	9	364	386
Line voltage regulator	38%	19	117	274	410
Power load conditioner	37%	20	21	277	318
Motor-generator	79%	37	88	94	219
UPS	100%	73	47	0	120

*Based upon the relative impact of disturbance on computer center.
†For a 100-kVA system ($1000s)

Supercapacitors as standby dc power supply. Electric double-layer capacitors achieve extremely high volumetric efficiency (capacitance per unit volume) at a given voltage—as much as 1 F in less than a cubic inch. With its low leakage, a supercapacitor lends itself to use as an efficient, reliable, and cost-effective temporary energy storage device. In fact, the capacitors can be used as standby power sources for very low power CMOS memories during power outages lasting up to 30 days.

The basic structure of the unit cell for a supercapacitor consists of two electrodes separated by a suitable porous material which has ionically conducting and electrically insulating properties. The cell's maximum charge voltage is limited by the electrolyte's decomposition voltage—about 1.2 V for the supercapacitor's sulfuric acid solution. If more than 1.2 V is applied, the solution gradually decomposes into small quantities of hydrogen and oxygen. For higher voltages, unit cells are stacked in series to obtain the desired working voltage.

Supercapacitors offer a lineup of benefits over batteries:

- They never need routine replacement, since they are not polarized.
- They cannot be damaged by being wired in backward.
- They can be mounted on printed circuit boards by conventional soldering processes along with other components.
- They can be charged and discharged at high or low current rates, from microamperes to amperes.
- They are safe; they will not leak or explode under any temperature extremes.

Thus, these batterylike capacitors minimize many of the disadvantages of batteries, such as lithium types, which provide no way of determining how much charge is still available to handle a power outage of unknown duration. Moreover, rechargeable batteries such as nickel-cadmium types exhibit a discharge memory, must have a controlled charge rate to limit the battery current, and eventually need replacing. The electric double-layer capacitor suffers from none of these shortcomings.

Although electric double-layer capacitors may be used in batterylike applications, they are still capacitors and therefore can be represented by the classical equivalent circuit.

11.3   Circuit Isolation

Traditional methods of isolation involve the use of such devices as *capacitors, relays, transformers,* and *optical couplers.* Capacitors and transformers isolate the circuit in the industrial noise areas and are effective and less expensive for isolation at lower frequencies. Relays are sufficient for isolation of office equipment from the outside line in low-speed operation. Optical couplers offer more reliable solutions to a wide range of circuit problems.

Capacitors

The equivalent circuit of a capacitor consists of three series impedances: capacitive reactance, inductive reactance, and the equivalent series resistance. A coupling capacitor is used to block the flow of direct current while allowing alternating or signal current to pass. A coupling capacitor, also known as a *blocking capacitor* or *stopping capacitor,* is widely used for joining two circuits or stages. A decoupling capacitor prevents transfer or feedback of energy from one circuit to another.

Using capacitors for reducing the line noise that comes from switching transients internal to an IC chip requires low inherent inductance within the decoupling capacitor and effective board design. When a capacitor is mounted on a board, lead lengths are a major source of inductance. This inductance must be minimized to obtain good decoupling performance under high-speed transient conditions. In a typical memory board, a 50-μF aluminum capacitor is used to counter the effects of the backplane wiring connecting the memory array board to the power supply; 6.8-μF tantalum capacitors are required to supply the bulk refresh current; multilayer ceramic capacitors are used to reduce the high-frequency noise components.

Relays

All relays, other than solid-state relays, utilize one or more coils to generate a magnetic flux which is then used as the prime force to actuate one or more electrical contacts. When the magnetic force acts upon a mechanical linkage which in turn acts upon the contacts, this relay is classified as an *electromechanical relay* (EMR). If the magnetic force acts directly upon magnetic contact members, the relay is classified as *electromagnetic*. A *solid-state relay* is a semiconductor switching or isolating device with input terminals isolated from the output switch path.

Electromechanical relays. A distinct electromechanical relay advantage is the ability to simultaneously actuate contacts with a common motor (coil and mechanical linkage), thus providing isolated and isolating functions at low cost per pole. To simplify the identification of the various relay contact arrangements and operating sequences, the United States of America Standards Institute (USASI) has assigned alphabetic symbols for the various relay contact combinations which are given in Fig. 11.20.

Several specialized terms apply to relay specifications.

Electromechanical relays are designed to operate from direct or alternating current. The power required to energize these relays is frequently expressed in volt-amperes (VA).

Contact ratings (in amperes) are given for both ac and dc voltages. They also are frequently specified in power handling ability—for ac ratings in volt-amperes and for dc ratings in watts.

Dielectric strength or breakdown voltage is specified in terms of rms ac voltage across open contacts. Breakdown voltage is also generally specified between the contacts and the coil, as is insulation resistance.

Relay life is specified in terms of the number of contact closures expected before failure and as the number of operations a relay's mechanical structure can make before failure. The latter number is invariably much larger than the former.

Nonresistive load switching can destroy unprotected relay contacts. Some relay contact protection schemes are given in Fig. 11.21.

Finally, pickup voltage is the value at which a relay's contacts initially close, and operating voltage is the nominal maximum voltage at the point where the full coil current and full operating contact pressure are established.

Operating times depend on the relay type and the applied voltage or current, but typically range from 1 to 10 ms at nominal ratings. Release times generally are shorter than times for actuation. In relays

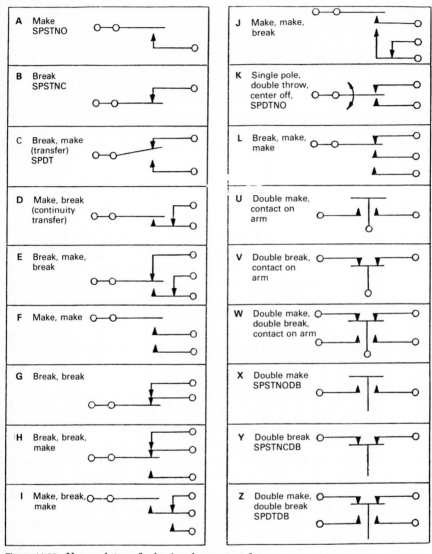

Figure 11.20 Nomenclature for basic relay contact forms.

used for low-level switching, contact arcing is usually not a problem. A silver alloy with an overlay of gold is most suitable for low-level switching and is therefore employed in many popular relay types. One major problem is contact bounce, i.e., the intermittent opening of a closed contact or closure of an open contact. The duration of the bounce after contact actuation or release can extend from a fraction of a millisecond to several milliseconds. This action often severely disrupts the intended switching function. Using mercury-wetted contacts is one way to overcome the problem.

Speed, life, and contact reliability in industrial environments often rule out the conventional electromechanical relays. For several critical applications, the electromechanical relay with glass-sealed contacts is ideally suited.

Electromagnetic relays.   There are three distinct glass-sealed electro-

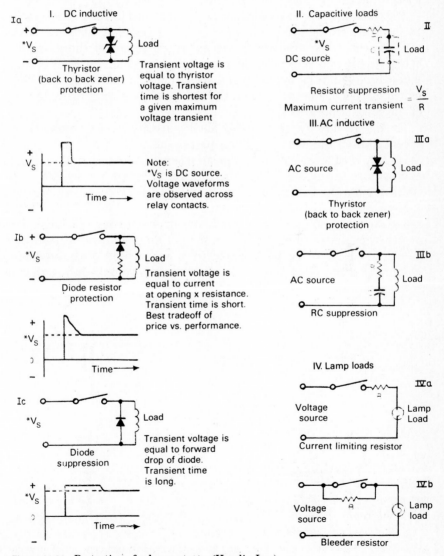

Figure 11.21   Protection of relay contacts. (Hamlin Inc.)

magnetic relay categories: mercury-wetted contact, dry reed, and mercury-wetted reed relays.

Mercury-wetted contact relays can switch wide ranges of signal and power levels without having the load affect either life or performance. The contacts are mercury-to-mercury surfaces with a capillary system that renews the contact surfaces during each operation. All mercury-wetted relays have a common orientation requirement, i.e., they must be mounted within 30° of vertical for proper operation. However some specially built mercury-wetted relays can operate in any position.

The basic dry-reed relay consists of two flattened ferromagnetic reeds. In the glass-sealed type, the reeds are sealed, one at each end of the tube, so that their free ends overlap in the center of the assembly. When this switch is introduced into a magnetic field, the reeds become flux carriers and the overlapped ends become opposite magnetic poles which attract each other. When the coil is deenergized, spring tension of the reeds separates them.

The dry-reed relay is an almost ideal switching device because of its speed, limited number of moving parts, and contamination-free contacts. Dry-reed relays are economical, insensitive to transmitted noise, and operate in the low millisecond range. They are not position-sensitive devices and therefore can be mounted in any convenient location.

Mercury-wetted reed relays consist of one or more mercury-wetted relay capsules mounted in a miniature dry-reed relay package. The switch capsule (see Fig. 11.22) consists of an armature, a fixed pole piece, and a mercury pool sealed in a pressurized glass envelope. Mounted on the fixed pole piece is a mercury-wetted contact that is

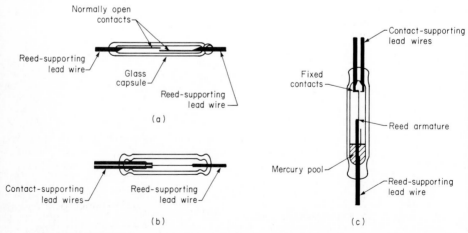

Figure 11.22   Reed relays come in dry- and mercury-wetted contact versions. Shown are: (*a*) form A; (*b*) form C dry-reed types; and (*c*) form C mercury-wetted unit.

engaged by the movable armature. The mercury flows up the reed by capillary action and wets the reed's contact area. If a magnetic field is produced by a coil around the capsule, the armature deflects and closes the contact. Removal of this field allows the spring-biased armature to open the contacts. The switching action is achieved by mercury-to-mercury contact surfaces, which provide bounce-free switching with low and stable contact resistance. Like mercury-wetted contact relays, mercury-wetted reed relays must be mounted within 30° of vertical and may require up to 30 s to clear the flooded area after inversion.

Note the difference between the mercury-wetted contact relay, in which the armature makes contact, and the mercury-wetted reed relay, in which reeds carry flux and are opposite magnetic poles when energized. Power switching with mercury-wetted reed relays requires arc suppression for best life.

Reed relay sensitivity ranges from a few milliwatts to hundreds milliwatts. Operation times range from approximately 0.5 ms to 2 ms.

A limitation of the dry-reed switch (but not the mercury-wetted version) is its contact bounce upon closure. For some applications the relay coil is suppressed by using an RC network or zener diode to limit the inductive kick upon release that might damage interconnected low-voltage solid-state circuitry. Insulation resistance across the open contacts of an assembled reed relay is typically 10^{10} to 10^{13} Ω. Typical maximum voltages across open contacts range from 200 to 500 V ac. Terminal-to-terminal capacitance ranges in the tenths of a picofarad.

An undesirable feature of the reed relay is that noise appears between terminals of a switch for a few milliseconds following closure, because of voltages generated in the reeds by magnetostrictive effects. For fast, low-level applications this noise must be taken into account.

Mercury-wetted units are available in high-power contactor-type versions with ratings of 50 to 100 A or more. Among the limitations of the mercury-wetted reed relay are poor resistance to shock and vibration and the need to mount the device within 30° of vertical. Another limitation is that mercury freezes at $-39°C$. Recently, mercury-wetted relays which operate in any mounting position have been introduced to the market.

Reed relays withstand vibrations and shocks better than EMRs, except that the frequency of vibration must differ from the reed's resonant frequency, which is in the voice-frequency band. In fact, if you place a leaf spring in a magnetic field oscillating at the resonant frequency of the spring, the spring will vibrate. If the mechanical properties of the spring are optimum, you have a relay that will respond to only one frequency to provide a pulsed output. This is the basis of operation for the *resonant-reed relay*. Note that contacts are not glass-sealed. The physical construction of a typical resonant-reed relay resembles a conventional relay, having a coil, a relay armature (resonant reed), and a fixed contact.

The reeds respond to almost any frequency in the audio range. For practical operation, the range of 100 Hz to 10 kHz can be considered useful for exciting resonant-reed relays. Harmonic rejection is usually quite good within this range, and simultaneous tone sensing is possible under most circumstances.

Noise spikes that could be dangerous to semiconductor circuitry will have little effect on these devices, and therefore, elaborate filtering precautions are not necessary. Resonant-reed relays have disappeared because the same function can be performed with compact solid-state devices.

Solid-state relays

A *solid-state relay* (SSR) is an electronic switching device, utilizing either discrete circuitry or microelectronic techniques, that provides electrical isolation between the control circuit (input) and the load circuit (output), and that otherwise performs essentially the same remote switching function as an electromechanical relay (EMR).

SSRs are available with switching speeds ranging from 8.3 ms down to the low microsecond region for lower-current ac/dc or bidirectional dual in-line package (DIP) SSRs.

AC SSRs offer the capability of withstanding high surge currents for relatively short durations, which makes them ideal for switching loads such as motors, transformers, and lamps. Most ac SSRs have a 1-cycle peak nonrepetitive surge current rating of 10 times the steady-state rms rating.

DC SSRs can be designed to provide overcurrent surge capability; surge ratings of over 400 percent for short durations (10 μs) have been achieved in some dc SSRs.

An SSR consists basically of an input control/isolation circuit (analogous to the coil of an EMR) and a solid-state output switching device (analogous to the EMR contacts). The output switch may be an FET for low-level switching; a bipolar device for medium and power switching, or a triac for ac power switching. Input/output isolation is typically achieved by means of an optocoupler or an oscillator/transformer combination. A typical isolation-voltage rating for an ac SSR is 1500 V rms. Higher ratings up to 3750 V rms are being specified where compliance with European specifications (such as those of the West German VDE) is required.

Comparison of solid-state and mechanical relays. Moving-contact relays, including EMRs and reeds, are seeing more use than ever despite the availability of solid-state devices; and relay users advance several reasons for this popularity. First, the solid-state devices are more expensive. Second, they are usually limited to one form: A [single-pole, single-throw normally open (spst NO)] or B [single-pole, single-throw normally closed (spst NC)] versions, so increasing the number of poles calls for buying more units. Electromechanical relays, on the other hand, can be specified for multiple operation at a minimal cost.

In applications requiring good open-circuit isolation, EMRs and reeds are superior. This is because solid-state units exhibit some degree of conduction when off.

Another drawback of solid-state relays is that when they are on, their resistance has some small value, larger than the milliohms characterizing mechanical-relay contacts. Additionally, a solid-state relay is nonlinear.

Electromechanical units can withstand high input-line transients to a greater extent than solid-state devices. And when properly protected, they can also shed output transients better. Further, although the indefinitely long life of solid-state relays is an advantage, electromechanical units have a predictable life under given load conditions; they provide satisfactory life over their design period, typically 100,000 to 1,000,000 operations.

Solid-state relays do exhibit several advantages in certain applications. For example, they suit use where high power and heavy duty cycles are required. Their high rates of contact and pickup make them much better for numerical machine-control applications than either EMRs or reeds.

Fast switching speed, freedom from contact bounce, contact degradation due to arcing, reduction of electromagnetic interference (EMI), high surge capability, high resistance to shock and vibration, and low power requirement are the advantages of SSRs.

Optical couplers.   Also called *optoisolators* or *photon couplers,* optical couplers offer reliable solutions to a wide range of circuit problems. They provide an ideal combination of speed, dc response, high common-mode rejection, and low input/output coupling capacitance.

Optoisolators normally consist of a light-emitting device (such as a neon or tungsten lamp, LED, or solid-state lamp) whose electromagnetic radiation is directed through air, glass, gas, or fiber optics toward a light sensor. Any light-sensitive device can be used as a sensor, but photoconductive cells (cadmium sulfide or cadmium selenide) or silicon light-sensitive devices like photodiodes, phototransistors, photo-Darlingtons, or photo-SCRs are most common (Fig. 11.23).

In the device that is called an *optocoupler,* both the light source and detector may be housed in a single package and sealed against external

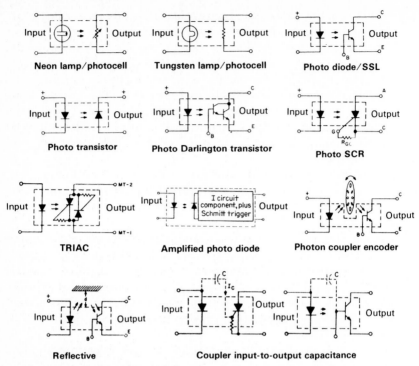

Figure 11.23 Optical coupler symbols.

light. Optocouplers can function as excellent alternatives to integrated circuit line receivers in digital data transmission applications. For example, a conventional line receiver is limited to ±20-V common-noise rejection at best, from dc over its operating frequency range, while an optocoupler can achieve rejections of ±2.5 kV at 50/60 Hz.

Solid-state lamps (SSLs) or *photodiode couplers* usually contain some version of a *silicon photodetector* and commonly operate in the infrared region.

Photodiode couplers have the highest speeds of any available type, in the 10- to 20-ns range, and the lowest current transfer ratio CTR (the ratio of input to output current). A typical CTR value is 0.15 percent.

The coupling resistance of an optical coupler is very high; generally 10^{11} Ω or higher. This level of isolation is excellent for most applications, such as dc level shifting and ground-loop prevention. Optoisolators are able to take surge voltages, typically 2500 V, at least 100 times during their life. The temperature coefficient of an optical coupler is defined as the change of output current due to a change of temperature with a constant input current. The SSL has a negative time constant, while detectors have positive coefficients. The photodiode type has a net negative coefficient, while the phototransistor has a net positive time constant. The photo-Darlington is also positive. Switching speed is influenced by load current in the output device, load resistance, input signal pulse widths, etc.

In the near future optoisolators with more output power and efficiency, more than 6 million hours life expectancy, and speeds to 20 Mb/s will be available. Also, built-in digital-to-digital or digital-to-analog converters will enhance the versatility of optoisolators.

Isolation transformers. An isolation transformer is designed to provide magnetic coupling between one or more pairs of isolated circuits, without introducing significant coupling of any other kind between them.

One simple way of protecting transistorized equipment from longitudinal surges on open wire and cable is to use a balanced transformer between the equipment and the line, as shown in Fig. 11.24. Some degree of protection can also be built into the circuit itself by taking advantage of the properties of the components used. For instance, line isolation transformers may be designed to have poor response to frequencies below the signal frequencies, thus sharply attenuating 60-Hz power voltages acquired by induction or contact. Transformers also provide efficient coupling between circuits of different impedances or between balanced circuits and unbalanced circuits.

Power taken from a typical ac power line is inherently noisy. This noise may affect other sensitive equipment sharing the same power source. To a degree every transformer isolates one circuit from another electrically while simultaneously coupling the two through magnetic induction. When the transformer must power a high-gain circuit, sensitive instrumentation, or data processing systems, primary noise must be blocked to prevent degraded or inaccurate performance. Such isolation can be carried out in four steps:

1. Separation of primary and secondary coils

2. The Faraday shield

3. The box shield

4. The high isolation

Physical separation of coils placed side by side or on separate legs of the magnetic core of a transformer will provide far less capacitive

Figure 11.24 Line isolation transformer.

coupling than coils wound directly over one another. Although greater physical separation of coils produces less noise coupling, it also increases leakage inductance and results in reduced power transfer. A grounded single turn of conductive foil placed between coils will divert much of the primary noise current to ground. Capacitance around the Faraday shield will still couple enough noise from primary to secondary to cause problems in sensitive equipment. A box shield completely encloses the winding with a conductive foil. The box shield provides a ground for primary circuit noise and has the advantage that a much smaller capacitance exists between primary and secondary coils than in a simple Faraday shield. The ultimate step in noise isolation is the triple-box-shielded transformer with coil separation. They are called *high-isolation transformers* (or *high-isolators*) in order to distinguish them from regular isolation transformers. Each coil is completely enclosed in a wrapped-foil-box shield. The transformer enclosure and special separator plates provide a second level of complete box shielding. In addition, transformer coils are separated physically for greater noise attenuation.

Comparison between high-isolation transformers and RFI filters.   Attempts to cure noise problems on power lines by installing RFI filters are better served by high-isolation transformers, although they are more expensive.

Lightning storms cause high voltage transients which can start RFI filters ringing and lengthen the noise duration. High-isolators attenuate lightning frequencies without ringing.

RFI filters generally attenuate voltage spikes in the 10–100 kHz frequency range. They have no effect on oscillatory decaying transients between 400–5000 Hz. High-isolators, however, attenuate all these frequencies.

RFI filters are designed primarily to reduce common-mode noise by shunting it to ground; common-mode noise is attenuated more effectively by the low effective interwinding capacitance of high-isolators, while transverse-mode rejection compares favorably to that of the RFI filters.

Furthermore, high-isolators eliminate hazards when the equipment is not fully isolated from the power line.

11.4   Static Electricity in the Electronics Industry

Static electricity is an excess or deficiency of electrons on a surface. The total number of deficient or excess electrons determines the charge on that surface. A surface exhibiting an excess of electrons is said to be charged negatively, and an electron-deficient surface is positively charged.

Static damage of components by operating personnel is fast becoming one of the most significant problems in the electronics industry. Technological advances in IC manufacture, such as ion implantation, ion-beam milling, and electron-beam direct writing, make possible devices with higher circuit densities, higher unit performance, and quite often higher static susceptibility.

Some chips have circuitry only 5 μm wide on 5 μm spacing, and these dimensions are growing smaller. A particle of dirt attracted by static electricity can destroy the chip during the manufacturing process.

It is predicted that the number of components per chip will continue to double every year; refer to Fig. 11.25.

Many sensitive devices are damaged by potentials that the discharging person cannot even feel. For all practical purposes, if potentials in the work environment can be maintained at less than 100 V, static problems should not exist.

Static damage of a component assembly can cause increased leakage, altered functional characteristics, or otherwise weakened device performance.

Static electric charges are brought about by the movement of similar materials against one another. A common observation of static electrical charge generation is summarized in the partial triboelectric series shown in Table 11.4. (Triboelectricity pertains to electric charges generated by friction between different materials.) The triboelectric series is a list of materials in order of static-charge-generation potential. Materials which are furthest apart on the list generate the greatest static charge when rubbed together. The material nearest the top retains the positive charge. Thus, polyethylene and human hair will generate a greater static charge than nylon and cotton.

Static charges are generated in numerous ways. For example, a man walking on a dry carpet (at a low relative humidity) can generate up

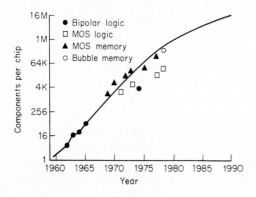

Figure 11.25 The number of components per chip doubles every year.

TABLE 11.4 Triboelectric Series

Positive	Air
(+)	Glass
	Human hair
	Nylon
	Wool
	Lead
	Silk
	Aluminum
	Paper
	Cotton
	Steel
	Nickel
	Brass
	Acetate rayon
	Polyethylene
Negative	Vinyl
(−)	Polytetrafluoroethylene

to 5000 V of static charge. Similarly, automobiles traveling on dry pavement or conveyor belts running over pulleys generate substantial static charges.

Protection from static electricity

The basic concept of complete static protection for electronic components is the prevention of static buildup where possible and the quick, reliable removal of existing charges. The means by which these charges are removed depends on whether the charged object is a conductor or a nonconductor (insulator). Both types of materials coexist throughout the electronics manufacturing environment.

Because charge cannot flow through an insulator (by definition), it cannot be removed by contact with a conductor; grounding a nonconductor will do nothing. Therefore, if the item to be discharged is an insulator, such as a worksheet holder, a plastic box, or even a person's clothing, ionized air is required.

An ionized-air blower neutralizes static charges on nonconductive items by supplying them with a constant stream of both positive and negative air ions. The charged object attracts the oppositely charged ions, thereby neutralizing itself. The unused ions or those having the same sign as the charged surface are repelled and eventually recombine with other ions or are themselves neutralized by contact with a grounded conductive surface such a machine frame, floor, etc.

Two of the most common treatments used to enhance the conductivity of static charged objects involve the addition of humidity into the work environment and the deposition of salt or detergent-based liquids, sprays, or powders. Unfortunately neither method is completely effective and does not work with all materials. Besides, high humidity can create new problems. Rusting, water spotting, and damage to test equipment are common results.

If, however, the charged object is a conductor, such as a metal tray, a conductive bag or person's body, complete discharge can be accomplished by simply grounding it.

The voltage on the discharging body at any time t is given by the relation

$$V = V_o e^{-t/RC}$$

where V = voltage at time t, V
   V_o = initial voltage on body, V
   t = elapsed time, s
   R = effective resistance to ground, Ω
   C = capacitance of the body being discharged, F

Personnel capacitance varies widely from one industry source to another. Values of 100 pF to 4000 pF have been reported, 200 pF being about average.

Although the initial voltage to be dissipated can vary, it has been well-documented that personnel in a manufacturing environment commonly attain potentials of 5000 V or more just walking across the floor. Therefore, to be effective, conductive surfaces must have a low enough resistance to ground to allow discharge from 5000 V down to a 100-V safe level in 1 s. A simple calculation with $C = 200$ pF gives a resistance to ground for either a conductive floor mat or table mat of 10^9 Ω (1000 MΩ).

It has been found that a portable megohmmeter can be used to give a reliable measure of the resistance to ground of the workstation, since these devices are capable of reading resistances on the order of 10^9 Ω at potentials above 100 V.

A completely static-safe workstation, therefore, includes a grounded conductive table top, wrist straps, and floor mat to discharge conductors as well as an ionized-air blower to remove the static from nonconductors.

Whenever static-sensitive devices leave the safety of such controlled environments, they must be packaged or held in containers offering that same high degree of static protection. High-resistivity materials, generally referred to as antistatic materials, are capable of preventing triboelectric (friction) charge generation. Protection from outside static charges, such as charged personnel, requires an additional set of electrical properties. In order to provide the necessary Faraday cage protection (electrostatic shielding), the packaging film must have at least one highly conductive surface or overwrap.

TABLE 11.5 Comparison of Floor Surfaces

	Static decay time, s	Static charge generation	Surface electrical resistivity, Ω/square	Static charge decay from personnel (step test), s
Ideal	<0.1	Zero	10^9	<1
Plastic film	0.08	100 V	10^9	<1
Vinyl asbestos tile	0.36	2–3.5 kV	10^{13}	10
With wax	0.90	4–7 kV	10^{13}	10
With topical antistat	0.36	0.5–1.2 kV	10^{11}	10
Conductive polyethylene	0.01	2–4 kV	10^8	<1
Conductive multilayer	0.1	2–3 kV	10^9	<1
Antistatic polyethylene	10.0	1–3 kV	10^{13}	10

General considerations on controlling static electricity

1. Keep relative humidity between 40–60 percent.

2. Specify hard-surface floor coverings with no greater than 10^9 Ω/ft^2 resistivity and not greater than 10^9 Ω to a grounded supporting structure such as concrete or a raised floor. A comparison of floor surface values is given in Table 11.5.

3. If carpeting is to be used, specify that the static electricity generated by walking upon the carpeting will not exceed 2000 V at 40 percent relative humidity.

4. Exercise some control over occupants' footware and clothing. Some shoes with crepe rubber soles, for example, will generate static in walking on a steel floor, and much more on a carpet or pressure-laminated floor. Clothing can often be treated with antistatic products during laundering. Nylon may still give problems.

5. Avoid furniture upholstered with plastic or fabrics which cannot be treated to reduce static problems.

6. Use antistatic mats with or without a grounding conductor in work areas with static problems. Ground the mats in high traffic areas.

References

Boutros, Kamal: "Filtered connectors fight the EMI gremlins," Electronic Products, July 2, 1984.

Batra, Vinod: "Grounding Electronic Switching Systems," Telephony, May 6, 1974.

Coyle, Michael J.: "Designers' Guide to Circuit Protectors," EDN, Nov. 5, 1973.

Technical Application Reference for Mercury-Wetted Contact Relays, Dry Reed Relays, Mercury-Wetted Reed Relays, 2d ed., C. P. Clare and Co., Chicago. May 1973.

RFI Power Line Filters, Curtis Industries Inc., Milwaukee, catalog no. 481.

Yenni, Donald M., Jr.: "Basic Electrical Considerations in the Design of a Static Safe Work Environment," 3M Company, St. Paul, Minn.
General Electric, Auburn, N.Y.: *Transient Voltage Suppression Manual*, 2d ed., 1978.
Lenkurt Electronic Co. Inc., San Carlos, Calif.: The Lenkurt Demodulator, "Shielding and Grounding," vol. II, no. 10, 1962.
Mendelsohn, Alex: "Transient Suppressors," *Electronic Products Magazine*, March 1979.
RCA Solid State Division, Somerville, N.J.: "Avalanche Transistor," Application Note AN-6215.
Topaz Electronics Div., San Diego, *Noise Suppression Reference Manual*, LT89, Sep. 1979.
Waterman, John J., Jr.: "Uninterruptible Power Systems," *Digital Design*, February 1980.

Chapter
12

Local-Area Networks

A local-area network (LAN) can be described as a private high-speed communications system that allows a broad range of independent automated devices to communicate with each other within a geographically limited area. Distances covered range from 0.1 km (328 ft) to 10 km (6.2 mi). Data rates on a local-area network also vary over orders of magnitude, from 100 kb/s to 10 Mb/s and higher. Messages are sent over the communications medium with a destination address included. Only the intended receiver is expected to respond, although other stations have the capability of listening in. Thus no security is present unless cryptographic techniques are used. Local networks are meant to be highly reliable, so that any failing station will simply be unavailable, without interrupting the communications between the remaining stations. Similarly, it is possible to add new stations without disrupting the ongoing communications flow.

LANs are being installed today as electronic data processing (EDP) systems with intraoffice extensions, using newly designed terminals that easily interface to a network, and as private branch exchange (PBX) systems with data sets. There are also a growing number of hybrid approaches: EDP-based networks with attached digital PBX systems, general-purpose microcomputer systems bundled with networks and software, and simple disk-storage systems designed to serve a cluster of microcomputers.

Because of the limited-distance nature of local networks, another standard feature is the ability to interconnect dissimilar networks. This internetwork link, called a gateway, may be a high-speed link for networks that are close to each other, or it may depend on a more conventional telecommunications network for reliably transmitting data from city to city, or around the world.

Because of the multiplicity of emerging network technology and the variety of communications protocols in use, gateways must be provided to permit stations on one type of network to exchange information with others on a different type of network. Both electrical and software protocols must be converted when data pass through these gateways.

The most significant contribution in the LAN field is not the communications aspect, but the development of a whole way of building computer systems. The fundamental organization assumes a fully distributed control mechanism with all nodes of the network communicating and cooperating with one another. Any node can be configured to act as a *server* to provide special services to other nodes that request service, called *clients*. Typical server functions are mass storage of files, printer support, time-of-day clock, translation of symbolic names into physical addresses, data-base management support, gateways to other networks or computers, and other specialized hardware support. Servers may also be clients of other servers on the network.

Servers are distinguished on the network merely by the software they run, the special hardware they contain, and the higher-level protocol they use. At present, there are no standardization efforts regarding server-client protocols.

In order to maintain a high level of reliability, the logic functions of the servers are usually implemented by separate physical computers. One could merge all of the above services into one larger computer, but in doing so would end up with something resembling a conventional central computer system.

All LANs are susceptible to transmission errors. The use of CRC techniques reduces error rate to acceptable levels (10^{-12}).

12.1   Beginning of Local-Area Networks

Local-area networks evolved from the large-scale telecommunications networks developed in the 1960s. As universities and research labs began to install computers, the need arose to permit the flow of information among them. The underlying communications protocols (packet transmission) came from the long-distance networks. The communications mediums (twisted pair or coaxial cable) were developed to support very high speed direct coupling between computers.

One experimental scheme (called the Aloha system) was elegant and operated in a manner very similar to the way that telephone party lines work. Each station would first listen to see if anyone else was transmitting, a procedure called *carrier sensing*. If not, the station would transmit its message, including error detection bits. As long as the total fraction of available transmission time used was low, everyone got a turn eventually. If two stations found the channel clear and started transmitting simultaneously, the two packets would collide. This collision would scramble the information, but the error-detection logic would throw away the bad data. If the stations did not receive an acknowledgment by a certain time, they would simply send the packet again.

Studies of this scheme quickly revealed a number of problems, one of the more serious being that, as the number of messages grew, many collided and only a small fraction of the true communications bandwidth was used for valid data. Even more serious was the fact that if enough stations tried to transmit, less and less data got through, and the result was continuous collisions.

12.2 Network Topologies and Protocols

Most early LANs used a star topology (see Fig. 12.1); a central node was connected via a radial cable to each of the other stations. The star arrangements are most like those used in time-sharing of central computers; data and text processors only occasionally share resources. Star arrangements also are used in hierarchial master/slave networks in which network control is centralized.

Telephone exchanges are organized as star networks, and many companies already have PBXs. By using the PBX as a LAN for data as well as voice communication, companies can take advantage of the already existing wiring; this is most suitable for low-data-rate information, such as that for video terminals.

Unfortunately, this system suffers from the consequences of a central failure. The entire system goes down if the center fails.

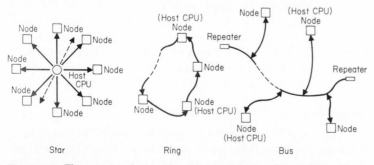

Figure 12.1 Three major classes of architecture for Local Area Networks.

Ring topology connects its stations in a closed network. Messages circulate in one direction, often being amplified and repeated at each node they pass through. Again a station failure can interrupt the entire message flow, but in some cases two alternative parallel loops are provided for reasons of reliability. Rings use a form of control strategy called a *token*. A token is a special bit pattern.

Bus topology is quite simple, a bus being merely a long cable that runs past each station. Stations are connected to it at the nearest point and can be added or removed without affecting any other station. A station can be added in two ways: the bus can be split, temporarily disrupting communications, and a new station inserted, or more commonly, taps can be installed while stations are transmitting. The tapping technique uses devices developed by the cable TV industry that pierce the cable from the outside, making contact to the inner and the outer shields. Even temporary shorts will garble only some packets, and they will be retransmitted once the short is removed.

Protocols

The functioning of the network is becoming critical, especially in light of the LAN's primary responsibility: to allow users of many different types of data processing equipment to plug into a network without having to worry about compatibility. This is possible only if all the equipment adheres to the same set of protocols that governs their communications on the network bus. Eventually, as the use of networks expands, particularly at the local level, the need to standardize at all seven protocol levels will become very important.

Refer to Fig. 12.2 and Chap. 7 for detailed information on seven-layer ISO-OSI protocols.

Several committees are attempting to develop an industry-wide standard for LANs. The IEEE in the United States has been developing an 802 standard that attempts to accommodate many diverse application, area, and functional requirements. The framework for defining a communications network is based on a layered series of ISO-OSI protocols. IEEE 802 standards are focusing on specifying layers 1 and 2 (link and physical levels) and offer many alternatives within one framework. The U.S. National Bureau of Standards has proposed a series of transport and higher-level protocols.

12.3   Link Access Procedures

The network topology chosen will strongly influence the method of accessing the network. Bus networks generally employ CSMA/CD ac-

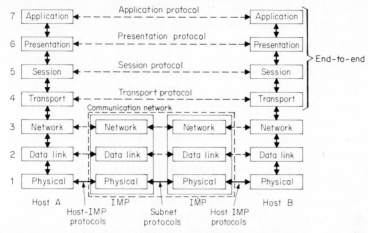

Figure 12.2 Protocol levels. IMP = Interface Message Protocols.

cessing, while ring networks employ token passing. (CSMA/CD stands for carrier-sense multiple-access with collision detection.) There is a third alternative, time-division multiplexing, where dedicated time zones or slots are allotted each nodal message. IEEE Standards currently available for LANs are

802.2   Logical Link Control

802.3   CSMA/CD (also known as Ethernet)

802.4   Token Bus

802.5   Token Ring

These standards have also been adopted by the ISO.

CSMA/CD is a random scheme in which a node accesses the bus on a contention basis. Before transmitting a message, the node listens to the data channel to make sure the channel is not busy. It does this by detecting the presence of a signal (carrier sense). If the channel is busy, the node is prevented from transmitting a message until the channel is clear. As soon as the transmission starts, the transmitting node monitors the channel over which it is sending a message by listening to its own transmission. Should the transmitted message collide with other messages (transmission garbled) on the bus, transmission is aborted (collision detection), and the node waits or backs off for a random period of time before attempting to retransmit.

CSMA/CD accessing offers two major advantages: extreme simplicity and suitability for integration into inexpensive LSI chips. It works well for lightly loaded systems, yielding better than 90 percent channel capacity utilization and low access delays. The probability of collision for lightly loaded systems (channel busy) is typically less than 1 percent.

For heavily loaded systems, CSMA/CD has some serious drawbacks. The greater the channel traffic, the greater the probability of messages colliding. This leads to unpredictable transmission delays. Thus the delivery of a message to its destination in a predictable time interval cannot be guaranteed. However, the main CSMA/CD drawback is the lack of a built-in priority mechanism. Messages with different urgency levels receive the same treatment when contending for the bus.

Collisions during the free-flow mode cause all other contending nodes to enter the higher-level priority mode to resolve the contention. Priority is assigned a node by determining the signal-propagation delay on the cable multiplied by the distance between the node and the closest node to it. This product, known as a unit-time transmission slot, is placed in one of three priority classes—alert, normal, or background—each of which is scanned by the network for slots. Once transmission ceases, the network returns to the free-flow mode.

In token-passing LANs, a message token is passed from node to node in one direction. Each node has a specific time during which it can remove the token, strip a message from it, and/or add a message to it. At this time, all other nodes can only listen. The sending node, which is also the receiving node for acknowledgment in a ring, makes this type of accessing highly reliable, a necessity for applications such as process control. In addition, token passing is not constrained by packet size or data rate, but works just as well under varying message size and data-rate conditions. One disadvantage of token passing in a ring architecture is its unidirectionality; any break in the ring causes a node to lose access privileges, since any message sent by a particular node must complete the circle in one direction and come back to that node. And being a synchronous scheme (a contention-based scheme is essentially asynchronous) makes token passing vulnerable to errors. An access control message could be destroyed or even erroneous, thus requiring a node to make up another message or delete the erroneous message, a difficult task to implement in a decentralized environment.

Token-passing access is not confined to ring architectures. In a bus architecture, a token is passed onto each node in much the same way as it is done in a ring network. The token passes from node to node (in a predetermined manner for the bus topology), where each node knows from which node the message came and to which node the message must next be sent. Indeed, token passing can be used in a free-form architecture that can include star and bus topologies.

12.4   Transmission Mediums for LANs

Multiconductor cable, twisted-pair wire, coaxial cable, fiber-optic cable, and laser beams are all suitable for LANs. Here, only brief information is given regarding LANs; refer to Sec. 1.4 for more information on transmission mediums. Baseband (digital) or broadband coaxial cable and fiber-optic cable are most often selected to handle these transmissions. Table 12.1 and Fig. 12.3 compare the transmission mediums.

Twisted-pair wire

Multipaired twisted copper wire is the simplest of the LAN transmission mediums. The most common type used is two-pair wire, which simply consists of two pairs of plastic-sheathed copper wire twisted around one another, then wrapped with a protective outer sheath. Twisted wire is also the least expensive medium. Twisted-pair wire can be used with any of the basic topologies, and typical networks contain up to 255 user devices. Figure 9.7 gives a good idea about signal quality on twisted-pair cables.

Baseband and broadband coaxial systems

Baseband coaxial cable has many of the capabilities required for computer-to-computer, multidrop applications but has a lower throughput than broadband coaxial systems. Baseband implementations employ techniques to increase the capacity of single-channel cable. The frequency spectrum occupied by baseband depends on the number of channels being transmitted and the type of modulation used, but is generally a small fraction of the spectrum available on the cable although the digital signal occupies 100 percent of the bandwidth. A negative aspect of baseband coaxial cable is that signals require regeneration at about 2500 m.

The baseband and broadband technologies use coaxial cables that are physically similar. The total bandwidth can be 150 MHz; in CATV cables the bandwidth reaches 440 MHz.

In broadband, the signals are FDM and occupy any selected portion of the frequency spectrum. Therefore broadband coax has a large capacity supported by a high multidrop capability for data distribution networking. It is also extremely flexible; the single coaxial spine of a LAN can carry voice, video, facsimile, and other traffic in two directions throughout a plant or plant complex. Many channels operate simultaneously and independently. Interconnect options are as varied as applications. With low-cost signal splitters and taps, cables can branch.

TABLE 12.1 Comparison of Transmission Mediums

	Twisted-pair wire	Baseband coaxial cable	Broadband coaxial cable	Fiber-optic cable
Topologies supported	Ring, Star, bus, tree	Bus, tree, and (rarely) ring	Bus, tree	Ring, star
Maximum number of nodes per network	Generally up to 255	Generally up to 1024	Up to about 25,000	Currently 2; in experimental tests, up to 8
Maximum geographical scope	25 km	10 kilometers	80 kilometers	10 kilometers
Maximum distance between adjacent nodes	4 km	10 kilometers		
Type of signal	Single-channel, unidirectional; analog or digital, depending on type of modulation used; half- or full-duplex	Single-channel, bidirectional, digital, half-duplex	Multi-channel, unidirectional, RF analog, half-duplex (full-duplex can be achieved by using two channels)	One single-channel, unidirectional, half-duplex, signal-encoded light beam per fiber; multiple fibers per cable; full-duplex can be achieved by using two fibers
Maximum bandwidth	Generally up to 10 Mb/s	Generally up to 10 Mb/s	Up to 400 MHz (aggregate total)	Up to 50 Mb/s in 10 kilometer range; up to 140 Mb/s in 6 to 8 km range; up to 5 Gb/s in experimental tests
Major advantages	Low cost	Low cost	Supports voice, data, and video	Supports voice, data, and

	(Twisted pair)	(Baseband coaxial)	(Broadband coaxial)	(Fiber optic)
	May be existing plant; no rewiring needed	Simple to install and tap	applications simultaneously Better immunity to noise and interference than baseband More flexible topology (branching tree) Rugged, durable equipment; needs no conduit Tolerates 100% bandwidth loading Uses off-the-shelf industry-standard CATV components	video applications simultaneously Immunity to noise, crosstalk, and electrical interference Very high bandwidth Highly secure Low signal loss Low weight/diameter; can be installed in small spaces Durable under adverse temperature, chemical, and radiation conditions
Major disadvantages	High error rates at higher speeds Limited bandwidth Low immunity to noise and crosstalk Difficult to maintain/troubleshoot Lacks physical ruggedness; requires conduits, trenches, or ducts	Low noise immunity (can be improved by the use of filters, special cable, and other means) Bandwidth can carry only about 40% load to remain stable Limited distance and topology Conduit required for hostile environments Not highly secure	High cost More difficult to install and tap than baseband RF modems required at each user station; modems are expensive and limit the user device's transmission rate	Very high cost, but declining Requires skilled installation and maintenance personnel Experimental technology, limited commercial availability Taps not perfected Currently limited to point-to-point connections

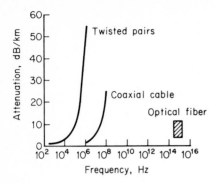

Figure 12.3 Comparison of transmission media.

In broadband transmission, as shown in Fig. 12.4, the total bandwidth available on the cable is divided into "forward" and "reverse" frequency bands, with a guard band separating the two. Analog and digital signals are interfaced to the cable through modems which transmit on a frequency in the reverse band and receive on a frequency in the forward band. Full-duplex (FDX) transmission is thus carried on a single coaxial cable. In addition, because of the large bandwidth available, many channels can be carried at one time on the same cable.

A simplified diagram of a broadband network is shown in Fig. 12.5. The head end contains a frequency translator which receives all the signals contained in the reverse band, converts them to corresponding signals in the forward band, and broadcasts them to the entire network. Modem 1A would then communicate with modem 1B. A modem placed at any point in the network can thus communicate with its mate located anywhere else in the network.

As shown in Fig. 12.5, taps and splitters are used to establish branches in a tree topology. Additional taps may be added to either the trunk or the drops to produce a large variety of network topologies.

Loss in the cable and in the splitters is compensated by two-way amplifiers, the locations of which are dictated by the network configuration. The two-way amplifiers are made up of filters, which separate the reverse frequencies from the forward frequencies, and two independent amplifiers, one for each direction.

LANs are now being used in both public and private sectors for efficient, cost-effective communications. In the public sector, broadband coax networks have recently become a standard offering of cable TV companies. These networks, called *institutional trunks*, are separate two-way cable systems provided by cable TV franchise holders, intended solely for municipal, industrial, and commercial use.

One of the key concerns to all network operators is that of reliability. The network components used in the cable installation (amplifiers, taps, etc.) have been designed for field use and generally have a long

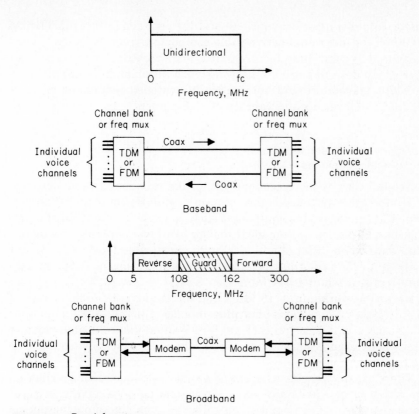

Figure 12.4 Coaxial systems.

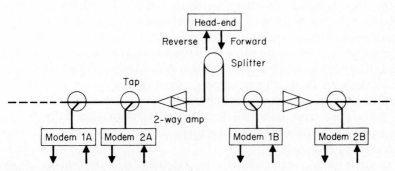

Figure 12.5 Typical broadband network.

history of proven performance. Mean time between failures (MTBF) of 40,000 h for individual active cable components reportedly have been measured by some manufacturers. It is not unreasonable to expect that a properly designed private network with automatically switched redundant translators and automatically switched redundant modems would have a service availability of 99.8 percent.

Comparison of baseband and broadband techniques

Baseband coax is more economical; unlike broadband cable systems, baseband cable systems require no data modulation onto an RF carrier, which keeps expensive equipment such as modems out of the picture. Baseband systems appear ideal for applications involving low aggregate data rates (3 Mb/s and less) over short cable lengths (22 km or less); up to 255 nodes may be attached to a cable length of 4500 m with data transmitted at 1.544 Mb/s.

Baseband works up to 16 Mb/s and has an acceptable error rate of (10^{-7}). Baseband systems offer plug-in ease of installation, as long as the number of devices on each cable is limited and real-time video or high-speed graphics are not required. They are relatively trouble-free and easy to repair.

There are drawbacks to baseband too; it is still just a single channel on which users must take their turns sending or receiving voice or data messages; an automatic controller assigns places on the queue, holding up traffic as necessary to prevent clashes between users' data. Furthermore, interfacing baseband with other networks requires special equipment.

For higher data rates and longer distances, broadband coaxial cable is more practical. Furthermore, broadband coaxial cable can easily be modified to handle additional services like video and voice and their dedicated bandwidths.

A broadband communications network has all the advantages of a baseband network and goes beyond baseband by eliminating many of its drawbacks. Broadband can carry information on up to several hundred channels over a single cable-TV-type coaxial cable; this capability eliminates the competition factor that limits baseband. The wide 440-MHz bandwidth of broadband allows simultaneous accommodation of hundreds of voice, video, and data channels along with widely dispersed data processing terminals. All broadband networks are fully transparent to user devices and other communication systems because they use dedicated channels.

A broadband system can easily be extended well beyond 40 mi by placing standard, low-cost CATV amplifiers every 600 m. BER in broadband networks is excellent (10^{-9}); data security is also enhanced with broadband, because potential "tappers" must know which channel they want as well as the encoding scheme being used. As a general rule, broadband has proven to be very cost-effective in networks that encompass multiple floors or buildings.

Transmission via optical cable

Extremely high data rates severely limit the length of coaxial links. The high speeds over long distances possible with optical links should make them a popular choice for video and other complex signal transmission. Fiber-optic links also offer secure transmission, as they are not easy to tap without noticeable signal loss.

It is predicted that fiber will not be a large factor in local networks in this decade. There are several economic and technical problems in using fiber optics for area networks, although operational systems are proving reliable and fiber-optic networks are commercially available in industrialized countries. Immunity to interference in industrial automation and process control applications are already making fiber-optic networks a reality.

Detailed information for fiber-optic cables is given in Chap. 10.

12.5 Applications, Benefits, and Future of LAN

Nearly any application currently implemented on a conventional point-to-point local network can be converted to LAN. In addition, depending on the LAN technology selected, support for any of a number of new applications not generally supported by conventional networks may be available to the LAN user.

Implementing a LAN based on today's commercially available technology allows a building to be rewired to interconnect all existing equipment, eliminating the point-to-point connections, relieving the overcrowded conditions, and allowing for easier reconfiguration and expansions. The new interconnection mechanism remains totally transparent to the user's applications.

The following list characterizes the general types of applications targeted by the LAN vendor community as the most suitable LAN candidates.

- *General business data processing.* File access, storage, and transfer; resource sharing (e.g., peripherals, services, applications); computer-to-computer and computer-to-peripheral interfacing at nearly bus speeds; distributed processing; retail point-of-sale operations; terminal-to-terminal communications; distributed data-base management; management planning (e.g., financial modeling); and network administration.

- *Office automation.* Document access, storage, and transfer; store-and-forward digitized voice; facsimile; electronic mail and message services; and word processor communications.

- *Laboratory, factory, and industrial automation.* Real-time process control; CAD/CAM; automated manufacturing and processing operations; and on-board interconnection of video, voice, and data processing equipment on large ships and aircraft.

- *Real-time voice and video.* In-house telephone switching, closed-circuit TV, security and surveillance, and automated building management.

- *Personal computers.* Processor, storage, and peripheral sharing; file access, transfer, and storage; software development and distribution; and centralized coordination and control.

- *Home.* A "wired household" in which temperature, lighting, appliances, security systems, intercom, telephone, television, home computer, and other functions are controlled over an in-home LAN.

Baseband coaxial cable LANs seem best suited to general business data processing and automated office environments. In the future, designers of systems for substantial voice or video applications would be well-advised to go with a broadband or fiber-optics LAN from the start. The real-time, high-reliability, high-performance needs of a laboratory or factory automation environment are more likely to be best served by a token-passing access method and ring topology, whereas the light but bursty traffic and need for easy expansion found in an office environment is more suitable to a CSMA/CD access method and bus topology.

Benefits and future of LAN

The future of local-area networking rests with users, not with technological advances that will drive this market. All the promises of the "office of the future" can be achieved only if users perceive them as reasonable, practical, useful, and cost-justifiable.

The assumption that most users are potential LAN candidates gains support from a recent study showing that a LAN may be able to support up to 90 percent of a user's current applications. In addition, a LAN can theoretically provide numerous benefits that may or may not be available in the current environment. Here are some possible advantages to be considered:

- *Resource sharing.* Users can share access to high-speed printers, large-capacity disk drives, high-speed telecommunications facilities, data-base management systems, and other resources that would be too expensive to justify for each system alone.

- *Added-value applications.* Because of its full-interconnectivity feature, a LAN can support terminal-to-terminal communications, applications switching, and related functions not generally available in most point-to-point environments. A LAN can also be used as a convenient medium for information exchange; for example, it can provide access to user documents and data bases and support for electronic mail applications.

- *Equipment compatibility.* A LAN can serve as a common interface between equipment of different types and/or manufacturers, thus freeing the user from dependence on a single vendor. It can also integrate devices based on older technologies with equipment of newer generations, thus extending the useful life of existing systems.

- *Distribution of hardware.* Equipment can be dispersed to the most convenient physical locations within a facility, or nearer the source of the user application, rather than being contained in a centralized area.

- *Integration of hardware and coordination of functions.* Previously unconnected computers and terminals can be integrated into a single network, and previously divergent information handling functions can be tied into a cohesive whole. Network statistics and other network management information can be centrally collected, and networkwide fault isolation, diagnostics, and error reporting can be centrally performed.

- *Distributed processing.* A decentralized processing environment can provide many benefits. It can eliminate the central host as a potential source of total network failure, extend the expansion limitations and improve service on a network that is reaching its growth maximum, provide redundancy for applications that require high reliability, and accommodate a degree of user independence. Users can determine the balance between centralized control and user autonomy. For example, in a network of otherwise independent microcomputers, certain major applications and data bases can be maintained and distributed from one system designated for this purpose, while others can be created and used locally by each user station.

- *Higher speed, lower error rate, longer distance than conventional point-to-point networks.* LAN throughput ranges from 200 kb/s to 50 M b/s per channel, rates much higher than traditional point-to-point networks. Error rates have tested out in the range of 1 in 10^8 to 1 in 10^{-3}. Distances can range up to 80 km without involving common-carrier facilities.

- *Simplicity, flexibility, ease of expansion.* Once the wiring is in place, adding a user device to a LAN can be as simple as plugging it into a special wall outlet. User devices can be transported from one physical location to another without reconfiguring the network.

- *Lower cost and/or better price/performance.* Some LAN vendors are claiming that their networks can present direct or indirect cost savings over installing and using a conventional point-to-point networks because of lower wiring costs, sharing of expensive resources, reduced need for operations personnel, terminal multifunctionality, lower interconnect costs, simpler network control operations, and accommodation of older and incompatible equipment.

12.6 Personal Computer Networks

While manufacturers of high-performance local-area networks continue to debate the wisdom of their approaches and try to establish meaningful standards, personal computer (PC) networks are moving into the spotlight. They are the simplest, most intelligent way for a series of small computers to share relatively expensive resources such as a letter-quality printer or a Winchester disk drive efficiently.

Most personal computers need neither the speed nor the traffic volume of high-performance networks. Comparison of $1200 to $1500 for connecting a computer to a LAN with about $300 to $600 for connecting a personal computer to its own network makes obvious one of the chief reasons why personal computer networks are thriving.

Today's personal computer networks have been sensibly planned and built to optimize the low or moderate performance levels expected of the machines. Operating at relatively slow data rates of 2.5 Mb/s or less, the networks represent an amalgam of technologies, from the system topology and transmission medium to the accessing scheme and software support. Of course, the type of machine involved and the least expensive hardware-software solution for a given level of performance are the most critical concerns when considering the assortment of personal computer networks and technologies.

There is no standard approach to the topology of a personal computer network to the transmission medium, or to the accessing technique. If twisted-pair wiring, token-passing accessing, and a bus topology have what it takes to get the job done, then so be it. That relatively simplistic approach may exhibit some technical shortcomings but will likely be the most cost-effective solution.

For the most part, personal computer networks are easy to install and use. Many, for example, employ twisted-pair wiring, which is found in virtually every office environment. That medium eliminates the cost and delays of installing coaxial cable.

Though twisted-pair wiring cannot carry data as far as coaxial cable, it proves more than adequate for moderate-performance networks dealing with distances of several hundred meters. In fact, data-grade twisted-pair wiring can be used for transmission of 1.5 Mb/s over distances of up to 1 km (refer to Figs. 9.7 and 12.3).

Many personal computer networks employ unshielded twisted pairs, whereas others opt for shielded wiring. As many office network users are discovering, shielding can be a big help, chiefly because it minimizes random noise emanating from fluorescent lights, elevator controls, and the like.

In harsher environments than the office, shielded wires are used and transformers couple the personal computers to the network wire, enabling faulty nodes to be completely isolated. Coaxial cable is also used in the personal computer networks; it has a higher immunity level to noise than twisted pairs and can operate over longer distances.

Accessing a personal computer network

Just as there is no standard transmission medium in personal computer networks, there is no uniform way for the computers to access the network. The three most popular accessing schemes are:

CSMA/CD (carrier-sense multiple-access with collision detection)

Master-slave polling

Token passing

A few personal computer networks modify or mix certain aspects of the techniques.

In a network employing CSMA/CA (collision avoidance) or CSMA/PA (positive acknowledgment), the node controller computes a random starting time for a message so as to minimize the probability of two nodes accessing the network at once. The technique not only eliminates costly collision-detection hardware and software, but also operates with a relatively high data rate that keeps transmissions reliable. For example, with data transferred at 800 kb/s to keep message collisions below 0.1 percent, a personal computer network can operate with gate-

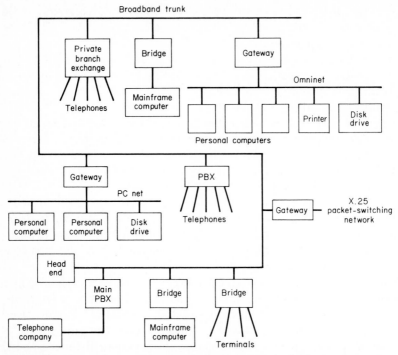

Figure 12.6 Personal computer network that incorporates bridges and gateways. It can hook up with other small computer networks as well as with local area networks, over public telephone lines via the X.25 packet switching network.

way interfaces and will allow access to other networks through the public telephone system (Fig. 12.6).

Another popular accessing scheme for personal computer networks is *master-slave polling*. Unlike CSMA or token passing, polling does not distribute control. In a master-slave arrangement, a hard-disk-based computer, which acts like a file server, controls other slave computers. (In a CSMA or token-passing ring or bus network, there are no slaves; each node is its own master.) The master controller polls each node, or computer, to see if any messages are ready to be sent over the network, since the slave nodes cannot initiate communication. The failure of the master controller might render the entire network useless, however. For that reason, systems employ an optional controller that backs up the primary controller in real time.

Though most personal computer networks were implemented with the CSMA/CD technique, recently installed token-ring nodes have exceeded CSMA/CD nodes in number. For instance, one network distributes control by using token passing, which is the most popular network configuration. This network accommodates up to 16 nodes and

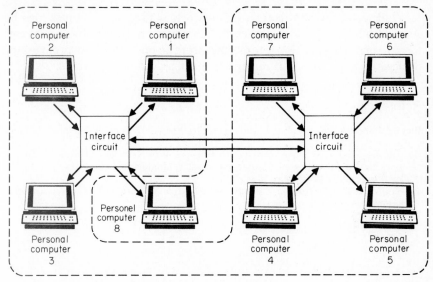

Figure 12.7   Some token-passing networks outwardly sport a star topology yet they effectively operate like logical rings.

transmits data at 750 kb/s. Though it relies on twisted-pair wiring as the transmission medium, the computer nodes are separated by as much as 600 m.

Another network uses token passing in a star structure, though the topology is effectively a logical ring because of the sequential order in which a token passes from one node to the next (Fig. 12.7). Each system, for instance, clusters about 30 computers around an interface circuit (called a line-isolation device), which is connected to another interface circuit that also has a series of computers surrounding it. Because a token travels sequentially through the stations—say, from the third station to the fourth—it passes between clusters via the interface circuits, regardless of the station location, before returning to the originating cluster.

Several personal computer networks are supported by software packages, handling either a single user and single task or multiple-users with multitasking capabilities. These networks may offer transparent operation and detect errors in messages and retransmit correct messages.

Some network manufacturers supply packages composed of hardware, software, and transmission medium, but others furnish only disk and print server hardware, letting the user add the software and missing hardware elements. Without the appropriate integration of hardware and software, the computers cannot talk to one another, much less benefit from each other's processing power.

Whether a personal computer network is proprietary must also be considered. The growth of personal computer networks has, however, forced some local network manufacturers to open up their proprietary designs to popular small machines built by other companies.

References

Barden, Robert A.: "Coax cable, a local access alternative," *Telecommunications,* October 1982.

Datapro Research Corp.: "An Introduction to Local Area Networks," CS20-450, 1983.

Geiser, Charles: "Considerations that you must evaluate in choosing the best LAN," *Communications News,* May 1984.

Jones, J. Richard: "Emerging Trends in Local Area Networks," *Telecommunications,* December 1983.

Organizations Involved in Telecommunications

This Appendix briefly discusses those regulatory organizations that were referred to in the preceding chapters. Table A.1 lists international and domestic organizations involved in making standards.

United States

Companies in the United States which furnish communication services to the public are referred to as *common carriers*. The telecommunication common carriers offer facilities for the transmission of voice, data, facsimile, television, telemetry, and telephoto pictures. Some of these are now offering on-line computer services, and it is possible that their business could branch out widely in this direction. There are more than 2000 telecommunication common carriers in the United States. (Other countries have only one organization, which is run by the government.) Most of the common carriers are small. Only about 250 of them have more than 5000 subscribers.

The AT&T System

The *AT&T System* refers to the vast network of telephone and data circuits with many switching offices and to the television and other links

TABLE A.1 Standards-Making Organizations

Organization and geography	Affiliation	Membership and representation	Influence
CCITT (International Consultative Committee on Telegraphy and Telephony) International	Part of International Telecommunications Union (a U.N. treaty organization)	Private companies; scientific and trade associations; postal, telephone, and telegraph administrations. U.S. representative is Department of State	"Recommendations" which are law where communications in Europe are nationalized
ISO (International Standards Organization) International	Voluntary, nontreaty	Standards bodies in participating nations. U.S. representative is ASNI; ECMA is observer	Responsible for Open Systems Interconnection 7-layer model; close relationship with CCITT
ECMA (European Computer Manufacturers Association) Western Europe	Computer suppliers selling in Europe; includes some U.S. companies	Trade organization of suppliers; small, with about 20 members	Contributes to ISO and also issues own standards; known for fast movement
ANSI (American National Standards Institute) United States	Voluntary	Manufacturers, organizations, users, and communications carriers	U.S. voice in ISO
NBS (National Bureau of Standards) United States	Government agency	Government agencies and network users; much work done by Bolt, Berenak & Newman, which is largely responsible for DOD's Arpanet	Issues Federal Information Processing standards for equipment sold to federal government; Department of Defense need not comply
EIA (Electronic Industries Association) United States	U.S. trade organization	Manufacturers	Contributes to ANSI; known for physical layer's RS-232-C standard
IEEE (Institute of Electrical and Electronics Engineers) International	Professional society	Dues-paying individuals	Contributes to ANSI and issues own standards, such as IEEE-488 bus

that are operated across the United States by the American Telephone and Telegraph Company (AT&T) and its subsidiaries and associated companies. AT&T leases private lines of a wide range of capacities and provides terminal equipment for data transmission.

The Federal Communications Commission (FCC). With the number of common carriers, many of which monopolize the services they offer, it is necessary to have a regulatory authority in the United States. The FCC is the authority regulating interstate lines and foreign facilities originating in the United States. It is an independent federal agency which regulates radio, television, telephone, telegraph, and other transmissions by wire or radio.

Telecommunication organizations in other countries

In many countries the job of delivering mail and providing telecommunications is undertaken by the same organization. Britain's General Post Office (GPO) handles mail, telecommunications, and broadcasting. It has the status of a government-regulated commercial company.

Most countries of the world have government-controlled monopolies providing their telecommunications and offering or planning to offer facilities for data transmission. In Germany it is the Deutschen Bundespost and in France the Postes Téléphonique et Télégraphique (PTT).

The International Telecommunication Union (ITU)

The International Telecommunications Union, an organization with headquarters in Switzerland, has 162 member countries throughout the world (as of March 1987). Its consultative committees carry out very detailed studies of world communications and issue recommendations for standardization. The recommendations are placed into practice widely throughout the world with some dissensions.

There are three main organizations within the ITU:

1. The International Frequency Registration Board, which attempts to register and standardize radio-frequency assignments

2. The International Radio Consultative Committee (CCIR), which deals with other standards for radio, especially long-distance radio telecommunications

3. The International Telegraph and Telephone Consultative Committee (CCITT).

The CCITT, based in Geneva, is divided into a number of study groups which make recommendations on various aspects of telephony and telegraphy. There are study groups, for example, on telegraphy transmission, performance, telegraph switching, alphabetic telegraph apparatus, telephone channels, telephone switching and signaling, noise, and several others. The recommendations are reviewed at plenary assemblies held at approximately 4-year intervals and are then published in sets of books referred to by color. The last four issues of CCITT books are

Green Book, Vth Plenary Assembly, Geneva, 1972

Orange Book, VIth Plenary Assembly, Geneva, 1976

Yellow Book, VIIth Plenary Assembly, Geneva, 1980

Red Book, VIIIth Plenary Assembly, Malaga-Torremolinos, 1984

CCITT Recommendations frequently referred in this book are in the following volumes of the *Orange, Yellow,* and *Red Books:*

Volume III. International telephone networks; analog carrier systems, digital networks, transmission of nontelephone signals. Series G, H, J, I Recommendations.

Volume IV. Maintenance of international systems and specifications of measuring equipment. Series M, N, O Recommendations.

Volume VI. Telephone Switching, Signaling, and Languages. Series Q and Z (for languages) Recommendations.

Volume VII. Telegraph transmission and switching. Series R, S, T, U Recommendations.

Volume VIII. Data communication over the Telephone network, Series V, and Data communication networks (services, facilities, interfaces, transmission, signaling, switching, network aspects, maintenance, interconnection), Series X Recommendations.

The study group which is perhaps the most concerned with the subject of this book is the Special Committee on Data Transmission. Its reports providing recommendations for data transmission standards are widely accepted.

International Telecommunications Satellite Organization (Intelsat)

Intelsat was established in 1964, whereby it became possible for all nations to use and share in the development of one satellite system. Its prime objective is to provide, on a commercial basis, the space segment for international public telecommunications services of high quality and reliability, to be available to all areas of the world. The Intelsat organization had grown to 114 investor members as of February 1988. Communications Satellite Corporation (Comsat) is the American signatory of Intelsat.

Apart from its global system, Intelsat is currently leasing satellite transponders to European PTT authorities for their domestic communications.

Dedicated satellites. Specific national requirements have prompted several countries to start dedicated satellites for their own domestic systems. Dedicated satellites offer technical advantages whereby it is possible either to increase the transponder's traffic capacity or to reduce the cost of the earth segment by simplifying the earth station with the use of smaller antennas.

Inmarsat. An international marine satellite communications system, Inmarsat, is also in operation. Comsat is the designated American participant. A European consortium has proposed the Marots system as the first stage of Inmarsat, interfacing with Marisat. Inmarsat has 53 member nations. Future Intelsat V satellites may include maritime communications capability.

Aerosat. Clearly there are other potential mobile users for satellite communications besides ships. An aeronautical satellite system, Aerosat, had been planned by the United States, Canada, and several European countries. Although the project came to a standstill because of economic and institutional obstacles, considerable work has been done on defining the Aerosat system and this may eventually bear fruit.

European Communications System (ECS). ECS will provide satellite communications services to as many as 31 nations after 1983. The space segment of ECS will be managed by the European Telecommunications Satellite (Eutelsat) organization.

Telephone Signaling

A switched telephone network connects and disconnects subscribers via signaling. Signaling also provides status information, like a busy tone, dial tone, ringing, congestion, and call charge data. Signaling can be considered in two parts which operate differently: signaling between the subscriber and the local telephone exchange and signaling between switching offices. The signals between automatic exchanges (trunks) are entirely machine-to-machine signals and are related to multiplexing and carrier methods that are in use.

Signaling may be broken down into two categories: *supervisory* and *address*. Supervisory signaling conveys information regarding on-hook (idle) and off-hook (busy) conditions. Address signaling routes the calls through the switching equipment; it is the signaling containing the dialing information. The supervisory function is carried out when a call is set up and when it is terminated; thus it is not continuous.

Signaling between exchange and subscriber

This signaling consists of the following:

- Two-state dc signal to indicate whether the telephone handpiece is on the rest or not (on-hook, off-hook)
- Audible tones intended for the ear of the user (dial tone and busy signal)
- A means of dialing (rotary or Touch-Tone)
- An interrupted dc signal which makes the telephone ring

TABLE B.1   On-Hook and Off-Hook Signals

DC telephone line	Trunk
On-hook signifies the loop is open to direct current supplied from other end.	If idle, signals on-hook to other end. Seizure at calling end signals off-hook to called end. While calling end awaits answer, called end signals on-hook to calling end.
Off-hook signifies the loop is closed, allowing relay at other end to operate. Signaling in reverse direction is ring-down.	Answer results in signaling off-hook from called end. If called end is not ready to receive address signals when seized, it signals off-hook to calling end until ready.

When a subscriber lifts the handset the dc voltage on the local loop changes and informs the exchange that the subscriber wants to dial a call. The central exchange puts a dial tone on the line telling the subscriber to dial. Dialing generates the train of dc pulses which consists of makes and breaks of 48-V loop voltage. These pulses correspond to the digits dialed and cause the local switching equipment to operate. E (ear) and M (mouth) signals are based on conditions of on-hook and off-hook, representing the condition of blocked or flowing direct current on the subscriber's line. Their extension to trunk signaling is given in Table B.1. Either condition is continuous and may be detected at any time. On the other hand, discontinuous signals must be recorded, and the condition represented is presumed to continue until a new signal is sent. Supervisory signaling in a backward direction (toward the calling end) is also needed in automatic working. It is also described as on-hook or off-hook, although on two-wire metallic circuits the signaling condition is usually a reversal of flow of the direct current rather than an interruption. Continuous supervisory signaling over longer distances is done by use of signaling paths distinct from the voice path. These signaling paths may be telegraph legs of a composite telegraph system, simplexing of voice pair, or special tones inside or outside the voice channel. Whatever the paths, they are extensions of separate dc leads from the trunk circuits, known as E and M leads. The relation between the conditions of these leads and the on-hook or off-hook signaling conditions they represent is shown in Fig. B.1.

Extension of E and M signals over tone channels may be done by in-band or out-band signaling.

Two basic categories of access circuits are *loop start* and *ground start*. The names refer to the methods of seizing the circuit for dialing or ringing.

Dialing.   Subscriber dialing generates the train of dc pulses or tones. The pulse rate is nominally 10 per second and varies between 7.5 and 12; the pulse lasts from 58 to 67 percent of the time interval. To increase

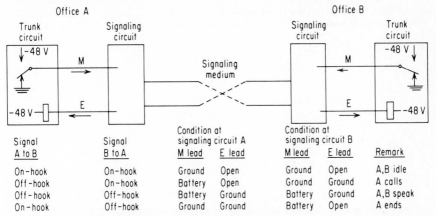

Signal A to B	Signal B to A	Condition at signaling circuit A		Condition at signaling circuit B		Remark
		M lead	E lead	M lead	E lead	
On-hook	On-hook	Ground	Open	Ground	Open	A,B idle
Off-hook	On-hook	Battery	Open	Ground	Ground	A calls
Off-hook	Off-hook	Battery	Ground	Battery	Ground	A,B speak
On-hook	Off-hook	Ground	Ground	Battery	Open	A ends

Fig. B.1 E and M signaling. Notes: (1) The E lead receives open or ground signals from the signaling circuit. (2) The M lead sends ground or battery signals to the signaling circuit. (3) REMARK represents normal calling procedures.

the speed of service and reduce holding time on telephone exchange registers, a tone-signaling technique for subscriber lines has been introduced. At the subscriber set, the conventional dial is replaced with a set of pushbutton keys which, when pressed by the subscriber, cause transmission to the telephone exchange of combinations of two audiofrequency tones, one combination serving for each numerical digit. A total of 8 tone frequencies is provided. The excess combinations over the 10 required for numerics are reserved for special signals. See Table B.2.

The train of tones is received by special equipment in the telephone exchange, which interprets them and stores the digits in a register with the same functions as that in which ordinary telephone dial pulses are stored. Thus the major switching equipment of the exchange is not different when pushbutton dialing is used; only that part for interpreting the signal is different.

CCITT recommendations on *technical features of pushbutton telephone sets* are given in Vol. VI, Rec. Q.23.

Ringing. The ringing tone on a subscriber loop is a 20-Hz signal of 75 to 150 V. Where the signal must travel over a carrier channel, a frequency of 1000 Hz modulated by a frequency of 20 Hz is used.

The level of tones on international circuits must have a nominal value of -10 dBm0. The recommended limits are not more than -5 dBm0 or less than -15 dBm0 measured with continuous tone. For detailed information about tones refer to CCITT Rec. E.180.

Data on standard audible tones for private lines in North America are given in Table B.3.

TABLE B.2 Pushbutton Multifrequency Signaling Code
(Frequencies in hertz)

Signal	697	770	852	941	1209	1336	1477	1633*
0				x		x		
1	x				x			
2	x					x		
3	x						x	
4		x			x			
5		x				x		
6		x					x	
7			x		x			
8			x			x		
9			x				x	

*1633 Hz is used in combination with the other seven frequencies
for special-category signals.

Signaling over trunks

Signaling over long-haul intertoll trunks uses techniques whereby signaling information is transmitted at audio frequencies within the voice-channel spectrum (in-band signaling) or just above the voice-channel spectrum (out-band signaling). Levels are comparable to speech levels.

In-band and out-band signaling. In-band signaling accomplishes both supervisory and address signaling inside the operative voice-band spectrum, i.e., 300 to 3400 Hz. On most signaling systems, signals between offices travel inside the voice bandwidth.

TABLE B.3 Standard Audible Tones in North America

Use	Frequencies, Hz				Power per frequency at exchange where tone is applied, dBm0	Cadence
	350	440	480	620		
Dial tone	x	x			-13	Continuous
Busy tone			x	x	-24	0.5 s on 0.5 s off
Reorder tone			x	x	-24	0.2 s on 0.3 s off or 0.3 s on 0.2 s off
Audible ringing tone		x	x		-16	2 s on 4 s off
High tone			x		-16	Varies according to use
Pre-emption tone		x		x	-18	Single 200/500-ms pulse
Call-waiting tone		x			-13	Single 500-ms pulse

TABLE B.4   2600-Hz Line Signal Codes
(CCITT Vol. VI, Rec. Q.311, Table 1.)

Signal	Signal direction[1,2]	Transmitted (sending) duration	Transmitted state[5,6] Originating end	Terminating end
Idle	⇆	Continuous	0	0
Connect (seizing)	→	Continuous	1	0
Delay dialing	←	Continuous[3]	1	1
Start dialing (proceed-to-send)	←	Continuous[3]	1	0
Answer	←	Continuous	1	1
Hang up (clear back)	←	Continuous	1	0
Disconnect (clear forward)	→	Continuous	0	0 or 1
Ring forward (forward transfer)	→	65–135 ms	0	0 or 1
Busy, reorder (congestion)[4]	←	—	Off	On

[1] →, → indicate forward signaling states 0 and 1, respectively.
[2] ←, ← indicate backward signaling states 0 and 1, respectively.
[3]The durations of these signals are variable and depend upon when the succeeding signal occurs. To ensure proper registration of these signals, the transmitted signal durations should not be less than 140 ms.
[4]Busy and reorder (congestion) conditions are indicated by audible tones.
[5]0: tone on, or signaling bit state 0 in PCM systems.
[6]1: tone off, or signaling bit state 1 in PCM systems.

The CCITT R1 system is regional and uses 2600 Hz in both directions, continuously. It is called SF (single frequency) and is the most common type in use in North America. Some countries use 2280 Hz in both directions. In-band signals most often are selected purposely in the higher end of the voice band because in normal conversation less speech energy is concentrated in that portion of the voice-channel spectrum. This provides added assurance that talk-down will not occur.

CCITT Rec. Q.311 on 2600-Hz line signal codes is given in Table B.4.

In-band supervisory signaling frequencies may be of the 1VF or 2VF types. This means that it could be SF signaling or two-tone signaling. Two-tone can be used either simultaneously or singly. For instance, CCITT No. 4 signaling uses 2040 and 2400 Hz in both directions and it is a pulse type.

Refer to CCITT Vol. VI, Supplement No. 3, for "Voice-frequency signaling systems" used in different countries.

A major problem with in-band signaling is the possibility of talk-down. *Talk-down* refers to the activation or deactivation of supervisory equipment by an inadvertent sequence of voice tones through normal speech usage of the channel. One approach is to use slot filters to bypass the tones as well as a time-delay protection circuit to avoid the possibility of talk-down.

With out-band signaling, supervisory information is transmitted out of band; here we mean above 3400 Hz. Supervisory information is binary, either on-hook or off-hook. Some systems use tone-on to indicate on-hook and others use tone-off. One expression used in the industry is "tone-on when idle." When a circuit is idle, it is on-hook. The advantage of out-band signaling is that either system may be used, tone-on or tone-off when idle. There is no possibility of talk-down occurring because all supervisory information is passed out of band away from the voice.

CCITT R2 line signaling (supervisory signals) is also regional and is out-band, low-level continuous tone-on-idle signaling. The most common out-band signaling frequencies are 3700 (North America) and 3825 Hz (CCITT Rec. Q.21 gives "Systems Recommended for Out-Band Signaling").

In the short run, out-band signaling is attractive from an economic and design standpoint. One drawback is that when patching is required, signaling leads have to be patched as well. In the long run, the signaling equipment required may indeed make out-band signaling even more costly owing to the extra supervisory signaling equipment and signaling lead extensions required at each end and at each time the FDM equipment demodulates to voice. The advantage is that continuous supervision is provided, whether tone-on or tone-off, during the entire telephone conversation.

CCITT Rec. Q.20 gives "Comparative Advantages of In-Band and Out-Band Systems." Refer to Recs. Q.20, 21, 22, and 25 for in-band and out-band signaling.

Multifrequency trunk signaling.   To increase the speed of setting up interoffice connections, multifrequency signaling is often applied to trunk circuits for transmission of switching information. Digital information is transmitted by combinations of two of the following five audio frequencies: 700, 900, 1100, 1300, and 1500 Hz. A sixth frequency of 1700 Hz is used in combination with the 1100-Hz frequency at the start of pulsing and in combination with the 1500-Hz frequency at the end of the pulsing signal. Table B.5 gives the standard R1 multifrequency signaling code, used in North America, per CCITT Rec. Q.320. Signal level is -7 ± 1 dBm0 per frequency.

System R2 is designed to use six signaling frequencies (1380, 1500, 1620, 1740, 1860, and 1980 Hz) in the forward direction and six signaling frequencies (1140, 1020, 900, 780, 660, and 540 Hz) in the backward direction. The interregister signaling is performed end-to-end using a two-out-of-six in-band multifrequency code with forward and backward compelled signaling. Detailed information for R1 and R2 signaling is given in the CCITT *Orange Book,* Vol. VI.3, *Yellow Book,* Fasc. VI, and *Red Book,* Fasc. VI.4 (Regional).

TABLE B.5   Register Signal Code of System R1

Signals	Frequencies (compound), Hz
KP (start-of-pulsing)	1100 + 1700
Digit 1	700 + 900
Digit 2	700 + 1100
Digit 3	900 + 1100
Digit 4	700 + 1300
Digit 5	900 + 1300
Digit 6	1100 + 1300
Digit 7	700 + 1500
Digit 8	900 + 1500
Digit 9	1100 + 1500
Digit 0	1300 + 1500
ST (end-of-pulsing)	1500 + 1700
Spare	700 + 1700
Spare	900 + 1700
Spare	1300 + 1700

SOURCE: CCITT Rec. Q.320.

Signaling and data transmission

In-band signaling may cause a problem with modems. The data system recognizes an in-band control signal by the fact that it has substantial energy at the signaling frequency. This is quite different from a human voice, which delivers less energy at that portion of the frequency band. To transmit data we must ensure that when there is energy at the signaling frequency there will always be sufficient energy at other frequencies to prevent the data from being mistaken for a control signal. In North America, 2400- and 2600-Hz signaling frequencies (1VF or 2VF) are used. The British Post Office uses 2280 Hz; and 2040 and 2400 Hz is used in the rest of Europe.

Utilized modulation methods in modems prevent energy concentration in that portion of the signaling frequencies. Care also has to be taken that intermodulation products from other channels do not have strengths to interfere with the signaling. These restrictions do not in general apply to leased communication lines because these do not carry the signals needed for switching purposes.

Channel-associated and common-channel signaling.   Two types of channel signaling are in use. In *channel-associated signaling* the signals travel with the voice channel. The techniques discussed in preceding paragraphs all are channel-associated signaling.

In *common-channel signaling,* a completely independent signaling channel carries the signals for many traffic channels. Common-channel signaling is more complex than sending signals with the channel, but as computer circuits drop in cost it becomes increasingly attractive. Furthermore, many switching offices are now becoming computerized and common-channel signaling can be controlled by these computers. Common-channel signaling gives much faster signaling speeds and a greatly enhanced signaling capacity. It can be used for network management functions such as diagnostics and the varying of call routing as traffic patterns vary. Furthermore the network is immune to talk-down.

International signaling systems are standardized by the CCITT and are applicable for general use in automatic and semiautomatic telephone operations.

CCITT Signaling System No. 4 is a Europe-only system for operator-controlled and full-automatic international services on unidirectional circuits. It uses 2040-Hz and 2400-Hz tones in pulses 100 ms, 150 ms, or 350 ms long for line and supervisory signals, and a four-element code using 2040-Hz pulses, 35 ms each, with 35-ms gaps between pulses.

CCITT Signaling System No. 5 is one of the most widely used systems. It uses two in-band frequencies for line and supervisory signals (2400 Hz and 2600 Hz). In this system, four-wire circuits are essential and the system is usually directly associated with a four-wire international transit exchange. Refer to *Yellow* and *Red Books,* Fasc. VI.2, for Signaling Systems Nos. 4 and 5.

CCITT Signaling System No. 6 is an international specification for common-channel signaling. The AT&T version is called CCIS, *common-channel interoffice signaling,* and it is designed for signaling between computerized switching offices. With these switching offices, telephone calls are set up in much less time than previously. The signaling data are built up of units of 28 bits, of which 8 are error-detection bits. These data are sent over a speech channel using a four-phase modem operating at 2400 b/s. Refer to *Yellow* and *Red Books,* Fasc. VI.3, for Signaling System No. 6.

CCITT Signaling System No. 7 is a common-channel signaling system for use between stored-program-controlled exchanges. Designed for use in a digital environment, it is the preferred CCITT system between integrated digital network exchanges and within integrated services digital networks. It can be used for the control of data transmission and telephone networks. All line, interregister, maintenance, and management signals are digitally encoded and formed up into signal units which are transmitted in binary form. Operation is optimized for a digital bearer at 64 kb/s, but operation at lower speeds on analog bearers is possible. Refer to *Yellow Book,* Fasc. VI.6, and *Red Book,* Fasc. VI.8, for Signaling System No. 7.

PCM Signaling. In-band signaling can be transmitted over PCM links easily, since the signals are simply digitized along the voice. It would, however, be advantageous to implement digital signaling systems for PCM links that employ the spare bits in the voice channel which were left available for signaling. A special version of the CCITT Signaling System No. R2 is designed to do this, and PCM versions of Signaling System No. 6 are being considered. Figure 5.4 shows the CCITT recommendations for common-channel signaling and channel-associated signaling with PCM transmission. For more information refer to CCITT. Recs. G.732 and G.733.

CCITT Recommendations for satellite signaling.

Q.35   Special Information

Q.48   Demand Assignment (DA) Signaling System

Q.60   Interworking of the Terrestrial Telephone Network and Maritime Mobile-Satellite Service

Q.62   Interworking with Signaling System No. 5

ITU 1982 Radio Regulations, Art. 1, No. 71, No. 73.

References

CCITT, Geneva: *Orange, Yellow,* and *Red Books.* Volume VI, "Telephone Switching and Signaling."

ITT: "Telephone Signaling," *Reference Data for Radio Engineers,* 6th ed., Sams, New York, 1975, p. 2–13.

Glossary

Acceptance Angle   The maximum angle, measured from the core centerline, within which light may be coupled into a fiber.

Access Time   (1) The time interval between the instant at which a control unit initiates a call for data and the instant delivery of the data is completed. (2) The time interval between the instant at which data are requested to be stored and the instant at which storage is started.

Acknowledgment   A character or group of characters generated at a receiving device to indicate to the sending device that information has been received either correctly or incorrectly.

Acoustic Coupler   A device that converts electric signals into audio signals (and vice versa), enabling data to be transmitted over the public telephone network via a conventional telephone handset.

Acronym   A word formed from the first letters of the words in a name, term, or phrase.

ACS   Advanced communications service. A shared, switched network service that provides for data transmission by using a broad range of data communications functions.

Active Satellite   A satellite carrying a station intended to transmit or retransmit radiocommunication signals.

Adapter   A device that matches operation between different parts of one or more systems or subsystems.

ADCCP   Advanced data communications control procedure. ANSI version of bit-oriented data-link control; specified in Publication BSR X3.66. See also HDLC.

Address   (1) A character or group of characters that identifies a register, a particular part of storage, or some other data source or destination. (2) To refer to a device or an item of data by its address.

ALGOL   Algorithmic language. An international problem language designed for the concise, efficient expression of arithmetic and logical processes and the control of these processes.

Algorithm   A prescribed set of well-defined rules or processes for the solution of a problem in a finite number of steps.

Alphabet No. 2, International 5 unit + start + stop telegraph code for tele-typewriter, defined by CCITT.

Aphabet No. 5, International 7 bits + parity code for information interchange, defined by CCITT (similar to ASCII).

Alphanumeric Information consisting of alphabetic and special characters and numerals.

Ambient Temperature The average temperature of the surrounding medium such as air, water, or earth into which the heat of the equipment is dissipated.

Amplification (1) Strengthening of a weak signal. Contrasts with attenuation. (2) The ratio between the output signal power and the input signal power of a device. (3) Gain.

Amplitude The strength of a signal.

Amplitude Modulation (AM) A method of transmission whereby the amplitude of the carrier wave is modified in accordance with the amplitude of the signal wave.

Analog Pertaining to data in the form of continuously variable physical quantities. Contrast with Digital.

Angle Modulation Modulation in which the angle of a sine-wave carrier is the characteristic varied from its reference value. Frequency modulation and phase modulation are particular forms of angle modulation.

ANSI American National Standards Institute.

Answerback (1) A signal or sequence of signals from a receiving business machine indicating that it is ready to accept or acknowledge receipt of data or to identify itself. The signal may be received audibly through a loudspeaker at the transmitting end for manual operation or electronically for automatic operation. (2) The act of transmitting a signal as described in (1).

APCM Adaptive pulse-code modulation.

APL A programming language. A language with a syntax and character set designed for mathematical applications, especially those involving numeric or literal arrays.

ARPANET Advanced research projects agency computer network. Resource-sharing system through a multicomputer network in the United States.

ARQ Automatic request for repeat of transmission.

ASCII American standard code for information interchange. A standard code used by many computers, video-display terminals, teleprinters, and computer peripherals in which 128 numerals, letters, symbols, and special codes are each represented by a 7-bit binary number.

ASCR Assymmetrical silicon controlled rectifier.

Assembler Language A low-level computer language used for implementing higher-level functions. One assembler statement produces one machine instruction.

Asynchronous Transmission   Transmission in which each information character or sometimes each word or small block is individually synchronized, usually by the use of start and stop elements. The gap between character or word is not of a necessarily fixed length.

ATPG   Automatic test program generator.

Attenuation   Decrease in magnitude of a signal.

Audio   Frequencies that can be heard by the human ear, usually between 20 and 20,000 Hz.

AUTODIN   Automatic digital network (U.S. military).

AUTOVON   Automatic voice-operating network (four-wire) (U.S. military).

Auxiliary Channel   A secondary channel whose direction of transmission is independent of the primary channel and is controlled by an appropriate set of secondary control interchange circuits.

Avalanche Transistor   In a common-base connection, when a voltage is applied between collector and base, a depletion layer or space charge is formed at the collector junction and spreads out into both the collector and base regions. Avalanche multiplication takes place in this depletion layer when a high electric field is present. Avalanche breakdown differs from zener breakdown in that no multiplication takes place because no free carriers are present in the zener condition.

AWG   American wire gage. A means of specifying wire diameter. The higher the number, the smaller the diameter.

Backward Channel   A secondary channel whose direction of transmission is constrained to be always opposite to that of the primary channel.

Band   A range of frequencies between two defined limits.

Bandwidth, Nominal   The maximum range of frequencies, including guard bands, assigned to a channel.

Baseband   (1) The band of frequencies occupied by the signal in a carrier system before it modulates the carrier frequency. (2) Digital signals used between stations of LAN.

Baseband System   A system whereby information is directly encoded and impressed on the transmission medium of a LAN.

Baseband Transmission   Transmission of data pulses over short distances on private cable or wire pairs which usually requires line drivers and receivers on each side of the line.

BASIC   Beginner's all-purpose symbolic instruction code. A simplified computer language intended for use in engineering applications.

Batch Processing   A method of data processing in which a number of similar input items are accumulated and processed together.

Baud (Bd)   A unit of signaling speed equal to the number of discrete conditions or signals per second of a character.

Baudot Code   A code for the transmission of data in which 5 bits represents one character.

BCC   Block check character. The result of a transmission verification algorithm accumulated over a transmission block and normally appended at the end of the block, e.g., CRC or LRC.

BCD   Binary-coded decimal. A coding system in which each decimal digit from 0 to 9 is represented by four binary digits; e.g., 23 is represented by 0010 0011.

BCP   Byte-control protocols.

Bend Loss   A form of increased attenuation caused by bends radiating from the side of the fiber. The two types of bend losses are (1) those occurring when the fiber is curved around a restrictive radius of curvature and (2) microbends caused by small distortions of the fiber imposed by externally induced perturbations.

BER   Bit error rate. The proportion of the number of digital errors to the total number of observed digits.

Bias   The dc voltage applied to a transistor or a relay to establish a desired operating point.

Bilateral Control   A synchronization control system between exchanges A and B is bilateral if the clock at exchange A controls that at exchange B and the clock at exchange B controls that at exchange A.

Binary   Numbering system based on 2s rather than 10s. The digits used in the binary numbering system are 0 and 1 only.

Binary Digit   The smallest of information in a binary notation system. A binary digit (or bit) is either a 1 or a 0.

Bipolar   (1) One of several fundamental processes for fabricating integrated circuits. A bipolar IC is made up of layers of silicon with differing electrical characteristics. Current flows between the layers when a voltage is applied to the junction or boundary between the layers. (2) A type of MLB pulse coding.

Bistable   The capability of assuming either of two stable states, thus of storing one bit of information.

BISYNC   See BSC.

Bit   Abbreviation of binary digit; it can have a value of either 0 or 1.

Bit Error Ratio (Rate)   See BER.

Block   A set of associated words, characters or digits handled as a unit.

Boolean Algebra   (1) Shorthand notation for expressing logic functions dealing with on-off circuit elements; associated by operators as AND, OR, NOT, thereby permitting computations and demonstration as in many mathematical systems. Named after English mathematician George Boole. (2) Algebraic rules for manipulating logic equations.

BOP   Bit-Oriented Protocols.

Break   A long space on an asynchronous line that is intended to alert the receiving CPU. Minimum duration is one character time.

Bridged Tap   Portion of the transmission facility that does not form the direct transmission path.

Broadcast   (1) A television or radio transmission intended for public reception. (2) A class of media for a LAN in which all stations are capable of receiving a signal transmitted by any other station. Also describes the mode of usage of such a medium by the data link layer in which all stations are instructed to receive a given frame.

BSC   Binary synchronous communications. A uniform discipline, using a definite set of control characters and control character sequences, for synchronized transmission of binary-coded data between stations in a data communications system. Also called BISYNC.

Bubble Memory   When an external magnetic field of appropriate intensity is applied perpendicularly to a thin film of a ferromagnetic single crystal, small cylindrical domains normal to the film surface are produced within the thin film. These small magnetic domains are called magnetic bubbles. The magnetic bubbles can be moved within the thin film by changing the external magnetic field appropriately. This phenomenon can be utilized to produce a memory function by assigning the presence of or absence of a bubble at a given position in the thin film to the binary digit 1 or 0. A magnetic-bubble memory is thus obtained.

Buffer   (1) A storage device in which data are assembled temporarily during data transfers. It is used to compensate for a difference in the rate of flow of information or the time occurrence of events when transferring information from one device to another. (2) A circuit inserted between other circuit elements to prevent interactions, to match impedances, to supply additional drive capability, or to delay the rate of information flow. Buffers may be inverting or noninverting. (3) The material that covers and protects fiber but has no optical function.

Bundle   A group of fibers for transmitting a single optical signal.

Bus   One or more conductors used for transmitting signals, data, or power. An example of some special buses are data and flag buses. A data bus transmits data or information. Often the bus acts as a common connection among a number of locations.

Byte   A sequence of adjacent bits operated upon as a unit for information exchange between devices; sometimes shorter than a computer word. Eight-bit bytes are most commonly used in the industry.

CAD   Computer-aided design.

CAM   Computer-aided manufacturing.

Capacity, Circuit   (1) The number of communication channels that can be derived from a given circuit at the same time. (2) The information capacity measured in bits per second of a circuit.

Carrier   A continuous frequency capable of being modulated or impressed with a signal.

Carrier Sense   A signal provided by the physical layer to the data link layer to indicate that one or more stations are currently transmitting on the channel of LAN.

Carrier System   A means of obtaining a number of channels over a single path at the originating end, transmitting a wideband or high-speed signal and recovering the original information at the receiving end.

Cassette Recorder   A magnetic tape recording and playback device for entering or storing programs.

CAT   Computer-aided test.

Cathode-Ray Tube   See CRT.

CCCI (C³I)   Command, control, communications, and intelligence.

CCIR   International Radio Consultative Committee. Branch of the ITU.

CCITT   International Telegraph and Telephone Consultative Committee. An agency of the United Nations International Telecommunications Union (ITU). Its purpose is to promote compatibility between communications practices and performance standards of various nations.

CCSA   Common-control-switching arrangement. Switching facilities connected by the telephone company to a corporation's network so that switching of leased lines of the network is accomplished by common-control-switching equipment. All stations in the network may dial one another without using toll facilities.

CDMA   Code-division multiple access. Multiple-access technique that utilizes full satellite bandwidth and whole time slots by employing a special coding-decoding technique.

CELTIC   Computer exploiting the idle time of circuits; a fully digital system.

Central Office   Location where communications common carriers terminate customer lines and house the equipment that interconnects these lines.

Central Processing Unit (CPU)   Portion of a computer which directs the sequence of operations, interprets the coded instructions, and initiates the proper commands to the computer circuits for execution.

Channel   A single path for transmitting electric signals.

Channel, Analog   Refers to a channel that will pass alternating current but not direct current. A switched-voice channel is an analog channel. If an analog channel is said to carry digital data, it is actually carrying the analog representation of the digital data in the form of various frequencies.

Channel, Digital   A channel capable of carrying digital current as opposed to analog channels.

Channel Logic   The logical functions provided between a transceiver cable and a data link which support the defined interface between the data link and the physical layers.

Channel, Telegraph-Grade A communications path suitable for transmission of signals at speeds up to approximately 180 Bd, but not suitable for voice due to restricted bandwidth; a narrow-band channel.

Channel, Voice-Grade (1) A common telephone connection between points. (2) A channel suitable for transmission of speech, digital or analog data, or facsimile generally with a frequency range between 300 and 3400 Hz.

Channelize To subdivide a channel into multiple channels of lesser bandwidth.

Character A symbol as used in a writing system; it could be a letter, a number, a period, or a space.

Character, Check A parity character added to a group of characters to assist in error detection or error correction.

Character, Control (1) A character whose occurrence in a particular context initiates, modifies, or stops a control operation or function. (2) A character used to initiate functions such as line feed, carriage return, etc. (3) In the ASCII code, any of the 32 characters in the first two columns of the standard code table. (4) Synonymous with function code.

Character Count Protocol (CCP) A protocol which specifies the number of data characters in the information field.

Characteristics, Signal The basic characteristics of a signal wave form are its amplitude, frequency, and phase.

Character-Oriented Protocol (COP) General term for BCP or CCP.

CHILL, CCITT. High-level language. Designed primarily for programming SPC telephone exchanges; however, it is considered to be general enough for other applications, e.g., message switching, packet switching, modelling etc. See CCITT *Yellow* and *Red Books* Z.200.

Chip A small piece of silicon impregnated with impurities in a pattern to form transistors, diodes and resistors. Electric paths are formed on it by depositing thin layers of aluminum or gold.

Circuit, Four-Wire A system in which the transmitting and receiving paths are separate channels.

Circuit, Multipoint A system consisting of a circuit connecting three or more terminals, any or all of which may simultaneously receive information flowing in the common circuit.

Circuit, Phantom A third circuit derived from two physical circuits by means of repeating coils installed at the terminals of the circuits.

Circuit, Two-Wire A system in which all transmitting and receiving is performed over one pair of wires.

Circular Orbit A satellite orbit in which the distance between the centers of mass of the satellite and of the primary body is constant.

Cladding The low-refractive-index material which surrounds the core of the fiber and protects against surface-contaminant scattering. In all glass fibers the cladding is glass. In plastic-clad silica fibers, the plastic cladding may also serve as the coating.

C language   A structured language designed to give efficient control of machine resources while enabling device-independent programming. Used for the Unix operating system.

Clock   An electric circuit that generates timing pulses to synchronize the operation of a computer or a digital system.

CMOS   Complementary metal-oxide semiconductor. Although it refers to an IC manufacturing technology, the term is almost always used to describe an IC logic family with low power dissipation.

CO   Central office.

COBOL   Common business-oriented language. Used to express problems of data manipulation and processing procedures in the business field in English narrative form.

Code, Five-Level   (1) A term frequently used as a synonym for Baudot code. (2) Any code using five elements, or bits, to designate one character. Such a code has 32 possible discrete combinations of the five-code elements.

Code Conversion   Conversion of character signals or groups of character signals in one code into corresponding signals or group of signals in another code.

Codec   An assembly comprising an encoder and decoder in the same equipment.

Coder   A device for converting data from one notation system to another.

Coding   Preparation of a set of instructions or symbols which, when used by a programmable controller, have a special external meaning.

Collision   The result of multiple transmissions overlapping in the physical channel resulting in garbled data and necessitating retransmission (refers to a LAN).

Collision Detect   A signal provided by the physical layer to the data link layer to indicate that one or more other stations are contending with the local station's transmission. It can be true only during transmission (refers to a LAN).

Common Carrier   A company recognized by the U.S. Federal Communications Commission or appropriate state agency as having a vested interest in furnishing communications services to the public.

Common-Mode Noise   See Noise, Common-Mode.

Compandor   A device for improving the signal-to-noise ratio of a communication link and for decreasing the absolute levels of noise when no signal is being transmitted. It consists of a compressor at the transmitting end and an expandor at the receiving end. Derived from compressor-expandor.

Comparator   Digitally, an arrangement of gates that checks two signals or numbers for equality and usually indicates equality, less than, greater than.

Compelled Telephone Signal   A line supervisory signal tone that is not sent as a pulse of specified length but rather on a continuous basis, until the distant end recognizes it and sends back an acknowledgment; when this answer has been received and recognized by the originating end, transmission of the first signal is stopped.

Computer   Any device capable of accepting information, applying the prescribed process to the information, and supplying the results of these processes.

Comsat   Communications Satellite Corporation. Comsat acts pursuant to general policies of Intelsat in the United States.

Concentrator   A communications device that provides communications capability between many low-speed, usually asynchronous, channels and one or more high-speed, usually synchronous, channels.

Conditioning, Channel   The electrical balancing of a channel to reduce attenuation distortion and delay distortion.

Contention   Interference between colliding transmissions in a LAN. Resolution of occasional contention is a normal part of distributed link management procedure (see CSMA-CD).

Control, Error   (1) An arrangement that will detect the presence of errors. In some systems, refinements are added that will correct the detected errors, either by operations on received data or by retransmission from the source. (2) A periodic or continuous check of such channel characteristics as delay distortion, frequency response, and noise in an effort to reduce or eliminate the causes of errors.

Control Character   See Character, Control.

Control Procedure   The means used to control the orderly communication of information between stations on a data link. Also called line discipline.

Copy, Hard   See Hard Copy.

Copy, Soft   See Soft Copy.

Core   The light-conducting portion of the fiber, defined by the high-refractive-index region. The core is normally in the center of the fiber, bounded by the cladding material.

Core Memory   A memory that uses small magnetic cores as the storage element and is characterized by low-cost storage and a relatively slow memory-operating speed.

Counter   A device capable of changing states in a specified sequence upon receiving appropriate input signals.

CPI   Computer-to-PBX interface.

CPU   See Central Processing Unit.

CRC   Cyclic redundancy check. An error-detection scheme in which the check character is generated by taking the remainder after dividing all the serialized bits in a block of data by a predetermined binary number.

Crossbar Switch   A switch having a plurality of vertical paths, a plurality of horizontal paths, and electromagnetically operated mechanical means for interconnecting any one of the vertical paths with any of the horizontal paths.

Crosstalk   The unwanted transfer of energy from one circuit to another circuit.

CRT   Cathode-ray tube. A high-speed device, similar to a television picture tube, which provides a visual, nonpermanent display of system input-output data.

CRT Terminal   A terminal containing a cathode-ray tube to display programs as ladder diagrams which use instruction symbols similar to relay characters. A CRT terminal can also display data lists and application reports.

CSMA-CD   Carrier sense multiple access with collision detection. The generic term for a class of link management procedure used in LAN operation. So called because it allows multiple stations to access the broadcast channel at will, it avoids contention via carrier sense and deference, and it resolves contention via collision detection and retransmission.

CVSD   Continuously variable slope delta modulation. A type of digital compression method. A form of waveform coding that encodes the difference in magnitude of adjacent samples. It is suited to speech waveforms because of the large amount of adjacent sample redundancy. Adequate production is achieved at 32 kb/s, with severe degradation lower than 16 kb/s.

Cycle Time   Time interval at which any set of operations is repeated regularly in the same sequence.

DAA   Data-access arrangement. Arrangement for isolation of customer's equipment from Bell equipment.

D/A Converter   Digital-to-analog converter. A unit that converts a digital signal into a voltage or current whose magnitude is proportional to the numeric value of the digital signal.

DAMA   Demand-assigned multiple access. A type of satellite operation; automatic assignment of carriers on an as-needed basis.

Dark Current   The current that flows through the photodiode biasing circuit when no light is incident on the photodiode.

Data   Any representation such as characters or analog quantities to which meaning might be assigned.

Data Link Control (DLC)   A uniform discipline for the transmission of data over a single communication link. DLCs include byte-controlled protocol (BCP), character count protocol (CCP), and bit-oriented protocol (BOP).

Data-Phone   A service offering in which various types of data are transmitted over the message network using data sets to connect business machines to the network.

Data Processing   Pertains to any operation or combination of operations on data.

Data Service Unit (DSU)   Interfacing unit between digital transmission network (DTE) and digital communication equipment (DCE).

Data Set   A circuit termination device used to provide an interface between a data communication circuit and a data terminal. A modulation and demodulation function is typically performed in a data set. See also Modem.

Data Terminal   A class of devices characterized by keyboards and CRT displays.

DCE   Data communications equipment. The equipment that provides the functions required to establish, maintain, and terminate a connection, the signal conversion, and coding required for communication between data terminal equipment and the data circuit. The data communication equipment may or may not be an integral part of a computer (e.g., a modem).

DDCMP   Digital data communications message protocol, by Digital Equipment Corporation (DEC). The best example of a character count protocol.

DDD   Direct distance dialing. A telephone service which enables the subscriber to call the other long-distance subscriber without operator assistance.

DDS   Data-Phone digital service. Digital data service in the United States.

Debug   To detect, locate, and remove mistakes from a program.

Decimal Digit   A character used to represent one of ten digits in the numeration system with the base of 10.

Decode   To determine the meaning of individual characters or groups of characters in a message through the reversal of some previous coding. Also called decrypt.

Dedicated Line   A line permanently assigned to specific data terminals not part of switched networks. Also called a private line.

Deference   A process by which a data link controller delays its transmission when the channel is busy to avoid contention with ongoing transmissions.

Delay   The difference in time between a cause and its effect.

Delay, Absolute   The real-time interval from the transmission to reception of a signal over a circuit. Also called transmission time or circuit delay.

Delivery Time   The time interval from the start of transmission at the transmitting termnal to the completion of reception at the receiver terminal. (Also used for a noninteractive system.)

Demodulation   The process of retrieving an original intelligence signal from a modulated carrier wave.

Diagnostic Program   Special program for checking a computer's hardware for proper operation.

Dibit   A group of 2 bits. In a four-phase modulation, each possible dibit is encoded as one of four unique carrier phase shifts. The four possible states for a dibit are 00, 01, 10, 11.

Differential-Mode Noise   See Noise, Differential-Mode.

Diffraction   (1) The bending of radio, sound, or light waves as they pass through an object or barrier. (2) The phenomenon whereby waves traveling in straight paths bend around an obstacle.

Digit   A character that stands for an integral.

Digit, Check   A redundant digit (or digits) carried within a unit item of information (character, word, block) which provides information about the other digits in the unit in such a manner that if an error occurs the check fails. Also see Parity Check.

Digital   (1) Data in discrete quantities; contrasts with analog. (2) Pertaining to data in the form of digits.

Digital Line Path   Two or more digital line sections interconnected in tandem in such a way that the specified rate of the digital signal transmitted and received is the same over the whole length of the line path.

Digital Switching   A process in which connections are established by operations on digital signals without converting them to analog signals.

Diode-Transistor Logic (DTL)   Logic employing diodes at the input with transistors used as amplifiers and resistor pull-up on the output.

DIP   Dual in-line package. A package for electronic components that is suited for automated assembly into printed-circuit boards. The DIP is characterized by two rows of external connecting terminals or pins which are inserted into the holes of the printed-circuit board.

Direct Memory Access   See DMA.

Dispersion   The cause of bandwidth limitation in a fiber. Because dispersion causes a broadening of input pulses along the length of the fiber, this mechanism is usually referred to as pulse spreading. The two major types of dispersion are mode and material dispersion.

Distortion   An unwanted change in waveform that occurs between two points in a transmission system.

Distributed Processing Network   Networks containing both programmable and nonprogrammable units connected in various ways, both locally and remotely, to communicate with each other.

DLE   Data link escape. The first control character of two-character-sequence signals used exclusively to provide supplementary line control signals.

DMA   Direct memory access. A method of gaining direct access to a memory location in order to store data.

DMI   Digital multiplexed interface.

DMOS   Double-diffused MOS.

DNI   Digital Noninterpolated unit. Interface unit between satellite system and terrestrial system used for small-capacity links; preassigned data can be accommodated.

Dot-Matrix Display   A display format consisting of small light-emitting elements arranged as a matrix.

Driver   (1) A program or routine that controls either external devices or other programs. (2) An element which is coupled to the output stage of a circuit to increase its power- or current-handling capability.

DS 1   Digital signal 1. The telephone industry primary standard digital signal used by the United States common carriers at 1.544 Mb/s.

DSI   Digital speech interpolation unit. Interface unit between satellite system and terrestrial system which makes the most efficient use of the satellite capacity. DSI takes advantage of the intermittent nature of speech by assigning satellite channels only to active voice channels.

DSU   See Data Service Unit.

DTE   Data terminal equipment. (1) The equipment comprising the data source, the data sink, or both. (2) Equipment usually comprising the following functional units: control logic, buffer store, and one or more input or output devices or computers. It may also contain error-control, synchronization, and station-identification capability.

DTL   See Diode-Transistor Logic.

DTWX   Dial teletypewriter exchange. Is used to describe the dial mechanization of the teletypewriter exchange service.

Dwell   The usually adjustable time length of an output pulse that is independent of input signal duration. Pertains to a pulsed logic amplifier output, either immediate or delayed.

EBCDIC   Extended binary-coded decimal interchange code. An 8-bit character code used primarily in IBM equipment. The code provides for 256 different patterns.

Echo   A wave which has been reflected or otherwise returned with sufficient magnitude and delay for it to be perceptible in some manner as a wave distinct from that directly transmitted.

Echoplexing   A checking system; characters received at a central processor are echoed back to the terminal which originated them, and this terminal prints the received echo so the operator may check for any errors.

ECS   European Communications System.

Eddy Currents   Those currents induced in the body of a conducting mass or coil by a rate of change in magnetic flux.

EDIF   Electronic data interchange format.

EDP   Electronic data processing.

Efficiency, Quantum   See Quantum Efficiency.

EIA   Electronic Industries Association. An association in the United States providing standards, including those for interfaces designed for use between manufacturers and purchasers of electronic products.

Electronic Mail   Delivery of messages from sender to receiver in some visual or digital form via electronic means.

ELF   Extremely low frequency; 30 to 300 Hz megametric waves.

Elliptical Orbit   A closed satellite orbit in which the distance between the centers of mass of the satellite and of the primary is not constant.

Emulate   To imitate a computer system by a combination of hardware and software that allows programs written for one computer to be run on another (compare with Simulator).

Encode   Conversion of a character into its equivalent combination of bits. Also called encrypt.

ENQ   Enquiry. Used as a request for response to obtain identification and/or an indication of station status. In binary synchronous communication (BSC) ENQ is transmitted as part of an initialization sequence in point-to-point operation and as the final character of a selection or polling sequence in multipoint operation.

EOA   End of address.

EOC   End-of-conversion signal.

EOM   End of message.

EOT   End of transmission. Indicates the end of a transmission, which may include one or more messages, and resets all stations on the line to the control mode.

EPROM   Erasable programmable read-only memory. A PROM that can be erased and reused indefinitely. Most EPROMs are erased under ultraviolet light and can be recognized by the clear cover over the silicon chip.

Equalization   The process of correcting a channel for its transmission deficiencies.

Equatorial Orbit   A satellite orbit whose plane coincides with that of the equator of the primary body.

EROS   Emitter-receiver for optical systems. Diode that can serve either as a transmitting LED source or as a receiving photodiode.

Error   Any discrepancy between a computed, observed, recorded, or measured quantity and the true, specified, or theoretically correct value or condition.

Error Control   An arrangement which detects the presence of errors. In some systems, error correction or recovery circuits are included.

ESS   Electronic switching system. The common-carrier communications switching system which uses solid-state devices and other computer-type equipment and principles.

Ethernet   Xerox's baseband local network.

ETS   Electronic tandem switching.

ETX   End of text. Indicates the end of text. If multiple transmission blocks are contained in a message in BSC, ETX terminates the last block of the message. The block check character is sent immediately following ETX. ETX requires a reply indicating the receiving station's status.

Eutelsat   European Telecommunications Satellite Organization.

Exchange   A unit established by a communications common carrier for the administration of communication service in a specified area which usually embraces a city, town, or village and its environs. It consists of one or more central offices together with the associated equipment used in furnishing communication service.

Execute Time   The time required to interpret a machine instruction and perform the indicated operation on the operand. Critical for evaluation purpose.

Execution   The performance of a specific operation such as would be accomplished through processing one instruction, a series of instructions, or a complete program.

Expandor   A transducer which for a given amplitude range or input voltages produces a larger range of output voltages.

Facsimile (FAX)   A system for the transmission of images. The image is scanned at the transmitter, reconstructed at the receiver, and duplicated on some form of paper.

Fading   The fluctuating in intensity of any or all components of a received radio signal due to changes in the characteristics of the propagation path.

Fast Fourier Transform   A method of efficiently calculating the Fourier transform of a signal.

FCC   Federal Communications Commission. A board of seven commissioners, appointed by the President under the Communication Act of 1934, having the power to regulate all interstate and foreign electrical communication systems originated in the United States.

FDM   Frequency-division multiplex.

FDMA   Frequency-division multiple access. A type of satellite operation.

FDX   Full-duplex.

FEC   Forward error correcting. Used to describe equipment that corrects transmission errors at a receiver. The technique provides additional information with the original bit stream so that if an error is detected, the receiver can create the correct information without a retransmission.

FED STD   Federal Government Standards (United States).

FED STD 1001   High-Speed Synchronous Signaling Rates between Data Terminal Equipment and Data Circuit–Terminating Equipment

FED STD 1002   Time and Frequency Reference Information

FED STD 1003   Bit-Oriented Data-Link Control Procedures

FED STD 1005   2400 BPS Modem

FED STD 1006   4800 BPS Modem

FED STD 1010   ASCII Bit Sequencing for Serial-by-Bit Transmission

FED STD 1011   Character Structure for Serial-by-Bit ASCII Transmission

FED STD 1012   Character Structure for Parallel-by-Bit ASCII Transmission

FED STD 1013   Data Terminal Equipment to Data Circuit–Terminating Equipment Synchronous Signaling Rates using 4-kHz Circuits

FED STD 1020   Electrical Characteristics of Unbalanced Voltage Digital Interface Circuits

FED STD 1030   Electrical Characteristics of Balanced Voltage Digital Interface Circuits

Feedback   The signal or data fed back to the PC from a controlled machine or process to denote its response to the command signal.

FET   Field-effect transistor. A transistor whose internal operation is unipolar in nature and widely used in integrated circuits due to small geometries, low power dissipation, ease of manufacture, and low cost.

FIFO (First In First Out) Buffer or Shift Register   A shift register with an additional control section that permits input data to "fall through" to the first vacant stage so that if there are any data contained, they are available at the output even though all the stages are not filled. In effect, it is a variable-length shift register whose length is always the same as the data stored therein.

Filter, Bandpass   A wave filter that blocks all frequencies outside a designated bandwidth but does not inhibit those frequencies within the bandwidth.

Firmware   A program placed into ROM.

Flag   (1) Any of various types of indicators used for identification. (2) A character that signals the occurrence of some condition, such as the end of a word.

Flip-Flop   A bistable device capable of assuming either of two stable states and of storing one bit (either 1 or 0) of information. Often used to establish parity.

Floating Ground   A reference point or voltage in a circuit that is not tied to an actual external ground.

Flowchart   A graphical representation for the definition, analysis, or solution of a problem. Symbols are used to represent a process or sequence of decisions and events.

Formatted Display   Standardized data arrangement to make data entry faster and more organized.

FORTRAN-Formula Translator   The language for a scientific procedural programming system.

FORTH   An extendable, stack-oriented, threaded language developed for data acquisition and radio-telescope orientation at an astronomical observatory. All system software except a kernel of low-level routines is written in FORTH.

Forward Channel   A data transmission channel in which the direction of transmission coincides with that in which information is being transferred.

Forward Error Correcting   See FEC.

Fourier Transform   A mathematical operation which decomposes a time-varying signal into its complex frequency components (amplitude and phase or real and imaginary components).

Frame   A set of consecutive time slots in which the position of each digit time slot can be identified by reference to a frame-alignment signal. The frame-alignment signal does not necessarily occur in whole or in part in each frame.

Frame Alignment   The state in which the frame of the receiving equipment is correctly phased with respect to that of the received signal.

Frame Check Sequence   An encoded value appended to each frame by the data link layer to allow detection of transmission errors in the physical channel.

Front-End Processor (FEP)   A communications computer associated with a host computer. It may perform line control, message handling, code conversion, error control, and applications functions such as control and operation of special-purpose terminals.

FSK   Frequency-shift keying.

FX   Foreign exchange.

Gate   (1) A device having one output channel and one or more input channels such that the ouput-channel state is completely determined by the input-channel states, except during switching transients. (2) A combinational logic element having at least one input channel.

Geostationary Satellite   A stationary satellite having the earth as its primary body.

Geosynchronous Satellite   A satellite that travels around the earth in exactly the earth's rotation time.

Graded-Index Fiber   A fiber whose index of refraction decreases radially from the center of the core; offers wideband capability with moderate coupling efficiency.

Graphic   A written or printed letter or symbol.

Ground   A conducting path, intentional or accidental, between an electric circuit or equipment and the earth or some large conducting body serving in place of the earth (a voltage reference).

Ground, Logic   A level that is used as a reference for digital signals in a system. Not necessarily at the same potential as earth or safety ground.

Handshaking   Exchange of predetermined signals when a connection is established between two data-set devices.

Hard Copy   A printed copy of a machine output.

Hardware   The physical equipment or devices forming a computer and peripheral equipment. Contrast with Software.

Hard-Wired   Interconnected by electric wiring.

Harmonic   A sinusoidal component of a periodic wave, having a frequency that is an integral multiple of the fundamental frequency.

HDLC   High-level data-link control. ISO version of bit-oriented data-link control. Functionally identical to ADCCP.

HDX   Half-duplex.

Header   The control information prefixed in a message text, e.g., source or destination code, priority or message type. Also called heading or leader.

HEMT   High-electron-mobility transistor.

Hertz   A unit of frequency equal to one cycle per second; abbreviated Hz.

Hexadecimal Number System   The number system with the base of 16. In hexadecimal notation the first ten values are represented by the digits 0 through 9 and the last six by the letters A through F. Each hex number represents a 4-bit binary number.

Hit, Line   An electric interference of very short duration causing the introduction of unwanted signals on a circuit. Also called a spike.

Holding Time   The length of time a communication channel is in use for each transmission. Includes both message time and operating time.

Hollerith Code   A widely used code for representing alphanumeric data on punched cards, named after Herman Hollerith, the originator of punched-card tabulating. Each card column holds one character, and each decimal digit, letter, and special character is represented by one, two, or three holes punched into designated row positions of the column.

Holography   The optical recording of an object wave that is formed by the interference pattern of two mutually coherent component light beams; produces a three-dimensional image of the object. By moving the head up and down and from side to side, a viewer can look around the object. This means that the light arriving from the hologram into the viewer's eyes is physically the same as light emitted from the original object.

Homodyne Detection   A system of detection using a locally generated carrier.

Host Computer   A computer attached to a network providing primary services such as computation, data-base access or special programs, or programming languages.

Hybrid Circuit   Any circuit made using a combination of the following component-manufacturing technologies: monolithic IC, thin-film, and discrete-component.

Hybrid Coil   A single transformer, having effectively three windings, that is designed to be connected to four branches of a circuit to render these branches conjugate in pairs.

IC   Integrated circuit. An interconnected array of active and passive elements integrated within a single semiconductor substrate or other compatible material and capable of performing one complete electronic circuit function.

IGES   Initial graphic exchange specification.

Impulse Noise   A noise characterized by nonoverlapping transient disturbances.

Incandescent Lamp   See Lamp, Incandescent.

Inclined Orbit   A satellite orbit which is neither equatorial nor polar.

Index of Refraction   The ratio of the velocity of light in a vacuum to the velocity of light in a specified medium. Also known as refractive index.

Information Bit   A bit which is generated by the data source and not used for error control by the transmission system.

Infrared   The electromagnetic-wavelength region between approximately 0.75 and 1000 μm. For fiber-optic transmission the near-infrared region between 0.75 and 1.3 μm is the most relevant because glass, light sources, and detector techniques are most nearly matched in this wavelength region.

Injection Laser Diode   A semiconductor device in which lasing takes place within the *pn* junction. Light is emitted from the diode edge.

Input   (1) Data to be processed. (2) The device or devices used to bring data into another device. (3) The process of transferring data from an internal or local device; can be automatic or manual. (4) Paper tape, punched cards, or the media containing data to be transferred to a distant location.

Insertion Loss   A loss inserted by an equipment between the connection points in series.

Instruction   A group of bits that defines a computer operation.

Integrated Digital Network   A network in which connections established by digital switching are used for the transmission of digital signals.

Intelligent Terminal   A programmable remote terminal with processing capability. This requires memory and logic capability. For example, an intelligent CRT terminal features insertion or deletion of lines and individual characters to occur in the remote terminal; equipped with extended capabilities of a smart terminal. See also Smart Terminal.

Intelsat   International Telecommunications Satellite Consortium. The international consortium formed in August 1964, which through an intergovernmental agreement and an operating agreement established the interim arrangements for the initial global commercial communications satellite system.

Interactive System   A system in which it is possible for the human user or the device serviced by the computer to communicate directly with the operating program. For human users, this arrangement is termed a conversational system. The opposite is a noninteractive system.

Interface   A common boundary between automatic data processing systems or parts of a single system. In communications and data systems, may involve code, format, speed, or other changes as required.

Interface Circuit   A circuit that links one type of device with another. Its function is to produce the required current and voltage levels for the next stage of circuitry from the previous stage.

Interframe Spacing   An enforced idle time between transmission of successive frames to allow receiving data link controllers and the physical channel to recover.

Interleave   (1) To send blocks of data alternately to two or more stations on a multipoint system. (2) To put bits or characters alternately into the time slots in a TDM. (3) In a computer, to insert segments of one program into another program so that they can be executed simultaneously.

Intermodulation   The modulation of the components of a complex wave by each other, as a result of which waves are produced that have frequencies equal to the sums and differences of integral multiples of those of the components of the original complex wave.

Inverse Fourier Transform   A mathematical operation which synthesizes a time-domain signal from its complex spectrum components. If a time-domain signal is Fourier-transformed and then inverse-Fourier-transformed, the original time function is reconstructed.

Inverter   (1) A circuit that takes in a positive pulse and puts out a negative one, or vice versa. (2) A circuit that changes DC into AC.

IS   International standard.

ISDN   Integrated services digital network. End-to-end digital network where services and other networks are plugged into the central office time-division digital switch. With ISDN all data (such as voice, video, facsimile, and keyboard) will be digital and can flow through the same two-wire (192 kb/s) or four-wire (2048 kb/s) local loops and the same central office digital switch. The signaling for all of the communication channels flows separately through a high-speed secure packet-switching network (CCITT Signaling System No. 7). ISDN's packet-switching network will interwork with the analog telephony network via analog/digital converters and out-of-band signaling to in-band tone conversion.

ISO   International Standards Organization. ANSI reports to the ISO.

Isochronous   A signal is isochronous if the time interval separating any two significant instants is theoretically equal to the unit interval or to a multiple of the unit interval.

Isochronous Distortion   For synchronous signaling, the ratio of the unit interval to the maximum measured difference between the actual and theoretical significant instants. The isochronous distortion is then the peak-to-peak phase jitter of the data signal expressed as a percentage of the unit interval.

Isochronous Transmission   Is a combination of both synchronous and asynchronous transmission. The data are clocked by a common timing base, and bytes are also framed with start-stop bits.

ITB   Intermediate text block. In binary synchronous communications, a control character used to terminate an intermediate block of characters. The block-check character is sent immediately following the ITB, but no line turnaround occurs. The response following ETB or ETX also applies to all the ITB checks immediately preceding the block terminated by ETB or ETX.

ITU   International Telecommunication Union. The telecommunications agency of the United Nations, established to provide standardized communications procedures and practices including frequency allocation and radio regulations on a worldwide basis.

Jam   An encoded bit sequence used for collision enforcement in LANs.

Jitter   Short-term variations of the significant instants of a digital signal from their ideal position in time.

K   A shorthand notation meaning 1024 bits, bytes, or words of digital data. A 64K memory, for example, contains 65,536 bits.

Keyboard Entry   (1) An element of information inserted manually, usually via a set of switches or marked punch levers called keys, into an automatic data processing system. (2) A medium as in (1) above for achieving access to or entrance into an automatic data processing system.

Keypunch   A keyboard-operated device that punches holes in a card to represent data.

KSR   Keyboard send and receive. A teletypewriter equipped with keyboard and printer but with no tape-handling capabilities.

Lambertian Emitter   An optical source which has a radiance distribution that is uniform in all directions of observation.

Lamp, Incandescent   A device in which an electrical current is passed through a resistance-wire filament (usually tungsten) to heat it to incandescence.

LANCE   LAN controller for Ethernet.

Language   A set of symbols and rules for representing and communicating information (data) among people or between people and machines.

LAPB   Link-access procedure, balanced. Point-to-point subset of HDLC for packet switching.

Laser   Acronym of light amplification by stimulated emission of radiation. A laser is a cavity, with plane or spherical mirrors at the ends, that is filled with lasable material. This is any material, crystal, glass, liquid, dye, or gas, the atoms of which are capable of being excited to a semistable state by light or electric discharge. The light emitted by an atom as it drops back to the ground state releases light from other nearby excited atoms, the light being thus continually increased in intensity as it oscillates between the mirrors. If one mirror is made to transmit 1 or 2 percent of the light, a brilliant beam of highly monochromatic, coherent radiation is emitted through the mirror. With concave mirrors the beam appears to emerge from a point source near one end of the cavity.

LATA   Local access and transport area (LAN).

Latch   To lock into a certain location or state.

Leakage Current   An undesirable small value of current that flows through or across the surface of an insulator, dielectric of a capacitor, or a reverse-biased *pn* junction.

Least Significant Digit   That occupying the extreme right-hand position in a number of words.

LED   Light-emitting diode. A solid light source that emits visible light or invisible infrared radiation.

Level   The apparent signal amplitude as indicated on a standard measuring scale.

Line Printer   A high-speed printing device that prints an entire line at one time.

Linear Circuit   A circuit whose output is a continuous amplified version of its input. That is, the output is a predetermined variation of its input.

Linear Predictive Coding (LPC)   A method that encodes the parameters of mathematical model describing the shape of the vocal tract at fixed analysis intervals. This provides satisfactory reconstructed speech quality at a moderate bit rate of 0.8 to 3 kb/s. LPC speech is characterized by an overriding buzzing sound and has diffficulties with the voices of women and children.

Link, Communication   (1) The means of connecting one location to another for the purpose of transmitting and receiving information. (2) A channel or circuit intended to connect other channels or circuits.

LISP   Computer language in which data and programs are represented as list structures using Church's lambda calculus, extended with a variety of program and data structures to a general-purpose language. Used widely in artificial intelligence research, symbolic mathematics, and computing theory.

Listener Echo   Echo which reaches the ear of the listener.

Load   (1) To put data into a register or storage. (2) To put a magnetic tape onto a tape drive, or to put cards into a card reader. (3) The electric power consumed by devices connected to an electric generating system.

Local-Area Network (LAN)   A high-data-rate communications network that covers a limited geographical area and allows a number of independent services to communicate with each other.

Logic   (1) The systematic scheme that defines the interactions of signals in the design of an automatic data processing system. (2) The basic principles and application of truth tables and interconnection between logical elements required for arithmetic computation in an automatic data processing system.

Logic Level   The voltage magnitude associated with signal pulses representing 1 and 0 in binary computation.

Loop, Local   That part of a communication circuit between the customer's premises and the central office (either two-wire or four-wire).

LRC   Longitudinal redundancy check. A system of error control based on the formation of a block check following preset rules. The check-formation rule is applied in the same manner to each character. In a simple case, the LRC is created by forming a parity check on each position of all the characters in the block. (For example, the first bit of the LRC character creates odd parity among the 1-bit positions of the characters in the block.)

LSI   Large-scale integration. The accumulation of a large number of circuits (say, 500 or more) on a single chip of a semiconductor. Characteristic of many CPU circuits and memories introduced since 1970.

Magnitude   The absolute value, independent of positive or negative signs.

MAN Multiple-area network. Links multiple networks and multiple locations.

Manchester Encoding A means by which separate data and clock signals can be combined into a single, self-synchronizable data stream, suitable for transmission on a serial channel.

Mark-Hold The normal no-traffic line condition whereby a steady mark is transmitted. This is a strap selectable option in most DCE and DTEs. Compare with Space-Hold.

Master Clock A clock which generates accurate timing signals for the control of other clocks and possibly other equipments.

Master Station A unit having control of all other terminals on a multipoint circuit for purposes of polling and/or selection.

Material Dispersion The spreading of a light pulse caused by the different delays imposed on different wavelengths by the fiber material.

Matrix A two-dimensional array of circuit elements, such as wires, diodes, etc., which can transform a digital code from one type to another.

Medium-Scale Integration (MSI) The accumulation of several circuits (usually less than 100) on a single chip of semiconductor.

MEDLARS Medical literature analysis and retrieval system.

Memory The capacity of a machine to store information subject to recall, or the component of the computer system in which such information is stored.

Memory Capacity The number of bits that a memory can hold; a 1-kb semiconductor memory can store 1000 bits (actually 1024 bits).

Message (1) Group of words, variable in length, transported as a unit. (2) A transported item of information.

Message Switching The technique of receiving a message, storing it until the proper outgoing line is available, and then retransmitting it. No direct connection between the incoming and outgoing lines is set up as in line switching.

MFLOPS Millions of floating-point operations per second.

Microcomputer A class of computer having all major central processor functions contained on a single printed circuit board constituting a stand-alone module. Generally refers to microprocessor systems including memory and I/O circuits.

Microprocessor A single LSI circuit that performs the functions of a CPU. Some characteristics of a microprocessor include small size, inclusion of a single integrated circuit or a set of integrated circuits, and low cost.

Microscope A device that focuses, magnifies, and if necessary converts into visible radiation the image produced by the refraction, reflection, or diffraction of a beam of incident energy by a specimen.

Microscope, Electron A device utilizing an electron beam for the observation and recording of submicroscopic samples with the aid of photographic emulsions or other short-wavelength sensors. With the electron microscope the maximum useful magnification is over 3,000,000.

Microwave   Any electromagnetic wave in the radio-frequency spectrum above 890 MHz.

MIMD   Multiple-instruction multiple-data.

Minicomputer   A class of small mainframe-type digital process control computers sized generally around a 16-bit word, with stored programs and various memory options for data acquisition and monitoring, supervisory, or direct digital control in systems having no more than 20 or 30 control loops.

MIS   Management information system. A communication process in which data are collected, recorded, processed, and distributed for operational purposes.

MISD   Multiple-instruction single-data.

MISO   Master-in slave-out pin.

MLS   Modulated light source. A photoelectric control that operates on modulated infrared radiation and responds to modulating frequency rather than to light intensity.

MML   Man-machine language; also called CCITT-MML. Can be used to facilitate operation and maintenance functions of SPC switching systems of different types. Refer to CCITT Recs. Z.311–318.

Mnemonic Code   Instructions for a computer written in a form that is easy for the programmer to remember. A program written in mnemonic code must later be converted to machine language.

MOCVD   Metal-organic chemical vapor deposition.

Modal Dispersion   The spreading of a light pulse caused by the differences in optical path lengths in a multimode fiber.

Mode   A condition or method of operation.

Modem   A contraction of modulator-demodulator. A data set that both transmits and receives data and control and clock signals; utilizes modulation-demodulation process.

Modem, Null   A device that will allow two pieces of data equipment configured as either data terminals or data sets to communicate with each other.

Module   An interchangeable "plug-in" item containing electronic components which may be combined with other interchangeable items to form a complete unit.

Monitor   (1) A device that observes and verifies the operations of a data processing system and indicates any significant departure from the norm. (2) Software or hardware that observes, supervises controls, or verifies the operations of a system.

Monolithic   Single silicon substrate in which an integrated circuit is constructed.

MOS Metal-oxide semiconductor. A class of insulated-gate field-effect transistors (FETs). The gate is insulated from semiconductor substrate material by using an oxide (or nitride) dielectric to form a unipolar device.

MOSFET Metal-oxide semiconductor field-effect transistor.

MOSI Master-out slave-in port.

Most Significant Digit That occupying the extreme left-hand position in a number of words; it contributes the greatest value to the number.

MOV Metal-oxide varistor. A device also used for protection of solid-state circuits from transients.

MSI See Medium-Scale Integration.

MTBF Mean time before failure. The average time that a system is operational before a failure occurs.

MTBR Mean time before repair. The average time required to repair a system failure.

Muldem Multiplexer-modulator/demodulator-demultiplexer.

Multicast An addressing mode in which a given frame is targeted to a group of logically related stations.

Multidrop Line Line or circuit interconnecting several stations; also called a multipoint line.

Multimode Fiber A fiber that supports the propagation of more than one mode of a given wavelength.

Multiplex The process of transmitting multiple signals from different sources over a common cable or transmission line.

MUMPS A text-oriented language with built-in data-base facilities and string and pattern matching. Used in hospitals and other large organizations for unified accounting.

Mutually Synchronized Network Each synchronizing clock in the network exerts a degree of control on all others.

N.A. Numerical aperture. Measure of light acceptance of a fiber cable.

Narrow-Band Channel Sub-voice-grade channel characterized by a speed range of 100 to 200 b/s.

NEP Noise equivalent power. Figure of merit, defines the minimum incident power required to generate a photocurrent equal to the total photodiode noise current.

Neutral Transmission Method of transmitting teletypewriter signals whereby a mark is represented by current on the line and a space is represented by the absence of current.

Newton The unit of force in the MKS (meter-kilogram-second) system, equal to the force which will impart an acceleration of 1 meter/second^2 to a 1-kilogram mass. Symbolized N. Formerly known as large dyne.

Node   (1) Also called junction point, branch point, or vertex. A terminal of any branch of a network, or a terminal common to two or more branches. (2) Also called nodal point. The point, line, or surface in a standing-wave system where some characteristic of the wavefield has essentially zero amplitude. The appropriate modifier should be used with the word *node* to signify the type that is intended (e.g., pressure node). (3) Provide data entry-exit points in computers and terminals and switch or process data. Smart terminals and smart programmable controllers—the ones based on microprocessors—also have true processing capability and qualify as nodes. Each node is potentially capable of performing application-oriented tasks.

Noise   Any condition that interferes with the desired signal to be detected by the control. Commonly understood to be electric noise, it can also be an interfering optical condition caused by ambient light.

Noise, Common-Mode (or Line-to-Ground)   Interference which is present as a common potential between ground and an entire power line.

Noise Current, Photodetector   The total noise current present at the input of the preamplifier.

Noise, Differential-Mode (or Line-to-Line)   Interference which is present as a potential between the individual power lines.

Normally High   A device in which the output is high in voltage in the rest condition.

Normally Low   A device in which the output is low in voltage in the rest condition.

Notation   The act, process, or method of representing facts or quantities by a system or set of marks, signs, figures, or characters.

npn **(transistor)**   A transistor consisting of two n-type regions separated by a p-type region.

NRZ   Nonreturn-to-zero pulse code. Pulses in alternating directions for successive 1 bits; no change from existing bias for 0 bits.

Null Modem   See Modem, Null.

Numerical Aperture   See N.A.

Nyquist's Theorem   See Sampling Theorem.

Octal   Pertaining to a characteristic or property involving a selection choice or condition in which there are eight possibilities.

Off-Line   Describes equipment or devices which are not connected to the communications line.

One-Shot Logic   Output energized when input is signaled and deenergized after dwell time, regardless of input signal duration.

On-Line   Equipment or operations that are in direct contact with other points on a circuit. An on-line teleprocessing system eliminates the need for human intervention between information input at the source and ultimate processing by a computer. Contrast with off-line.

Optical Coupler   A device that couples signals from one electric circuit to another by means of light, usually infrared or visible, as LED and phototransistor.

Optoelectronics   Technology dealing with the coupling of functional electronic blocks by light beams.

Orbit   (1) The path, relative to a specified frame of reference, described by the center of mass of a satellite or other object in space, subjected solely to natural forces, mainly gravitational attraction. (2) By extension, the path described by the center of mass of an object in space subjected to natural forces and occasional low-energy corrective forces exerted by a propulsive device in order to achieve and maintain a desired path.

OSI   Open systems interconnection. Provides the basis for connecting open systems for distributed applications processing. The term *open* denotes the ability of any two systems conforming to the reference model and the associated standards to connect.

OTDR   Optical time-domain reflectometer. Measuring system for characteristics of optical fiber.

Output   The useful energy delivered by a circuit or device.

Overhead Bit   A bit other than an information bit, e.g., a check bit, a framing bit.

PABX   Private automatic branch exchange.

Packet   A group of binary digits including data and call control signals which is switched as a composite whole. The data, call control signals, and possibly error-correction information are arranged in a specific format.

Packet Switching   A data transmission process utilizing addressed packets, whereby a channel is occupied only for the duration of transmission of the packet.

Packing Fraction   The ratio of the active core area of a fiber bundle to the total area at its light-emitting or receiving end.

PAD   Packet assembly-disassembly facility. Applies to exchange of serial data streams with the character-mode terminal and the packetizing-depacketizing of the corresponding data exchanged with the CCITT X.25 terminal.

PAR   The ratio of the peak to average voltage of a received pulse to that of a transmitted pulse.

Parallel Transmission   Method of data transfer in which all bits of a character or byte are transmitted simultaneously.

Parameter   A definable characteristic of an item, device, or system.

Parity Check   Addition of noninformation bits to data, making the number of 1s in a grouping of bits either always even or always odd. This permits detection of bit groupings that contain single errors. It may be applied to characters, blocks, or any convenient bit grouping.

PAR Measurement   An analog measurement to measure the quality of circuits for data transmission. Repetitive pulses sent by transmitter are processed at the receiver to determine how loss and distortion in the system reduces the pulse envelope peak (E_{pk}); the ratio of E_{pk} to full-wave average (E_{FWA}) serves for PAR rating:

$$\text{PAR} = \left(2\,\frac{E_{pk}}{E_{FWA}} - 1\right) \times 100$$

Pascal   A high-level programming language derived from ALGOL and developed intensively by a group at the University of California at San Diego (thus, UCSD pascal). In many ways simpler to use than BASIC, Pascal can be made machine-dependent or transportable. (Named for the French physicist Blaise Pascal.)

Passive Elements   Elements incapable of power gain (resistors, inductors, diodes, etc.).

Passive Satellite   A satellite intended to transmit radiocommunication signals by reflection.

PBX   Private branch exchange.

PC   Programmable controller; also see Personal Computer.

PCM   Pulse-code modulation. A process in which a signal is sampled and the magnitude of each sample with respect to a fixed reference is quantized and converted by coding to a digital signal.

Peak-to-Peak   The amplitude difference between the most positive and the most negative excursions of a signal.

Peripheral Equipment   Units that work in conjunction with a computer but are not part of the computer itself.

Personal Computer (PC)   A self-contained desktop microcomputer intended for one user.

Phase   The position of a point on the waveform of an alternating or other periodic quantity with respect to the start of the cycle, usually expressed in degrees.

Phase Modulation (PM)   A method of transmission whereby the angle of phase of the carrier wave is varied in accordance with the signal.

Phoneme   The set of basic sounds that are used to produce the words in a language. There are 40 to 50 phonemes in English.

Photometry   The science of the measurement of light intensity where "light" refers to the total integrated range or radiation to which the eye is sensitive.

Photon   A quantum of electromagnetic energy carried in small amounts by the energy and moving with the speed of light. Optical photons are photons having energies corresponding to wavelengths between 120 and 1800 nanometers.

Phototransistor   A transistor whose electric output current is proportional to the intensity and wavelength of a beam applied to its input.

Photovoltaic   A device capable of generating a voltage when exposed to visible or other light radiation.

Physical Address   The unique address of a given station on the network.

Physical Channel   The implementation of the physical layer.

Physical Layer   The lower of the two protocol layers of the LAN design, or the lowest level of upper-level network protocols.

Pilot   (1) The language created for computer-aided instruction (CAI); has basic facilities for interactive input and output, pattern matching, and conditional branching. Extended with various data types and structures. (2) In a transmission system, usually a single frequency, transmitted over the system to indicate or control its characteristics.

PL-1   A common programming language that looks and behaves like an extension of FORTRAN but is simpler than FORTRAN.

PM   See Phase Modulation.

Polar   A situation in which a binary 1 is represented by current flow in one direction and a binary 0 by current flow in the opposite direction.

Polling   A process in which a number of peripheral devices, remote stations, or nodes in a computer network are interrogated one at a time to determine if service is required.

Posistor   A thermistor which has a positive temperature coefficient.

Power Spectral Density (PSD) Function   A measure of the power distribution of a signal as a function of frequency. It may be obtained as the square of the magnitude of the Fourier transform of a signal.

Preamble   A sequence of (say 64) encoded bits which the physical layer transmits before each frame to allow synchronization of clocks and other physical layer circuitry at other sites on the channel.

Primary Block   A basic group of PCM channels assembled by time-division multiplexing.

Primary Block A   A basic group of PCM channels derived from 2048 kb/s PCM multiplex equipment.

Primary Block μ   A basic group of PCM channels derived from 1544 kb/s PCM multiplex equipment.

Primary Channel   The data transmission channel having the highest signaling-rate capability of all the channels sharing a common interface connector.

Program   A set of instructions that determines the series of steps to be followed by a computer system or other devices.

PROM   Programmable read-only memory. Type of memory that is not recorded during its fabrication but which requires a physical operation to program it. Some PROMs can be erased and reprogrammed through special physical processes (EPROMs).

Protocol   A formal set of conventions governing the format and relative timing of message exchange between two communicating processes.

PSDN   Packet switched data network.

Pseudorandom Digital Signal   A sequence of blocks, with lengths determined by some defined arithmetic process, that is satisfactorily random by satisfying one or more of the standard statistical tests for randomness. Utilized in transmission test sets.

Psophometer   A noise-measuring set which includes a CCITT weighing network.

PSPDN   Packet-switched public data network.

PTT   Posts, Telegraphs, and Telephones. European government departments responsible for national telecommunications.

Pulse   A momentary sharp change in a current, voltage, or other electric quantity that is normally constant. A pulse is characterized by a rise and fall and has a finite duration.

Pulse Code   A code giving the equivalence between the quantized value of a sample and the corresponding character signal.

Pulse Spreading   The increase in pulse width in a given length of fiber due to the cumulative effect of material and modal dispersion.

Quadbit   Data stream to be transmitted in a 9600 b/s modem is divided into groups of 4 consecutive data bits; each data bit is called a quadbit.

Quadrature Amplitude Modulation (QAM)   A modulation technique used in 7200 and 9600 b/s modems, combining phase- and amplitude-modulation techniques.

Quantizer   A device with a restricted quantity of possible output values that will assimilate any range of input values into its limited range.

Quantizing   A process in which samples are classified into a number of adjacent intervals, each interval being represented by a single value called the quantized value.

Quantizing Distortion   The distortion resulting from the process of quantizing.

Quantizing Noise   Noise introduced when analog signals are encoded into digital form and reconverted into analog form.

Quantum   The smallest amount into which the energy of a wave can be divided. The quantum is proportional to the frequency of the wave. See Photon.

Quantum Efficiency   (1) The ratio of emitted photons to injected electrons of a light source. (2) The ratio of primary photoelectrons generated to photons incident on the detector.

Queue   (1) A waiting line or area. (2) The contents of a waiting line or area.

Radiance   Radiant power per unit source area per unit solid angle, expressed in watts per square meter per steradian ($W/m^2/sr$).

Radio Astronomy   The detection and analysis of naturally formed extraterrestrial electromagnetic radiation within the radio-frequency range of the spectrum.

Radiometry   The science of radiation measurement. It is concerned with the detection and measurement of radiant energy, either at separate wavelengths or integrated over a broad range of wavelengths, and the interactions of radiation with matter, such as absorption, reflection, and emission.

RAM   Random-access memory. A data storage device that can retain and produce on demand any data placed in it.

Random Noise   Thermal noise generated from electron motion within resistive elements of electronic equipment.

Ray   A geometric representation of a light path through an optical device; a line normal to the wavefront indicating the direction of radiant energy flow.

Real Time   (1) Pertaining to the actual time during which a physical process transpires. (2) Pertaining to the performance of a computation during the actual time that the related physical process transpires in order that results of the computations can be used in guiding the physical process.

Redundancy   In a protocol the portion of the total characters or bits that can be eliminated without any loss of information.

Redundancy Check   An automatic or programmed check based on the systematic insertion of components or characters used especially for checking purposes.

Redundant Code   A code using more signal elements than necessary to represent the intrinsic information. For example, a five-unit code using all the characters of International Telegraph Alphabet No. 2 is not redundant; a five-unit code using only the figures in International Telegraph Alphabet No. 2 is redundant; a seven-unit code using only signals made of four space and three mark elements is redundant.

Reference Clock   A clock of high stability and accuracy which is used to govern the frequency of a network of mutually synchronizing clocks of lower stability. Failure of such a clock does not cause loss of synchronism.

Reflection   The phenomenon in which a wave that strikes a medium of different characteristics is returned to the original medium with the angles of incidence and reflection equal and lying in the same plane.

Refraction   The change in direction of propagation of a wavefront due to its passing obliquely from one medium into another in which its speed is different. Refraction may also occur in a single medium of varying characteristics.

Refractive Index   The ratio of light velocity in a vacuum to its velocity in the medium of interest.

Regeneration   The process of recognizing and reconstructing a digital signal so that the amplitude, waveform, and timing are constrained within stated limits.

Register   (1) A device that stores one word of data; often consists of several flip-flops. (2) In switching, the apparatus which receives dialed impulses and controls the subsequent switching apparatus.

Reperforator   A device that automatically punches a paper tape from received signals.

Resistor-Transistor Logic   See RTL.

Resolution   The magnitude of the smallest output step changes (expressed in percentage of full-scale output) as the measurement is continuously varied over the range.

Response Time   The time it takes for a device to respond to an input signal. (Also used for interactive devices.)

Responsivity   (Or sensitivity of a photodiode.) Minimally required input light power needed to achieve a given performance level.

Retrieval, Information   The methods and procedures of recovering specific information from stored data.

Reverse Channel   A channel used for transmission of supervisory or error-control signals. The direction of flow of these signals is in the direction opposite to that in which information is being transferred. The bandwidth of this channel is usually less than that of the forward channel.

RG/U   Radio guide universal. In MIL-C-17, RG is the military designation for coaxial cable, and U stands for general utility.

Ring Network   A computer network where each computer is connected to adjacent computers.

Rise Time   A measure (10 to 90 percent) of the time required for the output voltage to rise from a state of low-voltage level to a high-voltage level once a level change has been started.

ROM   Read-only memory. A device that has data permanently entered into it to be outputted on demand.

Routine   A series of computer instructions that performs a specific, limited task.

RPG-II   A limited and convenient report generator with some arithmetic and file-handling capabilities. Many word processors are more competent at all of its functions. One of the most widely used languages.

RS   Recommended standard (EIA).

RS 232C   Interface between data terminal equipment and data communication equipment employing serial binary data interchange (August 1969).

RS 269B   Synchronous signaling rates for data transmission (January 1976; identical to ANSI X3.1.1976).

RS 334   Signal quality at interface between data processing terminal equipment and synchronous data communication equipment for serial data transmission.

RS 357   Interface between facsimile terminal equipment and voice-frequency data communication terminal equipment (June 1968).

RS 363 Standard for specifying signal quality for transmitting and receiving data processing terminal equipment using serial data transmission at the interface with nonsynchronous data communication equipment (May 1969).

RS 366 Interface between data terminal equipment and automatic calling equipment for data communication (August 1969).

RS 404 Standard for start-stop signal quality betwen data terminal equipment and nonsynchronous data communication equipment (March 1973).

RS 410 Standard for electrical characteristics of Class A closure interchange circuits (April 1974).

RS 422A Electrical characteristics of balanced-voltage digital interface circuits (December 1978).

RS 423A Electrical characteristics of unbalanced-voltage digital interface circuits (December 1978).

RS 449 General-purpose 37-pin-position and 9-pin-position interface for data terminal equipment and data circuit–terminating equipment employing serial binary data interchange (November 1977).

RS 455-5 Standard test procedures for optical fibers and fiber-optic cables, transducers, and connecting and terminating devices (September 1982).

RT Reperforator-transmitter. A teletypewriter unit which perforates received data on a tape and retransmits it; consists of two separate units, reperforator and transmitter.

RTD Resistance-temperature device; a passive transducer based on the principle that the resistance of a pure metal is proportional to its temperature. Thus a small, stable excitation current forced through the RTD produces a voltage which is proportional to the resistance. It is a temperature-sensitive resistor.

RTL Resistor-transistor logic. An early form of semiconductor logic in which the basic circuit element is a resistor-transistor network.

R/W Read-write. A control output of the microprocessor that indicates if data are being transferred from the microprocessor to memory, or vice versa.

RZ Return to zero. Short positive current for 1 bits, negative for 0 bits; return to zero current after every bit.

SADT Structured analysis and design technique.

Sample The value of a particular characteristic of a signal at a chosen instant.

Sampling Rate The number of samples per unit time.

Sampling Theorem (Also known as Shannon's or Nyquist's theorem.) States that a signal is completely described by a sampled version of it, if it is sampled at a rate that is at least twice as great as the highest frequency contained in the signal. This theorem is based on having the input signal data band-limited with no energy contained above the highest frequency. Since this is not possible to implement because of the finite roll-off characteristics of practical filters, it is therefore necessary to sample at more than 2 times the highest frequency of the signal.

Satellite   A body which revolves around another body of preponderant mass and which has a motion primarily and permanently determined by the force of attraction of this body.

SCAN   Examine sequentially part by part.

SCF   Satellite control facility.

Schottky Diode   Schottky diodes are used to eliminate charge storage in the base region of transistors. A substantial portion of the propagation delay in a logic gate results from the stored charge caused by saturation of the transistor; when base input current is interrupted, the transistor continues to conduct until the charge dissipates.

SCK   Serial clock signal.

SCPC   Single channel per carrier. A satellite operation technique where one carrier is assigned to a voice or data channel.

SCR   Silicon controlled rectifier. A three-junction semiconductor device that is normally an open circuit until an appropriate gate signal is applied to the gate terminal, at which time it rapidly switches to the conducting state. Its operation is similar to that of a gas thyratron, which conducts current in one direction only.

Scrambling   A coding technique applied to digital signals that produces a random data pattern. In this way a more nearly constant transmitted power level is maintained which makes receiver timing recovery insensitive to the data pattern.

SDCU   Satellite delay-compensation unit.

SDD-1   A distributed data-base management system developed by Computer Corporation of America. SDD-1 is a system for managing data bases whose storage is distributed over a network of computers. Functionally SDD-1 provides the same capabilities that one expects of any modern data-base management system (DBMS) and users interact with it precisely as if it were not distributed.

SDL   Specification and description language by CCITT; designed to suit the specification and description of logic processes in telecommunication switching systems, but capable of wider application. Refer to CCITT Rec. Z.102–104.

SDLC   Synchronous data-link control. Bit-oriented protocol of IBM.

SDMA   Space-division multiple access. A type of satellite operation.

Secondary Channel   The data transmission channel having a lower signaling rate capability than the primary channel in a system in which two channels share a common interface connector.

Selective Calling   The ability of the transmitting station to specify which of several stations on the same line is to receive a message.

Self-Diagnostic   The hardware and firmware within a controller which allows it to continually monitor its own status and indicate any fault which might occur within it.

Sensitivity (Photodiode)   See Responsivity.

Serial Transmission   A system in which the bits of a character occur serially in time.

Service Digits   Digits which are added, normally at regular time intervals, to a digital signal to enable the equipment associated with that digital signal to function correctly, and possibly to provide ancillary facilities.

Sideband   The frequency band on either the upper or lower side of the carrier frequency within which fall the frequencies produced by the process of modulation.

Signaling   The exchange of electrical information (other than by speech) specifically concerned with the establishment and control of connections and management in a communication network.

Signaling System No. 4, CCITT   A Europe-only system for operator-controlled and full-automatic international services on unidirectional circuits.

Signaling System No. 5, CCITT   One of the most widely used systems. It uses two in-band frequencies for line and supervisory signals (2400 and 2600 Hz).

Signaling System No. 6, CCITT   An international specification for common-channel signaling.

Signaling System No. 7, CCITT   A common-channel signaling system for use between stored-program-controlled exchanges; designed for use in a digital environment.

Signal-to-Noise Ratio (S/N)   Relative power of the signal to the noise in a channel, usually measured in decibels.

Significant Digit   A digit that contributes to the precision of a number. The number of significant digits is counted beginning with the digit contributing the most value, called the *most significant digit*, and ending with the one contributing the least value, called the *least significant digit*.

Significant Instants of a Digital Signal   The instants at which the successive significant conditions recognized by the appropriate device of the modulation or restitution begin. Each of the instants is determined as soon as the appropriate device takes up the significant condition usable for a recording or a processing.

SIMD   Single-instruction, multiple-data.

Simulator   Software simulator used in the debugging process to simulate the execution of machine language programs using another computer (often a time-sharing system). Simulators are especially useful if the actual computer is not available.

Singing Point   A point that could be made to "sing" by slightly increasing the gain of some four-wire or two-wire portion of a circuit.

Single-Mode Fiber   A fiber that permits only one mode to propagate.

Sink   (1) A device which drains off energy from a system. (2) A place where energy from several sources is collected or drained away. (3) Anything into which power of some kind is dissipated. (4) The component or network into which energy (usually current) flows.

SIP   Single in-line package. A package of electronic components that is suited for automated assembly into printed-circuit boards. The SIP is characterized by a single row of external connecting terminals or pins which are inserted into the holes of the printed-circuit board.

Skew   Refers to time delay or offset between any two signals in relation to each other.

Slew Rate   Voltage-changing speed of a digital signal; expressed in volts per microsecond.

SLICE   Source language in-circuit emulator. A language that can switch directly from assembly code to a higher-level language and back without restarting the program and disturbing the user's software.

Smart Terminal   A terminal equipped with capabilities to edit and store data. However, capabilities are limited in comparison to an intelligent terminal. See also Intelligent Terminal.

SMDR   Station message detail recording.

SNA   System network architecture. IBM's formal definition of its data communications networking philosophy.

SNOS   Silicon-nitride-oxide-semiconductor.

Soft Copy   Report appearing on a medium that is not permanent.

Software   All programs and routines used to extend the capabilities of computers. If a particular bit of data manipulation is done through a program rather than by special circuitry, it is said to be in software. Doing things in software is cheap and flexible, since a program can be easily changed. Contrast with Hardware.

SOH   Start of header. A communication control character used at the beginning of a sequence of characters which constitute a machine-sensible address or routine information. Such a sequence is referred to as the heading.

Solid-State Devices (Semiconductors)   Electronic components that control electron flow through solid materials such as crystals, e.g., transistors, diodes, integrated circuits.

Solid-State Switch   A no-contact switch that completes a circuit by means of solid-state components.

Spacecraft   A vehicle which is intended to go beyond the major part of the earth's atmosphere.

Space-Hold   The normal no-traffic condition whereby a steady space is transmitted. Compare with Mark-Hold.

SPADE   Single channel per carrier pulse-code modulation multiple-access demand-assigned equipment. SPADE permits use of the satellite system on an occasional as-needed basis.

Spectroradiometry   The science of measuring the radiant energy from a source throughout the spectrum. An energy receiver such as a thermocouple or photomultiplier is employed for detection.

Spectrum   A continuous range of frequencies, usually wide in extent, within which waves have some specific common characteristic.

Spectrum Analysis   Generally used to refer to the process in determining the magnitude of frequency components of a signal, i.e., magnitude of the Fourier transform.

SPI   Serial peripheral interference.

SSR   Solid-state relay; an electronic switching device utilizing solid-state techniques and performing essentially the same switching functions as an electromechanical relay.

Standby Facilities   Facilities furnished for use as replacement in the event of failure or faulty operation of normally used facilities.

Start Element   In start-stop transmission, the first element in each character, which serves to prepare the receiving equipment for the reception and registration of the character.

Start-Stop Transmission   Asynchronous transmission in which a group of code elements corresponding to a character signal is preceded by a start element and followed by a stop element.

Station   (1) One of the input or output points of a communication system. (2) A single addressable site on LAN, generally implemented as a computer and appropriate peripherals.

Stationary Satellite   A synchronous satellite with an equatorial, circular, and direct orbit. A stationary satellite remains fixed in relation to the surface of the primary body.

Status   Information pertaining to the current state of a device.

STD   Subscriber trunk dialing. European version of direct distance dialing.

Step-by-Step Switch   A switch that moves in synchronism with a pulse device such as a rotary telephone dial. Each digit dialed causes the movement of successive selector switches to carry the connection forward until the desired line is reached.

Step-Index Fiber   A fiber whose index of refraction changes sharply at the interface of its core and cladding. The core material has a high uniform refractive index, while the cladding material's is low.

Stop Element   In start-stop transmission, the last element in each character to which is assigned a minimum duration, during which the receiving equipment is returned to its rest condition in preparation for the reception of the next character.

Storage   A device to which data can be transferred and from which they can be obtained at a later time.

Stunt Box   A device to recognize line control characters.

STX   Start of text. A communication control character which precedes a sequence of characters that is to be treated as an entity and entirely transmitted through to the ultimate destination. Such a sequence is referred to as text. STX may be used to terminate a sequence of characters (heading) started by SOH.

Substrate   The supporting material upon or within which an integrated circuit is attached.

Supergroup   A group of 60 voice-grade channels (five 12-channel groups) with a bandwidth of 240 kHz.

Supervisory Signals   Signals used to indicate various operating states of circuit combinations.

Suppressed Carrier Transmission   Method of communication in which the carrier frequency is suppressed either partially or to the level permissible. One or both of the sidebands may be transmitted.

SWIFT   Society for World Interbank Financial Telecommunications.

Switched Line   A communication link for which the physical path may vary with each usage, e.g., the dial-up telephone network.

Switching, Packet   See Packet Switching.

Switchover   To switch to an alternate component when a failure occurs in the equipment.

Synchronous   Two signals are synchronous if their corresponding significant instants have a desired phase relationship.

Synchronous Idle (SYN) Character   Character used as a character fill in the absence of any data to maintain synchronization.

Synchronous Network   A network in which the clocks are controlled to run at identical rates or at the same mean rate with limited relative phase displacement.

Synchronous Satellite   A satellite for which the mean sidereal period of revolution is equal to the sidereal period of rotation of the primary body about its own axis. (The sidereal period of rotation of the earth is about 23 h, 56 min.)

Synthesis   Construction of speech waveforms by combining the fundamental speech sounds (phonemes and allophones). It produces aesthetically unpleasing "robot" speech, but has a low bit rate—80 to 200 b/s. Synthesis is flexible because any word in the language can be constructed.

Synthesizer   A device that can generate a number of crystal-controlled frequencies for multichannel communications equipment.

System   A collection of units combined to work as a larger integrated unit having the capabilities of all the separate units.

Tariff   The published rate for a specific unit of equipment, facility, or type of service provided by a communications common carrier.

TASI   Time assignment speech interpolation. A system to utilize idle voice-transmission periods; switching equipment connects party to an idle channel and disconnects when speech stops.

TCM   Trellis code modulation.

TD   Transmitter-distributer. Paper tape transmitter of a teletypewriter terminal.

TDM   Time-division multiplex. A means of multiplexing channels over a single path by time-dividing the path into a number of time slots and assigning each channel its own slot.

TDMA   Time-division multiple access. Communication devices at different geographical locations share a multipoint or broadcast channel by means of a technique which allocates different time slots to different users in a satellite system.

Telecommunications   The transmission of information over a distance, usually by electrical means.

Telemetry   (1) The science of sensing and measuring information at some remote location and transmitting the data to a convenient location to be read and recorded. (2) The transmission of measurements obtained by automatic sensors and the like over the communications channels. (3) The practice of transmitting and receiving the measurement of a variable for readout or other uses. The term is most commonly applied to electric signal systems.

Teletex   Supertelex service. Terminals provide high-quality output (typically with multiple character sets), permit simultaneous preparation and receipt, and offer transmission rates up to 300 characters per second.

Teletype   Trademark of AT&T, usually referring to a series of different types of teleprinter equipment such as tape punches, reperforators, page printers, etc., utilized for communication systems.

Television   The electronic transmission and presentation of pictures and sounds.

Telex Service   A dial-up telegraph service enabling its subscribers to communicate directly and temporarily among themselves by means of start-stop apparatus and of circuits of the public telegraph network. The service operates worldwide. Baudot equipment is used. Computers can be connected to the Telex network.

Terminal   (1) A point in a system or communication network at which data can either enter or leave. (2) An input-output device capable of transmitting entries to and obtaining output from the system of which it is a part.

Termination   (1) The load connected to the output end of a transmission line. (2) The provisions for ending a transmission line and connecting to a busbar or other terminating device.

Text   (1) A sequence of characters forming part of a transmission which is sent from the data source to the data sink, and which contains the information to be conveyed. It may be preceded by a header and followed by an end-of-text signal. (2) In general communications usage, a sequence of characters treated as an entity if preceded by a start-of-text and followed by an end-of-text control character.

Thermal Noise (1) Random circuit noise associated with the thermodynamic interchange of energy necessary to maintain thermal equilibrium between the circuit and its surroundings (also called resistance noise). (2) Noise generated by the random thermal motion of charged particles.

Thermistor A passive transducerlike RTD that requires an excitation voltage or current, which should be kept to a minimum to prevent self-heating. Unlike RTDs, thermistor resistance changes exponentially with temperature.

Thermocouple A device that converts thermal energy directly into an electrical voltage when a temperature gradient exists between the two end junctions of a pair of dissimilar metal wires. It is a kind of transducer.

Thick Film A method of manufacturing hybrid circuits by screen deposition of conductive, resistive, or insulating films thicker than 0.01 in (0.25 mm).

Thin Film A method of manufacturing hybrid circuits in which evaporation or sputtering techniques are used to deposit very thin films of material onto a substrate.

Threshold The signal level at which a change in logical state is encountered in a circuit, such as 1 to 0 or a 0 to undefined transition.

Throughput (1) The rate at which information can be accurately delivered when averaged over a long period of time. (2) The time required to perform an operation from the time it begins until the time it is successfully completed.

Thyristors A family of semiconductor switching devices of which the silicon controlled rectifier (SCR) and the triac are the most commonly used. Thyristors are fabricated from four alternate layers of positive (p) and negative (n) semiconductor material.

Tie Line A private-line communications channel of the type provided by communications common carriers for linking two or more points together.

Time-Derived Channel Any of the channels obtained from multiplexing a channel by time division.

Time-Sharing A specific method of operation in which a computer facility is shared by several users for different purposes at the same time. Although the computer actually services each user in sequence, the high speed of the computer makes it appear that the users are all handled simultaneously.

Time Slot Any cyclic time interval which can be recognized and defined uniquely.

Timing Signal A cyclic signal used to control the timing of operations.

TLP Transmission Level Point. A reference level point on a voice-band circuit numerically equal to the algebraic sum of gains and losses at 1000 Hz (800 Hz CCITT) from a reference point (0TLP) to the point of measurement.

Toll Center Basic toll-switching entity; a central office where channels and toll-message circuits terminate.

Train Time The period required to equalize the line and recover timing from the received data on synchronous modems. This time is often referred to as RTS/CTS delay or poll response.

Transceiver   A terminal that can transmit and receive traffic.

Transducer   An energy converter that converts one form of energy to another. The energy may be in any form, such as electric, mechanical, acoustical, etc. This term is often restricted to a device in which the magnitude of an applied stimulus is converted into an electric signal proportionate to the quantity of the stimulus.

Transfer Function   A characterization of a system (for example, a mechanical structure or filter) by determining how the system responds to input energy at different frequencies.

Transients   In electrical usage, usually refers to an unwanted, temporary, large increase or decrease in a current or supply voltage that only occurs occasionally. Almost always due to reactive components during rapid changes in a voltage or a current.

Transistor   A tiny chip or crystalline material, usually silicon, that amplifies or switches electric current. It is a three-terminal semiconductor device.

Translate   To transform information from one code to another or from one language to another in a way that preserves meaning.

Transmultiplexer   An equipment which transforms signals derived from frequency-division-multiplex equipment (such as group or supergroup) to time-division-multiplexed signals having the same structure as those derived from PCM multiplex equipment, and vice versa.

Transparent   The property of being insensitive to the meaning of a code of information being manipulated. If a device interprets and reacts to the coded information it is handling, it is said to be not transparent.

Transponder   Satellite equipment which receives a signal, amplifies it, changes its frequency, and retransmits it.

Transputer   A computer on a chip (derived from *transistor* and *computer*).

Triac   A General Electric trade name for a gate-controlled full-wave ac silicon switch designed to switch from a blocking state for polarity-applied voltage with either positive or negative gate triggering.

Triboelectricity   Electrostatic charges generated by friction between different materials.

Trigger   A timing pulse used to initiate the transmission of signals through the appropriate circuit signal paths.

Trunk   A circuit between two telephone exchanges or switching centers or from an exchange to a customer's switchboard.

Truth Table   A matrix which describes a logic function by listing all possible combinations of inputs and by indicating the outputs for each combination.

TTL, T²L   Transistor-transistor logic. A family of integrated-circuit logic in which the multiple inputs on gates are provided by multiple-emitter transistors. TTL is characterized by high speed, low power dissipation, and low cost and is widely used in modern computers.

Turnaround Time   (1) The time required to reverse the echo suppressors on a switched telephone circuit. (2) The time required for a system to transfer from the receive mode to the transmit mode, or vice versa, in an HDX operation.

TWX   Teletypewriter exchange service. A public teletypewriter exchange service in the United States and Canada. Both Baudot- and ASCII-coded machines are used.

UART   Universal asynchronous receiver-transmitter. An LSI circuit for start-stop serial data transfer.

Ultrasonics   The technology involved with sounds that are too high in frequency to be heard by the human ear.

Unilateral Control   A synchronization control system between exchanges A and B is unilateral if the clock at exchange A controls that at exchange B but B does not control A.

Unipolar   (1) Refers to transistors in which the working current flows through only one type of semiconductor material, either n- or p-type. In unipolar transistors, the working current consists of either positive or negative electric charges, but never both. Unipolar transistors operate more slowly than bipolar IC transistors but take up much less space on a chip and are much more economical to manufacture. (2) Pulse code with single polarization.

Unit   (1) Basic element. (2) A device having a special function.

Up Time   The accumulated time that a system is operational during its life. Relative up time = [MTBF/(MTBF + MTBR)] × 100%.

USART   Universal synchronous-asynchronous receiver-transmitter.

USRT   Universal synchronous receiver-transmitter.

V   CCITT code designation for "Data communication over the telephone network."

V.1   Equivalence between notation symbols and the significant conditions of a two-condition code.

V.2   Power levels for data transmission over telephone lines.

V.3   International Alphabet No. 5.

V.4   General structure of signals of International Alphabet No. 5 code for data transmission over public telephone network.

V.5   Standardization of data signaling rates for synchronous data transmission in the general switched telephone network.

V.6   Standardization of data signaling rates for synchronous data transmission on leased telephone-type circuits.

V.7   Definition of terms concerning data communication over the telephone network.

V.10 (X.26)   Electrical characteristics for unbalanced double-current interchange circuits for general use with integrated-circuit equipment in the field of data communications.

V.11 (X.27)   Electrical characteristics for balanced double-current interchange circuits for general use with integrated-circuit equipment in the field of data communications.

V.15 Use of acoustic coupling for data transmission.

V.16 Medical analog data transmission modems.

V.19 Modems for parallel data transmission using telephone signaling frequencies.

V.20 Parallel data transmission modems standardized for universal use in the general switched telephone network.

V.21 200-Bd modem standardized for use in the general switched telephone network.

V.22 1200 b/s duplex modem standardized for use on the switched telephone network and on leased circuits.

V.22bis 2400 b/s duplex modem using the frequency-division technique standardized for use on the general switched telephone network and on point-to-point two-wire leased telephone-type circuits.

V.23 600- to 1200-Bd modem standardized for use in the general switched telephone network.

V.24 List of definitions for interchange circuits between data terminal equipment and data circuit–terminating equipment.

V.25 Automatic calling and/or answering equipment on the general switched telephone network. This includes disabling of echo suppressors on manually established calls.

V.26 2400 b/s modem standardized for use on four-wire leased circuits.

V.26bis 2400–1200 b/s modem standardized for use in the general switched telephone network.

V.26ter 2400 b/s duplex modem using the echo cancellation technique standardized for use on the general switched telephone network and on point-to-point two-wire leased telephone-type circuits.

V.27 4800 b/s modems with manual equalizer standardized for use on leased telephone-type circuits.

V.27bis 4800 b/s modem with automatic equalizer standardized for use on leased telephone-type circuits.

V.27ter 4800–2400 b/s modem standardized for use in the general switched telephone network.

V.28 Electrical characteristics for unbalanced double-current interchange circuits.

V.29 9600 b/s modem standardized for use on leased telephone circuits.

V.31 Electrical characteristics for single-current interchange circuits controlled by contact closure.

V.31bis Electrical characteristics for single-current interchange circuits using optocouplers.

V.32   A family of two-wire duplex modems operating at data signaling rates up to 9600 b/s for use on the general switched telephone network and on leased telephone-type circuits.

V.35   Data transmission at 48 kb/s using 60–108 kHz group band circuits.

V.36   Modems for synchronous data transmission using 60–108 kHz group band circuits.

V.37   Synchronous data transmission at a data signaling rate higher than 72 kb/s using 60–108 kHz group band circuits.

V.40   Error indication with electromechanical equipment.

V.41   Code-independent error-control system.

V.50   Standard limits for transmission quality of data transmission.

V.51   Organization of the maintenance of international telephone-type circuits used for data transmission.

V.52   Characteristics of distortion and error-rate measuring apparatus for data transmission.

V.53   Limits for the maintenance of telephone-type circuits used for data transmission.

V.54   Loop test devices for modems.

V.55   Specification for an impulsive noise-measuring instrument for telephone-type circuits.

V.56   Comparative tests of modems for use over telephone-type circuits.

V.57   Comprehensive data test set for high data-signaling rates.

V.100   Interconnection between public data networks (PDNs) and the public switched telephone network (PSTN).

V.110   Support of data terminal equipments (DTEs) with V series of interfaces by an integrated services digital network (ISDN).

VAN   Value-added network. Communications service companies that lease channels from the common carriers or specialized carriers and then resell specialized services that were not available from the original carrier. Among the advantages they offer are lower error rates and increased efficiency of line usage.

Variable   A quantity that can assume any set of values, and is subject to change.

Varistor   (1) Two-terminal resistive element that has nonlinear volt-ampere characteristics. (2) Two-terminal semiconductor device having a voltage-dependent nonlinear resistance. Varistors may be divided into two groups, symmetrical and nonsymmetrical, based on the symmetry or lack of symmetry of the volt-ampere curve.

VDR   Voltage-dependent resistor. Often referred to as a MOV (metal-oxide varistor); a device also used for protection from transients.

Video   Pertaining to electric currents and phenomena of frequencies corresponding to the variation in electrical levels of samples obtained by scanning a scene or image. (These frequencies are approximately from 0 to 10 MHz in the United States.)

Virtual Circuit   A connection between a source and a sink in a network that may be realized by different circuit configurations during transmission of a message.

VOGAD   Voice-operated gain-adjusting device.

Voice-Grade Channel   A channel suitable for transmission of speech, digital or analog data, or facsimile, generally with a frequency range of about 300 to 3400 Hz.

Volatile Memory   A memory that loses its information if the power is removed from it.

VRAM   Variable-rate adaptive multiplexing.

WATS   Wide-area telephone service. A service provided by telephone companies in the United States which permits a customer, by use of an access line, to make calls to telephones in a specific zone on a dial basis for a flat monthly charge.

Waveform Coding   Direct digital sampling of an analog waveform recording the absolute value of the waveform at each sample. Provides the most accurate reconstruction of the original waveform, but requires a data rate of at least 56 kb/s.

WDM   Wavelength division multiplexing.

Weighted Value   The numerical value assigned to any single bit as a function of its position in the code word.

Wideband   Communications channel having a bandwidth greater than a voice-grade channel; characterized by a data transmission speed of 10,000 to 500,000 b/s.

Word   (1) In telegraphy, six operations or characters (five characters plus one space). (*Group* is also used in place of *word*.) (2) In computing, a sequence of bits or characters treated as a unit and capable of being stored in one computer location.

WPM   Words per minute. A common measure of speed in telegraph systems.

Write   The process of loading information into memory.

X   CCITT Recommendation designation for "Data communication networks." Refer to Vol. VIII, Fasc. 2.7.

X3 . . . year   American National Standard code designation.

XMT   Transmit.

Zener Diode   A voltage-control diode; it is placed in reverse direction directly across the voltage it is designed to control, with a series resistor between source voltage and the zener diode connection point.

Index

Absorption, atmospheric, 14
Accuracy, oscillator, 188, 194
Acoustic coupler, 125
ACU (automatic calling unit), 118, 131
Adaptive delta modulation, 268
Adaptive equalizer, 131, 198
Adaptive pulse-code modulation (APCM), 144
Added-value circuit, 403
Aerosat, 413
AFC (automatic frequency control), 267
AGC (automatic gain control) circuit, 109, 172, 267
Aggregate bit rate, 18, 135, 174
Alarm:
    audible, 285
    major, 303
    minor, 303
    pilot, 171, 172
Alerting in interface circuit, 220
Aloha system, 390
Alphabet No. 5, International, 240, 243, 244
Alternate voice-data (AVD) operation, 22, 116
American Navy, Marisat system and, 279
American Standard Code for Information Interchange (see ASCII)
American Telephone and Telegraph (AT&T) Company, 409, 411
Amplitude distortion (see Distortion, amplitude)
Amplitude jitter, 67, 292
Amplitude modulation (see Modulation, amplitude)
AMVFT (amplitude-modulation voice-frequency telegraph), 165
Analog carrier system, 26, 81, 165–171
Analog channels, 16, 165–170

Analog-digital network, mixed, 185–187
Analog facsimile, 126, 207
Analog signal, 16, 18, 96, 97, 315
Analog system, optical, 325
Analog system operator, 304
Analog technique, 138, 144
Analog testing, 285, 286, 295
    control center for, 302–305
Analog-to-digital conversion, 186, 187, 198
Analog transmission, 16, 82, 133, 174, 184
Analog voice, compression of, 138, 139
    figure, 139
Analytic routing method, 138
Angle:
    acceptance, fiber-optic, figure, 316
    propagation, fiber-optic, 315
        figure, 316
Angle modulation (see Modulation, angle)
Anisochronous transmission, 184
Answering mode, 104
Antijamming, 274
APD (avalanche photodiode), 324–327
APL (programming language), 308
ARQ (automatic request for repeat):
    continuous, 252, 253, 276–278
    go-back-N, 278
    operation of, 116, 146, 158, 246, 250, 252, 253, 278
    selective repeat, 252, 278
    stop-and-wait, 252, 276, 278
Arrestor, 355
ASCII (American Standard Code for Information Interchange), 134, 159, 183, 235, 239, 240, 244, 245
    control character, 159
    table, 244

Assignment techniques, satellite
  multiple-access, 268
Asynchronous channel, 129
  multiplexing, 155, 156, 162
Asynchronous communication, 214
Asynchronous modem, 183, 305
Asynchronous transmission, 118, 182,
  245
Attenuation:
  in fiber optic, 317, 334
  overall (insertion loss), 23–31, 80
  signal, 123, 136
Attenuation compensation, 151
Attenuation distortion (*see* Distortion,
  attenuation)
Attenuation-frequency characteristics,
  31–35, 286
Attenuation-frequency measurements,
  32, 33, 35
  figure, 33
Attenuation values, marginal, 23
Attenuator, optical, 339
Automatic calling unit (ACU), 118, 131
Automatic frequency control (AFC), 267
Automatic gain control (AGC) circuit (*see*
  AGC circuit)
Automatic monitoring system, 301–306
Automatic request for repeat (*see* ARQ)
Avalanche diode, 362
Avalanche photodiode (APD), 324–327
Avalanche process, 324
Avalanche suppressor, 363
Avalanche-type zener diode, 363
AVD (alternate voice-data) operation, 22,
  116

Backup capability, DCE, 224
Balanced demodulator, 109
Balanced interchange circuit, 201–205,
  207, 213–216, 353
  tables, 202, 216
Balanced line, 124, 341, 342
Balanced modulator, 108, 109
  in facsimile transmission, 126
Balancing network, 37
Band, ripple in, 32
Band-edge roll-off, 32
Baseband, binary (*see* Pulse code)
Baseband equipment, 274
Baseband signal, 18, 27, 91, 93, 121, 136,
  270, 273, 395, 400
  return-to-zero, 254
  synchronization quality of, 102, 104

BASIC (beginner's all-purpose symbolic
  instruction code), 308
Batch transmission, 2, 116
Batch time-encoding technique, 141
Battery:
  gelled cell, 370
  lead acid, 370
  nickel cadmium, 370
  solar, 13
  wet cell, 370
Baud (Bd) rate, 133
  versus bits per second, 133, 134
  table, 121, 134
Baudot code, 183, 245
BCD (binary-coded decimal) code, 245
BCP (byte-control or -controlled protocol),
  234–238, 305
Bell System, 82, 152, 409
  modems, 112, 113, 118, 119, 227
  multiplexing, 170, 174
BER (bit error rate), 15, 116, 158, 271,
  297, 306, 326, 327, 400
BER tester, 297, 305
  figure, 296
Bias:
  external, 322
  negative (space), 78
  positive (mark), 78
  in receiver circuit, 291
Bias distortion, 77, 291
Binary, multilevel (MLB; pseudoternary),
  pulse code, 98, 103
Binary baseband(s) (*see* Pulse code)
Binary-coded decimal (BCD) code, 245
Binary data, 208, 214
Binary digits, 145, 198
Binary representation:
  of analog signals, 93–97
  of characters, 245
Binary sequence, random, 198
BISYNC (BSC, binary synchronous
  communications), 208, 211–213, 231,
  235–238
Bit, 16
  aggregate, 154, 156
  control, 231
  error-detection, 250, 422
  filling, 154
  least significant, 245
  most significant, 245
  parity, 130, 248
  redundancy, 252, 278
  6-bit transcode, 245

Bit (*Cont.*):
  start-stop, 124, 177
Bit count, 178
Bit error rate (*see* BER)
Bit interleave (*see* TDM, bit-interleaved)
Bit-oriented protocol (BOP), 234–238,
  305
Bit rate:
  aggregate, 18, 135, 174
  requirements, table, 97
  table, 97, 121, 134, 135, 138
  (*See also* Information rate)
Bit stuffing, 154, 231, 274
  figure, 155
Block error rate, 297
BOP (bit-oriented protocol), 234–238, 305
Bridging:
  circuit, 87
  conference, network, 87
Broadcasting, 123, 411
  satellite, 13, 280
Buffer storage (buffer synchronizer), 111,
  120, 145, 154, 157, 159, 162, 163,
  187–190, 197, 238, 271, 276, 278
  elastic, 116, 278
  figure, 189
Byte, 124, 134
Byte-control or -controlled protocols
  (BCP), 234–238, 305
Byte stuffing, 231

C line conditioning, 27–30
C-message filter, 51, 52, 82
C-notched filter, 52, 82
Cable:
  carrier, 44
  coaxial, 10, 31, 124, 167, 173, 213, 294,
    334, 342, 348, 349, 391, 395, 405
  interface, 187, 188
  low-capacitance, 122
  optical-fiber, 3, 14, 21, 125, 313–320,
    333–337, 395, 401
    installation, 329–333
    loose-tube, 319
    refractive index of (*see* Refractive
      index of optical-fiber cable)
    tight-buffer, 319
  submarine, 9, 65
  telephone, 9, 332
  trunk, 142
  twisted-pair, 9, 21, 204, 293, 391, 404
  underground, 127
  wire, 331, 332, 395

Capacitor:
  blocking, 372
  coupling, 372
Carrier:
  common, 145, 409, 411
  digital, 174–178
  microwave, 44
  residual, 172
Carrier channel, 77, 165–170
Carrier current, 127
Carrier disconnect, soft, 114
Carrier-frequency shift, 66
Carrier sensing, 391
Carrier system:
  analog, 66, 82, 165–170
  translation error in (*see* Error,
    translation, in carrier systems)
Cartridge, 306
Cathode-ray tube (CRT), 295, 300, 305,
  308, 309
CCIR (International Radio Consultative
  Committee), 269, 272, 282, 411
CCITT (International Telegraph and
  Telephone Consultative Committee)
  (*see* Standards and recommendations, CCITT)
CDMA (code-division multiple access),
  268–274
Central network control station, 272
Central office (*see* Office, central)
Central processing unit (CPU), 143, 306
Channel(s):
  analog, 16, 165–170
  asynchronous, 129, 155, 156, 162
  auxiliary, 112
  backward (reverse), 112, 120, 121, 250
  basic, 21, 27, 28
  carrier, 77, 165–170
  characteristics of, 22
  data, disturbance in, 366
  digital, 156, 173–175
  erect, 165
  forward, 250
  full-duplex (*see* Full-duplex channels)
  group (*see* Group, channel)
  half-duplex (*see* Half-duplex channels)
  inverted, 165
  leased (*see* Leased line)
  message, 165
  multiplexing, 158, 164
  narrow-band, 20, 138, 141
    figures, 150–152
    table, 166

Channel(s), narrow-band (*Cont.*):
  (*See also* Low-speed channel;
    Telegraph channel, power of;
    Teleprinter channel)
  primary, 111
  printer, 141
  satellite, 261, 264, 265
  secondary, 111, 305
  simplex, 4, 115, 128
  synchronous, 129, 155, 161, 162
  types of, 4
  voice, 23, 96, 138–142, 165, 421
  voice-grade, 161, 185, 303, 336
Channel service unit (CSU), 253, 254
Channel unit:
  basic, 270
  office (OCU), 254
Character:
  ACK, 235, 244, 246, 250, 252, 277
  block check (BCC), 248
  communication, 235, 243
  control, 159, 236, 243
  ending, 183, 235
  error control, 183
  graphic, 236
  idle, 238
  longitudinal redundancy check (LRC),
    237, 248, 249
  NAK, 235, 244, 246, 250, 252, 277
  nonprintable, 237, 245
  opening PAD, 178
  peripheral control, 235
  phasing, 178
  sync (SYN), 163, 178, 183
Character frame, 151
Character interleave (*see* TDM,
  character-interleaved)
Characteristic(s):
  of amplitude distortion, 32, 33
  attenuation-frequency, 31–35, 286
  channel, 22
Characteristic distortion, 79, 80
Characteristic impedance, 204, 214
Characteristic resistance, 290
Characters per second (cps), 134
  table, 134, 135
Circuit:
  automatic gain control, 109, 172, 269
  balanced interchange (*see* Balanced
    interchange circuit)
  clock, 103
  control, 47, 110, 210
  dedicated (*see* Leased circuit)

Circuit (*Cont.*):
  four-wire, 5, 22, 35, 37, 120, 131, 257,
    263
  integrated, 337
  interface, 183, 200–220, 240
  leased (*see* Leased circuit)
  limiter, 92
  receiver bias in, 291
  remote-tail, 191
  satellite, 54
  switched, 5, 21
  talker, 112
  two-wire, 5, 21, 35, 37, 109, 119
  unbalanced, 5, 131, 349, 353
  unbalanced interchange, 205, 206
  voice-grade, 27–29, 80
  wire-line, 275
Circuit assurance, 225
Circuit isolation, 372
Circuit protection, 345
Cladding layer, fiber-optic, 315
Client node, 390
Clock:
  common, 190
  Data-Phone digital service (DDS), 185,
    186, 188, 254
  external, 104, 185, 187
  internal, 178, 185, 189
  local, 185
  master, 194, 254
  modem, 184
  reference, 194
Clock phasing, 186
Clock signal (pulse), 48, 154, 177
Clocking, 99
  self-, 177
  (*See also* Timing)
Coaxial cable (*see* Cable, coaxial)
COBOL (common business-oriented
  language), 308
Code(s):
  detection, in satellite link, 276
  error-correcting, 22, 252, 278
  fixed-length, 160
  information, 183, 243
  pseudorandom noise (PN), 271
  pulse (*see* Pulse code)
  sync, pattern of, 181, 182
  variable-length, 160
  (*See also specific codes*)
Coding:
  convolutional, 274
  dibit, 91

Coding (*Cont.*):
linear predictive, 141
tribit, 91, 121, 136
variable-length, 159
variable-quality, 144
of wideband signal, 175
Collision, 391
detection, 393, 405
Common carrier, 145, 146, 409
Communication(s):
asynchronous, 155
intersatellite, 281
message, 1
optical, 13
satellite, 13, 130, 187, 259
synchronous, 155
verbal, 1
video, 281
written, 1
Communication characters, 235, 243
Communication-link configurations, 14
Communication security, 129, 336, 401
Communication speed versus transmission speed, 133, 134, 183
Communications management center, 258
Compandor, 48, 51, 81
syllabic, 48
table, 55
Compression of signal (*see* Signal, compression of)
Computer(s):
communications between, 155
host, 147, 164, 211, 233, 237, 238, 306
Comsat General Corporation of United States, 279, 413
Concentrator, 143, 146, 155, 163, 164
Conditioning, line, 22, 27–30, 257
specifications, 27
(*See also* Equalization)
Conduit system for fiber-optic cable, 330
Connector:
CCITT V.35, 202
EIA RS 232C, 202
EIA RS 449, 208
fiber-optic, 337
filtered, 350
interface, 111, 121, 208, 257
Winchester, 215
Contention, 394
Continuously variable slope delta modulation (CVSD), 141
Control bit, 231

Control center, technical, 302
for demand assignment in satellite system, 260
Control circuit(s):
crosstalk between signal circuit and, 47
EIA, 210
timing, 110
Control protocol(s):
byte, 235, 305
data-link, 231
network, 238
user, 239
Convolutional encoding, 274
Core of fiber-optic cable, 315
Coupler:
acoustic, 125
directional, optic, 338
hybrid, 37, 38
figure, 37
CPU (central processing unit), 143, 306
CRC (cyclical redundancy check), 158, 235, 237, 248–250, 390
Crosstalk, 9, 47, 68, 139, 150, 201, 207, 214, 336, 341
near-end, 47, 200, 205, 207
CRT (cathode-ray tube), 295, 300, 305, 308, 309, 334
Cryptography, 129
CSMA/CD (carrier sense multiple access with collision detection), 392, 402, 405
CSMA/PA (carrier sense multiple access with positive acknowledgment), 405
CSU (channel service unit), 253, 254
Current:
dark, optical detector, 322
eddy, 348
Current loop (*see* Loop, current)
CVSD (continuously variable slope delta modulation), 141
Cyclical redundancy check (*see* CRC)

D line conditioning, 29, 257
DAA (data-access arrangement), 118, 125
DAMA (demand-assigned multiple access), 266, 271
Data:
binary, 208, 214
wideband (high-speed), 165, 171
Data-access arrangement (DAA), 118, 125
Data block, 142, 163
variable-length, 163

Data channels, disturbance in, 366
Data encryption, 129, 139
Data entry, 308
Data-link control protocol (*see* DLC protocol)
Data network, public, 147, 238, 240–243
  (*See also* Switched network)
Data-Phone digital service (*see* DDS)
Data-Phone II service, 257, 301
Data rate, 135, 142, 174, 205, 208, 275, 279, 288, 337
  table, 121, 133
Data service unit (DSU), 162, 185–188, 254
Datagram service, 7
dB (decibels), 23
dB meter, 45
dBm, 24
dBmO, 25, 80, 81, 128
dBmOp, 54, 55, 80, 83
  table, 55
dBrn, 52
dBrnC, 52
dBrnCO, 52–54, 83
DDD (direct-distance dialing), 38
DDS (Data-Phone digital service), 119, 185–188, 253, 254
  clock, 186
  off-net extension, 187
Decision threshold (slicing point), 77
Decoding threshold, 274
Delay:
  envelope (*see* Envelope delay)
  propagation (*see* Propagation delay)
  in satellite transmission, 13, 62
  transmission, 96, 146, 152, 162, 214, 225, 242, 256, 270, 282, 334
Delay distortion, 10, 27, 29, 59, 82, 127
  characteristics of, 286
  measurement of, 61
Delay figures in various mediums, 62–64
Delay modulation (DM, Miller) code, 102
Delta modulation, 139, 140, 268
Demand-assigned multiple access (DAMA), 266, 271
Demand-assignment control center in satellite system, 259
  figure, 260
Demodulation (*see* Detection)
Demodulator:
  balanced, 109
  capability of, 124

Detection (demodulation), 92
  coherent (homodyne, synchronous), 92, 97, 271
  envelope, 92
  error (*see* Error detection)
  phase modulation, 93
Detector:
  envelope, 138
  optical, 313–315, 322–327, 334
  phase, 61
Deutschen Bundespost, 411
Diagnostic capability, EIA RS 449, 211
Diagnostic center, digital, 305
Diagnostic system, 273
Dial-up network (*see* Switched network)
Dialing, 5, 415–417
  direct-distance (DDD), 38
  pulse, 118, 416
  Touch-Tone (pushbutton), 118, 416
Dibit, 108, 120, 135, 136
Dibit coding, 90, 91
Dibit modem, 120
Dibit pattern, 109
Differential phase-shift keying (DPSK), 90, 91, 107, 120
Digital-analog network, mixed, 185–187
Digital bit rate, table, 97, 121, 134, 135, 138
Digital channel, 156, 173–175
Digital control system, 305
Digital diagnostic center, 305
Digital equalization, 65, 66, 113
Digital equipment, high-speed, 366
Digital exchanges, 175
  (*See also* Switching)
Digital filter, 65, 105, 141
Digital interface, 189, 275
Digital link, high-speed, 280
Digital magnetic recording, 99, 102
Digital modulation, 97
Digital multiplex equipment, 175
Digital network, 185, 188, 194
Digital noise interference, 141
Digital operating area, 354
Digital parallel transmission, 19
Digital receiver, 205, 215
Digital repeater, 18, 19, 46, 103, 174
Digital short-distance interconnection, 122
Digital signal, 16, 133, 315
  figure, 16, 17
Digital simulation, 141
Digital system operator, 305

Digital test facility, 303
Digital-to-analog conversion, 186, 187, 198
Digital transmission, 16, 46, 65, 139, 173, 184
  satellite, 274
Digital voice, 141, 144, 153
  compression of, 139
Diode:
  avalanche, 362
  injection laser (ILD), 315, 320, 324
  laser (*see* Laser diode)
  light-emitting (*see* Light-emitting diode)
  photo (*see* Photodiode)
  zener, 362–364
    figure, 361
Diode protectors, 362
Direct-distance dialing (DDD), 38
Disabler of echo suppressor, 40
Discrimination between satellite channels, 261
Dispersion:
  material, fiber-optic, 317, 325
  modal, fiber-optic, 317, 325
  of signal, 32, 62
Distortion:
  amplitude, 31, 65, 82, 324
    characteristics of, 31
    figure, 34
    (*See also* attenuation, *below*)
  attenuation, 22, 29, 286
  bias, 77, 291
  in cable, 62
  characteristic, 79, 80
  delay (*see* Delay distortion)
  harmonic, 75, 286
    measurement of, 75
  isochronous, 290, 291
    figure, 64, 291
  measurements on digital circuits, 288
  nonlinear, 76, 286, 324
    measurement of, 77
  phase, 76, 286
  in power supply line, 368
  radio, 11
Distributed communications network, 144
Distribution frame, main, 332
DLC (data-link control, level 2, line discipline) protocol, 147, 177, 199, 231, 241
DM (delay modulation, Miller) code, 102

Doppler effect, 276
DPSK (differential phase-shift keying), 90, 91, 107, 120
Driver, 41, 207, 290
  current density of, 322
  line (cable), 109, 123, 197, 293
Dropout, 58
Drum, facsimile, 126
DSU (data service unit), 162, 185–188, 254
DTMF (dual-tone multifrequency) signaling, 263
Duplex (*see entries beginning with the terms:* Full-duplex; Half-duplex)

E (ear) signal, 416, 417
Earth station, 13, 259, 260, 262, 270, 280
  digital, 275
  standard A, 268
  standard B, 268
  unmanned, 274
EBCDIC (extended binary-coded decimal interchange code), 183, 235
  table, 246
Echo(es), 34
  listener, 35
  microwave, 12
  talker, 35
Echo canceller, 40
  figure, 41
Echo control devices, 38
Echo delay tolerances, figure, 38
Echo return loss (ERL), 38, 41, 96
Echo suppression threshold, 39
Echo suppressor, 39
  disabler of, 40
Echoplex, 5, 197, 249
ECS (European Communications System), 413
Eddy current, 348
EDP (electronic data processing), 389
EIA (Electronics Industries Association):
  interchange connector, 202, 209–211
  RS 232C, 122, 156, 188, 192, 200, 214, 216, 221, 305, 306
  RS 357, 128, 207
  RS 422A, 156, 200, 201, 203, 205, 207, 209, 213, 293, 306
  RS 423A, 122, 205–212, 293, 306
  RS 449, 208–211
Elastic buffer storage, 116, 278
Electromagnetic (magnetic) field, 336, 342, 344, 347

Electromagnetic interference (EMI), 313, 336, 343
Electromagnetic pulse (EMP), 343
Electromagnetic radiation (EMR), 343
Electronic data processing (EDP), 389
Electronic mail, 3, 280, 402
Electronics Industries Association (see EIA)
Electrostatic field, 342, 347
ELF (extremely low frequency), 11
EMI (electromagnetic interference), 313, 336, 343
Emitter-receiver for optical system (EROS), 338
EMP (electromagnetic pulse), 343
EMR (electromagnetic radiation), 343
Encoder-decoder, 254
Encoding:
    A-law of, 96
    convolutional, 274
    digital speech, 141, 144, 145, 153
    μ-law, 96
    phase (see Phase-encoded binary baseband; Phase encoder)
Encryption, data, 129, 139
End of transmission code, 256
End-to-end link, circuit, 142, 145, 241
End-to-end performance, 274
End-to-end protocol, 238
End-to-end tests, 61, 296, 297, 301, 303
End-to-end transmission delay, 146
Envelope delay, 22, 28, 59, 76, 96
    distortion of, 59, 82
    measurement of, 61
Envelope detection, 92
Envelope detector, 138
Equalization, 21, 62, 102, 111–114, 289
    adaptive, 66, 113
    automatic, 66
    delay, 76
    digital, 65, 66, 113
    loop, 254
    middle-point, 65, 114
    in modem, 66, 112–114
    predistortion, 66, 113
    (See also Conditioning, line)
Equalizer, 62
    adaptive, 131, 198
    amplitude, 62
    automatic, 29, 113, 121, 131
    digital, 65, 113
    fixed, 113, 121
    manual, 65, 120, 131
    misadjusted, 32

Equalizer (Cont.):
    in modem, 109, 111, 112
    phase delay, 63
Erect channel, 165
ERL (echo return loss), 38, 41, 96
Erlangs, 264
EROS (emitter-receiver for optical system), 338
Error(s):
    performance, in modulation techniques, 89
    probability of, 22, 274
    translation, in carrier systems, 66, 80, 85, 125
    measurement of, 67
    (See also Frequency drift)
Error acknowledgment, 277
Error checking, 248
Error-checking field, 237
Error control, 199, 241
    forward (see Forward error control)
Error control character, 183
Error-correcting code, 22, 246, 247, 278
Error correction, 145, 247, 278
    forward (see Forward error control)
Error detection, 11, 98, 101, 112, 231, 247, 278, 391, 407
Error-detection bits, 247
Error-detection code in satellite link, 277
Error-free second, 299
Error rate, 6, 8, 67, 110, 116, 253, 274, 278, 287, 400, 404
    bit (see BER)
    block, 297
    long-term, 22
    in satellite link, 277
European Communications System (ECS), 413
Exchanges, digital, 175
    (See also Switching)
Extended binary-coded decimal interchange code (see EBCDIC)
Extremely low frequency (ELF), 11
Eye pattern, 66, 99, 115, 138, 288

Facsimile, analog, 126, 207
    figure, 126
Facsimile facility, 260
Facsimile service, 279, 409
Facsimile transmission, 89, 126–129, 395
Fading:
    in high-frequency radio transmission, 11

Fading (*Cont.*):
  in microwave transmission, 12
FCC (Federal Communications Commission), 27, 347, 411
  figure, 27
  table, 28
FD/CDMA; FD/TD/CDMA; FD/TDMA, 268
FDM (frequency-division multiplexing), 47, 77, 149, 150, 161, 171, 273, 395, 420
  in telephony, 282
FDM carrier, 265
FDM/FM, 274
FDM/FM/FDMA, 265
FDMA (frequency-division multiple access), 265, 268, 273
FDX (*see* Full-duplex channels; Full-duplex mode)
FEC (*see* Forward error correction)
Federal Communications Commission (*see* FCC)
FEP (front-end processor), 300
Fiber optic (*see* Cable, optical-fiber; Transmission, optical-fiber)
Field:
  address, 234
  control, 234
  electromagnetic (magnetic), 336, 342, 344, 347
  electrostatic, 342, 347
  flag, 234
  information, 234
FIFO (first-in, first-out) buffer, 116
Fill factor, 266
Filter, 59, 150
  bandpass (slot), 108, 419
  C-message, 51, 52, 82
    figure, 52
  C-notched, 52, 82
    figure, 52
  digital, 65, 105, 141
  flat, figure, 53
  integrated, ac, 367
  low-pass, 181
  monochromatic, 334
  notch, 92, 105
  optical, 339
  psophometric, 53
    figure, 51
  resonating, 141
  slot (bandpass), 108, 419
Firmware, storage, microcomputer control, 164

Fixed-length code, 160
Floppy disk, 306
FM (frequency modulation), 26, 127, 136, 279, 282
  figure, 90
FM carrier system, signal-to-noise, 46
FMVFT (frequency-modulation voice-frequency telegraph), 26, 30, 31, 165
  tables, 26, 55
Focal point, compandor, 48
Formant, voice, 139, 141
FORTRAN (programming language), 308
Forward error control (FEC, forward error correction), 116, 253, 268, 274, 278
Fourier spectrum, 198
Frame:
  character, 151
  distribution, main, 332
  variable, 158
Frame period, 269
Frame size, 276
Frequency, fundamental, 75, 141
Frequency control, automatic (AFC), 267
Frequency-division multiple access (*see* FDMA)
Frequency-division multiplexing (*see entries beginning with the term:* FDM)
Frequency drift, 80, 181
Frequency error, 80
Frequency frogging, 151
Frequency modulation (*see* FM; FM carrier system, signal-to-noise)
Frequency-modulation voice-frequency telegraph (*see* FMVFT)
Frequency-selective voltmeter, 75
Frequency-shift keying (FSK), 90, 92, 101, 119
Front-end processor (FEP), 300
FSK (*see* Frequency-shift keying)
Full-duplex (FDX) channels, 4, 15, 113–115, 131, 142, 200, 237, 255, 398
Full-duplex mode, 200

Gain control, automatic (AGC), circuit, 109, 172, 267
Gaseous recording lamp, 127
Gateway, 390
Geneva, Switzerland, CCITT assemblies in, 411, 412
Geostationary satellite, 259, 264, 270, 282

Go-back-*N*, ARQ and, 278
GPO (General Post Office) of Britain, 411, 421
Graded-index fiber, 317, 325
Graphic-display tasks, 122
Ground, 353, 360
  protective, 202, 203, 210
  signal, 202, 203, 210, 361
Ground rod, 357
Ground system, 357
  figure, 352
Grounding, 350, 354, 357
  in digital interfacing circuits, 353
    figure, 353
Group, channel, 165
  delay (*see* Envelope delay)
  figure, 168
  inverted, 167
  pilots on, table, 172
G/T (gain-to-temperature) ratio, 261, 272
Guard band, 398
Guard time, 270, 272

Half-duplex (HDX) channels, 4, 115, 177
Half-duplex mode, 115, 200, 237
Half-duplex operation, 112, 256
Half-duplex transmission, 15
Handset, 125, 415
Handshaking function, 200, 224
Handshaking signal, 197, 219
Harmonic(s):
  distortion in (*see* Distortion, harmonic)
  human voice, 141
HDX (*see entries beginning with the term:* Half-duplex)
Header (heading), 236
Hexadecimal representation, 245
High-fidelity music, 96
  table, 97
Hits, phase and gain, 58
  figure, 58
Holding tone, compandor, 51
Hollerith code, 245
Hook, off- and on-, in telephone network, 415, 417
Hybrid, measurement with, 42
Hybrid coupler, 37, 38
  figure, 38
Hybrid technical control center, 305

ICs (integrated circuits), 338
Idle period, utilization of, 133, 142

IEEE (Institute of Electrical and Electronics Engineers): Standard 488, 217–220
  Standard 802, 392
ILD (injection laser diode), 315, 320, 324
Impedance:
  characteristic, 204, 214
  measurement of, 44, 291
Impedance matching, 34, 37, 42
Impedance-matching network, 41
  (*See also* Repeating coil)
Impedance mismatch, 34, 36, 41, 42
Impulse noise (*see* Noise, impulse)
Information, communication, 271
  supervisory, 271
Information code, 183
Information control, 172
Information rate, 133
  (*See also* Bit rate)
Infrared range, 318, 323
  figure, 318
Injection laser diode (*see* ILD)
Inmarsat (International Maritime Satellite Organization), 413
Integrated circuits (ICs), 338
Integrator, 140
Intelligent terminal, 306
Intelligent time-division multiplexer (ITDM), 142, 156
Intelsat (International Telecommunications Satellite Organization), 412
  frequency plan, 266
Interactive operation, 307, 308
Interface:
  computerized, 146
  core-cladding, fiber-optic, 317
  current loop, 297, 306
  data service unit (DSU), 186, 254
  digital, 189, 275
  EIA circuit-fiber-optic, 125
  for host computer and data terminal equipment, 238
Interface cable, 187, 189, 192
Interface circuit, 183, 220–230, 240
Interface-circuit indicator, 297
Interface-circuit operations, 220
Interface connector, 111, 121, 208, 257
Interface protocol (*see* Protocol, level 1)
Interface signals, 107
Interface standards (*see under* Standards and recommendations)
Interference, 12, 341, 342, 348
  digital noise, 141

Interference (*Cont.*):
  electromagnetic (EMI), 313, 336, 343
  from high-frequency radio, 348
  intersymbol, 79, 99, 104, 290
  power-supply, 105
  single-tone, 70, 80
  sources of, 342
  from terrestrial systems, 262
  two-tone, 71
Interference problems of remote terminals, 122
Interleave:
  bit (*see* TDM, bit-interleaved)
  character (*see* TDM, character-interleaved)
  time-slot, 271
Intermodulation, 273, 421
International Frequency Registration Board, 411
International Telecommunications Union (ITU), 118, 411
Intersatellite communications, 281
Intersymbol interference, 79, 99, 104, 290
Inverted channel, 165
Inverter, 370
Ionized-air blower, 384
Ionosphere, 11, 12
ISO-OSI, 199, 392
Isochronous data, 154
Isochronous distortion, 290, 291
  figure, 64, 291
Isochronous NRZ signaling, 99
Isochronous transmission, 184
Isolation device, 407
Isolation transformer, 366, 367
Isotropic radiated power, effective, antenna, 263
ITDM (intelligent time-division multiplexer), 142, 156
ITU (International Telecommunications Union), 118, 411

Jitter, 35
  amplitude, 67, 292
  digital, 72
  figure, 58, 67, 292
  in NRZ signaling, 102, 289, 290
  phase (*see* Phase jitter)
  in PST (pair-selected ternary) signaling, 104
  tolerance in modems, 111
  transition, 289, 290

Jitter rate, eye pattern and, 288
Junction, *pn*, 320

Keypunch layout in data input unit, 307

L1 coaxial system, 171
  figure, 169
L3 carrier, 171
L4 carrier, 171
L600 mastergroup, 171
LAP (link-access procedure), level 2 protocol, 241, 392
Large-scale integration (LSI), 105, 393
Laser, 14, 321, 334, 336, 337
Laser beam, 281, 395
Laser diode, 336
  injection, 321, 324, 325
Layer, cladding, 315
LDM (limited distance modem, local modem), 123
Leakage current, zener diode, 363
Leakage path in carbon-block protector, 360
Leased (dedicated) circuit, 7, 38, 240, 241
  figure, 29
  international, 22, 80, 81
Leased line (channel), 15, 89, 118, 131, 145, 421
Least significant bit, 245
LED (*see* Light-emitting diode)
Level(s):
  in FMVFT system, 26, 30, 31
  for frequency-modulation phototelegraph transmission, 71, 81
  signal: measurement of, 301
    in modem, 110
  transmission, 24, 26, 39
Level calculations, 30
Level control (regulation), 171
Level variations, 23, 34, 80
Light-emitting diode (LED), 315, 320, 325, 334, 336
  two-color, 294, 305
Light-emitting-diode indicator, 285, 294, 295, 297, 307
Lightning, 344
Limited distance (local) modem (LDM), 123
Limiter circuit, 92
Line(s):
  balanced, 124, 341, 342
  characteristics of, 123
  leased (*see* Leased line)

Line(s) (*Cont.*):
  subscriber, 151
  twisted-pair, 9, 206, 293
  unbalanced, 124, 341
  unconditioned, 112
  voice-grade, 150, 162
Line conditioner, ac, 336–368
Line conditioning (*see* Conditioning, line)
Line discipline protocol (*see* DLC
    protocol)
Line (cable) driver, 109, 123, 197, 293
Line-matching transformer, 109, 381
Line-of-sight transmission paths, 313
Line protection, 111, 117
Line transients, 59, 343, 368
  figure, 58
Linear amplifier, 150, 338
Linear predictive coding, 141
Link:
  digital, high-speed, 280
  fiber-optic, 325
  microwave, 11, 47, 174
  satellite, 13, 54, 250, 253
  satellite down-, 262, 281
  satellite up-, 262, 281
  terrestrial (*see* Terrestrial link)
Link-access procedure (LAP), 241, 392
Link configurations, 14
Liquid-crystal device, 338
Listener:
  active, 219
  on IEEE 488 bus, 219
Listener echo, 35
Local (limited distance) modem (LDM),
    123
Local subscriber loop, 21, 123, 415
Long-haul telecommunications transmis-
    sion, 260
Longitudinal (horizontal) redundancy
    check (LRC), 155, 237, 248, 249
Loop:
  current, 126, 200, 342
    interface, 297, 306
    polar, 200
  digitally controlled, 110
  phase-locked (PLL), 117, 183, 335
  resistance, 209
  subscriber, local, 21, 123, 415
Loop testing and tests, 115, 118, 295,
    297, 304
Loop voltage, 416
Loopback, 21, 255, 296
  local line, 155, 208, 255

Loopback (*Cont.*):
  remote, 155, 208, 255
Loopback tests, 61, 295, 301, 303
Loss:
  insertion (overall attenuation), 23, 80
  in optical-fiber cable, 317, 328
    measurement of, 339
  radiation, 32
Loss distortion, 286
Low-speed channel, 150
Low-speed terminals, 149
LRC (longitudinal, horizontal redun-
    dancy check), 237, 248, 249
LSI (large-scale integration), 105, 393

M (mouth) signal, 416, 417
Magnetic (electromagnetic) field, 336,
    342, 344, 347
Magnetic tape, 308
Mail, electronic, 3, 280, 402
Manchester code, 102
Manholes, cable in, 328, 332
Marisat system, 279
Master station, 172, 271
Mastergroup, 166, 169, 175
  figure, 168, 169
Measurements:
  attenuation-frequency, 32, 33, 35
    figure, 33
  with BER tester, 297, 305
    figure, 296
  of delay distortion, 61
  on digital circuits, 288
  of impulse noise, 56, 80, 85
  levels and, reference frequencies: 800
      Hz, 22, 33, 82, 115
    figures, 29, 30
    1000 or 1004 Hz, 22, 23, 32, 52, 82,
      115
  loop, 61, 295, 298
  noise, 50, 80, 82
  in optical-fiber cable, 339
  out-of-service, 303
  peak-to-average-ratio (PAR), 286–288
  (*See also* Testing)
Memory disk, 102
Metal-oxide varistor (MOV), 362
  figure, 362, 363
Meter, analog, 309
  digital, 309, 310
Microphone, handset, 125
Microprocessor, 142, 257, 307
Microwave carrier, 44

Microwave link, 11, 47, 174
Microwave portable equipment, 12
Microwave radio, 11, 12, 21
Microwave transmission, 130
Military speech channel, 142
Military standards, 205, 215
Miller code (delay modulation, DM),
    101, 102
Milliwatt (mW), 24
Minicomputer, 142, 143, 305
MLB (multilevel-binary, pseudoternary)
    pulse code, 98, 103
Mobile radio, 142, 268
Mode:
    answering, 104
    check, 182
    free-flow, 394
    full-duplex, 115, 200, 237
    half-duplex, 115, 200, 237
    multi-, fiber-optic, 316, 338
    originating, 104
    packet, 243
    search, 181
    single-, fiber-optic, 316, 338
    synchronous, 243
Mode dispersion, 317
Modem(s), 14, 15, 33, 66, 91, 107–124,
    139, 211, 227–233, 257, 292,
    295–301, 421
    asynchronous, 183, 305
    Bell System, 112, 113, 118, 119, 227
    block diagram of, figures, 17, 108
    channel assignments for: figure, 113,
        151
        table, 119, 121
    control, 301
    dibit, 120
    equalization in, 66, 112–114
    features of, 111
    local (LDM, limited distance), 123
    scrambling in, 115, 178, 198, 199
    standards, 118–121, 130
    synchronous, 117, 183, 305
    timing diagram of, figure, 108
    tributary, 301
    wideband, 117, 123
Modulation, 69, 89
    adaptive delta, 268
    amplitude (AM), 69, 90, 273
        figure, 90
        vector diagram for, 70
        (See also pulse-amplitude;
            quadrature-amplitude, below)

Modulation (Cont.):
    angle, 68, 69, 273
        vector diagram for, 70
        (See also frequency; phase, below)
    continuously variable slope delta
        (CVSD), 141
    delay (DM, Miller) code, 101, 102
    delta, 139, 140, 268
    digital, 97
    frequency (FM), 26, 127, 136, 279, 282
        figure, 90
    multilevel, 183
    phase (PM), 91–93, 136
        figure, 90
    pulse, 93–96
        figure, 94
    pulse-amplitude (PAM), 50, 93–96,
        273
    pulse-code (PCM), 18, 47, 50, 72, 94,
        103, 139, 141, 215, 423
        adaptive, 144
        demultiplexing and, 181
        multiplexing and, 153, 175
        in satellite communications, 268
    pulse-position (PPM), 94, 99, 273
    pulse-width [PWM, pulse-duration
        (PDM), pulse-length], 94, 99,
        273, 370
    quadrature-amplitude (QAM), 115,
        117, 131, 134, 137, 138, 292
        figure, 292
    in satellite transmission, 273
    vestigial-sideband (VSBM), 91, 126
Modulation rate, 99, 118, 119, 271, 290
Modulator, balanced, 108, 109
    in facsimile transmission, 126
Monitoring, 257, 260, 275, 285, 336, 343
    automatic, 301–306
    continuous, 301
    diagnostic, 301
    digital, 285, 294
    satellite, 13
Most significant bit, 245
MOV (metal-oxide varistor), 362
    figure, 362, 363
MTBF (mean time before failure), 400
Multifrequency signaling, 420
    table, 418
Multilevel-binary (MLB, pseudoternary)
    pulse code, 98, 103
Multilevel bit transmission, 135
Multilevel modulation, 183
Multimode fiber-optic cable, 316, 338

Multiple-access satellite communication, 268
Multiplex telephony in satellite service, 282
Multiplexer, 261, 339
  intelligent (statistical) time-division, 142, 156
Multiplexing, 133, 149, 198, 242, 273, 308
  efficiency, 157
  frequency-division (see FDM)
  in modems, 117
  protocol for, 238
  space-division, 150
  standards, 153, 154, 165
  techniques of, 149
  time-division (see TDM)
  variable-rate adaptive (VRAM), 144
  wavelength division, 339
Multipoint (multidrop, multiaccess) operation, 156, 181, 213, 226, 234, 240, 275
  centralized, 15, 226
  multi-, 16
  noncentralized, 227
  one-way only (broadcast), 226
Multipoint channel, 28
Multipoint communication link, 15, 114

N.A. (numerical aperture), fiber-optic, 315–317
  figure, 316
Narrow-band channel (see Channel, narrow-band)
Narrow-band telegraphy, 268
National Bureau of Standards, U.S., 130, 392
National Electrical Code, 352
NATO (North Atlantic Treaty Organization), 13
NEP (noise equivalent power) photodiode, 323, 326
Neper (Np), 25
Network:
  analog-digital, mixed, 185–187
  balancing, 37
  dial-up (see Switched network)
  digital, 185, 188, 194
  distributed communications, 144
  impedance-matching, 41
    (See also Repeating coil)
  integrated, 281
  multipoint (see Multipoint operation)

Network (Cont.):
  packet-switching, 145, 241
  public data, 147, 238, 240–243
    (See also Switched network)
  switched (see Switched network)
Network management functions, 422
Network organization, 272
Network protection, 118, 254
Node (junction point), 136, 259, 390, 406
Noise, 46, 68, 76, 139, 150, 201, 262, 292, 335, 341, 359, 360
  C-message, 51
  C-notched, 51, 77, 82
  common-mode, 212, 367, 379
  differential, 367
  idle channel, 262
  impulse, 22, 46, 56, 80, 85, 292
    figure, 57
    measurement of, 56, 80, 85
  interference, 262
  longitudinal, 213, 342
  measurement of, 50, 80, 82
  quantizing (see Quantizing noise)
  signal to, ratio of (see S/N ratio)
  in space communications, 54, 262
  thermal, 324, 341
  with tone measurement, 51
  white, 46, 141
Noise equivalent power (NEP) photodiode, 323, 326
Noise figure, 48
Noise margin, 289
Noise objectives for long circuits, table, 54, 55
Noise units, 52
Nonlinear characteristics of light source, 324
Nonlinear distortion (see Distortion, nonlinear)
NRZ (nonreturn-to-zero) pulse code, 98, 99, 181, 289–292, 325
  NRZI, 99
  NRZ-L, 99
  NRZ-M, 99
  NRZ-S, 99
Nuclear blasts, 344
Numerical aperture (see N.A.)
Nyquist method for measuring envelope delay, 61
Nyquist theorem, 96, 135

Ocean region satellites, 279
OCU (office channel unit), 254

Off-hook condition, 415–417
  figure, 417
Office:
  central, 103, 145, 146, 187, 295, 351,
      352, 359
    figure, 22
  central terminal (CTO), satellite, 259
  customer, 253
  domestic, 187
  of the future, 3, 402
  switching, 409, 415, 417, 422
Office channel unit (OCU), 254
Offshore facilities, services to, provided
    by satellite, 279
On-hook condition, 415–417
  figure, 417
Operation(s):
  in-plant, 247
  satellite, 264
Operation center, 285
Operator efficiency, 308
Optical beam, 14
Optical coupler, 379
Optical detectors, 313–315, 322–327, 334
Optical-fiber cable (see Cable, optical-
    fiber)
Optical-fiber transmission, 313
Optical filter, 339
Optical time-domain reflectometer
    (OTDR), 334
Optoisolator, 379
Order-wire system, 262
Originating mode, 104
Oscillator:
  accuracy, 188, 193
  master, 109, 173
  phase-locked, 173
  stability, 110, 188
  voltage-controlled (VCO), 109
Oscilloscope, 57, 67, 115, 288, 292, 334
OTDR (optical time-domain
    reflectometer), 334
Out-of-service measurement, 303

P_{BE} (probability of bit error), 274
Packet assembly-disassembly facility
    (PAD), 239, 242
Packet format protocol, 199, 241
Packet mode, 243
Packet size, 146, 394
Packet switching, 133, 145, 187, 238
Packet-switching network, 145, 241
Packet-voice communication, 145

Packetized speech, 144
PAD (packet assembly-disassembly
    facility), 239, 242
Pair-selected ternary (PST) signaling,
    104
PAM (pulse-amplitude modulation), 50,
    93–96, 273
  figure, 94
Paper tape, 308
PAR (peak-to-average-ratio) measure-
    ment, 286
Parity, 134, 245
  horizontal, 248
  vertical, 248
Parity bit, 130, 248
Parity check, 248
Parity elements, 240
Pattern recognizer, 182
PBX (private branch exchange), 389, 391
PCM (see Modulation, pulse-code)
PDM (see Modulation, pulse-width)
PE (phase-encoded) pulse code, 98, 101
Peak-to-average-ratio (PAR) measure-
    ment, 286–288
Peak-to-peak phase jitter, 69–72
Peak-to-peak transition jitter, 289, 290
Peripheral(s), 306, 308
  close-grouped, 122
Peripheral equipment, 135
Personal computer network, 404
  figure, 406
Phase:
  absolute, 137
  reference, 93
Phase arrangements for coding, tables,
    91
Phase change, 137
Phase decoder, 109
Phase detector, 61
Phase distortion, 76, 286
Phase-encoded (PE) pulse code, 98, 101
Phase encoder, 107, 108
Phase hit, 58, 59
  figure, 58
Phase jitter, 22, 30, 60, 67–74, 80, 85,
    137, 188, 290, 292
  figures, 58, 73, 290, 292
Phase-locked loop (PLL), 177, 183, 335
Phase-locked oscillator, 173
Phase modulation (PM), 91–93, 136
  figure, 90
Phase relation between signals, 35
Phase-shift keying (see PSK)

Phase splitter, 139
Phase wobble, long-haul circuit, 68
Phasing, facsimile transmission, 126
Photocell signal, 126
Photodetector (*see* Photodiode)
Photodiode, 315, 322, 338, 380
    avalanche (APD), 324–327
    photocurrent, 322
    PIN (positive-intrinsic-negative),
        323–327
Phototelegraph apparatus, 127
Phototelegraph transmission, 26, 80, 81,
    128
Photovoltaic effect, 322
Picturephone, 9, 174
    table, 97
Pilot tone(s), 171
    alarm, 171
    frequency and levels for group signals,
        table, 172
    for frequency synchronization, 172
    for level regulation, 172
    reference signal, 267
PIN (positive-intrinsic-negative)
    photodiode, 323–327
PLL (phase-locked loop), 177, 183, 325
PM (phase modulation), 91–93, 136
    figure, 90
PN (pseudorandom noise) code, 271
Point-to-point link and circuit, 15, 119,
    213, 224, 240, 401, 404
Polar circuit protection, 363
Polar current, 200
Polar signal (pulse code), 98, 103
Polarization, satellite antenna, 261
Poll response, 117
Polling, 16, 143, 231, 233, 235, 301, 405
Power:
    aggregate and single-channel, in
        telegraph transmission, 31
        table, 26
    effective isotropic radiated, 263
    output, subscriber equipment, 26, 81
    reflected, 37
Power units, signal and noise, 23, 52
PPM (pulse-position modulation), 94, 99,
    273
Pressure-type recording, 127
Printer, high-speed, 403
Printer channel, 141
Printer unit, 306, 308, 404
Private branch exchange (PBX), 389,
    391

Processing:
    computer, 274
    distributed data, 198, 306
    speed of, 307
Processor, 217, 307
    central, 123, 231
    data, 22
    word, 4
Programmable communication network
    analyzer, 305
Programmable read-only memory
    (PROM), 164, 307
Propagation angle, fiber-optic, 315
    figure, 321
Propagation delay:
    in cable, 214
    in satellite communication, 276, 280
Propagation time, 270, 276
Propagation velocity, 10, 31, 32, 35, 44
    figure, 32
Protection:
    ac supply, 364
    circuit, 345
        solid-state, 361
    line, 111, 117
    network, 118, 254
    overvoltage, 359
    system, 346, 359
Protector:
    carbon-block, 360
    circuit, 346
    gas-tube, 360
Protocol(s):
    ADCCP (advanced data communica-
        tions control procedure), 234
    BCP (byte-controlled), 234–238, 305
    BDLC (Burroughs data-link control),
        234
    BOP (bit-oriented), 234–238, 305
    BSC (binary synchronous communica-
        tions, BISYNC), 231, 235
    CCITT recommendations (*see* Stan-
        dards and recommendations,
        CCITT, protocols)
    DDCMP (digital data communications
        message protocol), 234
    HDLC (high-level data-link control),
        231, 234
    hierarchy of, 199
    high-level, 147, 199, 238
    level 1 (interface), 147, 199, 238, 241
        dedicated service, 225
        switched network, 227

Protocol(s) (*Cont.*):
    level 2 (data-link, line discipline), 147, 177, 178, 199, 231, 240, 241
    level 3 (network control), 147, 199, 238
    level 4 (message reconstruction), 239
    level 5 (session), 239
    level 6 (presentation), 239
    level 7 (application), 239
    levels, figure, 393
    SDLC (synchronous data-link control), 234
    terrestrial, 276
    testing of a system via, 299
Protocol analyzer, 379
Pseudorandom BER sequence, 275
Pseudorandom bit pattern, 297
Pseudorandom data word, 288
Pseudorandom noise (PN) code, 271
Pseudoternary (MLB, multilevel-binary) pulse code, 98, 103
PSK (phase-shift keying), 91, 273
    differential (DPSK), 90, 91, 107, 120
    four-phase, 274
    modulator-demodulator, 267, 271
    table, 121
Psophometric filter, 53
    figure, 51
Psophometric noise power, 53, 80, 83, 262
PST (pair-selected ternary) signaling, 104
PTT (Postes Téléphonique et Télégraphique), 411, 413
Public data network, 147, 238, 240–243
    (*See also* Switched network)
Pullback procedure, ARQ, 252
Pulse, pseudorandom noise (PN) code, 271
Pulse code(s), 97, 98
    Manchester, 102
    Miller, 102
    MLB (multilevel-binary, pseudoternary), 98, 103
    NRZ (nonreturn-to-zero) (*see* NRZ pulse code)
    PE (phase-encoded), 98, 101
    polar, 98, 103
    RZ (return-to-zero), 98, 99, 254, 325
    unipolar, 98
Pulse modulation (*see* Modulation, pulse)
Pulse rate, dialing, 118, 416
Pulse rounding, 123
Pulse spreading, 317, 325

Punched card, 308
Punched tape, 308
PWM (*see* Modulation, pulse-width)
pWOp (picowatts psophometric), 53, 54, 80, 262
    table, 55

Quadbit, 137
Quadrature-amplitude modulation (QAM) (*see* Modulation, quadrature-amplitude)
Quantized signal, 95
    figure, 95
Quantizing, 47, 96
Quantizing noise, 47, 50, 80, 96, 272
Quantum efficiency, 320, 323
Queuing, 198

R1 signaling system, CCITT, 419, 420
R2 signaling system, CCITT, 419, 420
Radio, 11, 21, 411
    high-frequency, interference from, 348
    microwave, 11
        antenna beam angle, 12
        link, 21
    mobile, 142, 268
Radio frequency interference (RFI), 343
Radius, bent, fiber-optic cable, 330
Random-access memory (RAM), 164, 307
Random data pattern, 115
Read-only memory (ROM), 307
Real-time interconnection, 271, 402
Receiver, digital, 205, 215
Recording lamp, gaseous, 127
Redundancy bits, 252, 278
Redundancy check, 155, 248
    cyclical (CRC), 158, 235, 237, 248–250, 390
    longitudinal (horizontal, LRC), 155, 237, 248, 249
    vertical (VRC), 248, 249
Redundant bits, 252, 278
Reflection, 13, 214, 328, 334
    microwave, 12
    signal, 32, 37
Refraction, 315, 316
Refractive index:
    atmosphere, 12
    optical-fiber cable, 315, 316
        graded, 317, 325
        step, 317, 325
Regeneration, optical-fiber system, 315

Regenerator:
  analog, 107
  digital, 46, 65, 79
Register, shift, 189
Regulator, voltage, 366, 367
Relay, 273
  dry-reed, 376
  electromagnetic, 375
  electromechanical, 373
  mercury-wetted, 376
  resonant-reed, 378
  solid-state, 378
Reliability of digital data system, 274
Remote job entry (RJE), 122
Repeater, 150, 336
  digital, 18, 19, 46, 103, 174
  satellite, 269, 272
  submerged, 10
Repeater protection, 361
Repeating coil, 42
Resistance, characteristic, 290
Resolution, facsimile system, 129
Responsivity (*see* Sensitivity)
Return loss, echo (ERL), 38, 41, 96
Return-to-zero (RZ) pulse code, 98, 99,
  254, 325
RFI (radio frequency interference), 343
Ringer, telephone set, 116
Ringing:
  modem, 118
  telephone, 417
Rise time, fiber-optic system, 325
RJE (remote job entry), 122
ROM (read-only memory), 307
Routing information, 270
RZ (*see* Return-to-zero pulse code)

Sample (sampling), 93, 150
Sample rate, 107
Sampling instant, 289
Sampling interval, 271
Satellite, 13, 187, 261
  geostationary, 259, 264, 270, 282
  ocean region, 279
  (*See also* Earth station)
Satellite broadcasting, 13, 280
Satellite communications, 13, 130, 187, 259
Satellite delay compensation unit
  (SDCU), 278
Satellite link (*see under* Link)
Satellite monitoring, 13
Satellite transmission, 13, 62, 262, 273,
  274

Scanning, facsimile, 126
SCPC (single channel per carrier), 187,
  188, 215, 265, 274, 279
  PCM, 267
SCR (silicon-controlled rectifier), 363
Scrambler, 119, 198
Scrambler synchronization, 117, 199
Scrambling in modems, 115, 178, 198,
  199
SDCU (satellite delay compensation
  unit), 278
Security in communication, 129, 336, 401
Sensitivity:
  of earth receiving station, 272
  of photodiode, 323
Server (node), 390
SF (single-frequency) signaling, 419
Shielding, 341, 346
Shielding materials, 348
Shift, frequency, table, 166
Shift register, 189
Ship communication facilities, 279
Sideband, 69, 91, 136
  double, 69, 136
Signal(s):
  analog, 16, 18, 96, 97, 315
  black, facsimile, 81, 127
  clock, 48, 154, 177
  compression of, 48, 98, 102, 117, 124,
    133, 138, 139, 159
  digital (*see* Digital signal)
  dispersion of, 32, 62
  E and M, 416, 417
  handshaking, 197, 219
  impairments to transmission of, 288
  interface, 107
  level of (*see* Level, signal)
  phase relation between, 35
  photocell, 126
  polar, 98, 103
  pulsing, 420
  quantized, 95
    figure, 95
  reference, pilot, 267
  service, 240, 242
  speech, 172, 341
  supervisory, 112, 418
  television, 18, 19, 167, 173, 174
    table, 97
  timing, 267
  white, facsimile, 127
  wideband, 175
  wideband data, 165, 268, 395

Signal power, 23
Signal reflection, 32, 37
Signal-to-noise ratio (*see* S/N ratio)
Signaling, 21
  address, 415, 418
  CCIS (common-channel interoffice),
    422
  CCITT, 422, 423
  channel-associated, 421
  common-channel, 421
  DTMF (dual-tone multifrequency), 263
  in-band, 418
  interregister, 420
    table, 421
  multifrequency, 420
    table, 418
  NRZ (nonreturn-to-zero), 98, 289
  out-band, 418
  PCM (pulse-code modulation), 423
  PST (pair-selected ternary), 104
  R1, 419
  R2, 420
  SF (single-frequency), 419
  supervisory, 112, 418
    figure, 153
  telephone, 415
  teleprinter, 162
  tone, 417
  trunk, 416, 420
  two-tone, 418
Signaling rate, 208
Silicon-controlled rectifier (SCR), 363
Simplex channel, 4, 115, 128
Singing, 37
Single channel per carrier (*see* SCPC)
Skew, 290, 291
Skin effect, 32, 350
Slave station, 172, 271
Slew rate, 200, 201, 207
  table, 209
Slicing point (decision threshold), 77
Smart terminal, 306
SMUX (statistical multiplexer, ITDM),
  142, 156
S/N (signal-to-noise) ratio, 18, 22, 46, 96,
  111, 137, 253, 323, 326
  C-notched, 29, 77
  definition of, 46
  in FM carrier system, 46
Soft carrier, 114
Software, 308
Solar battery, 13
Solar cell, 322

Solid-state circuit protection, 361
Solid-state components, 338
Solid-state devices, 151
Solid-state lamp (SSL), 380
Solid-state light source, 313
Solid-state optical detector, 313
Solid-state uninterruptible power system
  (UPS), 369
SOM (start of message), 267
SPADE (SCPC, PCM, DAMA) system,
  266
Spectrum:
  Fourier, 198
  modem signal: figure, 109, 151
    table, 121, 138
Speech:
  active, 142
  digital, 141, 144, 153, 173, 272
  male, 141
  plus data: equipment function, 21
    operation, 263
  (*See also entries beginning with the
    term:* Voice)
Speech signal, 172, 341
Splicing, fiber-optic cable, 328, 337
Spurious signal, 341
SSB (single sideband), 69
  with suppressed carrier, 59
SSL (solid-state lamp), 380
Stability:
  daily, transmission system, 23
  oscillator, 110, 188
Standards and recommendations:
  American Standard Code for Informa-
    tion Exchange (*see* ASCII)
  CCIR, 269, 272, 282, 411
  CCITT, 200, 422, 423
    interfacing, 212
    maintenance and control centers,
      311
    modems, 19, 118, 130
    multiplexing, 153, 165, 173
    noise, 53, 80, 83, 262
    packet-switching network, 147
    protocols, 200, 212, 215, 239
      table, 202
    pulse-code modulation (PCM), 96,
      153
    signaling, 419
    voice-grade circuits, 28, 30, 80
  EIA interfacing, 200
  FCC, line conditioning, 28
  IEEE 488, 217

Standards and recommendations (*Cont.*):
  IEEE 802, 392
  U.S. military interface, 205, 215
Standby facilities, 260
Start of message (SOM), 267
Start-stop bit timing, 124
Start-stop bits, 124, 145
Start-stop DTE, 240, 242
Start-stop operation, 240
Start-stop telegraph and data codes,
    table, 134
Static electricity, 344, 382
Station:
  earth (*see* Earth station)
  master, 172, 271
  primary, 15
  secondary, 15
  slave, 172, 271
Station equipment, 21
STDM (statistical time-division multi-
    plexer), 142, 156
Step-index fiber, 317, 325
Storage, 116, 143, 152, 188, 307, 389
  (*See also* Buffer storage)
Stuffing:
  bit, 154, 155, 231, 274
  byte, 231
Subscriber:
  in packet switching, 146
  signaling between exchange and,
    415
Subscriber dialing, 416
  table, 416
Subscriber line, 151
Supercapacitor, 371
Supergroup, 166
Supermastergroup, 166
Supervisory information, 271
  figure, 153
Supervisory message, 235
Supervisory signaling, 112, 415
  figure, 153
Surge arrestor, 355
Switched circuit, 5, 21
Switched facilities, 260
Switched multitap transformer, 367
Switched network, 38, 81, 118, 120, 130,
    147, 198, 221, 223, 225, 227
  packet, 6, 145
  telegraph, 58
  telephone, 33, 63, 118, 129, 136, 415
    figure, 63
Switched operations, 240

Switching:
  circuit, 6, 305
  of light energy, 338
  message, 6
  of packet, 133, 145, 187, 238
  of reactive load, 343
  store-and-forward, 6
Switching device, intelligent, 159
Switching equipment, 95, 146, 351, 359,
    417
Switching information, 420
Switching office, 409, 415, 417, 422
Symbolic names, 390
SYN (sync character), 178, 183, 193
Sync code pattern, 181, 182
Synchronization (synchronizing), 177
  bit, 104, 153, 177, 271, 274
  burst, 272
  in byte-control protocols, 235
  character (word), 160, 178, 244
  of data equipment in different
    networks, 184
  in demultiplexed signals, 181
  frame, 181, 271, 272
  via interface control circuit, 224
  intrinsic, RZ code, 99
  loss of, 103, 104, 163
  of message, 178
  modem, 110
  national system, 194
  pilot frequency for, 172
  scrambler, 117, 199
  techniques in data equipment, 177
  time-division multiplexing (TDM), 153
Synchronization information, 270
Synchronization pattern, 154
Synchronizer (PCM signal conditioner),
    181
  buffer (*see* Buffer storage)
Synchronizing system, 275
Synchronous channel, 129, 161, 162
  multiplexing, 155
Synchronous (sync) character (SYN), 178,
    183, 193
Synchronous communication, 155
Synchronous data, 183
Synchronous idle, 193
Synchronous mode, 243
Synchronous modem, 117, 183, 305
Synchronous motor, 126
Synchronous operation, 240
Synchronous orbit, 275
Synchronous system, 254, 257

Synchronous transmission, 118, 177, 182, 257

T carrier:
  T1, 103, 148, 152, 155, 174, 274
  T2, 155, 174
  T3, 155, 174, 335
  T4, 155, 174, 335
Talk-down, 419, 422
Talker echo, 35
Talker on IEEE-488 bus, 218
TASI (time assignment speech interpolation), 10, 144
TD/CDMA (time-division/code-division multiple access), 269
TDM (time-division multiplexing), 149, 151, 153, 161, 174, 175, 253, 273, 279
  bit-interleaved, 151, 155, 162, 174
  character-interleaved, 151, 156, 162
  figure, 152
  table, 161
TDMA (time-division multiple access), 269, 279
Technical control center, 260, 302
Teleconferencing via satellite, 280
Teleconferencing system, 4
Telegraph, 58
  codes for, table, 134
  voice-frequency, 23, 26, 30, 31, 55, 155, 165
    table, 166
  (*See also entries beginning with the term:* Teleprinter)
Telegraph channel, power of, 31
  table, 26
Telegraph link, 8
Telemetry, 409
Telephone cable, 9, 332
Telephone line, 149
Telephone network, switched (*see* Switched network, telephone)
Telephone signaling, 415
Teleprinter channel, 139, 141, 162, 260, 263
  (*See also* Channel, narrow-band)
Teleprinter equipment, 258, 307
  (*See also entries beginning with the term:* Printer)
Teleprinter message from ship, 279
Television, transoceanic, 280
Television channel, 12
Television facilities, 409

Television monitor, 307
Television network, cable, 337, 400, 402
Television signal, 18, 19, 167, 173, 174
  table, 97
Television transmission, 11, 12, 41, 253, 282, 395, 411
Telex transmission, 247, 279
Tensiometer, 333
Terminal, intelligent, 306
  smart, 306
Terminal equipment, 178, 186
Termination, proper, 33
Terrestrial interconnection, 274
Terrestrial link, 13, 54, 62, 146, 176, 260, 277
Terrestrial network, 281
Terrestrial protocol, 276
Terrestrial radio relay, 273, 275
Terrestrial system:
  interference from, 262
  telephone plant, 38
Test facility:
  analog, 303
  built-in, 294
  digital, 303
Testing:
  analog, 285, 286, 295, 302–305
  disruptive, 301
  end-to-end, 61, 296, 297, 301, 303
  local, 295
  loop, 115, 118, 295, 297, 304
  loopback, 61, 295, 301, 303
  nondisruptive, 301
  remote, 295
  (*See also* Measurements)
Threshold:
  decision, 77
  level, 77, 110
  receiver, 289, 290
Threshold point, 262
Throughput efficiency, 276, 279
Thyristor, 362
Time:
  guard, 270, 272
  turnaround, 4, 40, 177, 178, 277
Time assignment speech interpolation (TASI), 10, 144
Time-division multiple access (TDMA), 269, 279
Time-division multiplexing (*see* TDM)
Time interval modification, 144
Time sharing, 391
Time slot, reference, 271

Timing:
  data-derived, 110, 111
  duration of, 270
  external, 104, 109
  transmitter, 109
  (*See also* Clocking)
Timing control circuit, 110
Timing signal, 267
Timing source, 124
TLP (transmission level point), 25, 31,
    52, 54
  table, 26
Token, 392
  passing, 394, 402, 404
Tone:
  busy, 415
  dial, 415
  holding, 51, 58
Topology, 391
  bus, 392
  ring, 392
  star, 391
Training period, 66, 117
Transducer, 125
Transfer block, 147
Transformer:
  ferroresonant, 370
  isolation, 366, 367
  line-matching, 109, 381
  switched multitap, 367
Transient(s):
  elimination of, 359
  line, 59, 343, 368
    figure, 58
  noise, 59
  sources of, 344
  suppression of, 363, 364
  tests for, 304
  (*See also* Noise, impulse)
Transient disturbance, 292
Transient trap, 355
Transient voltage, 361
Transition:
  data, figure, 79
  mark-to-space, 77
  space-to-mark, 77
Transition jitter, peak-to-peak, 289, 290
Translation error in carriers (*see* Error,
    translation, in carrier systems)
Transmission:
  analog, 16, 82, 133, 174, 184
  asynchronous, 118, 182, 245
  batch, 2, 116

Transmission (*Cont.*):
  digital (*see* Digital transmission)
  facsimile, 89, 126–129, 395
    stability of, 127
  half-duplex, 15
  isochronous, 184
  long-haul telecommunications, 260
  microwave, 130
  multilevel bit, 135
  optical-fiber, 313
  phototelegraph, 26, 80, 81, 128
  satellite, 13, 62, 262, 273, 274
  synchronous, 118, 177, 182, 257
  television, 11, 12, 41, 253, 282, 395,
      411
  telex, 247, 279
  tropo scatter, 12
Transmission delay (*see* Delay, transmis-
    sion)
Transmission level point (*see* TLP)
Transmission media, 8, 149
Transmission rate, 133, 277
Transmission signal, level of, 24, 26, 39
Transparency, 147, 149, 164, 197, 236,
    237, 239, 400
  definition of, 197
Transponder, 261, 268, 269, 273, 280
Traveling-wave tube (TWT), 261, 274,
    281
Triac, 363
Tribit coding, 91, 121, 136
Triboelectricity, 383
  table, 384
Tropo scatter transmission, 12
Troposphere, 12
Troubleshooting, analog testing for, 287
Trunk cable, 142
Trunk signaling, 416, 420
Turnaround sequence, 256
Turnaround time, 4, 40, 177, 178, 277
TWT (traveling-wave tube), 261, 274,
    281

U600 mastergroup, 169
  figure, 169
Ultraviolet spectrum, 323
Unbalanced circuit, 5, 131, 349, 353
Unbalanced interchange circuit, 205, 206
Uninterruptible power system (UPS), 369
Unipolar pulse code, 98
UPS (uninterruptible power system), 369
USASI (United States of America
    Standards Institute), 373

Utilization:
  channel, 143, 394
  of idle transmission periods, 133, 144,
    163

Variable-length coding, 159
Variable-length data block, 163
Variable-quality coding, 144
Variable-rate adaptive multiplexing
  (VRAM), 144
VCO (voltage-controlled oscillator), 109
VDE (Verband Deutscher
  Electrotechniker), 346
Vertical redundancy check (VRC), 248,
  249
Vestigial-sideband modulation (VSBM),
  91, 126
Video communication, 281
Video facility, 260
Vinyl in facsimile transmission, 127
Virtual call service, 241
Virtual circuit service, permanant, 241
Voice:
  digital, 139, 141, 144, 153
  human, 421
  simulation of, 141
  (*See also* Speech)
Voice band, 19, 155, 418
Voice channel, 23, 96, 138–142, 165,
  421
Voice compression:
  analog, 138, 139
    figure, 139
  digital, 139
Voice-data operation, alternate, 22, 116
Voice-frequency telegraph, 23, 26, 30, 31,
  55, 155, 165
  table, 166
Voice-grade channel, 161, 185, 303, 336
Voice-grade circuits, 27–29, 80
Voice-grade facilities, 185
Voice-grade line, 150, 162

Voice-operated device antisinging
  (VODAS), 37
Voltage-controlled oscillator (VCO), 109
Voltage regulator, 366, 367
Voltmeter, frequency-selective, 75
Volume indicator, 310
Volume unit, 310
VRAM (variable-rate adaptive multiplex-
  ing), 144
VRC (vertical redundancy check), 248,
  249
VSBM (vestigial-sideband modulation),
  91, 126

Waveguide, 10, 315
  circular, 11
  optical, 13
  rectangular, 11
Wavelength, 322, 323, 327
  emission peak, fiber-optic system, 327
  figure, 327
Waveshaping, 212
Waveshaping component, 208, 216
Wideband, 20
  facsimile, 128
Wideband data signal, 165, 268, 395
Wideband modem, 117, 123
Wideband signal, coding of, 175
Winchester connector, 215
Wire, open, 9, 21, 33
Wire cable, 331, 332, 395
Wire circuit (*see* Circuit, four-wire;
  Circuit, two-wire)
Wire-line circuit, 275
Wire pair, 9
Wireway (conduit) system, 330
Word processor, 402
WPM (words per minute), 134
  table, 134, 135

Zener diode, 362–364
  figure, 361

ABOUT THE AUTHORS

DOGAN TUGAL, a communications consultant, recently retired after 24 years at RCA Global Communications Inc. in New York. He has also held positions at NATO and the United Nations, specializing in telecommunications.

OSMAN TUGAL, formerly a project engineer with RCA Global Communications, is currently developing strategic and tactical plans for the telecommunications department of Goldman, Sachs, and Company.